D0435000

UNCOMPROMISING
HONOR

IN THIS SERIES by DAVID WEBER

HONOR HARRINGTON

EDITED BY DAVID WEBER

MANTICORE ASCENDANT

THE STAR KINGDOM

**To purchase all of these titles in e-book format,
please go to www.baen.com.**

UNCOMPROMISING HONOR

DAVID WEBER

UNCOMPROMISING HONOR

This is a work of fiction. All the characters and events portrayed in this book are fictional, and any resemblance to real people or incidents is purely coincidental.

Copyright © 2018 by Words of Weber, Inc.

A Baen Books Original

Baen Publishing Enterprises
P.O. Box 1403
Riverdale, NY 10471
www.baen.com

ISBN: 978-1-4814-8350-6

Cover art by David Mattingly

First printing, October 2018

Distributed by Simon & Schuster
1230 Avenue of the Americas
New York, NY 10020

Library of Congress Cataloging-in-Publication Data

Names: Weber, David, 1952– author.
Title: Uncompromising honor / David Weber.
Description: Riverdale, NY : Baen, 2018. | Series: [Honor harrington ; 19] |
    "A Baen Books Original."
Identifiers: LCCN 2018023334 | ISBN 9781481483506 (hc)
Subjects: LCSH: Harrington, Honor (Fictitious character)—Fiction. | BISAC:
    FICTION / Science Fiction / Military. | FICTION / Science Fiction /
    Adventure. | GSAFD: Fantasy fiction. | Science fiction. | War stories.
Classification: LCC PS3573.E217 U63 2018 | DDC 813/.54—dc23
LC record available at https://lccn.loc.gov/2018023334

10 9 8 7 6 5 4 3 2

Pages by Joy Freeman (www.pagesbyjoy.com)
Printed in the United States of America

For Elijah Dimas and Bill Berden,
two of the faces we've lost.
God bless, guys.

JULY 1922 POST DIASPORA

Unicorn Belt
Manticore B
Star Empire of Manticore

THE SHUTTLE DRIFTED THROUGH starlight and emptiness, a minnow threading through a pod of dead leviathans.

If there was a sadder sight in the entire universe, Captain Philip Clayton couldn't imagine what it might be. He sat in the pilot's couch, his copilot silent beside him, gazing out through the cockpit's armor-plast at a Sargasso Sea of starships, and wondered yet again what he truly felt.

It shouldn't be that hard to figure out, really. He'd fought hard enough to create this mass of murdered ships, after all. Yet it *had* been an act of murder, not war. Not really. Not when the Solarian League Navy had been so utterly outclassed.

And not when it had been offered the opportunity to survive... and rejected it.

"I never get tired of seeing it, Sir," Lieutenant Kalet said. Clayton looked at his copilot, and the tall, broad shouldered Manticoran shrugged. "It's...it's like nothing else in the galaxy," he murmured, looking back out from his own side of the cockpit. "I mean, *look* at it."

"I know," Clayton said quietly.

Two hundred and eleven warships—or what had been warships a T-month ago—floated in their lonely parking orbit, keeping deathwatch station on Manticore-B's Unicorn Belt. A hundred and thirty-one superdreadnoughts—sixty-nine *Scientist*-class ships and sixty-two of the newer, marginally more powerful *Vegas*—lay like vanquished titans at the heart of that huddle of beaten ships. Sixty of them were completely undamaged; the others ranged from near-total wrecks to ships which might actually have been repairable...if there'd been any reason *to* repair them. They were accompanied by twenty-nine battlecruisers, twenty-three light cruisers, and twenty-eight destroyers, which actually represented a higher percentage of Eleventh Fleet's original roster of lighter units. Probably because there'd been no reason to waste missiles on such insignificant foes.

The superdreadnoughts alone massed over 900 million tons. Compared to that, the battlecruisers and lighter units were a mere nothing, barely thirty-two million tons. And here they lay, abandoned—aside from caretaker crews on half a dozen of the undamaged SDs—waiting.

Waiting, as it happened, for Phil Clayton, and he wondered again how he'd drawn the duty. Oh, he had the engineering background for it, but so did a lot of other officers, and he hated his new assignment. Maybe they had been enemy vessels, but they'd been *ships*, and he'd loved the inner magic of ships for as long as he could recall.

His earliest memories were of standing with his nose pressed to the window on the south side of his parents' modest house, watching the atmospheric counter-grav freighters drive across the heavens, splashed in sunlight and cloud shadow, gleaming like the Tester's own promise of beauty. Pygmies compared to the doomed ships outside his shuttle at the moment, but enormous for pre-Alliance Grayson.

And even more so for the imagination of a little boy who'd realized even then that ships had souls. That anything that lovely, that graceful—anything that many men had given so much of themselves to—*had* to be alive itself. He'd watched them summer and winter, in sunlight, in driving rain, in snow. He'd watched them at night, roaring low overhead in a bellow of turbines, flanks gleaming with their own private constellations of running lights. By the time he was ten, he'd been able to identify every major class by sight. And when he'd climbed up into the attic (which he'd been able to do only when all of his moms assumed one of the others had him in sight), he could actually get an angle down onto Burdette Port's docks, where those massive constructs landed.

Oh, the cargoes he'd summoned from dreams of other steadings! The pallets and boxes, the containerized cargo, the nets of fruit and vegetables. He'd watched stevedores unload the cavernous holds—there'd been far more muscle power and far less automation at the time—and wished he was one of them. And he'd devoured everything he could find in print and on vid about not just the atmospheric ships, but about the freighters that called on Grayson, however rarely, from far beyond his own horizons. He'd ingested anything and everything, from the ballad of the *Wreck of the Steadholder Fitzgerald* to the mystery of the colony ship *Agnes Celeste* and her vanished crew, and he'd known what he wanted.

Not that there'd ever be much chance he could have it.

His parents had been relatively well-off, by Grayson standards, but certainly not wealthy, and like all too many Grayson families, he'd been the only boy. Besides, Grayson was the backside of nowhere. The atmospheric freighters that fascinated him so spent their time hauling purely Grayson products and produce, because there was none from anywhere else. What chance did a boy from Burdette Steading have of ever seeing another star, smelling the air of a planet that didn't try to poison him every day of his life?

That had been his father's opinion, at any rate, and all of his mothers had loyally shared it, although Mom Joan had seemed just a little less convinced than the others. She always had appreciated that stubborn streak of his.

He never had gotten aboard one of the atmo-freighters. For that matter, he'd never gotten aboard a space freighter. But he'd gotten into space, anyway, and now, as he gazed at that endless vista of captive warships, looked at the torn and shredded armor—at the ink-black holes punched deep into core hulls and the blown out scabs of armor where life pods had erupted into space—he remembered another ship, in other battles. He remembered GMS *Covington* and the Battle of Yeltsin, the Battle of Blackbird. He remembered the stench of smoke and burning flesh through the ventilators, the scream of damage alarms, the incoming missiles and the indescribable shockwave of hits lashing through her hull.

He remembered a young lieutenant, who'd known he was about to die defending his planet.

But that lieutenant had lived, instead, because a foreign-born woman, already wounded from the battle which had saved his Protector's life, had flung her ship and her crew between someone else's world and those who would have killed every human being on it without her. Which was how a considerably older captain of the Grayson Space Navy, serving in the Protector's Own, found himself here, playing sorter of the slain to the Solarian League Navy.

"What's the latest from Seven, David?" he asked Lieutenant Kalet.

"They're about ready for the first tranche," Kalet replied, keying up the report on his uni-link, and grimaced. "They're due to finish the last of the Yawata Strike wreckage by Tuesday."

"I don't know which is worse—that, or *this*." Clayton waved at the silently waiting starships.

"Believe me, Sir, it's the Yawata wreckage." Kalet's expression was grim. "These people," he twitched his head at the same starships, "got hammered because they frigging well deserved it. We didn't go looking for them; *they* came looking for *us*. I'm sorry it got so many of them killed, but that's what happens when you attack somebody without bothering to declare war first. And at least every damned one of those ships was at battle stations, with everybody aboard in skinsuits. Not so much for the Yawata Strike."

The lieutenant turned to stare out at the barely visible cluster of working lights that marked the enormous Unicorn Seven asteroid complex. The Hauptman Cartel's Unicorn Salvage Yard and the Unicorn Seven refineries had been repurposed as one of the Manticore-B reclamation centers, processing the wreckage from the orbital infrastructure which had been torn to pieces in the Yawata Strike less than five T-months ago.

"The reclamation crews are still finding bodies Search and Rescue missed," he said. "Last week, one of the Seven crews found their own forewoman's cousin." His nostrils flared. "I'm sure we'll find a few bodies when we start scrapping these, too, but at least they won't be our damned *relatives!*"

Clayton nodded. He was grateful he'd been spared from the cleanup after the Blackbird Strike, but he knew enough men—and women, now—in the GSN who hadn't been.

"There was a curse back on Old Earth," he said. "I don't know if you Manties have it, but we still have it back on Grayson. It goes 'May you live in interesting times.'"

"'Interesting times,' is it?" Kalet snorted. "Well, that's one way to put it, Sir. More 'interesting' for some than for others, though."

"Look at it this way," Clayton turned back to the flight controls, "one day we'll all be in the history books and some idiot child—just like the idiot children you and I were, once upon a time—will dream about how exciting and glorious it all must have been. Maybe they'll be luckier than we are and not find out how wrong they are."

HMS *Imperator*
Manticore A
Star Empire of Manticore

FLEET ADMIRAL LADY DAME Honor Alexander-Harrington, Duchess and Steadholder Harrington, commanding officer, Grand Fleet, finished tucking in her white, turtleneck uniform blouse and reached up to pull the pins which had confined her hair on top of her head while she showered. The long braid fell almost to her waist, and she allowed herself to luxuriate in the sensual silkiness of it as she unbraided it, then brushed it into a shimmering tide. She usually kept it braided when in uniform, but there was no sense pretending she hadn't grown to love the way it felt loose. Besides, she was scheduled for a state dinner groundside later that evening, and she'd be attending in her persona as a Grayson steadholder, not an officer of the Queen.

She finished brushing, slid the brush into its storage slot, and gathered the hair at the back of her head with a hairband of Harrington green. She cocked her head to assess the effect, then frowned slightly and leaned closer to the mirror while the fingers of her right hand explored the tenderness of the skin under one almond-shaped eye.

"Darn," she muttered as she realized it was going to bruise after all.

The long, sinuous, cream-and-gray treecat stretched along the bulkhead perch behind her bleeked a laugh, and she turned to glower at him.

"*Not* funny, Stinker!" Her tone was admirably stern despite the slight twitch of her lips. "You know how much grief Hamish is going to give me across the canapés if I turn up sporting a shiner!"

Nimitz only laughed harder, and the fingers of his true hands flickered.

"It was *not* my own fault!" she told him. "Spencer's still getting better, and I can't block *all* his hits."

More finger-flicker, and she snorted.

"The way my schedule's packed, I have to schedule sparring bouts whenever I can, and you know it. It's not my fault Elizabeth decided to throw this shindig tonight!"

Nimitz considered that for a second or two, then nodded grudgingly, and she laughed and scooped him off the perch. She cradled him in her arms, pressing her face into his silky, clean-smelling coat for a long moment, then carried him out of her palatial quarters' head into her day cabin. She crossed to the desk, let him flow out of her arms onto the perch above it, and settled into the body-conforming chair.

She touched the darkening bruise under her right eye again and shrugged. She'd just have to take a little extra care with her cosmetics, she decided. With luck, Hamish wouldn't even notice... which would spare her the unmerciful ribbing he'd administer if he did. She'd have been less worried if Emily had been going to be present to help divert his fire, but their wife was staying home at White Haven with the kids. That probably said something positive about her sanity.

She thought about that for a moment, then sighed and brought her terminal online for the first item on today's installment of her unending paper chase.

I really hate to think of the number of photons we slaughter every day on personnel reports, she thought glumly. *Talk about* genocide!

Her lips twitched in amusement, but then she shook her head and began skimming rapidly through the report before her.

✧   ✧   ✧

"Excuse me, My Lady, but that report you asked for is here."

"Don't you mean that *other* report I asked for?" Honor asked wryly, looking up from the readiness report on her desk display.

"Well, yeś," Commander Angela Clayton acknowledged. She wore the blue-on-blue of the Grayson Space Navy with the salamander flash of the Protector's Own, but her accent was Manticoran. In fact, it was pure Gryphon Highlands. "You *did* ask for it, though," she pointed out with something close to a twinkle.

Commander Clayton was a new addition to Honor's staff, serving both as a liaison with High Admiral Judah Yanakov and as Grand Fleet's logistics officer. A sturdy, no-nonsense sort, Commander Clayton. Although she'd been born in Rearson, the same barony as Anton Zilwicki, she'd become a citizen of Harrington Steading following five years of "loaner" service with the GSN, which explained why she habitually addressed Honor with the "My Lady" of a steadholder rather than the "Your Grace" of a Manticoran duchess.

It could get... confusing, sometimes.

"And what does Phil have to report?" Honor asked now.

"His survey crews are finished with the first half-dozen superdreadnoughts, My Lady," the commander replied. The almost-twinkle in her eye had faded and she sighed. "He purely hates the assignment. Says it makes him feel like a swamp grubber."

Honor grimaced at the simile. She knew Captain Clayton, just as she'd made it her business to know all of the Protector's Own captains, so she understood what Angela was saying, but he was being grossly unfair to himself. The Grayson swamp grubber was one of the more loathsome carrion eaters in the explored galaxy, and it was none too picky about how its meal turned *into* carrion.

"That aside, his report's about what we expected, except that his techs are a bit more impressed by the Sollies' current graser mount than anyone anticipated." Clayton shook her head. "I glanced at the specs, and he's right; that *is* an impressive piece of hardware, My Lady."

"Nobody ever said the Solarian League doesn't have good tech," Honor pointed out. "Their problem is they don't always have the *right* tech when they need it."

"Coupled with the fact that they think they *do*," Clayton agreed.

"Point," Honor conceded. She tipped back in her chair. "So, Phil's impressed by it?"

"Yes, My Lady. He did point out that he can't imagine what we'll do with all of them, though."

Honor nodded. No doubt quite a few people were wondering the same sorts of things, but they had to do *something* with the wreckage of Massimo Filareta's Eleventh Fleet. That was why its surviving units had been moved to Manticore-B after the Second Battle of Manticore. The *Massacre* of Manticore, really, she thought, eyes darkening in memory.

Under normal circumstances, they might have been parked somewhere as a potential bargaining chip to be returned to the other side following successful peace negotiations. Nobody seemed likely to be doing any negotiating anytime soon, however, and even if they'd been inclined to, no one would want Filareta's orphans back. In an era of pod-launched missiles, they were deathtraps, hopelessly obsolete both tactically and conceptually, however good the technology with which they'd been built.

Failing the possibility of repatriation, they'd normally have been sent to the ship breakers to be sawn up into chunks and run through the smelters and refineries for reclamation and separation. No one would have worried too much about the *technology*; all they would have wanted were the raw materials from which Manticore's voracious orbital industry would have built the newer and far more useful technology the Star Empire needed.

But that orbital industry had been hammered into ruin by the Yawata Strike in February. Five months later, it remained less than a shadow of a memory of what it once had been. The fabricating plants to *use* the raw materials were only beginning to be rebuilt, and even with every gram of assistance Beowulf and the Star Empire's new Havenite allies could provide, it would be at least six months before the fabricators and nano farms were back online once again. Even then, they'd possess only a fraction of their pre-Yawata capacity for a long time to come. Which was why Phil Clayton and his combined Manticoran-Grayson-Havenite salvage crews were crawling all over the captured Solarian ships. Their internal systems might be of Solarian manufacture, with all the compatibility headaches that promised, but they already existed. Under the circumstances, it made sense to see what could be removed for reuse—from fusion plants to reconfigurable molycircs to point defense lasers—before the gutted hulks were consigned to the reclamation platforms.

For that matter, Sandra Crandall's surviving units were Manticore-bound with minimal passage crews to share exactly the same fate. Hopefully they could find someone besides Captain Clayton to deal with them when they arrived.

"Well," she said now, "if nothing else, we could probably use the grasers for hellacious wormhole 'minefields.' Have you seen the design Admiral Foraker came up with for that?"

"No, I haven't, My Lady. I'll bet it was...interesting, though."

"Admiral Foraker does have a tendency to think outside the box," Honor acknowledged with a smile. "In this case, though, what she's suggested is basically an array of remotely deployed energy weapons. *Capital ship*-sized weapons, as a matter of fact. She's thinking something like Moriarty, not Mycroft. In fact, she's already worked out the quickest way to run up a remote platform tied into the central fire control system of a standard terminus fort."

"I thought that was what the minefields we already have were for, My Lady."

"Oh, they are! But those are basically one-shot—either bomb-pumped platforms or IDEWs that get one shot, then have to recharge between engagements. She's talking about feeding these things with broadcast power for the plasma capacitors. If her numbers hold up, they'd be good for at least five or six full-power shots each before the platforms had to shut down until the maintenance crews could recharge the capacitor reservoirs. So if these Solly grasers are as good as Phil seems to be suggesting, and given the fact that a *Scientist*-class SD mounts—what? sixty-four? sixty-five?—grasers, stripping a couple of hundred of them could let us build a really nasty defensive array, don't you think?"

"Yeah, I think you could call it that," Commander Clayton said, her expression suddenly very thoughtful indeed. The thought of what nine or ten *thousand* ship-of-the-wall-sized grasers could do to any target emerging from a wormhole terminus—when it could have neither wedge nor sidewalls for protection—was...sobering.

"I'm not sure how well it'll work out in the end," Honor said, "but

I've observed that Admiral Foraker tends to get what she goes after. And now that Admiral Hemphill's finally taken the *Weyland* R&D staff out to Bolthole..."

Clayton nodded. The notion of sharing the Star Empire's latest technology and research projects with a star nation with which it had been at war—cold or hot—for the better part of a T-century had... sat poorly with quite a lot of the RMN. In fact, there'd been enough passive resistance and foot-dragging to provoke a display of the famous Winton temper. Clayton hadn't been present for the meeting at which Empress Elizabeth had made her feelings on the subject abundantly, one might almost have said *super*-abundantly, clear, but Duchess Harrington had. And it was remarkable how quickly things had begun moving after that little interview.

On the other hand, the commander thought with a mental smile, it would appear there'd been just as much foot-dragging on the Havenite side when it came to telling their erstwhile enemies and present allies exactly where Bolthole itself lay. Not surprisingly, since it was so much closer to the Manticore System than to the Haven System. In fact, it was the next best thing to six hundred light-years from Nouveau Paris... and less than three hundred and fifty from Landing City.

No wonder ONI never found it, she thought. *We were busy looking for something in the Republic. It never even occurred to us to look on the far side of Manticore for it. And even if it had, a "lost colony" would've been the last thing we looked for!*

Still, Bolthole's location did explain why the Legislaturalists had selected it as a site for their secret naval base once the system more or less fell into the People's Republic's lap. And as a Gryphon Highlander—not to mention someone who'd married a Grayson—Angela Clayton had a better idea than most of what it had taken for the people of the planet Sanctuary to survive until Haven's survey crew rediscovered their existence at the end of the J-156-18(L)-KCR-126-06 warp bridge.

And how they found the place is a lot less important than what they've done with it since, she reminded herself. After the Yawata Strike's devastation here in Manticore, Bolthole had become easily the largest single shipbuilding facility of the entire Grand Alliance, not to mention the site of the redoubtable Shannon Foraker's R&D command.

So if there's one place in the galaxy none *of us want the people behind the Yawata Strike to find, it's damned well Bolthole!*

"Do we know how Bolthole's coming on Mycroft, My Lady?" she asked, and Honor smiled as she followed the commander's obvious chain of thought.

"It's going to be a while before they get the system fully up and running," she said, "but Admiral Hemphill's taking along an entire squadron of *Invictuses* to provide Apollo and Keyhole-Two coverage in the meantime. And I understand Admiral Foraker's already rung in some new variations on her sensor platforms. Once she and Hemphill sit down and put their heads together, the rest of the galaxy better hang onto its socks!"

"A thought that doesn't break my heart at all, My Lady," Clayton said. "Not one little bit."

SLNS *Québec*
Dzung System
Solarian League

"WELL, SIR, ALL I can say is that it's about frigging time," Captain Gabriella Timberlake growled, standing at Admiral Vincent Capriotti's shoulder as they gazed at the latest dispatch on Capriotti's display. The fact that the Dzung System was just under seventy light-years from Sol meant Task Force 783 had gotten the new general order sooner than most of the rest of the Solarian League Navy, and Capriotti wondered how the Navy's other flag officers were going to react to them.

For that matter, he wasn't entirely certain how *he* felt about them.

"I can't say I disagree, Gabby," he said finally. "On the other hand, if the stories about what happened to Eleventh Fleet and Admiral Crandall are anything to go by, this could get...interesting."

"One way to put it, Sir," Timberlake agreed. "On the other hand, I think I like the thinking behind this. The bastards can't have those killer missile pods and their damned superdreadnoughts *everywhere!*"

"They don't need to have them 'everywhere' to ruin our whole day," Capriotti pointed out. "They only have to have them wherever *we* turn up."

"I know, Sir." The admiral's flag captain shrugged. "Sooner or later, though, we've got to take it to them. And given what they did to Admiral Filareta, it looks like fleet engagements are going to be a really bad idea until our tech people can figure out how to match their damned missiles."

Capriotti nodded soberly. The Solarian League *did* need to "take it to" the Manties after the series of massive black eyes the Star Empire and its allies had handed the SLN. Despite any misgivings he might feel, he agreed with the captain about that. He just wished to hell he was more confident those in charge of the taking in question had at least a vague notion of what they were doing.

He wasn't prepared to wholeheartedly accept the Solarian news reports' version of what had happened to Massimo Filareta. According to the Manties, Eleventh Fleet had opened fire after being summoned to surrender. According to the "usually reliable sources" talking to the newsies "speaking off the record" because they weren't "authorized to disclose classified information," Filareta had *accepted* their surrender terms, then been blown out of space in an act of cold-blooded mass murder. And according to any official ONI analyses, no one in Old Chicago could find his arse with both hands and approach radar well enough to give one Vincent Capriotti a single damned clue which of those diametrically opposed analyses the Navy shared.

Not a good sign, he thought again. *Of course, Intelligence has been caught with its trousers around its ankles every step of the way* this *far. Maybe the* real *bad sign would be for the idiots to actually think they* did *know what happened!*

Vincent Capriotti was Battle Fleet from the ground up, and he'd known dozens—scores—of men and women in the ships Crandall and Filareta had lost. Like Timberlake, he wanted payback, and not just out of bloody-minded vengeance, although he was honest enough to admit that was a great deal of his motivation. In addition to that, however, he had a rather better idea than many of his Battle Fleet compatriots of just how critical the Office of Frontier Security's unofficial empire of "client star systems" truly was. And along with that, he recognized that OFS's arrangements were far more fragile than they might appear. The Solarian League literally couldn't afford what would happen to the federal government's cash flow if Frontier Security started shedding clients, and unless they demonstrated that they could stand up to the Manties, that was precisely what was going to happen.

On the other hand, the one thing of which Capriotti was certain was that if the Battle—or massacre, or whatever—of Manticore had been as short as both sets of reports suggested, he did *not* want to tangle with the sort of defenses Manties seemed to think were appropriate for major star systems.

Fortunately, judging from the synopsis of "Operation Buccaneer," that wasn't what Admiral Kingsford had in mind. So maybe someone in Old Chicago *did* have a clue what he was doing.

Maybe.

"All right," he said finally, turning away from the dispatch to gaze at SLNS *Québec*'s main astrogation plot. "I need to get Admiral Helland and Admiral Rutgers up to speed on this. I'm sure they'll both have useful input. Once Rutgers stops warning us not to be overly optimistic, of course."

His lips twitched and Timberlake actually chuckled. Rear Admiral Lyang-tau Rutgers, Task Force 783's operations officer, had started out in Frontier Fleet and transferred to Battle Fleet barely twenty years ago.

That hadn't been long enough to completely free him of the basic Frontier Fleet attitude that Battle Fleet would have made an excellent paperweight, especially if that got it out of the way of the people doing the Navy's *real* work. Along the way, he'd been known to offer pithy analyses of just how out of date Battle Fleet's strategic and tactical thinking might have become and he'd argued strenuously that training simulations and fleet problems should be restructured to match the Navy against true peer competitors, despite the fact that "everyone knew" there were none in real life. When confronted with that fact, he'd suggested that it might be better to train against an opponent *better* than anyone one might actually have to fight. At least *that* error was unlikely to get anyone killed. Not, as his attitude had made evident, that he'd expected anyone in Battle Fleet to give much thought to that possibility.

The flag captain was pretty sure that attitude explained why an officer of Rutgers's obvious competence and with the Rutgers family's military and political connections was still only a *rear* admiral. But it was rather refreshing in a lot of ways, recent events had sure as hell validated his warnings, and she knew Capriotti both respected and genuinely appreciated his contrarian viewpoint.

Vice Admiral Angelica Helland, TF 783's chief of staff, on the other hand, reminded a lot of people of a smarter Sandra Crandall. Of course, she could hardly have been a *stupider* Sandra Crandall, now that Timberlake thought about it. The contrast between her aggressive near-arrogance and Rutgers's voice of caution made for occasionally fractious staff meetings, but it also offered Capriotti a robust debate between differing viewpoints. That was something he'd valued even before anyone started shooting at the SLN, which had been rare, to say the least, among Battle Fleet four-star admirals.

At the moment, Helland and Rutgers were in transit back to *Québec* from observing a training simulation aboard the battlecruiser *Bavaria*, the flagship of TG 783.12. Thanks to the classification level of the dispatch, they had no idea why they'd been summoned home so abruptly.

Be interesting to watch their reactions, the flag captain thought.

"Just between you and me, I'm all in favor of our not being 'overly optimistic,' Sir," she said aloud, and Capriotti nodded.

"You and me both," he agreed. "Please have me informed as soon as they come back aboard. In the meantime, I'm going to the flag briefing room. I want to go through this ammunition manifest. And I especially want to review ONI's most recent estimate of Manty missile capabilities."

He shook his head, his expression turning grimmer, and Timberlake raised an eyebrow at him.

"I've only skimmed it so far," he said, "but I'm inclined to think it's still...over optimistic, let's say."

The flag captain's raised eyebrow segued into a slight frown. She, too, had skimmed the new estimate. There'd been no time to go through the analysis itself, but the conclusions section had been depressing. Intelligence's current metric gave the Manties and their allies a three-to-one advantage in throw weight, a thirty percent advantage in penetration aids, and a maximum powered envelope of thirty million kilometers. That was more than enough to be going on with, in her opinion.

"I'm not saying Manties are ten meters tall, Gabby," Capriotti said wryly. "And the new Cataphracts can match any range they've got...if we incorporate a ballistic phase. But you and I both know Lyang-tau is right on the money when he says we totally underestimated what the Manties could do to us. Shouldn't have taken a genius—or so damned long—for ONI to realize that, either, which says some pretty unfortunate things about our prewar analysts. Since the shooting started, though, the Manties've made Lyang-tau's point for him painfully enough not even our brilliant masters can miss it. I'm delighted they've sent us these new missiles, and I understand that Technodyne's tweaked their performance again. But until I've got something just a little more solid than 'our best guess' about enemy capabilities from the same idiots who brought us Sandra Crandall and Eleventh Fleet, I'm not going to make any rash assumptions about miraculously level playing fields."

"Works for me, Sir." Timberlake shook her head. "Better we over-estimate them than *under*estimate them!"

"Fortunately it sounds like someone back in Old Chicago's figured that out, too." Capriotti twitched his head at the dispatch they'd just finished viewing. "I can't say I'm delighted at the notion of blowing up anyone's star systems. That's not what I joined the Navy to do, and I have friends living in Cachalot, for that matter. But whoever came up with this idea, whether it was Admiral Bernard or Admiral Kingsford himself, I think it's the best one available to us at the moment. If we can cause enough pain to their peripheral star systems or the independent star nations trading with them, they'll have to disperse at least some of their forces to commerce and infrastructure protection. And the more we can keep them dispersed, the more likely we are to encourage a certain...circumspection on their part until Technodyne finally figures out how to build a genuine multidrive missile of our own."

Timberlake nodded, although both of them understood the additional point Capriotti had chosen not to make. Operation Buccaneer wasn't just about forcing the Manties and their allies to spread themselves thinner. In fact, that wasn't even what it was primarily about. Its *real* purpose was to warn anyone who might even think about signing up with the Manties, whether as ally or simple trading partner, that the decision would be...unwise. That the SLN would consider that anyone who sided with Manticore had just sided *against* the Solarian League, and that the consequences would be dire enough to discourage anyone else from following her example.

In fact, it was a terror campaign, directed against those unable to defend themselves. And if anyone might have missed that little point, TF 783's assigned target would make it abundantly clear.

The Cachalot System, 50.6 LY from Dzung and only 49.6 LY from Beowulf, was an independent system which had opted against joining the Solarian League when it was initially founded. It was also a prosperous, heavily populated system which had been a Beowulf trading partner for the better part of a thousand years...and depended on the Beowulf System Defense Force to provide its rapid response security force. Its organic "military forces" consisted of no more than a couple of dozen frigates and LACs, because no one would be insane enough to attack someone so closely associated with one of the League's founding and most powerful star systems.

Until now, at least.

She wondered just how explicitly Kingsford or Brenner, the CO of Strategy and Planning, had admitted Buccaneer's true objectives in the detailed operational orders. And, while she was wondering, she wondered how many of those independent and nominally independent star systems would recognize that the League was choosing to target *them* because it dared not attack the members of the "Grand Alliance" directly.

Bit of a potential downside, there, Gabby my girl, she reflected, then shrugged mentally. *Maybe that's another reason to pick Cachalot. It's close enough to Beowulf that systems farther out in the Fringe may not realize how lightly defended it is. Even if they do, we've got to do something, though, and thank God no one is planning on sending us after one of the Manties' primary star systems! Given how quick they smashed up Filareta...*

Her thought trailed off, and she nodded again, more firmly.

"I just hope Technodyne—or somebody—gets its thumb out and moves right along with that multidrive missile of yours, Sir!"

GSNS *Protector Oliver I*
Manticore Binary System
Star Empire of Manticore

"HONOR!"

Michael Mayhew turned with a smile as Honor and Mercedes Brigham followed the earnest-faced young ensign who'd been their escort from *Protector Oliver I*'s boat bay. Soft music played in the background, stewards circulated with trays of finger food and wine glasses, and conversation hummed in the background as he held out his hand. Honor gripped it firmly, smiling back at him, and Nimitz chittered a greeting of his own from her shoulder. Mayhew laughed and extended his hand to the treecat, in turn, and Honor chuckled.

Even as she did, though, she couldn't avoid the reflection that Mayhew, who was twenty years her junior, looked at least ten years her *senior*. That was the difference between the third-generation prolong she'd received as a child and the *first*-generation prolong he'd received when he was already adult. And even so, he looked far younger than his older brother, Benjamin.

"It's good to see you," Mayhew continued, then grimaced. "I know—I know! We see each other a lot, either on the com or in person, but that's always official business. I suppose this is, too, in a way, but at least the two of *us* don't have to talk shop tonight!"

"That will be something of a relief," she acknowledged. "There are times I find myself forgetting I'm an honest spacer, given all the time I spend in conferences, discussions, planning sessions, *worry* sessions..."

She shrugged and Mayhew nodded.

"I know. And it'll get even worse after the Beowulf referendum is certified. Getting them integrated into the Alliance is going to take some doing."

"With all due respect, My Lord, not as much as you might be thinking," another voice said, and Honor turned with a smile as a blue-eyed man in the uniform of a Grayson rear admiral joined the conversation.

"Michal!" she said. "I was wondering where you were."

"Well, I wouldn't want to say anything about the heirs of a planetary

18

ruler short-circuiting proper military etiquette or anything like that," Rear Admiral Michal Lukáč, commanding officer of First Battle Division, Sixth Battle Squadron, GSN, said. "But as I'm sure you and Commodore Brigham understand perfectly, the correct procedure is for you to be greeted by Captain White first."

Honor looked around quickly, then back at Lukáč.

"At least you waited until that poor ensign wasn't around to hear you," she said severely. "It wasn't his fault Michael here shortstopped me!"

"Excuse me," Mayhew said with a smile, "but unless I'm mistaken, I'm the brother of a planetary despot. That means I get to jump the queue when I feel like it."

"The fact that you're in a position to abuse your authority doesn't make it right," Honor told him. "And Michal is completely correct." She craned her neck, looking for Captain Zachary White, *Protector Oliver*'s commanding officer and Lukáč's flag captain. Since White was easily six centimeters taller than she was, he was seldom hard to spot. This time, though—

"Where *is* Zach?"

"Actually," Lukáč said, "at this particular moment, he's helping Misty deal with a slight emergency. Edward and a tray of canapés were in a head-on collision."

"Oh, my!" Honor shook her head. "I am *so* not looking forward to Raoul turning eight!"

"Young Edward is actually very well behaved, especially by the standards of Grayson males," Michael Mayhew told her.

"Yes, and this wasn't his fault," Lukáč said. "Despite Zach's centimeters, Edward's still not very tall, you know. The steward just didn't see him. In fact, the real reason Zach's helping deal with it is that Edward's upset. He thinks he ruined his dad's party, so I told Zach to nip off to reassure him and that I'd hold the fort until he got back. I think I remember reading somewhere that a good flag officer always has his flag captain's back."

"That's what I'd heard, at any rate," Honor said. "But what was this about 'not as much as you might be thinking'? From where I sit, getting Beowulf fully integrated's going to be something like Hercules and the stables."

"I don't think so," Lukáč disagreed respectfully. "Oh, it's going to take a lot of work, and a lot of details will need hammering out, but the truth is that Beowulf's already effectively part of the Alliance. I mean, whose ships do you think are out there helping rebuild after Yawata? And unless I'm mistaken, Beowulf's also who's building the Mark 23s in our magazines. So what we'll really be doing is regularizing something that's been going on on a de facto basis for months now."

"That's actually true, in a way," Michael Mayhew acknowledged. "It's the regularizing and the hammering out I'm not looking forward to."

"No reason you should, My Lord," Lukáč told him. "And, in fairness, it'll be a lot easier for us 'honest spacers' who only have to worry about shooting at the enemy. Besides—"

"Is Michal already bending your ear, My Lady?" another voice asked, and Honor turned as Captain Lenka Lukáčová joined the conversation. Lukáčová was about four centimeters shorter than her husband. She wore GSN uniform with the four golden cuff bands of a captain, but she also wore the Chaplains Corps's crosses on her collar, not the sword insignia of a line officer.

"He promised he wouldn't do that," she continued, gold-flecked green eyes dancing.

"And he isn't, Lenka, as you know perfectly well!" Honor told her. "In fact, he's hardly started making his points forcefully at *all* yet."

"Give him time," Lukáčová suggested.

"I'm sure. And how are *you*? Any problems adjusting?"

She'd tried to stay in the loop as Task Force Three, the Grayson component of Grand Fleet, settled into place. It helped that Manticorans and Graysons had been serving—and dying—together for two T-decades. But there were still differences between them and a much larger percentage of the entire Grayson Space Navy had been permanently stationed here in Manticore following the Yawata Strike and the emergence of the Grand Alliance. Despite the enormous strides Honor's adoptive homeworld had made, Grayson remained a highly religious, theocratic society. The Manticore Binary System as a whole had less experience than the RMN's officer corps with Graysons, and quite a few thousand Grayson civilians and dependents had arrived in Manticore to help support TF 3. Sliding them comfortably into a society whose basic constraints were sharply at odds with those of the society which had produced them was a nontrivial challenge. Lukáčová, as the senior officer of the Chaplains Corps assigned to TF 3 had a ringside seat for that sliding.

"Quite well, actually," the captain said now. "Archbishop Telmachi couldn't have been more helpful, although I think most of your fellow Manties are still a little ... bemused by the entire notion of official shipboard chaplains. Fair's fair, though. Most of our people still have problems with the notion that the archbishop is only the senior prelate in a society which specifically *rejects* the notion of a state church. Some of my chaplains seem to have a little trouble understanding he can't simply wave his crucifix and make all of our stumbling blocks go away. You really *are* a deplorably secular bunch, aren't you?"

"We stagger along as best we can," Honor said. "And let's not forget that it was the example of our 'deplorably secular bunch' that got Father Church to reconsider his position on priests who didn't have Y chromosomes."

Michal Lukáč flung up his hand in the gesture of a Grayson judge at a fencing match, and his wife laughed.

"I've *missed* you, My Lady," she said. "But you're right, of course." She rolled her eyes. "I can still remember all the apoplexy when Reverend Sullivan ordained me. I thought at least three of the Elders would be carried off to glory that afternoon." She smiled in fond memory. "And the way they waffled about titles!" She shook her head. "Do you know how close I came to being *Brother* Lenka? The Sacristy had actually written a learned dissertation about the 'sanctity' of the title. Thank the Tester the Reverend cut them off at the ankles!"

"For some reason," Michael Mayhew said to no one in particular, "for the last twenty years or so Grayson seems to have been producing an unconscionable number of uppity females. Can't imagine how that happened."

"Well, it's certainly not *my* fault," Honor said austerely. "In fact, it's probably more Mercedes' fault. Or hers and"—Honor looked over Lukáč's shoulder as two more officers approached—"Captain Davis's."

"Whatever it was, I didn't do it," the dark-haired captain—one of the *two* dark-haired captains—approaching the small conversational group said.

"Her Grace was just explaining that it's not *her* fault Grayson females are getting out of hand," Brigham said dryly, holding out her hand.

"Oh, no!" Captain Elizabeth Davis, Lukáč's operations officer said. "How could anyone *possibly* think *that*?"

"Not enough we have to produce them in a homegrown variety, but we go around *importing* them," Mayhew observed, still to no one in particular, and Davis laughed.

Her own accent marked her as a native of the Star Kingdom's capital planet, but like quite a few of the officers who'd been "loaned" to the modern Grayson Space Navy in its infancy, she'd decided she liked Grayson. In fact, she'd become a Grayson citizen almost ten T-years ago. Lord Mayhew rolled his eyes at her laugh, but he also held out his hand.

"And we've been damned lucky to get them—*all* of them," he said in a quieter tone. "Homegrown or imported."

"I have to agree," Honor said. "But you know, the really remarkable thing to me, even after all these years, is how well Grayson's grappled with all the changes."

"Part of that's the example we've been given," Lukáčová said. "And Reverend Hanks's input at the very beginning was huge." Her eyes darkened, and so did Honor's as she recalled how the gentle Reverend had given his life for hers. "And Reverend Sullivan's been just as strong in his own way. But the bottom line is that unlike those lunatics on Masada, we haven't forgotten the Book is never closed. They not only refused to stop *listening* to God, they started lecturing Him on the way things were *supposed* to be." She shook her head. "We've had our own iterations of the Faithful to deal with, but by and large, they did us a huge favor. All we had to do was look at them to see exactly what God *didn't* want us doing." She shrugged. "With that example, how could we not get it right...mostly, anyway."

"I think you're probably right," the officer who'd accompanied Davis said. He was a good twenty centimeters taller, stocky and very squarely built, with a ship's prow of a nose and a ponytail that reminded Honor of Paul Tankersley's. Unlike Davis, he spoke with a pronounced Grayson accent.

"It's good to see you, James," Honor said.

"And you, My Lady." Captain James Sena, BatDiv 1's chief of staff said. "Actually, though, I'm even happier to see Commodore Brigham. I was wondering if—"

"Stop *right* there," Rear Admiral Lukáč said, raising an index finger.

"But, Sir, after that exercise yesterday, we've got to figure out—"

"You're on dangerous ground, James," Lukáč said solemnly.

"Sir?" Captain Sena regarded his superior with a suspicious eye, and Honor's lips twitched.

James Sena was one of the GSN's outstanding administrators. Although he was an excellent combat officer—one of the best—he was far more valuable in his current position. He didn't *like* it, because he would far rather have been on a battlecruiser's command deck somewhere, but he wasn't the sort who complained. He was a no-nonsense, focused, very much to the point individual, however, and there were times when he found his admiral's puckish sense of humor more than a little trying.

"Lord Mayhew just informed us, immediately before your arrival, that we are *not* to talk shop tonight," Lukáč said firmly, blue eyes twinkling. "And as obedient subjects, it behooves us to obey him."

"It's a good thing it's my *brother* who's the despot—and owns all the headsmen—and not me," Mayhew observed.

"Oh, I'm sure!" Honor said.

In fact, everyone in the GSN knew Michael Mayhew had been "navy mad" since childhood. Only the fact that it had taken his older brother so long to produce the male heir the Grayson constitution required had kept him out of uniform before Grayson had joined the Manticoran Alliance. And only the fact that Benjamin had needed him so desperately as his personal envoy had prevented him from seeking a naval career afterward. That was the real reason officers like Lukáč and Sena were prepared to be so informal with him. He was one of their own, and he'd always had a very special, very personal relationship with the GSN and its personnel. They knew how deeply he loved the Navy, and they loved him right back.

"Ah!" Mayhew said now as an extraordinarily tall officer approached them. "Captain White!"

"My Lord." Zachary White bowed to Mayhew, and then to Honor. "My Lady." He shook his head. "I'm sorry I wasn't here to greet you, Lady Harrington. My son—"

"Admiral Lukáč told us about it, Zach," Honor said, shaking her head as she held out her hand to the much shorter woman who'd accompanied White across the crowded compartment. She was one of the relatively few civilians present, and on her, the traditional Grayson gown looked good. Although her particular version of it wasn't quite as "traditional" as many. Honor doubted she was wearing more than three petticoats.

"Is he all right, Misty?" she asked, and Madam White smiled.

"I think he's pretty much indestructible," she said. "He was just *so* upset over 'messing up Dad's party.'"

"He really was," Captain White agreed, and looked at Lukáč. "I really appreciate your taking over the host's duties, Sir. His mom could *tell* him I wasn't mad at him, but he was upset enough with himself that I think he needed the paternal reassurance."

"Lenka and I may not have any of our own, Captain, but I've got five siblings," Lukáč said dryly. "And thanks to Skydomes and our little population explosion, the last time I looked, I've got somewhere around—the number is subject to change without warning, you understand—thirty-seven nieces and nephews, at least four of whom have started producing children of their own!"

White chuckled, and nodded greetings to the other officers clustered around Mayhew.

"How's he doing overall—here in Manticore, I mean?" Honor asked Misty, and she shrugged.

"He misses his friends and his classmates, My Lady," she said, "but it's not like he's not making new ones, and he's actually ahead of his age-mates academically." Her smile might have held a slight edge. "I don't think those new classmates of his expected that. And the experience of actually *living* somewhere besides Grayson is going to be really, really good for him." She shrugged. "Besides, the truth is that everyone here in Manticore is bending over backward to make all of us Graysons welcome. It shows, believe me."

Honored nodded. As a steadholder—and, aside from Mayhew, the *only* steadholder in the Manticore Binary System—she'd felt a personal responsibility to represent the Grayson dependents who'd accompanied the GSN. Unfortunately, she couldn't. There simply weren't enough hours in the day, and so she was enormously relieved by how well things seemed to be going. And one reason they were going so well was the smiling woman standing beside her towering husband.

In many ways, Misty White was Lenka Lukáčová's civilian counterpart. While Lukáčová dealt with the Chaplains Corps's issues, Madame White was attached to the Grayson Family Support Command. Technically, that was a military organization, headed by Captain Leonard Fitzhugh and she was only a "civilian advisor." Fortunately, Fitzhugh was smart enough to stay out of the way when Misty White rolled up her sleeves and went to work.

"I'm glad it's going well," Honor said now. "I'd heard reports that it was, but I'm behind the curve on a lot of things."

"I can't imagine how that could possibly be the case, My Lady," Misty said.

"I'm sure you can't," Honor said warmly, slipping her left arm through Misty's right. "But unless my eyes deceive me, it looks like Michal's flag lieutenant is headed this way to tell us that now that the two of you have rejoined us, it's time for dinner. And as you may have heard, I'm from Sphinx." She smiled at the others. "Which is to say, I'm hungry...again."

"My Lady," Lukáčová said frankly, "I would *kill* for your metabolism. I really would."

"Oh?" Honor gave Misty a conspiratorial smile. "Well, if you think three o'clock feedings are bad for most children, you should think about trying to keep somebody with the Meyerdahl mods fed! My mom's made a few...pithy comments on that task over the years. They include references to somebody named Sisyphus."

"Oh, my!" Misty laughed. "I hadn't even *thought* of that, My Lady!"

"Trust me, Raoul's going to be repaying my karmic debt to my parents for the next—oh, seventeen or eighteen T-years. There are some aspects of parenting I look forward to less than others."

"Maybe, My Lady," Misty said, smiling as a petty officer came forging through the press of senior officers, towing a small, spotlessly clad boy child towards them. "But trust me, when the dust settles, it will have been worth every minute of it. Every single minute."

"Oh, I believe you," Honor said softly as she and Misty moved to greet young Master Edward White. "I believe you."

Hillary Indrakashi Enkateshwara Tower
City of Old Chicago
Sol System
Solarian League

"EITHER THERE ARE AN awful lot of these moles, or our search algorithms need some serious tweaking."

Lieutenant Colonel Weng Zhing-hwan sat back from the terminal, rubbing tired eyes with her left hand, and her tone was as sour as her expression. Then she inhaled deeply and reached for her cup of tea. She sipped, grimaced at the way it had cooled, and refreshed it from the pot at her elbow.

That pot had come from her own apartment. The dingy little office buried in the bowels of a building the Commerce Department used primarily for storage had been sealed and unused for over thirty T-years before Major Bryce Tarkovsky discovered it a couple of years ago. At the time, he'd planned to put it to use as a spot for friendly interservice games of chance at which he and his fellow spooks could talk shop without any inconvenient superiors catching them at it. Under the circumstances, he'd decided she and her coconspirators needed it rather more badly, and she supposed she was grateful. It would have been nice if it had come with at least *some* amenities, though.

And the dust had been pretty bad, too.

"The interesting thing," Captain Daud al-Fanudahi replied in a more philosophical voice, tipping back in his chair and resting his heels on one end of the desk between them, "is how long how many of our potential moles have been in position. Or working their way into it, at any rate."

"Assuming they really are bad guys," Weng pointed out. "Even if they are, getting into some of these slots—" she waved her teacup at the neat columns of names on her display "—was bound to take a while. And if they *aren't*—bad guys, I mean—then what looks like 'working their way into position' is simply the normal pursuit of an open and aboveboard career."

"Which is exactly how any defense counsel would present it." It was al-Fanudahi's turn to look sour.

25

"It has occurred to you, I trust, that we may all be suffering from paranoia?" Weng asked.

"Upon occasion." He snorted. "On the other hand, I'm not in favor of finding out whether or not we're paranoid by going public. What about you?"

"Not just yet, thank you," she said dryly.

"Pretty much what I thought." He shrugged. "And apropos of that point, and bearing in mind your comment about search algorithms, I'm a little nervous about our potential exposure. I really appreciate Brigadier Gaddis's support, but if anybody happens to look over his shoulder at the computer runs involved in all this..."

He let his voice trail away, and Weng nodded. Her expression seemed rather less concerned than his, though.

"He's been playing this game—well, this *sort* of game—for a long time, Daud," she said. "He got the Criminal Investigation Division because he's damned good at his job and because he's interested in really catching bad guys, and no one gives him any crap because he knows where way too many bodies are buried. Metaphorically speaking, of course."

"Oh, of course!" al-Fanudahi agreed.

"Well, I thought it was an important distinction."

She sipped more tea while he chuckled, then lowered the cup once again.

"My point is that people—especially people with something to hide—tend to stay far, far away from anything that might draw his attention. Given the...summary fashion in which he's dealt with anyone poking into one of his investigations in the past, snooping around in one of his data searches is what I believe you military types call 'contraindicated.'"

"Under normal circumstances, I'd feel reassured by that," al-Fanudahi said soberly. "But if we're anywhere close to right about what's going on, the people we're looking for this time around are the sort who've never seen a problem they weren't willing to kill. I don't see any reason they wouldn't be willing to apply the same prescription to him. In fact, I'm pretty sure they'd be perfectly happy to kill him and however many other people it took if they got even a hint of what he's looking for."

"CID is the last place anyone would expect to find a counterintelligence op. That's Noritoshi Väinölä's bailiwick...and exactly the reason neither Lupe Blanton nor I went anywhere near him with this. And it's a pain in the arse, too, because I'm pretty damn sure Väinölä's as straight as they come in the Gendarmerie." She grimaced in obvious frustration. "The problem is—"

"That if he *is* straight, and if this is the kind of operation he'd normally be in charge of, then he's the one our bad guys are going to keep the closest eye on," al-Fanudahi finished for her, and she nodded.

"Exactly. Simeon, on the other hand, always has at least a dozen sensitive investigations underway at any given moment. Adding one more's a lot less likely to trigger any alarms than sudden activity on Väinöla's part would."

"I can see that." Al-Fanudahi nodded, and he sounded a bit less worried, although his expression still wasn't what anyone would have called happy.

"The other thing he's got going for him," Weng continued, setting her cup back on the saucer and paging ahead through the file on her display, "is that he's spent the last twenty or thirty years assembling a team whose primary loyalty is to *him*. He calls them his Outcasts because the only thing they give a solitary damn about is catching the bad guys, *whoever* they are and whatever the consequences to their careers might be."

"Like Okiku?"

"Not so much, really." Weng frowned for a moment, obviously looking for exactly the right way to explain. "Okiku's got exactly the same attitude, but he's kept her outside the Outcasts. Pissed her off a time or two, too."

"Why?" Al-Fanudahi's eyebrows arched. "I'd think she'd be a perfect fit!"

"Oh, in so many ways, she would," Weng agreed, and smiled. She'd come to know Lieutenant Colonel Natsuko Okiku rather better in the past few weeks, and in the process, she'd come to appreciate exactly why Simeon Gaddis had kept her away from his "Outcasts." In fact—

"Why did you tell Irene to keep her mouth shut and let *you* take the heat for being right about the Manties' capabilities?" she asked.

Al-Fanudahi looked at her, then nodded.

"Point taken," he said. "He thinks she's too valuable down the road for him to burn her career at this point."

"Which makes it sort of ironic that she was so busy sneaking around behind his back when Bryce brought her into your little conspiracy." Weng chuckled. "She didn't want to risk any of it splashing on her boss, and now her boss is keeping her outside his circle of analysts to keep anyone from linking her with them."

"I don't have any problem with that," al-Fanudahi told her. "Especially if anyone's noticed that she's been talking to me and Irene—or you and Lupe, for that matter. The last thing we'd need would be for someone to connect her to us and then connect her to some supersecret research project over at CID."

"Exactly." Weng said again. "But my point is that unless one of his Outcasts is working for the bad guys, nobody's going to get a look inside his data searches. If someone's keeping a really close eye on him, they may be able to figure out what kind of information the Outcasts are looking at, but none of it's really all that unusual for a CID investigation, and there's a complete air break between their computers and the rest of the universe. That's pretty much standard, too."

It was al-Fanudahi's turn to nod again. The computer upon which he and Weng worked in their sessions here in their dingy little office was a portable unit completely isolated from Commerce's—or anyone else's—central core and processors. Nor was any of their data stored on it. All actual work was done on external memory chips, and he, Weng, Lupe Blanton, and Natsuko Okiku each had custody of a single chip biometrically coded to their personal DNA. That meant at least one of them was usually out of date, but it also meant no one could compromise their data without their knowing about it.

Of course, it also means that if it does *get compromised, it'll probably be because at least one of us is dead*, he reflected. *Still, if it was easy, anyone could play!*

"Well, like I say, either there are more of these people than we'd hoped there were, or else these Outcasts of his are pretty bad shots," he observed.

"One way to look at it." Weng tipped back her own chair and rotated it to face al-Fanudahi fully. "But let's not get too carried away just yet. What the Outcasts are telling us is that the names on this list all appear to be *associated* with at least one of the people we've already concluded is *probably* working for the bad guys. It's still way too early for us to conclude any of them are working directly for the bad guys. Or, for that matter, that they even realize the bad guys are out there!"

"Maybe it is, but we've got to get off the centicredit, Zhing-hwan. After what happened to Eleventh Fleet, I don't even want to think about what these people's next production's going to be like!" Al-Fanudahi shook his head, his dark brown eyes haunted by the thought of the hundreds of thousands of Solarian League Navy spacers who'd already died.

"Agreed. But until we have at least some idea of just what the hell is going on, nobody's going to take us seriously, and especially not if somebody they trust is telling them we're a bunch of lunatics."

"I know. That's why we've got to really drill into this. We think we know *what* they're doing, but until we've got that idea about *why* they're doing it we can't expect to convince anyone else we *aren't* lunatics. I'm beginning to think Bryce may have a point!"

"Major Tarkovsky is a very fine Marine," Weng said with a crooked smile, "and a superior analyst. He is, unfortunately, still a *Marine*. And there are occasions—difficult though I know he finds that to accept—when something moderately more subtle than a pulser dart or a KEW is called for. Especially since Simeon's probably right about just how bright our pool of suspects actually is. Like our friend Rajmund, for example. I know it pained Lupe when Simeon suggested Rajmund might not really be the unimaginative, corruptible clod she—and I, to be fair—always figured he was. For that matter, I'm still not thoroughly convinced he *isn't*. But it's a lot smarter for us to assume he isn't stupid than it is for us to assume he is. Because as successfully as these people seem to have set up their networks, the one thing they aren't is *dumb*. So while the notion of grabbing one of them and sweating her in a quiet little room somewhere possesses a certain appeal, I suggest we hold off on it at least a little longer."

"I know," al-Fanudahi repeated, then puffed his cheeks and exhaled noisily. "I know! But we're not going to get any official warrants on the basis of any 'probable cause' we can share with anyone higher up the food chain. That means the time's likely to come when we have to do it Bryce's way."

"Of course we are. I'm not looking forward to it, for a lot of reasons, but you're probably right about where we're going to end up. But if we've got to go entirely off the reservation and grab someone without benefit of due process, then I want to make sure we grab the *right* someone. Someone who really is the link we need between people like Rajmund and whoever the hell he's working for. Which is exactly what *this*"—she jabbed a finger at the columns of names—"is going to give us. Somewhere in all these names, Daoud, there's a handler. Somebody has to be managing their communications and coordinating their operations, and that probably means that whoever's doing it is in contact with more than one of their agents in place. That's who Simeon's Outcasts and their numbercrunching is going to find for us. And once we've found her, I'm likely to be just a little more inclined to give Bryce his head."

Office of Frontier Security HQ
Interior Department Tower
City of Old Chicago
Sol System
Solarian League

"YES, MARIANNE?" ADÃO UKHTOMSKOY tried not to sound impatient as Marianne Haavikko's image appeared in a window in the notes he'd been reviewing before his scheduled meeting with Nathan MacArtney, the Permanent Senior Undersecretary of the Interior.

Haavikko had been his secretary for a long, long time, and he knew she wouldn't have interrupted him on a whim. At the same time, she knew his schedule better than anyone else in the universe...including him. That meant she knew how important his review and preparation for this meeting was. As the CO of Frontier Security Intelligence Branch, Ukhtomskoy was MacArtney's senior "spook," and as the confrontation with the Star Empire of Manticore and its allies went further and further into the crapper, his meetings with his superior had become less than pleasant affairs. The permanent senior undersecretary had always had a tendency to take out his frustrations on his subordinates. He was also a micromanager, the sort who demanded detailed reports. Worse, he knew what he wanted—and expected—to hear before the reports were ever written. He could be counted upon to break the kneecaps of any subordinate who gave him the "wrong" details, but was equally vindictive with people who told him what he expected to hear...and were wrong about it. That made working for him challenging at the best of times, and with so many wheels coming off in the Fringe and Verge, there was no way to get reports *right* no matter how hard someone tried.

"I'm very sorry to disturb you, Sir," Haavikko said, and he realized she wasn't speaking into her hush phone. "I'm afraid Mr. Nyhus is here. I told him you're reviewing for an important meeting, but he insists on speaking to you."

He must really have pissed Marianne off for her to be making certain he can hear her. That was Ukhtomskoy's first thought. The second was: *And he'd better have a damn good* reason *for pissing her off, too. The bastard knows I'm meeting with MacArtney in less than an hour!*

"Did he say what he needs to speak to me about?"

"No, Sir. Just that it was urgent."

"I see." Ukhtomskoy frowned. Then he shrugged. If Nyhus was wasting his time, he was just likely to get his head ripped off this time. But if he *wasn't* . . .

"Send him in," he said.

"Yes, Sir."

His office door opened, and Rajmund Nyhus came through it. He was tall, with very fair hair and a dark complexion, and his expression was far from cheerful.

"I apologize for barging in this way," he said quickly, before Ukhtomskoy could speak. "I wouldn't have, except that I know you're supposed to be talking to MacArtney this afternoon. Under the circumstances, I thought I'd better bring you this immediately. And, frankly, it's sensitive enough I wanted to brief you on it personally."

Ukhtomskoy's eyebrows rose, despite himself. As the head of OFS Intelligence Branch's Section Two, Nyhus was responsible for analysis of internal threats to Frontier Security's operations. He was also deeply in bed with several of the Solarian League's more corrupt transstellars, and in most star nations, that would have been considered a conflict of interests. The Solarian League wasn't "most star nations," however.

"Brief me about what?" Ukhtomskoy said, waving the other man into one of the comfortable chairs in front of his desk.

"I got a pair of very disturbing reports this morning." Nyhus sank into the indicated chair. "One's about a problem we've been keeping an eye on for some time, but it's not really our responsibility, thank God. In fact, it was copied to me 'for information' from the Gendarmerie, not because anyone expects us to take any sort of action about it. According to the Gendarmes' sources, though, all indications are that the Hypatia referendum's going to come out with a clear majority for secession and political association with Beowulf. That's going to have some nasty implications for us—for the entire League—down the road, I think. But scary as it is, it's not nearly so worrisome, from our perspective, as the one I've received from the Maya Sector."

Ukhtomskoy frowned. He didn't like the sound of that at all, especially not if Nyhus thought whatever was happening in Maya was worse than the notion of a member system of the League deciding to follow Beowulf's example, kick the League to the curb, and sign on with the Manties. True, Hypatia was only modestly prosperous by Core World standards, but like its interstellar neighbor Beowulf, it had been a member of the League since the day it was founded. Its defection would have *major* implications for the League's cohesion, and Nyhus thought the Maya report was *worse?*

The Maya Sector had been one of Frontier Security's success stories for well over a T-century. In fact, in most ways, Maya was the crown jewel of the Protectorates: a highly prosperous, nine-star system sector, which had actually petitioned for Solarian "protection" a hundred and fifty T-years earlier. That was...unusual, to say the least, but the Mayans had seen Frontier Security coming for some time. Recognizing that OFS clienthood was clearly in their future, they'd begun preparing well ahead of time to make clienthood as tolerable as they could.

They'd understood they needed bargaining chips, so they'd actively courted investment by Solarian transstellars. But they'd simultaneously put local protections and controls into place—the sort of protections and controls Frontier Security clients were seldom in a position to hold out for. They'd wanted their investors to make a healthy profit, and they'd been willing to cooperate to make that happen, but they'd also wanted to be sure they retained a powerful voice in *how* those profits got made.

Their object had been to make the sector even more attractive to the League but in a way which would give them a certain leverage when the moment came. They'd made themselves into a golden goose, with such valuable preexisting relationships with so many transstellars that no one really wanted to destabilize them. In fact, they'd succeeded in turning the transstellars in question into their champions, ready and able to protect their existing relationships against interlopers when OFS started looking their way. At the same time, they'd made quiet contact with many of the bureaucrats who really ran the Solarian League. They'd understood discreet gifts could buy a lot of friendship, and they'd been careful to get on the career bureaucrats' good side.

And then they'd offered OFS a deal. They would accept Frontier Security protectorate status and an OFS-appointed sector governor, but they would retain local self-government *and* the appointee would have to be confirmed by a majority of the sector's voters. If he was rejected, OFS could always select another one, until a mutually acceptable candidate was reached, but whoever it was would have to be *mutually* acceptable. They would cough up the usual OFS "administrative fees," their transstellar "friends" would restrain the slash-and-burn rapaciousness which had devastated so many Fringe economies, and in return, they'd continue to manage their local affairs without infusions of Solarian Gendarmes or intervention battalions.

The arrangement had worked well for the last T-century and a half, although signs of increasing restiveness had begun to emerge among younger Mayans. For that matter, the Mayan business community was none too pleased by the way OFS had increased its fee schedules steadily for the last sixty or so T-years. Maya might not have been bitten as badly as many of the other Protectorates, but those "administrative fees" were taking a steadily bigger chunk of its revenues. Besides, whatever else they might be, Mayans were Fringers. They didn't much care for OFS's progressively uglier exploitation of other Fringe star systems.

Fortunately, Governor Oravil Barregos had proved capable of gentling a restive mount. He'd barely squeaked through the Mayan Assembly when he was first appointed as governor in 1912, probably because of the mounting local unhappiness with OFS's fee demands. But five years later, he'd been reconfirmed for a second term with sixty-eight percent of the vote. And in 1920, he'd won yet a third term—this time with a seventy-six-percent majority. In an era in which OFS governors considered themselves popular if no one was actively trying to blow up their air cars, Barregos genuinely *was* popular. Not only that, he seemed to be in the process of wooing Erewhon—and its wormhole—back into the Solarian fold from its alliances with first Manticore and then Haven.

At a time when the entire galaxy seemed to be catching fire, Maya represented a welcome corner of tranquility.

For the moment, at least.

"What sort of report are we talking about?" Ukhtomskoy asked unhappily. If he had to tell MacArtney Barregos's popularity was starting to wane and the days of Maya's tranquility might be numbered...

"I have two separate sources who each tell me Barregos has met directly with representatives of Manticore," Nyhus said flatly.

For a moment, Ukhtomskoy was certain he'd misunderstood. Then he straightened in his chair.

"What did you say?"

"I said I have two separate reports that Barregos is meeting with the Manties." Nyhus shook his head, blue eyes worried. "*Separate* reports from two different sources, Adão. And neither one of the sources knows about the other."

Ukhtomskoy's jaw tightened at the implication.

"I wouldn't have been in such a rush to tell you about it if it was only one report," Nyhus continued. "But when I've got two separate channels confirming each other, I've got to take it seriously."

"Are you suggesting *Oravil Barregos* is contemplating *treason?*"

"I don't *know* what he's contemplating," Nyhus shot back with an unusual note of frustration. "All I know is that I have usually reliable sources telling me he's talking to Manties. And, frankly, it worries me a lot more than it might have otherwise because of all the *other* reports I've been getting—and sharing with you—about Manticoran involvement in stirring up the Fringe."

Ukhtomskoy glared at him, but Nyhus looked back steadily. And, Ukhtomskoy was forced to admit, he had a point. Almost a year ago, Brigadier Noritoshi Väinölä, Ukhtomskoy's counterpart with the Gendarmerie, had kicked across a report of what appeared to be orchestrated restiveness across wide stretches of the Fringe. Ukhtomskoy had been inclined to write it off as a case of too much imagination, until Nyhus had come to him six or seven months ago with a report of his own. One that suggested not only that Väinölä's analysts might be onto something but that the Star Empire of Manticore might be behind it.

To date, any corroborating evidence had been thin, to say the least, and entirely too much of Nyhus's information came from "confidential sources." At Ukhtomskoy's insistence, he'd sent urgent queries back to his agents in place, demanding IDs on those sources in hopes of gaining some insight into their reliability. Field agents were always reluctant to reveal sources' names to higher authority, for a lot of reasons, however, and sheer distance complicated the situation because of the built-in data transmission delays. So far, only a tiny handful of those sources had been positively identified and the process of evaluating their trustworthiness was only beginning.

"And would it happen that this time we at least know who those 'reliable sources' are?" he asked tartly.

"As a matter of fact, I do know who *one* of them is," Nyhus said. "I know both agents—one of them personally, and one only by reputation—pretty well. Keiran MacQuilkin, the senior agent in our Landing office in Sprague, is the one I know personally. I sent her out to keep an eye on things when the Havenites and Manties started shooting at each other again. One of her stringers on Smoking Frog is a security guard on Barregos's staff in Shuttlesport. And he got this."

Nyhus tapped his uni-link, and a holo of a dark-skinned, strong jawed face appeared in Ukhtomskoy's display. He glanced at it, then looked back at Nyhus.

"And 'this' is who, exactly?" he asked.

"We're not entirely positive," Nyhus conceded. "Whoever he is, though, he's met very privately with Barregos in his office well after normal hours. That struck me as ominous, given all the recent...agitation in the Fringe, so I had that"—he twitched his head in the direction of the holo—"put through a full facial recognition pass."

Ukhtomskoy arched an eyebrow. Given the sheer, staggering quantity of imagery, a "full facial recognition pass" could take weeks, sometimes months, even at modern data processing speeds.

"I got a hit...sort of." Nyhus tapped his uni-link again and a second holo appeared beside the first one. This one was much poorer quality, although it was obvious it had been digitally enhanced. "I'm sorry it's no sharper," he said, "but it's only a part of the original imagery. The newsy who took it was using a concealed camera and trying to get pictures of Baron High Ridge."

"The Manty prime minister?" Ukhtomskoy looked up sharply, and Nyhus nodded.

"The ex-PM now, of course," he said. "The newsy was doing an undercover piece on High Ridge's meetings with some of his more camera-shy donors. He shot this outside the Manties' Parliament and just caught the fellow we're interested in in one corner of the frame."

A flashing cursor appeared in the image, above the head of a tall, broad shouldered, deep chested individual. The camera had caught him in three quarters profile, his head turned as he spoke to a much shorter uniformed man beside him.

"We're not sure who the shorter guy is," Nyhus said. "Whoever he is, he's wearing a Manty commodore's uniform, though. And the computers call it a ninety-three percent probability that the taller one is the man in MacQuilkin's holo of Barregos's midnight visitor."

SLNS *Québec*
Dzung System
Solarian League

ADMIRAL CAPRIOTTI TIPPED BACK his chair, holding his coffee cup in both hands, and looked around the briefing room table aboard SLNS *Québec* at the senior members of his staff.

"All right," he said. "Now that we've covered the bare essentials, does anyone have any immediate brilliant observations?"

The expected chuckle ran around the table, and he smiled. Then he sipped coffee, lowered the cup, and allowed his expression to sober.

"Seriously," he said, "this whole thing is coming at us pretty damned fast. I know all of you have a lot of i's to dot and t's to cross—and, if I haven't mentioned this, I'm very happy with all of you for the way you've already dug in on that—but we all know perfectly well that the people who planned this must've missed something. Hopefully, it's something minor, but it might not be. So I want each of you to spend the next twelve hours or so going over your individual parts of the ops plans. If there's anything—anything at all—you think could, should, or might be tweaked to our advantage, I want to hear about it before we leave Dzung. The one thing we know for certain about what happened to Eleventh Fleet is that it got the holy living hell kicked out of it. I have no intention of allowing that to happen to *my* task force. Is that understood?"

He let his eyes circle the table again in a brief bubble of silence, and then Vice Admiral Helland replied.

"Yes, Sir," she said. "I think I can speak for all of us when I say we have no more intention than you do to put on a repeat performance of that disaster. I believe you can safely conclude we'll be thinking very hard about ways to make sure we don't."

"That's what I wanted to hear, Angelica." Capriotti smiled. Then he nodded at the briefing room hatch. "So that's about it for now, people. Go see about finding some supper. Angelica, I'd like you, Lyang-tau, and Jason to stay behind for a moment."

"Of course, Sir," Helland replied as the remainder of the staff stood, came respectfully to attention, and saluted. Capriotti, with his customary deplorable lack of formality, waved his coffee cup in general acknowledgment and the staffers filed out of the compartment. The hatch slid shut behind them, and he let his chair come back upright and set the coffee cup back down on it saucer.

"The truth is," he said, "I'm not entirely happy about this entire operation. I don't expect that to go beyond the four of us and Gabby, but I want to be sure we're all on the same page."

"May I ask in what way you're unhappy, Sir?" Helland asked in a careful tone.

"From a purely military perspective, I have two concerns, only one of which our orders explicitly approach. The first is that Cachalot is only fifty-seven light-years from Beowulf. Strategy and Planning are busy assuming, on the basis of intelligence data they haven't seen fit to share with us, that neither Beowulf nor the Manties have seen any reason to station a naval picket there, and I'm a little less confident on that head than Admiral Bernard. As nearly as I can follow the logic, Cachalot is seen as safely in their column, so there's no need for the 'imperialists' to coerce the system, on the one hand. On the other hand, especially with the Beowulf plebiscite still up in the air, they don't want to look like they're strong-arming Cachalot. I'm inclined to think Strategy and Planning's probably right about the absence of a major Manty picket, for whatever combination of reasons, but I'm a long way from *certain* of it."

"Sir," Commodore Jason Schlegel said, "you know I'm not a big fan of the analyses we've seen coming out of Old Chicago. Having said that, I think the odds are good S&P is right about this one." He shrugged. "There aren't many things I'd put past Beowulf at the moment, but they do seem to be bending over backward to present themselves in the most favorable light. And the Manties are generating enough bad press in the League by this wormhole offensive of theirs that they're unlikely to up the ante by effectively occupying a neutral system as populous and wealthy as Cachalot."

Capriotti considered the younger man thoughtfully. Schlegel was TF 783's intelligence officer. He was also an extremely bright officer and, at only fifty-six T-years old, young for his rank, even in the gold braid-heavy SLN. Unlike altogether too many of his ilk, he brought a skeptic's eye to any intelligence report that crossed his desk, and Capriotti normally valued his input. He did in this case, as well, actually, but he also remembered that Schlegel considered Beowulf guilty of treason. The commodore fully accepted the argument that Imogene Tsang's prong of Eleventh Fleet's disastrous attack would have suffered an even worse slaughter than Massimo Filareta if Beowulf hadn't stopped her ships from transiting the Beowulf Terminus. However, he also believed—probably with reason, in Capriotti's opinion—that Beowulf was the source of Manticore's original intelligence about Operation Raging Justice. And he also believed Beowulf's "complicity" in Manticore's obvious swing to a rawly imperialist foreign policy and its evident intention of seceding posed an existential threat to the Solarian League.

"I said I was inclined to think Bernard's people are right, Jason," he pointed out mildly. "Since we don't have any actual pre-attack reconnaissance to confirm that, however, I'm certainly not going to operate on the assumption that they *have* to be."

"Of course not, Sir."

"However, the possibility that they aren't brings me to my second military concern—the one where we have clear direction: what we do if it turns out there *is* a Manty picket."

His tone was considerably grimmer, and his three staffers glanced at one another.

"Sir, I know you won't like what I'm about to say," Admiral Helland said after a moment, "but Strategy and Planning have a point. We can't afford to look...ineffectual, especially after what happened at Spindle and Manticore." She did not, Capriotti noticed, mention other events at places with names like Zunker and Saltash. "Under the circumstances, pulling back at what we all know the newsies would label 'the first sign of resistance' would undercut Buccaneer's entire strategic premise."

Lyang-tau Rutgers stirred but said nothing.

"I'm fully aware of that, Angelica." Capriotti's voice was a bit frostier than the one in which he normally spoke to his chief of staff. "I'm also aware of the reported loss of life in that mysterious attack on the Manties' home system. I know there are some who believe their officially released casualty numbers are inflated. Given what obviously happened to their industrial base, though, I doubt they were. And if it hadn't been for Spindle, how do you think League public opinion would have reacted to them?"

Helland started to reply, then paused. After a moment, she nodded slightly. One thing about her, Capriotti thought. She'd subscribed fully to Battle Fleet hubris—at least before the Battle of Spindle—and she still considered both Manticore and the Republic of Haven "uppity neobarbs" who needed to be taught their manners. Despite that, her brain actually worked.

"Point taken, Sir," she said. "If it hadn't come so close on Spindle's heels, the 'Yawata Strike' would've gotten an enormous amount of sympathetic play on the boards."

"And with damned good cause." Capriotti leaned forward, planting his forearms on the briefing room table. "That was a sheer, wanton slaughter, with no attempt at all to minimize civilian loss of life. Leave the kinetic impact damage on Sphinx completely out of the equation, and it was still unconscionable."

"Sir," Rutgers said cautiously, "should we gather from where you're going with this that you're . . . not in favor of Parthian?"

"I believe that would be a safe assumption on your part, Lyang-tau." Capriotti smiled thinly. "I always was a transparent, easily read sort."

"Sir, I understand your concerns—and your repugnance. I really do," Helland said. "But as I just said, if Parthian's taken off the table, then Buccaneer's fundamental strategic premise is compromised."

"It *may* be compromised," Capriotti corrected her. "A lot would depend on *how* it was taken off the table. If there is a Manty—or Beowulfan—naval presence in Cachalot, and if I choose to avoid Parthian on the basis that it would result in unnecessary and *avoidable* civilian deaths and make it clear that that's the *only* reason I'm not executing Parthian, we come off looking restrained, not ineffectual. Especially in the aftermath of all the contradictory stories about what happened to Eleventh Fleet."

Helland looked less than convinced, but she clearly recognized that this wasn't a good place to push. Capriotti gave what he'd just said a few seconds to sink in, then sat back once more.

"I don't see any need to discuss this particular concern with the rest of the staff," he said. "If S & P's right and there's no picket to get in our way, it will never arise. If there is, then the final decision on Parthian will be mine, anyway. I want all three of you, though, to be thinking about the possibility that S & P *isn't* right and considering what I suppose you might call a partial Parthian. The outer system's infrastructure, especially in the Snapper Belt, has a much lower population, and the people in it are much more lavishly equipped with life pods and small craft. Given even a few hours' warning, they should be able to evacuate almost totally. Going after Snapper would make Buccaneer's point, I think, and if I emphasized to the system government that we were deliberately avoiding heavier casualties, we should get credit for showing restraint, as well."

Helland nodded with what might have been a bit more enthusiasm.

"All right," Capriotti stood. "I think we could all use some supper of our own. Why don't the three of you join me in my dining cabin?"

"Of course, Sir. Thank you," Helland said, and the three staffers followed him from the briefing room.

Angelica has a point about Buccaneer's premises, Capriotti thought, as they headed for the lift shaft. *She's not the only person who's going to make it, either. For that matter, it's a virtual certainty that sooner or later somebody is going to execute Parthian, whatever I do.*

He hid a mental grimace. Parthian was the one part of the detailed ops plan with which he'd totally disagreed from the instant he read it.

The new, improved Cataphracts in the pods which had been delivered along with TF 783's instructions, had effectively unlimited range. Well, *all* missiles had effectively unlimited range, really, but the Cataphract's second stage meant it was capable of terminal maneuvers at the end of its run as opposed to a purely ballistic weapon coasting helplessly through space after its impellers burned out. That meant, in theory, that missiles launched from well outside the 15.84 LM hyper limit of the Cachalot System's K4 primary were fully capable of hitting targets in the vicinity of Orca, the system's inhabited planet, despite the fact that Orca's orbital radius was less than three light-minutes. For that matter, Orca's orbital infrastructure wasn't what one might call an elusive target. Capriotti had no doubt that Lyang-tau Rutgers and his tactical officers would be capable of taking out every bit of it without ever crossing the limit inbound.

But there were two things no tac officer could possibly guarantee if Capriotti ordered them to do that. First, they couldn't guarantee Orca wouldn't suffer exactly the same sort of collateral catastrophe which had destroyed the Manticoran city of Yawata Crossing. And, second, and even worse, if he executed Parthian—essentially a hit-and-run strike from extreme range to avoid entering the Manties' missile envelope—there would be no time for an orderly evacuation. They'd probably save more lives than the Manties had managed to save in the Yawata Strike, but almost a billion of the Cachalot System's 6.9 billion citizens lived and worked in that infrastructure.

In the course of his career, Vincent Capriotti had done more things he hadn't liked than he cared to contemplate. Committing mass murder wasn't going to be one of them, *whatever* Operation Buccaneer called for.

But sooner or later, someone will, *Vincent,* he thought. *It's the next best damned thing to an Eridani violation, but someone will. And what the* hell *do we do when the* Solarian League *starts violating the Edict?*

He didn't like that thought.

He didn't like it at all.

SLNS *Leonhard Euler*
Unicorn Belt
Manticore B
Star Empire of Manticore

"SIR, I THINK I'VE got something here you need to look at," Midshipman Dimas said.

"That would make a nice change."

Commander Bill Knight sounded more than a little sour, although that was scarcely Dimas's fault. In fact, Knight liked Dimas quite a bit more than an evaluating officer was supposed to admit to a midshipman on his snotty cruise. Dimas was smart and competent...and so bouncy he reminded Knight irresistibly of a Labrador retriever he'd had when he was a kid himself. That dog had been smart, too...and despite what some people might think was possible, he'd *definitely* had a sense of humor. One that had gotten both him and his youthful master into what his mom had always referred to as "a heap of trouble" more than once. Dimas's humor never got him into trouble—or not, at least, with his superiors; his fellow snotties might have disputed that value judgment—but he loved practical jokes and he was an accomplished amateur ventriloquist. His ability to mimic sounds and throw his voice into unlikely places had kept Midshipman Styles running around the compartment looking for his "lost" uni-link for almost fifteen minutes a couple of days ago.

Young Dimas had also won the Lester Allen Kovalenko Prize as the top math graduate in his senior class, however. He'd been the starting goalie on the Saganami lacrosse team during his junior and senior forms, as well, and he took the team's motto—"Live life fearlessly!"—to heart. In short, he was an outstanding young man who was going to be an outstanding officer.

None of which made Bill Knight any happier about their current duty.

There were a lot of things he'd rather be doing than sitting on the command deck of yet another hulked Solly superdreadnought. Unfortunately, he wouldn't be doing any of them for the immediately foreseeable future.

He grimaced at the thought and shoved up out of the captain's chair at the center of *Leonhard Euler*'s bridge. He wasn't certain who Euler had been—a mathematician, he thought—but his namesake had seen better days. Less damaged than a lot of her consorts, she'd still suffered over four hundred casualties, and lucky it hadn't been worse. Not that anyone looking around her pristine bridge and smelling its cool, fresh air, would have imagined how severely damaged she was.

He crossed to the communications officer's station, where Dimas was ensconced. Knight had been forced to concede that young Dimas had a better touch with Solly computers than he did. He hoped that didn't say anything about unfortunate, hidden character flaws on the young man's part. But what had started with Dimas "riding shotgun," shadowing the older and more experienced Knight while he learned his way around, had segued into something a lot more like a partnership, and the boy had more than held up his end. Along the way, they'd discovered that the com system actually had the best reach into the ship's computer net, although no one was quite certain why the com officer had needed more access than, say, the tactical officer or the astrogator.

Probably because there's a right way, a wrong way, and the Solly *way to do just about anything,* he reflected as he came to a halt at Dimas's shoulder. *Although, come to think of it, "wrong way" and "Solly way" is probably redundant.*

"So, what've you got, Elijah?" he asked.

"I've got the standalones running the deep core analysis, Sir," the middy said, looking back and up at him, and Knight nodded.

The reason he and Dimas were currently parked aboard *Leonhard Euler* was that—for their sins—they were among the better of the Royal Manticoran Navy's cyberneticists. In fact, both of them had been assigned to HMSS *Weyland* prior to the Yawata Strike. Knight had been aboard the space station for almost two T-years before the strike, assigned to the R&D side of its complement because of his expertise. Dimas had been sent aboard for his snotty cruise deployment to give him the hands-on, real world experience his Academy instructors had been unable to provide, and he'd ended up under Knight's mentorship. They were alive today only because Vice Admiral Faraday, *Weyland*'s CO, had called an emergency evacuation drill which had left the entire R&D staff planet-side when the deadly sneak attack tore the space station apart.

Technically, Dimas's snotty cruise had ended five days ago, but things were still badly unsettled following what had been dubbed the Second Battle of Manticore. The lad had been left where he was, assigned to Knight's team, for the forensic examination of the wreckage. The commander hadn't told him he'd specifically asked to be allowed to keep "his" midshipman a little longer because he was so good at his job. Nor did young Elijah know about the glowing efficiency report Knight had already composed. But the same gift for computers and—especially—for deep-diving into the cyber depths which had made Dimas so useful aboard *Weyland* made him even more valuable aboard a hulk like *Euler.*

One of the conditions upon which Massimo Filareta's survivors had been allowed to surrender had been the preservation of their computer cores. Several commanding officers had scrubbed their computers anyway, which was why those particular COs were spending their current confinement in somewhat less than palatial conditions. Most, however, had honored their promise. A lot of them had figured—quite reasonably, in Knight's opinion—that after what the RMN had done to Sandra Crandall it already had plenty of classified computer banks to play with. There were unlikely to be any shattering new intelligence landfalls in Eleventh Fleet's memory.

At the moment, Knight and Dimas were busy probing the memory of their twelfth superdreadnought, and they weren't the only team involved in the effort. And, so far, no shattering new intelligence *had* come to light, which tended to suggest those captains had had a point.

Dimas's "standalones" were designed to carry out a point by point comparison between *Leonhard Euler*'s memory and the computers they'd already stripped. There was far too much data for any mere human to sort through, and—in theory, at least—the standalones would make sure anything that wasn't already in the database was added.

The communications logs were another matter, however. Computers did a wonderful job of searching for things they were told to look for, and they were doing just that with all of the com traffic. But in something that tended to be as...free-form as inter-human communication, telling them where to look could sometimes be a nontrivial challenge. That was why he and Dimas had made it a point to at least skim the traffic for the last couple of hours before the Solarian surrender. The computers were looking at the same timeframe, but it was entirely possible they'd miss something.

"Should I take it the standalones have found something earth-shattering?" Knight asked now, with a smile.

"Actually, Sir," the middy said seriously, "I think I really *may* have found something."

"Like what?"

"A fragment of a com conversation between *Leonhard Euler* and *Philip Oppenheimer* from about the time the Sollies opened fire. From her flag bridge." Knight's eyebrows rose, and Dimas nodded.

"You're kidding," the commander said.

"No, Sir." Dimas shook his head, and Knight's eyes widened.

They'd been searching for some window into whatever insanity had led Filareta to open fire in an absolutely hopeless situation. Unfortunately, none of Eleventh Fleet's surviving units had been in direct communication with Admiral Filareta or his staff at the critical moment, and *Philip Oppenheimer* herself was not among the survivors. They'd found a few megs of recorded com traffic between *Oppenheimer*'s CO and other units of the fleet from that time window, but nothing that came from her *flag bridge* . . . or that shed any light on his decisions. So if his middy—

"Somebody on this ship was actually in communication with Filareta when everything went to hell?" he demanded.

"Not quite, Sir." Dimas shrugged. "What I've got here is part of a conversation between *Leonhard Euler*'s com officer and one of her cousins, Captain Sedgewick."

Knight's eyes narrowed. Captain Reuben Sedgewick had been Filareta's staff com officer.

"It's from the com officer's private files, not part of the official logs," Dimas continued. "Maybe that's because there wasn't time to worry about anything like that before everything hit the fan. Or it might be because they were violating regs tying up bandwidth on personal matters at a moment like that."

"I could see that." Knight nodded, trying to imagine what would have happened to a Manticoran communications officer who'd been gabbing away with her cousin at "a moment like that."

"It's not quite as bad as you may be thinking, Sir," Dimas said. "They weren't on any of the active command net channels; they were talking on one of the redundancy sidebands."

"Marginally better, I suppose," Knight allowed grudgingly. "But if this wasn't part of the official fleet traffic, why do you think anyone's going to want to see it?"

"Well, I sort of doubt that Captain Clarence—she was *Leonhard Euler*'s com officer—has any idea there was anything significant in what she had here, Sir. For that matter, I'm not even certain she realized she'd recorded it in the first place. If she did, though, I can see why she's kept her mouth shut since we started beating the bushes trying to figure out why Filareta opened fire."

"What are you talking about?" Knight demanded a bit more impatiently, and Dimas gave him a crooked smile.

"Let me show you, Sir," he said, and hit the playback button.

HMS *Imperator*
Manticore A
Star Empire of Manticore

"—AND AFTER THAT, YOUR Grace, you're scheduled for the state dinner at Mount Royal," Lieutenant Luca Tomei said. "Under the circumstances, I think it might be better if you attended as Steadholder Harrington rather than Duchess Harrington."

Honor Alexander-Harrington tried very hard—and almost successfully—not to roll her eyes. It wasn't Tomei's fault, but she'd managed her entire career without a dedicated public information officer. Partly, she acknowledged, that was because she'd avoided the limelight as much as possible. More of it was that she'd held primarily combat commands, where providing public information had not been high on her list of priorities. And still more of it was the fact that, unlike some officers she could have named, she vastly preferred to get on with whatever the current job in hand might be and let other people worry about who got public credit for it.

And not just because I'm such a naturally modest and self-effacing type, either, she thought, remembering the bitter political infighting after the Battle of Hancock and following Paul Tankersley's death and her own duel with Pavel Young. Then there'd been all the vicious innuendo about her and Hamish during the High Ridge premiership. And that didn't even count the Mueller dome collapse back on Grayson!

If there was anyone in the entire Star Empire of Manticore who wanted the spotlight less than she did, she'd never met her.

Unfortunately, she'd had to accept years ago that she couldn't avoid it, and she had to admit Tomei made it a less excruciating experience. A year and a half younger than Waldemar Tümmel, he was far more comfortable than the flag lieutenant when it came to social events, like tonight's state dinner to bid Benjamin Mayhew an official farewell. He was less adroit than Tümmel on the purely military side, but between the two of them—with prodigious assistance from James MacGuiness—they got her most everywhere she needed to be *almost* on schedule.

And in between dinners, meetings, interviews, baby-kissings, ribbon cuttings, and photo sessions, I actually get to spend a little time thinking about how to fight the Solarian League! she thought wryly.

"I think you're probably right about that, Luca," she said now. "Of course," she gave him an amused look, "there's still the question of whether I go in uniform or civilian dress, isn't there?"

"I suppose there is, Your Grace, but—"

A soft chime interrupted him, and Honor touched the stud on her desk.

"Yes?" she said.

"I hate to interrupt you when I know you're so deeply involved in something you enjoy so much, My Lady," Major Spencer Hawke, Honor's senior armsman, said over the intercom, "but Captain Reynolds would appreciate a moment of your time."

"Gosh," she said, giving Tomei a wicked look, "I really hate to break this off, but if Captain Reynolds needs to talk to me, by all means send him in!"

"You do realize I'll be back as soon as the Captain leaves, Your Grace?"

"But if I'm quick enough, I can sneak out the back way before you get here!" she said, and Nimitz bleeked a laugh from his bulkhead perch.

"There *isn't* a back way, Your Grace." Tomei's lips twitched, but his tone was admirably grave.

"You just *think* there isn't," she told him, then looked up as the cabin door opened and George Reynolds, her staff intelligence officer, stepped through it.

"George! *Just* the man I wanted to see!" she said enthusiastically.

Reynolds smiled, but it was a brief and fleeting expression, and her own eyes narrowed.

"What is it?" she asked in a rather different tone.

"Your Grace, I've got something you need to hear."

Office of the Second Space Lord
Admiralty House
City of Landing
Manticore
Star Empire of Manticore

"SORRY IT TOOK ME so long, Pat," Hamish Alexander-Harrington, Earl White Haven and First Lord of Admiralty, said, as he followed Commander Terry Lassaline, Admiral Patricia Givens's new chief of staff, through Givens's office door. Tobias Stimson, his personal armsman, peeled off outside the door. "We were in transit when your message came in. So what's this all about? I assume there's a reason I'm here instead of talking to the Select Committee, where I'm *supposed* to be?"

"Actually, Hamish," a familiar soprano said from the office's smart wall, "I'm the one who's messed up your schedule. Sorry about that. I'm sure you're looking forward to talking to the Committee *almost* as enthusiastically as I'm looking forward to that state dinner tonight."

"Honor!" White Haven's incipient frown disappeared as he turned to face the smart wall. "If you needed to talk to me, there are simpler ways to do it."

"I'm aware." His wife shook her head with a certain resignation as Lassaline touched White Haven's elbow and pointed at one of the armchairs facing the smart wall. "Unfortunately, this call isn't a social occasion. There's something you need to see."

"Me as in First Lord, I presume?" he asked, settling into the indicated chair with a nod of thanks to the commander. Lassaline smiled, then raised an eyebrow at Givens.

"We're good, Terry," the second space lord said. "But grab a seat. You should hear this, too."

"Yes, Ma'am." Lassaline found a chair of her own, and White Haven turned his attention back to the smart wall.

Honor stood at one end of her desk aboard *Imperator*, and he recognized Mercedes Brigham, her chief of staff; Andrea Jaruwalski, her ops officer; and George Reynolds, her intelligence officer, behind her. Captain Rafe Cardones, *Imperator*'s CO stood with them, and White

Haven's eyebrows twitched slightly. That quartet represented the most trusted core of Honor's staff, and their expressions were a strange mix of eagerness and...trepidation? No, that wasn't quite the right word, but it was headed in the right direction.

"Absolutely. One of our forensic teams pulled something very interesting out of a Solly superdreadnought's com records. It may shed a little light on Filareta's actions. Of course," she grimaced, "I think it probably poses as many new questions as it answers."

"Wonderful." He shook his head, then glanced at Givens. "Seems to work that way more often than not in intelligence matters, doesn't it?"

Givens, who commanded the Office of Naval Intelligence in addition to her other duties, snorted, and he looked back at Honor.

"Show me," he said simply, and Honor looked at Reynolds.

"George?"

"Yes, Your Grace." The newly promoted captain faced White Haven from the smart wall. "My Lord, what you're about to see was pulled out of a personal com exchange between Admiral Filareta's communications officer and the com officer aboard *Leonhard Euler*. We've abstracted the relevant material, stripped away the rest of the message, and enhanced what we kept. I'd like to recommend Midshipman—I'm sorry, it's *Ensign* now; Her Grace's authority—Elijah Dimas for some well-deserved recognition for spotting it, too. I'm not sure it would have popped the filters before we scrubbed and enhanced it."

White Haven nodded his understanding.

"We don't have any visual of the critical speakers," Reynolds continued. "They were outside the pickup's field of view, but the voice recognition software is ninety-nine-point-nine percent confident in its IDs."

"That could be a problem down the road, Hamish," Givens put in, then shrugged when he looked at her. "If we go public with this, there are going to be plenty of Sollies ready to point out how 'convenient' for us it is that all we have are disembodied voices."

"Maybe yes, and maybe no, Pat." Honor's voice drew Givens and White Haven's eyes back to her. "We've got all the rest of the message with this embedded in it. Anybody who wants to can do her own forensics on it. Not," she grimaced, "that anyone in Old Chicago's likely to be interested in determining whether or not it's genuine."

"You're probably right," White Haven said. "So why don't you go ahead and show it to me?"

"George?" Honor said again, and Reynolds nodded. Then he pressed a button, and another voice spoke against a background the admiral in Hamish Alexander-Harrington recognized only too well: the clipped, disciplined voices of a flag bridge at battle stations.

"Very well," it said. It sounded flat, wooden, and a caption on the smart wall identified it as Fleet Admiral Massimo Filareta. "Strike our wedges and send the pod self-destruct command, Bill."

White Haven's eyebrows shot up and he turned to dart an astonished glance at Givens. The admiral only shook her head and held up an index finger.

"Yes, Sir," another voice said, and the caption identified this one as that of Admiral William Daniels, Eleventh Fleet's operations officer.

"I suppose you should go ahead and get Harrington back, Reuben," Filareta's voice continued. "She'll want—"

There was another sound, one White Haven couldn't quite make out. It sounded almost like a muffled cry of protest. Then—

"What the *fuck* d'you think you're do—?" Filareta's voice shouted.

It cut off in mid-syllable, and White Haven's gaze moved from Givens back to Honor.

"That's all we've got," she said softly, "but the time chop's a perfect match. Filareta's last words synchronize exactly with Eleventh Fleet's pod launch. We've always known the launch order came from Filareta's flag bridge—the launch codes and sequence confirmed that—but nobody on his staff said a word to anyone outside *Oppenheimer* afterward. *Oppenheimer* was destroyed in our first-wave launch, of course, but time of flight was a hundred and sixty seconds, so there was ample time for them to have talked to *somebody* outside the flagship. And I'm particularly struck by how it breaks off so suddenly. *Leonhard Euler*'s com officer is the only person we know of who was in contact with Filareta's flag bridge at that moment, and she tried for almost three minutes to reestablish contact while her captain tried to find out what the heck was going on when those missiles launched. She couldn't, and that matches with everything we've heard from all of Eleventh Fleet's survivors. *No one* could raise Filareta's flag bridge. I'm inclined to wonder if that's because something happened to it right after they launched."

"But, if that's really Filareta, it sounds like he *did* decide to surrender!" White Haven said.

"I think that's exactly what he did," Honor said, and her voice was grim, her dark brown eyes cold. "I think he understood precisely what we wanted him to understand: that his only option was to surrender. And I think the bastards on the other side of this took precautions to prevent him from doing anything of the sort."

"You're saying this was another example of that killer nanotech of theirs?" It was technically a question, but it didn't sound like one.

"I'm saying that's exactly what it was, and that the people who planted it on him used me and my people to kill another quarter million Solarian spacers," his wife said harshly. "Nobody on Old Terra who wasn't already prepared to believe us will believe a word of it, but *we* know now, and these people—whoever they are—are running up quite a bill with me."

She smiled a hexapuma smile.

"I'm looking forward to presenting it."

Forge One
Refuge System

"I'M IMPRESSED, ADMIRAL," SONJA Hemphill said as she and Admiral Shannon Foraker stepped out of the lift car and walked down a short passageway. Foraker's yeoman popped to attention as they entered the admiral's outer office. She waved a casual hand at him, but he held the position and cut his eyes briefly sideways to his superior's guest.

The pause in Foraker's stride was barely perceptible, but then she cleared her throat.

"At ease, Jean-Louis," she said.

He dropped into something rather more like parade rest, and Hemphill stifled an inappropriate urge to giggle.

Her own career was checkered with...occasional lapses in military punctilio. In her own case, she acknowledged, they usually had something to do with losing her temper with someone who seemed to have become part of the problem instead of the solution. She'd been forced to admit—indeed, she'd recognized at the time—that tantrums were often counterproductive, and she'd worked on her temper for decades. Really she had! And it helped that so many—not all, but many—of the causes she'd championed since King Roger had instituted Project Gram had paid off handsomely in the war against the People's Republic. Partly, that was because people tended to argue with her less, which she'd discovered wasn't always a good thing. More of it, though, she'd come to realize, was because she no longer had to prove herself *to* herself. The truth, she'd discovered, was that quite a lot of her more youthful anger had been directed at the fact that she hadn't been certain she was on the right track, herself. She'd known *exactly* how badly the Star Kingdom needed some sort of technological equalizer against the stupendous People's Republic. It had been her job to find one, and her anger had been directed as much at her own never-admitted uncertainty as it had been at the obstinacy of those arguing with her.

The treecat on her shoulder made a soft sound and patted her right cheek with a gentle true-hand, and her eyes softened.

Hunts Silently had assigned himself as her bodyguard when Sphinx's

51

treecat population decided it was time to provide bodyguards for the "two-legs" fighting to protect Sphinx and all the rest of the Star Empire's planets against the enemies behind the Yawata Strike. That attack had massacred an entire treecat clan, and as the 'cats themselves had put it, they knew how to deal with "evildoers." The telempathic treecats also knew about the way in which humans had been turned into programmed assassins, and their ability to sense the unwilling killers' horror and panic when the programming took control made them the only defense against them anyone had yet discovered.

Quite a lot of the Grand Alliance's leadership, Sonja Hemphill among them, had acquired furry, adorable, highly intelligent, and very, very deadly protectors as a consequence of the 'cats' decision. What she hadn't fully appreciated was the speed with which Hunts Silently would become perhaps the closest friend she'd ever had. And she was pretty sure he'd had more than a little to do with her ability to understand the roots of the anger which had been so much a part of her for so long, too.

Shannon Foraker's lapses in military formality, on the other hand, stemmed from very different causes. In certain key aspects of her life, Admiral Foraker was the most focused, intense individual Hemphill had ever met, herself included. Outside those key aspects, however, she often seemed to inhabit a different universe. Despite that—or because *of* it, perhaps—her staff and subordinates were utterly devoted to her. It was rather touching to see the determination of people like Senior Chief Jean-Louis Jackson to protect her against the sort of lapses in formality which might embarrass her in front of her no doubt super-cilious, judgmental Manticoran guests.

Hemphill's thoughts carried her through the hatch into Foraker's inner office aboard *Forge One*, the oldest—and largest—of the four major space stations orbiting the planet of Sanctuary. They'd just completed a guided tour of the enormous platform, and she'd been deeply impressed by what the Republic of Haven and the Sanctuarians had accomplished. Individually, *Forge One* and its three consorts were little more than a quarter as large as Manticore's *Hephaestus* or *Vulcan* had once been, but the four of them together exceeded even *Hephaestus's* solo output. In many ways, that was what Hemphill found most impressive about Project Bolthole, because Haven had managed to build that capacity—from scratch—with a substantially less capable tech base...and in only four decades.

Of course, the woman whose office they'd just entered had spent the last several T-years working to make that tech base one hell of a lot more capable than she'd found it.

Foraker waved at the comfortable conversational area in one corner of the spacious compartment. The chairs, coffee table, and couch were arranged in a semicircle, facing a waterfall that poured down across a cascade of natural stone into an oval 3.5-meter pool. A flash of color caught Hemphill's eye as a spectacularly striped and banded fish with long, featherlike fins—she wondered if the species was native to Haven or to Sanctuary—leapt briefly above the pool's rippling surface.

"Sit down, please...Baroness," Foraker almost managed to conceal her grimace at having almost forgotten to add Hemphill's aristocratic title, and the Manticoran chuckled. Foraker looked at her as they sat, and she shook her head.

"Don't worry about any 'Baronesses' or 'Miladies,' Admiral Foraker," she said as Hunts Silently flowed down to curl in her lap. "They're not necessary, and I don't usually use my title back home, anyway."

"You don't?" Foraker sounded a bit relieved, and Hemphill chuckled again.

"I suppose I really should, but I've been plain old 'Sonja Hemphill' for a lot of years. I don't have time for much of a social life and I'm not that interested in politics, so I've never taken my seat in the Lords. I let one of my cousins sit there with my proxy." She shrugged. "Besides, Low Delhi's basically just a one percent arc of the Gorgon Belt in Manticore-B. That comes to about three-point-one quadrillion cubic kilometers, but those kilometers contain an awful lot of empty space. Mind you, some of the rocks floating around in it are pretty valuable, but I think its total population was nine hundred and twenty—or maybe it was twenty-*one*—the last time I looked. And most of my 'subjects' are asteroid miners who could give treecats stubborn lessons." She gave another shrug, then smiled. "Besides, I think the two of us will be working closely enough it should probably be 'Sonja' and 'Shannon,' at least in private."

"Oh, good!" Foraker sighed, then looked contrite. "Sorry! That didn't come out just the way I wanted. I suppose they warned you I'm not real good about the social stuff?"

"I think you can assume the odd word or two of...caution was dropped into my ear," Hemphill said wryly. "Should I assume the same sort of words were dropped into your ear about *me*?"

"Actually, the word Admiral Lewis used in your case was 'touchy,' I think." Foraker's tone was even drier than Hemphill's had been, and Hunts Silently laughed as the two of them sat back and smiled broadly at one another.

"To quote a line from one of Duchess Harrington's favorite ancient entertainment holovids, Shannon, 'I think this is going to be the beginning of a beautiful friendship,'" the Manticoran said.

✧　　✧　　✧

"—so from our analysts' perspective, it looks to me like we're in pretty good shape right now," Sonja Hemphill said much later that night, sitting across the supper table from Foraker with an after-dinner glass of brandy in hand. "I doubt the Sollies fully appreciate the powered ranges our MDMs can reach—we've tried hard enough to keep them from figuring it out, at any rate—and I'm almost positive they can't really appreciate the accuracy Apollo makes possible at those ranges. That doesn't mean they don't feel a desperate need to increase their own ranges, but until they can figure out how to build multiple impeller rings into the same missile body, they won't be able to match our performance. And as far as we can tell—and we've had a *really* good look inside their current tech, thanks to Filareta—they're only a little ahead of where we were twenty years ago, at First Yeltsin, on the grav-pulse coms."

Foraker sipped from the cup of coffee in her own hand and nodded slowly. The two of them had spent the last several hours bringing one another up to speed—in general terms, at least—on Bolthole's actual capacity and their separate R&D programs' current projects.

"That's probably true," she said now. "And given how long it took us to reverse-engineer the splitter technology even after we 'acquired' a few specimens to work from, I doubt they'll figure it out next week. But I think everyone needs to remember the Solarian League has plenty of really capable scientists and engineers. And the fact that they already know *we* can do it will give their researchers an enormous leg up."

"Agreed. Agreed!" Hemphill nodded back, much more vigorously. "Our current estimate is that it ought to take them at least a couple of years—more probably three or four, bearing in mind that we're pretty sure *they* haven't 'acquired' any samples—but we're well aware that it's only a guesstimate. And that it might be overly optimistic. I think it's going to take them a lot longer to match Apollo, though."

"Probably," Foraker said again. "I hope you won't take this the wrong way, but it's always seemed to me that you Manticorans have a tendency to build in what one of my staffers calls 'all the bells and whistles.'" She smiled wryly. "Mind you, if I had as many whistles and bells as you people do, I'd damned well build them in myself! But that hasn't been the case for us, which is why Five gave me that a couple of years ago."

She waved her cup at an old-fashioned frame on the bulkhead. It contained a quotation from "Anonymous," and Hemphill had smiled as she read it earlier.

"Perfect is the mortal enemy of good enough," it said.

"That's what we had to bear in mind for *years* after the head start you people got on us," Foraker said very seriously. "If we'd waited until we'd figured out how to duplicate *everything* you were doing to us, we'd never have gotten anything done. Not in time to do us any good, anyway."

"We haven't exactly waited until we were convinced everything was 'perfect' before we committed it to action ourselves," Hemphill pointed out.

"No, I'm sure you haven't. But my point is really looking from the perspective of the...technological underdog, let's say. We couldn't do the things you were doing the *way* you did them, so we had to figure out how to do what was 'good enough' to let us at least stay in shouting range. And I'd like to think that, every so often, we handed you a surprise or two of our own."

"Oh, you certainly did *that!*" Hemphill shook her head. "There were quite a few surprises along the way, like Moriarty and those 'donkey' missile pods of yours!"

"Exactly." Foraker set her cup down, folded her hands on the edge of the table, and leaned forward over them, her expression intent. "Exactly," she repeated. "You had the technological edge, both in weapons already in the pipeline and in terms of your basic infrastructure. *We* had the edge in sheer numbers and *size* of infrastructure, but we were well behind you in terms of deployed technology and even further in terms of the educational system which might have let us recoup our disadvantage.

"But the Solarian League is *huge*, even bigger in relative terms compared to the entire Grand Alliance than the People's Republic was compared to the original Star Kingdom. It's got the biggest, most broadly dispersed manufacturing infrastructure in the entire galaxy. Despite the situation on many of the Fringe and Verge planets—and a couple of the Core Worlds; let's be honest here—it has a first-rate educational system. And outside its warfighting hardware, its applied tech is about as good as it gets. I think you people clearly have the edge in several critical areas, but outside FTL bandwidth, that edge is pretty damned thin, and I'm willing to bet there are areas in which *they* have the edge, if they just sit down, take a deep breath, and think about it. And when they do that, if they decide to settle for 'good enough' instead of holding out for 'perfect'..."

"If they do, God only knows what *they'll* come up with as an equalizer," Hemphill finished for her when she allowed her voice to trail away. The Manticoran admiral's expression was grim as she recalled the Janacek Admiralty's hubris...and what that had cost the Royal Manticoran Navy in dead ships and personnel.

"That's *exactly* what I'm worried about," Shannon Foraker said quietly. "Given their performance to date, it's tempting to think every Solly's an idiot. But they aren't, and if some of those not-idiots convince the Mandarins to *listen* to them, our current technological edge could disappear a lot sooner than anyone wants to think it could."

The Golden Olive Restaurant
City of Old Chicago
Sol System
Solarian League

"SO WHAT DO *YOU* think of Rajmund's latest revelation?" Lupe Blanton asked as she and Weng Zhing-hwan finished punching their orders into the privacy-screened booth's terminal. "From where I sit, if there's really anything to it, we may need to rethink our position on who the Other Guys really are. Or if they exist at all, for that matter!"

"First, let's remember we're talking about *Rajmund*," Weng observed, pouring tea into her cup from the self-warming pot which had been waiting in their booth when they arrived. "That automatically means there's an agenda behind it. You know that even better than I do, since you, unfortunately, have to work with him—or around him—on an ongoing basis. Second, we know damned well that all of his patrons—or the ones we've been able to identify, at least—have strong vested interests in 'proving' the Manties are behind *anything* that goes south in the Fringe. And, third, I don't believe for one second that Oravil Barregos would be careless or stupid enough to be caught talking to the Manties—or anyone else—if he seriously contemplates anything of which your esteemed superiors might disapprove."

"A masterly summation." Blanton smiled thinly. She sat back on her side of the table, playing with a fork, and, despite the smile, her eyes were dark. "What really worries me is that Adão doesn't have any option but to take his reports seriously. I'm pretty sure he doesn't trust the...disinterested impartiality of what Rajmund's reporting any farther than I do, but there's so *much* of it."

"And he's upping the ante if he's handing over genuine photos of Manticoran naval officers," Weng agreed. "Especially if they turn out to be *genuine* Manticoran officers. And I'm assuming from Ukhtomskoy's reaction that they did?"

"Of course they did," Blanton said. "Frankly, though, that worries me less than some other aspects of it. Imagery—especially *bad* imagery that has to be digitally enhanced as much as this did—is easy enough

57

to fake. And there's no telling who may have slipped file imagery of completely nonexistent Manticorans into Frontier Security's databases for it to be compared to. I doubt Rajmund did it, because there'd be too much risk of that blowing up in his face if anyone starts fact-checking his reports. He's been around the block way too many times to leave a trail of breadcrumbs that might lead back to him. But do either of us really think he's the only mole someone like the Other Guys have in place? Assuming they exist, that is," she added piously.

"Of course not. Doesn't make me any happier contemplating what we're up against, though. Assuming they exist."

Weng's smile was even thinner than Blanton's had been.

"Actually, I'm more intrigued by your third point," Blanton said after a moment. "The bit about Barregos not being careless or stupid if he does 'seriously contemplate' anything that might piss off MacArtney. Or Kolokoltsov and the rest of the Mandarins, for that matter. Do you think he really *could* be contemplating something?"

Weng gazed down into her teacup for several seconds, lips pursed while she considered her response. Then she looked back up to meet Blanton's gaze.

"Last year," she began, "Noritoshi had me send one of my most trusted people—Jerzy Scarlatti; he's a major, I don't think you know him—out to Maya."

She arched an eyebrow at Blanton, who nodded. Brigadier Noritoshi Väinölä, CO of the Solarian Gendarmerie Intelligence Command, was Weng's immediate superior, Adão Ukhtomskoy's Gendarmerie counterpart.

"Officially, Jerzy was there to conduct an inspection of the local Gendarmerie Intelligence operations because he'd heard reports that the . . . complex relationship between Erewhon, Haven, and Manticore was spilling over onto Maya. Actually, we'd had reports that Barregos and/or Rozsak were skimming—skimming more than usual, I mean—off all the contracts they'd been placing with Erewhon. And the reason I chose him was that he and Philip Allfrey, Barregos's senior Gendarme, go back a long way. I figured Allfrey would be more likely to cooperate with a friend. And if he *didn't*—if there *was* something going on and Allfrey was part of it—Jerzy knew him well enough he'd probably pick up on it."

Blanton nodded again. It was a given that *any* sector governor, and the vast majority of Frontier Fleet sector commanders, would find . . . extra-curricular ways to line their pockets. In fact, that had been going on for so long the systematic graft was factored into their salaries. There were, however, limits to how blatant their superiors could permit them to be.

"Anyway, Allfrey assured Jerzy there was no significant peculation going on. In fact, there was less than usual, and he showed Jerzy his

own internal documentation to prove it. I'm pretty sure from what Jerzy said in his off-the-record report to me that he thinks Allfrey has a very comfortable relationship with Barregos, but his documentation checked out after the best analysis we could give it.

"On the other hand, he was there during the Congo Incident."

"He was?" Blanton's fingers stopped turning her fork over and over and her eyes narrowed.

The Congo Incident was the label the newsies had pinned on Admiral Luiz Rozsak's defense of the planet of Verdant Vista.

The League was officially ambivalent about Verdant Vista, known to its current occupants as Torch. The Congo System had never been claimed by the League, nor had it been an OFS protectorate system, so its original Mesan claimants had possessed no official League recourse to reclaim it when its population, backed by an astonishing united Manticoran-Havenite front, rebelled against their ownership in August 1919. Even if they'd tried to call on their many friendly Solarian bribe-takers, the fact that ninety-plus percent of the Verdant Vistans had been genetic slaves would have...complicated Solarian public opinion. Genetic slavery was something of which all "right-thinking" Solarians disapproved, even if only a tiny percentage were willing to get off their comfortable posteriors and do anything about it, so even Solarian bureaucrats had to be careful about anything that smacked of collusion with Manpower, Inc. On the other side of the ledger, the strong ties between the rebels, the new Torch government, and the Audubon Ballroom had allowed its detractors to suggest it would inevitably become a haven for terrorists. But that had been offset in turn by the Antislavery League's vociferous agitation in favor of officially recognizing Torch as a haven and homeworld for any liberated genetic slave.

Overall, it had seemed a situation tailor-made for the Solarian League to stay well clear of. Which had made Oravil Barregos's decision, as the Maya Sector's governor, to enter into a defensive agreement with Torch the cherry on top for some of Frontier Security's policymakers here in Old Chicago.

But Barregos had strenuously, plausibly—and successfully—argued in favor of the agreement as a way to minimize Manticoran and Havenite influence in the system. Nothing could completely freeze them out, he'd acknowledged, especially since the Queen of Torch was the adopted daughter of the infamous Anton Zilwicki and even more infamous Catherine Montaigne. But given the fundamental tension between Manticore and Haven, the united front they'd presented at the time of the rebellion couldn't last, and drawing the newly independent star system into the relationship he was currently cultivating with Erewhon

would position the Maya Sector to step into the gap when it inevitably occurred. His prediction about the Manty-Havenite relationship's stability had been proven correct barely two T-months later, when Haven resumed hostilities against Manticore, and judging by Torch's scrupulous official disavowal of the Ballroom's terrorist tactics, his accompanying argument that he'd be better able to moderate Torch's behavior through a policy of constructive engagement had seemed to make a lot of sense.

But then, the preceding October, after less than two T-years, Frontier Fleet had been forced to make good on that defensive agreement. Luiz Rozsak and his men and women had paid a heavy price to protect Torch against what certainly looked like an intended Eridani Edict violation financed by "parties unknown." The actual culprits had been renegade members of the People's Republic of Haven's State Security, although no one had been prepared to explain exactly what their motives might have been and it was obvious that only a very well-heeled patron could have provided the logistical support the attack had required. Their survivors had been handed over to Eloise Pritchart's Republic for trial, so the League's courts had taken no official cognizance of exactly who might have backed their effort, but there wasn't much question in anyone's mind, and public opinion had shed very few tears over anything that happened to Mesan proxies.

"I wondered about the official accounts," Blanton said now, her voice ending on a questioning note, and Weng snorted.

"You're not alone in that," she said, "and I've actually discussed that a little bit with Daud in light of Jerzy's reports. He—Daud, I mean, not Jerzy—was pretty bitter about the fact that no one higher up the chain of command had paid any attention to the reports he and Irene put together after it on the basis of Rozsak's after-action report.

"He says Rozsak's been telling people for *years* that the Manties and Havenites were outstripping the Navy in terms of both weapons and technique, and nobody's paid any damned attention. In fact, it turns out that for at least three T-years, Rozsak's reports were being suppressed before they ever got to *Daud*, much less went farther up the tree, and it looks like, in the absence of any direction from Old Chicago, the people on the ground have been trying to do something about it.

"Officially, Barregos has been buying locally produced warships from Erewhon as a way to inveigle the Erewhonese back into our sphere of influence, and that seems to have been working. But it's painfully evident that another reason Barregos's done it is to get some kind of window into the new technologies. Erewhon's only a minor power compared to Manticore or Haven, and its navy is outside the loop on

these latest, god-awful weapons the Manties are deploying against us. But it's pretty clear the investment in new hardware is the only reason Rozsak was able to defend Torch, although his losses were still pretty damned brutal. More brutal, I think, than was ever officially announced, although Jerzy didn't have any confirmation of that at the time and Daud hasn't found any since. But what pisses Daud off is that he worked up an analysis that strongly recommended Vice Admiral Hoover and the Office of Technical Analysis go through Rozsak's reports with a fine-toothed comb. If they had, even they would probably have figured out the Haven Sector was producing exactly the sort of innovations Hoover's analysts had systematically dismissed for *decades*. Nothing in them hinted at the missiles they used against Crandall and Filareta, but at least we might not have gone into this with such *total* complacency."

Blanton made a harsh sound of agreement, and Weng shrugged.

"At any rate," she went on, "Jerzy's report officially cleared Barregos of any financial wrongdoing. After reading it and discussing it with him, I think it raised some fresh questions about just how tight he's gotten with Erewhon, but not *financially*."

"Are you suggesting you're worried Maya might be...fertile ground for someone to plant seeds of disunity, whether it's the Manties or the Other Guys?" Blanton asked in a careful tone, and Weng shrugged again.

"I wouldn't say I've been worrying about *that*," she said. "Obviously, with the entire galaxy hell-bent on coming unglued, I'm not prepared to categorically rule it out, but Jerzy didn't come home with anything that set off any alarms in that respect. My impression of Barregos— and I hasten to add that this is only *my* impression; he's one of your people, not ours, and I don't think anyone else in the Gendarmerie's really thought about it that much—is that he's the sort of fellow who considers all possibilities. He's living in a dangerous neck of the woods, on the periphery of the longest lasting, most destructive war in galactic history—so far, at least—and I think he's a historian. I think he saw the possibility of something like our confrontation with Manticore coming a long time ago, and I think his relationship with Erewhon's designed to provide as close to a pocket of stability as he can create if all the rest of the galaxy goes to hell in a handbasket. How far he's prepared to go to make that happen is an entirely different question, and I don't have anything like enough information to offer an informed opinion on that."

"But it's the sort of situation, assuming you're right, that could make someone else regard him as either potentially susceptible to seduction or as someone who could be credibly *passed off* as being susceptible to seduction."

"Exactly. But if I *am* right, then he's been doing this tap dance of his for a long time without anyone figuring it out. I admit Maya's a long way from Sol, but that's still an impressive accomplishment. From everything Jerzy had to say, he has a genuine knack for attracting personal loyalty, too. So does Admiral Rozsak, apparently, and that can be a dangerous capability. Leaving that aside, though, someone able to keep so many balls in the air without anyone back home noticing would never be clumsy enough to let *anyone*, far less one of Rajmund's people's paid stringers, discover that he was meeting secretly with Manty representatives."

"You're right about that," Blanton said thoughtfully, beginning to play with her fork again. "Especially since he'd take particular precautions against anyone in *Frontier Security* finding out about it. I imagine he'd be a lot more worried about in-house leaks than about your people."

"You probably have a point."

Weng sipped tea. They sat in silence for twenty or thirty seconds, then she set the cup down and sat back.

"I think we'd better find out about this," she said. "And I can only think of one way to do that."

"Assuming there's time," Blanton pointed out, and Weng nodded. The travel time to Maya was fifty-one days, one way.

"I know," she said. "But I don't see another option."

"Neither do I. Can't be one of my people, though. Even at the best of times, I'd be poaching in Rajmund's preserve. And these are hardly 'the best of times.' If we're right about him, the last thing we need is to warn him anyone—especially *me*—might be looking in his direction. Send your Scarlatti back again?"

"I don't know," Weng replied, answering Blanton's professionally thoughtful tone. "On the one hand, I trust him and he was the one who first suggested Barregos's relationship with Erewhon was closer than most people here in Old Chicago thought it was. He wouldn't have done that if he'd been in Barregos's pocket. On the other, he *is* Allfrey's friend, and if Barregos *is* up to something, Jerzy didn't get a clear sniff of it—or report it, anyway—the last time he was there. And," she added, "coming up with a plausible reason to send him back again so soon without making someone as smooth as Barregos suspicious could be a nontrivial exercise."

Blanton's expression showed her agreement with Weng's thought train.

"I've got at least a half-dozen other people I could send if I don't send Jerzy back," the colonel said with a shrug. "And if I need to, I'll go to Noritoshi and get him to let me pick one of Simeon's people from CID. Either way, I can get someone off to Smoking Frog within a couple of days, outside."

"The sooner the better," Blanton said. "Even if she leaves tomorrow, it's going to be mid-September by the time she gets there."

"And the soonest she could get back would be the end of November," Weng agreed. "And that's assuming someone's stupid enough to leave that 'smoking gun' lying around for her to stumble over the instant she steps off the landing shuttle! Not going to happen."

"So we're probably really looking at not hearing back before the new year." Blanton's expression was sour, and Weng snorted.

"Any dinosaur's nervous system has a certain amount of built-in delay," she pointed out, and Blanton grimaced.

"Under the circumstances, I wish you'd picked a different metaphor," she said.

"Why?"

"Because the dinosaurs are extinct," Blanton replied grimly.

AUGUST 1922 POST DIASPORA

SLNS *Québec*
Cachalot System

"YOU CAN'T BE SERIOUS!"

The woman on Vincent Capriotti's com display was platinum-haired and dark skinned. It was a striking combination, and she was so photogenic he suspected she'd been the recipient of quite a lot of biosculpt. Politicians, as a rule, found physical attractiveness a valuable asset—far more valuable, in fact, in Capriotti's opinion, than simple competence. On the other hand, Cachalot System President Miriam Jahnke had amply demonstrated her own competence over a forty-T-year political career.

And, at the moment, the fury blazing in her brown eyes honed her attractiveness in much the same way lightning honed a thunderstorm's.

Or a hurricane's, perhaps.

"I'm afraid I'm quite serious, Madame President," he said in reply, then sat back to wait out the six-minute communications lag.

At the moment, TF 783 was almost 56,000,000 kilometers from the planet Orca, just over ten light-minutes inside the Cachalot System hyper-limit, closing with the planet at 18,119 KPS and decelerating at a steady 300 G. Given that geometry, they would reach Orca orbit in another hour and forty minutes, and their recon platforms had been swarming around the inner system for the last couple of hours. ONI had grudgingly admitted that stealth systems were another area in which the Manties had somehow acquired a commanding lead, but *nobody's* stealth was good enough to hide warships—even completely shut down warships—from the horde of drones he'd sent speeding ahead of his ships.

Which means there's absolutely no reason I can't carry out Buccaneer... damn it, he thought grimly. *The odds are we'll be the first task force to execute it, too, which means I'm the one going down in the frigging history books. I don't think I'm going to like that.*

At least it also meant there'd be no need—or any possible excuse—for Parthian. There'd be ample time for an orderly evacuation, and thank God for it!

He'd waited until he was positive that would be the case—and until the com lag was at least semi-manageable—before contacting Jahnke's office and telling her why he was here. Her response had been pretty much what he'd anticipated.

"You have no conceivable justification for this!" she snapped now from his display. "It's a blatantly illegal action against an independent and neutral star system! It violates at least a half dozen interstellar treaties—treaties the Solarian League both negotiated and *guaranteed*—and every conceivable canon of interstellar law!"

All of which was absolutely true...and had nothing at all to do with his orders, Capriotti thought.

"I'm very sorry you feel that way, Madame President," he said. "And, speaking as an individual and not as an officer of the Solarian League Navy, I understand why you do. I deeply regret the orders I've been given, but I have no option but to carry them out, and I intend to do so. At the same time, my orders emphasize the vital importance of minimizing any possible avoidable loss of life." Which was also true, as long as Parthian wasn't on the table. "That's why I'm speaking to you now to inform you that you have seventy-two hours to complete your evacuation of the infrastructure in question."

He waited for his words to reach her, and saw her expression when they did. If she could have reached him in that moment, she would have ripped out his throat with her bare hands, he thought.

"This system has maintained cordial and cooperative relations with the Solarian League since the year the League was created," she told him flatly. "We have never, in all those centuries, been anything but your star nation's friendly neighbor. And we certainly aren't participants in any aggression against the League! We're not Solarians, we aren't Manticorans, and we've been scrupulously neutral. We don't even have a navy, only a system *police force*! What you propose is not only blatantly illegal but an atrocity carried out against the life's blood of my star system!"

She had an excellent point, he reflected. Not that he intended to admit that Cachalot's *lack* of a navy was one of the main reasons he'd been sent here.

"Madame President, I'm prepared to grant that you haven't been military participants in the so-called Grand Alliance's aggression against the Solarian League," he said.

He knew he was speaking for the record, that this entire com exchange was probably going to wind up on the public boards throughout the League, and he forced himself to sound calm, measured, and—above all—reasonable. It was hard when what he actually felt was bitter shame. But he was a senior officer of the SLN and he had his orders.

"Even though you may not have aided the Manticorans and their allies *militarily*, however," he continued, "you've certainly aided and abetted them in other ways. As your government is well aware, Manticore began its campaign against the Solarian League by way of its blatantly illegal interference with freedom of astrogation and the Solarian economy. In effect, Manticore has weaponized interstellar commerce and directed it against the Solarian League because of my government's refusal to simply stand aside and enable its raw, unbridled imperialism through our passivity. And, Madame President, your star system has transferred virtually the entirety of its own trade to Manticore and the other star nations who, by their own declaration, are now actively at war with the League. That's hardly the action of an even-handed neutral, and my government has no option but to consider active collaboration with outlaw regimes which have killed hundreds of thousands of Solarian military personnel and citizens an act of aggression."

He met Jahnke's eyes steadily, even though both of them knew just how tenuous the connection between reality and what he'd just said truly was.

"The Solarian League takes no pleasure in the destruction of property, and my government is well aware of the economic hardship this will create for the people of your star nation," he went on in a tone of implacable regret, filling the transmission lag with the rest of the "talking points" with which the Navy and Foreign Affairs had seen fit to provide him. If he gave her the opportunity to respond, she'd probably point out that Manticore's version of commerce warfare meant the Star Empire and its allies were the only people with whom Cachalot *could* trade at the moment, and his lords and masters could never have *that* as part of the official record, now could they?

"However, it's clear Manticore has embraced an imperialism which is as much economic as territorial. Not content with the commanding position it already enjoyed, it's now set out to secure dictatorial control of the entire inhabited galaxy's economic life. The Solarian League cannot—and *will* not—allow any star nation to acquire that sort of power, of control and coercion, over its star systems and their citizens. And, since it's evident that raw aggression and economic domination are the only languages the 'Star Empire' understands, the League has no option but to respond to it in its own terms. Much as I may regret the mission which has brought me to your star system, your complicity in Manticore's assault upon the Solarian League has left my government with no other alternative.

"Again, I inform you that you have seventy-two hours in which to organize an evacuation of your orbital infrastructure. Obviously, I must also insist on the surrender of the armed units of your System Patrol. Vice Admiral Angelica Helland, my chief of staff, will be in contact with the System Patrol's commanding officer to arrange that surrender in as peaceful and orderly a fashion as possible. I'm sure I've presented you with a great many unpleasant decisions and actions. Again, I regret the necessity of doing so, but I will leave you to deal with them. I will contact you again when my flagship enters Orca orbit. Capriotti, clear."

He pressed the stud to kill his com and swiveled his chair to face Commodore Anthony, his staff communications officer.

"Until I contact her again, I'm unavailable, Roger," he said. Anthony's eyebrows rose ever so slightly and it was obvious from his expression that he didn't look forward to fending off Jahnke's inevitable fiery demands to speak to Capriotti. But the commodore only nodded.

Capriotti returned the nod, then turned back to the master plot as *Québec* and the rest of the task force decelerated toward Orca. He watched the moving icons and wondered how much of his unavailability stemmed from the PR requirements and psychological warfare aspects of Buccaneer...and how much of it stemmed from shame. He remembered his words to Captain Timberlake in their first discussion of the ops order, and they were bitter on his tongue. This *wasn't* the reason he'd joined the Navy, but if he had it to do, then he'd damned well do it.

✧   ✧   ✧

"We're ready, Sir," Lyang-tau Rutgers said quietly.

Capriotti nodded without speaking. He stood with his hands clasped behind him, gazing into the flag bridge plot. It had been reconfigured for visual display, showing him a needle-sharp vista of the planet Orca and the massive orbital infrastructure about it.

Cachalot had been settled for a long time, but it wasn't the best real estate in the known galaxy. Despite the relative dimness of the system primary, whose luminosity was less than fourteen percent that of Sol, Orca's close orbit—the planetary year was less than three T-months long—produced a mean temperature significantly higher than Old Terra's. Its tropical zone was virtually uninhabited, and its axial inclination was only nine degrees, which meant it had minimal seasonal variation even outside the all but unendurable tropics. There were, however, almost five billion human beings in its temperate zones...and another *three* billion in its orbital habitats.

That was a lot of people to turn into implacable haters, he thought.

At least the Cachalotians had opted for a sharper segregation between their industrial platforms and their habitats than happened in most star systems. That had probably started, initially, because so many of them had opted for the habitats' controlled climates in preference to the planet's from the very beginning. That meant the inhabited neighborhood had grown up even before its industrial base really developed, and separating them had protected their orbital population from the sorts of industrial accidents that could have unfortunate consequences. It had to create commuting problems for a lot of their labor force, but they clearly thought it was worth it, and their building codes had officially enshrined the separation for several centuries now.

Of course, they'd never seen an "industrial accident" like Buccaneer coming.

They were still going to lose one orbital habitat—and the homes of over five million of their citizens—anyway. There simply wasn't any way to demolish the Siesta Three platform's industrial capability without taking out the entire habitat. Three more major habitats were going to take significant damage, but Rutgers's demolition crews were confident the housing sections would survive unhurt.

Not so confident that Jahnke—or me—was going to leave those people aboard when the charges go off. Capriotti snorted mentally. *It's a lot easier to be "confident" about somebody else's homes*, he thought harshly.

Even without minor considerations like that, destroying the platforms in Orca orbit without creating catastrophic debris strikes on both the planet and the remaining habitats was a nontrivial exercise in its own right. The Snapper Belt platforms, better than fifty light-minutes from the primary, were a much simpler proposition. Snapper's 644,000 inhabitants had simply been moved en masse to Orca's surface and a dozen of Capriotti's destroyers would take out the belt's entire infrastructure with targeted missile launches. Closer to the planet, that was a nonstarter, however, and he considered the battlecruisers positioned around the first of Rutgers's targets.

"Very well, Lyang-tau," he sighed finally. "Proceed."

"Yes, Sir."

Capriotti stayed where he was, watching the visual, as the battlecruisers brought up their impeller wedges. The three major platforms—two fabrication centers and one of Orca's six primary freight platforms—remained clearly visible from *Québec*'s more distant orbit. The activated wedges completely enclosed them on three sides, however, cutting off direct visual observation from the planetary surface or any of Orca's other near-planet habitats or space stations.

"Detonation in fifteen seconds…mark," Rutgers said clearly behind him. "Fifteen…ten…five…four…three…two…one—"

The nuclear charges detonated simultaneously, in bursts of brilliance which hurt the eye. That had to be purely psychosomatic, Capriotti thought, even as he blinked against the brightness. The display automatically filtered their intensity more rapidly than mere organic nerves could respond to it, after all. Maybe it was just that he *knew* what they must have looked like to the unshielded eye.

Not even a nuclear blast could completely vaporize several billion tons of space station. That was why he'd placed his battlecruisers' impeller wedges to intercept any debris. They'd hold their stations until he was positive nothing could get through to Orca or any of the other platforms. Then they'd move on to the next targets on their list.

He stood for another fifteen seconds, gazing at the spot where the next best thing to two millennia of investment—and the livelihoods of 1.7 million people—had just been wiped from the cosmos. Then he drew a deep breath and looked over his shoulder at his staff.

"Keep me informed, especially about any debris fields," he said. "I'll be in my quarters."

"Of course, Sir," Vice Admiral Helland responded for the entire staff.

He nodded to them and walked from the flag bridge in silence.

Hillary Indrakashi Enkateshwara Tower
City of Old Chicago
Sol System
Solarian League

"THIS IS THE REASON Irene and I needed someone like you, Natsuko," Daud al-Fanudahi said in a tone of profound satisfaction. "We wouldn't have had a clue how to find something like this!"

"Well, don't go assuming we've really found what we all *think* we've found," Lieutenant Colonel Okiku replied. Al-Fanudahi stood looking over her shoulder as she sat at one of the desks in the office which had become their private HQ. Now she waved one hand at the display in front of her. "We've got plenty of evidence of corruption on all these people, but God knows there's *always* corruption—tons of it—here in Sol. So it's still entirely possible we're seeing connections that don't exist. Or connections that do exist but aren't the ones we *think* they are, at any rate."

"Understood." Al-Fanudahi nodded. "Same thing happens on our side of the shop. One of the things that's hardest to avoid—and one of the things that's biting the Navy on the butt right now, for that matter—is mirror-imaging. Interpreting what the other fellow's doing through the lens of how *you'd* do it. If their operating assumptions are different, their decisions and actions are going to be different, too, and it's hard to check your own fundamental concepts at the door."

"There *are* some similarities with that," Okiku acknowledged. "It's a little bit different, from a cop's perspective, though. It's not so much our fundamental 'operational concepts' as it is our effort to assess someone else's motivations when we can't just open a window and peek inside their heads. We know a lot about *what* these people are doing now; what we have to be careful about is assuming we know *why* they're doing it."

"And who they're doing it *for*," Bryce Tarkovsky put in sourly. Al-Fanudahi looked at him, and the tall Marine, another charter member of the group Okiku had dubbed the Ghost Hunters, shrugged. "Like Natsuko says, there's so much normal garden-variety corruption that

73

demonstrating exactly who's paying off whom and for what is the kind of challenge that would make Sisyphus weep."

Al-Fanudahi grinned and shook his head. Tarkovsky delighted in dredging up obscure references to ancient Old Earth legends. Partly that was because he genuinely loved them and had spent years studying them. But al-Fanudahi suspected his interest had begun as a deliberate response to the stereotypical view of Marines.

Personally, al-Fanudahi had never believed the stereotype. He knew at least a dozen Marines who could so read. Why, some of them could even *write!*

"Bryce is right," Okiku said. "That's why this is like chasing ghosts. And don't forget we have to be able to demonstrate whatever we finally do find well enough to convince *someone else*, not just to our own satisfaction. Someone who won't *want* to be convinced the way we do."

"And someone who'll quite possibly have his own reasons to not want any rocks turned over even if he thinks we may be on to something. Or *especially* because he thinks we may," al-Fanudahi agreed. He sat back in his own chair and puffed his cheeks, less cheerful than he'd been a moment before, but that didn't mean they hadn't made a lot of progress.

Simeon Gaddis's "Outcasts" had crunched their way through exabytes of reports, contacts, security camera video, social media, travel patterns, bank accounts, cash transactions, and intercepted and decrypted personal conversations and correspondence. They still didn't know exactly what he had them looking for, although there was no way to keep his personal cybernauts from speculating—probably with a high degree of accuracy—about what he was after.

As the correlations began to pile up, Gaddis had opened an official investigation into corruption within the Gendarmerie and wherever it might lead in the federal government generally. It wasn't the first time he'd gone a round or two with that Goliath, so no one was especially surprised by it. Cynically amused by its *futility*, perhaps, but not surprised.

Under cover of that investigation, however, he'd directed a small army of Gendarmes into the investigation without giving them the slightest hint of what they were really looking for, and the Outcasts had tapped into the flood of information that army had turned up. Armed with all that data, their accomplishments dwarfed anything al-Fanudahi and Irene Teague might have conceivably achieved on their own.

To date, the Ghost Hunters had identified almost a dozen individuals— exclusive of Rajmund Nyhus—who they strongly suspected were tools of what Lupe Blanton had christened "the Other Guys." They were certain Nyhus belonged on the list, but so far, they'd been unable to tie him to anyone else. Which had led both Blanton and Weng Zhing-hwan to fundamentally reassess their estimate of Nyhus's intelligence. Or, more specifically, their estimate of his lack thereof.

They'd had better luck in a few other cases, however, and he reached over Okiku's shoulder to indicate one of the names on her list.

"I think we need to be taking an even closer look at this one," he said, and she tapped the name to open the database associated with it.

"Ms. Bolton," she murmured. "I can see why you're interested in her, Daud. What did you have in mind?"

"Well," he said, "we've linked her to two of the other people on our list. If there's anything to the Outcasts' suggestion that she's also linked to Laughton, we need to nail that down. For more than one reason."

Tarkovsky had straightened in his chair at the sound of Bolton's name. Now he stood and walked around to join al-Fanudahi, and his expression was unhappy.

"I don't disagree with you," he said. "I wish I could, but I don't."

Al-Fanudahi rested one hand lightly on the Marine's shoulder, but Okiku only shook her head. Probably because she was a cop at heart, the captain thought. She drew a sharp line between good guys and bad guys, and anyone who found himself on the wrong side of that line was a target to be taken down as expeditiously and completely as possible. The way she saw it, if someone she'd thought was a friend turned out to be a bad guy, then he'd never been quite as much a friend as the colonel had thought he was.

Intellectually, al-Fanudahi agreed with her, and he knew Tarkovsky did, too, but Colonel Timothy Laughton had been Bryce Tarkovsky's colleague and personal friend for over fifteen T-years. In fact, he'd been on Tarkovsky's short list of potential recruits to the cause...until the Outcasts turned up his connection—his *possible* connection—to Shafiqa Bolton. There was no doubt that Laughton was "in a relationship" with Bolton, although the precise nature of that relationship had yet to be defined. It appeared to be purely social and not terribly close, but the number of peripheral and "coincidental" contacts between them was... statistically improbable.

And the Outcasts' algorithms insisted that Shafiqa Bolton was definitely linked to two other individuals—a Navy captain and a diplomat—they were almost certain were working for the Other Guys.

"I have to say she's got the classic earmarks of a handler," Okiku said after a moment as she scrolled through the database. "I might be less suspicious if her contacts with both Nye and Salazar hadn't spiked the way they have. There's no social or business reason for her to be 'running into' the two of them as much as she has, and the frequency of contacts is still trending upward."

"That's a little thin, Natsuko." Tarkovsky wasn't arguing so much as playing devil's advocate, al-Fanudahi thought.

"That's how these things work, Bryce," she said. "You pick at it until you find a thread you can unravel, and it's usually something small that starts the process. But look at this." She highlighted a section of the data. "Over the last two T-years, the frequency of her contacts with Nye has gone up almost eighteen percent, and most of that increase has occurred since Byng got himself blown away at New Tuscany last October. In fact, over half of it's occurred in the last six months. But his transactions are actually *down* seven percent over that same time period."

Tarkovsky nodded. Bolton, one of the senior partners of Nuñez, Poldak, Bolton, and Hwang, was a financial advisor, and a very good one, judging by her client list and their success rates. Stephanos Nye, a senior policy analyst in Innokentiy Kolokoltsov's Ministry of Foreign Affairs, was one of those clients, but he'd never been a heavy investor. He had lucrative arrangements with several well-heeled lobbyists, and his bank balance was more than comfortable, but he'd always tended to splash around in the shallows of the waters Bolton routinely navigated. Statistically, she spent a disproportionate amount of her time with such a relatively modest player. She always had, actually, although the disproportion had been far smaller up until about the time Haven resumed hostilities with Manticore. If there'd been some sort of personal relationship between them, the uptick probably wouldn't have been noticeable at all, but outside their meetings to discuss possible financial opportunities, they *had* no relationship the Outcasts could discover.

Only the closest scrutiny could have picked that discrepancy out of the hundreds of clients with whom Bolton met on a regular or semi-regular basis, but it was definitely there. Whether it was truly *significant* was another matter, but the fact that Nye's policy positions had steadily hardened against Manticore almost in tandem with Rajmund Nyhus's reports to Ukhtomskoy suggested that it was.

Then there was Captain Mardyola Salazar, one of Fleet Admiral Evangeline Bernard's staffers in the Office of Strategy and Planning. She had no business relationship with Bolton at all and her work schedule at S&P had become steeply more demanding as the confrontation with Manticore progressed from simply adversarial to disastrous. Despite the way that cut into her personal free time, however, she and Bolton kept "running into" one another in social settings. The uptick there was almost twenty-three percent in just the past two months, and al-Fanudahi's sources indicated Salazar had been one of the lead planners for Operation Buccaneer. Of course, al-Fanudahi wasn't supposed to know Buccaneer even existed, far less who'd been tasked with putting it together, but he *was* in intelligence, and recent events had pretty thoroughly validated warnings he'd issued over the years about events in the Haven Sector. As a result, the people at Strategy and Planning were actually talking to him these days. How much *attention* they paid him was debatable, but at least they were asking questions. The nature of those questions had enabled him to piece together a depressingly good picture of the thinking—such as it was—behind Buccaneer, and it was evident Salazar's contributions had strongly shaped the operations plan. In fact, she'd been an early—if not simply *the* earliest—proponent of the Parthian Option.

And then there was Timothy Laughton, the question mark of the moment.

Like Bryce Tarkovsky, he worked for Brigadier Meindert Osterhaut, the CO of Marine Intelligence under Admiral Karl-Heinz Thimár's nominal command as part of the Office of Naval Intelligence. He'd spent twelve T-years seconded to Frontier Security, during which he'd acquired a deep familiarity with the complexities of the Protectorates and the Fringe in general, and Osterhaut had come to rely on that familiarity. He was smart, hard-working, and insightful. He also played one hell of a poker game, as Tarkovsky had learned the hard way. Aside from an occasional—and profitable—foray at the poker table, however, he'd always been a bit...standoffish. He and Tarkovsky liked one another and had considered each other friends for a long time, but they'd never built the sort of close relationship Tarkovsky and al-Fanudahi enjoyed.

Which might turn out to have been fortunate, under the circumstances. Because, like Salazar, Laughton had been "bumping into" Bolton quite a bit recently. And *unlike* Salazar, he'd had no contact at all with her prior to about ten T-months ago...which was about the time his analysis of events in the Fringe—not simply in the Talbott Quadrant but much more broadly—had begun suggesting an increasingly militant and expansionist attitude on Manticore's part.

Under the circumstances, inviting him to become another Ghost Hunter might have had negative consequences for all concerned.

"The Outcasts can't get a lot closer to Bolton, Daud," Okiku said now. "They're still digging into her financials, and they're bird dogging all of her electronic communications to us. Anybody as smart as these people isn't going to do a lot electronically, though. If she's what we think she is, that's the reason she's meeting with people personally. So unless we want to go hands-on, we're not likely to get beyond the suggestive stage. Mind you, Simeon and I would both be confident enough to ask for warrants on the basis of what we've already got, except that we *can't* ask for warrants without going public with what we suspect."

"What do you mean by 'hands-on'?" Al-Fanudahi asked.

"One possibility's to feed at least one of these people something we figure the Other Guys are going to want or that they think they could use. Then we see if they go running to Bolton. If they do, and if the Other Guys act on whatever we gave them, then I think we've proved there's a direct link."

"If we're talking about some kind of vast interstellar conspiracy, that'd take a lot of time we may not have," al-Fanudahi pointed out. "Our suspect would have to get the information to Bolton, and then Bolton would have to get it to her superiors—through whatever chain of communications they use—and her superiors would have to act on it and then send their new orders back down the same chain. I don't think we've got that kind of time. And even if we did, God only knows how many more people would get killed while we waited!"

"Okiku said that was 'one possibility,' Daud," Tarkovsky pointed out. "I'm not sure it's the one she actually had in mind, though."

Something about his tone made al-Fanudahi look at him sharply, and the Marine gave him a crooked smile. Then he looked down as Okiku looked up over her shoulder.

"You were thinking about something a little more . . . proactive, weren't you?" he asked.

"Well," she replied, "you're right about how badly time constraints would work against the planted information approach, Daud. If the Navy's really going ahead with Buccaneer, it's the kind of escalation that's likely to provoke a painful response from the Manties. The kind of response that gets a lot of people killed. And even if that weren't the case, just think about how much damage Buccaneer's going to do—physical damage, I mean, much less the way it's likely to poison public opinion in the Verge and Fringe against the League for decades to come.

"If we're going to accomplish anything inside that time loop, it may be time for some of that proactiveness Bryce is talking about."

"How?"

"One possibility is to take his original suggestion, grab one of these people—like Bolton, maybe—and sweat them. It has the drawback that without a warrant, it's strictly illegal and morally questionable. And if it turns out we're wrong about whoever we grab, we end up facing what you might call a quandary. Do we assume we're wrong about everything and turn her loose with apologies, or do we assume we were wrong about *her*—not about the Other Guys in general—in which case we *can't* turn her loose. Which means we have to do . . . something else with her."

Al-Fanudahi's jaw tightened, but he had to respect her willingness to face the implications, and he nodded in unhappy understanding.

"And another possibility is for us to present a threat they have to honor. Something to make them react in a short timeframe. Something we can see and track."

Al-Fanudahi's nostrils flared.

"You mean present them with *someone* they'd see as a threat," he said, his tone flat.

"That may be our only option, Daud," Tarkovsky said. "There's only so far we can go without either directly questioning a suspect or trying to manipulate one of them into giving himself away. If you can think of another way to do that, I'm all ears. But if you can't . . ."

His voice trailed off and he shrugged.

Harrington House
City of Landing
Planet of Manticore
Manticore Binary System

"HONOR!"

Dr. Allison Harrington's smile was huge as Duchess and Steadholder Harrington entered the Harrington House foyer with Spencer Hawke and Clifford McGraw at her heels. Corporal Anastasia Yanakov, Allison's personal armswoman, nodded respectfully to Major Hawke and then smiled as she watched Allison throw her arms about her daughter. Honor Alexander-Harrington hugged her back, fighting the reflex urge to bend at the knees so she didn't tower over her diminutive mother quite so badly. She'd managed to break that habit about the time she turned sixteen, but the reflex still asserted itself from time to time.

Especially when her mother was pregnant.

"Mother," she replied a bit more sedately, then stood back with her hands on Allison's shoulders. "There have been some changes I see," she added, looking down at her mother's abdomen. "You could have mentioned something about this, oh, a month or so ago."

"I suppose I could have." Allison smiled up at her. "On the other hand, dear, while I wouldn't want to call you *unobservant*, or anything of the sort, it did seem to me that giving you the opportunity to... improve the acuity with which you view the universe might not be out of order."

"I see." Honor shook her head as Corporal Yanakov smiled and Major Hawke and Sergeant McGraw found somewhere else to look. "We do seem to have these little moments without proper warning, though, don't we?"

"At least in my case I knew I *could* get pregnant," Allison observed with a devilish smile, watching Hawke and McGraw from the corner of one eye. Then her expression sobered. "Although, to be honest, I had to think long and hard about deactivating my implant." Her lips trembled ever so slightly. "It was hard for your father. For me, too, I guess. But losing that many people we loved..." She shook her head, the eyes which matched Honor's dark. "It was almost like we couldn't decide whether we were reaffirming that life went on, creating the additional child we'd discovered we wanted—especially after Faith and James were born—or trying to replace the ones we loved. It was that last bit that made it hard. It felt almost *disloyal* somehow. In the end, though, we just said the hell with any philosophical questions."

"And I'm glad you did." Honor hugged her close again. "To be honest, if I had the time, I think Hamish, Emily, and I would be doing exactly the same thing. For all the reasons you just listed, really. And why shouldn't we?" Her embrace tightened for a moment. "Life does go on, we do want more kids, and we are creating more people to put into the holes in our hearts. I wouldn't be a bit surprised to see an uptick in births all across the system, but especially on Sphinx." She released her mother and smiled sadly. "It's one of the things that happen in wars."

"Well, on that topic," Allison said in a brighter tone, "I happen to think it's time you provided me with additional grandchildren. Not that Raoul and Katherine aren't perfectly satisfactory, you understand. There's a certain security in numbers, though. And while I realize *you're* busy at the moment, Emily's available."

"Mother, you're incorrigible!" Honor laughed and shook her head. "And, to be honest, I think Emily may be thinking in that direction, too." Her smile turned warm. "Hamish and I will never be able to thank you enough for getting her past that particular block."

"Even if I was pushy, insufferable, and meddlesome?"

"No! Were you really?" Honor gazed at her in astonishment. "I didn't realize. I thought you were just being your normal self." She paused a beat. "Oh! That's what you *meant*, wasn't it?"

"It's really a pity I never believed in corporal punishment," Allison observed, then grinned as her daughter giggled.

"Mother, I wouldn't change you even if I could," Honor said then. "Which, thank God, nobody in the universe would be capable of, in the first place."

Nimitz bleeked in amusement and nodded his head in emphatic agreement with that statement.

"Well, I certainly hope not," Allison said serenely, tucking her daughter's hand into her elbow and leading the way towards the private family section of Harrington House. Their bodyguards fell in astern, like escorting destroyers.

"And thank you for letting us use the house tonight," Allison continued as they started up the magnificent winding staircase. "We really appreciate it."

"Mother, this is your and Dad's house now, a lot more than it's mine. I believe I've told you that no more than, oh, five or six *thousand* times. It's got more rooms than most hotels, and as long as Hamish, Emily, and I have a modest little six or seven-room suite in which to hang our berets, I think we can consider our housing needs adequately met whenever two or three of us happen to be in Landing at the same time. Which, unfortunately, isn't happening all that often just now."

"I understand that. No, really—I do!" Allison waved her free hand as Honor bent a skeptical eye upon her. "But it's also Steadholder Harrington's official residence and Harrington Steading's embassy in the Star Empire. Under the circumstances, I don't think we should be throwing any drunken orgies without clearing it with you first."

"Your very own drunken orgy? How exciting! Are Hamish and I invited?"

Something very like a smothered chuckle escaped one of the Graysons behind her.

"No, dear." Allison patted her hand. "The drunken orgy is *private*, after the party. I was only using it as an example."

"Darn. And I was so looking forward to it."

"I see Hamish and Emily have been good for the Beowulf side of you," Allison said, and Nimitz laughed again, then raised his right hand—fingers closed to spell the letter "S"—and nodded it up and down in agreement.

"I'll admit they've helped me face my inner Beowulf," Honor acknowledged. "It's even possible the rest of the universe will forgive them for that . . . someday."

❖   ❖   ❖

Music drifted from the quintet of live musicians in the corner of the ballroom. The night was warm and clear, so the crystoplast wall had been retracted, extending the ballroom out across the terrace and increasing its normal six hundred square meters of floor space by a third. For the present, that additional floorspace was unavailable for dancing, however. Instead, spotless white tablecloths fluttered on the land breeze blowing outward across Jason Bay while the Harrington House staff, augmented for the evening, prepared to serve supper.

Nor was anyone dancing in the ballroom itself, despite its size, the splendor of its brilliantly polished marble floor, and the invitation of the music. Possibly because the music in question was a bit odd by Manticoran standards. Allison and Alfred Harrington had fallen in love with classical Grayson music during their time on Grayson, but the planet's ancient dancing traditions, which centered on something called the "square dance," weren't familiar to most Manticorans. The lack of dancers was subject to change, however, and Honor suspected that it would after dinner.

At the moment, she stood between Hamish and Emily Alexander-Harrington's life support chair, gazing out across the bay.

"Honor, I'd like you to meet someone," a voice said, and she turned as her father—one of the few people present who was actually taller than she was—walked up behind her.

Since Harrington House was technically Grayson soil, and Honor tended to dress in her persona as Steadholder Harrington whenever she was officially "home," she wasn't in uniform tonight. But her father, for the first time since her childhood, was. Rather than the four golden pips of his preretirement rank, however, his collar bore two gold planets. A single broad gold band had been added to the three bands of a commander, and the unit patch on his left shoulder showed the Rod of Asclepius under the word "Bassingford." In the newly reactivated Commodore Harrington's case, both the staff itself and the single serpent were embroidered in gold rather than the silver of other Bassingford Medical Center shoulder flashes.

Which was rather the point of this evening's festivities, she reflected. Her father hadn't simply gone back onto active duty. Effective tomorrow, he was Bassingford's one hundred and third commanding officer. Officially, that was because he'd been recalled by the Navy, and that was fair enough, because the Navy had wanted him back at Bassingford virtually from the day he retired and resigned his post as Head of Neurosurgery. In reality, though, it was the Yawata Strike which had returned him to active duty. He'd needed a few months to make up his mind. The process had begun shortly after the strike, but it had taken the Battle of Spindle and—especially—"Operation Raging Justice" to complete it. One thing was sadly obvious; if the Mandarins persisted in their current policies, Bassingford would need far more beds...most of which would be filled by Solarians. Alfred Harrington needed to be part of dealing with all those broken bodies and lives. That was what had finally pushed him back into uniform.

That and the need to do something *healing* rather than succumb to the part of him which had once been Sergeant Harrington, Royal Manticoran Marine Corps.

Now he smiled at his daughter, indicating the much shorter woman—no more than fifteen or sixteen centimeters taller than Allison Harrington—at his side. She had dark hair, ten or twelve centimeters longer than Honor had once worn her own, dark eyes, and a lively, mobile face. She, too, was in uniform with the Bassingford shoulder flash, although in her case, only the staff of the rod was in gold.

"Honor, this is Captain Sara Kate Lessem," Alfred said. "Sara Kate, my daughter, Duchess Harrington. She's—"

"*Sara Kate!*" Honor smiled broadly and enveloped the shorter woman in a hug.

"Ah, should I assume my introduction was a bit . . . superfluous?" her father asked after a moment while Hamish and Emily chuckled.

"Daddy, I've known Sara Kate for—what? Thirty T-years, Sara Kate?"

"I'm afraid it really has been about that long," Captain Lessem replied with a smile. "It's good to see you again, though. It's been too long!"

"I'm sorry I missed the wedding," Honor said, shaking her head. "I was . . . occupied at the time."

"You mean you were off blowing things up again," Captain Lessem observed.

"Well, yes, I suppose." Honor smiled. "And how do you like being a respectable married woman?"

"Honor, it's been three T-years now. How do you expect me to remember what it was like before? And speaking of respectable married women—?" Captain Lessem raised her eyebrows in Hamish and Emily's direction, and Honor chuckled.

"Mom and Dad really did teach me better manners than that," she said. "Sara Kate, this is my husband, Hamish Alexander-Harrington, and this is my wife, Emily Alexander-Harrington. Both of them have long, tiresome lists of titles we'll leave to one side right now. Hamish, Emily, this is Sara Kate Lessem. I first met her when she was Sara Kate Tillman."

"*They* have long tiresome lists of titles?" Captain Lessem shook her head, then shook hands with both of Honor's spouses.

"At least half of which come from our association with *her*," Emily told her with a smile. "May I ask how you and Honor come to know one another?"

"Uncle Jacques introduced us," Honor replied before Lessem could, and it was her father's eyebrows turn to rise.

"*Jacques* introduced you?" he said. "Wait a minute. Would this have anything to do with those anachronisms of his?"

"Of course it does. Sara Kate's another member of the Society. Her particular interest is in what they called ballroom dancing from the last couple of centuries Ante Diaspora. It's not what most people do today. Actually, I like it a lot better. So, Sara Kate, you're at Bassingford these days?"

"I am," Lessem confirmed.

"She means she's the Assistant Director *and* Head of Nursing and Physical Therapy," Commodore Harrington put in.

"And I've had a lot more patients than I'd like since that business with Filareta." Lessem's expression was much less cheerful than it had been. "They may all be Sollies, but a broken body's still a broken body."

"I know," Honor sighed. "And I hate it. If I could've avoided it—"

"If you could have avoided it, we'd be calling you God and lighting candles to you," Lessem interrupted. "And if it had occurred to me that you were going to go off on a guilt trip, I never would've opened my mouth about it, either."

"Oh, I *like* you, Captain Lessem!" Emily said enthusiastically. "Please! Kick her again!"

Lessem gave her a startled glance, then snorted in sudden understanding.

"Been brooding about it, has she?"

"Only sometimes," Emily replied in the judicious tone of someone trying to be scrupulously fair. "Not more than every other time I see her."

"Then consider her kicked," Lessem promised.

"Oh, thank you both *so* much." Honor rolled her eyes while Hamish and her father chuckled. "And you two aren't helping this, you know," she told the male component of the conversation severely.

"Not my responsibility to help when Captain Lessem and Emily are doing such a splendid job," Hamish informed her. "Not that either of them's likely to tell you anything I haven't."

"Acknowledged." Honor nodded. "And I'll try."

"Good." Lessem reached out to squeeze her upper arm gently. "That's good, Honor."

"I see Mistress Thorn's minions are about ready to serve," Hamish observed, looking back towards the ballroom. "Will you join us, Captain?"

"I'd be honored, My Lord."

"On social occasions, it's 'Hamish,' Captain."

"Only if it's also Sara Kate, *My Lord*," Lessem replied a bit pointedly.

"Then would you join us... Sara Kate?"

"Thank you... Hamish."

He smiled and offered her his arm while Honor took Emily's hand and the four of them headed for the head table. Alfred looked around until he located Allison. As usual, she was at the center of a cluster of admirers—most of them male—and he headed across to rescue her and escort her to the same table.

She smiled happily as he swooped down upon her, ruthlessly exploiting his position as both husband and guest of honor, since the evening was the official announcement of his return to duty, and she tucked her hand into his elbow and squeezed gratefully as he led her away.

"I don't know what you were thinking to leave me exposed that way." Her tone was teasing, but there was an edge of seriousness to it. "My God, Alfred! You didn't tell me we were inviting George Brockman!" She shuddered. "That man doesn't have the faintest concept of what 'monogamy' means."

"And if I'd thought for a moment that you weren't perfectly capable of cutting him off at the knees—or at any other appropriate point on his anatomy—I'd have been there in an instant," her husband assured her, and looked down at her with a faint twinkle. "Tell me with a straight face that you didn't enjoy doing exactly that when—as I'm sure happened—he gave you the chance?"

"You may be able to throw me heartlessly to the wolves, but you can't make me lie!" She lifted her nose with an audible sniff, then smiled wickedly. "I'm pretty sure the bleeding will stop in another hour or so."

"Good for you!" Alfred laughed. "And while we're talking about social lapses, were you aware Honor and Sara Kate Lessem—and Jacques, now that I think about it—all know one another?"

"Of course I was." She looked up at him again with a devilish smile. "Dear me. Did I forget to mention that to you?"

"Out of consideration for your delicate condition, I will defer the proper response to that."

"Oh, no, you won't!" she told him pertly. "I've already had the peach preserves sent to our room."

"You're incorrigible," he said, smothering a laugh.

"I don't know why you and Honor keep *saying* that. I'm the most *en*couragable person I know!"

✧   ✧   ✧

"It's good to see him laughing again," Emily Alexander-Harrington said quietly as her mother- and father-in-law headed towards the table.

"Agreed," Honor said, equally quietly. "And I think—"

She paused for a moment, then shook her head.

"You think what?" Emily pressed.

"Oh, it was just a passing thought." Honor shook her head again, her expression sobering. "We're all having a few of those at the moment, I think."

"Yes, we are," Emily agreed, but she gazed at Honor speculatively, and Honor made herself look back with tranquil eyes as she tasted the curiosity in Emily's mind-glow. She also didn't mention what had spawned that "passing thought."

"Tell me, have you given any more thought to a brother or sister for Katherine and Raoul?" she asked instead.

"I have." Emily nodded, although the question seemed to have sharpened the focus of that speculation Honor had tasted. "In fact, I have an appointment to discuss it with Dr. Illescue at Briarwood tomorrow afternoon, before I go back to White Haven."

"Oh, good!" Honor beamed at her, bending over her chair to envelop her in a gentle hug. "I'm thinking about doing the same thing. Maybe this time we can time it even closer!"

"There's only a month or so between the two we have, dear," Emily pointed out drily. "What? You want to synchronize the deliveries to the same *minute?*"

"Well, if neither one of us is going to be in a position to do it the old fashioned way, we might as well take advantage of the opportunities we do have. Besides—" she straightened with a devilish smile "—twins *do* run in Mom's family, you know!"

Emily laughed, and Honor's smile turned more gentle. But then she straightened and looked at Hamish across Emily's head. She swiveled her eyes to one side, to where Sandra Thurston, Emily's nurse and constant companion, stood chatting with James MacGuiness while he kept an eagle eye on the evening's festivities. Her gaze came back to Hamish, and he shrugged ever so slightly, letting an edge of worry show in his own blue eyes.

Her mouth tightened as she put that together with the undertone she'd tasted in Emily's mind-glow, but then she drew a deep breath. She wasn't going to borrow any trouble, she told herself firmly. Not tonight. And not when all three of them had so much to be grateful for, including—

"You're right about how good it is to see Daddy laughing again," she said, looking back down at Emily and squeezing her good hand gently, then looked at Captain Lessem. "I think it's going to be good for him to get back to work, too."

"Well, I can tell you the entire staff's damned glad we've *gotten* him back to work," Lessem said frankly. "Lord knows we need him as a surgeon, but we need him even more on the administrative side." She shook her head. "I wasn't joking about how many patients we're going to have, Honor. It's bad already, and if those idiots in Old Chicago don't get their heads out of—" She paused, then grimaced. "Out of the *sand*, it's going to get a lot worse."

"I know. And we're trying to hold it to a minimum," Honor said, easing Nimitz off her shoulder to join Samantha in the double highchair between her and Hamish. "And speaking of trying to keep things to minimums, where's Martin right now?"

"I suppose, given your august connections I can tell you," Lessem said, smiling crookedly at Hamish. "At the moment, he's got a task group with Vice Admiral Correia. I don't know exactly where they were headed, but I know it's part of Lacoön Two."

"If he's with Correia, he's probably in Ajay or Prime about now," Hamish said.

"And just between you and me, I'm a lot happier with the thought of his facing off with Sollies instead of Havenites," the captain observed.

"So am I, for now, at least," Honor. "I just wish we had a clue about some way to convince the Mandarins to at least pretend they have a single functional brain amongst them."

"I seem to sense just a little acerbity?" Lessem teased.

"Just a bit, perhaps," Honor admitted.

"Tell me, Doctor—Sara Kate, I mean," Emily said. "Honor mentioned something about 'ancient' ballroom dancing. How did you ever get involved with that?"

"Blame it on my misspent youth," Lessem replied with a chuckle. "That and the fact that my mother knew Honor's Uncle Jacques when they were college students. He got her involved with the Society for Creative Anachronism, and she's a physical therapist, too. Dance is sort of a natural connection for therapists. Or it can be, anyway."

"Fascinating." Emily shook her head. "I've had quite a bit of experience with therapists myself, over the years, but for fairly obvious reasons, no one ever suggested dance to me. I can see its applicability, though, now that you've mentioned it."

"Oh, I do it much more for pleasure than professionally," Lessem said. "I even got Martin to take it up, and he's remarkably good at it. To be honest, I'm looking for a new challenge for him."

"You are, are you?" Honor smiled. "Well, in that case, you've come to the right place."

"I have?" Lessem's eyebrows arched, and Honor's smile grew broader.

"Oh, yes. Tell me, are you familiar with the phrase 'dosey doe'?"

George Benton Tower
City of Old Chicago
Old Earth
Sol System

"SORRY I'M LATE," PERMANENT Senior Undersecretary for Foreign Affairs Innokentiy Kolokoltsov told his colleagues as he stepped through the conference room's doors and they slid silently shut behind him. "I was ready to walk out of my office when one of my analysts—Stephanos Nye, I think I've mentioned him to you before—asked for an urgent appointment. He was right about the urgency, and one thing led to another. I had to make some immediate decisions, and it took a little while to get all the technical information I needed."

"You could've screened to let us know you'd be delayed." There was an unpleasant edge in Nathan MacArtney's reply. Then again, they'd expected him almost an hour earlier.

"It's not like we don't all have plenty of 'urgent appointments' of our own we could be using our time on instead of sitting twiddling our thumbs," MacArtney added.

Kolokoltsov frowned at him, his eyes cold. Of all the people in this room, MacArtney, as Permanent Senior Undersecretary of the Interior, bore the most direct responsibility for the unholy mess they faced. Kolokoltsov was prepared to admit he'd contributed his own fair share to the making of that mess, but none of the others could rival the string of disasters MacArtney and his ally, the late, unlamented Fleet Admiral Rajampet, had brewed up before Rajampet's overdue suicide.

"I decided it wasn't a very good idea to discuss highly sensitive matters over the com, Nathan," he said after a moment. "We've got enough alligators biting us on the arse without letting anything... unfortunate get leaked."

"Oh, don't be ridiculous, Innokentiy!" Malachai Abruzzi, the Permanent Senior Undersecretary of Information, shook his head. "Our coms are the most secure in the entire galaxy!"

"Really?" Kolokoltsov crossed to the table, settled into the chair at its head, and turned it to face the others. "You're confident of that, are you?"

"Of course I am!"

"Then perhaps you'd care to explain how the conversation you and Nathan had last month about how to handle the Hypatian situation happened to hit the public boards in Hypatia last week?"

The silence in the deeply buried, heavily shielded conference room was as total as it was sudden, and he looked around his colleagues' faces.

"What conversation was that?" Omosupe Quartermain asked after a long, still moment. MacArtney, in particular, had been on the Permanent Senior Undersecretary of Commerce's personal shit list ever since the situation in the Fringe began deteriorating, since she and her colleague Agatá Wodoslawski, the Permanent Senior Undersecretary of the Treasury, were the ones trying desperately—and unsuccessfully—to cope with the catastrophic fiscal consequences.

"The one in which they considered how much simpler things would get if we dropped an intervention battalion or two into Hypatia to 'encourage' President Vangelis to call off the referendum. Something about shooting every tenth senator until they got it right, I believe." Kolokoltsov's voice was even colder than his eyes, and Wodoslawski joined him and Quartermain in glowering at Abruzzi and MacArtney.

"Oh, come on, Innokentiy!" Abruzzi protested. "That was never a *serious* policy suggestion!" He shook his head, expression disgusted. "For God's sake, there are over two billion people on Hypatia, and another million-point-two in the Alexandria Belt! Someone really thinks a couple of intervention battalions are going to turn something like *that* around? Give me a break!"

"Of course *I* don't think that. That doesn't mean someone else might not. And let's be honest here, it wouldn't be all that different from quite a few interventions OFS has pulled off out in the Protectorates, now would it? Did it ever occur to either of you that with feelings running as high as they are—and enough people on the other side primed to jump on any opening we give them—finding out that two of the 'Mandarins' are even *talking* about what would amount to a coup against a legally elected system president would play right into the hysteria mongers' hands?"

"First, we were on a secure government com. Who the hell was going to hear about it?" Abruzzi demanded. "And, secondly, it should've been totally clear from the context of our entire conversation that we were venting our frustration, not recommending some kind of serious policy!"

"Malachai, you're the Permanent Undersecretary of Information! You know, better than anyone else in this room, how easy it is to strip something *out* of its context and turn it into a soundbite that says exactly the opposite of what whoever said it actually meant. And that's just what some bastard in Hypatia's done with your and Nathan's little conversational...faux pas."

Abruzzi had opened his mouth to respond. Now he shut it again, his expression thunderous, because Kolokoltsov was right. The Ministry of Information spent far more of its resources on "shaping the narrative"—what an earlier and more honest age might have called "producing propaganda"—than it ever did on straight news releases.

"How the hell did anybody get their hands on it in the first place?" MacArtney demanded, glaring at Abruzzi with a certain self-righteousness. *He* wasn't the one who'd just proclaimed the inviolability of their communications channels, after all.

"If I knew that, whoever's responsible for it would be roasting on a slow spit," Kolokoltsov replied grimly. "All I know is that the latest courier boat from Hypatia came in about three hours ago, and your conversation—shorn of anything that could conceivably suggest it *wasn't* a serious policy suggestion, or at least a serious *consideration*— had been on the boards for two days before it left. In those two days, according to Stephanos, it logged over nine hundred and seventy-two million hits. I've done the math, by the way. That works out to forty-nine percent of the total population of the star system, including every babe in arms. And for your information, that's *seventy-five* percent of the adult population. To say it isn't playing well with the voters would be something of an understatement, Nathan."

"Oh my God." Quartermain's tone couldn't seem to decide between disgust, anger, and resignation. "So how bad *is* the damage, Innokentiy?"

"Well it isn't good." Kolokoltsov popped a data chip into the terminal in front of him and the header of a report appeared on his colleagues' displays. "This is Nye's initial take on it. He's doing a more deliberate analysis, and the numbers may get a little better, but I doubt it'll make much difference in the end. And the conclusion he's reached is that what was going to be a squeaker that would *probably* go against us is in the process of turning into something just a bit more...emphatic. The word he used was 'tsunami,' actually."

"All over what couldn't be more than three or four seconds of a com conversation?" Wodoslawski looked as if she would have liked to be incredulous.

"Oh, it's more than three or four seconds." Kolokoltsov spared MacArtney and Abruzzi a fulminating glare, then looked at Wodoslawski. "It would seem there was quite a bit of 'frustration venting' in the conversation, and whoever handed it over to the Hypatian newsies must have edited all the choicer bits together, because the actual soundbite runs almost six minutes. Don't misunderstand me. I'm not saying this is the only thing driving Hypatian public opinion. There were already a lot of negative factors in the mix, and we all know it. But it looks as if this could be the emotional trigger that turns a vote that already looked dicey into an outright disaster."

"Shit." Omosupe Quartermain seldom used colorful language, but she'd clearly decided to make an exception, and Kolokoltsov didn't blame her.

With less than a third of Beowulf System's population, and perhaps a fifth of its gross system product, Hypatia was on the small size for what was technically a Core System of the League. For that matter, as a full member system, Hypatia's contribution to the Solarian League's federal budget was limited, aside from the relatively modest duties levied on its interstellar shipping. It was a useful bit of cash flow, but there were probably a dozen Protectorate systems which contributed at least as much. So from that perspective, Hypatia's potential defection was unlikely to make an already grim situation much worse.

But Hypatia, like Beowulf, had been a founding member of the Solarian League when the League Constitution was proclaimed right here in Old Chicago seven hundred fifty-seven T-years ago last month. Not only that, the system was only forty-four light-years—less than six days, for a dispatch boat—from Beowulf and the Beowulf Terminus of the Manticoran Wormhole Junction. If Hypatia opted to secede and, even more disastrously, to throw in its lot with its longtime neighbors, trading partners, and friends, it would expand the "Grand Alliance's" bridgehead at the very heart of the Solarian League dangerously. Worse, a successful secession—*another* successful secession, since Beowulf's was a foregone conclusion as soon as the Beowulfers got around to holding their own vote—would go a disastrously long way toward validating the *right* to secede in the court of public opinion.

And that could not be allowed.

"Perhaps you can see now why I didn't screen you about this," Kolokoltsov observed. "In fact, I know it's going to be an incredible pain, but in addition to assuming anything we say on our nice, secure com system is likely to be overheard and watching our tongues accordingly, I think any sensitive information will need to be couriered back and forth between us, at least for the next few days. For that matter, it'd probably be smart of us to handle *really* sensitive information that way for the foreseeable future."

"That'd make it almost impossible to coordinate properly," Wodoslawski objected.

"No, it won't." Kolokoltsov shook his head. "It'll make it *difficult*, granted, but all of us—except you—have our offices here in George

Benton. I don't know how they got to Nathan and Malachai's com conversation, but this conference room is only a lift shaft away from our private offices, and it's shielded against every form of eavesdropping known to man. For that matter, so are our offices. I've already found you twenty-four thousand square meters of floor space here in the tower, and if you need it, we can free up twice that much in seventy-two hours. I know moving your entire staff over would be a pain in the arse, but I don't really see an option if we're going to keep you in the loop."

"You're serious, aren't you?"

"Dead serious," he said flatly. "Look, maybe this is an exercise in paranoia on my part, but we're about to get handed our heads in Hypatia, people. So far, most of the Core Worlds aren't especially worried about all this, which is a mixed blessing. They're not champing at the bit to throw their support behind us, but we don't have a couple dozen Beowulfs bolting from the League...yet. But that's why we can't—we just *can't*—go on with this kind of crap hitting us in the face every other week."

He looked around the conference room for a long, silent moment and saw it in their faces. So far, the majority of Core Worlders still regarded the conflict with Manticore as only one more "escapade" in the Fringe. They were used to that sort of thing—so used to it that they took it for granted. True, this time the Manties' wormhole seizures were starting to pinch many of the inner member systems enough to hurt, but what was pneumonia for the federal government's revenue stream was little more than a minor cold for the various system economies, and that was especially true for those in the Core, who had plenty of domestic industry. And despite the enormous death tolls the SLN had suffered, there was little moral outrage, either. For one thing, the public at large didn't know how high those totals were. For another, the SLN was a professional military force which represented an incredibly tiny demographic of the League's total population. Those deaths simply weren't impacting any significant percentage of the civilian population—not yet, at least—and in many ways, he and his colleagues were just as happy about that. There were a few talking heads trying to "view with alarm" where the navy's losses were concerned, but they were gaining remarkably little traction, especially with Abruzzi managing the news flow so carefully. All of which meant the Manties were managing to strangle the Mandarins to death without enraging Solarian public opinion—outside the Sol System, where the professional governing class lived, at least.

That was both a good thing and a bad thing from the Mandarins' perspective, but so far, the good outweighed the bad. And if they went on shedding the member systems which *were* paying attention, some of those other fat-and-happy member systems were going to wake up and smell the coffee. And if *that* happened . . .

"I've talked to my tech people," he went on. "That's one of the reasons I was so late. And they say that if we're all here in the tower, they can run secure, shielded, *hardwired* com lines that could only be tapped with direct physical access to the cables. I know it sounds like Dark Ages technology, but if it'll work, I don't really give a damn how 'antiquated' it is. And if all the cable involved is here in the same tower, it'll be a lot easier for us to make sure nobody's getting that physical access to it."

Wodoslawski sat back, shaking her head, and Kolokoltsov couldn't blame her. In truth, he wasn't certain himself how much of his proposal was rational and how much was the product of his own increasing desperation. The worst thing about it, he thought, was that he proposed to turn Benton Tower into a fortress, and people living inside fortresses developed fortress *mentalities*. If he and his colleagues retreated into a bunker, even one as splendidly equipped as this one, it might encourage them to retreat into a deeper and deeper disconnect with the galaxy about them, as well.

But where's the option? he asked himself. *Whether we like it or not, somebody hacked our coms, and none of our techs have found any finger-prints pointing at who it might've been or how the hell they did it. And I don't have to explain all the implications to the others. They know as well as I do that if someone can hack our coms, God only knows what* else *they can break into! And really, the only one who'd be physically moving would be Agatá. The rest of us're already* in *George Benton! For that matter, most of the ministries have been here since the day it was built, so it's not even like the rest of the League will realize we're forting up in the first place!*

No, they wouldn't. George Benton Tower was indelibly associated in the public's mind with the might and majesty of the League's Federal Government. Moving the other ministries *out* of George Benton would have generated far more speculation than moving Treasury *into* it. But he and his colleagues would know, and so would their most senior and trusted subordinates. And from there, the awareness would seep downward with the inevitability of a winter freeze in Tarko-Sale, his hometown in ancient Siberia.

He looked around the shielded, guarded conference room once more and wondered how often his fellows reflected upon the name of the two-kilometer tall tower which housed the Solarian League's heart and brain. Thought about the fact that it had been named for one of the dozen or so most famous human beings in history, the man most responsible, in many ways, for the League's creation. The co-leader of the medical teams—the teams from *Beowulf*—which had preserved human life on Old Earth itself after the Final War. The man who'd seen the need for a coordinating authority that could span hundreds of light-years, recognized its necessity in the wake of the catastrophic damage he'd done so much to repair, and spent the last thirty-five T-years of his life bringing that authority into existence.

The man whose distant descendant headed the Beowulf System government which was about to stab the Solarian League in the heart. Of course, he must have literally billions of "distant descendants" after the next best thing to eight hundred years, and it was only logical for them to be concentrated in Beowulf and its closest galactic neighbors. Yet it was bitterly ironic that even as Chyang Benton-Ramirez prepared to oversee the referendum which would supply the dagger, yet *another* of those descendants commanded the "Grand Fleet" which might well drive it home.

It was, perhaps, fortunate so few Solarians were sufficiently aware of their own history to ask why *that* man's descendants had chosen to destroy all he'd built.

"All right," Wodoslawski said at last. "My analysts and accountants need more space than we've got over at De Soto Tower, anyway. We've been looking at possible solutions for the last couple of years, really, in a desultory sort of way. For that matter, we've already considered moving into George Benton, and it looks like I can free up everything they need back in De Soto by moving my administrative personnel over here. That should at least keep it from looking like some kind of...panic reaction."

"And how long is it going to take to install these 'hardwired' coms of yours?" MacArtney demanded. For someone whose loose lips had contributed so much to the need for those selfsame coms, he sounded remarkably belligerent, Kolokoltsov thought.

"They'll be running the first lines to all the offices here in the tower within two or three hours," he replied. "It'd be faster to just reprogram the wall molycircs, but a lot less secure, so they're running actual cable through the air ducts and service shafts. According to my security chief and the building executive, they should complete the installation within eight days or so. After that, we can probably go back to electronic conferencing for everything but the most sensitive data."

"'*Probably*,'" Abruzzi repeated sourly, then shrugged. "All right. I think you may be jumping at shadows—or, at least, closing the barn door after the cow's left—but I also didn't think a frigging *joke* with

Nathan would turn Hypatia into a damned disaster, either! So *I'm* not going to tell you you don't have a point, Innokentiy!"

Kolokoltsov nodded and turned his gaze on MacArtney.

"All right. *All right!*" The permanent senior undersecretary of the interior raised both hands. "If everyone else's ready to go along with this, who am I to argue? And," he added grudgingly, "Malachai's right. If something he and I tossed off in a casual conversation can have the kind of effect your analyst's describing, it's probably time we *all* got paranoid as hell!"

Not the most gracious assent in history, Kolokoltsov reflected, but he'd take it. Now if only he could figure out some way to toss MacArtney off the troika before he did something even more regrettable. Unfortunately, every single one of them knew where too many bodies were buried for the others to safely feed him—or her—to the wolves.

"In the meantime, though, and while we're here," MacArtney continued, "what the hell are we going to *do* about Hypatia?" He looked around the table, his expression grim. "It's bad enough we're about to lose Beowulf, but at least where Beowulf's concerned we've built the case that they must've decided years ago to throw in with the Manties' imperialist ambitions. We haven't done that in Hypatia's case."

Personally, Kolokoltsov had distinct reservations about how well they'd "built the case" for Beowulf's "long-planned treachery" against the League. God knew they'd given it their best shot, and the establishment newsies had embraced the narrative. But while the public opinion metrics (here in Sol, at least; trying to keep up with current public opinion in star systems hundreds of light-years distant was about as impossible as a task came) were favorable to the government's actions *so far*, there was no guarantee they'd stay that way. Even here in Sol, a lot of that "favorable" attitude was probably as much lack of the interest that might have led to opposition, which meant it was subject to change without much notice. And Beowulf had a tremendous amount of well-earned prestige within the League. Given time, that prestige was only too likely to reassert itself in the public's mind, and that could be...unfortunate. Despite which, MacArtney had a point about Hypatia.

Hypatia hadn't been on their radar when they first began looking at other star systems which might follow Beowulf's lead. It should have been, but the Hypatians had adopted a calm wait-and-see attitude which—he admitted it—he and his colleagues had misread as fundamental acceptance of the League's indissoluble nature. Unfortunately, that had changed when the Manties leaked news of Operation Raging Justice to the media long before Massimo Filareta ever reached Manticore. Hypatia's relations with Beowulf were closer than its relations with Manticore, but Hypatians had been marrying both Beowulfers and Manticorans for centuries. In a lot of ways, technical Core World status or not, their population's mindset was more closely attuned to the Fringers beyond the Manticoran Wormhole Junction than it was to Sol and Old Terra, and they hadn't reacted well to the dispatch of hundreds of superdreadnoughts to attack Manticore—and several million of their relatives—without so much as a formal declaration of war. And once the possibility of secession had been mentioned, they'd moved forward far more quickly than anyone could have imagined, aided by a system constitution which made it easy to call snap referendums to approve—or *dis*approve—proposed government policies. Kolokoltsov doubted the Hypatian Constitution's drafters had ever envisioned that provision being used for something like this, but their handiwork had let System President Adam Vangelis and his Attorney General, Thanos Boyagis, put the machinery into motion with astonishing speed.

Hypatia would actually vote over a T-month before Beowulf, and there was little question that the outcome of the referendum would impact the Beowulf vote.

It's not going to change *it, though,* he reflected. *There's not a doubt in the universe which way Beowulf's going to vote, and there hasn't been from the beginning. What Hypatia* will *do, unfortunately, is to increase the margin in favor of secession, and probably by a lot. And it'll also mean* Hypatia *will be the example all the hotheads in those Verge Systems cite when they start calling for* their *star systems to secede. Unless we can figure out a way to…defuse that particular threat, that is.*

He looked around the table again, thinking about the policy options Stephanos Nye had outlined in the conclusions section of his report. He'd provided half a dozen possible scenarios, but it was clear which one *he* favored, and Kolokoltsov wondered if the others would be as appalled by it as he was?

And whether or not *they'd* find themselves endorsing it anyway.

HMS *Clas Fleming*
Prime Terminus
Prime-Ajay Hyper Bridge

"THE REALLY SURPRISING DIFFERENCE is how much less... call it 'cosmopolitan,' I guess, than Manticorans they tend to be," Sara Kate Lessem said from the display. "I have to say that's not something I would've expected, and it took me a while to figure it out. But it finally came to me." She shook her head. "They're *Solarians*, and Solarians automatically know everything they need to know about the neobarbs inhabiting the outer dark beyond the League's borders. So why bother to look for more data, far less open their minds to new opinions? And, to be fair, even some of them who've spent their entire careers in the Navy haven't seen anywhere near as many foreign star systems as our Navy personnel, much less our merchant spacers! For that matter, we see a *lot* more visitors from other star systems right here in Manticore than most Solarians ever see. So I suppose I *can* understand—in a way—that they never get exposed to anyone from outside their 'bubble.' But that doesn't make it one bit less scary. If the people in the Solarian *Navy* are... unsophisticated enough, let's say, to never even question the nonsense the Mandarins are spewing, how's the Solarian woman-in-the-street supposed to realize it's all lies?"

Now that, Commodore Sir Martin Lessem reflected, pausing the letter for just a moment to refill his coffee cup, *is an excellent summation of the problem, sweetheart.* He smiled. *I always knew you were a sharp one, despite the fact that you decided to marry* me! *Too bad I don't have any better clue about the answer to your question than anyone else seems to have at the moment.*

He sipped coffee, gazing wistfully at his wife's frozen image. At the moment, he and Cruiser Squadron 912 were 387.7 light-years (and forty-five days' hyper-travel) from the Manticore System, and it was going to be a while before he got the chance to hold her again. Fortunately, letters were another matter—for the moment, at least. Despite the Prime System's distance from Manticore, it was "only" twenty-nine days' hyper-travel from Beowulf. As interstellar travel times went, that wasn't especially bad. It wasn't anything he'd call *good*, but he'd had to put up with far worse.

Of course, that hadn't been in the middle of a war against the largest star nation in human history. That put rather a different slant on things...and had quite a lot to do with how CruRon 912 came to be floating in interstellar dimness just over seven light-hours from the Prime System's G0 primary.

His squadron's only company was a single platform keeping station on the Prime Terminus of the Prime-Ajay hyper bridge. That platform, the home of Prime Traffic Control, was on the small side. Then again, the Prime-Ajay bridge wasn't very impressive, compared to the massive Manticoran Wormhole Junction, and saw perhaps five percent of the Junction's traffic. The Prime System, however, was also only 21.5 LY (and less than three days) from the Agueda System and the Agueda-Stine hyper-bridge. That made this unprepossessing, thoroughly depressing volume of nothingness far more valuable than first impressions—or simple economics—might have suggested, given Lacoön Two's strategy of seizing control of as many wormholes as possible.

CruRon 912's job was to see to it that the Prime Terminus stayed seized, particularly since Vice Admiral Correia had taken the rest of the task force off to Agueda en route to Stine. It would be...inconvenient if he returned to Prime and found he had to return to Manticore through hyper. That was a point worth keeping in mind, since eventually even the Solarian League Navy was bound to start trying to do something about Lacoön's consequences.

Lessem grimaced at the thought and scolded himself for it. So far, the Sollies had stepped on their swords with almost unbelievable thoroughness, but they weren't really all idiots. It was obvious the SLN's peacetime ossification had gone deeper than anyone in ONI had been prepared to suggest in his wildest dreams, but there were plenty of perfectly good Solarian brains. The Darwinian consequences of the SLN's obsolescent weapons and...less than ideal operational thinking were bound to push some of those good brains to the forefront far more rapidly than Lessem's more optimistic—and, in his opinion, chauvinistic—colleagues thought possible. They damned well ought to know better than that, but it wasn't really fair for him to fault them too severely for it. He found *himself* doing it too often for him to be casting any stones, witness the "even" of his own thoughts!

The good news, as his letter from Sara Kate reemphasized, was that those good brains had to start digging at the bottom of an awful deep hole. What had happened thirty-nine days ago made that painfully clear. He couldn't imagine why Massimo Filareta had been *stupid* enough to open fire when Duchess Harrington had so conclusively demonstrated the hopelessness of Eleventh Fleet's position, but what had happened to his ships was a clear example of that Darwinian process in action. And given her position at Bassingford, Sara Kate was better placed than most to see the human cost.

He sipped more coffee and touched the play button again.

"Another thing that's pretty obvious," she said, "is that an awful lot of them—even some of their senior officers—still outright refuse to acknowledge how outdated their hardware is. I know that's got to be hard for them, but I don't understand how they can stay in such deep denial after what happened to their fleet! Dr. Flint—I think I've told you about him before; he's the new Head of Psychology here at Bassingford—tells me that's exactly what's happening, that they're still in the 'denial phase,' and I suppose that makes sense. It's not exactly what I'd call a survival trait, though!" She shook her head on the display, and her expression had turned grimmer. "If they can't get past that pretty darn quickly, a lot more of their people are going to wind up under our care here at Bassingford . . . or dead. I'd like to think we'd be faster to ac—"

The display froze, Sara Kate's voice sliced off in mid-word by the sudden, shrill, unmistakable stridency of the General Quarters alarm. Lessem was still jerking erect in his chair when a very different voice came over the speakers.

"Battle Stations! Battle Stations!" it barked. "All hands, man Battle Stations! This is no drill! Battle Stations! Battle Stations!"

✧   ✧   ✧

"Talk to me, Lester," Commodore Lessem said crisply, two minutes later, as he strode out of the lift car and onto the flag bridge of HMS *Clas Fleming*, the *Saganami*-C-class flagship of both Cruiser Squadron 912 and Task Group 47.3.

"They came out of hyper just over three minutes ago, Sir," Commander Lester Thúri, CruRon 912's chief of staff replied, straightening and turning from the display over which he'd been bent. "The good news is, they're right on top of the outer platforms, so we had eyes on them as soon as they arrived. The bad news is, there's a hell of a lot of them."

Lessem made a "keep talking" motion with the fingers of his right hand, and Thúri gestured to the master display's rash of crimson icons.

"We're still putting the numbers together, Sir, but it looks like at least a hundred Solly warships. We've got four really big-assed impeller wedges. They're big enough to be superdreadnoughts, but they look commercial. CIC's best guess is that we're looking at somewhere around fifty battlecruisers, supported by another forty or fifty light cruisers and destroyers, and that the big signatures are transports or fleet support vessels."

"Who was it back on Old Earth that said quantity has a quality all its own?" Lessem asked whimsically, and Thúri snorted harshly.

"Think they're here because of us, Sir?"

"It's possible." Lessem rubbed his chin as he frowned at the master display. "It would be an awful fast reaction compared to anything we've seen out of them so far, but there's been time for someone to reach Wincote. We didn't *see* anyone leaving the system, but we all know how much *that* means. If that's what happened, though, they must've had these people sitting there ready to translate out the instant they heard about us."

Commander Thúri nodded, moving over to stand beside his tall, square-built commodore, and his expression was thoughtful. At the moment, Lessem had exactly ten heavy cruisers, only four of them *Saganami-Cs*, supported by six destroyers and HMS *David K. Brown*, one of the new *David Taylor*-class fast support vessels.

One might, the commander reflected, call that a *slight* force imbalance.

Lessem didn't know what his chief of staff was thinking at that moment, but if he *had* known, he wouldn't have disagreed. It was true that his *Saganami-Cs* and HMS *Ajax* and HMS *Honda Tadakatsu*, the pair of *Roland*-class destroyers attached to TG 47.3, had full loadouts of Mark 16 dual-drive missiles, but the *Rolands'* Achilles' heel was the class's limited magazine space. Each of them carried only two hundred and forty of the big, powerful missiles, less than half the number a *Saganami-C* stowed. And none of the rest of his ships' internal launchers could handle the Mark 16 at all.

Unfortunately, the Royal Manticoran Navy didn't have an unlimited supply of Mark 16-capable warships, and a lot of those it did have had been retained for the Grand Fleet or dispatched to Admiral Gold Peak's Tenth Fleet in the Talbott Sector. He did have six *Saganami-Bs*—*Shelly Ann Jensen, Margaret Mallory, William S. Patterson, Oliver Savander, Rich Rucholka*, and *Jennifer Woodard*—all of whom were armed with the extended range Mark 13, but that weapon's powered envelope was far shorter than the Mark 16's; it was a single-drive missile and couldn't incorporate a ballistic phase into its flight profile; and its warhead was lighter, to boot.

Which may be something of a moot point, he reflected as the red icons of the Solarian task force began accelerating towards the wormhole at a sedate 375 G.

Battles outside the hyper-limit of a star system were virtually unheard of, for several very good reasons. The most salient was that there was seldom anything outside the hyper-limit worth fighting *for*. Wormholes like the one at TG 47.3's back were the primary exception to that rule, and so was the occasional valuable resource or bit of system infrastructure, like a particularly rich asteroid belt, which lay closer to the primary but still beyond its hyper-limit.

But there was another excellent reason battles were seldom fought outside hyper-limits: any starship outside a limit could translate into hyper any time it chose to. And because no one ever willingly fought a battle he didn't expect to win, the weaker side in any confrontation outside a hyper-limit always chose to translate into hyper before the stronger side could engage it.

Unless there was some reason it couldn't, that was.

That was the true reason for the massive fortifications covering the Manticoran Wormhole Junction. They were designed to annihilate anyone foolish enough to attempt an attack through one of the Junction's secondary termini, of course, but in addition, they were intended to provide sufficient concentrated combat power to stand up against almost any conceivable attack through hyper-space.

None of those fortifications were present on the Prime Terminus, however. Prime's five billion citizens had never found it necessary to build or maintain deep-space forts or anything resembling an actual navy. Although the Prime System was nominally independent, it was "closely affiliated" with the Solarian League, which meant it could rely upon the largest navy in the galaxy for its defense and required only a handful of lightly armed units to police the system's internal volume. And since everyone knew the Prime Terminus was under League protection, there'd never been a need to fortify it. Anyone stupid enough to seize it would soon have found the SLN knocking on his home star system's front door.

Ajay, at the far end of the terminus, was *not* "closely affiliated" with the League. In fact, Ajay didn't much care for the League. Although it maintained a civil relationship with Old Chicago, it had been an independent star nation for the better part of three hundred and fifty T-years. It had, in fact, been settled by colonists from other Verge systems who hadn't cared for the way the League's foreign policy was evolving, and their descendants had a not unreasonable suspicion that the Office of Frontier Security would really have liked control of the Ajay Terminus. As a counterweight to those OFS ambitions, the system had cultivated cordial relations and a long-standing, robust trade relationship with both the Star Kingdom of Manticore and Beowulf.

Despite that, System President Adelaide Tyson had protested in vociferous terms when Task Force 47 arrived on her doorstep and announced it was taking possession of her star system's greatest natural resource as part of Lacoön Two. Lessem was pretty sure most of her protests had been in the nature of covering her star-nation's posterior if things went badly for the Grand Alliance. They put her officially on record as strongly opposed to the Star Empire's "patently illegal" seizure of every warp terminus in sight. Hopefully, that would be sufficient to protect Ajay from the League's ire in the event of an eventual Solarian triumph. For that matter, win or lose, the League would still be there the day after the peace treaty was finally signed. Ajay would still have to live with it, and Sollies had long memories. Letting word get back to Old Chicago that she'd told the RMN she was delighted to see it in her star system was likely to put a certain strain on that future relationship.

Under the circumstances, Commodore Lessem found it difficult to fault President Tyson, especially since however strongly she might have protested, she and her modest Ajay System Navy had stayed out of Task Force 47's way and the Ajay Astro Control services had cooperated smoothly—although only after protesting stringently—with the foreign navy which had illegally seized control of its wormhole.

System Director Gregor Cho had reacted rather differently here in Prime, however. He'd protested even more strongly than Tyson, and he'd ordered his Terminus Traffic Control Command to refuse any cooperation with the invaders. Vice Admiral Correia had expected that and brought along his own specialists, who now provided a skeleton crew for the Prime Traffic Control platform after the Primese crews had been evicted from it. The vice admiral had also taken it as a given that Cho would find a way to send word to the League as soon as possible, but neither he nor Lessem had anticipated this prompt a response.

Which brought Lessem back to the unpalatable odds headed his way.

"Should we call Captain Rice forward, Sir?" Commander Thomas Wozniak, his operations officer, asked quietly.

"No." Lessem shook his head. Captain Jessica Rice commanded CruRon 912's second division, the *Saganami-C*s' HMS *Peregrine S. Faye* and HMS *Lisa Holtz*, covering the Ajay Terminus...and the rest of TG 47.3's back.

"She wouldn't add that much to our firepower," the commodore continued, "and we may need them—and *Echidna*—right where they are." He rubbed his chin a moment longer, then inhaled sharply and turned from the display.

"George," he said.

"Yes, Sir?" Lieutenant George Gordon, his com officer, replied.

"First, contact Commander Aamodt. I want *So-po* to stand by to transit the terminus with a complete tactical upload for Captain Rice on my command. The rest of his division is to lift our people off the Traffic Control platform and evacuate them to Ajay immediately."

"Yes, Sir."

Thúri made a sound of sour amusement, and Lessem cocked an eyebrow at him. The commander shrugged.

"Aamodt isn't going to like that, Sir," he said.

"Maybe not, but I doubt it'll surprise him," Lessem replied, and Thúri nodded.

Commander Tearlach Aamodt wore two hats as the CO of HMS *Obusier* and the commanding officer of Destroyer Division 94.2. Like HMS *So-po*—and all DesDiv 94.2's other units—*Obusier* was a *Culverin*-class destroyer. The *Culverins* had been bleeding-edge technology when they were introduced in 1899 PD, but that had been twenty-three T-years ago, before anyone outside a few ultra-classified research programs had ever heard of anything called a multidrive missile. They remained capable platforms against anyone who didn't have MDMs or DDMs of his own, but they were thoroughly obsolete against modern weapons. That meant Lessem could dispense with them more readily than with any of his newer units. They'd also been built for larger crews than the bigger, more modern *Rolands*, which gave them the redundant life-support to take the Manticoran traffic control specialists off the PTC platform.

"While George is talking to Aamodt, Tom," Lessem continued, turning back to Wozniak, "tell Captain Amberline to begin deploying and enabling pods as per Pattern Able."

"Yes, Sir." The operations officer didn't sound very surprised by the order.

Harriet Amberline commanded *David K. Brown*, most of whose capacious cargo pods were stuffed with Mark 16s. One of the FSV's cargo modules was loaded with Mark 23 MDMs, which offered twice the Mark 16's powered envelope, but Mark 23s were in short supply, not to be wasted where the smaller Mark 16 would do the job. More to the point, the Mark 23's greater range would offer no real advantage in the sort of engagement Lessem saw coming. Pattern Able deployed only Mark 16 pods, and he considered sending *David K. Brown* (known as "*Brownie*" by her crew, despite the fact that that name officially belonged to a *Hydra*-class CLAC) back to Ajay after the *Culverins* as soon as Amberline completed the Able deployment. She was a valuable unit, although the Service Train units with Rice in Ajay carried many times the number of pods she did. Despite her size, however, she could easily out-accelerate anything in the Solarian inventory and she represented his missile pod piggy bank.

And I may need to dip into that "piggy bank" pretty damned soon, he thought grimly. *A lot's going to depend on what these people decide to do.*

✧   ✧   ✧

"CIC makes it ten or twelve cruisers, four destroyers, and what *could* be a dreadnought, Ma'am," Rear Admiral Barthilu Rosiak reported.

"A *dreadnought*?" Admiral Jane Isotalo, CO, Task Force 1027, Solarian League Navy, repeated with a raised eyebrow. No first-line navy had used dreadnoughts in twenty T-years. ONI said both the Manties and the Havenites had used them early in their wars, but they'd all been retired long since.

"Yes, Ma'am," Rear Admiral Lamizana, TF 1027's intelligence officer, said before Rosiak could reply.

Isotalo transferred her raised eyebrow to Lamizana, and the intel officer shrugged.

"CIC isn't saying that's necessarily what it *is*, Ma'am," she said. "But they're calling its mass around three million tons, which is too big for even one of the Manties' battlecruisers. It's too big even for a battleship, for that matter, but way too small for an SD. It could be some kind of collier or supply vessel—in fact, it probably is—but it's showing military-grade impellers. Until we know more, I think we have to assume it's a warship."

Isotalo considered that for a moment, then nodded. Unlike her, Lamizana was Frontier Fleet. Under normal conditions, that might have left Isotalo less impressed by her caveat. Little though the admiral cared to admit it, though, Frontier Fleet had demonstrated a better track record than Battle Fleet when it came to acknowledging the threat of Manticore's technological advantages.

Not that any *of us have precisely covered ourselves with glory*, she thought.

Still, Lamizana was smart and she'd invested a lot of effort in acquiring the best insight into Manty capabilities she could even before TF 1027 had been tapped for Operation Buccaneer and sent off to burn Ajay's orbital infrastructure to the ground.

"What to do you think they're doing here, Maleen?" Isotalo asked now. "More of this wormhole seizure strategy of theirs?"

"Most likely, Ma'am." Lamizana nodded. "I can't think of another reason for them to be swanning around three or four hundred light-years from Manticore or Beowulf. They haven't had time yet to learn about Buccaneer and start deploying interception forces, and if that's what these people were doing, I'd expect them to be in greater strength than this."

"Just our luck to run into them here," Rear Admiral Kimmo Ramaalas, Isotalo's chief of staff observed with a sour expression.

Like Lamizana, Ramaalas was Frontier Fleet, not Battle Fleet, and he'd been with Isotalo for less than three T-months. In fact, he'd been assigned over her protest when they took Rear Admiral Tirso Frederick away from her. Frederick had been her chief of staff for the better part of three T-years, but Winston Kingsford had made a point of breaking up established command relationships—and of cross-assigning Frontier Fleet and Battle Fleet officers—ever since he'd replaced Rajampet Rajani as Chief of Naval Operations. The new policy had infuriated Isotalo when it was initiated, and she'd scarcely been alone in that.

She'd told herself it wasn't Ramaalas's fault. And, given the sheer depth of the crap in which the SLN had found itself since Josef Byng's New Tuscan stupidity, the last thing anyone could afford was for her to create any avoidable friction with her new chief of staff. None of which had made her happy to see him aboard SLNS *Foudroyant*, her battlecruiser flagship.

It had helped that, also like Lamizana, Ramaalas was smart and tactful. That wasn't enough to endear him to his Battle Fleet fellows, but it helped, and he and Isotalo had established a firm mutual respect.

"It's inconvenient, Kimmo," she acknowledged now. "But I suggest we look upon it as an opportunity, not a liability." Ramaalas cocked his head at her, and she showed her teeth briefly. "I still don't know that I accept all the horror stories Maleen and Bart have been telling us about Manty missile ranges," she went on, twitching her head at Lamizana and Rosiak, "but I'm not about to assume they're wrong, either. The bastards've sure as hell been kicking the crap out of us with *something*! But however good *their* missiles are, we've got a hundred thousand pods worth of improved Cataphracts of our own just aboard the colliers. They can't possibly match the depth of our magazines, and an engagement way out here won't play to their strengths the way one inside the hyper-limit would. The question in my mind is whether they're here on their own or if they're here to hold the door open for someone else?"

"You're thinking they may have staged through Prime en route to Agueda, Ma'am?" Ramaalas said.

"It would make sense, given this wormhole-seizure strategy of theirs," Isotalo pointed out. "And if that's what's happening, kicking them off the terminus and keeping them off it could play hell with their logistics. It might even force whoever they sent to Agueda to fall back on Manticore the long way." She smiled nastily. "That'd take their entire force out of action for almost two T-months without anyone even firing a shot."

"Agreed, Ma'am." Ramaalas nodded. "But whatever else happens, they're bound to send a dispatch boat back through the wormhole to Ajay."

"That's true," Isotalo conceded. "I don't know how much good that will do them, though. I expect we'll get a read on that shortly. If they've got enough firepower in Ajay to give us a fight, they'll either call it forward to support their pickets here, or else they'll fall back through the terminus to concentrate their forces if we come through after them."

Which, she added silently, *I have no intention whatsoever of doing. The last thing I need is to send the task force through in a wormhole assault against a prepared defense!*

She thought about that as she contemplated the main plot. The range to the Manties was just over five light-minutes. At this distance, all *Foudroyant*'s onboard sensors could see were the enemy's impeller signatures. The recon platforms speeding ahead of TF 1027 would begin providing better data in another twenty minutes or so, but she was unhappily certain the Manties already had that "better data" on her own command. ONI had been forced to accept that the Royal Manticoran Navy and its allies truly did have an FTL com capability—with sufficient bandwidth for recon drones—over at least intra-system ranges. It seemed unlikely any Manty commander would allow herself to be caught with her trousers down, so there was undoubtedly a shell of sensor platforms exactly like that spread out around the wormhole.

"Time to the terminus, Magumo?" she asked without looking away from the plot.

"We're ninety-four million kilometers out, Ma'am," Commodore Magumo Saintula, her astrogator, replied. "At current acceleration, we'd make turnover for a zero-zero intercept in eighty-four minutes. Velocity at turnover would be one-eight-point-six thousand KPS."

"Thank you," she said.

That was the geometry for an n-space approach, of course. They could have micro-jumped the three hundred-odd light-seconds through hyper in a fraction of the same time, and if the Manties chose to stand and fight on this side of the wormhole, she suspected there'd be quite a few micro-jumps in the not-too-distant future. Astrogation was more than a little dicey on short-range jumps, though, and she didn't plan on making any of them she didn't have to. Besides, a normal-space approach would give Rosiak, Lamizana, and their light-speed-limited drones more time to pry loose additional tactical data.

She studied the plot's bland icons for another fifteen or twenty seconds, then shrugged.

"In that case, I imagine we'll be finding out what they have in mind in a couple of hours," she observed. She clasped her hands behind her, turned from the plot, and walked to her command chair. "In the meantime, Bart," she continued, "let's get the Huskies deployed and open the intervals between the task groups. Put Santini in the van, but I want at least three light-seconds between the groups."

Rosiak looked at her and she smiled.

"If they decide to stand and fight, I'm more than willing to help them waste as much ammunition as possible," she said. "So at the same time you're passing the order to open the intervals, inform Tsukahara, Bonrepaux, and Santini that I want their best astrogators—I don't care whether they're on the flagships or somewhere else in the group—ready to compute the tightest micro-jumps they can give me if I ask for them."

Rosiak's eyes narrowed. Then he nodded with a smile of his own.

"Understood, Ma'am," he said.

❖   ❖   ❖

"Sir, CIC is reporting something...odd," Commander Wozniak said.

Commodore Lessem turned from his conversation with Commander Thúri, raising an index finger at the chief of staff in a "hold onto that thought" gesture.

"What sort of 'odd,' Tom?"

"It looks almost like four or five thousand recon drones, Sir."

"Four or five *thousand* drones?" Lessem's eyebrows rose, and Wozniak nodded.

"That's what it looks like...almost, Sir, but I don't think it's what it is."

Lessem crossed the flag bridge and looked over Wozniak's shoulder at the ops officer's display. Given the scale of the plot, the impeller signatures of the "drones" Wozniak had reported formed a sort of haze around the deploying Solarian battlecruisers rather than registering as distinct point sources. A digital sidebar spun upward as the sensors aboard the Ghost Rider platforms keeping an eye on the intruders— well, he supposed, the most *recently arrived* intruders, if he wanted to be fair about it—detected and plotted the blossoming signatures.

"You're right," he said. "They can't be recon drones, not staying that tight in around their formation. I don't know what *else* they could be, though."

"You can't really tell from the display, Sir, but CIC says they're definitely forming constellations around the battlecruisers. Whatever they are, there are approximately a hundred of them associated with each battlecruiser. I guess they could be some kind of missile defense—maybe they've come up with new decoy platforms to replace or supplement Halo and they're establishing as dense a pattern of them as they can around our priority targets—but that doesn't feel right, either. Whatever else they are, though, they aren't stealthy enough for reconnaissance platforms. We're actually picking up a sniff of them on *Clas Fleming*'s shipboard sensors, even at this range. We're not resolving individual signatures clearly—not the way Ghost Rider is—but we can *see* them, and we shouldn't be seeing even Solarian drones at this range."

"Which doesn't even count the fact that there's no sane reason to launch recon drones and then keep them tied in that tight to your ships," Lessem said, nodding his head in agreement. He stood gazing at the display for ten or fifteen seconds, hands clasped behind him and lips pursed in thought, then shrugged.

"Well, I imagine we'll find out what they're up to in due time. And at least any discovering we have to do is going to happen outside anyone's hyper-limit."

✧　　✧　　✧

"Commodore Quigley's on station, Ma'am," Rear Admiral Rosiak said. "Thank you, Bart."

Jane Isotalo nodded as she leaned back in her command chair and studied the master plot. Millicent Quigley's TG 1027.4 was the real reason she was prepared to spend missiles like water against a Manty squadron outside a limit. Unless she somehow managed to close to a much shorter range than the opposing commander was likely to allow, she didn't expect to kill very many of the Manties—not when they could duck into hyper to avoid her fire. No doubt the Manty CO would be willing to let her waste a lot of missiles *trying* for kills, and under normal circumstances, Isotalo would have been concerned about the sorts of ammunition expenditures involved. In this case, however, Quigley's three 7,500,000-ton *Voyager*-class freighters gave her rather deeper magazines than usual.

Unfortunately, the *Voyagers* were part of the Navy's TUFT fleet: civilian vessels designated to be "Taken Up From Trade" in an emergency. The Federal Government subsidized the construction of TUFT units, which gave it first call on them if the Navy decided to call in its markers, but they weren't designed to military-grade specifications and the *Voyagers* were a civilian design. They were unarmed and carried no active defenses. They were also sluggish compared to warships their size, which was why she'd moved Quigley's freighters, the *Atlas*-class fleet repair vessel *Hercules*, and their escorting light cruisers and destroyers, to a position a half million kilometers astern of Vice Admiral Tsukahara's TG 1027.2, her trailing group of battlecruisers. That gave them more time to dodge if anything nasty came their way, but it left them close enough to deploy additional Huskies for Tsukahara's battlecruisers if they were needed.

She glanced at the plot's sidebar. TF 1027 had made turnover eight and a half minutes ago. The range had dropped to thirty-eight million kilometers, and the closing velocity toward the motionless Manties had fallen to 16,704 KPS.

Seventy-five minutes to a zero-zero with the terminus, she thought. *Wonder what's going through their heads over there?*

✧   ✧   ✧

"Goodness me," Sir Martin Lessem murmured. "I do believe those people want the wormhole."

"Do you really, Sir?" Commander Thúri asked. Lessem glanced at him and nodded. "What was your first indication, Sir?"

Lessem snorted in amusement, although, truth to tell, watching that many battlecruisers advancing towards his command wasn't the most amusing thing he'd ever done. Especially given their acceleration rate. The Ghost Rider platforms had confirmed class IDs on the Sollies, and even at standard peacetime safety margins, the *Indefatigable* and *Nevada*-class battlecruisers could have produced an acceleration of 3.83 KPS². They were showing only 3.68 KPS², however—fifteen gravities lower than their eighty-percent settings. That might not seem like a vast difference, but it had suggested—and the platforms had confirmed—just what those mystery "recon drone" impellers signatures were all about.

Each of the incoming battlecruisers was towing a chain of missile pods outside its wedge, and the pods in question appeared nowhere in Tom Wozniak's databases on enemy capabilities.

It was tempting to assume they represented a jury-rigged lash-up, improvised because of the Sollies' technological inferiority. Come to that, that might actually be accurate. But those pods looked suspiciously like the "donkeys" Shannon Foraker had devised for the Republic of Haven Navy before the Republic's attack on Manticore. There were far too many of them for the number of ships on his display to be towing on individual tractors, and the clustered deployment patterns strongly suggested something more like the donkey than Manticore's tractor-equipped missile pods. More to the point, although the Solarians' acceleration was on the low side, it wasn't as low as it ought to be with that many pods on tow. And the reason it wasn't was that unlike Manticoran or Havenite missile pods, these had impellers of their own.

From the modest strength of their wedges, it appeared the Sollies had probably grafted the impeller nodes of a standard recon drone onto them, which would explain CIC's initial confusion over what they were. Packing in those nodes had to have cut deeply into the pods' volume, and he doubted they could maintain their current acceleration level for an extended period out of onboard power. But if they were, indeed, the conceptual equivalent of Havenite "donkeys," they were equipped only with tractors of their own and power and telemetry relays. The squeeze on their volume wouldn't cost the Solly commander any missiles, since they'd never been intended to carry missiles in the first place, and their impellers would go quite some way towards reducing the SLN's acceleration disadvantage vis-à-vis the Grand Alliance. *Clas Fleming*'s eighty-percent acceleration rate was 5.697 KPS^2, sixty gravities higher than a *Nevada* could turn out with no safety margin at all. If both ships went to maximum military acceleration, *Clas Fleming*'s advantage would be over two hundred and forty gravities. Nothing was going to let a *Nevada* overhaul a *Saganami-C* from a standing start, but towing that many unpowered pods would have drastically reduced the Sollies' already sluggish acceleration rates. *With* the built-in drives, the battlecruisers' acceleration curves were only grossly inferior to his own, not *hopelessly* so.

Jury-rigged or carefully thought through, though, they had to be a response to what the Grand Alliance's missiles had done to the Sollies ever since New Tuscany. The SLN's system-defense pods—system defense was the only role in which the prewar Sollies had ever considered employing missile pods—had neither needed nor possessed impellers of their own. So these things had to have been designed and put into production since the shooting started. In some ways, that was a small thing, scarcely likely to affect the balance of combat power in any significant way. As a harbinger of possible Solarian activity, though, it was...worrisome to see it so soon.

And there were a *lot* of the whatever-the-hell-they-were out there. He didn't like the implications of that at all. What it said about the number of missiles which might shortly be fired in his command's direction was bad enough, although the Sollies' hit probabilities at extended range would still suck wind. The speed with which this new system had appeared was a lot worse, though. It would seem the Darwinian process he'd worried about had begun, and at least as bad, a single task force this far from home had deployed just under five thousand of them, and they were towing a total of what appeared to be 30,000 unpowered missile pods. Assuming six to ten cells per pod, that would represent between 180,000 and 300,000 missiles, and given the presence of what looked suspiciously like ammunition ships tagging along behind the battlecruisers, he suspected that was only the tip of the iceberg. So in addition to evidence of Solarian adaptiveness, he was looking at proof of the League industrial infrastructure's capacity to put a brand new system into production in staggering numbers very, very quickly.

Not good, he thought. *Not good at all.*

But those implications were for the future—and for the attention of better paid, more highly placed brains than his—he reminded himself. Best he focus his attention on whatever the Solly CO had in mind for TG 47.3.

The Sollies had opened their formation as they closed, and the deployment they'd adopted wasn't exactly standard. They'd split into three roughly equal-sized sub-formations—he suspected they represented the other side's task group organization—advancing almost in a column formation, or perhaps like beads on a string, towards the terminus. CIC had designated them Alpha One through Alpha Three, and they were spaced almost nine hundred thousand kilometers apart which suggested the Solarian commander had something clever in mind. Lessem was pretty sure he'd figured out what the "something clever" was, but he had no intention of getting too tightly wedded to his own cleverness. It was entirely possible the Solly had come up with something completely different.

"Current range, Palko?" he asked.

"Thirty-six million klicks, Sir," Commander Palko Nakada, TG 47.3's astrogator replied. "Closing at one-six-two-seven-seven KPS."

"Thank you."

"They seem confident, Sir," Thúri observed. "Of course, I expect Byng was pretty confident up until—"

"Missile launch," Commander Wozniak announced suddenly. "Multiple launches from Alpha One. Estimate six thousand—repeat, six-zero-zero-zero—inbound."

✧　　✧　　✧

"First launch away, Ma'am," Rear Admiral Rosiak announced.

"Thank you, Bart," Jane Isotalo said as courteously as if she hadn't already seen the outgoing missile tracks from Vice Admiral Elvis Tsukahara's TG 1027.2. It was Rosiak's job to tell her that, after all.

That familiar observation ran under the surface of her thoughts as she watched that first wave of improved Cataphracts streak towards the Manties.

Whatever the war might mean for the Solarian League in general, its timing had proved... fortuitous for Technodyne of Yildun. The huge transstellar had faced enough criminal charges to make survival doubtful, even for a mega corporation its size. Over thirty members of its senior management had been sentenced to actual prison terms in light of certain embarrassing revelations—like the minor fact that the Republic of Monica had come into possession of a number of fully functional SLN battlecruisers, with all classified tech systems intact and operational—which had been previously scrapped by Technodyne. In Isotalo's opinion, that "minor fact" had been a principal contributor—probably *the* principal contributor, come to that—to the unholy mess in which the League currently found itself, but any additional penalties against Technodyne had evaporated in the face of the "Grand Alliance's" demonstrably superior war-fighting technology.

They hadn't evaporated because all was forgiven, but rather because Technodyne was one of the Navy's more important suppliers—one might more accurately have said the *most* important supplier—and its R&D staff had hit the ground running in the face of the Manties' superiority. Indeed, Isotalo suspected Technodyne had been paying closer attention than the Office of Naval Intelligence to reports out of the Haven Sector for quite some time, given how speedily the first Cataphract multi-stage missiles had emerged from its workshops. The Cataphract was both outsized and crude compared to current-generation Manty technology—it was effectively no more than a standard missile with a laserhead-armed "counter-missile" glued to its nose—but at least it provided the Navy with a weapon which could actually *reach* the enemy.

Obviously, Technodyne hadn't managed to duplicate the Manties' targeting and fire control systems, which meant long-range accuracy remained pathetic, but a sufficiently dense salvo would still generate hits. And in order to provide that density, Technodyne had come up with what it had dubbed the "Dispersed Weapons Module, Mod 2" (which, interestingly, suggested there'd been a previous "Mod 1" which it hadn't mentioned to anyone), christened the "Husky" by the Navy's tac officers.

Each Husky was a specialized towing drone equipped with a small impeller drive, a power receptor antenna, a telemetry relay, and eight tractor beams, each capable of towing one of Technodyne's missile pods. The Husky's onboard power was sufficient only for limited—*very* limited—independent maneuvering, but it could always be towed by a mothership's tractors. As long as it could be hit by beamed power from that mothership, its endurance was effectively *un*limited, however. And it had been designed so that each Husky could "mother" eight *additional* Huskies. In theory, they could be daisy-chained four-deep, with the actual missile pods forming the fifth tier of an enormous stack. That meant—again, in theory—that a single tractor aboard a single warship could tow 1,024 missile pods. The latest, tweaked version of the Cataphract was somewhat bigger than the model Filareta had taken to Manticore, and the new pods were individually smaller, able to carry only six of Technodyne's latest mark. So in theory—*in theory*—that single shipboard tractor could have put 6,144 missiles into space. The power requirement would have far exceeded that of anything short of a superdreadnought, however—in fact, Isotalo doubted even a superdreadnought could have handled that many pods—and the best her battlecruisers could manage was just under a hundred Huskies and "only" 768 pods apiece, which meant the battlecruisers of the lightest of her task groups had almost twelve thousand missiles in its deployed pods.

Without the Huskies' impellers, their acceleration would have been that of an arthritic tortoise...at best. *With* the Huskies' impellers, the effect of all that mass outside the battlecruisers' impeller wedges was negligible. And, all told, that would let her bring over 36,000 missiles to the fight.

Which didn't even count the reserve aboard her colliers. They were packed with an additional 90,000 pods, even after deploying the Huskies in her first salvo. It seemed...unlikely...that a dozen Manty cruisers could stand up to over half a million Cataphracts.

On the other hand, the Manties had demonstrated a perverse propensity for doing "unlikely" things to the Solarian League Navy.

In addition to producing the Husky, the arms maker had tweaked its original Cataphract, increasing its first-stage acceleration by twenty percent, which upped its maximum powered envelope from rest from 13,650,172 kilometers to 19,370,400. Technodyne hadn't been able to do anything about light-speed fire control limitations, however, and the additional acceleration wasn't a factor, at least for this launch. Rosiak had been forced to incorporate a ballistic phase into the attack, since even with the tweaks and her closing velocity at launch, her maximum powered envelope remained less than thirty-two million kilometers. Direct hits, especially against Manticoran missile defenses, would have been few and far between even at twenty million kilometers; at *thirty-six* million, they were unlikely as hell, but that wasn't really what she was after.

Show me what you've got, she thought silently, leaning back in her command chair as the missiles tore towards their targets. *I don't care how good your missile defense systems are; you can't have a hell of a lot of them on that few platforms. So show me what they can do.*

✧　　✧　　✧

"Missile defense Reno," Commodore Lessem said calmly as he, too, watched the tidal bore of missiles sweep towards him, then glanced at the plot's vector analyses. Based on the performance of Massimo Filareta's missiles, CIC was projecting a total flight time of 406 seconds, including a 151-second ballistic phase, and he pursed his lips as he watched the time display tick downward. There was time—if not a lot of it—to consider his options, and his brain whirred behind his thoughtful eyes.

"Missile defense Reno, aye, Sir," Wozniak replied. "Missile Defense has good tracking data from the Ghost Riders, and bow walls are active . . . now." He looked over his shoulder and smiled at the commodore. "I think these people are in for a surprise, Sir."

"We can always hope." Lessem glanced at Commander Thúri. "I wonder what percentage of their total birds that represents?"

"CIC makes it about twenty percent, Sir." From the promptitude of his response, Thúri had been thinking the same sort of things his commodore had. "I'm inclined to think it was probably *exactly* twenty percent," he continued, "but Brent's not prepared to be quite that definite."

"Why am I not surprised?" Lessem chuckled, never taking his eyes from the tactical plot.

Commander Brent Krösche, *Clas Fleming*'s tactical officer, was very good at his job. Joanne O'Reilly, *Clas Fleming*'s CO, thought the world of him, and Lessem was inclined to agree. But Krösche was a precise sort. If he wasn't certain of his numbers to at least the tenth decimal point, the best he would give was a "probable." And a very occasional "*highly* probable" if he was confident to the *ninth* decimal point.

"Well, if this many birds are only eight percent of what they could've thrown, they probably don't expect—"

"Sir, there's something strange about their launch profile," Commander Wozniak said suddenly. Lessem turned from Thúri to look at him, and the ops officer frowned unhappily. "Sir, they're showing a *lot* more accel than they should. The missiles we analyzed from Eleventh Fleet maxed at seven-zero-one KPS squared; *these* birds are coming in at over eight hundred and forty."

Lessem inhaled sharply, remembering his earlier thoughts about Solarian innovation and productivity.

"Assuming the drive endurance on both stages is the same as on Filareta's, that gives them a powered envelope of almost thirty-two million klicks," Wozniak continued. "That drops their ballistic phase to barely four million klicks and roughly twenty-four seconds, which makes their *total* flight time only two-seven-niner seconds."

"I see." Lessem's voice was level, but his brain raced. His decision loop had just become 134 seconds shorter than he'd assumed it was, and he'd already lost ten of them finding that out.

His ships' hyper generators were at Readiness, which meant they could pop into the alpha bands on less than a minute's notice. Well, all of them except *David K. Brown*, that was. The FSV had military-grade impellers, inertial compensator, and hyper generator, but she also massed over seven times as much as *Clas Fleming*, and size was a factor in hyper generator cycle times, as well as acceleration rates. A

Saganami-C like *Clas Fleming* could translate into hyper from Readiness in 44.6 seconds whereas one of the larger Solarian *Nevada*-class battlecruisers would need 55.7. A three million-ton FSV, however, required 118.8, and would have needed better than three minutes, if she'd mounted a *civilian*-grade generator. Which posed at least one interesting question, since the three transports or freighters in company with the Solly battlecruisers massed more than twice that much and they appeared to have civilian-grade impellers. If they mounted civilian generators, as well, their minimum cycle time would be almost three and half times as long as "*Brownie*'s."

Hyper cycle times meant very little under normal battle conditions, since no one could enter or leave hyper inside a star's hyper-limit, anyway. They meant quite a lot this far *outside* a limit, however, as Genevieve Chin had discovered when she encountered Duchess Harrington's Apollo-armed superdreadnoughts outside Manticore-A's limit.

The People's Republic's analysts had radically underestimated Apollo's effective range, and all of Chin's intelligence briefings had told her she was well outside it when Eighth Fleet launched against her. The 44,000,000-kilometer ballistic phase Duchess Harrington had been forced to incorporate into her launch just to reach Chin's ships had confirmed that she was outside effective shipboard fire control range, and so she had been. But not very *far* outside it. Eighth Fleet had been close enough to update the Apollo control platforms in near real-time just before it released them to autonomous control, and that autonomous control had been enormously better than anyone in the PRH had believed it could be. Even with that update, the Mark 23s had been far less accurate than they would have been at three light-minutes, as opposed to the *four* light-minutes at which they'd been launched. They'd simply been far more accurate than the Peeps had anticipated.

To Chin's credit, her own tactical instincts had overridden her ONI briefing when Duchess Harrington's MDMs shut down and went ballistic. But it had taken a few seconds for the shutdown to be reported to her. Then it had taken fifteen or twenty more seconds for her instincts to overrule her briefing. That was really a remarkably quick response, all things considered, but the clock had been ticking, and it had taken several more seconds for her flagship to transmit the order to hyper out. Then it had taken several more seconds for her captains to receive it, and a handful more for their astrogators to respond and Engineering to begin the cycle.

She'd run out of seconds. The cycle time on her superdreadnoughts' hyper generators, the minimum time required to translate even from full Readiness, had been over four and a half minutes, and total flight time for Eighth Fleet's missiles from the moment their second stage drives shut down had been only 5.2 minutes.

A difference of less than forty seconds didn't sound like all that much, but its consequences for her command had been catastrophic.

The cycle times for Lessem's ships, even *David K. Brown*, were far shorter than that, and he'd thought he could wait over five minutes from the moment the Solarians launched and still get the FSV into hyper to avoid the incoming fire. For that matter, his lighter ships would have had over *six* minutes to play with.

Now, though . . .

"No need to panic just yet, I think," he said, crossing to stand behind Wozniak and rest one hand on his shoulder as he gazed past the ops officer to his displays. "Not until they're willing to show us more missiles in a single launch. Makes you wonder what *other* surprises they may have for us, though, doesn't it?"

✧   ✧   ✧

Task Group 47.3 sat motionless in space between the Prime Terminus and Jane Isotalo's battlecruisers, and evasion maneuvers from a base velocity of zero would be limited. Even with a *Saganami-C*'s maximum acceleration of 726.2 gravities, *Clas Fleming* could have changed her position by no more than 587,000 kilometers and attained a velocity of only 2,890 KPS in the 6.8 minutes Lessem had expected Task Force 1027's missiles to reach her. In the time he actually had, the best she could have managed was 277,000 kilometers and 1,980 KPS. That was less than one light-second, which was negligible against missiles coming in at eighty percent of light-speed. On the other hand, Lessem couldn't have generated a much greater base velocity and stayed between Isotalo and the terminus.

Nor did he really need to.

Yet, at least.

The Cataphracts were much too far downrange for Rear Admiral Rosiak to control effectively. For over sixty T-years, since the introduction of the laserhead, effective missile engagements had been managed via the missiles' telemetry links. In theory, it ought to have been simple for any missile to find something as glaringly obvious as an impeller-drive starship under power. In practice, things were a bit more complicated. It wasn't that missiles operating in autonomous mode couldn't find targets; it was just that they had a great deal of trouble finding—and hitting—the *right* targets.

True, seeing the impeller signature of a target really *was* technological child's play in many ways. Unfortunately, impeller-drive starships were extremely maneuverable, their wedges sharply limited the vulnerable aspects from which they could be successfully attacked, and they mounted both active and passive defenses designed to make the task of any attack missile's seekers as *un*-simple as possible.

Given the way in which a missile's own impeller wedge narrowed its onboard seekers' field of view (one RMN training manual likened it to steering an air car while looking at the outside world through a soda straw), the small size of its effective target (the narrow gap between the impeller wedge's roof and floor), the decoys and electronic warfare systems designed to defeat those seekers, and the target's ability to rapidly roll ship in order to interpose its own impeller wedge, the probability of a hit by any single missile had always been low. Higher for laserheads than for *contact* weapons, but still low. And prior to the introduction of the modern missile pod, salvo *densities* had also been low, which had made it essential to find a way to increase that probability.

The solution had been to turn every salvo into a network of dispersed sensor platforms. Any given missile might not see the target very well—if at all—during an attack run, especially when coming in on a profile designed to make it as difficult as possible for that target's active defenses to intercept it. But when all the seekers aboard every missile in the attack reported what they *could* see to the ship which had launched them, the data could be collated, combined, and analyzed. A far better tactical picture could be assembled; enemy electronic warfare tactics could be mapped and allowed for; probable decoys could be identified and excluded from the targeting queues; the other side's evasion maneuvers could be plugged in, tracked, and projected; and refined instructions could be sent back not simply to the missiles which had supplied the data, but to every other missile in the salvo. Not only did that increase accuracy against assigned targets, but it permitted tactical officers to adjust targeting queues on the fly, redirecting missiles as their original targets were crippled or destroyed or as newer, higher-value targets were discovered. As the range increased, transmission lag set in and grew steadily worse until it reached the point at which new instructions from the firing ship were inevitably out of date and actually began degrading its missiles' accuracy, at which point the links were cut and each missile reverted to onboard control.

And that was TF 1027's problem.

Missiles attacking targets 36,000,000 kilometers from their launch platforms were far beyond the effective control range of light-speed systems. Admiral Isotalo had no choice but to rely on her birds' internal seekers and targeting AI, and that AI had always been rudimentary because it was designed to work in tandem with shipboard direction. That was what truly made Apollo so lethal, although the SLN as yet had no clue of just how true that was. The Mark 23-E control missiles could accept shipboard telemetry at sixty-four times the range light-speed telemetry made possible, but the Echoes had also been designed specifically for use beyond even Apollo's shipboard control range, with every control missile in the salvo talking to every other control missile and acting as an individual processing node for the data even when relay to—and *through*—the mothership was unavailable. Its autonomous accuracy was no more than thirty percent or so of its accuracy under tight shipboard control, but that thirty percent was many times more accurate than any current-generation Solarian missile could achieve.

Sir Martin Lessem's Mark 16s weren't Apollo-capable, and neither were his cruisers. But the Ghost Rider platforms' FTL links cut the telemetry loop in half. They could see better than any missile's sensors, they could report what they saw at FTL speeds—just as they were doing now on the massive incoming Solarian salvo—and that meant TG 47.3's telemetry lasers could continue to update far longer than its Solarian opponents.

Despite that, he chose not to waste any of his fire on Isotalo's ships just yet. His opponent had a hell of a lot more missile pods than he did. In fact, he was pretty sure the Solly CO saw this salvo as a test, a way to get a better read on his defensive capabilities, rather than a full-blooded attempt to destroy his ships. Lessem couldn't keep him from doing that, but he wasn't prepared to waste any of his own ammunition on targets that could disappear into hyper before his fire ever reached them.

And under the circumstances, he had no objection to showing the Sollies that they'd have to get a lot closer before their fire posed any realistic threat to his command.

His cruisers and destroyers mounted a total of 520 counter-missile launchers and 672 point defense clusters, and range from rest for the Royal Manticoran Navy's Mark 31 counter-missile was 3,585,556 kilometers. The first of Lessem's CMs went out 205 seconds after Isotalo's launch, one second after the Cataphracts' second-stage impellers lit off. A second wave of Mark 31s launched ten seconds after that. A third launched ten seconds after that. Then a fourth. The fifth and final wave of counter-missiles launched forty seconds after the first—thirty-five seconds before the Cataphracts could reach attack range. And then, with 2,080 Mark 31s headed downrange, every one of TG 47.3's units rolled ship, turning up on their sides relative to TF 1027 to present only the bellies of their impeller wedges to the enemy.

❖   ❖   ❖

Jane Isotalo's jaw clenched as she saw the incredible waves of counter-missiles lashing outward from the Manties.

Should've expected it, she told herself harshly. *If the bastards routinely throw around missile salvos of their own this size, they've got to have been working on defensive measures, too. Damn it, you knew that going in!*

Indeed she had, and she and Ramaalas and Rosiak had done their damnedest to allow for it, but their worst-case estimates hadn't visualized something like *this.* No Solarian ship mounted that many CM tubes per ton of displacement, and the bastards were actually launching counter-missiles from both broadsides simultaneously. No Solarian ship could have done *that,* either.

Nor were counter-missiles all those ships had launched.

❖   ❖   ❖

"Dazzlers in five seconds, Sir," Commander Constanta Solis, CruRon 912's electronic warfare officer, announced, and Lessem nodded.

The Dazzlers had been originally devised as a penetration aid, designed to knock down and blind the sensors feeding a target's defensive fire control with massive spikes of electromagnetic and gravitic interference. They were especially effective against counter-missiles, which relied on their ability to home in on the impeller signatures of their targets, because counter-missiles were designed to be produced in the largest possible numbers, and the fact that they didn't *need* sophisticated seekers helped hold the price down. Nothing in the galaxy was more glaringly obvious than the impeller signature of a missile accelerating at 98,000 gravities, after all. Spotting one of them was rather like trying to see a million-candlepower searchlight in a darkened room. Only a blind man could have missed it.

But that was what the Dazzler produced: blind men. The counter-missiles' seekers couldn't possibly cope with those enormous bubbles of jamming. That meant they lost lock on their targets, and if it was timed correctly, both they and their targets were moving too rapidly for them to reacquire after the Dazzler's pulse. Even if they reacquired *something,* their onboard electronic brains were seldom up to the task of reacquiring the *proper* something without guidance from their human masters.

That was what the Dazzler had been *designed* to do, but as the Fleet's missile officers played around with it, they'd quickly realized it had another function. After all, *attack missiles* and the ships controlling them relied on their onboard sensors, too.

❖   ❖   ❖

"Ma'am!" Rear Admiral Rosiak said sharply. "The Manties—"

He broke off, looking over his shoulder at Admiral Isotalo, and Isotalo gave him a choppy nod as the tactical plot went momentarily berserk.

"What the hell *is* that?" she demanded.

"Some kind of jamming," Rosiak replied. "I don't know how they're doing it, though. We can't see shi— That is, we can't see *very much* through all the garbage, but CIC's computers say it's coming from at least a couple of dozen sources. That means it has to be some kind of independent platform. I don't see how they could sustain emissions at this intensity for very long without burning out any emitter you could put into a drone, though, and—"

He paused again, pressing the fingers of his right hand against the earbug in his right ear and listening intently. His lips tightened, and he looked back at Isotalo.

"CIC doesn't think they *are* sustaining emissions for more than ten to fifteen seconds per platform, Ma'am. But there are a lot of them, and they're running them in a cascade pattern. That's going to play hell with the attack birds' seekers."

✧   ✧   ✧

Task Force 1027's upgraded Cataphract-Cs were far superior to the Cataphracts Commodore Adrian Luft and the ill-fated People's Navy in Exile had taken to disaster at the Battle of Congo. They were longer-ranged, faster, equipped with heavier warheads, and fitted with seeking systems which relied upon both better sensors and more effective onboard software. They were far more capable of thinking for themselves, and their ability to differentiate between false targets and real ones and to penetrate enemy ECM was at least thirty percent better than Luft's had been.

But they still had to *see* their targets . . . and thanks to the Dazzlers, they couldn't for several long, long seconds. Their electronic brains knew where to look when the interference cleared, however, and eventually, it *had* to clear, since their targets had to be able to see *them* if they meant to intercept them. And so the Cataphracts' computers waited with uncaring, incurious patience for the range to clear and let them find their targets once more.

✧   ✧   ✧

"Decoys coming up . . . now," Commander Solis said calmly, and the fusion-powered Lorelei platforms keeping station on Sir Martin Lessem's cruisers and destroyers suddenly switched on their emitters. Powered by the same micro-fusion reactors that made Ghost Rider possible, Lorelei had a far higher energy budget than anyone else's ECM or EW platforms. With no need for beamed power from the ships they were protecting, however, the platforms could actually maneuver independently, mimicking moving starships almost perfectly. And even as the cruisers' stealth systems knocked back their emission signatures; the Loreleis' emitters deliberately *enhanced* theirs. They couldn't match the full power of a *Saganami-C* or *Saganami-B*'s actual signature but they could—and did—duplicate the signature of a *Saganami-C* or *Saganami-B* hiding under stealth.

And there were dozens of them.

✧   ✧   ✧

The master plot aboard SLNS *Foudroyant* cleared as the jamming platforms went down at last, and Isotalo found herself leaning forward in her command chair, eyes narrowed as she watched the icons of the Manticoran ships reappear upon it. *There* they were, and—

"Ma'am, we're picking up—"

"I see it, Bart." She cut Rosiak off and shook her head. "Not quite the same thing as *believing* it, I'm afraid," she added harshly.

The number of targets on her tactical plot had quintupled. From this range, not even her passive shipboard sensors could positively differentiate between the sudden rash of false targets and the real ones. Her shipboard sensors had lost lock thanks to the jamming, just as the Cataphracts had, and the Manties had used their temporary cloak of invisibility well. The energy budget on those decoys had to be much higher than the SLN's Halo platforms, and they were clearly maneuvering independently, so they obviously weren't using beamed power from their motherships. However the Manties were doing it, though, their decoys had come online when no one in TF 1027 could see a thing. There'd been no way to plot them and keep track of them as they came up, and once the jammers shut down, *Foudroyant* and her consorts found themselves trying—and failing—to tell which of the sixty "cruisers" on the plot were real and which were false.

Even as she watched, numbers flickered under each of the cruiser icons—percentage values, changing rapidly to reflect CIC's confidence as its analysis winnowed through the input to find the Manty starships once more. They were unlikely to accomplish that before her missiles reached attack range, unfortunately, and there was no way the less capable sensors the missiles themselves mounted would be able to.

That was...disconcerting, and she glanced across at Maleen Lamizana.

The intelligence officer looked back steadily, and Isotalo made herself nod. Lamizana had warned her and Rosiak that all their data on Manty EW was sketchy. "Problematic," was the way she'd delicately put it as they reviewed ONI's current guesstimates. Isotalo and Rosiak had tried hard to bear that in mind, but her intel officer had made it tactfully clear that she'd believed they were still underestimating the problem.

Now it would appear that even *Lamizana* had underestimated it.

✧ ✧ ✧

Commodore Lessem watched the plot with an expression which was rather calmer than he actually felt. Intellectually, he knew the 6,000 missiles sweeping towards his command were far less capable than a similar launch by the RMN's old Havenite opponents would have been. But 6,000 missiles were still 6,000 missiles, and it looked like all of them had been directed at his heavy cruisers.

What's to worry about, Martin? he thought sardonically. *That's only about four hundred birds per ship, isn't it?*

Neither *Clas Fleming* nor any of his other ships mounted the Keyhole-Two platforms which were the secret of Apollo. Without those—and without the Mark 23-E control missiles—he couldn't have taken full advantage of the Mark 23s aboard *David K. Brown*, which was why he'd decided against even trying to.

More to the point at the moment, however, Thomas Wozniak couldn't manage the defensive engagement nearly as effectively as he might have with Keyhole-One or Keyhole-Two available. His ability to hand off his interceptors between different control platforms was much more limited, and he couldn't establish direct telemetry links around the "dead spots" created by his own ships' impeller wedges. What he *could* do, however, was to spread his Ghost Rider drones as broadly as possible and use their sensors to track the incoming fire. He could also—albeit with a certain degree of risk—roll ship to bring *Clas Fleming*'s or one of her consorts' control links to bear on those dead zones and update the counter-missiles' targeting solutions. At the current range, the risk was small; as the range closed, and time to roll back up disappeared, it could get risky indeed.

Ghost Rider couldn't substitute for Keyhole's telemetry links to the CMs, but it could feed the cruiser's tactical section just fine, even in *Clas Fleming*'s current attitude, and the effect of the Loreleis was immediately obvious. At least a thousand of the incoming missile swarm peeled off, targeting one or another of the decoys. It was always possible some of them would reacquire one of his cruisers, or even lock onto one of the destroyers in default of its betters. That was unlikely, but unlikely things happened, and missiles which reacquired were often more dangerous than missiles which had never lost lock in the first place.

Missile defense was a game of probabilities, and one of the defender's critical objectives was to assess those probabilities. Missile defense officers had only a limited number of counter-missiles and point defense clusters, and those limited numbers were allocated dependent on the threat hierarchy established by analyzing the incoming fire. Those missiles most likely to hit were targeted first, working from most likely to least likely in descending order until the defenders ran out of CMs or PD, and missiles which had clearly lost lock were at the very end of the targeting queue. So when one of those missiles suddenly reacquired a target at the very last instant, there was seldom a counter-missile or point defense cluster available to deal with it.

On the other hand . . .

✧   ✧   ✧

Admiral Isotalo looked back at the plot just as the first wave of counter-missiles reached her oncoming attack. Then her jaw tightened in fresh consternation. Solarian interception probabilities on a first-launch, at maximum range, against the Cataphracts' accompanying electronic warfare platforms and penetration aids, would have been on the order of ten percent.

The Manties did just a bit better than that.

✧   ✧   ✧

The first wave of CruDiv 912.1's CMs ripped into the oncoming Cataphracts.

The improved Solarian missile drives were accompanied by better penetration aids than the RMN had anticipated based on BuShips' analysis of the contents of Massimo Filareta's magazines. The difference was slight, but quantifiable, and *Clas Fleming*'s CIC took due note of it for the squadron's after-action report.

In terms of the Mark 31 counter-missile's performance, however, it was a negligible factor.

Five hundred and twenty Manticoran CMs slammed into the oncoming Cataphracts. A first-wave counter-missile launch, intercepting at maximum range, was always the least accurate of a defensive engagement. That was true in this case, as well, and the 520 Mark 31s intercepted only 152 of TF 1027's Cataphracts . . . just under three times the kill ratio Barthilu Rosiak had estimated.

✧   ✧   ✧

Jane Isotalo's eyes narrowed and fury burned in their depths.

She'd thought the Manties' decision to remain at rest relative to the terminus had indicated they intended to translate out as soon as a serious attack came their way. And, to be honest, she hadn't intended her first salvo as a *serious* attack. She *had* expected them to either disappear into hyper or take some significant damage from it, however.

Not going to happen, Jane, she thought now, hands tightening on her command chair's armrests as the second wave of CMs, with more time to acquire their targets, intercepted 260 attack missiles.

They're still feeding at least some telemetry to those damned things, she thought grimly. *They have to be. But how in hell can they even* see *my birds through their frigging wedges?*

The third wave intercepted 300 attack missiles. The fourth intercepted 393, and the fifth took down 471, a staggering 90.5% interception rate. All told, the Manticoran counter-missiles intercepted 1,183 Cataphracts, almost twenty percent of her total launch, and like all good missile defense officers, the Manties had concentrated on the fire most likely to find a target. They'd done a remarkably good job of ignoring the hundreds of Cataphracts which veered off to chase decoys or simply went off on a vector to God only knew where when they lost both sensor lock and telemetry.

Still, of the 6,000 missiles she'd launched, just over 3,800 got past both the counter-missiles and the electronic counter measures and came screaming in on the Manticoran starships.

✧　　✧　　✧

"Forty-three seconds," Commander Wozniak said flatly. "Stand by Point Defense."

✧　　✧　　✧

Task Force 1027's missiles executed their programmed attack profiles, trying for "look down" shots through the Manticoran sidewalls as they passed "over" or "under" their targets, or seeking the even more deadly "down-the-throat" or "up-the-kilt" attack positions which were every tactician's dream.

The attack birds were up to a closing velocity of 240,319 KPS—0.802 cee—as they howled down on their targets, and Isotalo smiled grimly. The SLN had stopped tweaking the software for its point defense clusters to deal with the higher closing rates of multistage missiles and completely replaced it instead, and TF 1027 had trained hard with the new systems, in both sims and live fire exercises against inert laser-heads. The improvement was enormous...it just still wasn't anything Jane Isotalo would have called adequate against targets coming in at the sorts of velocities Cataphracts could produce. She didn't much like that. On the other hand, physics played no favorites. At *those* velocities, an awful lot of *her* missiles were going to get through even the Manties' defenses, she thought vengefully, and—

✧　　✧　　✧

"Point Defense engaging...*now!*" Wozniak snapped as the attack missiles swept through the squadron's formation, and the laser clusters went to maximum-rate fire.

Rods of coherent energy stabbed out, matching the speed of cybernetic reflexes against the attackers' incredible velocity as the Cataphracts cleared the shadow of their targets' impeller wedges. Missiles, unlike starships, couldn't generate sidewalls. That meant they could be taken down by laser fire even before they dropped their wedges, if the geometry was right.

The geometry was right for quite a few of the Solarian missiles, and the waiting lasers punched straight through them. Many of their fellows simply streaked across the vulnerable sides of the cruisers' wedges without ever finding a target in the fleeting moments their preposterous velocity gave their sensors. Others were more fortunate in that regard, and missile wedges vanished and laserheads rolled on incredibly powerful thrusters as they fought to align their lasing rods with their targets.

But the point defense was waiting for them.

✧　　✧　　✧

Jane Isotalo watched the display. At thirty-six million kilometers, the light-speed lag was just over two minutes. Impeller signatures were FTL, so Tracking could plot her missiles' inbound positions in near real-time—there was still a 1.89 second delay—but her sensors would need the full two minutes to detect anything else, including nuclear detonations. Because of that, she couldn't really "see" a thing once the missiles' impellers went down, and she waited impatiently, along with everyone else on *Foudroyant*'s flag deck, for the telltale flare of detonating laserheads.

✧　　✧　　✧

Manticore's electronically steered laser clusters cycled much more rapidly than the SLN's did. It was, Sir Martin Lessem reflected, a prime example of those Darwinian processes that worried him where the Sollies were concerned. The increasing deadliness of the missile environment in Manticore's long war with the People's Republic of Haven had given the Royal Manticoran Navy's R&D people no choice but to improve cycle time. In fact, *Clas Fleming*'s cycle time was almost fifty percent more rapid than that of an earlier flight *Saganami-C*, and each of her clusters mounted not the eight emitters of an early flight ship but twelve, almost twice as many as a *Nevada*-class battlecruiser's clusters.

Cycle time didn't matter all that much this time. The window of engagement was so brief that not even a Manticoran emitter could have fired two shots in the available time. On the other hand, each of *Clas Fleming*'s broadsides mounted twenty-four point defense clusters with a dozen emitters each. That was 288 shots from each broadside—576, in total—with the same from each of his other three *Saganami-Cs* and an additional 288 from each of his six *Saganami-Bs*, with fewer emitters per cluster but more total clusters per ship. In all, including his destroyers, his squadron mounted over three thousand emitters... already coached into waiting positions by the Ghost Rider tracking reports.

The tension on *Clas Fleming*'s bridge could have been chipped with a knife, because no one knew better than Manticorans that any ship could be killed, however good its defenses, however skilled its crew. But this was a deadly ballet the Royal Manticoran Navy had danced countless times in the last twenty T-years. Its officers and ratings knew its measures better than anyone else in the galaxy, and the space around Sir Martin Lessem's squadron was suddenly a tornado of disintegrating Cataphracts as the defenses picked them off with viper speed and metronome precision. Shattered missile bodies tumbled onward into the endless dark, broken and inert. But even in the midst of their destruction, scores of surviving laserheads disappeared in bubbles of intolerable brilliance and bomb-pumped X-ray lasers stabbed out at CruRon 912.

❖   ❖   ❖

They must have had even better tracks on the incoming fire than she'd thought from their counter-missiles, Isotalo realized as impeller signatures began vanishing too early for end-of-run detonations. Thanks to the light-speed delay, she had ample time to contemplate the implications of those... premature disappearances, and she didn't like them one bit. Her salvo hadn't melted like a sand castle, because there hadn't been enough *time* for that. One heartbeat it had been streaking towards its target... the next the Manty point defense had ripped it to shreds. She'd never seen anything like it, never imagined mere cruisers could produce that volume of defensive fire.

Yet not even that fire could have stopped all of them. There literally weren't enough places on ships that size to put enough laser clusters to take out *that* many threats. Dozens—scores—of them must have gotten through unscathed. Unfortunately, she knew, the defenders had concentrated on the ones that could have *hurt* them, and most of those surviving dozens and scores would have wasted themselves against their targets' wedges and sidewalls. But the missiles crossing ahead of the Manties would be another matter. A ship simply couldn't pack as many laser clusters into her fore and aft hammerheads, and it was obvious from the timing that a higher percentage of missiles attacking the throats of the Manticoran wedges had shut down their impellers rather than being picked off on the way in. By rights, most of the birds who'd reached shutdown positions should have gotten their lasers off before they could be destroyed, and the throat of a starship's impeller wedge was far deeper than its sidewalls. That made it a much, *much* bigger target.

✧   ✧   ✧

Seventy-three laserheads detonated directly ahead of HMS *Clas Fleming*, and seven hundred and thirty bomb-pumped lasers ripped down the throat of her wedge.

But unlike the Solarian Navy's warships, the throats of current-generation Manticoran warships were no longer the traditional gaping chink in their armor. The bow-wall and its smaller cousin, the buckler, had finally provided the equivalent of a sidewall—and a very *powerful* sidewall—to cover that lethally vulnerable aspect of the wedge. That was one reason Sir Martin Lessem had waited motionless in space. He couldn't accelerate with the full bow-wall up, and he didn't trust the smaller buckler to provide sufficient cover. But he also hadn't wanted to suddenly stop accelerating at the instant the wall went up lest the Sollies figure out that *something* was covering that aspect of Manticoran ships.

The laserheads detonating in front of *Clas Fleming* were never able to properly localize their target, because they simply couldn't see it clearly enough through the bow-wall's focused gravitic plane. All they could do was fire blindly, trying to saturate the entire volume in which the heavy cruiser *might* be located. That was an awfully wide volume for even seven hundred lasers to cover, and the bow-wall bent and degraded even those which had managed to find a target in the first place.

✧   ✧   ✧

Admiral Isotalo reminded herself to breathe as she waited for the laggard photons to tell her how many of her missiles had survived to attack...and how well they'd fared. The human eye was notoriously unreliable at moments like this, but CIC's uncaring, hyper-efficient computers' count had already confirmed that the Manties had picked off at least seventy-five percent of her total launch before the surviving missiles dropped their wedges to attack.

That was yet another conclusion she didn't much like, and she made a mental note to grab those over-optimistic idiots in the Office of Technical Analysis by their throats and choke some sense into them as soon as she got back to Sol. They had to start coming closer to realistic assessments, or the Manties were going to go right on kicking the Navy's arse. She had the numbers to punch out a force this small, despite the...flawed enemy capability estimates with which she'd been sent out, but somebody else was going to run into a proper Manty *task force*, and when they did—

The thought broke off and her lips drew back in a snarl of satisfaction as the light-speed sensors finally updated the plot and hundreds of laserheads erupted in bubbles of nuclear fusion. Even as she snarled, she knew her most pessimistic estimate of how many had gotten through had been overly optimistic, but her targets were only cruisers, and at least fifty or sixty laserheads detonated directly ahead of four of them.

They sent the deadly stilettos of their bomb-pumped lasers straight down the wide-open throats of their victims' wedges...and absolutely nothing happened.

✧   ✧   ✧

"We took one hit forward, Sir," Commander Wozniak told Lessem. "Graser One's gone, and so is Point Defense Four. Seven casualties, nonfatal." He looked back down at his display. "*Robert L. Gartner* reports one hit starboard, Frame Seven-Five. That one cost two counter-missile launchers, but Captain Reicher thinks he can get one of them back and reports no personnel casualties. *Michael Cucchiarelli* took two hits, but she was lucky. Captain Disall's lost both of his secondary grav sensor arrays, but he reports no personnel casualties or weapon systems damage. *Edward Dravecky* took two hits; one down her throat and one portside, Frame Two Hundred. The hit forward knocked out a beta node and the power surge killed two ratings in her forward impeller room. The portside hit destroyed Graser Eight and Counter-missile Thirty-Seven. Nine casualties there, two fatal, I'm afraid."

Lessem nodded heavily, his expression tight. Four hits and eighteen casualties, only four of them fatal, was a minuscule return for six thousand pod-launched missiles. He knew that, and knowing did absolutely nothing to make it hurt less, because those eighteen casualties were *his* people.

On the other hand, he thought grimly, *I have to wonder how the* other *side's reacting to this?*

✧   ✧   ✧

Isotalo heard Barthilu Rosiak inhale sharply, swallowing what probably would have been a curse, as the same shock lashed through the operations officer.

There should have been *some* sign of damage, she thought almost numbly. They'd just fired over eight hundred Cataphracts right down the Manties' throats, each with the warhead of a Trebuchet capital missile, and CIC confirmed that at least a quarter of them—more probably a third—of the crossing shots had detonated before interception. Call it two hundred and thirty to split the difference, and that was still *twenty-three* hundred lasers against perfect targets.

Hit probabilities at that insane crossing speed against a target which couldn't even be seen clearly until the attack missiles' sensors cleared that target's wedge and could look down its throat had to be tiny, despite the ideal geometry of any "crossing-the-T" attack. She and Rosiak had estimated no more than a one-percent hit ratio in such circumstances, rather than the thirty-eight percent ratio they would have expected at a pre-Cataphract crossing rate, but that was still twenty-three hits. That might not inflict crippling damage, scattered across ten ships the size of the Manty cruisers, but it damned well should have inflicted *some*, and the Manties' emissions hadn't even flickered.

"I see we're going to need heavier salvos," Admiral Jane Isotalo said coldly.

✧   ✧   ✧

"What do you expect them to try next, Sir?" Commander Thúri asked quietly. Commodore Lessem glanced at him, then returned his gaze to the tactical plot. He stood that way for several moments, hands clasped behind him, whistling soundlessly.

"The one thing I *don't* expect him to do is to try another long-range launch, unless he's able to put a hell of a lot more missiles into it," he said then. "We didn't expect their new accelerations, and their projected accuracy was better than we expected at that range, too," he acknowledged with a shrug. "But not enough better to offset our advantages in missile defense, and judging from their attack profile, they don't know about the bow-wall, either. But unless they're idiots—and, frankly, whoever this fellow is, he doesn't strike me as another Crandall or Filareta—he'll have figured out that something sure as hell knocked back the damage all those down-the-throat shots should've inflicted."

He turned away from the plot, pacing slowly across the flag bridge to his command chair. He sank into the chair and turned it to face the astrogation plot while the chair's displays deployed around him.

"He'll want to get closer," he said then, his eyes narrowing. "If we can take all those down-the-throat shots without showing more dam-age than we did, he needs every scrap of accuracy he can get. That means getting into effective telemetry range—*his* effective telemetry range. And out here, he just might pull that off."

The chief of staff nodded, his expression thoughtful, then smiled.

"In that case, Sir, it's probably a good thing that you're—and I say this with the utmost respect—a sneaky bastard."

"I'll take that as a compliment, Commander," Sir Martin Lessem replied with an answering smile.

✧   ✧   ✧

"—so Technodyne's accuracy estimates at extended range were *almost* on the money," Rear Admiral Rosiak said, using the hand unit to highlight a column of numbers on the briefing room's bulkhead smart wall. "We can't be positive, but the hot wash analysis suggests Technodyne's estimate was accurate to within five or six percent. Which—" he looked around the unhappy faces of Admiral Isotalo's staff "—was higher than the estimate Maleen and I plugged into our pre-battle planning. Unfortunately, ONI's estimate of the Manty missile defense's capabilities was nowhere near accurate, so even with the better-than-expected accuracy, the actual hit ratio still sucked vacuum."

"In fairness to ONI, Ma'am," Rear Admiral Lamizana put in, "nobody who's gone toe-to-toe with the Manties has gotten home again to tell us how good their defenses really are. The best anyone's been able to do is extrapolate from the loss ratios, using our own capabilities as a baseline." She shrugged ever so slightly. "It seems pretty clear that baseline was too optimistic, but it was the only one they had."

Jane Isotalo's jaw tightened at that unpalatable reminder, but it was exactly the sort of reminder Lamizana was supposed to give her, and she nodded in recognition.

"So your recommendation is what, Bart?" she asked after a second.

"We have two options, Ma'am, either of which has pros and cons," Rosiak replied. "One is to simply fire the biggest damned missile salvo the galaxy's ever seen. I don't care *how* good their defenses are on a ship-for-ship basis. Hit them with enough birds to completely saturate their counter-missiles and point defense, and *something*'s getting through. Assuming we're right about the blind fire hit probabilities, my people estimate that a thirty thousand-missile launch should produce a minimum of four hundred hits, despite their defensive capabilities."

"Assuming they've actually shown us all of those capabilities yet," Lamizana added in a carefully neutral tone.

"Assuming that," Rosiak acknowledged, nodding at the intelligence officer. "I think Maleen's right that we have to assume they may not have, although I also have to say I find it a little difficult to believe anyone could see *six thousand* missiles coming at him and not pull out all the stops against them, however good he thought his defenses were. Having said that, I don't have any desire at all to get caught with our arses hanging out the way certain other people have."

Two or three people, Isotalo among them, surprised themselves with smiles at his last sentence. Although it wasn't really funny, given how many of their fellows—officers and enlisted—those "other people" had gotten killed.

And Bart can say that when Ramaalas or Maleen couldn't, she reflected, *because he's Battle Fleet, just like Crandall and Filareta.*

And he does *have a point.*

"I realize we have deep pockets where missile pods are concerned," she said then. "I'd really prefer not to use them up at the rate of five or six thousand per heavy cruiser, though," she added in a desert-dry tone, "so let's hear option two, Bart. Should I assume you're thinking in terms of Two-Step?"

"Yes, Ma'am, I am."

Rosiak waved at the smart wall without looking away from Isotalo.

"On top of their active defenses and EW, *Foudroyant's* CIC agrees with my own people's conclusion that the Manties have to have found some way to protect against down-the-throat shots. Nobody's prepared to go out on a limb over exactly how they're doing that, but my own feeling is that they have to've found some way to create a sidewall to cover the ahead and astern aspects of a wedge."

"Not to dispute Bart's conclusion, Ma'am," Rear Admiral Ramaalas said, "but if they've managed *that*, they have to be playing even faster and looser with physics than our worst-case assumptions."

"Not...necessarily," Captain Malati Raghavendra said.

Foudroyant's captain sat at Isotalo's left elbow, directly across from Ramaalas, both because it was her right as the task force's flag captain and because Isotalo respected her levelheaded—one might almost have said phlegmatic—common sense. Like Isotalo and Rosiak, Raghavendra was Battle Fleet, but she'd started in Engineering, not Tactical, which helped explain why she had so far attained only captain's rank in the admiral-heavy SLN.

"What do you mean, Malati?" the admiral asked.

"Well, Ma'am, speaking as an ex-snipe, there's no real problem with generating a...call it a 'bow-wall,' for want of a better term. You'd need generators that were a lot bigger and more powerful to produce a wall with that much area, but that's pretty straightforward. Just a matter of engineering, really. The *problem*"—she nodded at Ramaalas—"is that every time you put it up and closed the front of the wedge, your ship wouldn't be able to accelerate. But these people *weren't* accelerating. In fact, if they have something like that, it might be the reason they weren't."

"They *were* rolling ship, Captain," Ramaalas pointed out, but his expression was thoughtful, not dismissive.

"Yes, and a lot faster than they could have on thrusters," Raghavendra agreed. "They have to be using their wedges for that. But we don't know how quickly they could put the thing up or down, and none of us were looking for any evidence of it at the time. One thing my tactical officer noticed, though, was that after they initially rolled up against our fire, none of their ships ever changed attitude twice in a row."

"Twice in a row?" Isotalo repeated.

"What I mean, Ma'am, is that they were obviously clearing telemetry or sensor channels to take peeks downrange at our birds, but they did it in a staggered sequence, using a different ship each time. I'm wondering if that was because of the time it took to deactivate and activate the 'bow-wall' generators. The actual engagement time was too short for us to draw any kind of conclusions, but I think it's worth bearing the possibility in mind."

"Agreed." Ramaalas nodded and returned his gaze to Isotalo. "And I think I see where Bart was going with this. For them to handle that much fire without any evidence of significant damage, whatever they're using to protect the forward aspect of their wedges must be a hell of a lot tougher than anything ships that size ought to mount. I wouldn't like to face that kind of beating with a *superdreadnought*'s sidewalls, to be honest, and as the Captain points out, the sheer area they're covering means they must have given up a lot of volume and power supply to cram the suckers in. You have to wonder if they can mount sidewall generators equally heavy, don't you?"

"That question did cross my mind, Sir," Rosiak replied. "If so, we may be looking at a flipped situation, one in which we can expect better penetration and more hits going for the other fellow's sidewalls rather than trying to cross his 'T.' And that's a much narrower target, which means we need more accuracy to hit it. Again, a big enough deluge of missiles would *probably* give us the hits we need through blind chance, but Admiral Isotalo's right about the number of birds we'd need on a per-ship basis. Expenditures like that would burn through even our ammo supply before we ever got to the primary missions, but to avoid them, we need to get close enough to maintain our control links right up to the terminal phase. Which," he pointed out, turning back to Isotalo, "is one of the things Two-Step is designed to do."

"Yes, it is," she acknowledged. She thought about it for a moment, then sat forward in her chair and tapped her index finger on the surface of the briefing room table.

"Yes, it is," she repeated more briskly. "To be honest, I still have reservations about the concept. God knows we've discussed it enough for all of you to know what they are. But I think Bart's right. We've got to shorten the control loop if we're going to hurt these bastards. In fact, I'd love to get close enough to be able to launch inside their hyper generator cycle loops, and only a drooling idiot would let us get that close with an n-space approach. So I'm afraid that only leaves Two-Step, Isadore."

She turned to Captain Isadore Hampton, the task force's staff astrogator. Hampton was a swarthy, dark-eyed fellow who normally radiated an impression of calm competence. He still looked competent, but calm would have been pushing it at the moment, she thought, and with good reason.

"I can't see another approach," she told him. "I realize it'll be putting a lot of pressure on you, but if anybody can pull it off, you can. And before we start, let me say that I don't see where the tactical situation's likely to be a lot worse even if your numbers are off in the end. What I'm saying—and this is for the record—is that I fully realize the difficulty of what I'm asking you to do. I've made my decision to try it anyway based on all the information available to me, but I don't expect or demand miracles. Having said that, I do expect you to do your damnedest to make it work anyway."

"Ma'am, we can do it," Hampton replied. "We'll have to come in on the 'far side' to avoid the resonance zone, though."

"Understood," Isotalo said. Every wormhole created a resonance zone in the volume between it and the n-space star with which it was associated. Translations out of hyper and back into n-space in those areas weren't merely risky; they were extremely dangerous. So TF 1027 would be forced to approach the terminus from the side farthest from Prime. That would extend the jump somewhat, but the Manties were also positioned "outside" the terminus. Probably because they knew she couldn't micro-jump into the area between them and the primary even if she'd wanted to.

"We figured that when we first started looking at Two-Step," she reminded him. "And at least the Manties seem to be cooperating."

"So far, Ma'am," Hampton acknowledged. "And I'm fairly confident of hitting the distance pretty close. Translation scatter's likely to turn formation keeping into a god-awful mess, though, especially that close to the terminus."

Several heads nodded, and she grimaced.

"I know," she said. "But somebody way back in one of the ancient wet-navies on Old Terra said something one time that I'm afraid applies here. To paraphrase: some things have to be left to chance in a battle. I know that's anathema to any good Battle Fleet CO, but in this case," she smiled tightly at Ramaalas and Lamizana, "I think we're going to have to try it the sloppy, make-it-up-as-you-go-along Frontier Fleet way."

A chuckle ran around the briefing room, despite the tension, and she sat back again.

"Instead of sending in one of the task groups, Bart, I want Bonrepaux and Tsukahara to take the lead together. We'll hold Santini back as the follow-through. And since we're talking about shortening our command loops, we might as well go whole hog on it."

This time, her smile could have been a shark's.

✧　　✧　　✧

"That's interesting, Sir," Commander Wozniak said.

"What's interesting, Tom?" Lessem asked, looking up from the tactical problem he'd been playing through on his command chair's repeater plot.

"It looks like those 'donkeys' of theirs may have more internal endurance than we'd thought," the ops officer replied. "With your permission—?"

He raised his eyebrows, a finger hovering over one of the icons on his touchscreen, and Lessem nodded. Wozniak's finger touched the icon and a time-compressed tracking recording appeared on Lessem's display. The commodore gazed at it, then grunted.

"Wonderful," he said sourly.

"Don't know how useful it'd be under normal battle conditions," Wozniak said, "but it does give them some interesting options, doesn't it?"

"One way to put it," Lessem acknowledged.

The Solarian task force had started decelerating hard after the dismal failure of its initial attack. In fact, they'd gone to 4.4 KPS^2, ninety-two percent power for a *Nevada*. He didn't think for a moment that they'd given up, though. If they'd wanted to do that, all they had to do was translate out. No, they were only buying themselves more time to think. Assuming they maintained their increased deceleration, they would reach a zero velocity relative to the terminus twelve minutes sooner—and 824,935 kilometers farther from it. And from a resting launch, a range of 2.7 light-seconds would give missile flight times of almost exactly forty-two seconds for the SLN's prewar standard missile.

Which was...interesting, given the 42.7-second hyper generator cycle time of a *Saganami-C*.

In the meantime, however, a host of tiny impeller signatures sped towards the decelerating battlecruisers from the far larger freighters following well behind them. Apparently the Solarian version of the donkey could forward-deliver itself—and, presumably, its missile pods—to a designated end-user. As Wozniak said, not something that was likely to be critically important under most battle circumstances, but irritating as hell, nonetheless.

And maybe more than just irritating, too, he thought. *I wonder...*

"Get me Captain Amberline, please, George," he said.

"Aye, Sir," the com officer replied, and three seconds later Captain Harriet Amberline appeared on Lessem's com display. Behind her, he could see the bridge of HMS *David K. Brown* and the FSV's tactical section.

"Yes, Sir?" she said.

"I don't trust these people," Lessem told her. "They've obviously picked their decel to get inside our hyper generator cycles in a normal-space approach. In fact, I think they've picked it a little bit too obviously. I really hope they don't think I'm stupid enough to let them actually get to that point without translating the hell out of here, and if they don't, that suggests they have something else in mind."

"A micro-jump that short's tricky as hell, Sir. At the very least they're likely to get a *lot* of scatter," she pointed out, and he nodded at the confirmation that she was thinking the same thing he was.

"Might not matter a lot," he pointed out in turn. "They've got ten times the hulls we do, and the *Nevadas* actually have more broadside tubes than a *Saganami-C*. I know we can fire off-bore and they can't, but that's still a lot of missiles if they can ever get into their effective range of us. For that matter, the *Nevadas* have half again our energy broadside, too. If they could get *really* close..."

He let his voice trail off, and Amberline nodded soberly. Just this once, she was delighted that his collar carried the twin planets of a commodore and hers carried only the four golden pips of a junior grade captain.

"Given how much slower your generator's going to cycle, I think it's time you went elsewhere," he continued. "I promise we'll look after your waifs, and I'm giving you *Minion* and *Lancaster* for escorts. They've got less of the astro control people on board than *Obusier*."

She nodded again.

"Randy will have the rendezvous coordinates for you in a minute." Lessem waved one hand at Lieutenant Commander Ranald Kivlochan, CruRon 912's staff astrogator. "Somebody will be along, one way or the other, to let you know how things work out."

"I'll be expecting good news, Sir."

"Then we'll try our best to give it to you. And your going away present's probably going to help in that regard. Lessem, clear."

✧   ✧   ✧

"That freighter or whatever of theirs just translated out, Ma'am," Rear Admiral Rosiak reported. "Looks like a couple of their destroyers went with it."

"Damn," Admiral Isotalo said mildly. "Obviously, she *isn't* a drooling idiot. Not a surprise, but one could always hope."

"Nothing wrong with hoping, Ma'am," Rear Admiral Ramaalas observed. The chief of staff stood beside her command chair, watching the master plot with her. "Not as long as you don't let yourself get wedded to building your plans *based* on what you hope will happen, and in this case, you haven't done that."

"Nice of you to say so, anyway."

Isotalo swiveled her chair thoughtfully from side to side while she pondered the plot. The icon of what she'd become privately convinced had to be a purpose-built fast support ship had just vanished from it, accompanied by two more impeller signatures CIC had tagged as destroyers, which suggested the Manty CO had figured out what she was up to. On the other hand, she might not have, too. The task force had been decelerating at its current rate for twenty-three minutes and its approach velocity was down to 10,179 KPS. In just over nine and a half minutes, it would enter the 7.6 million-kilometer maximum powered range of a standard Javelin missile. The chance of a Javelin scoring a hit at 25.3 light-seconds against the defenses which had turned a six-thousand-strong Cataphract launch into mincemeat was nonexistent, but the range was going to go on falling. She needed to get at least another ten or fifteen light-seconds closer if she hoped for a decent hit percentage, and the odds that the Manty CO would sit still for another fourteen minutes while she closed another 5.3 million kilometers struck her as . . . low. It was possible the Manty expected her to *try* it, but neither one of them expected Isotalo to get away with it.

On the other hand, Isotalo had already fired a six thousand-missile salvo at her, and she had to have seen the Huskies streaming forward from Isotalo's own supply ships to replenish TG 1027.3. That meant she knew Isotalo could fire a much, *much* larger salvo of Cataphracts if she flushed all of her task groups' pods at once. Nor would Isotalo need to incorporate a ballistic phase this time. The Manties were already inside her powered Cataphract envelope, with a total flight time of "only" 210 seconds. No doubt the Manty wished TF 1027 *would* fire a bazillion or so missiles in her direction. There'd be plenty of time for her damned cruisers to translate safely into hyper, laughing down their sleeves at the stupid Sollies as a couple of hundred thousand expensive Cataphracts saw their targets abruptly vanish and self-destructed at the end of their powered runs.

But the support ship's cycle time had to be close to two minutes, so it was at least possible the Manty CO was simply getting it safely out of harm's way before the Cataphracts got inside *her* cycle time. That didn't necessarily mean she knew what Isotalo was actually planning.

Sure it doesn't, Jane, she thought sardonically. *On the other hand, even if she does know what you're thinking, you may still get away with it.*

✧   ✧   ✧

"Any time now, I think," Commodore Lessem murmured, watching the range continue to fall.

"I beg your pardon, Sir?" Commander Thúri said, and the commodore shook himself and smiled crookedly.

"Just making a bet with myself about when this fellow's going to pull the trigger," he said.

"I'm wondering that myself, Sir," the chief of staff admitted.

"And the other thing *I'm* wondering is how cautious this particular rat is when it comes to sniffing the cheese." Lessem shoved back up out of his command chair and crossed the flag bridge to stand looking over Lieutenant Commander Kivlochan's shoulder. "I'd hate to have them leave before the party begins."

Thúri nodded, standing at Kivlochan's other shoulder and watching the plot.

The Sollies had been decelerating for thirty-four minutes. The range was down to seven million kilometers, and their closing velocity had fallen to 7,293 KPS. They were actually in extreme Javelin range now, and they couldn't expect CruRon 912 to let them close much further.

Under normal circumstances, at least.

Lessem considered the geometry a moment longer, then nodded decisively.

"Better to encourage them, I think," he said, and looked over his shoulder at Commander Wozniak. "Execute Picador, Tom."

✧　　✧　　✧

"Missile launch!" Rear Admiral Rosiak announced sharply. "Estimate eight hundred and twenty-four—repeat, eight-two-four—inbound at four-five-one KPS squared! Time-of-flight two-point-seven minutes."

Jane Isotalo's head snapped around from her conversation with Kimmo Ramaalas. She'd dreaded this moment—and, frankly, been astonished it hadn't happened earlier. But—

"Confirm that missile count!"

"Tracking's confidence is high, Ma'am," Rosiak replied, looking up from the master plot to meet her gaze.

"That can't be all they've got, Ma'am," Ramaalas said quietly.

"Maybe not, but it's damned well more than even those big-assed cruisers of theirs should be able to launch from internal tubes."

Isotalo's voice was equally low. She turned to the maneuvering plot, eyes focused and intense while her mind whirred. All the reports and analyses insisted that Manty capital ships routinely threw thousands of missiles at their opponents, and there was no way in hell these people weren't operating with pre-deployed pods of their own. Not when missiles were the Manties' Hammer of God! Admittedly, *these* Manties were only heavy cruisers, but that many missiles couldn't have come from ten cruisers' internal tubes. They *had* to have been pod-launched, yet the numbers seemed ridiculously low if they were coming from a huge stack of pods. Unless...

"Maybe they don't have enough control links," she said. Ramaalas cocked his head at her, and she shrugged. "So far, we don't have any hard evidence of how many birds a single one of their *cruisers* can manage, and all the really big launches we know about have been handled by capital ships. Except for Spindle, maybe, and that was a launch from planetary orbit. God only know how many platforms they had controlling *that* one."

"That's true, Ma'am, but don't forget the reports that they can launch off-bore. We just got confirmation they can launch counter-missiles that way, and that argues pretty strongly that they can launch shipkillers the same way. And if you crunch the numbers, this sounds like it could be a double salvo from each broadside—hell, maybe even their chase tubes, too. I'm wondering if they might've designed the damned things to handle double broadsides."

"Stack 'em, you mean?" Isotalo considered that, then nodded. "Could be. It'd be a logical steppingstone for heavier salvo density on something that can't carry their frigging pods internally, at least. They'd have to stagger the light-off sequence a bit, but we'd never see them at this range till their impellers went live, so how could we know they had?" Her eyes narrowed. "But if you're right, that might mean this *is* the biggest salvo they have the channels to manage, even launching from deployed pods."

And it would be nice if there was some *limit on their damned salvo densities*, she added mentally.

"Could be, Ma'am," the rear admiral agreed. "On the other hand, they might just not want to piss away any more birds than they have to out here." It was his turn to shrug.

"And maybe it's all they think they're going to *need*, too," she said more bitingly, then raised her voice and looked at Rosiak again. "Projected targeting?" she requested.

"Hard to say this early, Ma'am. It *looks* like they're coming in on Vice Admiral Bonrepaux, but that could be evasive routing."

"Probably is, actually." Her tone was almost absent this time, and she looked back at the maneuvering plot. Thirty seconds since the Manties' launch.

"Execute Two-Step in seventy seconds from...mark," she said. "All task groups will initiate translation, but if your projected targeting holds, Group Three will abort and hold position here in n-space."

✧　　✧　　✧

"I hope you're ready to punch that button, Randy," Commodore Lessem said as the squadron's missile launch slashed toward its target.

If he'd chosen to dip into the missile pods tractored to the hulls of his ships, the older cruisers could have added more than six hundred additional missiles to his attack, and he'd been tempted to do just that, on the theory that fifteen hundred Mark 16s would turn any Solarian battlecruiser squadron ever built into wreckage. Unfortunately, there was no way in hell he was going to hit anything under the current circumstances, unless the Solly commander guessed very wrong about his target selection, and *Picador* was specifically designed to help the other fellow guess *correctly*. Under the circumstances, he wasn't about to waste any of the pods limpeted to his ships, so he'd elected to rely solely on his cruisers' internal launchers.

The *Saganami-C* mounted twenty tubes in each broadside and its telemetry links were designed to "stack" forty-missile salvos of Mark 16s two deep, so ships like *Clas Fleming* routinely launched eighty missiles at a time. She'd also been designed with a sixty percent control link redundancy as a hedge against battle damage and to let her wring maximum utility out of the RMN's missile pods.

A *Saganami-B*-class cruiser actually mounted two more tubes than a *Charlie*, counting its chase armament, and had also been designed to stack salvos, which gave it stacked salvos eighty-four missiles "deep," although it had only about half the *Charlie*'s control link redundancy. The *Bravos* weren't equipped to fire the Mark 16, with its internal fusion plant, either, but they *were* armed with the Mark 14 Extended Range missile with its enhanced endurance impeller nodes. The Mark 14 had only fifty-six percent of the Mark 16's powered range, and its onboard power budget was much lower, which impacted things like ECM capability. But even with those limitations, it had eighty percent *more* powered range than the Cataphracts the RMN had discovered in Massimo Filareta's magazines. Inferior to the Mark 16 and the Mark 23 they might be, but they were superior to anything the Sollies had, and more than enough for his present purposes.

And it would be really nice if those people were clumsy enough to let us actually hit *them, too,* he reflected. *Not going to happen, though.*

❖   ❖   ❖

"Bastards *were* trying to sneak one in on us, Ma'am," Rear Admiral Ramaalas observed as the entire Manty salvo swerved at the last possible moment, shifting target from Vice Admiral Bonrepaux's TG 1027.1 to Vice Admiral Tsukahara's TG 1027.2.

"And it's going to bite them on the butt," Isotalo agreed, studying the attack's geometry with profound satisfaction. The Manty missiles' course change had placed Helmut Santini's TG 1027.3 well outside their envelope. Even at their acceleration, they couldn't reorient to acquire his ships, given the separation she'd inserted between her task groups.

"Com, confirm Two-Step abort to Admiral Santini," she said.

"Yes, Ma'am!" Commodore ad Kadidu, her communications officer acknowledged.

"I'll probably piss Helmut off by belaboring the obvious," Isotalo said quietly to Ramaalas, "but it never hurts."

"True, Ma'am," the chief of staff replied. The Manticoran missiles were barely fifteen seconds from detonation, but Ramaalas seemed unperturbed by the looming destruction of a third of TF 1027's battle-cruisers.

With good reason, Isotalo thought with a glance at the digital time display. In just about—

◇　　◇　　◇

"Why am I not surprised?" Commodore Lessem observed as two thirds of the Solarian warships disappeared into hyper five seconds before CruRon 912's missiles reached attack range. "George, send *So-po* and *Obusier* through to Ajay."

"Aye, aye, Sir," Lieutenant Gordon acknowledged, and Lessem turned to Commander Kivlochan.

"Start the clock, Randy."

"Aye, aye, Sir. Executing in . . . two-eight-zero seconds."

◇　　◇　　◇

Astrogators hate micro-jumps, which are defined by most of the galaxy's merchant spacers as any hyper-space trip which covers less than four or five light-minutes in normal-space. Actually, anything short of half a light-hour could be reasonably considered a micro-jump, but 72,000,000 kilometers is generally considered to be absolutely the shortest hyper "voyage" any reasonable person wants to make.

A large part of that is due to the fact that although a ship's maximum acceleration rate is identical in n-space and h-space—outside a grav wave, at least—its *apparent* acceleration rate to an observer in normal-space is much, much greater. In the Alpha bands, the differential is approximately 640 percent, which gives a Solarian *Nevada*-class battle-cruiser an apparent maximum acceleration of 32,112 gravities—over 370 KPS². That acceleration doesn't make an astrogator's calculations any more difficult, but it does mean any small errors have much larger consequences when the ship returns to normal-space. And some error is inevitable. The hyper log which keeps track of a starship's location in hyper, much the way ancient inertial navigation systems kept track of pre-space submarines' submerged positions, has to calibrate after any translation into hyper-space, and that calibration depends on a series of complex comparisons between the vessel's actual energy readings and those projected by a "perfect" model run over a period of time. There's not enough time for the hyper log to complete its comparisons in a micro-jump. Depending upon the jump's duration, the hyper log may be able to *refine* its accuracy; it can never achieve anything like *complete* accuracy.

And what creates problems for a single ship tends to create a lot more of them when multiple ships execute a micro-jump together. Even when a single ship runs the master clock for the jump and every ship initiates its downward translation simultaneously, there's some variance when they actually hit the alpha wall between hyper- and normal-space. Crossing the wall is akin to encountering atmospheric turbulence in an aircraft, and the wall fluctuates as the result of a complex interaction with any local n-space gravity wells or wormholes. The degree to which that fluctuation can be adjusted for depends upon how well the astrogation computers have analyzed it, and that, too, is a factor of how long they've had for the analysis.

Bearing all those factors in mind, merchant captains generally refuse to put wear on their alpha nodes and hyper generators for anything less than a half light-hour. Their schedules are seldom so time-critical as to make shorter micro-jumps worth the trouble, the effort, and the uncertainty. Naval astrogators, on the other hand, are specifically trained to make those shorter micro-jumps, although things can get tricky even for them if the total distance is much less than, say, *three* light-minutes.

Task Force 1027's micro-jump was only twenty-three *light-seconds*, however, and Isadore Hampton had the disruptive influence of the terminus itself to contend with, as well.

Inevitably, there was going to be a certain…sloppiness about it.

✧   ✧   ✧

"Hyper footprints!" Thomas Wozniak announced 4.5 minutes after thirty Solarian battlecruisers, twelve light cruisers, and twenty destroyers had vanished from CruRon 912's sensors. "Many footprints," he continued, studying the data. "The nearest is…seven hundred thousand kilometers!"

✧   ✧   ✧

The terminus's approaches were a storm of blue lightning, flashing against the Stygian dark as sixty-two starships returned to normal-space. Under the circumstances, it was a tight formation, Jane Isotalo thought as the hyper footprints flared upon SLNS *Foudroyant*'s master plot. "Tight," however was a relative term, and her two task groups

were still scattered over an enormous volume. One division of *Nevadas*
from TG 1027.2's BatCruRon 615 was over a million kilometers from
the rest of its squadron. That was the worst dispersal, however, and
she smiled fiercely as she saw how tight Isadore Hampton's astrogation
had actually been. He had, indeed, hit very close on the distance. If
four of her battlecruisers were 1.6 million kilometers from the Manties, eight more were barely beyond energy weapon range. Flight time
for a Javelin at 700,000 kilometers would be thirty-nine seconds, well
within the cycle time on a heavy cruiser's hyper generator, and the
communications lag would be only 2.3 seconds. At that range, all the
ECM in the universe wouldn't save the Manties.

She would have preferred energy range, but she'd settle for what
she had.

"Fire Plan Delta!" she snapped.

Delta relied solely on her ships' internal launchers, because there
wasn't time to redeploy the extended chains of Huskies and missile
pods which had been drawn in close enough for the battlecruisers'
hyper translation fields to extend around them. Still, the eight *Nevadas*—
including *Foudroyant*—closest to the Manties belched 224 missiles two
seconds after she'd given the order.

✧   ✧   ✧

"Not bad astrogation," Commodore Lessem observed as the master
plot stabilized. "Those bastards at zero-three-eight did especially well."

He twitched his head at the closely grouped clump of hyper footprints
off *Clas Fleming*'s starboard quarter. The Solarians weren't moving relative to his command—a ship translating out of hyper shed over ninety
percent of its velocity in transit energy bleed-off, and they hadn't been
moving especially fast through hyper even before they translated back
down—but those eight ships had maintained an extremely tight formation. In fact, he doubted very many Manticoran squadrons could have
matched their performance.

"Better than *I* expected, Sir," Commander Thúri admitted.

"Nobody ever said the Sollies weren't competent spacers," Lessem
pointed out. "We tend to forget that because—"

"Missile launch!" Wozniak said. "Two hundred-plus inbound from
zero-three-eight, one-six-three at niner-three-five-point-three KPS
squared. They look like Javelins, Sir. Time-of-flight...three-niner-
point-two seconds."

"Acknowledged," Lessem replied, never looking away from the plot.
"As I was saying," he resumed calmly, "we tend to forget that because
of how one-sided the actual fighting's been so far. But they're not
going to keep their heads inserted into their anal orifices on that front

forever, Lester. And when they get them extracted, they're still going to be competent in all those other areas."

"Point, Sir," Thúri said.

Lessem turned his head to smile at him, then glanced at Lieutenant Commander Kivlochan. The astrogator's expression was intense as he watched his console, but there was remarkably little concern on *Clas Fleming*'s bridge as the missiles accelerated towards her. And then—

✧   ✧   ✧

"Damn," Admiral Isotalo said as the entire Manticoran squadron disappeared into hyper fourteen seconds after her missiles had launched.

"Aborting salvo," Rear Admiral Rosiak said, and transmitted the destruct code to the Javelins which had been hurtling towards their foes. They self-destructed a second later, and Isotalo grimaced.

"I hate it when the other side has a brain," she said.

"All due respect, Ma'am, it didn't take a whole *lot* of brain to figure our options," Ramaalas pointed out. "Like you said, Two-Step was really our only chance to get into effective range before they bugged out, anyway. And I believe you were also the one who said only 'a drooling idiot' would let us get away with it. It was worth trying, but they had to have had their generators ready to cycle the instant they saw us go into hyper."

"I know. I know!" Isotalo snorted. "I guess I'm mostly pissed off at myself for letting them suck me into firing those missiles. Like you say, they had to've known when we'd be turning up and they could have hypered out four damn minutes before we translated back down. The only reason they didn't was because they wanted to sit here long enough to let me fire at them. It was a little...cheeky of them, but given the timing, we'd've had to hit n-space less than ninety thousand kilometers out to catch them with a missile launch. And at that range, we'd have been ripping them apart with energy fire, and damn the missiles! But what were the chances even Isadore could put us that close?" She shook her head. "No, the Manties did that on purpose. And they did it to make the point that they *could* do it."

"Beg your pardon, Ma'am?" Ramaalas's eyebrows furrowed.

"We could've fired ten times that many birds without making a hole in our internal magazines, much less what Quigley's got in the support ships. I think we can assume they're smart enough to figure that out, too. So they damned well didn't expect that convincing us to waste missiles chasing them into hyper was going to affect our combat readiness in any way. No, those people only waited because they were thumbing their noses at us before they ran away."

"Maybe so," Ramaalas acknowledged after a moment, "but that could end up costing them. Especially if they really can't fire salvos bigger than the one they already threw at us, Ma'am. *We're* on top of the terminus now, not them, and if they don't have the firepower to blow us back off of it, they're stuck on this side of it. At best—from their perspective—that would mean they'd have to go home the long way."

"You could be right, but I'm not convinced someone as smart as this wouldn't be a jump or two ahead of that logic. I'm thinking she probably *chose* to stay on the side of the terminus."

"Because he's expecting friends, Ma'am?"

"It's certainly a possibility." Isotalo turned and walked back to her command chair while the task groups' scattered units began accelerating back toward *Foudroyant*. Given the separation, it would take at least fifteen minutes for them to coalesce around the flagship once more. The Manties would probably translate back out of hyper well before that.

"They didn't have time to put that many ships through the terminus after we went into hyper," she pointed out, settling into her chair. A beckoning index finger summoned Rosiak to join her and Ramaalas and she leaned back. "Not in a *sequenced* transit, anyway. The minimum time for that would've been—what? A hundred and sixty seconds? And that would've been with all of them lined up in a tight transit queue. But if they'd intended to fall back on Ajay, they could've done that any time they wanted to before we translated out. For that matter, if they'd been planning on falling back, they could've been positioned for a simultaneous transit of their entire force. This terminus isn't as big as some, but it's more than big enough to handle that many cruisers simultaneously. And if they'd made transit to Ajay, we'd know they were sitting right on the other side of the terminus ready to rip our arses off with energy fire when we came through after them."

Her staffers nodded, expressions somber. A starship transited a wormhole under Warshawski sails, not impeller drive, and that meant it emerged with neither an impeller wedge nor sidewalls. It took several seconds—about eighty in the case of the Prime Terminus—to clear the wormhole sufficiently to reconfigure to wedge. During those eighty seconds, the ship in question was mother naked against defensive fire. That was one of the reasons Isotalo and her staff were quietly convinced that all the savage vituperation in the newsfaxes—and the Assembly—against Beowulf was completely unjustified in at least one respect. Colluding with the Manties or not, the Beowulfers had saved hundreds of thousands of SLN lives when they blocked the Beowulf Terminus of the Manticoran Wormhole Junction against Fleet Admiral Tsang. If Tsang *had* made transit into the teeth of the unshaken Manticoran defenses, her entire fleet would have been massacred even more completely than Filareta's had been. The politicians and the talking heads could say whatever they liked, but after what had happened to Eleventh Fleet, any naval officer with two brain cells to rub together knew what would have happened to Tsang would have been even worse. *Far* worse.

"There has to be a reason they didn't choose to do that," Isotalo went on. "And the most likely one that springs to my mind is that they are, indeed, supposed to be picketing this terminus while another of their task forces takes out the Agueda-Stine bridge. If that's the case, then they need to keep an eye on us to keep us from setting up an ambush to greet that other task force when it arrives." She showed her teeth. "Wouldn't it be sweet if *we* were the ones sitting on the terminus with a few thousand of *our* missile pods deployed in the area defense role when the Manties came back? They wouldn't have any of those damned invisible recon platforms deployed, and even their shipboard sensors would be degraded until the transit energy bled fully away. By the time they picked us up through our stealth, they'd probably be in range for a mass launch, and I would cheerfully use up a half million or so missiles to kick the shit out of one of their point-of-the-spear task forces!"

"That *would* be nice, Ma'am." Ramaalas sounded a bit wistful.

"And that's what they're primarily worried about, I think," Isotalo continued. "They want to maintain a sufficient force on this side of the terminus to play watchdog for their friends. An incoming task force wouldn't need recon platforms if there's already an entire damned cruiser squadron sitting here to tell them about us."

"What about protecting Ajay, though, Ma'am?" Rosiak asked. She raised an eyebrow at him, and he shrugged. "That has to be fairly high on their priority list, too, I'd think," he pointed out.

"I think we have two main possibilities," Isotalo said. "Either what we've been looking at here on the Prime side of the terminus is all they've got—or their primary force, at any rate—or it's not. Given how many missiles they threw at us in that one salvo, and given what we've heard so far about the kind of salvos Manty capital ships can throw, I'm inclined to think there can't be any wallers on the Ajay side. I don't care what some of our less brilliant colleagues might do if they'd brought a couple of those 'podnoughts' of theirs along, but all *I'd* have done would have been to run the hell away, and they'd have to assume any SLN admiral with a brain would be thinking exactly that. No way are we going to cross swords with something that can do what those damned things did to Filareta!"

Both her subordinates nodded in agreement—and profound relief—at that.

"From their perspective, maintaining control of this side of the terminus has to be more attractive than simply defending it from the other side, especially if they're operating against Agueda. So, again, if they'd had that kind of firepower available, I'm pretty sure they'd have brought it through to chase us off or at least make us keep our distance from the terminus. Given all that, I'm inclined to assume— provisionally, at least—that what we've seen is pretty much all they've got. It looks to me like they've decided it's more important to hold this terminus—and probably slam the door shut behind us, if we go through it—than it is to defend from the Ajay side."

"But that leaves everything in Ajay exposed, Ma'am," Rosiak said.

"It does, but think about it." Isotalo's expression had turned to stone. "What's it exposed *to*, as far as they know? Any of their shipping—or anyone else's in Ajay, for that matter—should have plenty of time to run for it before we turn up. Manties are damned good at commerce protection, everybody knows that, and that's what's going to be on their minds, because they don't know about Buccaneer. They can't."

Rosiak inhaled deeply, and Ramaalas's expression turned almost as stonelike as Isotalo's.

Of course it did, the admiral thought. *Kimmo doesn't like Buccaneer one bit more than I do. We'll do it, because those are our orders and because there's no other way we can hurt the frigging Manties at the moment. But he doesn't like it, and he and Bart both know as well as I do that no Manticoran naval officer would imagine for a moment that the* Solarian League, *of all star nations, would start systematically destroying entire star systems' industrial and orbital infrastructures.* Stopping *that sort of thing was one of the main reasons the League was created in the first place!*

The very thought revolted her, but she'd had plenty of time to get over that. And the critical point was that the Manties didn't know about—and would never expect—anything like Buccaneer. A commerce raid, yes. An attack on any Manty warships they encountered, the seizure of any merchant vessel they met—any and all of that, they would anticipate. And if anything in the galaxy was certain, it was that the Manty CO had sent one of her units back to Ajay to tell every single *legitimate* commerce-raiding target to get the hell out of the star system. That meant she'd cleared her responsibilities in Ajay, and *that* meant it would actually make strategic sense for her to let TF 1027 through the terminus into Ajay and then close it behind Isotalo, forcing *her* ships to take the long way home the way she'd anticipated forcing the Manties' Agueda force to do.

"Either way," she said, "we still have Buccaneer to carry out."

She settled herself in her chair, contemplating the consolidating icons on the plot, then looked at Rosiak.

"I want Quigley here on the terminus."

The operations officer looked startled, and she chuckled harshly.

"Not to *stay*, Bart," she reassured him. "Trust me, I want her task group in and out as quickly as possible. By the time she gets here, you're going to have put together a pod deployment plan that will let me detach Santini with enough firepower to give even a division of Manty superdreadnoughts something to worry about. Ideally, I want him to be able to hold the terminus against anything they throw at it long enough for us to withdraw from Ajay, hopefully with Buccaneer's mission objectives completed."

And, please, God, without Parthian *on my conscience,* she added silently.

"Everything we've heard about their operational stance suggests they're seizing the wormholes primarily with battlecruisers and cruisers," she continued serenely. "I think that's most likely the case here and that we won't be looking at superdreadnoughts whenever their Agueda force gets back. If we are, though, then Santini's orders will be to punch as many missiles at them as he can from as short a range as possible, accepting that they'll be blind fire, before he translates out and runs the hell back to Wincote. And before he does *that*, one of his tin cans will transit to Ajay and warn the rest of us what's coming up our collective backside.

"Frankly, given the combat differential, they probably wouldn't really need wallers to kick our butts," she said frankly. "A half-dozen of those big battlecruisers of theirs could do the job without breaking a sweat, especially since that logistics vessel of theirs is sitting out there somewhere with a load of additional pods for them. And, Kimmo, I want Santini's orders to be clear. I don't care whether it's superdreadnoughts, battlecruisers, or a horde of outraged gerbils, if the Manties turn up and start firing shit pots of missiles at him, then he had *better* get his arse into hyper and out of here before any of them get a chance to *hit* anything."

"Understood, Ma'am."

✦   ✦   ✦

"Well, so far, you seem to've read them pretty well, Sir," Lester Thúri said quietly as he and Commodore Lessem stood watching the master plot and Lessem's steward replenished their coffee mugs.

They'd been watching the Solarians through the Ghost Rider platforms they'd left behind for almost nine hours now. The wormhole and its approaches formed a zone three-quarters of a light-second across, defining a sphere with circumference of 2.36 light-seconds and a volume of over 5.9 *quadrillion* cubic kilometers. The Solarian warships were a handful of minute specks in that enormity, and it was impossible for the plot to show the individual missile pods they'd been busily deploying ever since they'd taken possession of it. The hidden recon platforms and the computers were keeping track, though, and according to them, the Solarian CO had placed approximately seventy thousand pods. Judging from the earlier firing pattern, each of those pods contained only six missiles, considerably fewer than Eleventh Fleet's pods at Manticore, but that still came to roughly 420,000 missiles, which would be enough to give just about anyone pause.

They'd also sent a quartet of destroyers through to Ajay, clearly probing the terminus with light units before their battlecruisers made transit into the face of something unpleasant. One of those DDs had returned five hours ago, so it would appear *So-po* and *Obusier* had executed Lessem's orders and kept right on accelerating away from the far side of the terminus. No doubt the other three Sollies were making sure the approaches to the Ajay Terminus stayed as clear as they were just then.

"Maybe," Lessem replied to the chief of staff's comment, his voice as low as Thúri's had been. "But I have to admit, there's one thing—*at least* one thing—I can't figure out, and that worries me."

"And what's that, Sir?"

"What the hell they're after." The commodore shook his head, eyes narrowed in thought. "I mean, there are only two reasons for them to be here. One is to take control of the terminus before we do, and they obviously didn't manage that. I don't care how many missile pods these people are deploying, they won't have enough—not without Ghost Rider and Apollo—to keep Admiral Correia from kicking their asses all the way from here to Old Chicago when *Pierrier* catches him with our dispatch."

He paused, quirking an eyebrow at the commander as if to invite a response, but Thúri only nodded. It was a given that the *Culverin*-class destroyer would bring back a quick response from the rest of the task force as soon as she reached it.

"Well, in that case, what we're seeing is an exercise in futility. If they'd gotten here before we did—before the Admiral headed for Agueda—then all this activity of theirs might make sense as a way to fortify the terminus against anything coming through from Ajay. If they're attacked from *this* side, though, not so much. So from that perspective, they should already have headed home. Or, if not that, I don't see any reason for them to invest this many missile pods on *this* side of the terminus in an effort to prevent the inevitable. Transit to Ajay and fortify hell out of the *Ajay* Terminus, sure. Failing that, hang around, make us maneuver against them, make *us* use up missiles the way we made *them* use up missiles—all of that I could see...sort of. But any of that would come in a piss-poor second to forting up in Ajay, and even if they can churn the things out like cookies, seventy thousand of them—the next best thing to *eighty thousand*—is an awful lot of industrial effort to just toss out the airlock."

He paused again, puffing his cheeks and frustration, then sipped coffee.

"But that brings us to the second reason for them to be here, and that's because they intended to raid Ajay. What it looks to me like they're doing is fortifying the terminus against *us*—our task group, not Admiral Correia—before they poke their noses into Ajay. They want to keep us from sneaking back in and re-taking the Prime Terminus to ambush them when they come home again while they move on Ajay. But they've got to know we've had plenty of time to evacuate all of our ships and personnel from the system, if that's what we've decided to do. So why raid an empty cookie jar? I mean, I suppose it would be an exercise in showing the flag, turning up in Ajay after they've 'chased the nasty Manties out of town,' but that'd be a purely cosmetic accomplishment. Again, stacking half a million missiles out where they're likely to lose them for little or no return, strikes me as a pretty stiff price tag for a symbolic 'victory'!"

"That's a valid point, Sir," Thúri said after gazing down into his own coffee mug for several thoughtful seconds. "And I don't have an answer."

"Neither do I, and that's why it worries me." Lessem waved his mug at the icons of the Solarian ships. "We're missing something. There's got to be a reason they're doing this, and I can't shake the suspicion that whatever it is, it represents a significant shift in their strategy."

"Well, maybe we can find out what it's all about from the survivors, Sir," Thúri said. "You're right about what's going to happen to them on this side when the Admiral comes back—assuming your own brainchild doesn't send them on their way even sooner than that. But whatever they've got in mind for Ajay, I think they're going to find it just a little more difficult to carry out than they think."

"Maybe." Lessem smiled briefly. It was remarkably cold, that smile. "We put enough effort into the cheese, anyway."

❖   ❖   ❖

"The Task Force is ready to proceed, Ma'am," Rear Admiral Ramaalas said formally, and Jane Isotalo nodded.

"I'm assuming that if we'd heard anything untoward from Captain Oglesby's division, you'd have brought that minor fact to my attention."

"Yes, Ma'am. I believe you could safely assume that."

"Very good," she said. "In that case, Admiral, proceed."

"Aye, aye, Ma'am." Ramaalas looked at Rear Admiral Rosiak. "Execute," he said.

"Aye, aye, Sir. Executing now."

Rosiak touched a macro, and the carefully orchestrated movement plan unfolded with metronome precision.

Isotalo sat back in her command chair, fingers of her right hand toying absently with the closure of her skinsuit while she did her primary job: radiating serene confidence as her subordinates executed her directives.

She still didn't like the idea of Buccaneer one bit, but she felt a deep sense of satisfaction as her task force rumbled toward its objective. After the seemingly unending tide of Manticoran triumphs and Solarian debacles, TF 1027 was about to execute its orders flawlessly. According to Captain Hieronymus Oglesby and his three destroyers, the far side of the terminus was just as naked as she'd hoped it would be. The destroyers' recon drones had confirmed—as she'd expected—that any Manticoran or neutral shipping in Ajay had cleared the limit and disappeared across the alpha wall long since, and that was a pity. But Buccaneer's true objective couldn't escape into hyper, and there wasn't a trace of a Manty warship to be found.

She reminded herself of how astoundingly good Manticoran electronic warfare had proved both against Eleventh Fleet and against her own missile salvo right here on the terminus. It was possible there were still Manty warships hiding under stealth somewhere in Ajay, but it would have required direct divine intervention to hide anything bigger than a frigate from her destroyers and their reconnaissance platforms within ten or twenty light-seconds of the terminus. The terminus itself was enough to interfere with sensors—enough to make it more difficult to detect gravitic and electronic emissions signatures in the first place, although not seriously enough to significantly degrade fire control once the target had been picked up in the first place—but it was also, for all its size, a limited volume. Any ship large enough to pose a threat to her battlecruisers that couldn't be picked up by Warshawskis or radar would have a hard time—a *very* hard time—hiding from visual and thermal detection.

No, she thought. *The henhouse door really is wide open . . . damn it.*

SLNS *Hindustan*, leading Lamont Bonrepaux's TG 1027.1 headed into the terminus and flickered into nonexistence on her way to join the destroyers in Ajay.

Ajay Terminus
Prime-Ajay Hyper Bridge

"SO, YOU STILL LIKING the odds Giselle gave you, Andy?" Commander Aaloka Menendez inquired, turning her command chair to face Andreas Bazignos, her executive officer.

Lieutenant Bazignos looked back without saying a word, and Sarah Chi, HMS *Boomslang*'s tactical officer, chuckled without taking her attention from her own displays.

"Should've known better, Andy," she told him. "First, because the Commodore... well, he's the *Commodore*. When was the last time you saw him get it wrong? Whenever it was, I'm pretty sure it was the *first* time, too. But even leaving that aside, nobody in his right mind bets against Giselle. And even if they did, nobody'd be—I hate to say it, but 'dumb' is the only word that comes to mind—to do it when she offers *odds*. What were you *thinking*?"

Bazignos maintained his dignified silence, but his lips twitched. Chi had a point. At forty T-years, Lieutenant Giselle Parkkinen, *Fire Snake*'s executive officer, was the "old woman" of the group, seven T-months older than Commander Menendez. Her relatively ancient age for her rank had nothing to do with lack of competence; she'd just been busy doing other things until the People's Republic of Haven's Operation Thunderbolt brought her a direct commission from the merchant service. If she didn't end up with an admiral's stars, it would only be because somebody managed to kill her along the way.

And, as his good friend Chi had just so kindly pointed out, Parkkinen never had the wrong end of the odds in a friendly wager. She also had a nasty—and expensive—knack for filling inside straights. For that matter, she was one of the best TOs he'd ever met, and her analysis of Plan Estocada—and what the hell was an "estocada," anyway?—had been spot-on so far. He didn't see much chance that was going to change anytime soon, and he wondered what he'd been sniffing when he took her bet.

"Well, I'd have to say it's not looking too good from your side," Menendez said now, twitching her head at the red icons of the three

Solarian destroyers on *Boomslang*'s smallish master plot. "Those three seem to be doing exactly what she—and the Commodore; let's not forget him—predicted."

"I know," Bazignos admitted finally. "And I knew it'd probably work out exactly that way from the beginning. But the odds were so *good*!"

"I only hope you're luckier in love than you are at cards and betting," Menendez told him.

"Oh, I am—I am!" he assured her with a broad smile.

"Funny," Chi offered, still watching the quiescent destroyers. "That's not what Sally Parkins down in Engineering said."

"You don't want to believe everything you hear from snipes," Bazignos warned her. "Besides, I think she was uncomfortable in my presence because of my godlike good looks." He shook his head sadly. "One of the crosses I bear. The women in my life realize they just can't compete with my superhuman physical beauty."

Both women guffawed, and Lieutenant (JG) Josh Whitaker, *Boomslang*'s communications officer, looked across the cramped command deck at him with round, admiring eyes.

"Is *that* what you call it, Sir?" he asked in awed tones. "And here *I* thought your last name derived from the...lordly dimensions of your proboscis."

Bazignos lifted the proboscis in question—which was indeed of "lordly dimensions"—with an equally lordly sniff.

"Alas, it's ever my fate to be maligned by the little people," he said. "But that's okay! I'm used to it." He heaved a deep sigh. "I've been dealing with it since high school, after all."

"Yeah, sure," Chi said. "Not the way *I* remember it," she added, and it was Bazignos's turn to chuckle. He and Chi had known each other since childhood, and she was probably his closest friend in the galaxy.

"That's because your mind is starting to go and—"

"Hyper footprint!" Chi snapped, cutting him off in midsentence. "Somebody transiting the terminus, Ma'am!"

"Acknowledged." Menendez's voice had turned crisp and coldly professional as quickly as Chi's had; she glanced at Whitaker. The com officer had been waiting.

"Hot mic, Ma'am!" he confirmed, and Menendez's finger stabbed the transmit key on her command chair armrest before he finished speaking.

"Typhon," she announced over the suddenly live network of short-range whisker communications lasers in that same cold, hard voice. "Typhon, Typhon." Then she released the key and looked around her command deck. "Here we go, boys and girls," she said. "Make it count."

As battle cries went, it lacked a little something in drama, she reflected, but that was all right. There'd be plenty of drama to go around without her adding to it.

✧   ✧   ✧

"Hyper footprint," Commander Patricia Richtmann, SLNS *Voltigeur*'s tactical officer, announced calmly. It wasn't as if the arrival was a surprise. They'd been expecting it for at least the last three hours, but they were waiting for *battlecruisers*, after all. Every destroyer officer knew that the time required for any task expanded geometrically in proportion to the tonnage of the ship involved.

Be fair, Pat, she scolded herself. *It wasn't just the standard transit prep this time. And unless you really want to walk home the long way, you should be happy they took the time to lay those pods. Because guess who'd be sent through to check for any Manty visitors if Admiral Santini wasn't watching the back door?*

"Got the transponder code?" Captain Oglesby asked.

"Yes, Sir," Richtmann replied. "It's *Hindu*—"

✧   ✧   ✧

"Firing . . . *now!*" Sarah Chi announced, and pressed the key.

HMS *Echidna* was a *Hydra*-class LAC carrier. The *Hydras* were 33,000 tons smaller than the *Minotaurs* which had preceded them, but they managed to pack in an additional dozen LAC bays. All one hundred and eleven of her serviceable LACs—one of the brood was downchecked by the group engineering officer because its stealth systems had a stubbornly persistent glitch—had been launched and left behind, hiding in the midnight depths of the Ajay Terminus when *Echidna* and the rest of the Ajay picket took themselves elsewhere in obedience to HMS *So-po*'s relayed order from Commodore Lessem. They'd sat there, waiting, watching the Solarian destroyers checking for defenders, and now it was their turn.

It wasn't Patricia Richtmann's fault no one had noticed them. She and her fellow tactical officers aboard *Chamberlin* and *Timberlake*, *Voltigeur*'s division mates, had searched diligently for any sign of warships. The problem was that no one in the Solarian League Navy who'd ever encountered the RMN's *Shrikes* and *Katanas* had gotten home to tell anyone else about it. As a consequence, no one in Task Force 1027 had ever imagined that something that small—a *Shrike* massed only twenty-one thousand tons and was barely seventy meters long—could possibly pose a threat to any genuine ship of war. *Voltigeur*, at 112,500 tons, had no business in a fleet engagement, and her officers and crew knew it. The thought that anyone should worry about something less than a fifth *their* size would have been absurd. There was a reason—in fact, there were a *lot* of reasons—no serious navy had built LACs for the past century or so, and even those which were in service were purely sublight system-defense or patrol vessels. Without Warshawski sails and hyper generators of their own, which no one could possibly fit into a hull that size—or the LAC *carriers* no Solarian knew a thing about—they couldn't have been here in Ajay space anyway.

And even if they'd known about CLACs *and* the new generation LACs, nothing else in the galaxy was as stealthy as a *Shrike* or *Katana*. Even active radar's effectiveness against them was hugely degraded at anything above very short range. The only way to really spot one of them, with its impellers down and its stealth systems up was for it to occlude a star, and Commander Menendez, who was *Echidna*'s COLAC as well as *Boomslang*'s CO, had made sure her deadly little ships were motionless relative to the terminus. The chance that something their size and holding that still might occlude a star (or anything else, for that matter) were . . . slight.

Had the Solarian destroyers looked hard enough and long enough, they might still have spotted them. Not even Manticoran EW could make them *invisible* to active radar with enough power behind it. But they were very *close* to invisible. Their radar return was far too tiny any represent any threat the SLN or its computers had ever heard of. People look for the threats they know about, and none of the men and women aboard those ships knew one damned thing about *Shrikes*.

For example, none of them were aware that in addition to the *Shrike-B*'s internal rotary missile launcher, it carried a single spinal-mounted graser as heavy as many a superdreadnought's broadside armament.

✧   ✧   ✧

"I have the destroyers' impeller signatures, Sir," Captain Absolon Badrani's plotting officer announced as SLNS *Hindustan* reemerged into everyone else's universe.

"Very good," Badrani acknowledged absently. His attention was on his helmswoman as the *Nevada*-class battlecruiser glided out of the terminus. *Hindustan*'s sister ship *Océan* was on her heels, and Captain Hackenbroch had an acid personality backed up by a scalpel-sharp sarcasm. She was bound to say something rude if *Hindustan* was clumsy about getting out of her way.

Not that *Océan* would be coming through *that* quickly. Admiral Isotalo had ordered a twenty-five second interval between transits. That was far longer than anyone would ever need. True, it would be another—he checked the display—fifty-three seconds before he could reconfigure from Warshawski sail to impellers, but those sails provided all the acceleration he'd need to keep *Hindustan* out of *Océan*'s way.

Not that Hackenbroch'll *see it that way. If not for the fact that she's just as competent as she is annoying, that mouth of hers would've—*

Twenty-four grasers, each designed to rip straight through a super-dreadnought's armor, slammed into SLNS *Hindustan* like the curse of God.

It was like hitting a puppy with a ground lorry, only worse.

Far worse.

Not one shot missed. There were no sidewalls to stop the fire coming from *Hindustan*'s flanks, and her side armor was woefully inadequate against graser fire that heavy delivered from such brutally short range. Even worse, half the fire came in from above, where there wasn't *any* armor, because designers didn't armor areas of the hull normally protected by the wedge that ought to have been there.

❖   ❖   ❖

"*Jesus Christ!*" Patricia Richtmann blurted as nine hundred thousand tons of battlecruiser—and twenty-three hundred men and women—disappeared in the titanic fireball of failed fusion bottles. She stared at her plot in stark disbelief, then sucked in a shocked breath.

"*Impeller signatures!*" Her professional voice was frayed and harrowed as the impeller wedges of Menendez's LACs sprang to malevolent life on her display. "*Many* impeller signatures! Estimate ninety-plus. Bearings—"

She broke off, slamming her heel on the button that locked her bridge chair's shock frame.

"Missiles incoming," she said flatly. "Estimate seventy-five—no, *eighty*—inbound. Time-of-flight, twenty seconds."

❖   ❖   ❖

Aaloka Menendez's eyes glittered with fierce satisfaction as the first Solly battlecruiser blew apart. Her *Shrikes'* heavy grasers could have blown through battlecruiser sidewalls at this range with contemptuous ease, but they didn't even have to do that. And while two of her squadrons dealt with *Hindustan*, three more of them launched against the Solarian destroyers who'd never seen them coming.

The *Shrike-B* carried fourteen shipkillers, and the attacking LACs' rotary launchers spat them out in a deadly stream. The range was so short they could easily have taken the Sollies down with graser fire, but the Achilles' heel of the *Shrike*'s massive energy armament was that its fission reactor couldn't recharge its plasma capacitors in battle. The energy budget simply wasn't there. That meant her units' energy fire was at least as limited as their magazine capacity, and she wanted all the graser shots she could bank against future need.

❖   ❖   ❖

"What the h—?" Captain Chayula Hackenbroch blurted, snapping upright in her command chair as *Océan* emerged on the Ajay side of the terminus. One moment the tactical display had shown only the calm, orderly line of battlecruisers queued up for transit. The next it was littered with missile traces, impeller signatures, and the homing beacons of a bare handful of life pods, speeding away from the fading fireball which must be all that remained of *Hindustan*.

"Impeller signatures! *Many impeller signatures!*" her tac officer screamed.

And then the holocaust which had hammered *Hindustan* came for *Océan*, as well.

✧　　✧　　✧

SLNS *Ohio*, *Neptune*, and *Minotaur* followed into the furnace one by one, emerging at neat twenty-five-second intervals into the devastating fire of LAC Group 117, and the fire in Commander Menendez's eyes grew cold and bleak.

They don't have a chance—not a chance. My God! It's not even shooting ducks; it's clubbing kittens! These poor bastards don't even know we're here until they sail right into our sights and we blow them to hell!

Her jaw tightened, and her nostrils flared. Whatever their high command and political masters might have done, surely the men and women aboard those dying ships were not so different from the men and women aboard *her* ships.

"Targeting change," she heard her voice say. "Go for the hammerheads, Sarah. Take out the impeller rings and the poor bastards are toast if they don't surrender as soon as we get back around to them." She grimaced. "Let's not make any more orphans today than we have to."

Prime Terminus
Prime-Ajay Hyper Bridge

VICE ADMIRAL HELMUT SANTINI accepted the cup of tea from his steward with a nod of thanks, but his expression was unhappy. He sipped the hot brew and gazed at the blandly uninformative tactical plot on SLNS *Colossus's* flag bridge for a handful of seconds. The comforting green icons of his task group floated in place, barring the Prime Terminus to all comers, and that was good. But then he flipped his eyes to the master astrogation plot and glared at the handful of *red* icons floating tauntingly twenty-seven light-minutes from the Terminus. He treated them to fifteen seconds of silent, fulminating bile, then turned to the tall, broad-shouldered rear admiral at his side.

"I don't like it, Jansen," he said—unnecessarily, he was sure. "I don't like it one damned bit."

"I don't like it either, Sir," Jansen Vasiliou, Task Group 1027.3's chief of staff, replied. "And I wish we had some kind of explanation for it."

"You and me both."

Santini sipped more tea, brooding at that damnable plot—*both* those damnable plots—and checked the time display . . . again.

Admiral Isotalo's scheduled update on Buccaneer's status was far overdue.

The Ajay Terminus was 342 LM from the system primary. A trip that long through normal-space would have required over twenty-three hours, allowing for a zero-zero arrival at the hyper-limit. But 5.7 light-hours didn't qualify as a "micro-jump" in anyone's book, and in hyper, going only as high as the Gamma bands, TF 1027's other task groups should have made the trip in just under thirty-seven minutes. By that calculation, Isotalo had crossed into the inner system over nine hours ago. Even assuming there'd been some reason she couldn't send a destroyer back to the terminus with dispatches, a light-speed message announcing her arrival in orbit around Elm, the system's only inhabited planet, should have reached the damned picket destroyers three and a half damned hours ago. At which point, one of them should damned well have returned to the Prime Terminus to give him some damned idea what was going on.

He wished—more than he could possibly have said—he could blame it on Isotalo's sloppiness, but the one thing Jane Isotalo *wasn't* was "sloppy." There was a reason—a *compelling* reason—she hadn't sent him that update, and he was unhappily certain he wouldn't have liked Vasiliou's explanation if they'd had it.

Not that *not* having it was inspiring any cartwheels of joy.

"Send one of the tin cans through to check with the picket, Sir?" Vasiliou asked, quietly enough no one else on Flag Bridge was likely to hear him.

"Tempting," Santini acknowledged. "But Admiral Isotalo took over fifty starships through that terminus. If there's something on the other side nasty enough to keep her from sending us even an update, what do you think it's going to do to a destroyer?"

"I thought about that, Sir." Vasiliou's voice was even softer, and although his expression remained merely calm and attentive, there was something very dark at the backs of his eyes. But they were unflinching, those eyes, and they met Santini's levelly. "The thing is, Sir, that that would be a message of its own, wouldn't it?"

Santini's jaw tightened and he clamped down on an urge to rip off his chief of staff's head for even suggesting the cold-blooded sacrifice of a destroyer and its crew. Unfortunately, it was an eminently sound suggestion. There was no way he could justify taking his entire task group through, even in a simultaneous transit, without *some* idea of what had happened to the rest of the task force. The one thing he did know was that there were—or had been, he amended grimly—three Solarian destroyers directly atop the far side of the terminus. If something had gotten close enough to prevent even one of them from escaping back to Prime, it was probably nasty enough to deal with sixteen battlecruisers, all but two of them the older *Indefatigable*-class, and fourteen destroyers if he was obliging enough to deliver them without impeller wedges or sidewalls.

So, yes, Jansen's right, he thought, *and he's got the guts to say it. If we send a tin can through and it doesn't come back, I'll have no choice but to conclude that the Admiral's been cut off from retreat through the terminus, at the very least. I can always assume that's what's happened without sacrificing a destroyer, but an assumption would be all it was. The truth is, I need some sort of confirmation, and paying the price of a destroyer would be a hell of a lot cheaper than losing the entire task group. But say I do send a tin can through and lose it, what do I do for my next trick?*

On the one hand, with the thousands upon thousands of missile pods deployed around the Prime Terminus and with his own battlecruisers' energy batteries poised to eliminate any hostile unit emerging from it, his position was a powerful one. Indeed, against any threat from the Ajay side, it was unassailable. So he could stay right where he was indefinitely, waiting to see if Isotalo could work her way around whatever was blockading her—and God, he *hoped* she was only blockaded!—in Ajay and return to Prime. For that matter, staying put would continue to keep the terminus corked against the Manty task force which had probably already been summoned back to Prime from Agueda.

At least until they turn up and deploy their *damned pods to blow us all to dustbunnies,* he reflected harshly, glaring once more at the heavy cruisers maintaining their prudent distance from his battlecruisers and the Cataphracts.

On the other hand, he was a vice admiral in the Solarian League Navy. Vice admirals weren't supposed to sit around with their thumbs up their arses hoping something would come along to save them from making the hard decisions. No matter what he chose, somebody far, far away in a nice, safe office was going to second-guess him. He knew that, and he didn't like it, but he cared one hell of a lot less about that than he did about the rest of the task force. The thought of leaving them unsupported turned his stomach into a vacuum flask. Yet there was nothing he could do *to* support them, not when the far side of the terminus was a hundred and three light-years away through Einsteinian space.

He sipped more tea, thinking about that distance. He could make the trip to Ajay through n-space in a bit over twelve and a half days, although he doubted there was much his single task group could do to reverse Isotalo's fortunes, even assuming she was still *in* Ajay the next best thing to two weeks from now. No, that was a non-option, for a whole host of reasons. But at the very least, he had to inform Old Terra about the rest of TF 1027's disquieting silence. Only he didn't really have anything to tell Admiral Kingsford, did he? "They went into the terminus and they didn't come out again" wasn't a hell of a lot of information.

No, it's not. But he does need to know about it, because if the Manties really did come up with some kind of mousetrap—a mousetrap so well hidden three destroyers posted specifically to watch for it never saw it coming—that could... prevent the Admiral from returning to Prime, this may not be the only place they've done it. And, his eyes grew grimmer, *she may not be the only one they've done it* to, *either.*

"We have to send a dispatch back to Wincote for the Admiralty," he said quietly. "I know there's damn-all we can tell them at this point, but if something *has* happened to Admiral Isotalo, they've got to know about it."

"Agreed, Sir. But do we send dispatches now, or wait a while longer in hopes somebody *does* come back to tell us what's going on?"

"I don't know." Santini sipped more tea, then grimaced. "No, I do know," he said. "We'll wait twenty-four hours. If we send anyone back to Wincote before that, some idiot somewhere along the chain of command'll decide we jumped the gun because we've had the shit scared out of us." He grimaced again, more deeply. "The fact that I think I *have* had the shit scared out of me doesn't make me any more eager to give the idiot in question any ammunition I don't have to. If we wait a T-day, that's a nice, solid interval. Long enough to show we thought it over carefully before we did what we already know we damned well need to do. And it's not like anything's going to sneak up on us here on this side of the terminus, is it?"

"No, Sir," Vasiliou agreed.

"Then have Sheila and Franziska put together a complete file for us, all the tac data from Sheila and the entire communications chain from Franziska."

Vasiliou nodded. Commodore Sheila O'Reilly was TG 1027.3's operations officer, and Captain Franziska Ridolfi was Santini's staff communications officer.

"I want the best analysis Sheila can give us, and I want to see it before I write my cover dispatch for it." He shook his head, staring into the plot again. "Actually, I'm hoping like hell the Admiral will come back in one piece before I have to send the thing.

"The problem"—he turned his head to meet Vasiliou's eyes once more—"is that I feel like I'm a kid back home in Faraday, whistling in a graveyard at midnight."

✧　　✧　　✧

"I think it's time," Sir Martin Lessem said.

Commander Thúri glanced at him across the table in his dining cabin, and the commodore shrugged.

"The fact that nothing's come back from Ajay suggests Commander Menendez and her people kicked their asses pretty conclusively." He paused, one eyebrow arched, and Thúri nodded. "Well, I'd hoped whoever they left in command on this side would be foolish enough—or impatient enough—to bash on through, trying to find out what happened. Clearly, he's too smart to do that. So if he's not going to oblige us by sticking his head into the noose, I suppose it's time for Descabello."

Thúri pursed his lips in thought, then nodded. He wondered if Lessem realized just how completely he'd revealed the revulsion underlying his professionalism when he named his ops plans. The *descabello* was the deathblow—the second, spine-cutting deathblow if the *first* one was clumsy and unsuccessful—in the ancient bullfighting tradition which had been revived on some of the more decadent Core Worlds.

Lessem had been dragged to one of them before the war, when he'd been assigned as the military attaché in the Sebastopol System, and "deeply disgusted" was a pale shadow of his response to it.

Which didn't mean "Descabello" wasn't a perfectly apt word for the ops plan to which he'd appended it.

Not that there'd been anything clumsy or unsuccessful about his actions so far.

"All right," the commodore said now. "Go ahead and tell Tom to execute in—" he checked his chrono "—twenty minutes."

"Yes, Sir," the commander said quietly, sliding his chair back from the table. "With your permission, Sir, I'll do that in person."

"Fine." Lessem nodded and Thúri came briefly to attention, then turned and left the dining cabin.

Lessem watched the hatch slide shut behind him, then picked up his wineglass and sipped again. The rich port seemed vinegary on his tongue, and he set the glass back down with a disgusted air.

I miss you, Sara Kate, he thought, looking at the light portrait on his bulkhead. *I miss you for* so many *reasons, but right now, I need someone I can talk to who isn't one of my officers. Somebody who lets me put my head in her lap and tell her I feel like a murderer.*

He closed his eyes, remembering his elation when he and his people danced rings around what was obviously a smart, competent adversary. Remembering how clever he'd felt when he realized Menendez and her LACs must have evaded detection by the destroyers the Solly CO had sent through. He'd predicted *exactly* what the Sollies would do, and they'd done it because it was what competent people who lacked critical knowledge did...and the fact that none of them had come back yet meant none of them ever would.

What must it have been like aboard those ships, in the fleeting seconds they had to realize what they'd just sailed into? They'd done everything right...and they were just as dead, in just as staggering numbers, as if they'd been commanded by Josef Byng or Sandra Crandall or Massimo Filareta.

And whoever might have commanded the LAC executioners, *he* was the one who'd killed them. That was almost the worst part of it, but not quite.

No, the worst part of it—the part he needed Sara Kate to save him from—was the fear that in the months and the years ahead, he'd learn to forget the horror...and remember the pride.

✧   ✧   ✧

The *Shrikes* and *Katanas* in Ajay weren't the only LACs the SLN had failed to detect. Three of *David K. Brown*'s interchangeable modules had been configured as ammunition holds stuffed with pods of Mark 23s and Mark 16s, but the fourth had been configured to support three full squadrons of LACs, in addition to the eight LACs of her under-strength organic squadron.

To be fair, there was an even better reason TG 1027.3 hadn't spotted the deadly minnows here on the Prime side of the terminus. The FSV had dropped all forty-four of her brood over seventeen million kilometers from the terminus, on the side farthest away from Lessem's heavy cruisers, on her way to the rendezvous point three light-days away in interstellar space. At that range, a *superdreadnought* would have been invisible with its wedge down, even without benefit of stealth, and *Shrikes* were far stealthier than any superdreadnought.

Now CruRon 912's FTL com sent them the single codeword "Desca-bello." It took over twenty-six minutes for even that message to reach them, but they knew what to do when it did.

✧   ✧   ✧

"Coming up on the mark, Sir," Commander Wozniak said quietly, sixty-one minutes after the transmission had been sent, and Sir Martin Lessem turned from the master plot and crossed to his command chair. He seated himself and methodically deployed his repeater displays. Then he nodded to Wozniak, and the operations officer looked at Ranald Kivlochan.

"Execute on the mark," he said.

"Aye, aye, Sir. Executing on the mark."

Everyone on *Clas Fleming*'s flag bridge knew that *precise* timing wasn't vital this time around, but they were the Royal Manticoran Navy, and that—by God—meant they would do this by the numbers.

"Standing by," Kivlochan replied formally.

"In ten," Wozniak said, reading the time display as the maneuver already locked into the ship's computers counted down. "Nine...eight... seven...six...five...four...three...two...one...*execute*."

Clas Fleming and her consorts disappeared into hyper.

✧   ✧   ✧

"Status change!" a tracking rating sang out in SLNS *Colossus*'s CIC. He turned to the officer of the watch, his expression tight. "Ma'am, the Manties just translated out."

✧   ✧   ✧

"After sitting there all this time, *now* he suddenly decides to move," Helmut Santini snarled. He'd been just about to step into the shower when the message from CIC reached them. Now he stood in his bath-robe, glowering at Vasiliou's image on his sleeping cabin's com display.

"I'm afraid so, Sir." Vasiliou looked at something outside his own visual pickup's field of view. "They translated out roughly three min-utes ago, Sir."

"And at an n-space accel of six hundred gravities?" Santini demanded. He and his staff had decided to assume that base acceleration for their calculations.

"Another eighteen minutes, Sir."

"All right. Spin the generators up for translation ten seconds after that." Santini smiled thinly. "I don't think he's going to want to bring cruisers into energy range of *battle*cruisers even if he can manage to hit his alpha translation that close. So, he's going to come back out somewhere in missile range, but if he can get missiles into space and hit us with them in ten frigging seconds, we better draw up the articles of surrender now!"

The chief of staff's expression showed he wasn't delighted by his admiral's turn of phrase, but he nodded.

"Yes, Sir. I'll see to it."

✧   ✧   ✧

Sixteen minutes later, an immaculately skinsuited Vice Admiral Santini strode onto his flag bridge. Officers and ratings came to attention, but he waved them back to their consoles, crossed to his command chair, and seated himself.

"Status, Admiral Vasiliou?"

"Ready to hyper in . . . ninety-five seconds," Vasiliou replied. "All ships closed up at Battle Stations."

"Good." Santini smiled thinly. "I'm looking forward to letting *them* waste some missiles this time!"

"Yes, Sir, and—"

"Hyper footprint!" Commodore O'Reilly called out from tactical. "Multiple hyper footprints at two-point-one million kilometers!"

"Already?" Santini looked down at the repeater deployed from his command chair and frowned. The Manties had botched their translation badly, if they'd been trying to get into range to hit him before he hypered out. In fact, they were well over a million kilometers short of his position. That was still deep inside their missiles' range basket, but at that range, flight time would be over sixty-eight seconds, twelve seconds longer than his *Nevadas* required to translate out from Standby readiness.

"Abort translation, but stand by to reinitiate!" he said sharply.

"Aborting translation, yes, Sir," O'Reilly acknowledged, and Santini gave Vasiliou a lopsided smile.

"It would appear even the vaunted Manties can screw up," he observed. "Do you think they'll go ahead and launch?"

"Don't know, Sir," the chief of staff replied with an answering smile. "Kind of embarrassing for them, I suppose."

Santini chuckled, although neither of them really thought the situation was especially humorous. Yes, the Manties had screwed up, but that didn't undo anything that had happened to Admiral Isotalo—*whatever* had happened to her. Still, at least it gave Santini's task group an opportunity to get a little of their own back. It might be only a moral victory, but the proof to his own people that even Manties could make mistakes wasn't anything to sneer at after what looked like being yet another debacle after all.

"Well, keep an eye on them," Santini told O'Reilly. "The instant they launch a missile or translate out again, start the generator clock."

"Yes, Sir."

"In the meantime, I think—"

SLNS *Kilkis* blew up with all hands.

✧   ✧   ✧

David K. Brown's LACs came out of the dark like demons.

They'd begun accelerating at a leisurely—for *Shrikes*—317.75 gravities the moment they received the codeword. At that rate, less than half their maximum accel, and given their stealth systems, they'd been effectively undetectable at any range much above a million kilometers, but they'd shut their wedges back down after only forty-five minutes. By that time, they'd attained a velocity of 8,143 KPS and traveled 11,358,050 kilometers, to a point almost exactly six million kilometers from Santini's battlecruisers. It had taken them twelve more minutes to enter attack range, and every bit of TG 1027.3's attention had been riveted to the maneuvers of the Manticoran *heavy cruisers*. No one had been looking in exactly the opposite direction for ships they didn't know existed and couldn't have seen if they *had* been looking.

There were only forty-four of them, but they streaked in on the non-evading targets they'd tracked continuously from the moment *Brownie* deployed them, thanks to the Ghost Rider platforms still monitoring the terminus. They knew exactly where their targets were, and they went for the kill without a shred of mercy.

Sir Martin Lessem watched the FTL plot as his piranhas swarmed their far more massive foes in a feeding frenzy of destruction. The tonnage imbalance was preposterous: 891,000 tons of LACs against *17.3 million* tons of Solarian warships, not to mention another thirty million tons of support ships. But tonnage didn't matter. What mattered was surprise, ferocity, and firepower, and the imbalance in those qualities did not favor the Solarian Navy this bloody day.

Eight thousand kilometers per second was not an enormous closing velocity by the standards of deep-space combat, but it was enough for the LACs to pass completely through their energy weapons envelope in under two minutes. They opened fire at five hundred thousand kilometers; sixty-one seconds later they passed directly through the heart of what had been Helmut Santini's formation, and those sixty-one seconds were a minute of unmitigated butchery.

In the end, seven of TG 1027.3 and TG 127.4's fifty starships—all destroyers—managed to cycle their hyper generators and escape before the LACs got around to such insignificant fare. A handful of their less fortunate consorts actually survived, albeit with brutal damage, but only because the LAC skippers had been tasked to immobilize rather than destroy as many Solarians as they could. They tried hard and did their job well, those skippers, but grasers with that kind of power were not precision weapons. Or, rather, they *were* precision weapons, but it was the precision of a chainsaw, not a scalpel, and their targets were only battlecruisers.

A certain amount of...breakage was unavoidable.

Commodore Lessem watched the carnage, watched the half-dozen Solarian escapees disappear into hyper-space, and heard his flag bridge's cheers. They rang in his ears, and he made himself smile in acknowledgment, but it was hard.

"Descabello," he'd called it, and he'd been right.

It was the perfect battle, from his perspective, actually. Not a single Manticoran loss—on this side of the terminus, at least—in return for total victory.

So why did he feel so much more like a butcher than a Queen's officer?

Maybe Sara Kate could help him answer that question...someday. But someday wasn't *this* day, and he raised his voice.

"All right, Randy. That was a beautiful micro-jump, but if it's all the same to you, I think we'll just mosey over to the terminus through n-space." He showed his teeth and chuckled. "I believe we have a few POWs to collect."

Office of the Director of Research
Gregor Mendel Tower
City of Leonard
Darius System

"SIR, MR. CHERNYSHEV IS here," the office AI announced.

"Good, Socrates! Send him in," Daniel Detweiler responded.

Most of his brothers—Everett was the exception—preferred a human receptionist. Partly that was because a human staffer was a prestige symbol, even on Mesa, but Daniel was willing to admit it wasn't just social snobbishness on their part. Like their father, Albrecht, they valued the intuitive and emotional feedback of a human interface while interacting with the other humans with whom they dealt on a day-to-day basis. Even the best AI wasn't as good a . . . focusing lens as a highly intelligent, trained, experienced, genuinely self-aware human being. The "highly intelligent" bit was the most important, of course, and Daniel had to agree that it worked for them. But he strongly suspected that the real reason it did was that most of them *liked* people. They were comfortable dealing with them. In fact, they actually enjoyed it. But he and Everett were the technology wonks of the family team, and neither of them was as good with human interrelationships as their siblings.

Daniel often thought that was a bit odd, since he and his brothers—and Albrecht, for that matter—shared exactly the same genes. Despite that, they'd developed different character traits—often strikingly different—as a gift from their parents. Albrecht and Evelina had taken pains to differentiate them from one another as children, and while Daniel hadn't exactly been groomed from the outset for his present duties, his interests in that direction had been encouraged from a very early age.

He'd personally designed the "brilliant software" which allowed Socrates, his office AI, to simulate self-awareness almost seamlessly. He might have been able to come even closer if he'd been a little better at inter-human interaction himself, but it was still an impressive accomplishment. It was that "almost" bit which dissuaded people like Collin and Benjamin, who had to work so intimately with their human colleagues, from ordering a Socrates of their own, however. Collin had toyed with the notion, since his role as the Mesan Alignment's chief of intelligence meant he had even more secrets to keep than his other brothers. The notion of telling his "staff" to forget something and knowing it was actually erased from memory was attractive to Collin. By the same token, though, Collin was the Detweiler who most needed to be aware of the human frailties of his subordinates.

The office door opened, and he stood, banishing the familiar train of thought and holding out his hand as Rufino Chernyshev, who had inherited Isabella Bardasano's duties as Collin's director of operations walked through it.

"Good morning, Rufino," he said.

"Good morning, Daniel," Chernyshev replied. The higher echelons of the Mesan Alignment didn't go in for a lot of formality. Not that there was any question of who stood where in the hierarchy. In fact, Daniel rather thought it was the clarity with which that was understood which allowed the informality to work so well. "Thank you for seeing me."

"You indicated a certain urgency," Daniel responded, pointing at the chairs in one corner of his spacious, high-ceilinged office.

Chernyshev obeyed the silent invitation, and the two of them settled into the almost sinfully comfortable chairs. The entire outer wall of Daniel's suite was one-way crystoplast, and the view out over the city of Leonard and its ten million inhabitants was breathtaking on a brilliant spring morning.

"Coffee?"

"Please." Chernyshev nodded. "Black, one sugar."

"You heard, Socrates?"

"Yes, Sir. It will arrive in one hundred twenty-three seconds."

"Thank you," Daniel said. Then arched an eyebrow at Chernyshev as the agent chuckled. "What?"

"Just thinking that your cybernetic friend might have just a *bit* too much precisionist in his code."

"Trust me, there's no such thing as 'too much precisionist' in my line of work. I imagine that, like Collin, you need a bit more…looseness. A little more freedom to encourage the synergistic association of thought processes I suppose. Brainstorming's important for R and D, too, but I think it's even more essential on that side that information be communicated as precisely and with as little ambiguity as possible."

"You know, I don't think I've ever thought about it exactly that way," Chernyshev said. "Clarity's important in my line of work, too, but you're right in at least one sense. Too *much* clarity means the people I'm talking to or whose reports I'm reading are trying to force the data into a neat—or at least clearly and concisely explainable—model, even if they don't consciously realize it themselves. And when that happens, the entire data set's contaminated."

"That's because you're dealing with human beings, and human beings are a naturally chaotic system," Daniel pointed out. "If you try to control for the chaos, you're automatically discarding data bits, and the ones you're discarding may be the ones you most need in the end."

"That's what I was thinking, and—"

Chernyshev broke off as the office door opened again and a silent counter-grav tray floated over to the conversational nook with a carafe of coffee, two cups, and all the condiments any caffeine addict might require. It settled neatly at Daniel's elbow, and he poured for both of them.

"Now," he said, sitting back with his own cup as his visitor added sugar, "what was it you needed to see me about?"

"Actually, I probably should have gotten this to you sooner," Chernyshev responded to his politely brisker tone. "With Isabella's death, Operation Janus, the Green Pines nuke, and now Houdini, I've had a lot on my plate. I haven't been reading all of those human-generated reports as promptly as I should have, I'm afraid, and this one just floated to the top of my stack."

"No need to apologize for *that*." Daniel shook his head, his expression momentarily bleak.

There were times he was even happier than usual to leave intelligence and covert operations to Collin, and this was definitely one of them. He couldn't argue with the need to expedite the evacuation of the inner onion—the leadership elements of the Alignment who knew the truth about the covert organization hidden within the larger covert organization—from the Mesa System. The annoyingly persistent survival of Victor Cachat and Anton Zilwicki had gone from the status of Severe Irritant to Oh Shit the instant they got home to Manticore and Haven with even anecdotal evidence of the Alignment's existence. With the military situation swinging in favor of Manticore and its allies so much more strongly, and sooner, than allowed for in their original projections, Cachat and Zilwicki's report meant it was only a matter of time—and probably not a lot of it—before the "Grand Alliance" got around to invading Mesa to drag the Alignment out of the shadows. It was fortunate Albrecht, Collin, and Benjamin had planned for exactly that contingency for so long, but executing Operation Houdini in such a compressed timeframe meant the "collateral damage" was going to run to hundreds of thousands—possibly even millions—of additional deaths.

Who was it back before the Diaspora who said "A single death is a tragedy; a million deaths is a statistic"? Intellectually, I can't argue the

*point. But emotionally? No. Collin and Dad can carry that part of it. I'll
wimp out and just design the weapons to turn as many as possible of the
other side into a statistic.*

"May be no need to apologize," Chernyshev said, "but that doesn't
mean we can afford to go around dropping stitches, either. Which is
what brings me to this."

He extracted a data chip from the inside pocket of his tunic and
handed it across.

"I could've emailed that to you, I know. I wanted to make sure it
didn't get stuck somewhere in the bowels of *your* Deal With Me Immediately queue the way it did with me. And I figured if you had any
questions off the top of your head I should be here to answer them."

"And what's on it?"

"That"—Chernyshev nodded in the direction of the chip on Daniel's
palm—"is a report from one of our agents in place in the Beowulf
System Defense Force. He's not senior enough to have access to the
technical specifications of what he's talking about, but his description
of what it does is probably enough to go on with. And what he's talking about is something called 'Mycroft.'"

"Mycroft?" Daniel repeated.

"Yes." Chernyshev's expression turned deadly serious. "Mycroft is
the reason the Manties and their friends will be able to pull their
battle fleets entirely out of Manticore, Beowulf, Haven, and Grayson
sometime very soon now."

"Excuse me?"

Daniel sat upright, both eyebrows rising. The majority of the
Grand Alliance's formidable striking power was gathered in its Grand
Fleet, currently stationed in Manticore with one powerful task force
advanced into Beowulf. Or, rather, covering the Beowulf Terminus
of the Manticoran Wormhole Junction and staying well clear of
Beowulf orbit to avoid any appearance of coercion in the star system's approaching plebiscite. Despite that, somewhere close to a third
of the Allies' total wall of battle was dispersed covering their home
star systems against a repeat of the Alignment's Oyster Bay attack
or a more successful iteration of Massimo Filareta's attempt on the
Manticoran Binary System. If they could call in and concentrate all
those additional ships-of-the-wall...

"Essentially, Mycroft's an updated version of the Havenites' Moriarty
system of pre-deployed missile pods and a dispersed constellation of
control stations," Chernyshev replied. "But it looks like they've mated
that concept with the Manties' Apollo and those damned Ghost Rider
platforms of theirs. I'm sure you can figure out for yourself what that

kind of fire control and, say, eighty or ninety thousand system-defense missile pods could do to any attacking force."

Daniel's jaw tightened. He could, indeed, figure that out. Words like "annihilation" came most readily to mind.

"Now, I know *we're* not planning on poking our noses back into Manticore or Haven anytime soon, even with the spider drive ships, but the Sollies are going to have to do just that. Kingsford's commerce-raiding notion was a good one, although I think our modest contributions to Buccaneer's operational thinking will bite him on the ass before very much longer. Eventually, though, they'll have to go into defended space again, and if they suffer another Eleventh Fleet debacle, the war may be over a lot sooner than we'd like. So when I mentioned this to Collin, he suggested I get on my two little feet and come over here and share it with you."

"He's thinking we need to combine what we know—and the Sollies don't—about Manty technology with this new information and come up with some counter, then pass it on to Technodyne?"

"Exactly. And there's also some information on that chip that I got Benjamin's people to pull up for me—a fairly detailed description of something the Manties came up with against Moriarty. They called it 'Mistletoe,' and Benjamin thinks that might be a good starting point for some of that brainstorming you mentioned a few minutes ago."

Tarducci Tower
City of Approdo
Genovese System

"SO, ADMIRAL," COMMISSIONER HIROKICHI Floyd said as his butler poured the after-dinner wine, set the bottle at his elbow, and withdrew, "I assume you're eager to depart and get on with it?"

"We're certainly ready, anyway, Commissioner," Vice Admiral Hajdu Győző replied. He lifted his wineglass and sipped, then set it back down with a rather tight smile. "Shifting targets at such a late date offered a bit of a challenge, since all our planning had focused on Exapia. But the truth is that there's not really much change in the *parameters* of the operation." He shrugged. "More a matter of plugging in new names and addresses than confronting any new threats or logistics issues. We've completed all of our preparations and pre-op planning and we'll translate out Thursday at zero-seven-thirty. After that?" He shrugged again.

"After *that*, Admiral," Floyd's piercing green eyes flashed, "Buccaneer will teach the frigging Manties and their arse-kissers that, as my Uncle Chojiro used to say, when you fuck with the bull, you get the horns."

"Indeed."

Admiral Hajdu produced another smile. It wasn't easy, because what he wanted to do was to roll his eyes. Unlike Floyd, who was a product of one of Old Terra's mega-urb towers, Hajdu had been born and raised on the planet Crişul Negru on a twelve thousand-hectare cattle ranch. He rather doubted "Uncle Chojiro" had possessed any personal experience with irate cattle of either sexual persuasion, and—having personally dealt with *very* irate, two-thousand-kilo, genetically-enhanced Chianina bulls upon more than one occasion—he'd always loathed that particular cliché and the people who seemed so fond of it.

Then again, there was a lot to loathe about Uncle Chojiro's nephew, too.

"The arrogant bastards have it coming," the commissioner continued. He drained his own wineglass in a single swallow and refilled it from the bottle without ever looking away from Hajdu. "God only knows how many people they've already gotten killed!"

172

"Indeed," Hajdu repeated. He found that noncommittal response useful in dealing with people who could be relied upon to interpret it as agreeing with whatever the hell it was they'd just said.

"I'm looking forward to your after-action report, Admiral." Floyd showed his teeth. "I don't think anybody in *Manticore*'s going to enjoy reading it, though!"

"Indeed," Hajdu said yet again, and shook his head mentally as the repetitions sailed right by Floyd. That was another thing the word was good for. The number of times in a row he could repeat it before it produced a reaction was a faithful barometer of his current audience's stupidity. And despite the misleading impression of mental acuity produced by the commissioner's piercing eyes, the admiral suspected he could set a new record with Floyd, if he really put his mind to it.

The commissioner only smiled broadly at him, but Hajdu reminded himself that just because Floyd was stupid didn't mean he couldn't be dangerous in the Byzantine infighting of the Solarian League's entrenched bureaucracy. Someone of his towering incompetency wouldn't hold a sector governorship, even of one as piss-poor as the Genovese Sector, unless he had the right gutter-fighter instincts and patrons at a high level. He was *not* the sort with whom a prudent flag officer engaged in pissing contests. Which was a pity, given his record to date.

I agree with him that the Manties need to be taken down a peg or three, Hajdu thought from behind his answering smile. *I'm not happy about the change in targets for* our *op—and neither were some of my staff people— but I'm not going to shed many tears for it at the end of the day. Any of the Manties' buddies who get run over along the way only have to look in the mirror to see who pasted the target on their backs, and looking after their interests is nowhere in my job description. I'm no more eager to trash star systems than the next man, but I'm a Solarian officer. My loyalty's to the League and its vital interests, not theirs, and anything that makes the Manties' supporters—any of their supporters—rethink their positions can't be all bad. And whatever I may think of Floyd, he's got a point about* this *op.* Hajdu's nostrils flared just a bit—a minute change of expression his staff would have recognized as his equivalent of a shouted profanity—at that thought. *Neobarb neutrals are one thing, but someone who chooses to stab the League in the back when it's his responsibility to* represent *it, deserves whatever the hell he gets. In spades.*

Still, even this cretin ought to realize it's not just the Manties getting people killed. The Manties may be the ones pulling the trigger, but fair's fair, Governor. It's idiots like you—and certain *other idiots in Old Chicago—who keep shoving our people in front of them before they do!*

In fairness, Floyd hadn't gotten anyone killed...yet. Not for lack of trying, though. And while no actual blood had been shed, there'd been plenty of other consequences, including the sudden end of one of Hajdu's personal friends' career. Liam Pyun had made Floyd look bad five T-months ago by showing the moral courage to disobey the governor's direct (and suicidal) orders in the Zunker System, and in the Solarian League, embarrassing a superior—especially one who deserved it—was the only truly unforgivable sin.

I'm sure he wishes we were headed back to Zunker to beat the hell out of the Manties who helped humiliate him, *but maybe even he's smart enough to realize the real basis for target selection has a hell of a lot more to do with hitting the Manties where they aren't than going toe-to-toe with them.*

Not yet, *anyway.*

"I suppose I shouldn't say this, Admiral," the commissioner continued, like a man confiding in a lifetime friend, "but there's a part of me that actually hopes they'll be stupid enough to refuse your demands. I'd just as soon not see anyone killed, but—" he tapped an index finger heavily on the table for emphasis "—it's about frigging time people figured out there are consequences for supporting rogue regimes like Manticore."

"Indeed," Vice Admiral Hajdu replied.

HMS *Phantom*
Task Group 110
Beowulf System

"I JUST GOT OFF the com with Admiral Truman," Rear Admiral Jan Kotouč told the men and women around the briefing room table aboard HMS *Phantom*.

A *Nike*-class battlecruiser, barely seven T-months old and built by Pardubice Shipbuilding in its *Hephaestus* module, *Phantom* was 2.5 million tons of lethality, the fastest and most deadly broadside-armed warship in the galaxy. The Royal Manticoran Navy needed about ten times as many of her as it actually had and, under other circumstances, it would have had most of them. Unfortunately, almost eighty of her sisters had died stillborn when the Yawata Strike tore *Hephaestus* and *Vulcan* apart.

Kotouč was even better aware than most of how sorely those dead ships were missed, since he'd been slated to command an entire squadron of them. That squadron had died with *Hephaestus*, however, along with entirely too many of the men and women he'd already come to know. Eighty-five percent of the squadron's six thousand personnel had been aboard ship or elsewhere on *Hephaestus*, preparing to take over their new ships from the yard dogs.

None of them had survived.

A charmed ship, he thought, looking at the shrouded, ghostly figure on *Phantom*'s bulkhead-mounted crest. *That's what they call her, anyway. And who knows? They may even be right.*

In the absence of the squadron's other *Nikes*, the Admiralty was building him a replacement out of *Saganami-Cs* and *Saganami-Bs*, with emphasis on the latter. The *Charlies* were in almost as urgent demand as the *Nikes* themselves, and he'd been warned that he'd be lucky to see a single full-strength division of them. Unfortunately, it would be at least two more T-weeks before he even knew how many of them he'd be receiving. Although he'd been formally named as Commanding Officer (designate), Task Group 110.2, which would ultimately become a vest-pocket task force—and one cut for a generous-sized vest—all he had at the moment was *Phantom* and the *Saganami-B*-class cruisers *Cinqueda*, *Shikomizue*, and *Talwar*, supported by a single *Roland*-class destroyer, HMS *Arngrim*. He'd been supposed to receive the CLAC *Vukodlak* last week, but she'd suffered a major impeller room engineering casualty two weeks before that, and the Beowulf yards would need at least another ten days to put her back in service. In fact, ten days would be something of a miracle, given that they'd been required to replace no less than four of her after beta nodes.

So at the moment, he was a task group commander with all of five ships under his command.

"The Admiral," he continued now, "had just finished a conversation with Director of State Longacre, and Director of State Longacre had just finished a conversation with Special Representative Lambrou and Special Representative Tsakabikou. Which is the reason Admiral Truman was talking to me and the reason that *I'm* talking to *you*."

He smiled without very much humor.

"We have our movement orders, people," he said, and several of his officers stiffened in obvious surprise.

"Movement orders, Sir?" Captain Jim Clarke repeated after the briefest of pauses, and Kotouč smiled a bit more broadly.

"Movement orders," he confirmed. "It would appear President Vangelis has changed his mind about an Allied presence in his star system."

Clarke sat back in his chair, eyebrows raised, and Kotouč shrugged.

"It's not really hard to understand why his administration didn't want us there to begin with, Jim," he pointed out. "We've been careful to keep any fleet units out of *Beowulf* orbit during the debate over the referendum. The Hypatian government had even better reasons to avoid any appearance that their referendum vote was coerced by foreign warships."

"Agreed, Sir." Clarke nodded. "I'm just wondering what's changed?"

"According to Lambrou and Tsakabikou, what's changed is that the most probable outcome of the referendum's become...abundantly clear."

The rear admiral paused and looked around the briefing room until every head had nodded. Brad Lambrou and Sofronia Tsakabikou were the designated Hypatian "special representatives" to Beowulf. Technically, they were simply observers of the Beowulfan plebiscite. Actually, they were Adam Vangelis's ambassadors to the star system with which he intended to seek formal political union as soon as his referendum validated his intent and Beowulf got its own, slower-paced plebiscite out of the way.

"Apparently," Kotouč continued, "something new has been added to the mix in Hypatia."

"That com conversation between MacArtney and Abruzzi, Sir?" Lieutenant Albamonte, Kotouč's electronic warfare officer, asked. News of the leaked soundbite—and the first intimations of Hypatia's fiery reaction to it—had reached Beowulf over a T-week ago.

"Sounds like it." Kotouč shrugged. "Never underestimate the pure fury that kind of talk can generate, Paul, whether there's any serious intent behind it or not. I really doubt even MacArtney or Abruzzi thought they could get away with any kind of decapitation of the Hypatian government. Mind you, they *are* Sollies—and Mandarins, for that matter—so anything's *possible*. But I'm pretty sure that if that's even really their voices, they never had any intention of pursuing that nonsense as an actual policy. Nobody in Hypatia seems inclined to give them the benefit of the doubt, however, which—let's face it—isn't such a bad thing from our viewpoint. A very... clarifying thing, moral outrage. If I had a dollar for every time emotion's trumped reason—or, for that matter, gotten behind reason and pushed like hell—I'd be Klaus Hauptman."

Several people chuckled, and he grinned. Then his expression sobered.

"Whether it was the mention of intervention battalions or something else, Lambrou and Tsakabikou told Director Longacre that it's no longer a question of whether or not the referendum's going to pass. It's not even a question of whether or not it'll be a landslide. The only real question in Vangelis's mind now is how *big* a landslide it'll be.

"At any rate, he's confident enough of the outcome—and, I think, that com conversation's made him nervous enough about how the Mandarins are likely to respond when they hear the vote total—that he's decided to go ahead and invite us now. The referendum's scheduled for next Wednesday. If we leave within forty-eight hours, we'll hit Hypatia sometime Thursday. That'll keep us out of the system until after the vote's counted—or until enough of it's been counted to project the outcome with certainty, at any rate—but also close up the window in which the Sollies can just waltz into Hypatia unopposed."

"Sir, I understand what you're saying," Commander Markéta Ilkova, TG 110.2's operations officer (designate) was five centimeters shorter than her admiral. She was also attractive, with red hair and sharp, intelligent blue-green eyes. Indeed, Kotouč had discovered she was rather more attractive than he might have wished, given the restrictions of Article 119. She was also at least as competent as she was attractive... and obviously less than delighted by the news of their impending departure. "But we're still all the task group you've got."

"And we're more than enough to beat the holy living hell out of any light Solly squadron that comes our way," Kotouč pointed out with just a bit more confidence than he actually felt. Then he sighed.

"Admiral Truman doesn't expect us to hold off a fleet the size of Filareta's or Crandall's, Markéta, but Director Longacre's made the point—and it's a valid one, people—that if Hypatia's willing to pin a big target on its chest by standing up beside the Alliance, the least we can do is provide President Vangelis's citizens with visible, tangible proof the Alliance will be just as determined to look after them as we are to look after our own star systems. Nobody in Hypatia's likely to mistake five ships—even *Queen's* ships—for a system-defense fleet. But what they'll see are the lead elements of the task group that *will* be capable of defending them when it's fully assembled. And it won't hurt a bit for us to be there, getting a feel for the system astrography and establishing a working relationship with Vangelis and his people, while we wait for the rest of the task group to join us."

"Understood, Sir," Ilkova said.

"Admiral Truman assures me she'll send forward at least four more *Bravos* within the next seven or eight days. And *Vukodlak* should be out of the yard dogs' hands a couple of days after that. As soon as she's finished testing her repairs, she'll be sent to join us along with a freighter load or two of system-defense pods. And by the time she gets to *Hypatia*, we'll have worked out the best way to use her and be ready to start deploying the pods."

Harrington House
Jason Bay
City of Landing
Manticore Binary System

ADMIRAL LADY DAME HONOR Alexander-Harrington, Steadholder and Duchess Harrington, kicked off her house shoes, folded her legs under her on the chaise lounge, and dropped a pair of marshmallows into her hot chocolate.

Manticore's small moon, Thorson, was low on the western horizon, touching the banked clouds in that direction with dramatic bands of silver and ebony. Lightning flickered very occasionally—and very distantly—along that cloud wall, but the weather sats all insisted the bad weather wouldn't reach Landing until sometime after dawn. In the meantime, there were no clouds over Jason Bay or the capital city, and the sky overhead glittered with a storm of stars. As always, there was a lot of orbital traffic, as well. In fact, it was much heavier than normal and the usual moving dots of the communication and solar collector satellites were accompanied by scores of other lights as near-Manticore space swarmed with repair ships, and temporary habitats for construction workers.

A *lot* of repair ships and construction workers.

The horrific damage and casualties of the Yawata Strike were barely six T-months in the past, but the replacement space stations' skeletons were already growing, far more quickly than they'd dared to hope for in their initial estimates of how long it would take to rebuild. Then again, their initial estimates hadn't included the full-fledged support of the Beowulf System...or of the Republic of Haven. For that matter, they'd seriously underestimated the amount of civilian infrastructure that could be repurposed. And Lacoön had produced an unexpected side effect. An unexpected *good* side effect, that was, she thought with a mental grimace.

At least three quarters of the Star Kingdom's civilian shipbuilding industry had been co-located with the Navy yards on the major space stations. From the perspective of efficiency and cost, that had been a no-brainer, and no one had ever anticipated something like the Yawata Strike. Attacks, yes, but not attacks nobody saw coming in time to take a single defensive measure. Just over half of all the rest of the Manticore Binary System's civilian industry had also been located aboard one of the stations or in close enough proximity to be destroyed when *Hephaestus* and *Vulcan* were taken out. So it wasn't all that surprising the immediate post-attack estimates had been so bleak.

Haven's return of the interned Grendelsbane construction force had been a huge help, as much from a morale perspective as from any other. The workers from the forty-seven percent of the civilian infrastructure which *hadn't* been co-located with the space stations had proved to be a far greater resource, however. And the fact that Lacoön had idled close to ninety percent of the massive Manticoran merchant marine had been another unexpected asset.

Lacoön's consequences for the Star Empire's economy had been less dire—a *little* less dire—than initially predicted because no one had expected the Republic of Haven's markets to be opened to Manticore. For that matter, they hadn't anticipated the addition of the Talbott Quadrant. That hadn't kept the loss of their markets in the Solarian League and—especially—their *carrying* trade in the League from being catastrophic for what had been by far the largest single component of Manticore's economy. Quite a few of the smaller cartels were unlikely to survive, and even the major cartels like Hauptman were looking at enormous losses. The "act of war" clause in standard insurance policies meant most of the commercial enterprises on *Hephaestus* or *Vulcan* would be unable to recover their losses, and the...uncertainty (to put it mildly) of the Star Empire's future relations with the Solarian League cast a serious cloud over the smaller shipping lines' futures. The last estimate she'd seen predicted at least a third and possibly as many as half of the independent lines were going to go under.

And then there were the enormous Manticoran investments in the Solarian League. No one knew where *that* was going, either, and she was frankly surprised the League hadn't simply seized their assets. There was no guarantee Quartermain and Wodoslawski wouldn't get around to it eventually, but unless the League won an unambiguous victory—which wasn't going to happen—one of Manticore's key peace demands was going to be the return of all sequestered assets, and Sir Anthony Langtry had made certain through "neutral sources" that the League was made aware of that.

Her own financial interests had taken a massive hit, although those had been centered far more in Grayson than here in Manticore. The Blackbird complex had represented a huge chunk of her portfolio there, but Blackbird had been almost exclusively a naval building complex. Ninety percent of the Grayson Space Navy's suppliers and subcontractors had been located there, but virtually none of the system's *civilian* industry had been affected. From Honor's purely selfish perspective, that meant Skydomes of Grayson had been untouched, which put her in a strong position to recover, especially with her Skydomes labor force redirected to rebuilding Blackbird. From the Graysons' perspective in general, it did nothing to lessen the brutal loss of human lives but provided a solid basis for reconstruction and recovery. And the Church of Humanity Unchained had thrown its stupendous resources into the recovery effort. There were entire star nations with less wealth than Reverend Sullivan commanded, and his instructions were clear. Where there was want, there also would be Father Church. Not one of the Tester's children would be allowed to suffer alone and unaided. They would worry about the consequences to the Church's investment portfolio later. And if they had to rebuild that portfolio from absolutely nothing, why they'd do that, too.

The good news—the *overwhelmingly* good news—from the Star Empire's perspective was that no financier in the galaxy failed to grasp that whatever happened politically, *astrography* wasn't going to change. The Manticoran Wormhole Junction wasn't going anywhere, and neither were its implications for the interstellar movement of goods, people, services, and data. That meant no one doubted the imperial government's ultimate solvency—as long as it survived its confrontation with the League—and Baroness Morncreek, at the Exchequer, and Bruce Wijenberg at the Ministry of Trade had capitalized on that fact.

The Exchequer had already instituted the largest program of low-interest government-guaranteed loans in Manticoran history, both to assist those whose losses hadn't been covered by insurance and to help finance new and replacement ventures. A lot of Havenite money would be looking for a home postwar, as well, which didn't even consider the opening of what had been closed Solarian markets in the Protectorates. For that matter, whatever the League might think about the Grand Alliance in military and diplomatic terms, *economically* it wouldn't have much choice about doing business with the Star Empire, thanks to the Junction. It seemed unlikely to Honor that the Star Empire's merchant marine would regain its totally dominant position within the League, but in absolute terms, it ought to recover fully to prewar levels.

Manticore's traditional fiscal challenge had been to find places to invest the revenues streaming into the Star Kingdom in a way that prevented a financial glut and its resulting inflation. Over the T-centuries, the government and private investors had learned to adjust that cash flow through out-system investment, most of it in the League. Their presence in Solarian markets wasn't an unqualified plus at the moment, but that pattern helped explain how the Cromarty Government had managed to avoid genuine deficit spending until only a very few T-years before the outbreak of open hostilities between the Manticoran Alliance and the People's Republic of Haven.

Since then, for obvious reasons, that had changed, yet until the Yawata Strike, the Junction's enormous revenue generation, coupled with the Star Kingdom's huge investment portfolio, had held the national debt within easily manageable dimensions. For the next several years, that wouldn't be true. Morncreek's analysts weren't happy about that, and they projected that it would take twenty or thirty T-years—at least—to pay that debt down, assuming prewar revenue streams. Unlike almost any other star nation in the galaxy, however, the Star Empire could *do* it, which was why there was remarkably little panic here in the Manticore System.

Which wasn't to say there wasn't a lot of *pain* or that the Manticoran economic safety net wasn't under unprecedented strain. On the other hand, the need to rebuild—and the number of skilled technicians who'd been killed in the attack—meant overall unemployment rates were astonishingly low, considering what had happened to the shipping industry. The government was pouring enormous sums into wages for the workers rebuilding *Hephaestus*, *Vulcan*, and *Weyland*, which was a not insignificant factor in its deficit spending. Those sums were being paid as *wages*, however, not direct transfer payments, which meant they didn't affect their recipients' eligibility to vote and that they represented taxable income, which allowed at least some recapture.

We've never—ever—been hurt this badly before, she thought. *But I suspect the people who did it to us overestimated* how *badly it would hurt us by at least as big a factor as we* did, *right after the strike. And in the end, that's going to hurt* them *one hell of a lot worse than they ever hurt us.*

She smiled up at that beautiful sky and the lights swarming across it with grim satisfaction...and more than a bit of proprietary pride. There were quite a few warships, freighters, transports, and naval auxiliaries to keep the rebuilding effort company, and *all* that overhead activity was directly or indirectly her responsibility, one way and another. But for tonight, she'd left it in the hands of her staff, with Admiral Alfredo Yu, her deputy CO in the Protector's Own, riding herd upon it.

The one good thing about being stuck here instead of out actually accomplishing *something is that I get to nip home for visits every so often*, she reflected, stirring the chocolate with an index finger and then licking it clean. Her mother had tried for years to break her of that particular habit before she'd finally thrown up her hands and admitted defeat.

And it is a gorgeous night for sitting on the deck drinking chocolate. The land breeze, blowing out across Jason Bay's cooling waters fluttered her kimono's flowing sleeves and molded its silk against her, and she inhaled deeply, gazing out over the bay's gently moving surface. *Wish there was time to spend tomorrow down here, too. I'd love to take the boat out after the front passes through, and I'm overdue for some time with Faith and James. They'd love that! But not with that exercise scheduled for Tuesday, I guess.*

"Excuse me, My Lady."

She turned her head as Major Hawke poked his head out onto the deck. That deck stood out from the seaward side of Harrington House, a good seventy meters above sea level, which made it totally inaccessible except through the house itself or from the air. Under the circumstances—given that Harrington House would have made an acceptable fortress on most planets and that Clifford McGraw and Joshua Atkins, the other members of her permanent detail, were undoubtedly parked in the shrubbery with shoulder-fired surface-to-air missiles and the odd vest-pocket nuke or three—Major Hawke had graciously consented to allow her a modicum of privacy.

"Yes, Spencer?"

"The Earl just commed, My Lady. He asked me to tell you he's about six minutes out. For some reason, he couldn't seem to reach you." Hawke raised an eyebrow. "Could it be you didn't take your uni-link with you?"

"Guilty as charged," she admitted while Nimitz bleeked in amusement from the chaise lounge beside hers. "After I got out of the pool and climbed out of the shower, I just threw on my kimono and came straight out here."

"I see."

Hawke gazed at her for a moment, and she looked back innocently. No respectable traditional Grayson lady would have suggested to anyone other than her equally respectable husband that all she had on was a thin, billowy silk kimono. Hawke had been with her long enough to know when she was pulling his chain, however, and his notion of just what "respectable" meant had been...expanded by contact with Honor.

And, especially, with Honor's mother.

"I'll just send His Lordship right out when he gets here, then, My Lady," the armsman said after a moment.

"Please do. And please ask Lucie to tell Mistress Thorn we're going to need a pot of coffee for him. For that matter, I'll bet he missed supper again, so ask Lucie to see about having some sandwiches sent up, too. After all," she smiled wickedly, "he'll need his strength."

"Of course, My Lady," Hawke replied just a bit repressively, and her smile grew broader as he withdrew. Then it faded again as she sat back, looking up at the stars, and thought about what she'd just requested. Or, rather, who she'd requested it of.

She hadn't wanted to fill the gaping wound Miranda LaFollet's death in the Yawata Strike had left in her household. It had seemed... disloyal. Worse, just thinking about it had reminded her how horribly she missed Miranda, Farragut, and—especially and always—Andrew. Yet she'd really had no choice. Not only did she need someone to assume the host of duties Miranda had fulfilled for her, but there were certain Grayson norms even her deplorably nontraditional Harringtons wanted observed, and having their Steadholder provided with a proper "personal maid" was one of them.

At only a hundred and fifty-seven centimeters and with brown hair and dark brown eyes, Lucie was very different physically from Miranda, for which Honor was grateful, but they were very much alike in other ways. Miranda had been far more than a "maid." In fact, she'd been a female James MacGuiness, acting as the general manager of Honor's affairs on Manticore whenever her Steadholder and MacGuiness were in space. Despite that, however, she'd always insisted on "looking after" Honor whenever Honor was home. Lucie, for all her social flexibility, was a chip off the same stubborn block of Grayson granite in that respect, and her feelings would have been hurt if Honor hadn't asked her to see to it that Hamish was fed.

And the chance to tease Spencer didn't have a thing *to do with it, either, did it?* she asked herself.

Herself chose not to answer, and she sipped her chocolate, enjoying the night, and waited for her husband.

✧   ✧   ✧

"Sorry I'm running so late," the Earl of White Haven said contritely as he stepped out onto the deck.

The instant he opened the door, a dappled, tawny treecat launched from his shoulder, bounced off the deck flooring once, and landed with precision and style beside Nimitz. She wrapped both her upper sets of limbs—and her tail—around him, buzzing a delighted purr, and Honor laughed.

"Way to go, Sam!" she congratulated the female 'cat. "Spacers don't make port often enough to let any opportunities go to waste."

"Oh?" White Haven dropped onto the chaise lounge beside her and did a pretty fair job of hugging her, despite the handicap of having only four limbs. "Should I assume from that observation that I'm going to get lucky tonight?"

"You should assume from that observation that *I'd* better get lucky tonight," Honor told him, pausing halfway through to kiss him thoroughly. "I don't know which is worse, to be in totally different star systems for months on end or to be in the *same* star system, just an hour or two apart, and unable to take advantage of it."

"The latter," White Haven said promptly. "*Definitely* the latter."

He smiled and kissed her again, choosing not to mention that he could think of quite a few flag officers who would have found ways to "take advantage of it" every other night or so. He'd never been one of them, and neither had Honor.

"Of course, when the opportunity *does* come along..." she murmured wickedly, nestling deeper into his embrace.

"Well, when *that* happens," he said with a pontifical air, "it's clearly our responsibility to...to give Samantha and Nimitz the opportunity to spend quality time together while we find some way to occupy ourselves, as well."

He elevated his nose, then "oofed" as an elbow jabbed him in the ribs.

"'Occupy ourselves,' is it?" She regarded him darkly. "If I hadn't been stuck in space so long, somebody would be sleeping on the couch tonight for that one!"

"Then thank God for sensory deprivation," White Haven said fervently, and kissed her again.

"Your Grace?" a voice said.

"Yes, Lucie," Honor replied, sitting up a bit straighter. "Come on out, we're both decent." She smiled at White Haven. "Your timing's just about perfect, as always. He hasn't even had time to muss my hair properly."

"I'm certain he'll get around to it, My Lady," Lucie Šárová said serenely.

She guided a counter-grav float with a large pot of coffee, a tray loaded with sandwiches—on seedless rye, White Haven's favorite bread—and a platter with one of Sue Thorn's hallmark pound cakes. Unlike Spencer, she simply looked at her Steadholder and Steadholder Consort with an eye of benign approval. In fact, she'd made it clear to Honor that, in her opinion and speaking for Harrington Steading in general, it was time Raoul Alfred Alistair Alexander-Harrington had a younger brother to keep him company. Despite her flexibility on other issues, Lucie was a Grayson, and there were never enough boy babies to go around on Grayson. Especially where a steadholding's succession was concerned.

It was, perhaps, unfortunate that her Steadholder's parents had provided additional grist for her mill, but at least Allison wasn't expecting *twins* this time.

Lucie parked the float between Honor's chaise lounge and the one occupied by Nimitz and Samantha. Then she whipped the cover off a third platter, and the treecats buzzed with delight as she revealed the plate of stewed rabbit and a dozen sticks of celery.

"You are a wicked influence, spoiling everyone shamelessly," Honor told her, and she smiled. Then Lucie nodded respectfully to White Haven and withdrew.

"Your Grayson henchmen—and hench*women*—do take good care of us," White Haven observed, sitting up to pour coffee. "And I hate to say this, given the delightfully salacious nature of our earlier conversation, but I'm starving."

"I figured you would be." Honor swung her own feet back onto the decking and reached for one of the sandwiches. She seldom passed up the opportunity to stoke her genetically modified metabolism. "You really do need to stop putting in hours that keep you from eating, though," she said more severely. "The last thing anyone needs is for the First Lord of Admiralty to work himself into a state of collapse."

"I'm a fair way short of that this far, love," he replied with a twinkle. "Not that you don't have a point, and I know it. For that matter, Emily's been beating me about the head and ears over the same minor point."

"Good!"

Honor's voice showed her firm approval of their spouse's attitude, but she also gave White Haven a thoughtful look. He was busy looking down to select a sandwich of his own and didn't notice, but Samantha looked back at her with solemn eyes, and Honor's lips tightened ever so slightly. Emily seldom visited Landing these days. She'd made an exception for the dinner party announcing Alfred's return to active duty, but she always preferred to spend her time at White Haven, with the children. Besides, she said Landing always made her tired. That was true enough for all three of them, really, but she seemed to get tired even more rapidly than she'd used to, and—

"I wish there'd been time to run home to White Haven tonight," White Haven went on a bit wistfully as he picked out his sandwich.

"So do I." Honor agreed, and this time he heard the questioning note and looked back up quickly. She looked at him levelly, and, after a moment, he sighed.

"I don't know what to tell you, sweetheart," he said. "You know her health's been up-and-down for the last two or three years. She tells me she's fine—'all things considered'—and Sandra's not telling me anything different. I don't like how tired she seems to be all the time, but she and I have been through patches a lot worse than this one, over the years." He sighed again and shook his head. "The one thing I can tell you for sure is that if either one of us starts 'hovering,' she'll kick us squarely in the ass, and you know it."

"Yes, I do," she said after a moment, and shook her own head with a smile. "In fact, she did just that the last time I seemed, um... overly solicitous."

"An experience we share," he said wryly, then shook himself, and she felt him deliberately shifting mental gears. "And if we *did* run home, she'd be perfectly right to read us both the riot act. By the time we flew up we'd be lucky to get three hours of sleep before we had to load up to fly *back* for Pat's intelligence brief tomorrow."

"Whereas *here*, we can get at least four or five hours of sleep... once I've had my way with you," Honor agreed with a smile, accepting the change of mood.

"Precisely!" He beamed at her, then took a bite out of the sandwich and sighed. "Does anything ever come out of Mistress Thorn's kitchen that *doesn't* taste good?"

"Oh, yes. I remember once—seven years ago, I think, though it *might* have been eight—she actually scorched some rice." Honor shuddered delicately. "Quite horrible, it was."

"I'm sure." White Haven's tone was dry, and he sipped coffee. Then he sat back with sandwich in hand and gazed up at the midnight sky. The light pollution of Landing's distant towers, on the far side of the house, was scarcely noticeable, and he inhaled deeply.

"Gorgeous, isn't it?" he murmured, unaware he was voicing Honor's earlier thought.

"Yes, it is. Of course, I have a slightly unfair advantage when it comes to enjoying it."

"I know. I hope you'll pardon me for saying I have somewhat ambivalent feelings over that particular advantage, though."

"I've had a few 'ambivalent' feelings about it myself, over the years," Honor acknowledged. She raised her left hand—her *artificial* left hand—to her equally artificial left eye. "On the other hand, I've been sitting here watching the work boats around *Hephaestus Alpha*. It's pretty impressive." She shook her head. "I'm astonished that they've accomplished so much so soon, really."

White Haven nodded in agreement. Without her cybernetic eye's telephoto feature, he couldn't make out details from here, but he spent more than enough time actually in space touring the projects to know she was right. Current estimates were that the first shipyard modules would be ready to begin construction again in no more than another eight to ten T-months, *far* sooner than anyone had dared project immediately after the strike, and the new stations—two of them in orbit around each of the Manticore Binary System's inhabited planets this time, not one—would boast ample active and passive defenses of their own.

Nothing like a burned hand to teach you what you should have seen coming all along, he thought grimly. And more than a little unfairly, he acknowledged. Without the "invisible" weapons someone—almost certainly the "Mesan Alignment" Victor Cachat and Anton Zilwicki had discovered—had used in the attack, *Hephaestus*, *Vulcan*, and *Weyland* would have been just fine.

"I wonder if Cachalot's going to be as lucky as we have," he said, then grimaced apologetically as he felt Honor stiffen beside him. "Sorry! Didn't mean to bring any business up tonight. Just slipped out."

"Nothing I wasn't already thinking about." She shook her head with a sigh. "I can't say I'm looking forward to hearing all the gory details from Pat tomorrow. What we've already heard is bad enough." She shook her head again. "You know, I realize we're talking about the Mandarins, and God knows nobody in the galaxy's better aware of how far the Solarian League's fallen from what it was supposed to be, but the idea that the League officially *sanctioned* something like this 'Buccaneer' abortion is just...just more than I can process, I guess. Or more than I *want* to be able to process, maybe. I know it's stupid of me, but I'd really rather this had been some rogue flag officer—another Byng or Crandall—acting entirely on her own."

"I know. But the truth is, we probably should've seen it—or something like it—coming. After what happened to Filareta, even the real idiots in Battle Fleet have to realize they can't face an Allied wall of battle. That takes any sort of fleet engagement out of their table of options, and you're a naval historian. You know *guerre de course* has always been the strategy of the weaker side. Hell, Honor! It's the strategy *you* were using with Eighth Fleet after the Havenites hit us with Thunderbolt."

"I know, and I hated it then, too," she said, both eyes bleak as she gazed up at the distant lights. "There's something obscene about destroying anything that's taken that long to build. Especially when so many people who never did a single thing to you or yours depend on it for a living."

"But we didn't have a choice, because at that point we were the ones who couldn't risk a decisive battle," White Haven pointed out. "And be fair to yourself, sweetheart. You *never* did the sort of job this Admiral Capriotti apparently did on Cachalot. I don't think the damage evaluation's going to get any better after we listen to Pat tomorrow, and it's pretty damned bad right now! I got a revised update just before Tom Caparelli and I decided to call it a night and head for home."

He shook his head. "It sounds like after he'd taken out every scrap of industrial infrastructure—and one major orbital habitat went with it; we're not sure *that* was intentional, but the damage they inflicted on three others damned well was—he rounded up every ship and small craft in the system bigger than a runabout and either took them with him or destroyed them."

"What?" Honor's head snapped around, eyes narrowed, and he nodded.

"We got a follow-on report from Captain Crouch this afternoon."

He cocked an eyebrow at her, and she nodded in recognition. She'd known John Crouch for years, ever since her time at the ATC, when he'd been a promising lieutenant commander on her staff. In fact, she'd recommended him for his current command, and his cruiser division had arrived in Cachalot on a routine port visit less than twenty-four hours after the Solarians had completed their work and departed once more. From the Cachalotians' description of the Solly task force, it was just as well that Crouch's four *Saganami-Bs* had missed it, but he'd immediately dug in to do what he could in the wake of such widespread devastation. He'd also sent HMS *Mortar,* one of his escorting destroyers, from Cachalot to Beowulf and straight on to Manticore. He clearly grasped how seriously the attack was likely to impact other neutral star nations' public opinion, which hadn't surprised her a bit. Nor did the fact that he'd sent another dispatch after the first one. Someone like Crouch was only too well aware of how the slow speed of interstellar communications could affect everything from tactical decisions by local commanders to the grand strategy of star nations.

"I haven't seen the actual dispatch, but Pat dropped us a preliminary synopsis," White Haven went on. "According to Crouch, they went after *everything,* Honor. When you were carrying out Cutworm, you were careful to avoid civilian collateral damage. Oh, it's not always possible to make a clean separation between military infrastructure and civilian infrastructure. We both know that. But you at least *tried* to, and you never took out civilian power sats or orbiting agro habitats. And you *damned* well never collected up every tugboat, repair boat, ore collector, and rowboat in the system and trashed them. There's no conceivable military justification for *that* kind of destruction. It's so . . . so *petty.* It's like a full grown adult punching out a twelve-year-old in a temper tantrum and then deciding to go through his pockets and steal his allowance, too!"

Honor nodded slowly, her expression tight. She *had* tried to minimize collateral destruction, and it hadn't always been possible. But this—!

"Capriotti made it clear the Mandarins were sending a message," she said after a moment, memory replaying the record of the com exchange between the Solarian and System President Jahnke, which Crouch had included with his initial dispatch. "From what you're saying, it's pretty obvious what the message *is*, too. Piss us off, and we'll turn your entire star system into a junkyard." Something dangerous crackled in the backs of her eyes. "And in answer to your earlier question, I don't see how Cachalot can be as lucky as we've been. Oh, they were a lot luckier about the *body count*." The fire behind her eyes turned cold and lethal with the memory of her own dead and how many millions of other Manticorans had joined them. "But they don't begin to have the depth of resources we have, even without Beowulf and Haven, and at least nobody systematically destroyed anything we might've used to *start* rebuilding!" She shook her head. "I know we'll do whatever we can to help, but I have to wonder how much we *can* do, given how much rebuilding we've got on our hands."

"President Jahnke's already recognized as much," White Haven said grimly. "She's asked for all the assistance we can provide—and she damned well should have, since we're the ones the Sollies are really trying to get at with this shit—but she obviously understands how constrained our resources are right now."

"And from Capriotti's statement, Cachalot's not the only system the bastards are going to do this to." Honor's voice was harsh, and White Haven could have counted the number of times he'd ever heard her call someone "bastard" on his fingers and toes without taking off both shoes.

"No, I'm sure it's not," he acknowledged. "That's one of things we'll be looking at with Pat tomorrow before you, Tom, and I have the ineffable joy of coming up with some kind of recommendation for Elizabeth. At the moment, I don't have a clue what that recommendation's going to be, either."

"I don't either." Honor's nostrils flared. "What I'd *like* to do is to announce a policy of reprisal. You come in and devastate one of our star systems, or somebody you accuse of tilting our way, and we devastate one of *yours*. Problem is, I'm pretty sure the Mandarins wouldn't object if we did that."

"That might depend on which system we chose for our reprisal," White Haven countered.

"Would it?" Honor settled back, resting her head on his shoulder and shaking it as she looked up at those star-strewn heavens. "I don't think it actually would, Hamish. This isn't really a military strategy; it's a *psychological* strategy. We're still well enough tapped into Old Chicago's internal dynamic to know how desperate they're getting, so maybe we should have seen this coming."

White Haven nodded. Despite Lacoön, the Grand Alliance had scrupulously allowed passage for mail, courier ships, and unarmed passenger vessels, and Manticore had *very* good relations with some of the worlds with which it was technically at war at the moment. There were more than enough unofficial leaks to keep Landing abreast of what was happening in the Sol System...always allowing for the time lag inherent in any interstellar communications loop. Personally, he shared the conclusion of both Special Intelligence and ONI that it was the fact that the Mandarins had to know that some of "their" planets—although, admittedly, not in the Core—were too well inclined towards Manticore to follow the party line which had prevented them from seeking a formal declaration of war.

On the other hand, they had to be getting desperate. Even accepting the analysts' least optimistic estimates, they couldn't keep funding the war effort for more than another T-year or so. The more optimistic ones measured their time window in months. And desperate people did desperate things. That was why Tom Caparelli and his staff were constantly updating plans to embrace an all-out offensive strategy. No one *wanted* to do that, because of the revanchism it was bound to create in the post-war League. A war against a behemoth that size after it had time to acquire matching weaponry was one no sane person wanted to face, yet they all realized the situation might change in a way which required them to roll the dice and hope the outcome was at least survivable.

Unfortunately, the *last* time someone had done that had been in a star system named Manticore, the dice had belonged to the Republic of Haven, and it...ended poorly for Lester Tourville and his fleet.

"They want to terrify people who might support us into backing away," Honor continued. "That's obvious. And it does have military *implications*, because they want us to do what we forced Tom Theisman to do with Cutworm and dissipate our forces. Spread them over as many potential targets as we can to prevent them from doing this over and over again. If they're willing to target Cachalot on the basis that it's simply been trading with us, though, their criteria for target selection's so broad there's no way we could separate *probable* targets from the merely possible ones. And if we can't identify or prioritize them, we couldn't really cover them, either, even if we didn't realize that was one of the things they wanted.

"But I have to say that, in some ways, I'm almost as worried about what they may be trying to tempt us into doing in response as I am about the actual attacks. If we start demolishing League star systems, we won't be punishing the people who actually ordered this thing, and we *will* be alienating League public opinion. Not only that, we'll be handing Abruzzi and the others a pretext they can use to go on whipping up a Solly war frenzy. Do you really think any of their pet newsies will suggest even for a moment that *our* attacks are a reprisal in response for *their* attacks? Especially when Capriotti's already equated 'Buccaneer' with Lacoön? Under their version of reality, we 'forced' them to adopt 'Buccaneer' when we began waging such brutal warfare against their citizens' 'economic lifeblood.' Nobody in the League's going to parse Abruzzi's news releases well enough to realize how absurd that comparison is."

"You're probably right." White Haven sighed, tucking his arm around her and drawing her in more tightly against his side. "But we *are* at war with them, love. Sooner or later, that's going to trump the 'public opinion' issue in my thinking, I'm afraid."

"I know. Mine too, really. But everything we're seeing says the Solly woman-in-the-street—especially outside the Sol System itself—is still a long way from being onboard with any of this. Or would be, if she had full information on what's going on. And as long as the League's shedding systems like Beowulf and Hypatia, we really don't want to give Abruzzi a bigger lever while he tries to push opinion the other way."

"Granted." He nodded. "But the flip side is that if we *don't* do something about it, our potential friends in the Verge and the Fringe are likely to wonder if that's because we can't or because we simply *choose* not to. And *that* could...adversely affect the trajectory of public opinion, as Tony's analysts so delicately put it."

"Of course other systems will wonder," she agreed in a disgusted tone. "Hard to blame them, too. Some of them will do the math and realize why we can't protect every inhabited star system in the galaxy, but how many people truly realize how many inhabited star systems there *are*? They know about theirs and maybe a half dozen others they've personally visited or where they have friends or family. Beyond that, it's all abstract...and the threat to their own star system is anything *but* abstract. It's another version of this false-flag operation Mike's turned up in Talbott. It doesn't matter whether or not what happens to one of the Fringe systems is our fault, because it's our job to keep it from happening *whoever's* 'fault' it is! It's illogical, it's unreasonable, and in some ways it's just plain silly, but it's also human nature, and somebody in Old Chicago knows it."

"Cogently reasoned," he told her, brushing the tip of her nose with his index finger. "Would it happen that the brain behind that analysis has any suggestions to make? Besides the delightful one we've already ruled out about burning a few Solly star systems to the ground in retaliation, I mean?"

"Actually, I have had *one* thought," she said, and his eyes narrowed at her serious tone. "Chien-lu was aboard *Imperator* for dinner the night John Crouch's first dispatch came in, so I shared it with him."

White Haven nodded. Chien-lu Anderman, Herzog von Rabenstrange, was Emperor Gustav's first cousin and third in the succession for the Andermani throne. He was also Gustav's representative to the Grand Alliance...and a personal friend of one Honor Alexander-Harrington. Theoretically, White Haven supposed, the information in Crouch's dispatch had been classified, but it wouldn't stay classified for long, and Honor and von Rabenstrange had a long history—one which had served both the Andermani and the Star Empire well, over the years—of working around formal restrictions.

"He was as furious about it as I was," she continued, "and we discussed the implications as well as we could, in light of what we knew at the time. And in the course of our discussion, we came up with a thought that may have some merit."

"What kind of thought?"

"Well, I don't think Gustav is overjoyed by the way Mike's been pushing the pace in Talbott, and I expect him to be even less overjoyed when he finds out we've sent Lester out to reinforce her and authorized operations against Madras. I think he figures our favorite loose-laserhead Winton's likely to have Mesa in her sights, as well, and you know how badly he wants to take the 'Alignment' down himself."

White Haven nodded. When Gustav Anderman learned of the Alignment's existence—and that the murder of his nephew in the attempted assassination of his younger brother and immediate heir had almost certainly been carried out using the Alignment's "killer nanotech"—there'd been no question about his idea of a proper response. At the same time, he had no desire to step into the Solarian League's sights, if only because he was a coldly pragmatic practitioner of interstellar *Realpolitik* who recognized the potential consequences for his own star nation after the shooting stopped and the League settled down to deciding how to even the score. That consideration wouldn't have stopped him from invading the Mesa System anyway, if not for the way in which Manticoran and Havenite allegations about Mesa had been incorporated into the narrative of their confrontation with the League. It was impossible to extricate the Alignment from the Mandarins' claims that Manticoran imperialism—compounded and driven, possibly, by paranoia about imaginary enemies—was the primary cause of the escalating conflict. Which meant any action Gustav might take against Mesa would be seen by both the Mandarins and by Solarian public opinion as a decision on his part to take Manticore's side against the League.

"Chien-lu didn't say so, but I think another factor in Gustav's thinking is the way the Talbott Quadrant sort of boxes the Empire in," Honor continued, and White Haven nodded again.

He'd spent quite a bit of time helping his brother, the Prime Minister, and Foreign Secretary Langtry worry about Gustav's possible reaction to the Star Empire's expansion. He doubted anyone in the Empire truly believed Manticore wanted to lock the Andermani up in their own little corner of the galaxy. For that matter, anyone who understood the realities of hyper travel knew they couldn't lock anyone up even if they *had* wanted to. But it was undeniable that the newly annexed Talbott Quadrant lay squarely athwart the hyper-space route between the Andermani Empire and the Solarian League. Given that the Manticoran Wormhole Junction already controlled the hyper bridges between the Andermani and the rest of the galaxy, a dynast like Gustav Anderman had to be experiencing at least a mild spasm of paranoia.

"Anyway," she said, "while we were bewailing the fact that Gustav can't join our formal declaration of war—and that we don't really *want* him to, in a lot of ways—we started looking for things the IAN might be able to do *short* of declaring war on the League. And that's when Chien-lu suggested that he could propose to Gustav that the IAN consider establishing 'neutrality patrols' down on our Talbott flank."

"'Neutrality patrols'?" White Haven repeated, and she nodded against his shoulder.

"What he's thinking is that not even the Mandarins are going to want to add the Empire to the Alliance. We've assumed from the beginning that they'll want the Andermani to stay neutral. And we've encouraged Gustav to do just that because it gives him so much more leverage with them. We've been looking to that as a card in the end game, a chance for him to step in and play the 'honest broker' when the idiots finally realize shooting at us is a losing game and start looking for some sort of peace settlement. But he could use that leverage for other things, as well. For example, he could announce a list of star systems with whom the Andermani trade regularly and warn everyone, including the Alliance, that he intends to station a few cruisers in most of them—just to keep an eye on pirate activity, of course. And if he happened to call that a 'neutrality patrol,' the Mandarins would probably recognize it as a tripwire they'd better not stumble over. If *we* want to deter attack on a system, we'll have to physically defend it, because we're already at war with the League and nothing's going to change that. But Chien-lu's thinking is that Gustav wouldn't have to come up with the strength to actually defend the systems, the way we would, because any attack on his ships would bring the Empire into the war as a full ally, and the Mandarins know it."

"Probably something to that," White Haven said thoughtfully. "Did von Rabenstrange suggest how many systems he thought Gustav might be able to get away with protecting that way?"

"No, and that's going to be a more delicate calculation. The Mandarins will go a long way to avoid provoking Gustav into declaring war, but if he's too obviously working with us, they may decide he's already *effectively* declared war. In which case he gets added to their hit list and the 'moral persuasion' aspect of his neutrality patrol goes out the airlock."

"Makes sense."

"I thought so. And there's another potential downside for us in the suggestion."

"Ah?" White Haven turned his head, looking at her, then smiled, remembering a very youthful, intensely focused Commander Honor Alexander-Harrington who'd been something of a blunt object...and not especially interested in the finer implications of interstellar diplomacy.

"Let me guess," he said. "You're thinking that if Gustav is so helpful and accommodating, he'll generate all kinds of goodwill in the systems he's protecting. The kind of goodwill that leads to things like, oh, most favored star nation trading status, military alliances, that sort of thing."

"Exactly." Honor shrugged. "It's a game the Andies have been playing for a long time, Hamish. It's how they've expanded their frontiers over the years without having to actually conquer anyone. They make themselves useful enough that they get *invited* in, and let's face it, as imperialist strategies go, that's about as benign as it gets. They've had a lot of practice and they've gotten *very* good at it, though. And the very things which would limit the systems Gustav could legitimately cover this way means they'd all fall naturally into the Andermani sphere of influence to begin with."

"Very true, unfortunately. On the other hand," White Haven pointed out, "they seem to be having rather more trouble absorbing their share of Silesia than we are. They probably need a while to digest that python lump before they look around for their next meal."

"Probably. But I can't help thinking Chien-lu—and you know how much I genuinely like him—sees this as a potential way to set the table. And maybe bribe the maître d' to make sure Gustav gets the best seat in the house."

"And that bothers you enough to turn the notion down?"

"I didn't say that." Honor shook her head again. "First, because you and I both know the Andies are going to go fishing in those waters sooner or later anyway. Like the old nursery rhyme says, fish gotta swim, birds gotta fly...and Andies gotta expand. We couldn't change that if we wanted to. But the real reason it doesn't bother me enough to say no?" Her lips tightened. "I'm in favor of anything that stops the sort of thing that happened to Cachalot *anywhere*, Hamish. We've lived through that right here, and I can't convince myself the Sollies will all be as careful about minimizing the loss of life as Capriotti apparently was. I've lost too many people I loved. Nobody else is living through another Yawata Strike on my watch. Not if there's one damned thing I can do about it!"

He gazed at her, hearing the iron in that promise. And, better than most, he *understood* that iron, knew how utterly she meant every word of it...and that she would follow those responsible for the Yawata Strike to the ends of the universe. Someday, Honor Alexander-Harrington would catch up with them, and what would happen then would be as sure as entropy...and just as cold. But the Solarian League had never met the Salamander. Not the way he had. And he doubted the Mandarins had any concept of the Juggernaut they would unleash if another Admiral Capriotti wasn't as careful about the careless butchery of someone else's civilians.

"I believe you," he said simply, and he did.

She'd told him once that a monster lived deep inside her, and he believed that, too. He'd seen it as she wept for Andrew LaFollet and her family after the Yawata Strike. He'd recognized it, known that for all his own outstanding military record, he wasn't even in her league when it came to sheer, focused deadliness. But that monster was chained by compassion, by the moral code of someone who'd devoted her entire life to protecting others. Who'd found a *use* for her monster and embraced it in a way which, conversely, made her one of the two gentlest, most loving human beings he'd ever met.

And I'm married to both of them, he thought wonderingly. *How does a man get* that *lucky?*

"What?" Honor asked in a rather different tone, her eyebrows furrowing.

"What 'what' would that be?" he said.

"The 'what' that's making you look at me the way Nimitz looks at celery," she replied tartly, and he laughed at her expression. She had a pretty darned good idea what was making him look at her that way, he reminded himself. His wife literally *could* read him—or his emotions, at least—like the proverbial book.

"I promise you, I don't think of you *remotely* the way Nimitz thinks about celery, Honor!" he told her in his most serious possible tone. "Or, let me rephrase. There is a certain...I don't know, resonance, perhaps, between the way I think of you and the way he lusts after celery. The end objective is rather different in my case, however."

"You're an idiot," she told him, shaking her head with a smile. "You know that, don't you?"

"Maybe I am, but I'm *your* idiot." He leaned closer, his kiss slow and lingering. "And you're stuck with me," he added in a whisper, nibbling the lobe of one ear.

"Oh, darn," she replied, putting her arms around him.

"It's a wonderful warm night," he pointed out. "It's even clear, with no rain in the forecast until midmorning, and this is a very large chaise lounge. Sturdy, too."

"I'd noticed that."

"Well, let me just go lock the door so we don't inadvertently scandalize Spencer and Lucie."

"I think that would be an excellent idea."

He gave her another kiss, climbed off the chaise lounge, and crossed to lock the old-fashioned door. It wouldn't stop Spencer Hawk or Tobias Stimson for a moment if a genuine emergency arose, but he smiled as he imagined their reaction if they happened to discover it was locked in a *non*-emergency situation. They'd snatch their hands away from the doorknob as if it were radioactive, he thought with a chuckle.

"You know," he said, sharing the thought with Honor as he pressed the locking stud and turned back towards her, "if Tobias or Spencer come along and—"

His eyes widened. Honor stood before him, gilded in starlight and moonglow, her kimono puddled about her feet.

"About that chaise lounge..." she said, and her eyes glowed as she opened her arms to him.

Solarian Gendarmerie Headquarters
City of Vivliothḗkē
Hypatia System

MAJOR INGRID LATIMER, SOLARIAN Gendarmerie, hid a quick frown as she stepped through the office door. Major Latimer was a little on the stocky side—a result of her homeworld's 1.25 g gravity—but she had dark red hair, gray eyes, and a quick-moving grace that the planet Hypatia's 0.93 g gravity only emphasized. In her impeccable uniform, she could have been used as a Gendarmerie recruiting poster any day. More than that, she was intelligent, dedicated, and just as good at her job as her appearance suggested.

She was also an unhappy woman, and the news accounts murmuring from the HD in one corner of Major Lawrence Kourniakis's office had quite a lot to do with the source of that unhappiness.

"Oh, hi, Ingrid!" Kourniakis greeted her, looking up from the paperwork on his desk display. "What brings you to the troglodyte side?"

"Hi, Larry."

Latimer smiled dutifully. She was the Gendarmerie's in-system third-in-command, head of the Criminal Investigation Division in Hypatia, and she thought of herself as an old-fashioned cop, because she vastly preferred catching crooks to wading around in the cesspool of politics and surveillance. Kourniakis, on the other hand, commanded the Security Division, charged with both cyber security and counterintelligence in the star system. He was senior to her—in fact, in addition to his security responsibilities, he served Colonel Ganesh Naran, the senior Gendarme in Hypatia, as his second-in-command—and she'd always thought his cheerful, extroverted nature was a less-than-perfect fit for someone with his responsibilities. He certainly didn't strike anyone as the sort of fellow who would hover in corners listening to private conversations. Which, she acknowledged, might be one reason he'd been so effective in what he liked to call his "troglodyte duties."

Now Kourniakis touched his display, turning the HD volume completely down, and cocked his head at her.

"To what do I owe the honor?" he asked.

"One of my people turned up something you need to take a look at," she replied.

"Shoot," Kourniakis said, opening a notepad on his display, and pointing at the chair by his desk.

"We've been investigating some smuggling activities down at the port." Latimer dropped into the indicated chair. "I wouldn't've been too worried about it, with all the other crap going on right now, except that these particular smugglers were bringing in 7H."

Kourniakis looked up from the note he'd been jotting with a quick, dark frown. "7H" was cop and street shorthand for "Seventh Heaven," a particularly nasty psychedelic nanotech which had developed a hefty pool of addicts despite the psychoses it produced in long-term users. Just last week, a lorry driver down at the port had experienced a psychotic event while driving and rammed his vehicle through two warehouse bays and a crowded pedestrian walk. Six people had died on the scene, and another fourteen had been med-evaced. There was a reason *nobody* wanted 7H on his world.

"You have proof of that?" he asked, and she nodded.

"Plenty of proof, already bagged up and in Evidence Impound. Eleven perps in lockup to go with it . . . and three in the morgue because they didn't want to come along when we knocked on their door."

"Pity about that." Kourniakis's smile was thin, and she smiled back. But then her expression sobered.

"While we were surveilling them just before the bust, though, something else turned up," she said. "We came across somebody else's hack. Not on our perps, but piggybacked through their system to hit the planetary AG's files."

"Attorney General Boyagis's office?" Kourniakis asked sharply, and she nodded.

"I think the perps were trying to keep tabs on any investigation by the VPD or the System Bureau of Investigation. Anyway, they'd managed to get into Boyagis's files—we think we've IDed the hacker they hired, if you want her name—but then someone else jacked *their* files to get to Boyagis's. I'm not sure who the 'someone else' was, but I know it wasn't my people, so I thought I'd better come and make sure it wasn't any of *your* people before we report it to Boyagis. Or, rather, before I report it to Colonel Naran and *you and he* report it to Boyagis."

"No clue at all who it was?"

"None," she confirmed. "And I assume from your question that it wasn't you?"

"Of course it wasn't me!" Kourniakis sat back in his chair. "Why the hell would I be hacking the Attorney General's files?"

She considered several possible responses to that question. None of them seemed very constructive, however.

Unlike her, Kourniakis was a native Hypatian. That was scarcely unusual in the SG. In fact, the majority of the Gendarmes in Hypatia were Hypatians, given the Gendarmerie's Core World staffing policies. Usually, Latimer thought that was an excellent idea. Core Systems weren't Protectorates. They were full-fledged, self-governing members of the Solarian League, so there'd never been any reason for the Gendarmerie to transfer in people who had no local connections to seduce them from the straight and narrow, and there were strong arguments in favor of using as many locals as possible. Latimer's own CID was living proof of that. Her best agents, most effective investigators, were all Hypatians, with the innate feel for their homeworld's social patterns and interactions which could be produced only by total submersion in their environment. They also tended to get the best results whenever CID had to interface with local law enforcement agencies—which happened a lot—because they weren't outsiders trying to cut in on someone else's turf. And, even if all that hadn't been true, assigning people light-years away from their friends and families when there were plenty of openings right in their hometowns had a powerful negative impact on personnel retention rates.

Right this moment, though, those personnel policies were contributing to something Latimer really didn't like. And not just with Kourniakis, although he was certainly a case in point.

She'd known Lawrence Kourniakis for over eight T-years. They were friends. He and her husband Carl were hunting and fishing buddies, and his twin girls attended the same school as her son Peter. She wasn't as close to Kourniakis's wife Angelika as Kourniakis was to Carl, but both of them loved landscape photography, and Angie knew all the best vistas and exactly when the lighting would be most spectacular.

And despite all of that, Ingrid Latimer couldn't say what she was thinking to Kourniakis. "Larry, you should be digging as deep as you can into the treasonous SOB's files to find out just how badly the bastard and his bosses are planning on screwing the League," wasn't something Kourniakis wanted to hear.

Of course it's not, she thought. *Larry's a hell of a nice guy, and I'd trust him with my life. But he's about as blind as any of these other Hypatians. And he doesn't think they're doing a single thing that's illegal.*

In fairness, Latimer wasn't certain the Hypatia System Unified Government's actions *were* illegal. On the other hand, she wasn't certain they *weren't,* and it seemed to her that a few precautions were in order. Unfortunately, Colonel Naran had taken the position that the entire referendum was a local government issue. It might have federal *implications*, but absent a formal decision from the League Judiciary that the constitutional right of secession was no longer operative, he had no authority to interfere in the process while the Hypatians sorted it out.

And by the time they finish "sorting it out," it'll be too late. Unless something turns around pretty damned quick, these people aren't going to just cross the Rubicon. They're going to cross it, blow up their bridges behind them, and throw the splinters back into the river with a rock tied to their ankles! In fact, maybe the metaphor I want has more to do with the Red Sea than any rivers.

"Well, if it's not you, then maybe it's one of the Liberty Committees," she said out loud. "They're making enough noise, and don't forget the injunction Allerton's asking for. The Committees could be looking for inside information about where Boyagis's thinking is on that."

"And it could also be some damned newsy wanting a scoop," Kourniakis shot back just a bit quickly. "It doesn't have to be one of the Committees, Ingrid. For that matter, it could be one of Allerton's people looking for exactly the same kind of info."

"It could," she conceded, although she didn't think for a minute that it was.

Senator Makiko Allerton had made her opposition to the referendum madness crystal clear. Her arguments against secession were just as emotional as the strident demands of the dozens of Liberty Committees which had sprung up to organize in favor of it and she was, in Latimer's opinion, a far more eloquent spokeswoman. But she was also badly outnumbered. She was fighting a losing battle, and that battle had gotten a hell of a lot harder when that never-to-be-sufficiently-damned Abruzzi-MacArtney soundbite hit the public boards here in Vivliothéké. The vote trend had been clear almost from the beginning, but opposition to the referendum had plummeted and support among the previously undecided had skyrocketed in the wake of that stupid, obviously—and heavily—edited scrap of private conversation.

Allerton and her small cohort of doggedly loyal fellows in Hypatia's unicameral legislature had fought hard against the referendum while it was still in the draft stage, and they hadn't stopped fighting since. The political cost for Allerton, who almost every pundit agreed would have been the next System President if the referendum had never come along, had been steep, but she'd refused to yield. Now, though, after the disaster of the Abruzzi-MacArtney clip and with only three more days until the actual vote, it must be obvious even—or perhaps *especially*—to her that she was destined for defeat. Even Latimer had to admit that her probably-doomed request for an injunction, postponing the referendum until the legality of secession was ruled upon by the Federal courts, was no more than a last-ditch, forlorn hope effort to avoid the inevitable.

Whatever else Makiko Allerton might be, though, she was a woman who believed in due process and the rule of law. She'd dedicated her entire life to that. The possibility that *she* might have hacked the Attorney General's office simply didn't exist.

Which, the major acknowledged unhappily, *doesn't mean one of her supporters couldn't've done it without her knowledge or approval. I hate to say it, but Larry's got a point about that. I just wish I felt more confident he's still trying to keep the playing field level in his own mind. And I hate even having to wonder about that, damn it!*

"Anyway," she said out loud, "I figured you needed to hear about it. Under the circumstances, I'm just as happy I don't have to make the call about whether or not to tell Boyagis about it, but I thought it would be a good idea to give you a heads-up before the official report lands in your inbox."

"I appreciate that." Kourniakis smiled at her. "And as soon as that official report gets here, I'm sure Colonel Naran will pass it on to the AG." He shrugged. "Until the referendum's actually voted on, all of the rules about jurisdictions still apply, and this is clearly in Boyagis's. Thanks for bringing it to me, Ingrid."

"You're welcome." She pushed up out of the chair and extended her hand across the desk. "Take care, Larry."

"You, too, Ingrid." Kourniakis stood to shake her hand. "And don't forget Friday night. Alethea and Alexia have informed me they intend to cook supper." He shook his head. "God only knows what it'll be, but I promise it won't poison anybody."

"That's what you say *now*," she replied with a smile, then nodded and headed back for her own office.

❖   ❖   ❖

Lawrence Kourniakis watched the door close behind Ingrid, then settled back behind his desk and turned the HD volume back up. The talking heads weren't saying anything he didn't already know, but he let them natter in the background as he tipped back in his chair, gazing at the closed door with a pensive expression, and ran the conversation back through his mind.

Ingrid had a point about how badly the Liberty Committees might have wanted a peek inside Attorney General Boyagis's files. And he didn't think for a moment that Makiko Allerton would have condoned any illegalities on behalf of herself or her anti-referendum crusade. The truth was, he didn't have a clue as to who it might have been, and he was just as happy it wasn't a federal matter—which meant it wasn't *his*—until and unless the system authorities requested the Gendarmerie's assistance.

Which they wouldn't do now if the Spíti tēs Gerousías *was burning down with the Senators inside it,* he thought sourly. *Never thought I'd see something like this, and I wish to hell I* wasn't *seeing it. But, damn it, it's time to fish or cut bait.*

Up until very recently, Lawrence Kourniakis had never wondered whether he saw himself first as a Hypatian or as a citizen of the Solarian League. Those identities had been identical, as far as he was concerned. But now, since this whole confrontation with first the Manties, then the Republic of Haven, and now even *Beowulf*...

If not for Beowulf, he'd probably still be inclined to give the Ministry of Information and the anti-Manty newsies the benefit of the doubt. Certainly all this nonsense about centuries-long Mesan conspiracies sounded like either the ravings of a lunatic or pure fiction. But he knew too many Beowulfers. For that matter, his wife's family was from Beowulf, and one of his uncles had married a Manticoran. He'd found it difficult to recognize any of his in-laws in the imperialistic, warmongering monsters the newsies were portraying. Of course, he'd also been prepared to admit that he'd never made a close study of Manticore's relations with the League or of any possible Mesan conspiracies. But he'd viewed Felicia Hadley's fiery denunciations of the "Mandarins" from the floor of the Legislative Assembly itself, and the worm of doubt had crept into his heart as she hammered the League's foreign policy.

Maybe it wouldn't have if he hadn't spent fifteen years seconded to Frontier Security before he returned to Hypatia, married Angela, and settled down. Most of those years had been out in the Protectorates, and he hadn't liked what he'd seen there. He hadn't liked the kind of deals he'd seen between corrupt Solarian transstellars and the local OFS commissioners. The sort of deals which lent a damning edge of plausibility to Manticore and Haven's claims about Mesa. He hadn't liked the façade democracies, or the way OFS propped up local despots and dictators, regardless of their human rights policies, as long as they kept the fee schedules moving. And he hadn't liked the way the League had operated to suppress any local opposition to those despots and dictators.

He'd told himself those sorts of operations were Frontier Security's business, not the Gendarmerie's, and there'd been a lot of truth to that. But nobody could witness it without being touched by it, and he'd still felt...dirtied by some of the things *he'd* witnessed. Some of the things in which he'd been forced to participate, if only at second or third hand.

Things that had left a scar.

And that scar was what had tipped him from ambivalence over secession into full-bodied support for it. People could argue all they wanted to that that conversation between Malachai Abruzzi and Nathan MacArtney had had never been serious. That it had been no more than venting, driven by their intense frustration as the Manticore Crisis escalated. But the fact that they'd said the words at all had reminded Major Lawrence Kourniakis of the things the Solarian League—*his* Solarian League—routinely *did* do in the Protectorates. And when he added that to the way the Mandarins and their surrogates had torn into Beowulf—accused it of *treason*, for exercising its legal rights where the Beowulf Terminus was concerned and probably saving hundreds of thousands of Solarian lives into the bargain—he'd realized he didn't really have to leave the League.

The League had already left him, long ago. *His* League had died somewhere out there in the Protectorates, and all the referendum represented, really, was the formalization of the death certificate.

He inhaled deeply, shook his head, and returned to his paperwork.

Proedrikḗ Katoikía
City of Vivliothḗkē
Hypatia System

"I HAVE TO SAY that while I'm very relieved to see you, your timing may be just a bit *too* expeditious, Admiral," System President Adam Vangelis said as he stood and walked around the desk to shake Rear Admiral Kotouč's hand. "We didn't expect you for another full-day or so."

"I'm pleased to be here, and I hope I can be of service, Mister President," Kotouč replied a bit cautiously as he shook the proffered hand.

He felt awkward out of uniform, and he'd wondered why the President's message had asked him to travel on a government-chartered, civil registry shuttle and wear civilian attire for his visit to the Proedrikḗ Katoikía. He'd wondered if Vangelis's request was a bad sign when the message was delivered, and the last thing he wanted to discover was that it had been.

"As for our arrival time," he continued, "my orders were to make the most expeditious passage I could. Is there some reason I shouldn't have?" He shook his head. "My instructions are to assist you in any way I can, and I'm afraid I'm not sufficiently familiar with the local political scene to be aware of any... timing issues. Ms. Goode's done her best to bring me up to speed on Hypatian politics, and I viewed her reports with great interest on our way here, but I'm sure you understand that I haven't had time to develop any sort of inside perspective."

"Of course you haven't!" Vangelis shook his head and smiled at the silver haired woman who'd accompanied Kotouč into his office. "It's remarkable that Kay's developed such an excellent understanding of Hypatia in the short time she's been here. I'll allow her, oh, eighty hours, let's say, to instill that same understanding in you."

"As always, Mister President, your generosity awes me," the Honorable Kay Goode responded in a pronounced Sphinxian accent, and the treecat on her shoulder bleeked a laugh.

"And that's enough lèse-majesté out of *you*, too, Dizzy!" Vangelis said, shaking an index finger at the 'cat... who seemed mightily undismayed by the admonition. Goode reached up and stroked his ears gently, shaking her head, and Vangelis chuckled.

Kotouč didn't know Goode personally, but he knew quite a bit about her, including the fact that she was distantly related to both Klaus Hauptman—the connection was *very* distant there—and also to Honor Alexander-Harrington, through the Zivoniks, one of the oldest families on Sphinx. He also knew she'd lost her husband and, although the Goodes as a family hadn't been hit nearly so hard as the Harringtons, several other close family members in the Yawata Strike. He doubted anyone would have realized that, given her serene expression, but no one who'd viewed her situation reports from Hypatia would make that mistake. The lava behind those gray eyes burned hot in those reports, and he'd wondered, viewing some of them, if she saw the Solarian League more as an enemy in its own right or as no more than an obstacle between her star nation and the people who'd murdered so many of its citizens.

He suspected it was the latter...and that her priorities only added a finely distilled vitriol to her hate and loathing for the Mandarins.

Whatever her feelings, and however much of them she'd revealed in her reports to her Manticoran superiors, he was sure she'd kept them under control here in Hypatia. She was Sir Anthony Langtry's special envoy to Hypatia, and everyone knew that as soon as the referendum's outcome was announced she would take off her special envoy's hat and replace it with that of the Star Empire of Manticore's Ambassador and Minister Plenipotentiary to the System Republic of Hypatia. It probably wouldn't change her personal relationship with Vangelis—which was obviously very good—a bit, but the legal implications of naming an ambassador to a newly independent star nation which had been a founding member of the Solarian League would not be lost on the galaxy at large.

"In the meantime, Admiral," Vangelis continued, ushering both of his guests over to stand at the office's floor-to-ceiling windows, looking out across the Proedriké Katoikía's beautifully landscaped grounds, "I didn't mean to imply that your arrival is in the least unwelcome. I don't believe I'm going to need your assistance to maintain order here in Hypatia." He smiled just a bit crookedly. "I'm sure there's going to be *some* 'buyer's remorse.' There always is, even in decisions nowhere near as monumental as this one! And the minority who opposed secession—it looks like around twenty-one percent actually voted against it—may produce a certain...restiveness. Overall, though, I'm not anticipating any significant domestic unrest."

"I'm relieved to hear that, Mister President."

Kotouč gazed out at the lacy, feathery leaves of the native trees along the ancient stone wall separating the Proedrikḗ Katoikía—the President's House; and the admiral hoped Vangelis wouldn't be offended when he used the Standard English translation instead of mangling the Greek—from a broad, smooth avenue. Hypatia was old enough that Vivliothḗkē had been built without counter-grav, and the original architecture had been lovingly preserved. The Old Town was walled about with the monolithic towers of a later tech base, but building codes had pushed them far enough from the ancient heart of the city to prevent the kind of overshadowing effect he'd seen on too many other planets.

"I'm relieved to hear it," he repeated, "and that assessment accords pretty well with what Representative Lambrou and Representative Tsakabikou predicted during the voyage from Beowulf. A little better than Mr. Lambrou predicted; not quite as rosy as Ms. Tsakabikou expected."

"I'm sure it does," Vangelis said a bit dryly. Kotouč raised an eyebrow, and the president chuckled. "Brad's been more of a 'wait-and-see-how-it-all-works-out' type from the beginning, Admiral. Sofronia... not so much."

"I'd have to say that fits my own observation of Ms. Tsakabikou," Kotouč acknowledged.

"I'm sure it does."

Vangelis stood between the two Manticorans—at 165 centimeters, he was shorter than either of them—looking out the window for several seconds. Then he drew a deep breath.

"I'm more concerned about the non-Hypatians here in the system, Admiral," he said, turning to look at Kotouč. "In particular, Rupert Chernikov—he's the Managing Director for Alexandria Belt Extraction Industries—fought the referendum tooth and nail. I've always gotten along well with Rupert, on a personal basis, but that doesn't mean as much as it used to, after what happened to Sandra Crandall and Massimo Filareta. And not just for people from outside the system, either. Makiko Allerton and I have been friends since we were kids, and she's scarcely speaking to me these days."

Regret darkened his brown eyes, but he went on levelly.

"I don't want to think Rupert would try any kind of actual sabotage, and it's not like we're one of the Protectorates. Alexandria Extraction's majority-owned right here in Hypatia, with less than a quarter of the voting stock held by out-system interests, and even if he was inclined to try something like that, ninety-five percent of ABEI's employees are Hypatian. I can't completely rule it out, though, and the fact that his employees are Hypatian, doesn't mean all of them supported the referendum.

"There are other assets and operations here in the system, however, that are owned primarily by one of the transstellars who're likely to think secession doesn't bode well for their long-term economic interests. My local law enforcement people are keeping an eye on all of the prospective problem children we've been able to identify, but it's been my experience that it's seldom the problems you see coming that do the damage. I assume it's that way in military operations, as well?"

"Oh, I think you could safely say that, yes, Mister President," Kotouč agreed. "Naval officers *hate* surprises, for a lot of reasons."

"Well, I don't really anticipate any armed resistance or major sabotage. What I'm more concerned about are people carrying tales to the League out of school, so to speak, and we've got a lot of privately owned hyper-capable ships here in Hypatia. There's no way we could keep someone from running to Old Chicago with the outcome of the referendum, and I'm fairly sure someone already has. I know." He waved one hand. "The results haven't been officially announced yet, mainly because we're still counting some of the absentee ballots from the belter habitats." He shook his head. "That's where our more anarchistic citizens hang out. The dinosaurs in some of those habitats still use *paper* ballots."

Both of Kotouč's eyebrows arched this time, and Vangelis snorted.

"The good news, from our perspective, is that they're even more… irritated with Old Chicago than most, so the only question is how much they'll inflate the margin of victory. But it's been my administration's policy from the beginning that we won't certify the result of the referendum until every single voter's been given ample opportunity to cast his or her ballot and have it counted." The president's expression sobered. "I very much doubt that early victory projections would actually have suppressed the vote against secession, but I didn't intend to let that happen. Nothing is going to taint this referendum or its results, Admiral. This is the kind of decision where a decent respect for history requires that it be arrived at openly, honestly, and transparently."

"I agree entirely, Mister President," Kotouč said, and Goode nodded. Her reports had prepared Kotouč for a system chief executive who took his responsibilities seriously, and everything he'd seen since arriving in Hypatia only confirmed that impression.

"The bad news is that we're still at least a day-half from actually certifying the count," Vangelis continued, and Kotouč nodded. At just over forty hours, Hypatia's planetary day was longer than the planetary days of most colonized planets, and its inhabitants had divided it into more manageable-sized "day-halves" and "full-days"—or, more commonly, simply "halves" and "fulls."

"I'd just as soon keep your arrival under wraps until those last ballots come in and get counted," Vangelis continued. "My official position—and my personal promise to Senator Allerton and her supporters—has been that no foreign warship will enter Hypatia orbit until the final vote's been certified by the Department of State and the Supreme Court."

"I wasn't aware of that, Sir," Kotouč said. "My orders were to proceed to Hypatia as quickly as possible to provide security here in the system after the referendum. And I'm afraid neither Mr. Lambrou nor Ms. Tsakabikou warned me about your 'dinosaurs' and any delays in the vote tally. I can understand why it might not have occurred to them to mention it, but I'd assumed the result would have been announced no later than yesterday."

"I realized that as soon as you turned up." Vangelis nodded briskly. "And certainly no one's faulting you or your people for how quickly you got here! For that matter, none of your ships *are* in Hypatia orbit, are they?"

"No, Mister President, they aren't," Kotouč acknowledged. *And now I understand why System Traffic Control sent us to the Alexandria Belt rather than to Hypatia, too.*

Fortunately, the Alexandria Belt was an inner-system belt, between Hypatia and its G4 primary but less than a full light-minute from the capital planet. The shuttle flight from *Phantom*'s current orbit to Vivliothékē Field had taken less than two hours.

"I know it's inconvenient," Vangelis said, "but I think it's important that I keep my promises. The real reason I asked you to come visit me today—and to come in what I believe you Navy people call 'mufti'— was to explain why we're keeping your arrival under wraps and won't be having any formal dinners to welcome you to Hypatia for the next half-day or so." He smiled. "I didn't want you thinking it was because you were unwelcome!"

SLNS *Camperdown*
Task Force 1030
Solarian League Navy

"DO YOU THINK THEY'VE announced the outcome yet, Admiral?" The Honorable Madhura Yang-O'Grady asked as the lift car slowed.

"I'm afraid your sources are probably better where that's concerned than mine are, Ms. Yang-O'Grady," Hajdu Győző replied. Which self-evident fact, he reflected, she should already have possessed.

"I know." Yang-O'Grady's tone carried a hint of apology as the lift car doors opened on the passage outside SLNS *Camperdown*'s flag briefing room. She was almost eighteen centimeters shorter than Hajdu, with green eyes, a dark sandalwood complexion, and naturally crimson hair which was quite striking, and he suspected that under more usual circumstances, she had a lively sense of humor.

"I believe that question comes under the heading of making inane conversation as a way to distract myself and keep my brain from wearing any more holes in itself," she added, as if to confirm his suspicion.

"I see." Hajdu's lips twitched. "In that case, Ms. Yang-O'Grady, I am enchanted to have been of service."

"Thank you."

Yang-O'Grady rewarded him with a smile, but there was a tautness—a darkness—behind her amusement. Given the nature of her assignment, a certain tension was not simply understandable but to be expected, Hajdu thought. In fact, only a moron—which Madhura Yang-O'Grady manifestly was not—wouldn't have been worried as hell by the job she'd been handed. But this seemed to go farther, he thought, and wondered about its possible implications for their mission.

They reached the briefing room hatch, and Hajdu courteously waved her through it. The command structure for their current operation was . . . complex. As Innokentiy Kolokoltsov's personal representative, it was Yang-O'Grady's job to convince the Hypatia System Unified Government to renounce the results of its referendum if, as all reports indicated was inevitable, the decision to secede had been sustained. It was Hajdu's job to float ominously in the background, lending weight

210

to Yang-O'Grady's arguments. Unless and until Yang-O'Grady failed in her own mission, that was all he was supposed to do.

At that point, however, Buccaneer came into play. From his staff's analysis, there was no way that *wasn't* going to happen in the end, and a part of the admiral wanted to simply get on with it. If Hypatia had chosen to betray its eight hundred T-years of loyalty and mutual obligations to its fellow League member systems, then it was time Hypatians were shown the error of their ways. Hopefully, their experience would make other potential traitors wise, and if he had to do it, he wanted it over and done as quickly as possible. The sooner Hypatia's experience became general knowledge, the less likely other traitors were to arise.

Besides, mixing politics and military policy was never a good idea. The result was usually an abortion, and the best one could normally hope for was that it wouldn't be a *total* abortion. To this point, he was cautiously tempted to believe their current mission might prove an exception to the rule, but it was early days yet.

For now, however, Yang-O'Grady was senior to him, which was why he'd waved her into the briefing room in front of him. It was her responsibility to determine the moment at which their mission transitioned from political to military. Until that moment, he was at her orders. *After* that moment, she became a passenger.

"Attention on deck," Commodore Fred Brigman, TF 1030's chief of staff, said as Yang-O'Grady and his admiral arrived. Under more usual circumstances, the staff would simply have risen respectfully until Hajdu was seated. With "guests" present, Brigman was being a bit more formal, and Hajdu walked across to his chair, waited until Yang-O'Grady had seated herself, then sat down and nodded to the commodore.

"Carry on," he said.

"Thank you, Sir."

The rest of the staff resumed their seats, but Brigman remained standing and keyed up the elevated display in front of him.

"As the Admiral already knows, Ms. Yang-O'Grady," he said courteously to the Foreign Ministry representative, "this is basically just a final readiness report. We completed our last scheduled exercise fifteen hours ago, and on the basis of that, Commodore Koopman"—he nodded to Daphne Koopman, TF 1030's staff operations officer—"and I have added a few tiny tweaks. The main purpose of this briefing is to apprise both Admiral Hajdu and you of our readiness estimate, based on the exercises we've conducted, and to examine our mission orders one last time in light of that estimate. The Admiral's made it clear to us that you need the most complete possible picture of our capabilities and the elements of Buccaneer and how they would play out in the unhappy eventuality of their becoming necessary. In addition, this briefing offers an opportunity for you—or the Admiral—to reconsider or more fully define any of those elements. From my own reading of the intelligence reports, unfortunately, I believe it's likely the Hypatians will have voted in favor of secession by the time we get there. If that's happened, the Task Force's primary mission is to enable you to accomplish *your* mission without a shot being fired, and the Admiral feels that makes it essential that you be as hands-on as possible with our planning process and operational options."

"I see," Yang-O'Grady said, when he paused. She glanced at the admiral sitting beside her. "And I appreciate it, Admiral." She grimaced. "Before I joined the Foreign Ministry, I spent quite some time with Interior and cut my teeth in Frontier Security. During those years, I had ample opportunity to watch what should have been coordinated military and diplomatic operations turn into fiascoes. I doubt you can fully imagine just what a relief it is to know that whatever happens in Hypatia, it won't be because your people and my people weren't on the same page going in."

HMS *Phantom*
Alexandria Belt
Hypatia System

"TALK TO ME, JIM!" Jan Kotouč said as he strode into flag bridge.

"Yes, Sir!" Captain Clarke turned from an intense discussion with Commander Ilkova. "We're still getting the details, but it doesn't look good. So far, CIC is reporting a minimum of a hundred and fifty hyper footprints."

"And we don't have a single Ghost Rider platform out there to keep an eye on them, do we?" Kotouč observed sourly.

"No, Sir. Sorry, Sir," Ilkova said, and Kotouč waved a hand at her.

"That wasn't a criticism, Markéta. Or, if it was, it was a *self*-criticism, not directed at you. I should have deployed a shell as soon as we made our hyper translation."

"My job to remind you, Sir," she said loyally, and Kotouč shook his head.

"If I recall my Academy classes correctly, the responsibility rests with the commanding officer."

His tone was almost whimsical, but his staff knew him well enough to recognize the intense self-anger buried within it. And Ilkova was correct; it *was* her job to "remind" her admiral about such things. But Hypatia was a friendly system with its own sensor net already in place. Kotouč had allowed himself to forget how unexpectedly things could change, and with him as an example, it was hardly surprising even a staff as good as his had done the same thing.

You told Vangelis Navy officers hate surprises, he thought acidly. *Maybe it would've been a good idea for you to do a little something to minimize this* one?

"All right," he said. "We screwed up—I'll grant you we both dropped the ball on this one, Markéta—so let's do something about it. Get the recon shell deployed now. Complete stealth. That many footprints can only mean this is the Sollies, and I don't want them to have even a sniff of our presence in-system."

"Yes, Sir." Ilkova turned to begin giving orders, and Kotouč moved his attention to Commander Jason Kindrick, his staff astrogator.

Kindrick was a bookish sort—his nose was usually buried in his reader or an old-fashioned hardcopy book whenever he was off duty—who rejoiced, for some reason Kotouč had never discovered, in the nickname of "Vulture." It was hard for him to think of a name less suited to someone's physical appearance, but Kindrick only smiled whenever he heard it. And wherever it had come from, or however fond of the printed page he might be, he was also one of the best astrogators Kotouč had ever served with.

"While Markéta's seeing to that, Jason," he said now, "I think we need to move—very cautiously—to a point farther from Hypatia. We've got a lot of room to hide in where we are, but we're also under a light-minute from the capital. If I were these people, I'd be looking that volume over very carefully, so I want to be somewhere outside it by the time they're close enough to start looking. Pick us a good spot to hide at least fifty or sixty million klicks from here."

"Yes, Sir," Kindrick replied, and Kotouč nodded and crossed to the master display, twitching his head to invite Clarke to join him there.

"You think this is some kind of armed attempt to suppress the referendum, Sir?" the captain asked quietly.

"Well, it's not a convoy of ice cream tankers," Kotouč replied tartly, then shook his head. "You know, the entire time we were rushing to get here, I never imagined anything this size coming over the hyper wall. This is a lot more escalation than I ever anticipated, especially in a Core System like Hypatia."

"I suppose it's at least theoretically possible they're only staging through Hypatia en route to somewhere else," Clarke said.

"No, you don't suppose anything of the sort." Kotouč shook his head. "You're just trying to find a silver lining. Best case scenario, whatever genius in Old Chicago sent these people out here is hoping a force this size will overawe Hypatia into backing down on their referendum. In that case, they're probably under orders just to be as visible and intimidating as possible, and I have to concede that a couple of hundred warships could do a pretty fair job of intimidating just about anybody. On the other hand, they're only forty-four light-years from Beowulf, and they know what Admiral Truman has sitting on the Beowulf Terminus. So if they're here to do any intimidating, they're probably under orders to do it pretty damned fast."

"And if that isn't why they're here, Sir?"

"About the only other reason they could be here is to...take steps if President Vangelis and his administration refuse to back down," the admiral said, flat-voiced.

Clarke started to ask another question, then visibly changed his mind, and Kotouč smiled grimly. His chief of staff was as capable of doing the math as he was, and neither of them liked the answers they were coming up with.

Nobody ever expected us to stand off a full-scale invasion, *damn it*, he thought harshly. *Nobody ever expected it, and we didn't come prepared to do it, either. No pods, no CLACs, no Mycroft. Just* Phantom, *three* Bravos, *and* Arngrim *and only what we have in the magazines.*

"Have Markéta make sure we have a Hermes buoy on the approach vector from Beowulf," he said. Clarke looked at him, and he showed his teeth. "Give us another seventy-two hours, maybe even only forty-eight, and the force balance in Hypatia will change rather significantly," he pointed out.

"Yes, Sir, it will," Clarke agreed. He nodded respectfully to Kotouč and turned to speak to Ilkova. The admiral watched him go, then clasped his hands behind him, squared his shoulders, and looked down into the plot while he waited out the no-longer-accustomed-to light-speed delay from the Hypatian sensor net.

Yes, the force balance will change, he thought. *But unless* Vukodlak *and a couple of missile colliers turn up—at a minimum—it's not going to change* enough, *and you and Jim both know it.*

He watched the plot, waiting, and prayed silently that whoever commanded those anonymous hyper footprints wasn't one of the SLN's hotheads.

SLNS *Camperdown*
and
Proedrikḗ Katoikía com center
Hypatia System

"I'M AFRAID THAT'S OUT of the question, Ms. Yang-O'Grady," the brown-haired man on Madhura Yang-O'Grady's com display said. "I regret the fact that you came all this way only to have me refuse your . . . request, but the referendum's results have been tallied and officially certified. As a consequence, I really have no choice in the matter."

System President Vangelis didn't sound very regretful to Yang-O'Grady, but she made herself smile at him. SLNS *Camperdown*'s parking orbit was low enough that there was no perceptible delay in com transmissions, and she leaned towards her com's pickup ever so slightly.

"Mister President," she said as calmly as she could, "I understand the Hypatian System Constitution mandates both the procedure for and the implementation of any referendum and its outcome. I also understand that under the letter of the law, you're technically correct that you have 'no choice' but to abide by the results of your system's most recent referendum. Obviously, the Federal Government and I differ with your system's interpretation of the *Solarian* Constitution, however, and that's what creates our present problem. The Interior Ministry believes Article Thirty-Nine, the so-called secession clause of the Constitution, is a legal archaism which has lapsed over the seven and a half *centuries*"—she emphasized the last word deliberately and allowed her eyes to harden just a bit—"since the original Constitution was ratified. I believe the relevant technical term is 'desuetude.' I can provide you with the legal definition if you need it."

She bit her mental tongue the instant the last sentence escaped her. Her tone had been, even to her own ear, what her mother had always called "snippy," and what her husband, Jason, called "insufferably bitchy." The fact that Vangelis was playing word games with her was no excuse for anything that might legitimately put up his back. And lecturing him on arcane legal terminology in which his own attorney general would have schooled him exhaustively before

216

the language of the referendum was ever drafted was a wonderful way to do that.

"I'm familiar with the term, thank you," Vangelis replied with false amiability. "As I understand it, however, it applies—in the established jurisprudence of the League—to statutes and regulations which have gone unenforced for a sufficiently long period for a new 'customary usage' to evolve—one clearly contrary to the original intent and purpose—which presents a bit of a problem for your argument."

He smiled back at her, showing just an edge of incisor.

"First, a clause of the Constitution is neither a statute nor a regulation; it's part of the fundamental law of the League, upon which all of those other statutes and regulations rest, and the Founders specifically stated in the preamble that it is alterable *only* by constitutional amendment.

"Second, Article Thirty-Nine's never gone 'unenforced' because up until the current...unpleasantness, no one ever felt compelled to resort to it."

His smile turned even thinner. If she'd been male, Yang-O'Grady could have shaved with it.

"And, finally, what the League is confronting today is, I'm afraid, the very reason Article Thirty-Nine was incorporated into the Constitution. And I also seem to recall that a majority—almost two thirds, including the Sol System, in fact—of the League's original member systems refused to ratify the Constitution *without* Article Thirty-Nine. While I understand Interior's position on this matter, Attorney General Boyagis and Chief Justice Varkas have concluded that, given the established history and current circumstances I've just described, 'desuetude' does not—and *cannot*—be legally applied to Article Thirty-Nine. And as the Hypatia System's chief magistrate, I have no option but to enforce the laws of this star system as interpreted by the judiciary *unless* those laws contravene the Federal Constitution or an overriding federal *statute*— not a regulation, and not a legal theory which hasn't been sustained by the League Judiciary."

"Mister President, the Judiciary is considering this very issue on an expedited basis. Until the Court's had time to rule, however, the Federal Government—and, in particular, the Interior Ministry—strongly dispute the interpretation of Article Thirty-Nine which you've just cited. And, as is the long-standing legal tradition of the League when constitutional ambiguity impacts on government policy, Interior Minister da Orta e Diadoro has sought and received an injunction against the exercise of Article Thirty-Nine until such time as the Court issues a definitive opinion in this matter."

She delivered her statement in the measured tone she'd rehearsed many times on the voyage from the Genovese System to Hypatia. She'd debated against inserting Jacinta da Orta e Diadoro's name into the conversation, despite her instructions from her superiors. Those instructions had been firm on that point, however. Vangelis knew as well as she did that da Orta e Diadoro had no more real authority than any of the League's other official cabinet ministers, but Innokentiy Kolokoltsov and his senior advisers had determined that every legal fiction must be scrupulously adhered to in this case. No doubt that reflected the Manties'—and the Beowulfers', damn them!—fiery denunciations of the "corrupt, kleptocratic bureaucracy" which had "usurped all legitimate authority" in the League.

From the flicker in Vangelis's expression, citing the Interior Ministry's figurehead had not strengthened her argument.

"Again, with all due respect, Ms. Yang-O'Grady," the System President said after a moment, "Article Thirty-Nine, by its nature, is exempt from any injunction. If that had not been the intention of the Framers, then the article would have become a dead letter, since any corrupt administration"—his eyes went very hard with the last two words—"could have prevented its ever being executed simply by seeking one spurious injunction after another from an equally corrupt and compliant Judiciary. Or seeking only a single injunction while the Judiciary 'takes the matter under advisement'... and keeps it there until a time more convenient for the administration in question."

"Are you implying that that's what's happened here, Mister President?" Yang-O'Grady inquired sharply.

"By no means, Ms. Yang-O'Grady. I'm simply suggesting that that *could* have happened, and that the Framers provided Article Thirty-Nine precisely against circumstances in which it might. The exact nature of the concerns which impelled their decision aren't really germane to the exercise of their clearly stated intent, however."

Yang-O'Grady's teeth pressed firmly together and she forced herself to pause, berating herself for rising to his bait in an exchange that was clearly being recorded by both parties.

I wish to hell they'd sent Jason or someone else from Interior to deal with this, she thought.

Jason Yang-O'Grady was a senior member of Nathan MacArtney's ministry, a Regional Commissioner in the Office of Frontier Security, and she knew why sending someone like him had been a total nonstarter. Despite the fact that Interior had to take point in this situation, no one remotely connected with OFS could possibly be sent out as the government's spokeswoman to a full member system of the League. That would have been true anywhere, but after the hacked conversation between

Abruzzi and MacArtney, the logic had become even more pointed in Hypatia. Under the circumstances, *anyone* attached to Interior in any way would be tarred with the Frontier Security brush by the lunatic hotheads like Vangelis who were ripping the League apart. That was the entire reason this radioactive potato had landed in Foreign Affairs' lap, despite all the potentially thorny aspects of sending an envoy from the ministry whose normal charge was dealing with the League's *foreign* affairs, not internal issues.

She understood that. Understanding, however, wasn't the same thing as liking it.

She kept her own expression serious and judicious, stepping down hard on the fury boiling up within her, and part of her wondered how much of that fury stemmed from the fact that she'd known from the outset how unlikely she was to succeed. Failing in a mission like this at a time like this was unlikely to be a career-enhancing accomplishment. That would have been more than enough to frustrate and anger any career Solarian bureaucrat for purely personal reasons. Watching the Solarian League swirl around the drain only made it infinitely worse.

You smiling, arrogant *bastard,* she thought at Vangelis. *Who the hell are you to be telling the* Solarian League *what it can and can't do? And what possible justification can you come up with for* splitting *it in the face of the first really serious threat it's faced in almost a thousand T-years?*

While she fully understood OFS's mission and supported its objectives, Madhura Yang-O'Grady was more than smart enough to realize that the policies which *supported* those objectives had provided any number of completely rational—and justifiable, damn it—reasons for any Fringe System to prefer association with the Manties and their "Grand Alliance." She didn't like it, and she hated and loathed the uppity Star Empire for creating a situation in which the Solarian government literally could not continue to function in the fashion which had evolved over the last half-millennium. No doubt it was at least partly the bureaucracies' own fault for having become so dependent on the cash flow from the Protectorates, but that couldn't absolve the Manties. They must have known—they damned well *had* known—how attacking OFS's ascendancy in the Protectorates would destabilize the entire Solarian League, the largest star nation in the history of humankind.

And now she had to deal with *this.* With the treachery of a full member system, a Core System which couldn't possibly claim *its* rights or interests had been stepped on by Frontier Security or any other arm of the Federal Government. She could understand, even accept, that a Fringer might legitimately hate and despise the distant overlords who controlled his star system; she could neither understand nor accept the disloyalty of a system like Hypatia which, along with all the rest of the League, had profited from OFS's thankless labors for so long.

"Mister President," she said finally, "you've made your position abundantly clear. Now, unfortunately, I need to make mine—the Ministry of the Interior's and that of the Federal Government as a whole—equally clear. The government's first choice, obviously, would be for you and your star system to renounce the secession referendum—the almost certainly *illegal* referendum, when the Judiciary finally rules—and void the vote. Failing that, the government's *second* choice would be for your government to voluntarily place the execution of the referendum on hold—as the injunction already granted against it requires—until the status of Article Thirty-Nine is fully determined by the courts. Since you refuse, for reasons I'm sure seem good from your perspective, to agree to either of those reasonable requests, I have no choice but to proceed to the government's third and least desired option."

She paused to look him square in the eye, then continued.

"No doubt you've observed the number of warships which have accompanied me to Hypatia, Mister President. These ships have been assigned to something called Operation Buccaneer, a commerce-raiding strategy directed against the Manticorans, their allies, and any star system complicit in lending the 'Grand Alliance' military, economic, or political support in their aggression against the Solarian League. Admiral Hajdu's original destination was the Exapia System. He was diverted from Exapia to provide a suitable escort for my own mission. It gives me no pleasure to point this out, but if Hypatia follows through on its threat to secede from the Solarian League, and—even more—on the referendum's express intention to seek political union with Beowulf, should Beowulf also secede and join its Manticoran friends in armed hostilities against the League—your star system will have placed itself in the category against which Buccaneer is directed."

She paused again.

"Believe me, Mister President," she said then, very softly, "Hypatia does *not* want to find itself in that category."

◇   ◇   ◇

"Do you think he really intends to poll his Cabinet about asking for a reconsideration?" Hajdu Győző asked as the stewards finished serving and withdrew. He and Madhura Yang-O'Grady sat in Hajdu's favorite spot in any *Nevada*-class battlecruiser. Theoretically, the armorplast dome over their heads represented a chink in *Camperdown*'s armor, but that was true only in the narrowest, most technical sense. The spacious compartment—listed on the ship schematic as "Flag Officer's Dining Cabin"—was located on the centerline of the big ship's dorsal surface. In combat, it was completely protected by the *Camperdown*'s impeller wedge. Or, if it *wasn't* protected by the wedge, the ship was already in so much trouble that lack of armor would be the least of her concerns.

The compartment was much too big for only two people. Had the larger tables been set up, it could easily have seated fifty, which meant a table for two seemed lost and tiny in its vastness, but Hajdu loved the view, and he'd discovered Yang-O'Grady shared his tastes in that respect. And while the limitless starscape would normally have made the compartment seem even vaster, that wasn't the case tonight. *Camperdown* was inverted, relative to the planet, and that gave Hajdu and his guest a magnificent view of Hypatia's white-and-blue-swirled sphere as it floated against the stars.

The view of Hypatia's low-orbit infrastructure was equally spectacular. Especially when he thought about what might happen to that infrastructure so shortly.

"I don't know," Yang-O'Grady sighed. "I think he probably took it to them but the real question is whether or not he'll abide by the result if they vote in favor of putting the referendum on hold."

She picked at the delicious *Fatányéros* on the traditional wooden platter in front of her. The grilled meats were surrounded by a frame of garlic mashed potatoes, rather than garnished with the traditional fried potato slices, and it smelled delicious. Unfortunately, she was in no fit mood to do justice to the admiral's chef, and she laid her fork aside and reached for her wineglass.

"And do you think he will?"

"Honestly?" Her eyes were dark as she gazed at the beautiful blue planet "above" them, and she shook her head. "No. I don't think he's going to give a centimeter. He pretended to be neutral during the secession campaign because that was what was legally required of him, but everyone knows he was one of the referendum's strongest supporters in private. I'm inclined to think he doesn't really believe Buccaneer might apply to *his* star system, and in a lot of ways, I wish he was right. But he's not, and in a lot of other ways, I'm perfectly all right with that if that's the way these people want it." Her lips tightened. "When you're fighting for your life and someone's announced she's going to help the people trying to strangle you, she doesn't have any kick coming when you break her arm before she can."

"I see your point," Hajdu murmured, and reached for his own wineglass. "So why do you think he took it to his Cabinet, then?"

"If he actually took it to his Cabinet at all—and I'm not sure he did; or, for that matter, that there'd be any *reason* for him to take it to them, since it seems pretty damned clear they all agreed with the referendum's outcome—then it's only to buy time."

"Time for what?"

"Time for the dispatch boat he sent off to Beowulf the instant we appeared to come back with an 'Alliance' fleet," Yang-O'Grady said flatly. "I told him Buccaneer specifies a seventy-two-hour grace period to evacuate system infrastructure. The only thing he could possibly be hoping for is to stall me—us—until the Manties arrive or he knows they're *going* to arrive in less than seventy-two hours."

"Actually, Buccaneer doesn't mandate any specific 'grace period,'" Hajdu observed, looking across the table at her, and she nodded.

"I understand that. For that matter, I was listening when Commodore Brigman briefed me on Parthian Shot. But these people are so damn sanctimonious, so full of the legalisms they think protect them from the consequences of their own actions, that if I hadn't told him your orders dictate a specific timeframe, they'd figure they could spin it out indefinitely by telling us they 'haven't yet had sufficient time' to complete the evacuation." She shrugged. "I had to give them a definite time window if I wanted to...focus their thinking properly."

"I see."

Hajdu considered what she'd just said and decided she was probably right. She was *definitely* right about the Hypatians' desire to defer and delay Buccaneer as long as possible, and it was hard to blame them for that.

No, he told himself after a moment, *actually, it's very easy to blame them for putting themselves in a position where they* need *to defer and delay anything. It's their own damned fault, and any pressure she can bring to bear to get them to swallow their pride—and stupidity—and crawl back off the ledge is all to the good. Besides, a seventy-two-hour window won't change things much from my perspective. It's the next best thing to hundred and thirty hours one-way to Beowulf. If they sent a dispatch boat off the instant we arrived, we could wait six more T-days and still give them their frigging seventy-two hours and be gone by the time anyone got here from Beowulf.*

And if it happened that somebody turned up sooner than that, he had an ops plan to deal with that, too.

He considered that thoughtfully for several seconds, then sipped wine and set his glass back down.

"I believe it was Gustav Anderman who observed that when a man knows he's going to be hanged in a week, it tends to concentrate his thinking."

"Was it Anderman?" Yang-O'Grady tilted her head, eyebrows furrowed. "I always thought it was Thomas Svartkopff." She considered it for a moment, then shrugged. "Well, whichever one of them said it, it's certainly true, and if there was ever anyone who needs to do a little concentrated thinking, it's those idiots down on Hypatia." Her smile was cold. "I'd have preferred to accomplish my mission without you having to accomplish *yours*, Admiral. If they decline to give us that option, though, I'm sure you and your people will be able to amply demonstrate why they shouldn't have."

"Indeed," Hajdu Győző murmured.

Gregatsoulis Park
City of Vivliothḗkē
Hypatia System

"MOM?"

Ingrid Latimer twitched as the plaintive sixteen-year-old voice summoned her back from her inner thoughts.

"Sorry, Peter." She managed a quick smile for her son, although he was old enough—and smart enough—for her to be pretty sure he'd noticed a certain artificiality to it. "What can I do for you?"

"I told you Alethea and Alexia've asked me if we can go to their soccer game Friday first-half. You said you'd let me know."

"Yes, I did, didn't I?"

She gave him another smile, then looked down the length of the picnic table, across the hot dog buns, the potato salad, the chips and hummus, at her husband. Carl Latimer looked back with no expression at all, and she fought back an urge to scream at him. Why couldn't he—he, of everyone in her entire universe—understand what was tearing her apart inside?

No, that's not the real reason you're so angry with him, she told herself bleakly. *The reason you're so pissed is that he* understands *you just fine. He just doesn't* agree *with you.*

Even when she was most furious with him, she knew Carl would never try to dictate to her conscience. Nor would he deny her right to act in whatever way that conscience demanded. But he'd been on Hypatia too long. That was the only explanation she could think of. He'd been here too long, become too accustomed to a Hypatia-eye perspective on the galaxy. He wasn't a Hypatian citizen, but he'd been a Hypatian *resident* long enough to recognize the justice of the referendum's position.

Well, Ingrid recognized its justice, too; it was its *legality* she questioned. That and what she knew were going to be the nightmare consequences for Hypatia if her friends and neighbors pursued this madness to its ultimate conclusion. She remembered a conversation with Larry Kourniakis, one from years ago, when they'd talked about the need—the moral responsibility—to take a stand. About the fact that sometimes men and women simply had to stand up for what they knew was right, regardless of the consequences, or concede the fight to the forces of barbarism.

But those were the forces of barbarism, *not the* Solarian League, *damn it!* a voice wailed deep down inside her. *And if Larry, and Angie, and all their friends carry through with this, the League is going to* hammer *this star system. It won't have any* choice, *not with the Manties already at its throat. Can't they* understand *that?*

Apparently, they couldn't. Or, even worse, they understood perfectly... and they were stubborn enough they were going to do it anyway.

"Friday first-half?" she repeated looking at Peter.

"That's what I said," he replied impatiently.

"Well, I don't see why not," she said. "Assuming nothing comes up between then and now, of course."

"Thanks, Mom!" Peter smiled so broadly that Ingrid wondered which of the Kourniakis twins—or which of their friends—had finally caught his eye.

The thought brought a little welcome and much-needed lightness to her day, but then she looked up at the cloudless afternoon sky, and any lightness disappeared.

Something, she suspected, was definitely going to "come up" between now and Friday first-half. That was the main reason she'd insisted on moving their scheduled picnic up. She'd wanted to get it in, put at least one last positive memory into the bank, before "something" came up. No one knew exactly what Madhura Yang-O'Grady had said to System President Vangelis, but the news that there was a deadline had leaked, and the existence of a deadline implied a threat of consequences if it wasn't met. Worse, if the leaks were accurate, that deadline fell on Thursday.

Major Latimer was a Gendarme, not a naval officer, and she didn't know exactly how much firepower had accompanied Yang-O'Grady to Hypatia. There was probably quite a lot of it, but she didn't know *how much*, and that was what was truly torturing her. The thing she hadn't so much as breathed to Carl. Because if she didn't know that, she *did* know something else.

"How about a little more potato salad?" she asked her husband with a smile.

SLNS *Camperdown*
Hypatia Planetary Orbit
Hypatia System

"HOW WOULD YOU ASSESS the reliability of this intelligence, Captain Adenauer?" Madhura Yang-O'Grady asked. She sat back in her chair, rubbing her eyes—it was the middle of *Camperdown*'s shipboard night, and she'd been in bed for less than an hour before she was dragged back out of it. "Obviously, we have to take it seriously, but do you believe it's reliable or simply a product of the rumor mill?"

"Ma'am, that's a question I can't answer," Hajdu Győző's intelligence officer replied. "It comes from a Gendarme who, according to the system datafiles they sent out with us, is both apolitical and a career investigator. On the face of it, that would incline me to believe she wouldn't be reporting rumors unless she thought there was a lot of truth in them, and that she's trained to recognize when there is. From the perspective of whether or not she's telling us what she really thinks, I don't think there's much question about her reliability. I might add that she was obviously stressed and unhappy in the data packet she encrypted and fired out to us. This is a woman who didn't like what she was doing but did it anyway, because that was her duty."

"So you think it *is* reliable?"

"Ma'am, the distinction I'm trying to make is between *truthful* and *accurate*, and the two aren't always the same. She's definitely not lying to us. The question is whether or not what she thinks she knows is accurate, and that's what I can't assess."

"We understand the line you're drawing, Denton," Hajdu said. "On the other hand, you have to have some sort of feel for whether or not it's *likely* to be accurate."

"Yes, Sir." Adenauer recognized Hajdu's fish-or-cut-bait tone. He didn't *like* it, but he did recognize it, and he inhaled deeply.

"First," he began, "it would make a lot of sense. If the Hypatians are going to secede from the League and ask for political union with Beowulf, it would be logical for them to take the next step and request a protective naval presence here in Hypatia. The system authorities would have to be careful about how they handled that, at least until the referendum vote was tabulated, because direct contact with the Manties or the 'Grand Alliance' would be treason, now that the Manties have declared war on us. Contact simply with *Beowulf* might not be construed that way by the Federal Government. Direct military talks with Manticore certainly would be, and the last thing they'd want would be to have the local Gendarmes arresting their System President, his cabinet, or members of the Yerousía—I mean their Senate—for treason on the eve of the referendum.

"So, from that perspective, an invitation to the Manties to send a substantial naval force *after* the referendum vote's been certified would be a logical step. In fact, our operational planning assumed that was exactly what they *would* do.

"That brings me to my second point, though." He looked around the briefing room table at faces showing different degrees of fatigue and hands clutching steaming mugs of coffee. "If they've been planning on inviting them in only after the referendum's been certified, which is what we'd assumed based on our prior intelligence on Hypatia, then the invitation couldn't have been sent more than about six hours before we made our alpha translation. So, in that case, we reasonably shouldn't expect to see any Manties for at least another five T-days.

"For them to arrive sooner than that—which is what Major Latimer says her source in the Hypatian Customs Service let drop—they would've had to have been invited before the referendum vote was taken. Now, if I were the Manties and an entire League member system told me it wanted to leave the League and switch over to my side—which, let's face it, is exactly what any union with Beowulf would mean, in the long run—then I'd damned well get my arse in gear and get my naval forces here in a hurry. I'm thinking that means they should already be here, *if* they were invited before polling began on the referendum. And we haven't heard a word about that."

"If Manty stealth systems are even half as good as the more pessimistic estimates suggest, finding them if they wanted to hide would be damned near impossible," Commodore Koopman pointed out. Hajdu looked at his ops officer, and she shrugged. "Sir, a star system's an awful deep pool for a single minnow. Shut down your impellers, go to emission-control, and maybe run your stealth field up to twenty or thirty percent, and somebody'd have to literally stumble across you to find you. We've got recon drones deployed to watch the entire hyper perimeter, so I'm pretty damn sure nobody's going to sneak in past us. I can't guarantee there's not *already* somebody in-system, though."

"Daphne has a point, Sir," Brigman said, and Hajdu nodded. Not only did she have a point, but she had the intellectual courage to admit that Manty technology might actually be as good as it was reputed to be.

"Yes, Sir, she does," Adenauer conceded, nodding respectfully across the table at the ops officer. "But when I said we 'haven't heard a word' about them, that's exactly what I meant. We've been monitoring their news channels ever since we got here, and I pulled up the 'faxes and the board archives for the last solid T-month. I'm pretty sure we got clean copies, without any editing from the locals, and I plugged in a data search after Major Latimer's message came in. There *are* some references to senators and—rumors and 'unidentified sources,' only, for this one—at least one Cabinet Secretary *suggesting* the Manties or Beowulf might be called upon for naval support. In response to every single newsie question about that, though, Vangelis's responded by reiterating his promise that 'there will be no foreign warships in Hypatia orbit' until *after* the referendum. It's possible he was lying when he said that, but that doesn't match his record. And there's been exactly zero reference to any 'foreign warships' actually arriving. Having a squadron or two of wallers drop in on your star system's the kind of thing it's not real easy to hide, Sir."

"Not easy, but not impossible, either," Hajdu replied. It was clear he wasn't rejecting the intelligence officer's analysis. He was simply expanding upon it, and Adenauer nodded again.

"No, not impossible, Sir."

"But it's your sense that if the Manties haven't arrived yet, they may not be delayed much longer?" Yang-O'Grady pressed, and there was something different about her tone. A harder, sharper edge, Hajdu thought. Something...hotter.

"If Major Latimer's correct about the locals' intentions—and I'm pretty sure she is—I can't rule that out, Ma'am." Adenauer shrugged. "The exact timing is another unanswerable question, though. If they asked for help as soon as Latimer's suggesting they might have, it could've been here already. *Should've* been here, really. So, assuming she's right about that, they could come over the hyper wall from Beowulf in the next fifteen minutes. Assuming they waited until after the vote was taken, as Vangelis's promises suggest they did, we've got five T-days, until sometime Thursday 'first-half.' That's absolutely the best assessment I can give you, Ms. Yang-O'Grady, Admiral." He shook his head, his expression taut. "With all possible respect, and no intention of being humorous at all, this is one time I'm just as happy someone farther up the chain of command than me has to make the call."

"Thank you for not waffling." Yang-O'Grady managed a tight smile. "And, by the way, I've sat in on enough intelligence briefings to know the difference between waffling to cover your arse and making a clear distinction between what you know and what you can only speculate upon."

Adenauer inclined his head at the compliment, and Yang-O'Grady sat silently for almost a full minute, gazing at the blank display in front of her. Then her nostrils flared, and she raised her eyes to Hajdu.

"Admiral," she said in formal, measured tones, "on the basis of this intelligence, I am certifying that the diplomatic aspect of our mission to Hypatia has failed. I think it's obvious we now know why Vangelis is playing for time. I think it's also obvious from what Captain Adenauer's just so capably laid out for us, that we don't know how much time we have. I am therefore authorizing you to proceed with Buccaneer."

"Yes, Ma'am," Hajdu replied. "May I ask if you have any suggestions about the timing of my actions?"

Her green eyes flickered just a bit when he asked for "suggestions" rather than "directives," but he met her gaze steadily. From the instant she'd authorized him to proceed, he was the one in command and she was the one who'd just become an advisor.

"No, Admiral," she replied. "None at all. Except," she added, and he suddenly realized he'd misunderstood why those eyes had seemed to flicker, for her voice was suddenly much harder and harsher than it had been, "that the sooner you teach these people what happens to traitors, the better."

HMS *Phantom*
Alexandria Belt
Hypatia System

"I DO HATE SURPRISES," Rear Admiral Kotouč said, gazing around the faces in the windows in his day cabin's smart wall.

"I think we all do, Sir," Captain Ellis Rupp, commanding the *Saganami-B*-class heavy cruiser HMS *Cinqueda* agreed. Rupp was Kotouč's senior ship commander, followed by Květa Tonová, *Phantom*'s captain, then Captain Jackson Ortega-Burns of HMS *Shikomizue* and Captain Ching-yan Lewis of HMS *Talwar*. Commander Megan Petersen, commanding the *Roland*-class destroyer *Arngrim*, was his junior CO, and he thought she looked surprisingly calm, given her youth and the circumstances.

"I think we all do," Rupp repeated, "but Jayson and I—" he twitched his head at Commander Jayson Stob, his executive officer, sitting beside him "—have been trying to figure out what kind of bee this Hajdu's gotten up his ass to do something like this. It *can't* be because he figured out we're here, or he'd be moving a lot faster even then this."

"An excellent point," Kotouč said and glanced at Lieutenant Commander Vyhnálek. "Any thoughts on that, Štěpán?"

"Aside from the fact that I wish whatever the hell it was had left him alone, Sir?" TG 110.2's intelligence officer shook his head. "I'm guessing—and it's only a guess—that somebody in-system finally got around to telling them the Hypatians had asked for a naval presence. Maybe somebody's been counting on his fingers and toes and realized that since we obviously aren't here yet, we may be getting here Sometime Real Soon Now, as they say on Grayson."

"Until the smoke clears, that's probably the best almost-answer we're going to get, Sir," Captain Clarke said, running the fingers of his right hand through his sandy hair.

And what makes you think that when "the smoke clears" we'll be around to find any *answers, Jim?* Kotouč wondered.

But that wasn't something he could say out loud.

"In the meantime, we have some decisions to make," he said out

230

loud, although everyone in his audience knew "we" didn't have to decide a damned thing. *He* did.

He leaned back in his chair, and as he did, his mind ran back to another time and place—to Saganami Island, almost exactly two T-years earlier. He'd been there to celebrate his nephew Ondře's snotty cruise at the traditional pre-deployment family dinner. But he'd gotten there a day early, and because he had, and because Vice Admiral Alb's brother John was one of his close friends, the baroness had invited him to attend Ondře's Last View.

And John had invited him to the family memorial after he became *Baron* of Alb when his big sister died in the Battle of Manticore, as well. That was an unpleasant reflection at the moment.

It had been thirty T-years since his own Last View, on the eve of his own snotty cruise, but he hadn't forgotten what it was like. Hadn't forgotten the chill down his spine, the ball of ice in his belly as he thought about what he was seeing, ingested what might be expected of *him* someday. But Ondře's Last View had been different. It had been different because the youngsters about to depart on the training and evaluation cruise which completed their Academy education were sailing not in time of peace, as he had, but straight into a renewed war with the Republic of Haven. And different because Baroness Alb had invited a very special guest speaker. Someone who'd known the full, grim reality of what the Last View merely promised the graduating middies *might* come to them. Who'd met that challenge not once, but repeatedly. Someone who was already spoken of as Edward Saganami's spiritual heir.

Lady Dame Honor Alexander-Harrington, the Salamander herself, had stood in that huge, darkened lecture hall, the treecat who'd shared and endured so much with her on her shoulder, and her soprano voice had rung out across the endless rows of midshipmen as she told them what they were about to see. And he remembered the lump in his throat, the bright, unshed—and unashamed—tears in his eyes, as the image of that very first Parliamentary Medal of Valor floated before him and that soprano sword of a voice had come out of the darkness, repeated the words, the oath—the *vow*—to which every graduating class for four hundred and ten T-years had dedicated itself.

"Ladies and gentlemen," the Salamander had said, *"the tradition lives!"*

And so, in the end, he already knew what his decision had to be, didn't he?

Proedriké Katoikía
Hypatia System

"AND I'M TELLING YOU, Admiral, that we can't possibly evacuate our entire orbital infrastructure in thirty-six hours!" Adam Vangelis snapped. "I'm not trying to *stall* you, damn it—it's physically impossible!"

"That's regrettable, Mister President," Hajdu Győző said from the com display above the conference table, his voice like interstellar space. "I advise you to evacuate as many people as possible, however, because I *will* execute my orders at the time I've given you."

"You'd be killing hundreds of thousands—*millions*—of innocent civilians!"

"On the contrary, Mister President. I may be the one giving the order; *you*—and your government—are the ones who have forced my hand. I'm simply obeying the orders of my legally constituted chain of command. You and your star system are the people who committed treason against the Solarian League, leaving me no option but to execute my contingency orders in the time window available to me."

"That's an utterly meaningless and specious attempt to evade the blood guilt for anyone who dies in this star system thirty-six hours from now." Vangelis's voice had turned even colder than Hajdu's. "Believe me in this, Admiral. This war—the war your 'legally constituted chain of command' began with an unprovoked attack on a sovereign star nation in time of peace—will end one day, and unless you're a lot stupider than I think you are, you know as well as I do that the Star Empire of Manticore and the Republic of Haven are way too big a mouthful for your navy to chew. So, when the inevitable day comes that a peace treaty is signed between the Solarian League and the Grand Alliance, be certain that your name, and the demand that you be extradited to an Allied court to face trial for premeditated mass murder, *will* be part of those terms. Even if, by some unimaginable turn of luck, the current clique running the League should survive in office, don't think they'll hesitate for one single instant before throwing you under the air lorry to save their own contemptible arses."

"My statement is neither meaningless nor specious, Mister President,
232

and I've already told you where the 'blood guilt' resides in this instance. As for the conclusion of hostilities," the admiral permitted himself a snort of contempt, "I'll take my chances on your neobarb friends' ability to force the Solarian League to do anything it chooses not to do. For the present, however, further discussion is pointless. I will be back in contact in twenty-four hours. I advise you to expedite your efforts in order to save as many lives as possible from the consequences of your star system's actions. Hajdu, clear."

The display went dark, and Vangelis turned to the men and women seated around the table in the Proedrikḗ Katoikía's Situation Room. His gaze circled the table, his eyes fiery, but his desperation was as obvious as his fury.

"My God, Adam." Kyrene Morris, the System Vice President, was white-faced, her eyes shocked. "My God, he's really going to . . . to *murder* all those people?"

"That's what he says, and I doubt he would've said it for the official record if he didn't mean it," Vangelis replied harshly.

"What if we were to renounce the referendum result?" Frederica Saraphis, the Senate Majority Leader sounded a bit hesitant. She raised her right hand, palm uppermost. "I know we don't have the legal authority to set it *aside*, but we could certainly delay—even suspend—its execution, under the circumstances!"

As the chairwoman of the Liberal Centrists, with a thirty-seat majority, Saraphis had shepherded the referendum—formally sponsored by the LibCents and all but one of the other major Hypatian political parties—through the Senate. She'd been one of its staunchest supporters, and her expression showed how little she liked making that suggestion.

"We can't, Freddie," Makiko Allerton said, her voice flat and hard. She sat beside Saraphis. Her Independent Democrats had been the only major party to oppose secession, and she'd fought her old friends Saraphis and Vangelis tooth and nail the entire way. But now she shook her head, her violet eyes dark and bitter.

"You're right that we can't set the referendum aside," she continued after a moment. "Even suspending its implementation would get us into all sorts of questionable waters, legally speaking."

Allerton glanced at Attorney General Boyagis, who jerked his head in a single, curt nod, then looked back at Saraphis, and now her expression held an edge of what could almost have been compassion.

"Completely aside from the legal aspects, though, there are the moral ones," she said. "I opposed secession. I thought that was the right decision. But I lost, and I happen to believe in the legal and political systems of Hypatia. I lost," she repeated, ". . . and if this man—this *monster*—is going to come into my star system and murder hundreds of thousands of my fellow citizens, of my *people*, and tell me his actions have been *approved* by the Solarian League, then thank God I did."

She looked around the table again, her eyes like iron.

"I don't know about this 'Mesan Alignment' the Manticorans and the Havenites are talking about. I don't know about an awful lot of things, but I just discovered how horribly wrong I've been about one thing I thought I *did* know. I thought I knew the Solarian League was worth saving."

"I'm sorry, Makiko," Vangelis said softly. "I know how much saying that had to hurt."

"So do I," Saraphis said, reaching across to squeeze Allerton's hand. "And I agree that Hajdu proves the Mandarins are even more corrupt than we'd thought they were. But think of all the lives we're talking about! I'm willing to risk the legal consequences of anything that would save that many people, so if suspending the referendum's execution—even indefinitely—will stop him, I say we have no choice but to do just that."

"Won't work, Freddie." Vangelis sighed. She looked at him, and he shrugged. "I already suggested that to Hajdu." Some of the others looked shocked, but he only shrugged again, harder. "Of course I did! Frederica's right. My first responsibility, as a human being and not just to my oath of office, is to save as many lives as I can. The only way I could save anybody today would be to convince Hajdu not to pull the trigger, and I am by God prepared to do anything that might possibly accomplish that! His response was that it's too late for that."

"Too late?" Saraphis stared at him. "*Too late* to save all those lives? *That's* what he said?"

"In almost exactly those words," Vangelis told her. "The conversation was recorded, if you want to view it yourself, but the short version is that by expressing our intent to leave the League and—especially—by even suggesting the possibility of some sort of political union with Beowulf, we've demonstrated our fundamental treachery and willingness to trample all over his version of the Constitution. As such, he's not prepared to delay the execution of his orders even if we promised we'd *never* secede, regardless of the referendum vote. After all, how could he possibly take the word of a bunch as traitorous as we've proved ourselves? No doubt we'd simply change our minds back again as soon as he left the system. Because of that, he has no choice but to carry out 'Operation Buccaneer' *before* he leaves."

Saraphis sat back in her chair, her face ashen, and this time it was Allerton squeezing *her* hand comfortingly.

"But why is he so insistent on his time limit?" Mildred Roanoke, the Secretary of Industry asked. "If he'd give us just an additional forty hours—even *thirty* hours—we could get almost everybody out, even from the Belter habitats!"

"Somebody must've told the cowardly bastard we're expecting Allied warships, Ma'am," Commodore Franklin Nisyrios, the senior uniformed officer of the Hypatia System Patrol grated. The red-haired commodore's gray eyes blazed and his lip twisted in contempt. "He may talk a good fight about how he thinks this war is going to end, but even if he believes that crap, he's a long way from any peace treaty that might save his sorry arse. And right now, he knows damned well what a squadron or so of Allied wallers would do to his task force. So he's shitting his skinsuit—pardon my language—to get the hell out of here before those wallers turn up!"

"I think Frank's right," Vangelis said. "I think someone must've told him—or given him enough information that he could extrapolate for himself—when we originally expected Admiral Kotouč to arrive. So he's going to execute his orders and run for it before then. Obviously he doesn't know the *exact* time we expected Kotouč, or he'd probably have given us the extra time we need. But that's got to be what's driving him right now."

"Speaking of Admiral Kotouč—" Bernard Yale, the Minister of Infrastructure began, but Nisyrios interrupted him.

"Forget it, Mr. Yale," he said. "The Manties are good, and Kotouč's ships are—well, the only way I can put it is that they're *totally* out of the SLN's class. I had time for a virtual tour of *Phantom*, and her capabilities..."

He shook his head, gazing off into his memories, his expression almost awed, then pulled his eyes back to focus on Yale's face again.

"That ship could take any Solarian superdreadnought one-on-one and kick its arse into next week without even working up a sweat," he said simply. "But Kotouč only has *one* of her... and Hajdu has ninety-five battlecruisers. Worse, Kotouč told me he doesn't have any of the missile pods that might help to even the odds. And even if he had them, according to my revenue cutters' sensors, Hajdu's deployed several thousand missile pods of his own."

He shook his head again, this time heavily.

"All Kotouč and his people could do would be to die gallantly, Mr. Yale. I don't doubt they'd do that in a minute... if it could stop Hajdu. But it couldn't. They might be able to hurt him badly first, but not badly enough to stop him from carrying out his orders in the end, and no military commander could justify throwing away his own people's lives when the sacrifice couldn't make any difference in the end."

"So what do we do?" Vice President Morris said after a moment.

"We go on doing what we're already doing," Vangelis replied heavily. "We've got every orbit-capable shuttle, cutter, runabout, and garbage scow in the system moving everyone we possibly can in the time Hajdu's so *graciously* given us. There's already been some panic—you just can't organize an evacuation on this kind of scale without telling people why you're evacuating them—but so far, it's manageable. Commodore Nisyrios's people are providing armed parties for the major habitats' boat bays to prevent—we hope—things from getting too out of hand, and we're beginning with the major residential habitats. We should—*should*, probably—be able to get between eighty and eighty-five percent of the residents down to the planetary surface in thirty-six hours. That's almost a hundred and nine million people."

"And it still leaves eighteen-point-seven million people up there," Morris said.

"And another one-point-two million in the Alexandria Belt," Roanoke said. "My God. We're talking about *twenty million* dead as our *best case* scenario!"

She looked around the conference room's frozen-helium silence, and the clatter of a falling pin would have been deafening.

SLNS _Camperdown_
Hypatia System

"DO YOU THINK THE Admiral will really keep to his timetable?" Captain Adenauer asked very quietly as he and Commodore Koopman worked to update his best estimate of the number of Hypatians who'd been evacuated to the planetary surface so far.

"What do _you_ think?" Koopman replied after a moment.

The sable-haired operations officer's eyes were a very dark brown under normal circumstances. Now they could have frozen oxygen as she considered him, and the intelligence officer reminded himself that Daphne Koopman was not a good person to get sideways of. She was smart, she was ambitious, she had lots of family connections, she'd made a habit of discovering the locations of as many buried bodies as possible, and rumor said she kept meticulous lists of those who'd helped her career, those who'd _harmed_ her career, and those who'd simply really, really pissed her off.

"I don't know what to think," the captain said after considering his options. "I just know that all of this"—he gestured at the displays full of intelligence data his remotes were pulling him from the system data-net, side-by-side with the results of Koopman's remote sensors—"says these people really are doing their dead level best to get their people evacuated. I mean, so far almost twenty of their System Patrol people have been killed in accidents because they're cutting the margins so fine. I'm just wondering if he's going to take that into consideration."

"Worried about what might splash onto you if the opposition groups back home get hold of the casualty figures?" Koopman didn't—quite—sneer, and Adenauer flushed.

"Maybe I _am_, some," he acknowledged with a defiant jut of his chin. "Mostly, though? Mostly, Commodore, I don't want to be a Solarian officer who's remembered for his part in killing fifteen or twenty million Solarian citizens."

Koopman started to say something sharp, then stopped herself, and what might have been a certain grudging respect showed in her eyes. It took more than a little courage for a member of a Solarian flag officer's staff to voice anything which could be taken as a criticism of the flag officer in question. And that was especially true when Admiral Hajdu had to know that, orders or no orders, billions of people who weren't here and hadn't had to make the decision were going to bitterly criticize whatever he did. He had a reputation as a ruthless survivor of the Solarian League Navy's Byzantine bureaucracies and turf wars, and he knew all about burying inconvenient witnesses. That meant the consequences for any officer he suspected of disloyalty, or whose opinions might help fuel the criticism, were likely to be...significant.

"It's a little late to be developing cold feet, Adenauer," she said, after a moment.

"I didn't say I was developing cold feet. On the other hand, that might be one way to put it," Adenauer admitted. "And it's not exactly like you or I were asked to volunteer when the orders were handed out. For that matter, I know the Hypatians voted to secede, which, I guess, means they *aren't* Solarian citizens anymore. It just...just bothers me, Ma'am."

"Well," Koopman returned her attention to the data on the display between them, "I guess if I'm going to be honest, it bothers me, too, and I'm the one who drew up the ops plan." She shook her head. "But exactly what he plans on doing when the time limit runs out—?"

She shrugged.

Prásino Phúllo Habitat
Hypatia Planetary Orbit
and
Hypatia System Patrol Shuttle *Asteria*
Hypatia System

"COME ON, PETRA!" KASSANDRA Tsoliao tried to keep the impatience—and fear—out of her voice. "We've *got* to go, Honey!"

"But I can't find *Mikhalis*!" five-year-old Petra protested tearfully. "We *can't* go without Mikhalis!"

"He'll be fine, Honey," Kassandra promised her.

She *hated* lying to her daughter. It was one of the things she and Sebastianos *never* did. But today, she didn't hesitate. Nor did she tell Petra that the reason she couldn't find the cat was that Kassandra had locked him in his carrier in the storage closet down the passageway from their apartment.

God, she'd hated doing it—*hated* it! She loved that cat, too, but she'd had no choice. The evacuation orders were harsh, uncompromising, and draconian. No pets—not even a parakeet—on the evacuation boats. No carry-on luggage beyond a single bag small enough to fit into its carrier's lap. No family treasures, no heirlooms, *nothing* that wouldn't fit into that single bag.

But she could never have explained that to Petra, and so she'd rubbed Mikhalis under the chin, kissed him between the ears one last time, and then dashed the tears out of her eyes with both hands as she left him purring comfortably in the familiar confines of his carrier and went back to the daughter she could never have convinced to leave him behind.

Forgive me, Mikey, she thought now. *I'm so sorry. But I know you love Petra, too, and I have to get her out of here.*

"Are you *sure* he'll be all right, Mommy?" Petra pressed, and Kassandra made herself smile.

"Of course I am, Honey. Tell you what, we've really got to run, but why don't you dash out to the kitchen and make sure there's water in his bowl?"

239

"Good idea, Mommy!" Petra beamed and scurried toward the kitchen while her mother covered her eyes with the palms of her hands and tried not to cry.

✧   ✧   ✧

"Prásino Phúllo Control, this is—"

Lieutenant Paulette Kilgore, Hypatia System Patrol, felt her exhausted mind blank completely. She jammed her thumb down on the mute button on her joystick and stared at the display, cursing herself as she realized she hadn't entered the flight number into her onboard computer when she lifted for the current run. Then she shook herself and twisted around to look over her shoulder at her flight engineer—they were so desperately pressed for people that she didn't have a copilot—Sergeant John Debnam.

"God, what number *are* we now, John? Don't tell me *you* didn't write it down either," she begged.

"One-Seven-Niner-Papa-Papa-Echo-Six," Debnam replied without looking up from his own panel.

"Thank you, *thank you!*"

The bearded sergeant only nodded, still without looking up, and Kilgore took her thumb off the mute button.

"Sorry about the com glitch, Prásino Phúllo Control," she said. "Had to deal with something. This is One-Seven-Niner-Papa-Papa-Echo-Six. Requesting approach to Bay Nineteen Bravo."

"One-Seven-Niner, Prásino Phúllo Control," a voice even more exhausted than she felt replied. "Negative Bay Nineteen Bravo. I say again, negative Bay Nineteen Bravo. You are cleared approach Bay Eighteen Bravo. I say again, *Eighteen*—One-Eight—Bravo. Confirm copy."

"Control, One-Seven-Niner confirms diversion to Bay Eighteen—I repeat, One-*Eight*—Bravo."

"That is correct, One-Seven-Niner. The holding beacon is Niner-Niner-Zero-Alpha. You are...seventh in the approach queue."

"Niner-Niner-Zero-Alpha and we are number seven," Kilgore replied.

"Confirm, One-Seven-Niner. Godspeed."

"Thank you, Prásino Phúllo Control." Kilgore started to key off the com, then paused. Stacking shuttles seven deep under the current conditions suggested a major snafu of some sort at a time when no one could afford snafus.

"Control, can I ask why we're being diverted?" she asked.

There was silence for several seconds. Then she heard someone sigh at the other end of the link.

"There was an...incident, One Seven Niner. I don't have the details, but there was some sort of explosion. Took out two shuttles and at least three hundred civilians. We're not getting Nineteen Bravo back today."

This time Sergeant Debnam looked up from his displays, his dark eyes meeting his pilot's blue gaze.

"Thank you, Control," Kilgore said quietly. "And . . . Godspeed to you, too."

"Appreciate it, One Seven Niner. Now get your arse over to Eighteen Bravo."

"On our way. One-Seven-Niner, clear."

Kilgore altered her heading, then leaned back in her couch, looking over her shoulder at Debnam again.

"An explosion," she said. "Don't like the sound of that, John. I don't like it at all."

"Don't much care for it myself, Ma'am."

They looked at one another for a handful of seconds, and then she turned back to her controls, thinking about that voice on the other end of the com. The voice which must have realized from the beginning that it wasn't getting out, whatever happened to the civilians it was trying to save.

Guts, she thought. *God, that takes* guts. *Look after him, Jesus. Look after all of them.*

✧   ✧   ✧

Sebastianos Tsoliao watched the icon alter heading away from the atmosphere-spewing wound in Prásino Phúllo Habitat's skin. He wondered if he'd ever met its pilot. The chances that he had were excellent; he'd worked with the HSP's pilots for a lot of years now. But never like this, and he wondered if the pilot of that shuttle knew how fervently he wished her "Godspeed."

He checked his displays. At least twenty seconds till the next incoming, he thought, maybe as much as a full minute, and he punched the button on his uni-link.

"Yes, Sebastianos!" his wife's beloved contralto said even before he'd heard the first buzz from his end.

"How are you and the baby doing?" he asked, trying to drag a little of the exhaustion out of his voice, trying to infuse a bit of energy. Of hope.

"We're fine." He wondered if she realized her chipper tone sounded as false as his own. "Petra didn't want to leave Mikhalis behind, but I told her he'd be fine until we get back and she checked his water bowl."

"Little pitchers have big ears?" he asked softly.

"Yep."

"Well, can you put me on speaker for just a few seconds? I don't have much time before the next inbound flight."

"You're on . . . now," she said, the sound of her voice shifting as she lowered the wrist unit so that Petra could hear him.

"How you doing, sweetheart?" he asked.

"*Fiiiiiine*, Daddy," she said, and his heart twisted as he heard the anxiety—the little-girl bravery—in her drawn out reply.

"I'm glad to hear it!" he said cheerily. "You're taking good care of Mommy?"

"Of course I am. *I'm* carrying both bags!"

"That's my big girl. I knew I could count on you. You stay close to Mommy, now, hear me? And you go on looking after her until—" his voice wavered ever so slightly, and he yanked it ruthlessly back under control "—until I see you again, all right?"

"Of course I will, Daddy. Are you coming soon?"

"Just as soon as I can, sweetheart. You know Daddy has a job to do. Sometimes it's more important than others, and this is one of those times. So it may be a little while. Just remember how much I love you and Mommy until I get there."

"Yes, Daddy. And do you think you can bring Mikhalis when you come? I know he'll be all right, but he's really kind of a small cat without his people there to look after him."

"I'll keep an eye on him for you," he promised. "Now Mommy and I need to do some grown-up talk for just a second, okay?"

"Okay, Daddy. Love you!"

"Love you, too, baby girl."

"We're off speaker," Kassandra told him a moment later, and he cleared his throat.

"What I wanted to say," he said more briskly, "is that there was some kind of explosion at Nineteen Bravo. I don't know exactly what it was, but it was pretty bad. So you're going to have to use *Eighteen* Bravo, instead. You've got plenty of time! The tube cars are still running. Go up to Deck Seven and take the Number Twelve line. That'll get you there without any problems, and I've already updated the passenger list. They'll be holding places in line for you and Petra."

"I understand."

He heard the fresh flutter of fear behind the two words. She kept her voice light for Petra's sake, but then she asked the question he'd dreaded. The question she *had* to ask, even with Petra listening.

"Will you be leaving through Eighteen Bravo, too?"

"No," he said. "They're pulling us out through Niner Charlie. You know it's a lot closer to Flight Control."

"I guess it is." She sounded a tiny bit less anxious, as if the reminder that Bay 9C truly was much closer to his duty station had reassured her. After all, he could get there in a hurry, especially with the high-speed tube cars reserved for station personnel's emergency use. "How much longer do you think?"

"Not much." He closed his eyes as he lied to the woman he'd loved for twenty-seven years. "Third shift's due to take over pretty soon. When they do, everybody on Second'll get a chance for some rest, and those of us with families will be sent on to join them."

"Thank God," she whispered, and he heard the tears quavering in the words.

"Yeah, I think He's working overtime for me today," Sebastianos said with absolute sincerity. "You just look after the baby for me till I catch up with you."

"We'll be waiting for you."

"I know you will, Honey. But I gotta run now. More shuttles incoming. Love you!"

"Love you, too," she said, and he killed the link.

Then he sat there, looking down at the uni-link. He could count the number of times he'd told her even little white lies on the fingers of one hand. Now he'd lied to her three times in less than ten seconds, because he had at least another ten or fifteen seconds before his scopes needed him again. But he'd had to go, before his voice failed him completely and she realized the truth behind the *other* lies.

He stroked the uni-link, his fingertip just brushing the call button, and drew a deep, shuddery breath.

"Love you, Babe," he whispered. "Look after the Moonbeam for me. I'll be waiting for both of you . . . but not today. Not today."

SLNS *Camperdown*
Hypatia System

"ARE YOU GOING TO adhere to your deadline, Admiral?" Madhura Yang-O'Grady asked, and Hajdu Győző looked up from the message board he'd been studying.

"If they can't get everyone off in time, are you going to adhere to your deadline?" she repeated.

"That depends," he said after a moment. "I meant every word I said to that traitor Vangelis. This is *their* fault, not ours, and I have zero interest in exposing my personnel to risk just to save the lives of a few thousand traitors and their families."

"I'd just as soon not see anyone killed if we don't have to kill them," she said, and he regarded her thoughtfully. That decision was no longer hers, but he supposed he did owe her the courtesy of a fuller explanation.

"As nearly as I can tell," he said, "they're working as hard and as fast as they can to get as many people as possible out of the residential habitats, at least. That tells me that whatever the arrival schedule they're predicting for the naval force they requested, they don't expect it to get here until after my original time limit runs out. I'm sure they'd want to get everyone they could out as early as possible under any circumstances, but the rate at which they're working right now—and, frankly, the number of accidents they've absorbed *because* of the rate at which they're working—tells me they're truly desperate.

"Because that indicates we have some time in hand, I'm more inclined to consider extending the deadline—possibly in five or six-hour increments—for as long as they *stay* desperate. I'm not about to give them more than another twenty-four hours or so, no matter what, given that there's no way to *know* when the Manties are going to arrive, but I'm not especially eager to kill anyone we don't have to, either. The instant it looks to me like they're relaxing a bit, though, I'm going to assume that means they expect help momentarily. And at that point," his voice was grim, "there won't be any extensions."

"But you will extend it at least once?"

Yang-O'Grady's fervor for punishing the traitors seemed to have ebbed a bit, he thought. Probably because she was a civilian. She'd thought all along in terms of the nice, clean destruction of deserted installations. Explosions that might do terrible damage to a star system's economy and standard of living, but wouldn't *kill* anyone. Now it looked as if quite a few "anyones" were about to be killed, and she didn't like it.

I don't like it, either, he thought. *But I knew something like this could be in the cards from the instant I read the precis of Parthian Shot. It didn't take a genius to read between the lines and know what* that *meant... and what's likely to happen to anyone who fails to come through in the crunch. Besides, this is my responsibility. Making the point to Hypatia—and everyone else in the goddamned galaxy—just became* my *job. So I'll do it, and these people had better by* God *believe I will. And so should the next system on the Buccaneer list. In fact, running up the death toll here just might help that "next system" see the error of its ways without having to* kill *anyone there.*

The truth was that every life lost here might well save dozens of lives later. He didn't like thinking in those terms—and recognized the sophistry of any comfort they might give him—but that didn't make them untrue. And what that meant for extended time limits...

"Not necessarily, Ms. Yang-O'Grady," he told her, his tone cold. "I'll make that call when I get there. So I guess we'll just have to see."

Prásino Phúllo Habitat
Hypatia Planetary Orbit
Hypatia System

CORPORAL HELIKE VASDEKIO WAS only twenty-nine T-years old, but she'd joined the Hypatia System Patrol when she was just seventeen, and she'd learned a lot in those twelve years. At 162.6 centimeters, and small-boned, she was no hulking giantess. Her mother had always insisted she was "no bigger than a minute" when she was a little girl, but she was a very muscular and solid "minute" these days. She was also a member of HSP's Alpha Seven, its elite Search and Rescue team, as well as a highly skilled cargo inspector with no less than nine major smuggling busts to her credit. So there was ample reason for her to feel confident and competent to handle any duty that came her way.

But she'd never expected *this* one.

She stood almost in a position of parade rest, with her hands clasped behind her. A pulser nestled in a shoulder holster under her left armpit, a stun baton hung from her belt, and the visor of her skinsuit's helmet was raised as her brown eyes watched the crowd. They were very still, those eyes, with something deep and dark lurking in their depths, yet she was unfailingly courteous. She smiled a lot, too. It wasn't easy, but reassurance was something Alpha Seven's teams learned to project early—people who needed rescuing were generally a little stressed, after all—and the last thing anyone needed was a panic in the evacuation queue.

Next month was her thirtieth birthday, and she wished she'd be there for the party her fiancé had planned. A lot of people weren't going to be where they'd thought they would, though, and there were a lot worse things someone could be doing just now. A *lot* worse ways someone could—

"Look, Mommy! It's Helike!"

Vasdekio's head snapped around. It took her eyes a second or two to pick up the tiny, dark-haired girl child who'd just appeared out of the crowd. Then she went down on one knee and opened her arms wide.

"Petra!"

The girl flung herself into Vasdekio's embrace, and the corporal hugged her back, careful of the way her lightly armored skinsuit could bruise. She looked up over Petra's shoulder at her mother and saw the recognition—the happiness at seeing a familiar face—flicker through Kassandra's expression. Then the relief disappeared, and Vasdekio sighed silently. Of course Kassandra was smart enough to realize why Vasdekio was here...and that she'd undoubtedly still be here, still be trying to save a few more lives, when the timer ran out.

"Kassie," she said, standing and holding out her hand.

"I wish I were happier to see you, Helike." Kassandra Tsoliao's tone, even more than her words, confirmed that she'd guessed the truth.

Vasdekio smiled at her, briefly but with more genuine warmth than most of her other smiles had contained, and flicked an inquiry into her uni-link. Then she nodded.

"You and Petra are on the list, Priority Gamma," she said. "That means you go to the head of the queue for the *next* shuttle, not this one."

She twitched her head sideways at the line of passengers—many of them weeping, one or two on the edge of hysteria...or with the glassy, drugged smiles of someone who'd already been there—creeping down the boarding tube to the shuttle in Bay Eighteen Bravo's Number Three docking buffers. It didn't look as if all of them were going to get on board, but she pointed at a line on the deck to one side.

"Over there," she said. "There are another couple of dozen Gamma Priority people already here. Go ahead and walk on over. We're due to start forming the line in another couple of minutes, anyway; might as well get the two of you close to the head."

"Thank you," Kassandra said softly.

She gave the corporal's hand one last squeeze, then twitched her head at Petra.

"You heard Helike, sweetheart. Let's go get in line."

✧   ✧   ✧

"Man, I don't like this," Alexandros Karaxis said. "Don't like it one bit, Apollo!"

"How about telling me something I don't already know, Xander?" Apollo Dukakis shot back, rolling his eyes in exasperation. At twenty-seven, he was eight T-years older than Karaxis...and *twelve* T-years his senior in Prásino Phúllo Grúpes—the Green Leaf Griffins—one of the more vicious gangs which made some places in Prásino Phúllo Habitat's bowels unsafe to visit.

"Man, they gonna put all these sheep onboard those shuttles and they ain't gonna do *shit* for us. Hell, they probably be just as happy to get rid of us once and for all!"

Despite Alexandros's less than stellar performance on the Hypatia Department of Education's standardized tests, there were moments when he grasped the essence of a situation with commendable clarity, Apollo thought. This was one of them. No doubt burning a house to the ground was an expensive way to get rid of the cockroaches, but if the place was going to burn anyway, you might as well make sure as few roaches as possible made it out. And he had to admit that from the perspective of Hypatia's law-abiding community, the Grúpes would make very nice cockroach briquettes. For that matter, he couldn't even blame them.

That didn't mean he had to go along with their plans in his own, personal case, however, and for his present purposes, Alexandros's size—he stood 195.6 centimeters in his smelly sock feet and had massive, powerful shoulders—offset his sad lack of mental acuity.

"Just be frosty," he said now, softly. "There's not enough time to get into position for this shuttle. But be ready when the sheep start boarding the *next* one. You know what to do, right?"

"Oh, *right!*" Alexandros smiled and slid his hands into his trouser pockets to touch the waiting knuckledusters. He did *so* like hurting people, and this time it would be for a much better cause than usual.

❖   ❖   ❖

The shuttle which had been loading when they arrived departed, and Kassandra watched the next one slide into the buffers and engage the umbilicals. The display lit with the flight number—179-PPE-6 and the name *Asteria*—and the window between its arrival and the previous shuttle's departure was far shorter than standard operating procedure would ever have permitted under normal circumstances. No one was likely to complain today, though, and she watched the light above the boarding tube turn green, signifying a good seal. The exhausted-looking young man in the same Traffic Control uniform Sebastianos wore on formal occasions—the sight of it sent a fresh pang of worry through her—held his uni-link to his ear, listening to it through the not-so-muted crowd-mutter of the packed concourse. Then he nodded.

"Ready to board!" he called. "Have your uni-links ready for the scanner, please! And remember, if you're not scheduled for this flight, you won't be allowed to board, but there are going to be plenty of additional flights!"

Kassandra checked her own uni-link, then gripped Petra firmly by the hand as the exhausted-looking young man stepped aside. He made a beckoning motion with his hand, and they started forward. It was going to—

"*Mommy!*"

She heard Petra scream at the same instant her daughter's hand was snatched out of her own. She turned frantically, then cried out and went to both knees, holding a suddenly bloody face as the hulking tough's knuckledusters smashed her to the deck with a brutal backhanded blow.

"All right!" the other ganger, the one who'd snatched Petra off the deck, shouted. He held the sobbing, terrified girl suspended by the neck of her coverall with one hand while the other closed upon the nape of her slender neck, and his face was hard. "We got no boarding passes," he snarled, "but we ain't staying on this fucking deathtrap, either! So you're letting us on the shuttle. And if you don't, this little girl? She's gonna need a new neck, 'cause I swear to God, I'll break it in a heartbeat."

"You realize," a single voice replied quietly into the sudden, ringing silence his threat had produced, "that if any of that happens the authorities will be waiting for you dirt-side? The instant you step off that shuttle, a dozen SWAT guys will bust your arse like a soft-boiled egg. And they'll enjoy it, too."

Dukakis, who was all of five centimeters shorter than Karaxis, turned toward the speaker, holding the sobbing little girl between them, and his lip curled. The HSP corporal was a good thirty centimeters shorter than he was and looked like she couldn't have weighed a whole lot more, without the skinsuit and the equipment belt, than the little girl in his hands. She stood eight or nine meters away from him, and she hadn't even drawn her stun baton. She simply stood there, arms folded across her chest, and cocked her head as she gazed up at him.

"Listen, mouní," he sneered, "nothing worse they can do to me down there than what's gonna happen if I don't get my arse off this hab. Me and my bud here? We be just as happy to surrender all sweet and gentle the instant we hit the ground. Can't hardly do anything like you're talking about to us 'thout violating our civil rights, if we don't resist arrest, now can they?"

Helike Vasdekio considered him with a calm, thoughtful expression that masked the fury raging inside her as she saw Kassandra kneeling on the deck, clutching her broken face while the second ganger twisted one fist in her hair and brandished the other one in promise of still more violence if anyone was stupid enough to approach him. Most of that fury was directed at the gangers, but a lot of it was directed at herself, as well. She should have spotted the tattoos on the younger thug's forehead and right cheek. And she certainly should have recognized the sinuous green griffin that covered the entire right side of the older one's face. She was exhausted, she was scared, and she knew she was going to die, but that was no damned excuse for not doing her job and sparing her friends at least this much of the nightmare.

"That's your last word on the subject?" she asked. "You figure you'll get your ride down, then get taken into custody, spend a little time in Eval, and then do—what? Five T-years? Ten?—for assault and kidnapping. Got it all worked out. Trade a few years in the slam for getting off the habitat before something nasty happens to it. Right?"

"For a mouní, you ain't so stupid after all," Dukakis told her. "Yep, that's 'bout the way it's gonna work. And if it don't?" He shrugged. "Well, in that case, I guess my arse gets locked up up here, instead, and somebody else gets this little bitch's seat, 'cause she won't be needing it." He shrugged. "Way I see it, I'm no worse off that way."

"Well, if that's the way you see it, then I guess the only thing for me to do is to spare you the cell time," she said, and he grinned in triumph.

Then her right hand moved. It had been tucked into the bend of her left elbow as she stood with her arms crossed. No one had been able to see it until it moved, and even then its movement was so smooth, so casual, so manifestly unthreatening, that it took Dukakis a moment to realize what he was seeing. Indeed, it was unlikely he ever did realize, because he was too busy dying to work it out as the pulser whined and his head exploded.

Petra screamed in fresh terror as the hurtful hands relaxed instantly. She tumbled to the deck. An instant later, Dukakis's corpse fell over her, crushing her with its weight. Somebody—a man—started to shout something. But then she heard the high, shrill whining sound a second time. He stopped shouting in mid-word, and she heard another voice, one she knew.

"*Petra!* Petra, it's okay, honey!" that voice said urgently. "Some of you help me get this bastard off her!" it snapped to someone else, and the weight crushing her was suddenly lifted away. She wailed in panic, then sobbed in relief as Helike Vasdekio's arms enveloped her.

"It's okay," Helike murmured in her ear again and again. "It's okay. I've got you. It's okay."

"Mommy! Mommy-Mommy-*Mommy!*"

"Your Mom's hurt, honey," Helike told her. "But she's going to be all right, I promise. And the man who hurt her, he'll never hurt anyone again. I promise you that, too. Do you believe me, Petra?"

Petra pushed back from Helike, bracing her hands on the corporal's shoulders and staring into her eyes through the curtain of her own tears. She stayed that way for several, eternal heartbeats. Then she nodded once, convulsively, and collapsed back against the side of her parents' friend's neck, sobbing.

"It's okay, Petra," Helike Vasdekio told the weeping child in her arms as she stepped across the bodies of the men she'd just killed. A couple of other evacuees and one of the habitat EMTs had helped Kassandra back to her feet. Now they steadied her, walking her down the boarding tube to the shuttle, and Helike paused at the entrance.

"You've got to go now, Honey," she said, handing Petra off to one of the shuttle flight crew. The girl tried frantically to cling to her, but she shook her head and disengaged the clutching hands as gently as she could.

"I've got her, Helike," a voice said gruffly, and she looked up in recognition.

"Take care of her for me, John," she said, feeling her eyes burn. "Her dad's a friend. And he's running Flight Control for this entire station quadrant."

Sergeant John Debnam met her gaze and nodded in understanding as he gathered the little girl who was about to lose her father into his arms.

"I've got her," he promised again, his weary voice softer. "I'll look after her and her mom. My word."

"Thanks," Vasdekio said even more softly, then looked down at Petra, frightened and tearful as she found herself in a stranger's arms.

"You go on with John now, Petra," she said. "He's a good friend of mine. He'll take good care of you and your mom. And you be brave, hear me? Your mom needs you, and she's going to need you even more in the next little bit. So you be there for her. Can you do that? Can you be brave for me?"

Petra sniffed, scrubbing her eyes with her fists, then nodded. Her lips trembled, but she actually managed a shaky smile.

"Good!" Vasdekio said. "I knew I could count on you! Now go on, because I've got to get back to work."

HMS *Angrim*
and
HMS *Cinqueda*
Hypatia System

"I DON'T LIKE THIS, Jayson. I don't like it at all," Commander Megan Petersen said. "If they're serious about something like this in Hypatia, what are they going to be willing to do somewhere *else?*" She shook her head, brown eyes worried. "I've got a really bad feeling about where this is going to end up."

It wasn't something she would have admitted to anyone under most circumstances. And as the captain of a Queen's ship, it was something she *couldn't* have admitted to any of her crew. A captain's job was to project the confidence, or at least the determination, her people needed from her. It was *not* to let those same people see the inner frailties any human being possessed. They knew they were there, but just as the rules of the game required her to pretend they weren't, those same rules required her crew to pretend she'd fooled them.

Her father had tried to warn her how lonely command was, and she'd believed him. She just hadn't realized how deep that loneliness could cut. Especially when the man she loved was so close at hand... and so far away.

"Can't say I'm too crazy about it, myself," Commander Jayson Stob told her from his cabin aboard HMS *Cinqueda*. "I'd like to think the bastards were only running some kind of elaborate bluff—or that this Hajdu's timetable was just designed to get the Hypatians to evacuate as quickly as humanly possible. The only problem is, I don't."

"It's just...I've already seen this before. I don't want to see it again. Not here, not anywhere," Megan said, and Jayson nodded.

Megan's previous ship, HMS *Nomad*, had made her hyper translation just outside the Manticore Binary System's hyper-limit less than forty-five minutes before the Yawata Strike had turned her elation and eager anticipation into nightmare.

She'd been *Nomad*'s XO, completing her final deployment before assuming command of a brand, shiny new destroyer. HMS *Arngrim*'s originally designated CO had been reassigned to the command of a *Saganami-C* completing at *Hephaestus*, and *Nomad* had been ordered to expedite her return to Manticore so Megan could replace him.

That's what she'd been looking forward to—seeing her new ship, meeting her new crew, assuming the hard-earned responsibilities of command. And instead, she'd spent the next ninety-six hours straight pulling scores of bodies and a tiny handful of survivors out of mangled wreckage. Jayson had been out-system at the time, spared the first-hand horror she'd confronted, but he knew others who'd been there, and it had left a mark on all of them.

That and an iron determination that something like the Yawata Strike would never happen again. A determination which had to be making the situation here in Hypatia enormously worse for her, he thought, wishing, not for the first time, that they weren't on separate ships.

And just what would you do about it if you were *on the same ship?* he asked himself. *You know what you'd* like *to do, but you also know what Article One Nineteen would have to say about it, don't you? Of course, Megan's probably smart enough to not transgress the sacred Articles of War—*one *of* you *should be, anyway—so it'd probably actually be worse, in the end.*

At least they were assigned to the same task group. It might be a pretty thin silver lining, since they probably wouldn't have been if he'd gotten his ship, but the Yawata Strike had changed that, too. He'd been designated to command the new *Roland*-class HMS *Laozi* almost five T-months before Megan had been ordered to *Arngrim*, and she'd twitted him mercilessly in the letters she'd recorded, crowing over the fact that she'd have her new ship a month and a half before he got his despite his "head start."

Neither of them had seen the Yawata Strike coming.

Arngrim had been two T-months ahead of *Laozi* in the building queue . . . which meant she'd been away from HMSS *Vulcan*, where both of them had been built, on a builders' trial of her impeller nodes when *Vulcan* was blown apart. And that was how Megan came to command her first destroyer while her fiancé remained an executive officer.

Jayson was scarcely the only Queen's officer whose career had been scrambled by the Yawata Strike, and he tried to keep his disappointment in perspective. It was harder sometimes than others, but he supposed that was human nature. And he was enormously relieved Megan had been spared at least that much. There were times he envied her magnificent new ship, but the nightmares she'd experienced during the brief leave they'd snatched together before this deployment killed any sense of resentment stone cold.

He could see the ashes of those nightmares behind her eyes even now as they spoke over the low-powered whisker lasers connecting the squadron's ships in a network no one could have detected from more than a very few thousand kilometers away.

"I know you've seen it, sweetheart," he said now. "We all have, but you had a ringside seat. I'm just as glad *I* didn't. That may be cowardly of me, but it's true. And I wish to hell there were some way to tell you it's not going to happen again here and make that be the truth, but I can't. Nobody can."

"I know. I know!" She shook her head, then kissed the fingers of her right hand and laid them gently against her display. His eyes brightened, and she smiled as he returned the long-distance caress.

"I know," she repeated. "And I guess what I'm really doing is just talking to someone who can listen to me carry on without its being prejudicial to discipline!"

"You're entitled, whenever I'm available," he pointed out. "One of the things I'm here for, now that I think about it." He lifted his nose. "Feel free to lay all of your concerns in my capable hands, my daughter."

"What I'm going to feel free to do is kick you in the ass the next time I see you," she replied with a chuckle, and he shook his head mournfully.

"Such a violent person," he sighed. "I don't really understand how I came to find myself in such an abusive relationship."

"You're an idiot," she told him. "*My* idiot, but an idiot."

"At your service."

He grinned, delighted by her gurgle of laughter. He didn't expect it to last, but for the moment, at least...

"I think what you need," she began, "is for someone to—"

She broke off as a chime sounded and the icon of an urgent message flashed beside the name "Thirunavu" in one corner of her display.

"Just a sec, Jayson," she said. "Rolf's pinging me."

She put the ship-to-ship link on hold and hit the message icon. A blue-eyed, dark-haired, dark-skinned face with a hawklike profile appeared in Jayson's place.

"Yes, Rolf?"

"Skipper, we've got an update from *Phantom*," her executive officer said without preamble. "President Vangelis just got formal notice from Hajdu." Lieutenant Commander Thirunavu shook his head, his eyes grim. "There won't be any more extensions. Anybody who can't get off before he opens fire is just out of luck."

Megan Petersen felt herself go cold. Until that very moment, she realized, some part of her had hoped Hajdu's threat to destroy the

Hypatian orbital infrastructure before it could be completely evacuated was only some sick bluff. Maybe she'd been able to do that because what he proposed to do instead violated so many laws of interstellar warfare. In fact, it was a violation of the fourth clause of the Eridani Edict, part of the League's very Constitution.

My God, she thought. *That's what this is, really, isn't it? This "Operation Buccaneer" was conceived from the beginning specifically as an Eridani violation. It's a* terror *campaign, and all Hajdu's really doing is coming out of the shadows to underline that for all its future victims!*

How had they gotten here? How had they reached a point where the Solarian League was willing to openly violate its own Eridani Edict? The edict specifically designed to prevent this sort of atrocity? Which required any military commander to take every possible precaution to limit collateral damage and preclude *any* avoidable civilian deaths? The League had executed more than one officer—military commander or brigand; it hadn't mattered—over the last eight hundred T-years for violating the fourth clause, and now it was prepared to violate it itself.

It has to go. The realization went through her like an icicle. *The League has to go. It's not enough to just negotiate peace with it again. Not anymore. Anything so corrupt it could embrace something like* this *has to go.*

"Understood, Rolf," she said. "I'll be on the bridge in ten."

"Yes, Ma'am," Thirunavu said formally, and she nodded, then punched back to her link to *Cinqueda.*

"We just heard from *Phantom,* and—"

"I got the word while you were talking to Rolf," Jayson interrupted her. "They need me in AuxCon."

"Understood." She stared at the display for a long, still moment, drinking up the sight of him, storing him away in her heart. Then she inhaled.

"Be safe, love," she said. "I'll see you later."

SLNS *Troubadour*
Hypatia System

"HOW ARE WE DOING, Ellen?" Commander Madison Echols inquired as he stepped on to the ridiculously spacious bridge of SLNS *Troubadour*.

The commander knew an officer with as little seniority as he had was fortunate to have a command at all in the Solarian League Navy. Despite its huge size, the SLN was rank-heavy—to put it kindly—and the decision against mobilizing the Reserve had only emphasized that. An awful lot of officers who should have been commanding squadrons, or at least divisions, during any shooting war had been forced to settle for individual ship commands. For that matter, some of those officers were on the beach, which made Madison Echols profoundly grateful to be in space.

Despite that, and given the human ability to infallibly recognize how much greener the grass was somewhere else, Echols would have preferred to command a *warship*. That was not to be, however, and so he'd been assigned to the TUFT fleet and given the 7,000,000-ton *Troubadour*. His new command was old and long overdue for a general overhaul. She was also slow, unmaneuverable, and totally unarmed. She was, however, all his, which made up for a lot. Despite which, he had yet to grow accustomed to the sheer size—and the sparse instrumentation—of her civilian-designed command deck. He could have played basketball in here!

"Captain Abshire's just finishing the pod deployment, Sir," Lieutenant Commander Ellen Riba, *Troubadour's* executive officer, replied.

Riba was seated in the rather worn captain's chair at the center of the bridge, and she unwrapped herself from it and saluted—sort of—still cradling her cup of coffee in her off hand. Not very shipshape and Navy style, Echols admitted as he acknowledged the salute with a nod, but *Troubadour* had that effect on people. Besides, anyone who hadn't made at least captain was a pretty junior tadpole by Solarian standards. They tended to adopt a sort of "what the hell, we're all in this together" attitude.

"I'll bet she's delighted about *that*," he said as he stepped past Riba and settled into the chair she'd just vacated.

Like himself, Florence Abshire was a mere commander, although both of them were entitled to the title of "captain" as starships' commanding officers. He'd known her a long time, though, and he had a pretty fair notion of how she must feel about this entire "Buccaneer" crap. He knew how *he* felt, at any rate. The term "buccaneer" had all sorts of glamorous connotations, the notion of a swashbuckler with the audacity to back his wit against the entire galaxy, take his chances against any foe. The operation to which it had been appended was anything but glamorous, and they certainly weren't taking any chances when they executed it.

He understood the logic behind it, and his sympathy for so-called neutral star nations who'd shown their hostility by embracing the Manties and their friends was limited. But he also knew the Solarian League Navy—*his* Navy—was deliberately picking victims specifically on the basis of who could—and couldn't—fight back. That his Navy had embarked on a systematic campaign of vandalism because it dared not face its enemies in combat. And so, what *he* felt whenever he thought about Buccaneer was shame.

And especially in this case, he thought grimly, settling himself in the command chair. *This isn't a hostile "neutral." This is a star system—these are* people—*that were Solarian just two T-weeks ago. That's whose infrastructure we're about to blow to hell...and God only knows how many of them are still aboard it.*

His stomach churned, although he was careful about his expression. Had to maintain the Navy's dignity, after all. And he supposed given the inclusion of an option like Parthian Shot, he shouldn't be all that surprised by Vice Admiral Hajdu's timetable.

Have to get our arses out of here before those nasty Manties turn up. Wouldn't want to have to face them, would we? So instead, we murder a few hundred thousand Solarians—excuse me, ex-Solarians—*and get the hell out while the getting's good.*

"I don't think Captain Abshire was delighted, no, Sir," Riba said in answer to his question. She shook her head. "For that matter, Sir, I probably shouldn't say it, but I'm just as glad *Merchant Mart* drew the assignment. I know it's got to be done, and I wouldn't mind smashing up a few Manties, but this..."

She shook her head, and Echols grunted in acknowledgment. He really shouldn't let her get away with comments like that on duty, but it would have been hypocritical to hand her her head when all she'd done was to say out loud the very things he'd been thinking. Spoken words were probably more prejudicial to discipline than private thoughts, but neither one was something upon which the Regs and the Navy smiled.

"Any word from the Flag?" he asked instead, and Riba shook her head again.

"No, Sir," and her tone—like his—said more than the simple words had.

"I see," he replied as he tilted the command chair to a more comfortable angle. So Hajdu wasn't going to grant any more extensions. Well, there'd never been much chance he would. He'd already given Hypatia an additional twelve hours, after all. How much more generous could an executioner be?

Stop that! he told himself sternly. *You've got your orders. He's got his, and he's your commanding officer. So shut the hell up and do your damned job, Madison!*

Easier said than done, he reflected. Easier said than done.

Still, he was guiltily aware that he agreed with Riba about where the actual duty had fallen. He supposed it didn't really matter whose ship had transported the missile pods about to be employed in such ruthless abandon, but at least he could cling to the illusionary innocence of arguing that they hadn't come from *his* cargo holds. And the truth was that Hajdu was being rather parsimonious in his ammunition expenditures. Not that they were going to *need* that many of them. The improved Cataphracts' laserheads were designed to take out capital ships; what they'd do to unarmored industrial platforms—*and residential habitats; don't forget* those, *Madison,* he heard his own voice say in the back of his brain—would be beyond devastating.

And what's going to happen to Hypatia when all that wreckage starts de-orbiting? He's not even trying to prevent that. I guess that's not his job when the only people down there are traitors. Bit hard on their kids, maybe, but who was it back on Old Earth said you couldn't make omelettes without cracking a few eggs? And then there's that other charming bit of wisdom about nits.

He closed his eyes. He *had* to stop this shit. Either that, or he had to request relief and resign his commission, and despite everything, he wasn't quite ready for that just yet. Not yet. But if this continued—

"Sir, I'm picking up something a little weird."

Echols's eyes popped open and he turned the chair gratefully towards Lieutenant Fedosei Castello, *Troubadour*'s electronics officer. "Electronics officer" was a bit of an ambiguous term, especially in *Troubadour*'s case. She wasn't armed, so she didn't have a *tactical* officer, nor was she equipped with even rudimentary ECM or passive defenses, so she didn't have an *electronic warfare* officer, either. If she'd had either of those things, Lieutenant Castello would have been in charge of them. Since she didn't, he doubled as communications officer and tracking officer, doing his best with *Troubadour*'s limited sensor suite.

It was a thankless task, but Castello was only twenty-three, young enough to retain a hefty dose of new-puppy enthusiasm for his duties.

"What do you mean, 'weird,' Fedosei?" Echols asked, glancing at the master plot.

Merchant Mart and SLNS *Stevedore*, Vice Admiral Hajdu's third missile collier, floated in formation, spaced about five thousand kilometers apart, practically on top of one another in space-going terms. The icons of Task Force 1030's actual warships were almost all between the freighters and the planet, and he saw absolutely nothing in the display that could have qualified for Castello's chosen adjective.

"I'm not quite sure, Sir. It's almost like—*Oh, my God!*"

Echols was still jerking upright in his chair when he discovered that he wouldn't be working out his feelings about Operation Buccaneer after all. He had one instant to see *Merchant Mart*'s icon vanish abruptly from the display.

And then, SLNS *Troubadour*, and every man and woman aboard her, did the same thing.

SLNS *Camperdown*
Hypatia System

"WHAT THE HELL JUST happened?"

"I don't *know*, Sir!" Daphne Koopman admitted, her brown eyes shocked. "Just one second they were—"

"Excuse me, Admiral," another voice interrupted, and Hajdu Győző wheeled towards Commodore Honoratus Valentini, his staff electronic warfare officer.

"What?" he demanded, in a voice that was almost normal again.

"I think...I think I know what happened, Sir."

"Well, don't keep it a secret," Hajdu said, and realized that whatever his voice might sound like, his own sense of shock was still growing. Not surprisingly. It was less than ten seconds since roughly twenty million tons of his ships had ceased to exist.

"Sir, I think it was a drone. Drones, plural, I mean."

"*Drones?*" Commodore Brigman repeated. "Are you serious?"

"I know it sounds crazy," Valentini told the chief of staff. "But just before *Merchant Mart*...came apart, we picked up an impeller signature. A small one. It came out of frigging *nowhere*, and it was awfully hard to localize even after we saw it. We only had about eight seconds to track it. Then it disappeared...along with *Merchant Mart*. I think it must've been a heavily stealthed recon drone, probably coming in ballistic, that brought its wedge back up for a terminal maneuver just before it rammed."

Hajdu stared at his EWO, and his mind raced. It was ridiculous! Nobody used *drones* as shipkillers, for God's sake!

But even as he thought that, he realized there was no reason someone *couldn't*. In fact, the majority of modern SAMs used their own impeller wedges to kill atmospheric targets, like stingships. The problem was that any warship's missile defense could kill any drone long before it could reach *ramming* range, and that was the only way a drone could attack something. But even though its maximum acceleration might be only ten or fifteen percent that of an attack missile's, a drone impeller wedge was thoroughly capable of destroying any starship ever built... if it could get through.

And they weren't maneuvering—didn't even have their wedges up. They were frigging sitting ducks, and I was so damned confident I held all the cards that I just let the fucking Hypatians kill a couple of hundred of my people and take out my entire un-deployed supply of missiles.

His teeth clenched so hard his jaw ached, and red-fanged fury pulsed deep inside him, but he forced himself to draw a deep, steadying breath.

He was enraged, but even in his fury, a corner of his mind knew no reasonable person could have faulted the Hypatians for striking back any way they could. Yes, they were traitors, and, yes, he'd fucking well cut them off at the knees for this. But if he'd had the ability to hurt the people about to massacre his own star system's orbital infrastructure and kill millions of his fellow citizens, he'd damned well have used it, too.

But where the hell did they get the capability? his mind asked him suddenly. *We never saw this coming, but we weren't exactly just sitting here! Our sensor net's up, so where the hell did Hypatia get something—at least three somethings—that got through our sensors completely undetected? That's not—*

"*Incoming!*" Koopman barked suddenly. "Missiles incoming—*many* missiles incoming! Range at launch, fourteen-point-six million kilometers. Initial closing velocity, fifteen thousand KPS. Estimate three hundred fifty-plus inbound at forty-five thousand five hundred gravities. Time-of-flight two hundred twenty-five seconds!"

HMS *Phantom*
Hypatia System

"ALL THREE TARGETS DESTROYED, Sir!" Commander Ilkova announced exultantly.

"Excellent!" Rear Admiral Kotouč replied. "Good work, Markéta. Now let's see how well the rest of the plan works."

"Yes, Sir!" Ilkova nodded crisply, but her blue-green eyes glittered with satisfaction. And with good reason, Kotouč thought.

So far, at least.

He'd hoped, when Vice Admiral Hajdu relented and granted the first extension on his truncated time limit, that the Solly would allow total evacuation, after all. Throwing his own people's lives into the scale to save "only" industrial platforms and the Hypatians' homes would have been an even harder decision. He might have made it in the end, after all, but if Hajdu had simply waited long enough for *Vukodlak* and some of the other promised reinforcements to arrive, he wouldn't have needed to. Under those circumstances, the Solly might have thought better of committing an act of wanton destructiveness on such a scale. It was always easier to make the right moral decision when there was somebody waiting to shoot you between the eyes if you didn't. So, yes, Hajdu might have opted to leave Hypatia intact if he'd seen a Manticoran squadron bearing down upon him with what *looked* like a superdreadnought leading the way.

Not that Kotouč had really expected it. If Hajdu was willing to coldbloodedly murder several million Hypatians who simply hadn't gotten out of his way in time, then the odds said he'd send off as massive a missile salvo as it took to ensure the system's infrastructure was destroyed before he disappeared into hyper. And unless *Vukodlak* had come along on exactly the right vector, not even Manticoran compensators could have overhauled him before he crossed the hyper-limit and escaped.

But it would've been nice, he thought almost wistfully. *I've always admired Edward Saganami; I never really wanted to be him, though.*

It had been clear that the Sollies had failed to detect Kotouč's ships, especially after he'd moved them so much deeper into the Alexandria Belt, away from the central node where they'd been quietly sequestered upon arrival. Given that head start, simply avoiding Hajdu's ships would have been child's play, even without the advantages state-of-the-art Manticoran stealth systems provided. Maneuvering into a position from which he could *attack* them, instead, had been a more ticklish proposition.

The good news had been that even if he'd been detected coming in, the Sollies could never have intercepted him against his will. His acceleration advantage was too great, and despite his position "inside them," he could have dodged around the inner system almost indefinitely, or else simply turned away and shown them his heels as he accelerated across the hyper-limit long before they overtook him. The bad news had been his certainty that if they'd detected him, they would have accelerated "Operation Buccaneer" to complete it before he got close enough to intervene. Although, to be fair, they might have been confident enough—given the numerical odds—to stand and fight, instead.

He certainly would have been.

But he'd managed to creep very cautiously, at a mere trickle of acceleration, from his hiding place in the Belt to a position considerably closer to Hajdu's task force. He, Clarke, and Ilkova had taken their time analyzing the Solly flag officer's dispositions, and the one thing Kotouč could fault him on—tactically, at least; there was quite a lot he could fault him on in terms of moral leprosy—was that he was so busy watching his back, it never seemed to have occurred to him that his adversaries might actually have beaten him to Hypatia. His remote platforms were spread along the hyper-limit, with much sparser, almost casual-afterthought coverage of the *inner* system. He didn't have enough overlap even along the hyper-limit to reliably defeat current generation Manticoran stealth, although that wouldn't have been an issue against a new arrival, since no stealth system could hide the energy flare of a hyper footprint. In the inner system, however, the lack of overlap had created chinks through which TG 110.2 could pick a surreptitious way.

Picking a spot to creep *to* had been a tad less simple.

Initially, his ships had been little more than nine million kilometers from Hypatia, but he'd moved them—slowly and carefully—all the way around the system primary from the capital planet to get them safely away from any Solarian sensors in orbit *around* the planet. That had seemed only prudent when the Sollies first arrived; it wasn't until Hajdu's Buccaneer ultimatum that he'd realized just how badly placed he was to intervene. Fortunately, he'd had a lot of star system to work with, and he'd moved to a point just over eighty million kilometers from Hypatia, then held that position relative to the planet for the next forty-five hours.

When the Ghost Rider platforms informed Kotouč that Hajdu had begun deploying the missile pods to execute Buccaneer he'd known he could wait no longer. So two and a half hours ago, his ships had begun accelerating toward the Sollies at a miserly 175 G and acquiring a closing velocity of just over 15,000 KPS in the process. He hadn't wanted to do that, but he'd had no choice. For the first time since Spindle, the SLN actually had the range advantage, thanks to the Cataphract's second drive. His Mark 16s could outperform them; the *Saganami-Bs'* Mark 14s couldn't. Despite their extended range, they had only a single set of impeller nodes, which made any ballistic phase impossible. That meant they had to close with the enemy. They had to come within his reach if they meant to reach *him*. But while they were doing that, Commander Ilkova had sent the final programming—by light-speed directional laser, to avoid any betraying FTL com grav-pulses—to the quartet of Ghost Rider platforms she'd maneuvered into position and parked unobtrusively in Hypatian orbit long before Hajdu approached the planet.

Wish I'd left more of them, Kotouč thought now. *And if I'd had a clue Markéta might come up with an off-the-wall inspiration like this one, I damned well would have! Of course, if I'd left enough to take a real bite out of Hajdu's task force, even the Sollies probably would've spotted them, whether or not they were actively emitting at the time. But there were only four of them, damn it, and those frigging missile colliers had to go.*

"First salvo should enter their CM basket in...twenty-four seconds, Sir," Ilkova said, unaware of his thoughts. "Penaids coming up in twenty seconds from...now."

"Very good," Rear Admiral Kotouč replied once more, and settled himself more firmly into his command chair's shock frame.

SLNS *Camperdown*
Hypatia System

"WHERE—*WHAT*—ARE THEY LAUNCHING FROM?" Hajdu Győző demanded as the first incoming missile salvo was followed by a second, equally massive, twenty seconds later.

"Sir, I don't *know*—not yet," Koopman replied. "We only know where to look because we caught the flare as their impellers came up, but we can't see a frigging *thing* out there! I've got half a dozen recon platforms closing on the launch locus, but until they get closer—"

The commodore shrugged. It was a gesture of frustration and anger—mostly *self*-anger, Hajdu knew—and the vice admiral nodded in unhappy understanding.

"Sir," Commodore Brigman said quietly, standing beside Hajdu's command chair. Hajdu looked at him, and the chief of staff leaned closer. "Sir, we've got to return fire."

"At *what*?" Hajdu asked tartly. "Do *you* see any targets out there? Until we can at least tell the missiles what to look for, our chance of hitting anything at this range doesn't exist."

"But if we throw enough birds into their faces, it might push them back onto defense long enough for Daphne's platforms to ID them. Or at least *find* them."

"And under normal circumstances, I'd do just that." Hajdu's tone was sharper, and he shook his head, lips pressed together and eyes glittering. It took him a second or two to regain command of his voice. Then he said, "These people—whoever the hell they are, and however they got here—knew *exactly* what they were doing when they went after the freighters. The pods that're already deployed are the only ones we've got now, Fred. That means we can't waste them on blind fire."

Brigman looked at him for a moment, then shook himself.

"Yes, Sir." He grimaced. "I hadn't thought that all the way through."

"Understandable, given the surprise quotient." Hajdu shrugged. "And don't think I enjoyed thinking about it myself."

Brigman nodded, his expression grim, and Hajdu nodded back, trying very hard not to think about the literally millions of missiles which had been eliminated along with the three TUFT freighters. He'd gone from an effectively bottomless pool of ammunition to the twenty thousand pods he'd already deployed plus his internal magazines...and only his battlecruisers could launch even first-generation Cataphracts internally. Of course, each of those pods contained six improved Cataphracts, and applying the adjective "only" to 120,000 missiles was patently absurd. Except that it wasn't. Not against Manty EW and Manty missile defenses.

Maybe not, he thought grimly, *but whoever these bastards are, and however they got here, there can't be very many of them. Not with salvos that size.*

Each of the incoming salvos—there were eight inbound now, and as he watched the display a ninth wave of impeller signatures blossomed upon it—was "only" about three hundred and sixty missiles strong. And they were spaced twenty seconds apart. That meant they were coming from internal launchers, because a pod-launched salvo would have been much heavier. He was realist enough to know his missile defense crews would be hard-pressed—at best—to stop the next best thing to four hundred Manty missiles. What had happened to Eleventh Fleet at Manticore was ample proof of that. But they'd be one hell of a lot more effective against four hundred than they would have been against four or five *thousand*, and the Manties had to know that as well as he did.

For that matter, even though they still hadn't managed to locate the Manties, the short range at which they were attacking was revealing. According to ONI's best guesstimate, their missiles really could reach a powered range of thirty million kilometers, yet they were attacking from less than half that. That put them deep inside his own range basket, and while he might have lost the pods still aboard *Troubadour, Merchant Mart*, and *Stevedore*, he still had the ones they'd already deployed in preparation for Buccaneer. So if he could only *find* them, and if there were as few of them as he thought there were...

"First salvo entering the outer zone in twenty seconds," Koopman announced. "So far—"

She broke off, then suddenly raised her right arm, pumping her fist exultantly.

"*Got* them, Sir!" she announced. "Seven—no, *nine*—bogeys at one-four-point-five-seven million klicks! Looks like at least two of those huge 'battlecruisers' of theirs. The others might be smaller battlecruisers or those outsized heavy cruisers. Either way, we've got them."

"Program an alpha launch," Vice Admiral Hajdu Győző said. "Let's see how the bastards like *that*."

HMS *Arngrim*
Hypatia System

"THE SOLLIES HAVE LAUNCHED, Ma'am!" Lieutenant Bill Berden announced.

The tactical officer's voice was crisp and professional, yet there was an odd softness to it, as well. Like everyone else aboard HMS *Arngrim*, he knew about his captain's engagement. In fact, he'd been the assistant TO aboard *Cinqueda* when it was announced, and he'd attended their engagement party aboard the heavy cruiser. In the wake of the Yawata Strike, it had been a welcome reaffirmation that life went on.

And now Jayson and *Cinqueda* were 60,000,000 kilometers from *Arngrim* and a tidal wave of missiles had just erupted from the Solarian battlecruisers.

"Estimate one hundred twenty thousand inbound, and they're turning out better acceleration than Filareta's Cataphracts showed at Manticore," Berden continued. "I'm reading eight-four-one-point-eight KPS squared. Time-of-flight," he finished quietly, "one-five-two seconds."

"Thank you, Guns."

Megan Petersen made herself sound calm as she sat very still in her command chair, her eyes on the tactical plot. It wasn't easy. She would far rather have been the target of those missiles herself, she realized. At least then the threat would have been to *her*, and not to the man she loved. And knowing that he would have felt exactly the same way, had the situation been reversed, only made her love him more.

She'd argued, when Admiral Kotouč gave her her orders. She didn't know whether or not the admiral knew about her engagement to Jayson, and she hadn't brought it up, either. She'd simply suggested, respectfully, that his logic was flawed.

Task Group 110.2 wasn't going to survive. That was a given, something every man and woman aboard every one of Jan Kotouč's ships knew as well as he did. This was their Saganami moment, the one every Manticoran officer knew might one day come to her, and as the Admiral had pointed out, it didn't matter that Hypatia was someone else's star system. It never had mattered, really. Ellen D'Orville had proved that in the Ingeborg System two centuries ago. Duchess Harrington had reaffirmed it in Grayson less than twenty T-years ago. And now it was their turn, here in Hypatia, to prove the tradition still lived.

Yet the fact that they were about to die didn't mean they couldn't accomplish their mission first. The odds were against it, but, like Edward Saganami himself, they *might* pull it off. Even if they didn't, they could be certain a lot fewer Solarian battlecruisers would go home to brag about the atrocity they'd committed.

And we will by God show every other star system in this galaxy that the Star Empire of Manticore and its Allies stand by their friends, come hell or high water, she thought now. *It's just that I've seen so much aftermath. I'm tired of it. I'm tired of picking through the bodies and the rubble. I'm tired of being the survivor who has to tell other people the ones they loved didn't make it. And,* God, *I don't want to lose Jayson!*

That, she knew, was the real reason she'd argued with Admiral Kotouč. She'd made the case that they were going to do need every launcher they had...and *Arngrim* had twenty-four of them, with twenty Mark 16s per tube. That made her a more effective platform than any of his three *Saganami-Bs*, with their Mark 14 tubes. That was the argument she'd made, when deep inside she'd known her real reason was her bleeding need to *be* there when the rest of the squadron—and Jayson—walked into the furnace at Kotouč's side. She'd known that, deep inside, and a part of her hated herself for it. Her pain was no excuse for throwing away the lives of *Arngrim*'s people, even though her entire crew shared her sense of betrayal, of having abandoned their fellows in the ships standing to die with their admiral.

But Kotouč had been correct in at least one sense. In the final analysis, the weight *Arngrim*'s magazines and missile tubes might have added to the task group's striking power would never change the final outcome. All she could really have accomplished would be to die beside her larger consorts, and there was no justification for sending another sixty-seven people to their deaths when that was true.

Especially not when he had another mission for her ship.

"The discussion is closed, Captain," he'd said flatly, his expression stern on Megan's com. "Someone has to bring Captain Acworth up to date when *Vukodlak* gets here. Acworth's a good man, not the sort to take chances, but that doesn't mean he can't sail straight into an ambush if there's not someone to keep him from doing that. Your ship is best equipped for that. You've got the speed, you've got the best ECM in the task group, after *Phantom* herself, and you *do* have Mark 16s to discourage anyone who gets too close to you, anyway. That makes it your job to be Acworth's eyes and ears here in Hypatia. Now go do it."

"Yes, Sir," she'd replied. It was the only response she could make, and so she'd watched the rest of the squadron—*Phantom* and the three heavy cruisers—get underway for their rendezvous with Hajdu Győző while *Arngrim* headed equally cautiously in the opposite direction.

And now she was doing her job. She was watching through the Ghost Rider platforms, downloading the Admiral's complete tactical feed through the Hermes buoys he'd deployed. She was seeing all of it, getting every instant of it for the record and for later tactical analysis...and unshed tears burned her eyes as that stupendous missile salvo streaked towards the man she loved.

HMS *Phantom*
and
SLNS *Camperdown*
Hypatia System

"CIC CONFIRMS IT, SIR," Captain Clarke said quietly, standing beside Jan Kotouč's command chair as they watched the master plot. "They're coming in almost eighty percent hotter than they should have. Must be a new bird, which makes our missile defense projections a lot more problematical. And they've flushed at least three quarters of their deployed pods at us. Looks more like eighty or ninety percent, actually." He smiled ever so slightly. "I suppose we should take that as a compliment."

"One way to look at it," Kotouč acknowledged.

"Might as well look on the bright side, Sir. While we can, anyway."

Kotouč only grunted in acknowledgment, his eyes on Commander Ilkova as she and her assistants bent over their consoles.

"Range at launch twelve-point-zero-two million kilometers. Time-of-flight one-five-two seconds," she announced, updating her initial projections. Her voice seemed preposterously calm, but it was the calm of concentration, not lack of understanding or imagination. The tension in her eyes showed that clearly enough. "At current acceleration, they'll enter the outer defense zone in...one-one-five seconds. First wave counter-missile launch in forty seconds."

Only twelve million kilometers, Kotouč thought. Judging by the timing, it must have taken the Sollies longer than he'd dared hope to localize his units. Each of his four ships had put ten double broadsides into space—and closed well over two million kilometers at their base velocity of 15,125 KPS—while the Sollies looked for him, and he had time for another nine launches before that massive wavefront of Cataphracts could reach him.

Of course, when it *did* reach him...

True, that hundred and twenty thousand-strong salvo had to be blind-fired. All the Solarian battlecruisers combined—they'd identified ninety-eight, all *Nevadas* and *Indefatigables*—could bring less than four

270

thousand telemetry links to bear, only three percent of what they'd need to control that many birds. But the numbers worked out to roughly 30,000 missiles for each of his ships. The five Lorelei decoys he'd deployed would thin that quite a lot—all the way down to a "mere" 13,300 or so. Assuming a mere three percent hit rate, that was almost four hundred per ship. Not even a *Nike* could shake off that kind of hammering, and the sheer volume of fire was guaranteed to swamp even Manticoran missile defense.

I believe this is what the analysts call "overkill," Kotouč thought wryly. *I'm actually surprised he didn't try to take us with just his internal tubes, given the numerical balance. Too bad he didn't. Missile defense probably could've handled a mere five or six hundred missiles per ship!*

He surprised himself with a faint but genuine smile, yet the truth was he hadn't wanted Hajdu to rely on his broadside tubes. Indeed, that was one reason he'd deployed only five Loreleis. Their ability to counterfeit the sensor signatures of all up warships was all but impossible to penetrate above very short ranges, even for Manticoran sensors which knew what to look for, but the one thing they couldn't do was actually launch missiles of their own. That was why he'd been unable to tempt the Solly admiral into wasting any significant number of missiles by simply showing him Loreleis to draw his fire. If the Loreleis weren't firing at *him*, then he'd have no reason to fire at *them*, and unless the actual firing platforms were close enough to the Loreleis to fool him, he probably wouldn't bite. At most, he'd probably toss a relatively limited salvo at them to see how they responded, and when that salvo of *Solly* missiles took out every target without *any* return fire, he'd know he'd been had.

That same inability to fire also limited the total number he could deploy to cover his approach without someone on the other side running the math and realizing that at least some of those targets had to be decoys. He didn't want that, but he *did* want to convince Hajdu that he faced an even more dangerous threat than he actually did. TG 100.2 could sequence its launches closely enough that the fact that they were double salvos might well not be noticed, and at missile ranges, it was impossible to tell which ship had launched which specific missiles...as long as there weren't too many platforms to produce them all. So he'd had to choose between offering as many targets as possible or offering as many as the Solly tac officers might find *plausible*, and the last thing he'd wanted was for the Sollies to think things through.

The truth was that he'd just succeeded in one of his two primary goals. It looked as if the Solly had thrown everything he could at TG 110.2 in his initial salvo...which meant he'd emptied all or almost all of the missile pods he'd deployed for the execution of Buccaneer. And when Ilkova killed his freighters, she'd also killed his ability to replenish those pods. No doubt the magazines aboard his battlecruisers and their escorts carried more than sufficient missiles to do the job anyway, but they'd be shorter ranged and less efficient. It would take them longer, and every extra hour of delay was another hundred thousand lives saved.

And if TG 110.2 succeeded in its second goal, there'd be one hell of a lot fewer of those magazines to go around, too. For that matter, if Hypatia wasn't the only star system on Hajdu's Buccaneer list...

"Penetration EW coming up in three seconds," Commander Ilkova said.

❖   ❖   ❖

Did I just let the son-of-a-bitch sucker me? Hajdu Győző wondered coldly.

He glared at the nine icons in his display, jaw clenched, as the stupendous wave of Cataphracts streaked towards them. He'd flushed the pods in near spinal reflex, without really analyzing his decision, and he kept all expression from his face as he did that analysis now.

Whoever was in command over there had gone unerringly for Buccaneer's jugular. Without those missile colliers, no Solarian flag officer dared to confront an Allied task force. That would have made killing them eminently worthwhile under any circumstances, but destroying them had also cut deeply into Hajdu's missile reserve here in Hypatia. And his decision to flush the deployed pods had just fired away everything that hadn't been blown to hell with *Troubadour, Merchant Mart*, and *Stevedore*.

And that, almost certainly, had been one of the Manty's primary aims.

Doesn't matter, he decided, watching the tenth salvo erupt from the Manticoran ships. *I've got enough birds left in my magazines to do the job. Hell, for that matter I can take out the targets with* energy *fire, if I need to! And one thing I damned well know is that I'd better take these bastards out fast...* however *big a launch that takes!* He grimaced. *Missiles in magazines won't matter if the ships those magazines belong to get their arses blown out of space before they ever launch.*

He didn't like thinking that, but there was no point denying the truth. The size of the incoming Manticoran salvos made it clear *they* had the telemetry links to actually coordinate their fire, because if those birds had been blind-fired, there'd have been one hell of a lot more of them. He *didn't* have those links, and he wasn't at all sure the weight of fire he *could* have coordinated would be sufficient to penetrate their defenses. Not only that, but they'd put well over three thousand missiles of their own into space before his people even *found* them.

Judging from the SLN's previous experience, that meant an awful lot of his ships were about to die. If they were given the chance to go *on* launching, the death toll could only skyrocket, which was exactly what made it so imperative to completely crush them as quickly as humanly possible.

If a hundred and twenty thousand missiles can't do the job, then nothing else can, either, he reflected grimly. *And one thing about it, we'll find out pretty damn quickly when the Alpha launch gets there. Of course,* he smiled thinly, *we'll have to survive five or six of* their *salvos first, won't we?*

✧　　✧　　✧

Task Force 1030's tactical officers were tight-lipped as they tracked the incoming Manticoran salvos. They seemed awfully tight, those salvos, packed much more closely together than the same number of SLN missiles would have been. Hajdu's TOs couldn't see any reason for the Manties to do that, and they didn't like not knowing what the sneaky bastards were up to. There *had* to be a reason they'd concentrated their fire into such a tight, easily targeted zone, but what the hell *was* it? Why give missile defense such an ideal target? The projected numbers in the tactical computers' constantly updated predictions spun steadily upward towards an incredible thirty-five percent interception rate, and the tac officers would have loved to believe those numbers.

Unfortunately, they didn't.

They'd been briefed, based upon the very best intelligence available on Allied missile capabilities, but the accuracy of those briefings' assumptions had never been tested. Worse, they were based—and every one of those TOs knew it—on little more than conjecture. Given the SLN's staggering losses, they should have amassed a huge amount of information on Manty missile capabilities and doctrine. They hadn't...because no ship which had been the *target* of Manty missiles had yet made it home with anything like hard sensor data, They'd all seen the imagery the Grand Alliance had provided of the destruction of Eleventh Fleet, but that imagery had been scrubbed of all useful tactical data before it was ever released. They knew that. Yet if there'd been no useful data in it, there'd been ample evidence of the horrific speed with which Massimo Filareta's wall of battle had been reduced to wreckage.

The effectiveness of their own missile defenses had been increased by a minimum of thirty percent by the tweaks and new software— and, hopefully, new doctrine—the SLN had rammed through following Sandra Crandall's debacle. Some of those tweaks had been in the pipeline for T-years, delayed by sheer bureaucratic inertia, although there'd been no time to get them to Eleventh Fleet before it hypered out for Manticore. Others, though, were brand-new, created on the fly by a navy not accustomed to improvisation and rapid adjustment. As a consequence, every predictive model was...questionable, and they knew that, too.

Now the first three hundred and ninety-six missiles came tearing straight into the very teeth of their defenses in a solid, unswerving phalanx, and they wondered why.

✧　✧　✧

"Counter-missile launch in five seconds," Daphne Koopman announced. "Four...three...two...one—launching!"

She made the announcement with fierce satisfaction, and SLNS *Camperdown* quivered as the first salvo of counter-missiles belched from her launchers. Hajdu sensed himself leaning forward in his command chair and scolded himself for showing his own tension so clearly. It was his job to project assurance, not worry, and—

Commodore Koopman twitched upright in her own command chair, her expression shocked, as the penetration platforms seeded throughout TG 110.2's lead salvo came up and her orderly displays disintegrated into chaos.

It was standard, absolutely predictable RMN missile doctrine. Any Havenite tac officer would have known what was coming the instant he saw that launch, saw how tight-packed the salvo was, how little clearance there was between the individual missiles' impeller wedges. The problem was that Solarian tactical officers *didn't* know that. No one in TF 1030 had ever seen that doctrine in practice. They'd seen theoretical analyses, projections based on assumed capabilities, but the people behind those analyses and projections had lacked hard data. In the absence of that data they'd extrapolated—and all too often mirror-imaged their own doctrinal assumptions into—the Manties' thinking. It wasn't because they were stupid; it was because they had no other base line assumptions to use, and so they'd done their best with what they had.

And because they had, their projections were deeply flawed.

Fifteen Dazzlers came up all across the salvo's front, perfectly timed to ten seconds behind the counter-missile launch. The huge spikes of jamming blasted the Solarian sensor picture into threshed ruin, and missile defense officers swore in shocked disbelief as the entire wave of Manticoran missiles simply disappeared behind that rolling wall of interference.

The counter-missiles lost lock as their onboard sensors were blinded. Perhaps a third of them wandered off on courses to nowhere, trying—and failing—to find new targets to acquire, but the remainder continued straight ahead. Some of them, still under shipboard control, steered towards the center of the missile swarm's last known position. Others followed their onboard protocols, spreading a bit wider, orienting to keep their seekers targeted on the zone where their computers told them—correctly—the missiles they'd lost track of had to be.

But then the jamming went down, and Daphne Koopman slammed her fist furiously against her console.

There'd been three hundred and sixty missiles on her plot before the jamming; after the jamming, there were *seven* hundred.

No SLN analyst had yet heard a single word about the RMN's Dragon's Teeth. And because they hadn't, Hajdu's missile defense officers were totally unprepared for an EW platform which could generate ten totally convincing false missile signatures. Nor had they realized that Markéta Ilkova had dedicated a full fifteen percent of her initial launch to penetration aids.

Three hundred and eleven attack missiles, covered and protected by their electronic siblings, streaked towards their targets, separating onto individual, evasive approach profiles at last, and TF 1030's missile defenses tried frantically to reacquire them as they came.

"Projected targets *Ontario, Enterprise, Edinorg, Marengo,* and *Re Umberto*," Koopman said flatly. "Tracking's confidence is not—repeat, *not*—high."

Hajdu's jaw tightened. If those projections were correct—and, looking at the hashed nightmare of the plot he understood exactly why Tracking's confidence in them was so low—all nine of the Manties had concentrated their fire on only five of his ninety-eight battlecruisers. That would produce a density of almost seventy missiles per target, assuming an even distribution, and that promised disastrous consequences. Seventy *Solarian* missiles would have been enough to wreck any battlecruiser, assuming they could get through its defenses. Looking at that plot, it was obvious a lot of them *were* going to get through, and one thing all OpAn's projections agreed upon was that Manticoran warheads were far more destructive on a bird-for-bird basis.

He's not even trying to target all of us, the vice admiral realized. *He's going to go for a handful of targets in each salvo, concentrate his fire to pound through their defenses, and rip them to frigging bits.*

Hajdu Győző's brain went through the remorseless math. There were fifteen salvos in space now. His Cataphracts were actually faster than the missiles coming at him—their time-of-flight was seventy-one seconds shorter than the initial Manticoran salvo's—but by the time they reached their target, the Manties would have fired a total of nineteen. If each of those salvos concentrated on five of his ships and even a third of them got through, they could reduce every single one of his battlecruisers to wreckage.

✧　　✧　　✧

Despite their confusion, the Solarian counter-missiles intercepted almost seventy of the incoming targets. Unfortunately, fifty-one of them were electronic ghosts generated by the Dragon's Teeth. Another fifteen were Dazzlers. Of Markéta Ilkova's three hundred and eleven shipkillers, two hundred and ninety survived to streak across the point defense envelope at thirty-eight percent of the speed of light.

SLNS *Enterprise*'s point defense clusters had time for one shot each before the missile storm was upon her. Under the circumstances, they did remarkably well, plucking nineteen shipkillers out of the chaos of her fire control, and "only" forty-five got through to attack her.

All of them were Mark 14-ERs, not Mark 16s. The inability of the *Saganami-Bs* to launch the Mark 16 had forced Commander Ilkova to step down *Phantom*'s Mark 16s' acceleration in order to maintain concentration. That density paid a major dividend when it came to penetrating the Solarian defenses, but the Mark 14 wasn't fitted with the Mark 16-G's improved laserhead. The Mark 16-G could kill super-dreadnoughts; the Mark 14 couldn't.

It was, however—unfortunately for *Enterprise*—quite capable of killing *battlecruisers*.

The *Nevada*-class ship heaved as bomb-pumped lasers punched through her sidewalls, ripped deep into her flanks. Men and women died, weapons disappeared. Her core hull was breached in at least seven places, belching atmosphere as it decompressed explosively. But bad as that was, the six laserheads which detonated directly ahead of her were far worse. Unlike Rear Admiral Kotouč's ships, *Enterprise* had no bow-wall. There was nothing to protect her forward hammerhead, aside from its armor and her particle screening, and neither of those was remotely enough.

X-ray lasers punched effortlessly through that armor. Three of her forward impeller nodes exploded, and two graser mounts, three counter-missile tubes, and two laser clusters went with them. A fraction of a second later, power bleed and ruptured plasma conduits turned her entire forward impeller room into a crematorium for its crew. The nine hundred thousand-ton ship staggered, yawing drunkenly as half her wedge went down, and two more of those hellish lasers ripped almost directly down her central axis, tearing deep into her essential systems.

She reeled under the savage assault and her *after* impeller ring went down, as well, proof of the chaos raging through her brutally wounded control systems. Acceleration gone, she coasted onward, out of the fireballs of the attacking missiles.

Fourteen seconds later, she disappeared in the glare of a failing fusion bottle.

Her sister *Marengo* and the *Indefatigable*-class *Edinorg* were more fortunate; they survived. But they survived as hopeless wrecks. *Edinorg* still had her wedge, although she'd lost half a dozen nodes, and she turned brokenly away, seeking cover behind her intact consorts' interposed wedges, while *Marengo* coasted onward, shedding life pods and small craft. *Ontario*'s back broke and her shattered hull tumbled wildly, and *Re Umberto* simply blew up under the pounding.

❖   ❖   ❖

"Good hits, Sir!" Captain Clarke reported as the numbers came up on his display. Commander Ilkova was too busy for reports at the moment. "Looks like we took out all five alpha targets!"

"Good!" Kotouč acknowledged, but his eyes were on Ilkova and the master plot. That massive Solarian salvo was only ninety seconds out, and he had few illusions about what was going to happen when it arrived.

Nor was he alone in that. He could see it in the tight shoulders, the masklike faces of his flag bridge personnel. Even Clarke's, despite his obvious satisfaction.

Only Ilkova seemed oblivious to it as her hands flew across her console. The range was forty light-seconds, but the Ghost Rider platforms reduced that to less than one. She'd already cut the control links to the next three salvos in the firing queue, but there was still time for her to refine the penetration ECM and targeting of the salvos behind that. She was totally focused on just that, her blue-green eyes fiery, and Kotouč glanced at Paul Albamonte.

The EWO was just as focused as Ilkova, but not on offense. The ops officer had assumed direct control of the attack birds' penetration EW so that Lieutenant Albamonte could concentrate on the squadron's *defensive* ECM. Just as the Ghost Rider platforms near the planet gave Ilkova a direct, real-time view of her targets, those between the task group and the Sollies had given Albamonte a real-time view of the incoming missiles. There was less he could do with it, but he wasn't sitting on his hands.

He hit a macro on his console and the missile control which had passed to him launched Dazzlers from every tube the task group had. They didn't travel far, and then they erupted squarely in the path of the incoming Cataphracts. There weren't enough of them and the shell wasn't dense enough to block all of the Solly missiles' sensors, but it was close enough to the task group and broad enough to block the vast majority of them, and Solarian missiles didn't talk to each other the way Apollo birds did. With Apollo, everything *any* missile in a salvo could see was available to *all* missiles in that salvo, but Solly missiles at this range would be on their own. Each of them knew where its target was supposed to be, but it had to be sure that target was really there before it attacked. That meant reacquiring if it lost lock for any reason, and if there happened to be anything to confuse its sensors at that moment...

Kotouč checked a secondary plot and smiled viciously as the Loreleis came to life upon it.

Suck on that *one, Hajdu,* he thought vindictively as his four ships suddenly became twenty-five... then thirty-nine.

Then the Dazzlers went down once more, clearing the task group's defensive sensor range, and *Phantom* quivered with the sawtooth vibration of counter-missile launchers in maximum-rate fire. They spat out thirty-two CMs every ten seconds, and his jaw tightened as the incoming salvo entered the outer intercept envelope. They'd be finding out shortly how many of those Cataphracts had been diverted to other targets.

He didn't expect it to be enough.

"Missile impact in sixty seconds," Albamonte announced as the squadron's defensive fire began tearing into that stupendous cloud of death. Dozens of Cataphracts—scores of them—disappeared, but there were *thousands* of them, and Jan Kotouč faced a far larger salvo with far less missile defense than Commodore Lessem had faced in Prime.

They're getting through, he told himself. *Accept it, Jan.*

Maybe so, but in the meantime...

                    ✧   ✧   ✧

"God *damn* it!" Hajdu Győző snapped. "Can't we *stop* those fucking things?"

Fred Brigman looked at his admiral from the corner of one eye but said nothing. It was obviously a rhetorical question...and the first time he'd ever heard such furious frustration from the unflappable Hajdu.

It was very unlike him, but it was also hard to blame him, Brigman thought grimly. Five of those hell-spawned salvos had smashed into TF 1030, and twenty-seven—*twenty-seven*—of Hajdu's battlecruisers had been blown apart or turned into crippled wrecks that would never move again under their own power. SLNS *Espana, Impero,* and *Libertad,* like *Edinorg,* retained enough nodes to limp away from the carnage, but none of them were effective units any longer. Of Hajdu's original ninety-eight battlecruisers, only sixty-seven remained in action.

A sense of shocked desperation enveloped the task force as those merciless salvos hammered home again and again, killing or crippling their battlecruisers five or six at a time, with mechanical precision. They seemed unstoppable, and whoever was behind them, he was using his electronic warfare advantages with merciless skill. The jamming patterns shifted and danced, there were more decoys in some waves, fewer in others, driving Tracking into near futility. They were knocking down more of the shipkillers in the inner counter-missile zone, and the laser clusters were claiming more kills as updated profiles on the attack missiles' terminal maneuvers and emission signatures were relayed throughout the task force, but they were actually getting even *fewer* kills in the outer and middle zones. It was as if the Manties had real-time data on their own tracking and EW shifts. As if they were programming adjustments into their missiles penetration profiles right up to the instant they actually hit the Solarian defenses.

And now this, Brigman thought, glaring at the display on which the false targets had suddenly appeared. They had to be decoys—although God only knew what sort of decoys could do what *these* were doing!—and they were going to play hell with the blind-fired Cataphracts' ability to find the real targets.

Well, maybe so, the chief of staff told himself grimly. *But there's only so much decoys* can *do against a salvo that size, and they only get one more of their own in before it's* our *turn to hammer* them!

"Impact in five seconds," Daphne Koopman announced hoarsely.

✧   ✧   ✧

"Three more hard kills," Clarke announced. "Looks like at least one additional mission-kill, too."

That makes...at least thirty-four, Kotouč thought, doing the math. *Over a third of them. These bastards frigging well know they've been kissed!*

No doubt they did, and by any objective standard, TG 110.2 had already achieved an overwhelming victory. At least twenty-seven Solarian battlecruisers, most of them *Nevadas,* had been destroyed outright. That was 24.6 million tons of warships, nine times TG 110.2's total tonnage, with 78,000 men and women aboard. TG 110.2's total personnel amounted to only 1,900, barely two percent as many, and the Sollies were going to lose still more ships. Ilkova had already updated the next four salvos in her firing queue and cut her links to them. That meant at least another sixteen dead Solarian battlecruisers, whatever else happened.

It was a pity so few of his own people would be around to see that happen.

Phantom, Cinqueda, Talwar, and *Shikomizue* had rolled ship thirty seconds ago. They could do that, because *Phantom*'s Keyhole platforms gave Ilkova and Albamonte uninterrupted sensor coverage, light-speed telemetry to the attack birds, and FTL links to the Ghost Rider drones, and it was going to make Kotouč's ships far harder targets than any Solly had ever dreamed of attacking. It just wasn't going to make them hard enough.

The CM zones were a holocaust. Counter-missiles sought out Solarian shipkillers, blotting them from existence in suicidal eruptions of wedge fratricide. Some of those strikes took out more than one attack missile at a time, but not even Manticoran missile defense computers could run meaningful threat analyses on that many missiles. The Solarian tactical officers had simply pointed them in the right direction. After that, aside from the thousands of EW platforms threaded throughout the missile swarm, every one of those birds was on its own.

The penetration aids had been better than projected, knocking back kill numbers by another fifteen or twenty percent. The Loreleis offset some of that by sucking the fire aside—not as much as he'd hoped they would, but more than he'd actually anticipated. Or it looked that way, in the fleeting moments he had to absorb the display. But there simply weren't enough of them, because the true killer was the sheer number of threats. There was no way to parse the incoming fire, no way to predict which missiles would go for the decoys, which would lose lock and go wide, and which were likely to acquire good firing solutions. The defenders had been driven to take whatever shots they could get, not the ones they would have cherry-picked with better tracking data, and it was a mathematical certainty that many of the successful intercepts had been wasted on attackers that never would have found a firing angle, anyway.

"Impact in five seconds," Commander Ilkova announced, looking up from her targeting displays at last. Her voice was surprisingly calm, Kotouč thought. Or perhaps the word he wanted was exhausted, because she was soaked with sweat. The sweat of concentration and determination, he thought, not fear.

"Helmets!" the quartermaster of the watch barked, and the admiral twitched. He'd forgotten his own standing orders, and his hands unhooked the helmet from his seat arm, lowered it over his head, and sealed it to his skinsuit's locking ring.

The possibility of its making much difference was remote.

✧   ✧   ✧

Megan Petersen's hands were claws on her command chair armrests as that mammoth wave of missiles roared down on Rear Admiral Kotouč's defiant handful. *Arngrim* was tied into the same recon drones as *Phantom*. The destroyer's tactical display showed the same information Jan Kotouč and his staff could see. But unlike the flagship—unlike *Jayson*—Megan was safe, her ship un-threatened.

She'd never realized what a curse safety could be, a distant corner of her mind thought.

The squadron's point defense lashed out as the incoming missiles streaked "above" and "below" those interposed impeller wedges. She knew hundreds of incoming missiles had just disappeared, ripped to pieces by those strobing laser clusters. But she couldn't see it; the globe of nuclear explosions completely enveloping TG 110.2 made it impossible.

She tasted blood from her bitten lip as that incredible, glaring ball of plasma erupted. Tens of thousands of warheads exploded, spawning their own bomb-pumped lasers, ripping at sidewalls, bow-walls, battle steel armor...and human flesh and bone. It seemed to take forever, although at a terminal velocity almost half the speed of light the actual attack was over in a heartbeat. In less than a second.

Jayson...

She never knew if she'd whispered that name aloud. She only knew her heart seemed to stop as the brimstone glare faded from the plot and she saw what was left.

✧   ✧   ✧

"*Got the fuckers!*" Daphne Koopman shouted.

It was scarcely a proper report, but Hajdu Győző wasn't going to call her on the carpet for it. Not when the light-speed sensors confirmed what the gravitics had already reported. The Manties' impeller wedges had disappeared from the FTL gravitic plot; now, forty seconds later, the light-speed data from the recon drones speeding outward in the shipkillers' wake showed him why they had.

Seven of their targets—*seven* of them!—were simply gone, vanished, probably the victims of their own failing fusion plants. The enormous "battlecruiser"—two and a half times *Camperdown's* size—had survived, but only as a shattered wreck, and she was accompanied by what looked like half of a heavy cruiser. It was hard to be sure about that, given the ship-fragment's splintered state.

Yet two more Manticoran salvos had slammed into TF 1030 while he waited for that confirmation. Those salvos had killed nine more of his own ships, and even as he glared triumphantly at his vanquished foes, eleven more were still inbound.

He looked at the damage sidebar, and his nostrils flared. SLNS *Friedland, Charles Martel, Potemkin, Dingyuan, Iéna, Barfleur, Custoza...* forty-six of his battlecruisers had been totally destroyed or hulked. *Belliqueuse, Ne Tron Menia,* and *Novgorod* had joined *Edinorg, Impero, Espana,* and *Libertad,* limping away from the carnage while all but essential damage control personnel evacuated the ships, and six more of their consorts showed varying degrees of damage.

He'd gone into battle with ninety-eight battlecruisers; he was down to forty-four, and the dying wasn't done yet.

"Finish them off," he heard himself say flatly, eyes hard and hating on the crippled, broken wrecks of his foes.

A sudden silence enveloped *Camperdown*'s flag bridge, even deeper and stiller somehow against the staccato background of combat chatter, and Commodore Brigman looked at the vice admiral, his face expressionless.

"Excuse me, Sir?" he said.

"Finish those bastards off," Hajdu grated. "*Now*, Commodore Koopman!"

"Yes, Sir!" If there'd been hesitation in Brigman's voice, there was none in Koopman's. Her hands raced across her panel, and she jabbed a final button. "Launching now, Sir."

✧   ✧   ✧

"Oh my God," someone said softly, and Megan Petersen's head snapped up from the visual display where she'd been trying desperately to determine which of Jan Kotouč's heavy cruisers hadn't been totally destroyed.

"Skipper," Lieutenant Berden said, "they've just launched again. Estimate sixteen hundred inbound. These are slower—I think they're the same Cataphracts Filareta had—but the range's down to five-point-four-four million klicks. I make it one hundred twenty-four seconds."

Megan inhaled sharply and her eyes darted back to the icons of the Solarian task force. They clung to its winnowed ranks, and shock flared in their depths as she realized Berden was right. The Sollies *had* fired again. Fired upon ships unable to move or maneuver in any way. Ships fighting frantically to evacuate survivors from shattered compartments and broken hulls. Ships specifically protected by the Deneb Accords... yet another interstellar protocol guaranteed by the Solarian League.

It's a war crime, she thought. *No, it's* another *war crime.*

The shock in her eyes turned into something else—something cold and deadly—as the missile icons speared out at those helpless targets. Even with Ghost Rider, it was impossible to see life pod transponders or small craft at this range, and even if anyone had gotten off alive, the collateral damage from that many missiles was bound to kill a lot of them.

Oh, Jayson, she thought. *Oh, Jayson.*

"Make sure we get every bit of this, Guns," she heard herself say, never looking away from the damaged ships with two more minutes to live. "We'll need the evidence at the trial."

✧   ✧   ✧

Rear Admiral Kotouč opened his eyes and shook his head.

It was a mistake.

Agony lanced through him, focused somewhere below his shoulders but radiating all the way up his spine to the top of his skull. It wasn't a dull, throbbing agony. This was sharp, brutal, stabbing at him in ragged spasms. His left hand fumbled, trying to find the med panel on the right sleeve of his skinsuit, but his arms didn't seem to be cooperating.

He blinked, fighting to focus through the waves of pain, and realized he was staring up at the overhead outside Flag Bridge. And he was moving. But how could he be moving? He couldn't even feel his legs.

Panic bubbled as he realized that was true. Despite that, his brain was starting to function once more, and he blinked again. If he couldn't walk but he was moving anyway, that could only mean—

He moved his head, craning around to look up past his shoulder. The HUD on the inside of his helmet glared with angry red medical warnings, but he looked past them, ignoring their import, and his eyes narrowed.

Commander Ilkova's left hand was locked on his skinsuit's shoulder-mounted purchase point. Her right arm hung at her side, and that entire side of her own skinsuit was seared and blackened as if by fire and splashed with blood. There was a lot of that, but not hers, judging from her movements.

"Others?" he got out.

"We're it, Sir," the ops officer replied, and his eyes closed again in a pain not of the flesh.

"What are—?"

"Flag Bridge's life pods are gone," she panted, dragging him down the passage in starbursts of excruciating pain. "So's the lift."

He frowned, trying to think through the sea of anguish. If the flag bridge's pods were crippled and the lift was out, then she must be...

"CIC?"

"Yes, Sir."

He shook his head. The Combat Information Center was as deeply buried as Flag Bridge. In fact, it was one deck farther down. It was also the only other compartment Ilkova could hope to reach that was fitted with the armored shafts through which a life pod could be launched. But getting there through this—the passage was clearly open to vacuum, judging by the thin haze of smoke racing along the overhead towards the hungry rents in *Phantom*'s hull, and God only knew what other damage there might be—would have been hard enough for someone who wasn't encumbered and didn't have a broken arm. Trying to drag him that far with only one working arm...

"Leave me," he got out through the ragged bursts of pain.

"No, Sir," she said flatly.

"Leave me!" he repeated. "Go see if...there's anyone left...in CIC. If there is...you can...send back...a rescue party."

"No, Sir." Her voice was even flatter.

"I—"

"Attention all hands!"

Another voice drowned his out, blaring from the all-hands circuit. He recognized Tonová and felt a stir of surprise that *Phantom*'s captain was still alive. But the surprise vanished into something else an instant later.

"They've launched again," Tonová said harshly. "We've got two minutes. Abandon ship. Everyone who can, abandon *now!*"

Those bastards. Oh, those bastards! *We're* done, *can't they* see *that?*

Of course they could, he realized. They just didn't give a damn.

"*Leave me!*" he snapped again. "You heard...Captain Tonová! Get... out *now!*"

"No, Sir," Ilkova grated through clenched teeth, yanking harder, hauling him along the air-bleeding passage at a faster rate.

"God damn it...that's...an order!" He twisted his shoulders, despite the agony in his damaged spine, trying to wrench out of her grasp.

"All due respect," she panted, "no."

"Let me go!"

"Not going to happen." Her voice was hammered iron. "Now stop *squirming*, damn it! You're slowing us down."

"But—"

"Sir, will you just shut the hell up?"

❖   ❖   ❖

Hajdu Győző watched Daphne Koopman's missiles race outward, then turned his attention to the next incoming salvo, grimly satisfied by what was about to happen to the bastards who'd murdered his task force. And when they were gone, he'd deal with the *rest* of the traitors in this damnable star system! If they'd thought—

"*Incoming!*" someone screamed.

Thirteen seconds later, Hajdu Győző and SLNS *Camperdown* ceased to exist.

And eighty-five seconds after that, so did HMS *Phantom* and HMS *Cinqueda*.

SLNS *Lepanto*
Hypatia System

IT WAS VERY QUIET on SLNS *Lepanto*'s flag bridge. The quiet of shock and stunned, absolute disbelief, Commodore Sandra Haskell thought within the cocoon of her own numbed incomprehension. As chief of staff for Battle Cruiser Squadron 4012, she'd had the best possible perspective, and she still couldn't understand, couldn't even start to process, what had just happened.

The entire engagement had lasted less than eight minutes. How could that be *possible?* How could TF 1030 have begun it with ninety-eight battlecruisers, forty cruisers, and thirty-two destroyers and have only ninety-three warships left—total—less than *eight minutes* later?

Yet it had happened . . . and the task force's current *effective* strength was even lower than that: twenty-nine destroyers, thirty-six cruisers . . . and eleven battlecruisers. She was pretty sure the four cruisers and three destroyers they'd lost had been accidents. The Manties' concentration on the battlecruisers had been obvious, crushing, and lethal. All of the combat effective survivors—aside from SLNS *Hamidieh* and *Lepanto* herself—had taken at least some damage. Technically, there were another seventeen whose hulks might have been repairable, if there'd been some way to get them home. There wasn't. Which meant they were effectively as dead as *Troubadour*, *Stevedore*, and *Merchant Mart*.

And as Vice Admiral Hajdu Győző.

That thought took Haskell's eyes away from the tactical display to the tall, powerfully built man in the command chair at the center of the flag bridge. Rear Admiral Martin Gogunov, CO, BatCruRon 4012. Aside from *Lepanto*, only two of Gogunov's original eight units survived: SLNS *Queen* and SLNS *Revanche*.

And despite its sixty percent loss rate, Gogunov's squadron had the most survivors of any of TF 1030's original *thirteen* battlecruiser squadrons.

Nine ships, Haskell thought, looking at the man who had just inherited what remained of Vice Admiral Hajdu's task force. *They did it to us with* nine ships.

She gave herself a mental shake. Yes, the Manties had done it with only nine ships, but those deadly eight minutes had been time enough for them to put nineteen salvos into space before TF 1030's enormous launch took them off the board. Seventy-five hundred missiles was barely six percent of the fire the Manties had taken, which made the loss ratio even more grotesquely unbalanced, but Haskell had come up as a tactical officer. As she'd watched those missiles, watched their ECM, those massive jammers and incredible decoy penaids, watched their attack profiles shift and adjust, she'd realized there truly had to be an FTL component to the Manties' fire control. It was the only way they could have adapted that quickly or maintained their telemetry links so long, and if she'd needed any proof, there was what had happened to the final incoming salvos. There'd been no one left to provide them with additional updates, and their accuracy and—especially—target selection had dropped markedly, despite the fact that TF 1030's missile-defense net had been torn to shreds by the earlier launches.

So when you come down to it, it's not really surprising somebody with that kind of range, that kind of EW advantage, and *FTL telemetry links kicked the living* shit *out of us. Especially not when you add complete and total surprise into the equation.*

Despite her shock, despite her chill awareness of what the technology revealed here portended, despite even the loss of *at least* a hundred and fifty thousand more SLN lives, she felt an unwilling admiration for those Manties. She hated what Vice Admiral Hajdu had done to any survivors aboard their ships, and she regretted it even more deeply as she contemplated the sheer courage it must have taken for just nine ships, however great their tactical advantage, to take on a hundred and seventy.

They couldn't have known how badly they'd hurt us, not really. They probably expected our losses to be heavy, but they couldn't have expected them to be this *heavy. And whatever they thought they might do to us, they damned well knew* they *weren't going home.*

And it wasn't even their star system.

She didn't like to contemplate what *that* might mean for the future, either. Nor did she care for the "Grand Alliance's" inevitable reaction to TF 1030's violation of the Deneb Accords. The Accords were pretty damn specific about not targeting obviously disabled ships while they evacuated their crews. It happened sometimes, of course. Often, it simply wasn't possible to abort an attack on a ship, however disabled it might have been, especially with missiles. But that wasn't what had happened here. The salvo which had finished off the Manty cripples had been launched only after it was obvious they'd been totally incapacitated.

There'll be hell to pay when the Manties and their friends find out about this *one*, she reflected grimly. *And there should be. There damned well* should *be. There's a reason the Deneb Accords were written in the first place, and—*

"I want updated ammunition totals soonest." Gogunov's voice was hard, flat, and his eyes were bleak. "I know most of our survivors've taken damage. Now that we've lost the pods, I need to know who's got what when we reassign the targets."

Haskell twitched inside. Surely he didn't mean—?

"We're going to proceed with Buccaneer, Sir?" she asked.

"Of course we are!" Gogunov's surprise was obvious, and he glared at her. "It's why we came! Vice Admiral Hajdu may be gone, but that doesn't change the mission!"

"Oh, of course not, Sir!" Haskell said quickly. "We'll get those numbers for you immediately." She nodded at Commander Gregory Ham, Gogunov's operations officer, and Ham begin punching queries into his panel.

"Good." Gogunov's expression relaxed . . . some, and he turned to Captain Alexis Choi, his communications officer. "While Greg's getting the numbers, raise Rear Admiral Yountz. Inform him he's now the Task Force second in command. Tell him I'm assigning him operational control of our cruisers and destroyers and that I want him to take personal command of search-and-rescue."

"Yes, Sir," Choi said quickly. She glanced at Haskell from the corner of one eye and began entering the code for SLNS *Yashima*, Rear Admiral Thomas Yountz's heavy cruiser flagship.

Haskell knew why Choi had darted that glance in her direction. If Gogunov was handing off responsibility for SAR with that many Solarian life pods and that many wrecked Solarian battlecruisers on his hands, it could only be because he expected to be too busy with something else to oversee it himself. And that meant—

"Sir," Commodore Ham reported, "the numbers are preliminary, but it looks like about two thousand birds aboard the battlecruisers. You were right about the damage. We've lost at least one magazine each aboard five of the ships that are still combat effective. I'll need at least five or six minutes to sort out a new queue for Buccaneer."

"Well, two thousand should be enough to do the job," Gogunov said. "Go ahead and start setting it up now."

"Sir," Haskell asked in a careful tone, "what timing do you want on the launch?"

"What timing do you *think* I want?" Gogunov snapped. "The one Admiral Hajdu gave them!"

Haskell swallowed hard. She hadn't liked it when Hajdu Győző refused to extend his final time limit for the Hypatians by one additional second. She didn't care what their mission orders said; as far she was concerned, an Eridani Edict violation was an Eridani Edict violation, whoever committed it and no matter who authorized it.

And she'd just discovered she liked Hajdu's decision even less now that its execution had fallen on BatCruRon 4012 and its staff.

On Sandra Haskell.

"Sir, I think we might want to consider—"

"Admiral Hajdu and Ms. Yang-O'Grady—both of whom, I remind you, are now *dead*, Commodore—did all the considering we're going to do," Gogunov said flatly, his eyes harder than ever. "The fact that those Manty bastards just ambushed us to try to stop us only makes it more important to prove they didn't. That they *couldn't.*"

Haskell sat very still while her mind raced like a hamster in an exercise wheel trying to find some way, some argument, that might change his mind.

The problem was, she didn't think one existed.

She'd never met a flag officer she respected more than Martin Gogunov. She'd been his chief of staff for almost five T-years, and his ops officer for two T-years before that, and she'd learned a lot from him over that time. But she also knew the Martin Gogunov she'd served for so long had become a driven man even before what had just happened to the task force.

His was a family with a proud naval tradition, and he, his sister, and all three of his brothers had graduated from the Academy and gone straight to service with the Fleet. Commodore Marguerite Gogunov, his sister, and Captain Allen Gogunov, his next-youngest brother, were both Frontier Fleet. His older brother, Vice Admiral Marshall Gogunov had gone into Battle Fleet...and died with Sandra Crandall in the Battle of Spindle. And she knew Gogunov had received confirmation just before they translated out for Hypatia that Captain Scott Gogunov, the baby of the family and another Battle Fleet officer, had been killed under Massimo Filareta at Manticore.

A lot of Solarian League Navy officers had lost family and close friends at Spindle and Manticore. Total casualties might be less than a statistical blip compared to the incredible total number of Solarian citizens, but for all its enormous size, the SLN was one of the smallest military organizations in history as a percentage of the population of the polity it served. Its peacetime strength was barely 155,000,000, and that included its entire uniformed dirtside establishment. In theory, that strength would more than triple on a wartime footing when the Reserve was fully mobilized, but no one was talking about mobilizing all those superdreadnoughts now, given their total obsolescence. The Navy's pre-Spindle peacetime shipboard strength—the men and women actually fighting this war so far—had been only 27,400,000, and losses to date in KIA, WIA, and POWs, not counting today's debacle, were already over *five* million. That was almost twenty percent of its total space-going strength, and despite its size, it was a tight-knit community, with many families like the Gogunovs—and the Haskells, for that matter—who'd served in the Navy for T-centuries. So, yes, a *lot* of Solarian officers were hurting, but few of them had been hit as hard as Martin Gogunov.

And even fewer were in a position to act upon their grief and hatred.

"Sir, I have a com request from President Vangelis." Captain Choi's tone was even more carefully expressionless than Haskell's had been.

"What does *he* want?" Gogunov bit off each word like a sliver of battle steel.

"Sir, he's offering to assist us in search-and-rescue."

"Oh, I'm sure he *is*," Gogunov sneered. "I suppose that's one way to try to run out the clock after he never bothered to mention to us that there were hostile warships in the system. The bastard knew they were there, knew they were planning to attack us, and all he did was keep whining about how he needed more time to get his damned people off the platforms! Hell, he was probably just stalling us until they could get into position to shoot us in the back!"

"Um, shall I transfer him to your display, Sir?"

"I can't think of a single reason in the galaxy why you should," Gogunov replied. "Please be good enough to inform the 'President' that I'm a little too busy to take his call just now and that I recommend he concentrate on expediting the evacuation of his own people. We'll look after ours."

Choi hesitated, her expression profoundly unhappy as she faced her displays, her back to her admiral. Then her shoulders sagged.

"Yes, Sir," she said softly. Then she cleared her throat, pressed a key, and spoke into her own microphone.

"I'm sorry, Mister President," she said expressionlessly. "Admiral Gogunov has instructed me to inform you that he's too occupied at the moment to speak with you. He recommends, however, that you concentrate on expediting the evacuation of your own people while we deal with our search-and-recovery efforts."

She paused for a moment, listening to her earbug.

"No, Mister President. I'm sorry. That's the only message I have for you." She listened again. "Yes, Sir. I understand." Another pause. "I regret that you feel that way, Sir. And, yes, it has been recorded."

She sat back as the connection with the planetary surface was broken, and Haskell could see her biting her lower lip.

The flag bridge's silence was as total as it had been after the final missile salvo, but it was very different now. The chief of staff felt it around her, felt the uncertainty, the unhappiness, the horror…and the countervailing tides of angry, vicious approval from some of Gogunov's staffers. She couldn't tell how many of them felt which way, and that mental hamster raced faster and faster as she tried to think of some way—*any* way—to deflect her admiral, the man she admired so deeply, from Juggernaut's course.

"Sir, I have a com request from Captain Turner," Captain Choi said suddenly, and Gogunov glanced at her, then nodded.

"Put her through."

"Yes, Sir," Choi replied, and Gogunov's petite, dark-skinned flag captain appeared on his display.

"Yes, Indira?" he said a bit impatiently.

"I understand from Tactical that we're reassigning the Buccaneer targets, Sir," she said.

"Of course we are."

Gogunov had specifically requested Turner as his flag captain. They went back a long way, to their Academy days, and Sandra Haskell knew how deeply he respected Turner's judgment. Despite that, his tone was testy, impatient.

I wonder if he already knows what she's going to say. What I hope to hell she's going to say, she thought. *I bet he does. I bet that's why—*

"May I ask how soon you intend to launch?" Turner asked.

"I intend, *Captain*, to launch on our previously announced schedule." The voice which had been testy was icy now.

"Sir, with all due respect, I believe we should delay launch."

"No."

Turner's gray-green eyes hardened ever so slightly at the flat, one-word reply. She gazed at him for a moment, then inhaled deeply.

"Sir," she said with unaccustomed formality, "I strongly urge you to reconsider that launch time."

"No," he repeated, his voice even harder.

"Sir, we're monitoring over eight thousand pod transponders." Turner's effort to keep her own tone reasonable and rational was obvious. "It's going to take time to recover them all, and God knows there are probably pods out there with dead or damaged beacons. We need all hands for search and rescue right now. And, frankly, we *really* need the assistance of every Hypatian shuttle we can lay hands on. If we push back the launch time, give them the additional time they need to complete their civilian evacuation"—she emphasized the word "civilian" ever so slightly—"they're a lot more likely to make those small craft available to us."

I wonder if she really doesn't know Vangelis just offered exactly that. Haskell thought. *It doesn't* sound *like she does, but—*

Whatever his chief of staff might have thought, Gogunov's suddenly fiery eyes showed what *he* thought had happened.

"We have ninety ships up here, Captain," he said coldly. "I feel confident we can find sufficient shuttles and cutters to pick up our own people. And if the local authorities are unable to evacuate all of their *civilians*"—unlike Turner's, his emphasis was anything but slight—"in time, then perhaps they should have thought about that before they became traitors to the Solarian League and invited in the miserable sons-of-bitches who just murdered almost two hundred thousand of *our* people." He glared at his old friend's image. "You'll pardon me if I don't shed many tears over their reaping the consequences of their own fucking treason."

"Sir, we don't know which of the civilians in those habitats supported the secession referendum," Turner replied unflinchingly, "but there are still over six million of them, and according to the Hypatians' announced totals, twenty percent of the system's population voted *against* secession. That means there are somewhere around a million Solarian citizens who never chose to secede—*and their children*—on those 'targets.'"

"That's too fucking bad," Gogunov said. "We didn't put them there."

"There's no military necessity for this." Turner's voice was as flat as Gogunov's had ever been. "There are, in fact, military arguments—like the rescue of our own personnel—against it, as I've just pointed out. Under the circumstances, Admiral Gogunov, I protest your decision in the strongest possible terms."

"What you're pleased to call *my* decision was made by Vice Admiral Hajdu, with the support and endorsement of the ranking civilian representative of the Federal Government in the system, Captain!" Gogunov snapped. "Both of them happen to be *dead* now, thanks to the attack launched with no warning whatsoever by a hostile task force the Hypatians knew was there and never mentioned. Since they're no longer available to alter the decision—and the timing—they laid down before they were murdered, I'm simply proceeding with the execution of the last legal order I was given. And that's precisely what this task force is going to do. Is that clear?"

"Your intent is clear, Sir," Turner replied in a measured, formal tone. "It is my belief, however, that it constitutes an illegal act under the Eridani Edict. As such, I must decline to carry it out."

Haskell inhaled sharply as the flag captain's steely words hit the deck like an ancient knight's gauntlet, and Gogunov's face darkened.

"You have no authority to refuse my orders, Captain! The Articles of War make that abundantly clear, and I remind you that the Solarian League is in a state of war. That makes mutiny a capital offense, Captain Turner!"

"Military and civilian courts have clearly established that military law does not override the Constitution, Sir," Turner said unflinchingly. "And the Eridani Edict constitutes a *Constitutional* prohibition of the action you propose to carry out. And, I would remind *you*, Sir, that the Articles of War themselves both require a serving officer to refuse an illegal order and specifically state that that obligation applies in time of war just as it does in peacetime."

"I'm not going to debate this with you, Captain. You *will* carry out your orders, or I will relieve you of command and place you under close arrest to await court-martial upon our return to base."

"Sir, I must respectfully decline to obey that order."

"Then you are relieved, Madam. Captain Yoshizaki will replace you as *Lepanto*'s commanding officer, and *you* will retire to your quarters and consider yourself under arrest. Now, are you prepared to obey *that* order, or do I need to send Marines to forcibly remove you from the command deck?"

"You have the authority to relieve me, and I will accept relief," she said coldly, but then her voice changed. "I'll accept relief, but speaking as someone who's no longer your flag captain—someone who's known you for forty years—*think* about this, for God's sake, Martin! Haven't enough people already died today?"

"Not the *right* ones!" Gogunov snapped, and stabbed the disconnect key.

"Where's that launch queue?" he demanded.

"Working on it, Sir," Commodore Ham said into the ringing background stillness.

"Good."

"Sir, Admiral Yountz is on the com," Captain Choi said.

"Put him on," Gogunov replied, then nodded to the pickup as Yountz appeared on his display. "Admiral." His voice sounded almost normal, despite the confrontation with Turner. "What can I do for you?"

"Sir." Yountz's eyes had an odd look, the look of a man trying to grapple with a nightmare...and failing. "May I have permission to request Hypatian assistance in search-and-rescue efforts?"

"No!" Those shadowed eyes widened at Gogunov's snapped response, and the task force's new commander shook his head sharply. "They have—" he checked the time display "—ninety-seven minutes before we execute Buccaneer." He showed his teeth in a thin not-smile. "I won't have it said we prevented them from evacuating as many of their people as possible before the deadline, even if they are traitors."

"But, Sir, I'm not sure we've got enough small craft to pick up our survivors and—"

"I don't want to hear any crap about our not having sufficient small craft." Unlike Yountz's, Gogunov's eyes burned like blue lava. "We're the fucking Solarian League Navy, Admiral. Now get the job done!"

"Yes, Sir," Yountz replied. "But, Sir, if I may finish, I don't have enough small craft to pick up the Manticoran survivors, as well. That's why I thought the system authorities might—"

"Pick up the *Manties?*" Gogunov erupted. "What the fuck do I care about the goddammed *Manties?*"

"But the Deneb—"

"*Screw* the Deneb Accords!" Gogunov barked, and his fiery eyes took on a sudden, icy glitter. "But you're right, Admiral. We can't just leave them floating around out there, can we? And their drift velocity means they'll enter Javelin range in about ten minutes."

"Sir—" Haskell began, unable to keep the horror out of her voice. Firing on life pods was a violation of every rule of war. Surely he couldn't intend to—

"Do you have hard locks on their transponders, Admiral?" Gogunov continued, ignoring her, his eyes locked with Yountz's.

"Well, yes, Sir." Yountz's expression had gone totally blank. "On some, at least. Are you instructing me to fire on them when they enter Javelin range, Admiral Gogunov?"

"That's exactly what I'm ordering you to do," Gogunov said flatly. "It's time someone taught these butchers actions have consequences. They're responsible for every drop of blood that's been shed from the moment they murdered Admiral Byng and every man and woman aboard his flagship. Now it's *their* frigging turn."

"Sir, are you *sure*—"

"Of course I am!" Gogunov roared. "What the fuck is *wrong* with you people? You've got your orders—*now carry them out!*"

"Yes, Sir," Yountz said woodenly.

"Sir," Haskell began again. "Admiral Gogunov, if we—"

"Missile launch!" Ham said suddenly. "Multiple launches at—" He paused for a moment, as if unable to believe what he was about to say. Then he looked over his shoulder at Gogunov. "Sir, the range at launch is sixty million kilometers. Acceleration approximately four-five-one KPS squared."

HMS *Arngrim*
Hypatia System

"I'M AFRAID HE MEANS it," Adam Vangelis said from Megan Petersen's com screen. The system president was haggard and his exhausted expression was like iron. "When Hajdu was killed, I hoped whoever replaced him might be saner, but this Gogunov won't even *talk* to me." He shook his head, his voice heavy. "After the price your people paid, I can't...I can't really fit my mind around all of this." He shook his head again, the movement weary and defeated. "Our people will never forget what Admiral Kotouč and your spacers did, Commander Petersen. *Never*. But it looks like all of them died for absolutely nothing."

Megan's heart was a stone. She looked at the com image, transmitted over a distance of 3.3 LM by the Hermes buoy Admiral Kotouč had left in place. They hadn't used it before, since its directional grav pulses could hardly have been concealed from the Sollies. There was no longer any reason to hide the presence of Manticoran warships in Hypatian space, however. Besides, the remaining Ghost Rider platform keeping it company had been transmitting FTL from the moment Kotouč launched his attack. That platform had showed her every brutal detail of what the squadron had done to TF 1030, and as she'd watched the carnage explode across her plot, realized Hajdu's flagship was among the dead, she'd hoped—like Vangelis—that whoever inherited command would show the sanity to back away from an Eridani violation. Yet now, as she looked reality bleakly in the face, she knew hope was all they'd ever had, and the taste of its failure was bitter on her tongue.

Admiral Kotouč had never expected to destroy the Solly task force. For that matter, he'd never envisioned inflicting anywhere near the losses the Sollies had suffered. None of them had. And he'd known—they'd *all* known—that if the Sollies were crazy enough to authorize something like this in the first place, their survivors might carry through with their act of mass murder.

But we had to try, she thought drearily. *We had to. Every single one of us would rather die trying to stop it than live knowing we'd stood by and let something like this happen.*

294

The stone in her chest spasmed as she thought about Jayson, wondered if there was any chance he might be aboard one of the handful of life pods whose transponder beacons they'd picked up. But there were little more than a hundred of those pods, and her brain had already worked the math with merciless precision.

And now this.

"He won't give you *any* more time, even after you offered to help rescue his own people?"

"Not a single second," Vangelis said heavily, seven and a half seconds later as the Hermes buoy relayed his light-speed transmission to *Arngrim*. The system president laughed bitterly. "He wouldn't even tell me that to my face. He's 'too busy.' And there's not one damn thing we can do about it."

"I wouldn't bet on that, Sir," Commander Megan Petersen said, and she didn't recognize the iron in her own voice.

She looked up from the display and met her executive officer's eyes. Lieutenant Commander Thirunavu looked back at her without speaking, then nodded ever so slightly. She pointed at Lieutenant Berden and Lieutenant Patrick Crouch, *Arngrim*'s electronic warfare officer, and Thirunavu nodded again, more sharply. He stepped across to Berden's tactical section just as Vangelis responded to Megan.

"What do you mean, Commander?" the Hypatian president demanded, then stiffened. "Your ship's the only one *left!* You can't possibly expect to stop *ninety* Solarians all by yourself! For God's sake, hasn't Manticore spent enough lives trying to stop what you can't stop in the end anyway?"

"It doesn't matter whether or not we *can* stop it, Sir," Megan told him flatly, her brown eyes were flint. "What matters is whether or not we *try* to."

"But...but you can't sacrifice all your people's lives for nothing," Vangelis said softly, seven seconds later, and she shook her head.

"We're not talking about 'nothing,' Sir.' We're talking about the reason we're here. We're talking about responsibility and *decency*." She squared her shoulders, meeting his gaze levelly. "Another Manticoran captain had to make this decision at a place called Grayson, Mister President. She made the same one Admiral Kotouč made, and for the same reason. You trusted us. Your *people* trusted us. And even if that weren't the case, Mister President, I can't go home and tell my Empress I stood by, watching an act of mass murder, and did *nothing*." She shook her head. "The Star Empire's honor—*her* honor—won't let me do that. Now, if you'll excuse me, I have a few things to do. Petersen, clear."

SLNS *Lepanto*
Hypatia System

"*MISSILES?*" MARTIN GOGUNOV DEMANDED.

"Yes, Sir," Commodore Ham confirmed. "At that range, we haven't got a solid count yet, but it looks like about thirty."

"From sixty *million* kilometers?" Gogunov glared at the plot as if he thought it was lying to him.

"Yes, Sir." Ham shook his head. "I don't have any idea what's out there, I'm afraid. We don't have anything in position to cover the launch locus. It's over seventy-five million kilometers from the point at which they originally launched against us."

"They must have detached an observer, Sir," Haskell said, praying that the distraction of a fresh enemy might divert Gogunov from his madness. He looked at her, and she shrugged. "We've just had proof their EW's good enough to hide from us in-system, Sir, but nobody could hide a hyper footprint at this kind of range. Besides, they're inside the limit and their missiles' initial velocity shows they launched almost from rest, relative to Hypatia." She gestured at the maneuvering plot, where the launch's approximate coordinates had just been added. Without a solid emission signature for the launching ship, they were a lot more approximate than usual, and the amber sphere indicating their possible position was almost two light-seconds across. "That means it can't be some new arrival."

"So they're more of the same bastards who bushwhacked us," Gogunov grated. That wasn't the verb Sandra Haskell would have chosen for anyone gutsy enough to engage at eighteen-to-one odds, but she nodded vigorously.

Gogunov glowered at the tactical display's sidebars. It was ridiculous! Even assuming someone—*anyone!*—could accurately target anything at almost three and a half light-minutes, sixty million kilometers was twice any range at which even the Manties had ever attempted an engagement without one hell of a lot of closing velocity. Assuming those incoming missiles were somehow able to maintain acceleration all the way in, it would still take them almost nine minutes to reach his ships. But they couldn't. No missile impeller node ever built could sustain that kind of accel that long, and unlike the multistage Cataphract, no Manty missile had ever demonstrated the ability to incorporate a pure ballistic phase into its attack profile. So was this some sort of insane *bluff*? Were the murderous bastards trying to divert him from his core mission to teach the Hypatians and the rest of the galaxy the price of treason?

Maybe it *was* a bluff, but he'd take no chances after what had already happened.

"Stand by missile-defense," he said. "And let's vector some recon platforms towards their launch locus."

"Yes, Sir," Ham replied. "Missile-defense is at Readiness One. And the closest platforms will be on their way in another . . . eighty seconds, as soon as the maneuver instructions reach them. I'm afraid it'll take another five or six minutes to get them close enough to burn through Manty stealth."

"Just find the bastards, Greg," Gogunov said. "Just find them."

Commodore Ham nodded, and Sandra Haskell sat back in her command chair, watching the missile icons accelerate towards her. Like her admiral, if she'd only known, she found it almost—*almost*—impossible to believe even Manticoran missiles could have that sort of range. Then again, even the early-generation Cataphracts in *Lepanto*'s magazines did, although it would require a ballistic phase 41,000,000 kilometers—and over eight minutes—long. Of course, the chance of their actually *hitting* anything at 3.3 LM was . . . poor, to say the least. But if—

"Wedge shutdown!" Ham announced suddenly. "Acceleration period was three minutes, Sir. Closing velocity at shutdown seven-point-three thousand KPS; range five-two-point-six million kilometers." He shook his head. "We've lost lock, I'm afraid."

Gogunov grunted. Of course they'd lost lock. No one could hold targets that small at that range on active sensors, and without impeller signatures, passives couldn't track them, either.

He considered the numbers. Three minutes equated to a maximum duration acceleration phase for a standard missile. The latest generation single-stage Solarian missiles had a slightly higher acceleration *rate*, but that three-minute acceleration *endurance* for missile impellers had been a tactical fact of life for every navy in space for the better part of a T-century. So the question became whether or not the Manties had the same multistage capability as the Cataphract after all.

Either they do, or they don't, *Martin*, he thought. *And either way, you'll have a little more information on the bastards' capabilities.*

"Assume they have a second stage with the same endurance," he said. "What's their profile then?"

"Under that assumption, Sir, total time of flight from shutdown should be right on nine-point-three minutes. They'll be ballistic for three hundred and seventy-nine seconds and light up again at about twenty-one-point-nine million kilometers, assuming they want maximum velocity for their final penetration profiles." Ham shrugged. "They could delay that just to be difficult, of course."

Gogunov nodded and checked the time display. Three hundred and seventy-nine seconds from shutdown meant they'd know one way or the other about any second-stage capability in another five and a half minutes.

"Do you have that targeting queue for Buccaneer?" he asked.

"Uh, no, Sir," the ops officer said. "I'm afraid—"

"I understand why you were distracted, Greg." Gogunov smiled thinly. "But we've got some time before those missiles get here—assuming they do—so we might as well put it to use, don't you think?"

"Yes, Sir." Ham seemed less than delighted at the prospect, Haskell noted. "I'll get right on it. It'll take—"

He broke off, pressing his earbug deeper into his ear, then looked up sharply.

HMS *Arngrim*
Hypatia System

"COMING UP ON SECOND stage initiation in five minutes," Lieutenant Berden announced, and Megan nodded.

Her decision to launch had been less spontaneous than President Vangelis might have assumed. She'd given a lot of thought to her orders as she waited for Admiral Kotouč and the rest of the squadron to make their sacrificial attack, and there was no question in her mind that she'd just violated them. She was supposed to be the Admiral's observer, his witness. She was supposed to record whatever the Sollies might do for posterity, as evidence in any postwar war crimes trials. She was supposed to look after any of the squadron's survivors, if the Sollies didn't pick them up. And she was supposed to be Captain Acworth's forward scout, the one who warned him and updated him if *Vukodlak* and her consorts miraculously arrived before the Sollies left.

And she was supposed to get *Arngrim*'s people home alive.

She knew all of that, just as she knew any board of inquiry would conclude that her orders left her no discretion to do anything else. But that was another way to say her orders would cover her ass. That with Admiral Kotouč's uncompromising instructions in *Arngrim*'s communications database, no one could fault her for not having done anything else.

Only there were some orders she couldn't obey. Not when Hajdu's successor was just as determined to drown the Hypatia System in civilian blood. She couldn't "observe" that and live with herself.

She'd wondered, when she made her actual decision, how much of it was because she'd lost Jayson. The bleeding wound of his death ripped at the heart of her, made even worse by the fact that it was unlikely—now—that she'd ever know for certain whether or not he'd actually died with *Cinqueda*. She'd run the numbers, she knew how infinitesimal that chance truly was, but given the odds against her single ship, it was only too likely she'd never know if he'd beaten those numbers. And if, by some miracle, he'd survived and she didn't, what would he think of her decision now?

299

He'd understand, she told herself. *He'd have made the same one. I know* he would have.

And she thought he would have approved of her tactics.

Arngrim's greatest weakness was her magazine capacity. With only twelve launchers and only twenty rounds per tube, she had a total of just two hundred and forty missiles, and a quarter of them were EW birds, primarily Dazzlers and Dragon's Teeth. That gave her exactly two laserheads for each of the surviving Solarian warships.

Not even Manticoran tech advantages could offset that sort of odds.

But the Sollies might not *know* that, and so she'd stacked a triple salvo, using a full fifteen percent of her total ammunition supply in a single launch. Thirty-six Mark 16s—eight of them Dazzlers and Dragon's Teeth—were *going* to get through what was left of the Sollies' defenses, she thought grimly, and she'd chosen her targeting with malice aforethought. As long as they didn't guess that she could do it only five more times before her tubes ran dry...

Oh, and it would be sort of a good idea to avoid running into any of their missiles, too, Megan, a voice that sounded remarkably like Jayson's said in the back of her mind, and she surprised herself with a small but genuine smile.

"Those recon drones are getting closer, Ma'am," Lieutenant Crouch said from his electronic warfare station. She glanced at him, and he looked up to meet her eyes. "They're likely to burn through our stealth in the next forty-five seconds or so."

"Then I suppose it's time for your little surprise, Pat."

"Yes, Ma'am!"

Despite the tension of the moment, Crouch actually grinned with youthful enthusiasm. Probably because at his age he truly did feel immortal, Megan thought. Not that he didn't have a right to a certain proprietary pride. He and Berden had given the possibility of Solarian recon drones quite a bit of thought after *Arngrim* had received Admiral Kotouč's orders.

Solly RDs were a lot less stealthy than the SLN thought they were. It wasn't that they ran around shouting "Here I am!" at the top of their lungs. In fact, compared to the remote platforms with which the Royal Manticoran Navy had begun its long war against the People's Republic, they weren't bad at all. Quite a bit better than the RMN had possessed at the turn of the century, as a matter of fact. Unfortunately for the SLN, that had been twenty T-years ago, and things had changed in the Haven Sector. The combination of *Arngrim's* shipboard sensors and the far more capable recon platforms she and her slain consorts had deployed before Admiral Kotouč's final battle had very little trouble keeping track of the incoming drones, and Berden and Crouch had spotted flights of Mark 31 counter-missiles along their most probable vectors. The CMs had launched ballistic, with their drives shut down, relying solely on the initial velocity imparted by the powerful mag drivers of *Arngrim*'s launch tubes. That was barely fifteen hundred meters per second, a *very* low velocity by the standards of missiles and counter-missiles, but they'd also been launched beginning the better part of an hour ago, in intervals along *Arngrim*'s track as she continued to put space between herself and the rest of the squadron's launch point. Even at their arthritic pace, the closest of them was 5,300 kilometers from the ship, and four of them were almost perfectly positioned to intercept the nearest recon drone. In fact *one* of them—

"Take them from the side," she said. "Number Twelve, I think."

"Aye, aye, Ma'am!" Berden replied. "Engaging with Number Twelve... *now*," and he pressed the button.

Two of the potential interceptors were almost directly between *Arngrim* and the drone. Another pair was well to one side of the shortest vector between her and the RD, however, and Megan had chosen the one *farthest* from *Arngrim*. Its trajectory wasn't as good, but if the second prong of Berden and Crouch's brainstorm worked...

She left them to it while she returned her own attention to the Mark 16s whose impeller wedges had just lit off once more.

The range was so extreme that even with the Ghost Rider platform parked almost on top of the Sollies, there'd be very little time for any sort of course correction over *Arngrim*'s light-speed telemetry links. She'd accepted that going in. But what that platform had done was allow her to fingerprint her targets' emission signatures with excruciating accuracy. Not only that, Crouch and Berden had come through for her on a second front. They'd identified the new Solly flagship after her birds had been launched but while there was still plenty of time to tell them who to look for.

I'm afraid it's about to rain all over your day, Admiral Gogunov, she thought. *And if my brilliant tac department* does *manage to kill your drones before you find us, I may actually get to rain on* your *successor before she can find me to launch her own damned missiles, too.*

She'd like that.

She'd like that a *lot*.

SLNS *Yashima*
Hypatia System

"SIR, I HAVE THAT firing solution," Captain Rochetti said quietly.

Rear Admiral Thomas Yountz turned to face his ops officer, and Rochetti cleared his throat.

"We don't have hard locks on the...targets. Not yet. The best we could do at this point is a saturation launch. It'd...take a lot of missiles, Sir."

His voice sounded almost hopeful, Yountz realized. That was his first thought. Then he had another one, and he opened his mouth.

He closed it again.

They didn't have "hard locks"?

"Sir, I've glanced over Maurizio's data," Commodore Dantas, CruRon 4018's chief of staff, said. "He's right. Without hard locks, we'd need a lot of missiles to cover a volume of space that big. It'll be at least another—" he glanced at the tactical display, where a digital time readout slid steadily downward toward the predicted arrival time of the incoming Manticoran missiles "—nine or ten minutes before their vector brings them close enough for us to get hard sensor returns."

No doubt it would, Yountz thought. Life pods were very small targets, after all.

Which was the reason they carried transponder beacons...just like the ones blinking on that same tactical display. Transponder beacons designed to help shuttles—or anything else—home in on them and their fragile cargos of survivors.

"Under the circumstances, Sir," Dantas continued, "I'd recommend we hold the launch until we have better numbers. The Task Force's already lost a lot of its missiles. Be a good idea not to expend any more than we have to."

His eyes held Yountz's for a long, still moment. Then the admiral nodded.

"An excellent point, Justin," he said. "We'll have plenty of time to carry out Admiral Gogunov's orders when the range's shorter. In the meantime, let's concentrate on picking our people up. I think—"

"Counter-missile launch, Sir!" Rochetti said suddenly. "The Manties just launched against the reconnaissance platforms!"

SLNS *Lepanto*
and
SLNS *Yashima*
Hypatia System

"COUNTER-MISSILE LAUNCH!" COMMODORE HAM snapped, and Gogunov's eyes darted to the icon which had just appeared in the plot. It came streaking out of nowhere, well to one side within the amber sphere—considerably greater in diameter than usual, at that insane range—indicating the Manty missiles' possible launch site. Given counter-missiles' extreme acceleration rates and the velocity the recon platform had built, flight time was very short. But it was long enough for the computers to nail down the point from which that counter-missile had launched.

And then, thirty seconds after the CM's impeller signature had been detected, the RD's final light-speed transmission reached *Lepanto.*

"Got them, Sir!" Ham said exultantly. "The signature's still weak, but—Correction, Sir: *signatures*, plural. CIC makes it a pair of those big-assed destroyers of theirs."

"Plot it and get the birds away!"

"Yes, Sir! Programming now."

"Very good. And once you've gotten them launched, set up the Buccaneer queue." Gogunov smiled viciously. "We've still got six minutes before their birds get here, even if our worst-case assumption is accurate. We might as well make use of them.

Ham flinched and his hands actually stopped moving for an instant before he completed the firing sequence. *Lepanto* quivered as a full salvo of Cataphract-As belched from her broadside tubes and the operations officer watched their outgoing tracks for a heartbeat or two, then looked at Gogunov. He didn't say a word, but the admiral saw the silent question—perhaps even the silent *protest*—in his eyes, and his hungry smile turned into a glare.

"I gave Vangelis Admiral Hajdu's complete time limit, despite the fact that the Manties attacked us well before we'd reached the end of it. Hell, for all they knew, the Admiral might have still relented and

303

extended it again! But they took that possibility off the table when they bushwhacked us. So if they've seen fit to attack us before the expiration of our time limit—*again*—any consequences will be on their heads. Now set up the launch, Commodore!"

"Sir, I—"

"Set it up, or you can join Captain Turner's court-martial!" Gogunov barked.

"Don't do it, Greg."

Sandra Haskell didn't realize she'd spoken until every eye on flag bridge snapped toward her.

"*What* did you just say?" Gogunov demanded, whirling towards her with incandescent eyes.

"I told Greg not to do it, Sir," Haskell said to the flag officer she'd served and respected for so long. "Please, Sir! You don't have to do this! Captain Turner's *right*, and somewhere inside, you have to know she is! This is what the Navy was created to *prevent*, Sir! Don't turn yourself into—"

"Shut your mouth and get the hell off this flag bridge!" Gogunov snarled. "You're relieved, Commodore, and I'll see you *rot* in prison! Get the hell out of my sight!"

"Sir—"

"*Now*, Commodore! And as for *you*, Commodore Ham, you can launch or face charges. And if you do, I'll personally demand the death sentence!"

Ham paled. His eyes darted to Haskell, but then they closed.

"Yes, Sir," he said tonelessly.

"*Please*, Sir," Haskell said. "I'm begging you. Don't—"

Gogunov punched a button on his command chair's armrest.

"Master at Arms, lay to Flag Bridge . . . and bring your sidearm," he grated in a voice of iron, his eyes never wavering from Haskell's face.

✧   ✧   ✧

"Oh, Jesus," Captain Rochetti breathed as the command codes scrolled across his display.

"*What?*" Yountz snapped.

TF 1030 had just launched on the Manties' coordinates. Unlike Hajdu Győző's mammoth pod-based salvo, there were under three hundred birds in this one, and even with the RD's latest information, accuracy at that range would be . . . less than stellar. He didn't need any fresh distractions at this point.

"The Flag is launching on the orbital platforms in four minutes, Sir," Rochetti said flatly.

Yountz stared at him. Surely he didn't mean it! Gogunov was launching *now*? He'd promised the Hypatians fifty more minutes!

"Sir, the Manty missiles' wedges just came back up!" Rochetti's assistant announced.

Yountz's eyes jerked back to the plot as the Manticoran shipkillers reappeared upon it. Obviously, they *did* have a multistage capability of their own.

"Impact in three minutes," Rochetti said harshly. "Counter-missile launch in one hundred seconds!"

"Squadron orders," Yountz heard himself snap. "Do *not* launch on the platforms!" He whirled to the chief of staff. "D'you understand me, Justin? Get that out *now. Do not launch!*"

"But, Sir—!" Rochetti began, and Yountz's glare snapped back around to him.

"Goddamn it, do it, Captain! Nobody in this squadron is going to *touch* that frigging launch button!"

HMS *Arngrim*
Hypatia System

"THEY FELL FOR IT, Ma'am!" Lieutenant Berden crowed exultantly. "Look at that *beautiful* plot!"

It was scarcely a proper report, Megan Petersen reflected, but under the circumstances, she wasn't about to complain. The Cataphracts speeding outward from Hypatia were obviously the older version, identical to the ones they'd found in Filareta's magazines at Manticore. Flight time at this range would be forty seconds longer than for her own Mark 16s, and her attack would reach its target over seven minutes before they reached theirs.

Despite which, she knew Berden was almost certainly right. There was still time for the situation to change, if the Sollies realized they'd been snookered, but they'd have to do it before their birds' first stages shut down. So unless they figured it out in the next two and a half minutes or so, they'd just wasted almost three hundred more missiles.

"You and Pat did good, Bill," she said. "It looks that way so far, at least," she added, throwing out a sheet anchor, just in case.

"I don't think they've got a clue what we just did to them, Ma'am," Lieutenant Commander Thirunavu said, shaking his head. "And they sure as hell don't have another platform close enough to tell them in time to do anything about it!"

"I don't think they've figured it out, either, Rolf," Megan replied. "I'm just remembering what pride goes before."

"Good point."

The XO nodded, although it was evident he didn't believe anything of the sort was going to happen here, and Megan honestly didn't blame him. At the same time they'd launched their counter-missiles with inert drives, they'd spotted all half dozen of their available Loreleis in strategic locations. One of those locations had been on the far side of the counter-missiles she'd used to take out the recon drone, but almost two hundred thousand kilometers farther away from *Arngrim*. From the Cataphracts' initial track, they certainly seemed to have been targeted on the pair of "*Rolands*" which were nothing of the sort.

306

I wish I could see Gogunov's face when—if—he figures it out, she thought with vicious satisfaction. *In fact, the only thing that would please me more would be if he never figures it out because he comes down with a serious case of* dead *first.*

SLNS *Lepanto*
and
SLNS *Yashima*
Hypatia System

MEGAN PETERSEN'S MISSILES CAME slicing in on what was left of TF 1030.

This time, the Dazzlers didn't come as a surprise. Nor did the Dragon's Teeth. The Solarian missile-defense officers had seen them before, knew what they were.

Unfortunately, knowing what they were wasn't the same thing as knowing how to *defeat* them.

There were far fewer missiles this time, only thirty-six rather than the three hundred and ninety-six in each of Jan Kotouč's salvos. On the other hand, Hajdu Győző's battlecruisers had been able to bring 1,568 broadside CMs and 1,960 point defense clusters to bear against those larger salvos. Against *Arngrim*'s, Gogunov's surviving battlecruisers had only 141 launchers and 176 clusters. Despite the paucity of lighter Solarian units' missile defenses, his cruisers and destroyers actually more than trebled his firepower as the Mark 16s tore into his formation.

It wasn't enough—not in the face of the Dazzlers and the Dragon's Teeth, and not when Lieutenant Brendan and Lieutenant Crouch had the detailed emissions signatures of every unit under Gogunov's command, relayed by the Ghost Rider platform they *still* hadn't realized was there. The range was too great for any last-second adjustments, but their missiles had been told precisely what to look for and where to find it.

The counter-missiles picked off five genuine shipkillers and twenty-six Dragon's Teeth "ghosts." Point defense stopped fourteen more shipkillers, which was a better performance than Megan Petersen had anticipated. In the end, only thirty-two percent of her birds got through everything the desperate defenders of TF 1030 could throw at it.

Just nine laserheads. But each of those Mark 16-G laserheads was more powerful than a Solarian Trebuchet capital missile, and every one of them was looking for the same target.

Its name was *Lepanto*.

✧   ✧   ✧

Sandra Haskell's shock frame hammered her savagely as the Manty laserheads ravaged her ship.

Only someone who'd actually experienced the reality of missile combat—and until today, Sandra Haskell hadn't, whatever she might have thought—could have truly imagined what it was like. The long, drawn out minutes while you knew dozens of missiles were driving towards you to kill you. The frozen ball of ice in your belly as you realized they were targeting *your* ship, not her consorts. The crisp commands, the voices that got more clipped, went higher in pitch, as the minutes turned into seconds, racing through your fingers. The heart-stopping terror when the incoming fire burst through the counter-missile zones and the laser clusters went to frantic maximum-rate fire.

And then the sledgehammer. The shock like Thor's hammer as the laserheads detonated and bomb-pumped lasers shredded battle steel and human flesh with demonic fury. It wasn't a series of detonations, not really. Oh, it *was* a series, but at those closing velocities, in the finely focused, impeccably sequenced attack that was the Royal Manticoran Navy's hallmark, no human brain, no human senses, could measure the sequence. It was one pitiless, pulverizing instant ripped from the heart of eternity and burned indelibly into the blood, bone, and brain of anyone who managed to survive it.

The universe heaved insanely. Damage alarms screamed, three quarters of the ship schematic on the after bulkhead simply flashed from green to lurid crimson, more quickly than the human eye could follow. Something ripped through Flag Bridge's heart—something so vast, so terrible, a mere mortal couldn't even start to grasp it. The bridge depressurized—not gradually, the way it did in simulations; instantly, with an explosive decompression, a hellhound howl that shrieked over her skinsuit helmet's pickups...and then went suddenly, abruptly silent.

And then it was over.

She felt the air sobbing in her lungs as she gasped for breath. As she realized she was still alive. That somehow, someway, she'd survived that holocaust.

So far, at least. There was still time for the ship to break up—or *blow* up. God knew she'd seen enough of *that* this horrific day!

The gravity died suddenly, and her nostrils flared as every primary lighting element went dead and the emergency lights came up. For an instant, she sat paralyzed before she realized that was probably a *good* sign. Losing power was far better than having a fusion bottle fail, and if there was no power to the grav plates, then there was no power to the impellers, either, and that meant a failing inertial compensator wasn't going to let *Lepanto*'s impeller drive turn all of her surviving crew into gruel.

It meant she might get to go on surviving...unless someone on the Manties' side was in the mood for reprisal after Vice Admiral Hajdu's Deneb Accords violation.

Nothing you can do about it if they are, Sandy, she told herself. *Best to be concentrating on what you* can *do something about.*

She unfastened her shock frame and pushed off from her command chair, pirouetting in midair—well, in mid-vacuum, she supposed—as her eyes took in the savagely maimed bridge and the drifting bodies who'd been friends of hers thirty seconds before.

"All hands channel," she told her skinsuit's computer.

"Shipboard all hands channel disabled," the suit's musical contralto told her.

"General skinsuit broadcast, then."

"General broadcast link opened," the computer said, and she drew a deep breath.

"All personnel, this is Commodore Haskell," she said as clearly and levelly as she could. "Flag Bridge has been hit hard. I need search and rescue personnel ASAP. I repeat, Flag Bridge has been hit, and I need—"

She broke off, barely managing to stifle a yelp of surprise, as something fastened on her left ankle. She looked down, and her eyes widened as she saw Martin Gogunov.

The rear admiral was still alive. In fact, he didn't appear to have been injured at all, which was remarkable, given the tangled wreckage to which his command chair had been reduced. His shock frame was buckled, broken, and jammed—she could see where he'd pulled the emergency release pin, and nothing at all had happened—and the panel on his skinsuit's right pauldron had been half torn away. It seemed impossible that it could've taken that much damage without ripping clear through the skinsuit, but it obviously hadn't. Looking through the crystoplast of his helmet, she could see the green glow that confirmed good suit pressure.

But there was no way they were getting him free without cutting gear.

That was her first thought, but then she wondered why he'd grabbed her ankle instead of calling for assistance over his com. It would have been—

He looked up at her, made eye contact, then released her ankle and thumped the side of his helmet with his right hand. He pointed through it at his right ear and nodded vigorously. Then he opened his mouth, obviously saying something, and shook his head with equal force.

Of course, she thought. The com was mounted behind the right shoulder in an SLN skinsuit. He could still hear her, but he couldn't transmit.

She nodded to show that she understood, but then he pointed again, and she frowned. He pointed a third time, harder than ever, and her eyes widened. He was pointing at the tactical section...where the corpse which had been Commodore Gregory Ham sat headless in his chair. She looked back at him, and his lips moved again, shaping a single word she couldn't hear, forming it slowly enough she could read it, instead.

"Launch."

She looked down at him for a handful of seconds, and then, slowly, shook her head.

He froze. For a moment, he didn't seem to react at all. Then his face contorted, dark with fury, and his mouth moved again. She knew he was shouting the command again and again, but only he could hear it. And when she didn't respond, his lips started shaping other words, a torrent of invective.

She gazed at him almost compassionately. As far as she could tell, he was uninjured, and that meant he was still in command. But to *be* in command, he had to be able to *exercise* command, and that required the ability to communicate.

The Articles of War were clear. She knew exactly what her commanding officer was ordering her to do, assuming she could somehow get the order out beyond *Lepanto*'s broken hull. That meant she had no option, as his chief of staff, but to see that order was relayed and executed.

"General skinsuit broadcast," she told the computer again.

"General broadcast link opened," the computer replied.

"All personnel," she said crisply, strongly, gazing down into Martin Gogunov's furious blue eyes, "Commodore Haskell. If anyone has access to a working intership com, contact Rear Admiral Yountz immediately. Inform him that he's in command. Repeat, inform Admiral Yountz that *he* is in command."

Gogunov twisted furiously, ripping at the imprisoning shock frame, roaring the curses no one could hear, and Haskell pushed herself down onto the deck beside him, just beyond the reach of his flailing arms. She switched to the flag command link built into her skinsuit com. If he could hear the general link, perhaps he could hear this one, too.

"I'm sorry, Sir," she said. "I'm *so* sorry. But I can't let you. I just *can't*. And I think Yountz won't, without your specific order. I'm sorry."

✧　　✧　　✧

"Sir, I have a com request," Commander Holečková said in an odd voice.

"I've got plenty of those already, Taťána!" Thomas Yountz snapped at his com officer, and God knew it was true. Including one he wished to hell he hadn't gotten, from Captain Indira Turner, relaying Commodore Haskell's message passing command to him.

He'd always wanted task force command, but not like *this!* The only good thing was that Gogunov hadn't had time to execute the Buccaneer launch before his flagship was taken out.

"Sir, this one's from the Manties," Holečková said, and Yountz froze.

From the Manties? It couldn't be! The salvo Gogunov had gotten off before *Lepanto* was crippled had taken out *both* Manties. They had positive confirmation of that from the second recon drone vectored in on their location! There wasn't even any wreckage left! But—

"You're sure it's not someone down on Hypatia trying to screw with our minds?"

"Sir, it's coming from about thirty thousand kilometers from *Yashima*. I suppose it could be a Hypatian trick, but it doesn't...well, it doesn't feel *like* that, Sir." Holečková shook her head. "I think it's genuine, Sir."

"Shit," Yountz muttered, softly enough Holečková could pretend she hadn't heard. Then he shook himself.

"In that case, I suppose I'd better take the call, shouldn't I?" He crossed to sit in his command chair again. "Put it up."

"Yes, Sir."

An instant later, the image of a sturdily built brunette with remarkably hard eyes wearing the skinsuit of a Royal Manticoran Navy commander, appeared on his display.

"I'm Rear Admiral Thomas Yountz, Solarian Navy," he said. "And you are—?"

He sat back to wait out the transmission lag, then twitched as she responded barely seven seconds later.

"Commander Megan Petersen, Royal Manticoran Navy." Her voice was as cold as her eyes were hard. "I assume Admiral Gogunov got my message?"

Yountz's jaw tightened. He'd wondered what freakish fate had selected *Lepanto* as that single salvo's target. But perhaps it hadn't been "fate," at all. Yet if she was seriously claiming to have deliberately targeted TF 1030's flagship—and if she was telling the truth—then how in *hell* had she pulled it off? And how did she even know who Martin Gogunov *was*?

Stupid damned question, he realized an instant later. *Even if we didn't take out the ships that launched, she's got to be at least three or four light-minutes from here, and it's sure as hell not taking six minutes for com turnaround, now is it? If they've got enough FTL bandwidth to relay through some kind of buoy or platform only thirty thousand klicks from here and we can't even see the frigging thing, she's probably been in communication with Vangelis the entire time! And if that's true, who the hell knows what* other *nasty little sensor platforms are floating around out there?*

He told himself he couldn't afford to ascribe supernatural capabilities to Manticoran technology. The last thing he could let this Commander Petersen do was convince him she could accomplish wonders beyond his imagination.

Of course, what she'd already accomplished was bad enough.

"Who's Admiral Gogunov?" he asked.

"The maniac who told President Vangelis he intended to murder six million Hypatian citizens in about thirty-seven minutes from now," Petersen replied icily. "The maniac aboard SLNS *Lepanto*, which is currently drifting without power and shedding life pods."

Yountz inhaled. So much for what other "nasty little sensor platforms" were keeping an eye on him. Vangelis could have told her who Gogunov *was*, but he couldn't have told her *Lepanto*'s current condition.

But you already knew that, really, he thought. *You knew it the instant you realized she'd deliberately targeted Gogunov's ship.*

"I don't know if the Admiral is dead or alive," he heard himself say in a flat tone. "At the moment, I've assumed command. So whatever you have to say, say it to me."

"All right, I will." She smiled ever so slightly. The expression reminded him of an Old Terran shark.

"The people of Hypatia have decided to secede from the Solarian League," she told him. "I realize the League denies their right to do anything of the sort. Obviously, my Star Empire and its Allies disagree with that...constitutional interpretation. Until this very day, however, it would never have occurred to me that the Solarian League Navy, that paragon of all virtues, that guardian of everything which is just and true, would undertake a deliberate Eridani violation. Then again," that smile disappeared into a battle steel expression, "I wouldn't have expected the SLN to violate the Deneb Accords quite so blatantly, either. I don't know why I wouldn't have. We all know what your Navy's done from time to time in the service of Frontier Security, don't we?"

Yountz felt his face go dark, but he couldn't deny her accusation. In fact, he realized, that was the real reason he was so angry. Because she was right about what the Fleet had done in the Protectorates all too often...and about what Hajdu Győző had done right here in Hypatia.

"I won't lie to you, Admiral Yountz," Petersen went on after a moment. "My ship is the only Manticoran vessel currently in the system...now, at least. But you've already seen what *four* Queen's ships can do to a *hundred* Solarian battlecruisers, and I've just demonstrated what mine can do to a single chosen, *targeted* battlecruiser. I can do it again. I can do it again as often as I have to, but unlike Vice Admiral Hajdu and Rear Admiral Gogunov, I really don't like killing people when I don't need to. Not even Solarians who've just finished killing two thousand of my friends."

Her eyes bored into him, and something inside him shriveled before their frozen menace.

"I can't compel you to do anything without killing more of your ships, Admiral," she said flatly, "and between the two of us, I think enough people have already died today. So here's my proposition. You take your surviving ships, and you get the hell out of Hypatia. I'm sure the Hypatians will take care of rescuing all your surviving personnel, assuming they can stop trying to save the civilians—the *children*—the Solarian League is willing to murder to make a political statement. If you don't want to do that, that's fine. You've got ten minutes to make up your mind. If you decide to stay, then I suppose you and I will find out how many more of your battlecruisers I can take out, one-by-one, until you—or *your* successor—finally figure out where I really am and manage to return fire. Of course, even when you do, *my* defenses are designed to stand up to *Manticoran* missile fire, aren't they? And, trust me, I'm one hell of a lot faster than anything you've got. You can't find me, you can't hit me, you can't catch me, and you damned well can't *outrun* me.

"So you make up your mind, Admiral Yountz. You tell me what you're going to do and whether or not I have to start killing more Sollies today after all."

HSP Shuttle *Asteria*
Hypatia System

PAULETTE KILGORE SHOULD HAVE been grounded by Flight Control. For that matter, she should damned well have grounded herself, and she knew it. Tired pilots made mistakes; *exhausted* pilots made catastrophic ones.

Screw it, she thought drunkenly. *There's nobody aboard but me and John, and he'd be even more pissed off than me if somebody did try to yank us.*

"Got something at zero-three-eight," Sergeant Debnam said, as if her thought had summoned the announcement.

"Like what?" Kilgore asked, automatically swinging the nose to the indicated bearing. The question came out slurred by fatigue, she realized, but Debnam appeared not to notice.

"Dunno," he said. "Could just be another chunk of debris—God knows there's enough of that," he added bitterly.

Got that right, *John*, she thought with equal bitterness. Four of the last five radar targets they'd intercepted had been just that: debris. The fifth had been a life pod, its transponder as dead as the young woman in the commander's skinsuit. Kilgore didn't like to think about how that young woman had died, alone in a dead pod, slowly bleeding to death from her internal injuries. But Debnam had gone EVA to bring her aboard and Kilgore had left her flight couch to help stow her, gently and reverently, in the passenger compartment beside the two skinsuited corpses they'd already recovered.

"Got no transponder, but it's about the right size," Debnam continued. "Range . . . forty-three-point-six thousand klicks. We've got an opening velocity of about two hundred KPS."

"What's that make our intercept time?"

The question was a dead giveaway of her exhaustion. That was the kind of solution she did in her head every day.

"'Bout . . . fifty seconds to match velocity at four hundred gravs, then three-point-eight minutes to actually catch it," Debnam replied.

"Well, let's go find out if somebody got a little luckier this time around," Kilgore said, and goosed the impellers.

✧   ✧   ✧

"Should be able to see whatever it is about now, Paulette," Debnam said four and a half minutes later, and Kilgore nodded.

She didn't take her eyes off of her own panel, though. The debris field traveling through the Hypatia System seemed tiny and forlorn as the last memorial to the two thousand or so men and women who'd given their lives so that six million might live, but its components were moving across the system at better than 15,000 KPS and spreading laterally at over ninety KPS. That meant it was actually over a million kilometers in diameter—a hemisphere with a volume of almost eleven cubic light-seconds. Despite its spread, the debris was dense enough to present a genuine hazard to navigation, and *Asteria*'s particle screens weren't as powerful as those of larger vessels. The good news, if it wasn't obscene to call anything "good" in the wake of such carnage, was that her shuttle was traveling *with* the debris. It had been for several hours, now—many of the other rescue craft had exhausted their endurance and been forced to break off after conducting SAR over such a vast space on top of their grueling efforts to evacuate the orbital habitats—but at least that meant the relative velocities weren't as high as they might have been.

She checked the chrono and shook her head, still unable to process all that had happened. Barely four hours since the Manty admiral launched his sacrificial attack. But during that time, the shattered wreckage—and life pods—of his ships had crossed the forty-eight light-seconds to Hypatia orbit and then traveled almost 11.3 light-minutes beyond it.

Search-and-rescue had devolved on the Hypatians even after the Solly CO—the most *recent* Solly CO, she reminded herself with vicious satisfaction—had thrown in the towel and headed for the system's hyper-limit. The single Manty destroyer left had to stay covert, hidden, the sword of Damocles hanging over the Sollies' head until they actually cleared the limit and translated out.

There were thousands of Solarian life pods far closer to Hypatia, and they were being picked up, too. Unlike people like Hajdu Győző, Hypatians weren't butchers. But those pods were near enough to the planet for over two thirds of them to make safe, independent reentry; the Manties weren't, and the Hypatia System *owed* the Star Empire of Manticore. That was why every single shuttle, like *Asteria*, had swarmed out to pursue the wreckage of Admiral Jan Kotouč's slain ships.

So far, according to the reports, they'd actually rescued fifty-seven Manties alive, most from the heavy cruiser *Cinqueda*. Under the circumstances, that was a near-miraculous number . . . but it represented less than three percent of the people who'd crewed the four Manticoran ships. They'd also intercepted almost forty life pods with live transponders which had either launched empty or whose passengers, like the young woman aboard the dead pod she and Debnam had recovered, had died of wounds in the end, despite escaping their doomed ships.

There were no live transponders left. There hadn't been, for almost an hour now. All the active beacons had been intercepted, and they weren't going to find any more of their star system's saviors alive. But it didn't matter. Not to Paulette Kilgore.

To the human eye, the system primary was little more than a brighter-than-usual star at this distance. Soon it would be impossible for any eye to pick out from the debris field's position, yet that wreckage's journey was only beginning. Her mind quailed from the thought of the debris' lonely, eternal trek across the bottomless void. No Odysseus would return to Ithaca from this Troy, and her heart ached as she imagined any bodies they hadn't recovered voyaging endlessly across the silent, unwinking, uncaring stars. Imagined those funeral lights, scattered across a tomb as vast as the universe itself.

Not going to happen, she thought drunkenly, eyes stinging. *Not on my watch. Not on John's. Any of these people who're still out here are going* home, *by God!*

She knew that wasn't really so. She was on the ragged edge of collapse, *Asteria* was low on fuel, and they were eleven light-minutes from home. Whatever she and Debnam wanted—*needed*—to do, they had to turn back soon. At least they knew the wreckage's vector, and System Patrol had planted huge radar reflectors and active transponder buoys in the heart of the field. Maybe the Manty Navy would be able to complete the work Paulette Kilgore would have to leave undone, after all. Maybe. She hoped so. But in the meantime—

"Got it!" Debnam said suddenly. "Coming up on your Number Three now."

Kilgore looked at the indicated display, slaved to the optical head Debnam had been using to search visually for their target. All she saw for a moment was the dim, almost imperceptible glow of reflected sunlight, but then Debnam zoomed in, and her weary eyes narrowed.

"It *is* a pod, Paulette!" Debnam said.

"Yeah, but it looks bad," she replied. Not only was there no beacon, but even the running lights designed to guide searchers visually to it were dead. Nor did their passives detect any EM signature from it at all.

Doesn't mean anything, she told herself doggedly. *Only been four or five hours.* Pod *may be dead, but Navy skinsuits're good for a* lot *longer than that on internal resources, and the pod's rad and heat shielding'd hide their signatures. If somebody got aboard it in the first place, she* might *still be*—

She chopped that thought off. There was no point fooling herself, and it would only make the inevitable hurt worse. In fact, she found herself hoping this was one of the pods which had launched empty. They had a sufficient honor guard of dead heroes aboard already.

She blinked as she realized that even as her mind had been churning through those thoughts, her hands had automatically brought the shuttle around to an intercept heading and sent it ghosting towards the life pod at ten gravities.

"You about ready, John?" she asked as she reached turnover and flipped to decelerate to rest less than fifty yards from her target.

"Moving into the lock now," he confirmed, and she felt the pressure in her eardrums and saw the red light blink as the pumps evacuated the lock's atmosphere back into the passenger compartment.

"Opening the hatch," he said a moment later, and then she saw him—tether trailing behind him—as his SUT thruster pack carried him across the vacuum.

His handheld tractor-presser unit locked onto the pod and drew him in, and he landed gently beside the inspection panel.

"LED's dead," he said over his skinsuit com. "Plugging into the auxiliary jack now, and—*Holy Christ!*"

Kilgore jerked upright in her flight couch.

"John?" She heard him breathing over the open com. "*John?*"

"Paulette—" For a second, she couldn't recognize his voice. It sounded so...broken. So hoarse. But then—

"Paulette, they're *alive!* Christ and all the Holy Angels, we've got *two* of them, and they're *alive!*"

"Oh my God," she whispered, and realized the strangeness hovering in his voice was tears. And then she realized *she* was weeping, and that she'd pressed both trembling hands to her mouth. "*Oh my God.*"

"I'm hooking my tether now." Debnam sounded much closer to normal. "I'm heading back."

"Understood."

Kilgore wiped her eyes brusquely, unstrapped, sealed her helmet, and headed for the passenger compartment. She'd cycled through the lock by the time Debnam got back to *Asteria*, and the two of them worked with practiced efficiency as power came on the winch, reeling in the cable the sergeant had attached to the life pod.

Getting it properly mated to the docking collar wasn't easy, but life pods had been built to standard models for over six hundred T-years for moments exactly like this. It took them less than ten minutes to establish a solid seal between the collars, and Kilgore made herself stand back and watch Debnam double check it—then check it again— lest they'd screwed up in their fatigue.

"Good seal," he announced finally, and Kilgore removed her helmet as air rushed back into the lock. She hit the hatch toggle, but she wasn't really surprised when nothing happened, given the pod's obvious loss of power. She drew a deep breath and reached out to the manual locking lever on the pod hatch, vaguely surprised to realize her hand was trembling.

She had to pull twice before the lever activated.

No surprise there, she thought, looking at the pod's scorched, scored, seared, and actually dented surface. *My God, they must've been right on the fringe of the fireball when their ship went up!*

Then the hatch opened, and she looked in at the unconscious passengers. Neither looked to be in very good shape, she thought, and activated the closer Manty's external med panel readout. It was impossible to read the woman's skinsuit nameplate. From her suit's blackened appearance, she'd been *way* too close to something nasty even before she boarded the pod. But the med panel came up, and Kilgore inhaled deeply.

"Broken arm, half a dozen broken ribs, and some internal bleeding," she told Debnam. "But the vitals look good." Her smile faded and she looked over her shoulder at the sergeant. "According to the readout, the only reason she's unconscious is that she tranked herself pretty much to the max from her skinny's pharmacope about an hour ago. 'Nough to keep her out till her suit's enviro ran out." Her mouth twitched. "Guess she'd figured out how unlikely anybody was to find them."

"Don't blame her," Debnam said softly. "Don't think I'd want to be awake under those circumstances, either." He shook his head. "Surprised she didn't go ahead and OD, really."

"Don't think you can with a Manty skinsuit," Kilgore replied absently, switching her attention to the other Manticoran. She keyed the second med panel, then inhaled again, much more sharply.

"Not good," she said. "Looks like the spine's gone in at least three places, and *his* vitals don't look good at all. And—" she looked back at the woman "—according to the time chop, she tranked him five minutes before she tranked herself." Her mouth tightened. "Probably wanted to make sure he was out before she put herself to sleep, too."

"Makes sense."

Debnam nodded, and Kilgore bent back over the savagely injured Manty. Unlike his companion's, his skinsuit seemed undamaged, despite his injuries, and—

"John," she heard herself say in a voice she didn't quite recognize.

"Yeah?" He looked at her, his exhaustion-lined face puzzled by her tone.

"Get on the com," that voice she didn't recognize said very, very calmly. "Tell them we just found Admiral Kotouč...and he's *alive*."

Governor's Residence
City of Shuttlesport
Smoking Frog
Maya System

"MR. ELLINGSEN, CAPTAIN ABERNATHY. It's good to see you again!" Oravil Barregos said, standing and extending his hand as Julie Magilen escorted the visitors into his office.

As in their previous visits, they'd arrived quietly in orbit aboard a small, fast, privately chartered transport whose crew had then shuttled them to the surface of Smoking Frog without imposing upon any of the commercial shuttle lines. Unlike their first two visits, however, this time their shuttle had landed directly on the Governor's Residence's private pad, where Magilen, Barregos's office manager, had met them and escorted them quickly and discreetly past the security checkpoints to his office.

There was another difference from their previous trips to the Maya System, too. This time Barregos was accompanied by his lieutenant governor, as well as Luiz Rozsak, the senior Solarian League Navy officer in the Maya Sector.

"It's good to see you, too, Governor," Håkon Ellingsen, the taller and much darker of the two said, reaching out to grip Barregos's hand.

He seemed surprised by Lieutenant Governor Brosnan's presence, but he took it in stride. He also bore a remarkable family resemblance to the Winton Dynasty, which probably wasn't too surprising in a senior—if covert—member of the Manticoran diplomatic corps. His family pedigree, as well as his diplomatic background, no doubt explained his calm response to Brosnan's inclusion in this very confidential meeting. The Wintons had been playing high-stakes interstellar poker for a long time now.

His companion was much smaller, at least twenty-six centimeters shorter than him, with a sandalwood complexion, and was clearly not quite as comfortable over the lieutenant governor's addition. Probably not too surprising in a serving naval officer who'd been seconded to the skulduggery section of the aforesaid diplomatic corps and felt a bit out of his depth.

320

"I wasn't certain I *would* be seeing you again," Barregos continued, waving his guests into the waiting chairs. The governor's bodyguard, Vegar Spangen, stood post in one corner and Jeremy Frank, his senior aide, began pouring coffee for all hands.

"Will there be anything else, Governor?" Magilen asked.

"I think not—not for a while, anyway. Thank you for being your usual efficient self and getting our friends here unnoticed."

"It wasn't really all that hard, Sir," Magilen pointed out with a smile. "It's only about four hundred meters from the pad, and there's plenty of shrubbery along the way."

"And four or five security posts, all of them manned by people we don't want asking any questions about our guests, if I'm not mistaken," Barregos replied.

"Well, yes," she conceded.

"Which is why I think you'd better hang around, now that I think about it. Somebody's going to have to get them back to the shuttle pad without being noticed, and who would have the temerity to notice *you* if you told them not to?"

"Oh, a veritable dragon, I am!"

She bared her teeth, and Barregos chuckled. Then he smiled warmly at her.

"Never a *dragon*! Maybe a hexapuma, given where our guests are from, though."

"Whatever you say," she replied, then nodded to Ellingsen and Captain Abernathy and withdrew.

"I can tell you two've been together a while, Governor," Ellingsen said with a smile.

"Almost thirty-five T-years," Barregos confirmed with a reminiscent smile of his own. "The pool sent her to me as a receptionist the first time, if you can believe it. She was *not* amused when she found out what I'd asked for. In fact, she really could have passed for a dragon that afternoon. Whoever made that spectacularly wrong personnel choice, though, did me an enormous favor. I couldn't run the place without her."

"I can believe it." Ellingsen nodded, then cocked his head politely at Lieutenant Governor Brosnan.

"If Gail hadn't been off-planet during your second visit, she'd have joined Luiz and me then." Barregos shrugged. "She's a huge improvement on her predecessor. I was pretty confident she wouldn't try to have me assassinated when I promoted her to acting lieutenant governor. Since then, she's become a trusted and valued member of the team. The *real* team."

"Ah. We'd missed that."

"I wouldn't want to say your intelligence services aren't excellent, but we've gone to some lengths to keep anyone from figuring that out. In fact, Gail's sending regular reports back to Intelligence Branch to keep Mr. Nyhus fully informed of our activities. Or, rather, of our total *lack* of activities."

"Very good." Ellingsen smiled his approval, and the sable-haired Brosnan nodded in acknowledgment.

"Since you've decided to include Ms. Brosnan in our conversations, should I take that as a sign you and Admiral Rozsak have finalized your requirements for naval support?" Ellingsen continued. "Captain Abernathy's been authorized to conditionally approve your needs, assuming they fall within the parameters we'd already discussed. If you've realized you need more firepower, it's probable we can cut a little additional tonnage loose. Unfortunately, the Captain can't guarantee that without running any fresh numbers past the Admiralty."

"Oh, I don't think there's going to be a problem about force levels," Admiral Rozsak said. "There has been a slight change in plans, however."

"Indeed?" Ellingsen raised his eyebrows, and Rozsak smiled.

"Yes," he said pleasantly. "I'm afraid the two of you are under arrest." Ellingsen stiffened.

"I don't understand," he said in the tone of someone who hadn't quite gotten the punchline of a joke.

"Oh, I think you do," Barregos said, and the governor's normally affable voice had turned hard and cold. "Unfortunately for you, we had a visit from a *real* Manticoran admiral shortly after your last visit. Her name was Givens—*Patricia* Givens. I found it quite remarkable that the woman who runs the Royal Manticoran Navy Office of Naval Intelligence had never heard of either of you. Perhaps you'd care to explain that?"

His eyes bored into the two men sitting on the far side of his desk, and Abernathy's right hand twitched.

"I wouldn't," another voice said, and the "captain" turned his head to find himself looking into the muzzle of the weapon in Spangen's hand. It wasn't a pulser. Instead, it was a stun gun, the modern descendant of the ancient Ante Diaspora Taser.

"Vegar's a very good shot, 'Captain Abernathy,'" Barregos said. "But if you think you can reach that pulser under your left arm—the one my security people picked up when you walked through the shuttle pad scanners—go right ahead. I understand being stunned is a very unpleasant experience, and just this moment, I'd really like to see you have one of those."

The office door slid silently open once more. Abernathy's head turned again, and his eyes narrowed as a brown-haired, brown-skinned man in the uniform of a Gendarmerie brigadier walked through it. He looked at the newcomer for a moment, and then his hand relaxed. In fact, he sat back in his chair with a curiously serene look and folded both hands in his lap.

"I assume you recognize Brigadier Allfrey," Barregos said.

"I do," Ellingsen said after a moment. "And should *I* assume from his presence that you have some suitable plan for our disposal?"

"Always nice to deal with a professional," Barregos replied. "We do have a few questions. I'm sure it'll be a fascinating conversation. After that, we'll be sending you to talk to some other friends of ours. I imagine you can guess where they live."

"I understand Landing's very nice this time of year," Ellingsen said almost whimsically, and Barregos's eyes narrowed. There was something about the other man's voice. Something odd that resonated somehow with Abernathy's relaxed body language.

"So I hear," the governor replied, and Ellingsen smiled.

"Pity I won't see it," he said . . . and slumped in his chair.

✧   ✧   ✧

"We don't have a clue," Philip Allfrey said several hours later. He looked more frustrated than surprised. "As far as the autopsy can tell, 'Ellingsen' had a massive heart attack and 'Abernathy' suffered an aneurysm. 'Natural causes,' both of them."

"Bullshit, Philip," Luiz Rozsak said pleasantly. The admiral was parked at one end of Barregos's conference room table with a large cup of coffee.

"Of course it is." Allfrey shrugged. "I'm just telling you what the ME said. And, by the way, he figured it was bullshit, too, given the fact that both those 'natural causes' deaths occurred in the same twenty-five-second span. He said something about lottery numbers when I asked him what the odds against that were."

"I have to say I find this disturbing," Gail Brosnan said. The others looked at her, and she shrugged, her expression worried. "Not the fact that they're dead. Given what they said to you the last time they were here, Oravil, I can't think of anyone who deserves to be dead more than they did. And I've always been a great believer in that old proverb about dead men and tales. But I don't like how . . . calm they were about it. Seeing somebody that relaxed just before she kills herself makes me wonder about exactly what we're up against here."

"I don't think they did kill themselves," Rozsak said. The others looked at him, and he waved his coffee cup. "I think they knew they were going to die, but I don't think they killed *themselves*," he amplified.

"If there's anything to what Givens told us about this 'killer nanotech' the 'Alignment's' supposed to have, it'd make perfect sense to install a version of it in their agents. There's always the chance even the most dedicated operative will decide against suiciding when the time comes. If you've got something like the Manties are describing, you can take that off the table."

"So you think all their agents are walking around with this stuff inside?" Allfrey asked.

"Yep. And so do you, don't you?"

"Yeah, I guess I do." Allfrey didn't look overjoyed by his own admission.

"As Gail just suggested, this may make any interrogations...difficult," Barregos said in a light tone that fooled no one. "And it makes me wonder just how motivated these people really are. I mean, if you and Philip are right, Luiz—and I think you are—they knew what was going to happen. That means they knew whatever it is had been implanted before they ever came to call on us the first time. I'm sure they expected to get in and out again, just like they'd done before, but these were obviously top-notch, smart people. I've been inclined towards assuming they were as mercenary as your average transstellar's covert operative, but it's hard to imagine a typical operative agreeing to carry an *involuntary* suicide switch around with him."

"I could see that," Rozsak demurred. "Offer somebody a big enough payoff, especially if the somebody in question's convinced he's smarter and quicker than anyone he's likely to come up against, and he might well agree. After all, his ego would tell him nobody was going to trip *him* up. Even if he admitted the possibility to himself intellectually, he'd still figure the odds were in his favor." He shook his head. "It's not the fact that they'd been rigged to die if they were caught that bothers me. It's not even the fact that they *knew* they were. What bothers *me* is that they were so calm about it." He shook his head, dark eyes shadowed. "That's the signature of a zealot. Whatever else they might have been, these two were true believers. And—" his voice turned harsher "—so was the crew of their damned transport."

Barregos grimaced. With "Ellingsen" and "Abernathy" dead, Rozsak had been forced to use his fallback plan. Instead of convincing one of them to order the transport to stand down, he'd tried for a covert boarding action, sending in Marine special forces operators in skinsuits on a ballistic intercept.

Individual powered-down skinsuits were extraordinarily difficult to detect, but the transport's crew obviously had. They'd allowed the twelve-Marine squad to make soft landings on their vessel's hull. Then they'd dumped their fusion bottle and blown themselves—and the Marines—into plasma. The sensor records made it abundantly clear that that was what had happened, and reactor bottles didn't dump spontaneously.

"So basically what we have to pass on to the Manties is a whole bunch of nothing," the governor said disgustedly.

"I think we got a little more than that, Oravil," Rozsak said. "If nothing else, we've got a pair of bodies, and if the Manties and Havenites have more experience with this nanotech, they may spot something our forensics people don't know to look for. At the very least, it would be confirmation our bad guys and their bad guys really are the same people. I don't think we need that confirmation, though. It's hard for me to imagine there's more than one galaxy-spanning conspiracy out to get Manticore at any given moment. Well, okay. Maybe more than one, but not more than *two!*"

Barregos lips twitched and he shook his head. But then he nodded, too.

"Point taken," he said. "And I think we've got confirmation we've been put on the same hit list."

"I'm still not completely sold on that part of it." Rozsak drank more coffee, then shrugged. "That's one of the reasons I really wanted to have a little heart-to-heart with those two. *Are* we on their hit list, or did they simply see us as one more club to use on the Manties and Haven?"

"Does it really matter?" Brosnan asked, and Rozsak nodded.

"I think it does, Gail. If they put us on their little list as a *target*, not as a potential weapon, it suggests they know more about our ultimate intentions than we thought anybody outside the Sector did. And if *they* know more about our plans, who knows who else does? For that matter, if they know, have they arranged to make that information available to our lords and masters in Old Chicago if something prevents their original plan from working?"

"That's…an interesting question," Barregos said slowly.

"And likely to affect our own timing?" Rozsak asked with a raised eyebrow.

"I'd say there's a distinct possibility." No one could have described Oravil Barregos's expression as eager, but there was very little indecision in it. "We have Givens's promise of naval support if we really need it, and this time we know the offer's legitimate," the governor continued. "The real problem's Erewhon. No one in Suds expected us to move before we had the first of our own podnoughts. Even with the Manties—the *real* Manties—promising to support us and provide their 'Mycroft' for system-defense, that could be a problem. We had enough trouble getting them to agree to accelerate the timetable last time. I'm afraid Havlicek, at least, may be less than delighted if we suggest moving it up even farther. She wasn't that enthusiastic last time, and I doubt she'll care for the notion of increasing the window of vulnerability between declaring our intentions and when the Manties can get Mycroft installed."

"No, she won't," Rozsak agreed. "We may not have a choice, though. Especially not if what Philip's telling us about the other systems out our way is accurate, and I think it is. These two were here to press us to act in the next couple of months, Oravil. I'm willing to bet they've had other people pushing the same schedule in Kornati and some of the other systems in our vicinity. If those other systems start going up in flames, that's likely to draw a response from Frontier Fleet. And when *that* happens—"

"When that happens, somebody will get a lot better look at what we've been building out here," Barregos finished. "At which point, the hammer comes down."

"Unless we get in before they do, with the Manties standing ominously behind us."

"That might make it just a bit harder for Manticore to sell the rest of the galaxy on the notion that they didn't have anything to do with it," Brosnan pointed out. "If we move and announce the Star Empire's supporting us, Abruzzi and his people will fall all over themselves arguing that that couldn't have happened if we hadn't coordinated it well ahead of time. And that'll lend an awful lot of credence to the notion that Manticore was the instigator all along."

"You may be right," Barregos said after a moment. "In fact, you probably are. But Landing and Nouveau Paris have to have thought about that before they sent Givens out here in the first place. And the bottom line is that we're not doing what we're doing to help their Grand Alliance." He looked around the table, his face hard. "We're doing it to protect the Maya Sector and the people who live here. If that's *inconvenient* for the Manties, I'm afraid they'll just have to live with it."

**Bassingford Medical Center
and
Mount Royal Palace
City of Landing
Manticore Binary System
Star Empire of Manticore**

MEGAN PETERSEN TURNED FROM the window as the waiting room door opened behind her. She expected a nurse or a doctor; what she got was a hard-eyed man in a green-on-green uniform with sergeant's stripes and a nameplate that read "McGraw." Those hard eyes swept the room with the precision of a laser tracker. Then he nodded courteously to her and keyed his uni-link.

"Clear," he said, and came to a parade rest to one side of the door.

It opened again, a moment later, and it was Megan's turn to come to attention as a very tall woman with a treecat on her shoulder came through the door. Two more green-uniformed men followed her.

"Your Grace!"

"Commander." Lady Dame Honor Alexander-Harrington crossed the room in three long strides and held out her hand. "I didn't expect to find you here. I'm glad I did, though. It gives me the chance to personally commend you for what you and all of Admiral Kotouč's people did in Hypatia. That was well done, Commander. *Very* well done."

"Your Grace, I appreciate the sentiment, but, really, *Arngrim* didn't do nearly as much as the others." Megan's face tightened with the memory of her helplessness as the rest of the squadron died. "We mostly just sat there and watched it happen."

Duchess Harrington cocked her head, her expression thoughtful, and her treecat mirrored the movement.

"I wondered if you'd feel that way," the duchess said after a moment. "I suppose it's natural you should feel you somehow let down the rest of your squadron. Allow me to point out, however, that *Arngrim* couldn't have improved on what her consorts accomplished. I mean that seriously, Commander." Those steady brown eyes held hers. "You literally *couldn't* have increased the damage the rest of your squadron inflicted

327

in that exchange, and your ship is alive today because Admiral Kotouč gave you an order—exactly the correct order, as it happens—and you obeyed it. And afterward, when yours was the only ship left, you and your people performed *brilliantly*, Commander."

"Your Grace," Megan felt her face heat and shook her head hard, "we were *bluffing*. We couldn't have stopped them if Yountz had been willing to pull the trigger!"

"I was never much of a poker player, myself, but my husband and my wife are fanatics." Megan blinked at the non sequitur, but the duchess only smiled. "According to them, a 'bluff' is when you raise on a busted flush, Commander Petersen. You had at least a pair of aces, and if Yountz had called, you would have hurt them badly."

"If they'd realized how little ammunition we had—"

"You're not listening to me," the duchess said more sternly. "No, you couldn't have destroyed his entire remaining task force. You couldn't even have destroyed all his remaining battlecruisers. But you didn't have to. After what Admiral Kotouč had already done to them, they didn't have the stomach to find out if you could. No." She shook her head. "What you did—what you and your *people* did—saved *at least* six million lives. You didn't do it in a vacuum, and you couldn't have done it if Admiral Kotouč hadn't made the hard call and decided to fight, but you *did* do it when it counted. And the prisoner interrogation we've already done makes it clear that if you hadn't intervened, Admiral Gogunov most certainly would have killed all of those civilians."

Harrington's brown eyes had gone bleak and cold, and the cat on her shoulder bared his fangs. Then she shook herself and gave another of those crooked smiles.

"I'd say we owe a vote of thanks to Commodore Haskell, too, although we probably wouldn't do her any favors if we were to publicly thank her for it just yet."

"No, Your Grace, we wouldn't," Megan agreed, recalling her own interview with Haskell...and the incredible hatred burning in Martin Gogunov's eyes when *he* spoke about his chief of staff.

"Actually," she went on after a moment, "I think what *Arngrim* may really have done was to give Yountz a pretext to avoid carrying out Buccaneer. I can't prove that, but we do know he specifically ordered the screen *not* to launch when *Lepanto* sent out the fire distribution orders. I'm pretty sure he'll downplay that in his after-action report, but that wasn't the decision of a man who wanted to murder people in job lots."

"Let me remind you of something I know they taught you at the Academy, Commander," Harrington said. "Battles aren't always—or even usually—won by killing everybody on the other side. They're won inside the other side's brains and wills. Given the right weapons, the right tactical situation, anyone can *kill* an enemy. Convincing her to yield, to do what you set out to compel her to do *without* killing her—that's harder. That's a *lot* harder, and it's also exactly what you and *Arngrim* did."

Megan looked at her, absorbing what she'd said. If there was an officer in Manticoran uniform who knew what she was talking about—knew exactly what the squadron had faced—that officer was standing in front of her. And if *she* said...

"I know people are going to compare Hypatia to Grayson," the duchess said, and Megan managed not to blink at the way the older woman's thought had followed her own. "I suppose that's inevitable, given the similarities. Of course, the *differences* are a lot more significant than any of those idiot newsies are going to realize!"

She grimaced, and Megan surprised herself with a chuckle. *Arngrim* had returned to Manticore with dispatches, accompanying the Hypatian transport carrying the squadron's survivors, barely two T-days earlier, and she'd already decided she'd rather face a salvo of Cataphracts than the Manticoran news corps any day!

"Better," the duchess said approvingly, then laid a hand on Megan's shoulder.

"I had a heavy cruiser to face a *single* battlecruiser," she said more soberly. "The tech imbalance was a lot narrower than the one you had, but in a way, that only made the situation simpler. I mean, there weren't a lot of fancy tactical options. You found a much more... elegant solution, and at least Hypatia doesn't have steadings."

"I beg your pardon?" This time, Megan did blink.

"After my own escapade, I got dragged kicking and screaming into the wonderful world of politics, Commander. Without any hereditary titles to hang on you, the Hypatians can't do the same thing to you. Speaking with the voice of experience, I advise you to count your blessings."

"I hadn't even thought about *that*, Your Grace!" Megan shuddered.

"Well, don't let your hopes get *too* high," the duchess advised her. "Hypatia may not have a toy chest full of steadings and titles and things, but Her Majesty does. And, still speaking with the voice of experience, she likes to open it up for people who accomplish the sorts of things you accomplished. And, to be honest," her expression softened and the hand on Megan's shoulder squeezed once, firmly, "you deserve it. Everyone in your entire *squadron* deserves it, and I'm pretty sure Her Majesty will make her own feelings in that regard abundantly clear."

"Your Grace, I've already got the only thing I could possibly have wanted," Megan said softly.

"I know. Believe me, I know." Harrington smiled oddly, and the treecat made a sound that seemed to fall somewhere between a soft croon and a laugh. "And I understand Commander Stob responds well to regen."

"That's what he's been telling me, anyway." Megan's smile turned a bit tremulous. "I wouldn't put it past him to lie about it, though."

She closed her eyes for a moment, jaw tightening as memory replayed the moment when the HSP told her they'd recovered Jayson's life pod... and another moment, the one in which she'd realized he'd lost both legs.

Sixty people. That was how many they'd recovered alive out of the 1,948 men and women aboard *Phantom*, *Shikomizue*, *Talwar*, and *Cinqueda*. Three percent. And one of them—miracle of miracles—had been the man she loved. At that instant, she hadn't cared about his legs; she'd cared about his *life*.

"As a matter of fact, he isn't—lying, I mean," the duchess assured her with a smile. "Personally, I don't regenerate at all, so I made a point of asking about all your people from the squadron. As it happens, I have pretty fair contacts here at Bassingford, so I didn't get any nonsense about patient confidentiality, and the only one who doesn't is Commander Ilkova. Mind you, Commander Stob's going to be in what my father refers to—somewhat inelegantly—as the 'body shop' for quite a while, but in the end, you'll get him back in one piece, I promise."

"Thank you, Your Grace," Megan said sincerely.

Somehow, coming from Duchess Harrington, that reassurance went deeper than it had coming from mere doctors or even Jayson himself. Was that because she knew Harrington had paid the price of combat more than once herself? Or was it simply something about the woman the newsies called the Salamander?

"Well, I just wanted to tell you how incredibly well I think you performed." The duchess's voice was brisker, and she patted Megan's shoulder once, then stood back. "Until my pinnace grounded, I didn't realize you'd be here so I could tell you that in person. I'm glad I had the chance, but my real motive in coming dirt-side was to have lunch with my parents, and my dad, especially, doesn't have a lot of flex in his schedule anymore, so I'm afraid I have to get a move on. Especially since I need to drop in on Admiral Kotouč while I'm here." She shook her head. "He's going to be in the shop even longer than your fiancé, I'm afraid."

"I'm just glad he's here to *be* in it, Your Grace," Megan said frankly, and Harrington nodded.

"You and me, both," she said. "And I imagine he's at least as prone to 'survivor's guilt' as you are." The duchess's nostrils flared and her lips tightened for just a moment. "Trust me, that's something else I know a little about, Commander. Fortunately, I had Nimitz. You don't, but be smarter than I was. Talk to the counselors here at Bassingford."

"I'm already talking to them, Your Grace."

"Good woman!" Harrington smiled broadly and this time, she punched Megan lightly on the same shoulder. "Not only a good tactician, but a *wise* one, too! I see great things in your future, Commander. And at the risk of sounding rude, would I be too far out of line if I invited myself to your wedding?"

"To *our* wedding?" Megan managed to get her mouth shut again after a moment. "We'd be *honored!* It never occurred to me that—"

Words failed her, and the duchess chuckled, but her expression was serious when she spoke again.

"The honor will be mine, Commander. Trust me, the honor will be mine."

✧　　✧　　✧

"There you are!" Crown Princess Consort Rivka Rosenfeld-Winton exclaimed as Honor stepped out of the old-fashioned elevator in King Michael's Tower with Spencer Hawke on her heels.

"Your Highness," Honor replied with a faint smile.

"I'll 'Your Highness' you!" Rivka said, reaching out to take both of Honor's hands in hers and squeeze. "I've got a ribbon cutting in Haynes Port I'm already late for, so I can't stay right now, but Roger and I would love to have you join us for supper! How long will you be in Landing?"

"Only about another six hours, I'm afraid." Honor grimaced. "I'm on my way to Admiralty House from here for a conference, and as soon as it's over, I've got to head back to *Imperator*. Now that you're an experienced married woman, you can *probably* figure out why I'm not especially happy I won't be able to spend the night dirt-side."

"Actually, I can't imagine why," Rivka said innocently, and Honor snorted.

"Of *course* you can't. Tell me, have your loving subjects started talking to you about heirs to the Crown the way my loving steaders have been talking to *me* about heirs to the Key?"

"Not yet, but I'm sure it's coming." Rivka shook her head. "You'd think that as long as we've had prolong..."

"Hah!" Honor snorted again, this time with magnificent disdain. "Maybe someplace where they don't think in terms of dynasties! Although, at that, Manticorans aren't quite as... obsessive about it as

Graysons. Trust me, no one's cutting *me* a pass in Harrington Steading! Not," she added with a judicious air, "that the preliminaries to produce heirs don't make up for a lot, now that I think about it."

"True," Rivka agreed with a smile. "Very true. Thank you for helping me keep this in perspective."

"One of the things I'm here for," Honor reassured her. "And now, I believe I have an appointment with your mother-in-law."

✧   ✧   ✧

"And how was lunch with your parents?" Elizabeth Adrienne Samantha Annette Winton inquired as the lieutenant from the Queen's Own opened the sitting room door and ushered Honor through it.

Honor nodded her thanks to their guide—not that she'd actually needed guiding after so many years—and Major Hawke peeled off to join the sergeant standing post outside the door.

"Lunch was good, if a little on the hurried side," she said, crossing the room to hug the woman who was arguably the most powerful monarch in the explored galaxy. "I thought I'd allowed plenty of time, but Admiral Kotouč was conscious. He wasn't much in the mood for small talk, but Nimitz and I needed to have a word with him." Her expression sobered. "He's not taking what happened to his squadron well, Elizabeth."

"I'm not surprised." The Empress waved her into one of the worn, comfortable armchairs. "After the last twenty odd T-years, I've had entirely too much experience with people who have to deal with something like that. And I've discovered that being the Queen—or even the Empress—doesn't make *me* feel one bit better when people go out and die for me."

She sighed, her eyes sad, then shook herself.

"Still," she said in a brighter voice, "I'm sure you and Nimitz did him a world of good."

"Not us so much as Commander Ilkova," Honor said.

"Oh, really?" Elizabeth's eyebrows rose.

"Oh, *definitely* 'really'!" Honor rolled her eyes. "Not that either of them is saying a word about it yet to the other one. Trust me, though, they're both picking up on what the other one isn't saying, if you take my meaning. I think they're probably smarter than Hamish and me, too."

"Is Article One-Nineteen going to be a problem for them?"

"Not as far as *I'm* concerned," Honor said. "One thing I've never had a taste for is hypocrisy, Elizabeth! But from Ilkova's mind-glow, I'd say there's not much chance of her letting Kotouč get away. And from *his* mind-glow, he won't be trying to!"

"Wise man."

Elizabeth's tone was even drier than Honor's had been. Then she leaned back in her own chair, her eyes darker.

"I've been keeping tabs on his condition myself," she said. "We need him back, and I can't tell you how glad I am that he seems to be doing so well. But this whole 'Operation Buccaneer' has me worried, Honor. Worried a lot."

"It should," Honor replied. Nimitz flowed from her chairback. He sat upright in her lap, leaning back against her, and she wrapped her arms about him and rested her chin between his ears. "It should. This was a lot uglier than I expected it to get, even after Cachalot. Than any of us expected, I think. Which probably says something about our own wishful thinking, in the end."

"Don't be too hard on yourself. *I* never saw it coming, either."

"Maybe that's because not even the People's Republic at its worst went around casually embracing Eridani violations. Of course, we're not dealing with the Peeps anymore, are we? We're dealing with the *Solarian League*, the shining beacon to which all the rest of the galaxy aspires!"

Elizabeth winced at the bitterness of Honor's tone.

"Is it confirmed that the Mandarins *did* sign off on Hajdu's decisions?" the Empress asked after a moment.

"Not on his *time limit*, but, yes. They sent him out with specific authorization to execute 'Buccaneer' against Hypatia. We pulled his orders out of what was left of *Lepanto*'s computers. They've upgraded their security software since we hammered Filareta, but we'd gotten too good a look inside first, and *Arngrim* brought back *Lepanto*'s actual data core. It was in pretty bad shape, but our cyber people cracked its security protocols within six hours of getting their hands on it. I think the Sollies need better cybernauts of their own."

"I'm sure they'll come up with them entirely too soon to make any of us happy," Elizabeth observed, and Honor snorted in agreement.

"Anyway, we've got what we believe is a complete copy of the Buccaneer ops plan and orders," she continued, "and even if Hajdu wasn't sent out with a specific timeframe for his response to Vangelis's rejection of Yang-O'Grady's ultimatum, I doubt anyone in Old Chicago would have objected to the one he picked."

"Are you sure about that?" Elizabeth's brow furrowed. "It wasn't just a case of an out-of-control admiral reinterpreting his orders to suit himself?"

"Elizabeth, I haven't had time to sit down and discuss this in detail with Pat or anybody else at Admiralty House yet. That's where I'm going from here, and Tom Theisman and Tom Caparelli will be joining us. But we've been tapped in well enough to know they were getting desperate even before they came up with Buccaneer. Just based on that and what I've already seen of the ops plan, I'm pretty darn sure he didn't do much 'reinterpreting.' In fact, he may not have done any at all. There's something in the basic Buccaneer plan called 'Parthian Shot.'"

"'Parthian Shot'?" Elizabeth repeated, and Honor nodded.

"It's a reference to an ancient Old Earth cavalry tactic." She grimaced. "Apparently, the SLN isn't very good at picking deceptive codenames. I doubt it would even occur to them to name a decisive offensive operation 'Buttercup,' for example! But, the Parthians—and quite a few other light cavalry forces—used a tactic in which they turned in the saddle and fired arrows at their pursuers while fleeing at a full gallop."

"They—?" Elizabeth began, then broke off, her eyes widening, and Honor nodded again.

"Exactly," she said grimly. "Their task force commanders are specifically authorized to 'launch and leave' in the face of anything like serious opposition. No delays to let civilians evacuate... and if they happen to deorbit a few megatons of wreckage onto an inhabited planet, well, that's just too bad."

Elizabeth sat back, shaking her head slowly, and it was Ariel's turn to flow down into her lap. The two women sat there, hugging their 'cats while the horrific potential consequences of the tactic flowed through them.

After the Yawata Strike, it didn't take much imagination.

"What's worse, in some ways," Honor continued, "is that we have an at least partial list of their objectives. Cachalot's on it—we already knew that, even if Capriotti's obviously a very different breed of cat from Hajdu and Gogunov—but so are half a dozen other star systems, Elizabeth. Most of them are neutrals where we don't have any naval presence to do anything about it, too. I guess the one good side of that is that if we don't have anybody there to reprise Kotouč's accomplishment at Hypatia, that ought to at least deprive their COs of any excuse to resort to 'Parthian.' But it's going to be ugly when the other reports start coming in, and we'll have to respond to it somehow. That's another thing both Toms and Hamish and I will be kicking around at Admiralty House."

"How *can* we respond?" Elizabeth demanded. "Unless we want to start breaking up Grand Fleet, at least!"

"Mycroft will be completely up and running in Beowulf by early next month," Honor replied. "It's already up here in the home system, and Nouveau Paris will be covered in another couple of months. That'll let us free up at least a half-dozen additional squadrons of wallers, if we need to. But, frankly, superdreadnoughts aren't what we need. Oh," she waved one hand as Elizabeth's eyebrows rose, "they'd do the job, all right, but deploying superdreadnought divisions for area coverage would be like using a sledgehammer to crack walnuts. It *works*, but there's a certain degree of overkill involved. Besides, if the Sollies see two or three podnoughts waiting for them, that'll almost certainly trigger 'Parthian.' And even with Mycroft, we don't begin to have enough SD(P)s to be spreading them broadcast around the galaxy. We probably have enough to cover the most strategically important neutral systems, the ones whose trade with us makes them *obvious* Buccaneer targets. That may be what we need to do, however little I like the thought, but I'm going to fight tooth and nail against any more diversions from Grand Fleet than we absolutely have to make."

"Why?"

Elizabeth's tone was honestly curious, and Honor gave a short, sharp laugh.

"Well, whatever Hamish may say when he's feeling feisty, it's not because they're 'my' superdreadnoughts and I don't want to share!"

"He *would* say something like that, wouldn't he?"

"Only to me—thank God!" Honor shook her head. "However, I do have several reasons for resisting dispersal. One is the need to maintain a concentrated striking force—we've already sent a substantial chunk of fighting power off with Tourville to reinforce Mike and the Talbott Quadrant, and I'd just as soon not get into the habit of frittering away our 'mailed fist.' If we decide the strategic balance is shifting enough that we have to rethink our stance and take the offensive, I want as much striking power concentrated in one place as we can get. But that's secondary, really. My main objection is more psychological than anything else, to be honest."

"Psychological?" Elizabeth seemed surprised.

"I don't want the Mandarins to think they've succeeded in compelling us to significantly redistribute our battle fleet, Elizabeth. That's the primary objective of a strategy like this one. I don't believe for a moment that they have the technological and tactical wherewithal to take advantage of our response if we *were* to weaken ourselves here by redistributing Grand Fleet. And absent some new hardware we don't know about yet, I'd be surprised if anyone on *their* side's stupid enough to think they do—now that Rajampet's dead, at any rate. It's possible that the Alignment might try to take advantage of any dispersal, but everything we've seen from the Yawata Strike analysis says we have to worry about stealth, not massive firepower, where they're concerned. Mycroft and Apollo are more than capable of killing anything the

Alignment could possibly send in; we just have to *see* it first, and stacking superdreadnoughts up in heaps won't expand our sensors' reach. So I don't see a defensive downside to spreading our capital ships out a bit.

"But if the Mandarins believe they're compelling us to dance to their piping, it's likely to give them a greater sense of self-confidence. There was a general back on Old Earth who was a great proponent of maintaining what we call 'psychological dominance' these days. *He* called it 'putting the scare' into the other side, and when we're up against something the size of the Solarian League, we need them as scared of us as possible. What we don't need is them convincing themselves they *don't* need to fear us. Or even simply that they don't need to fear us as much as they did. Because if they decide that's the case, they're likely to start thinking in terms of more operations as stupid as Raging Justice, at which point the death toll—most of it Solly—will skyrocket again."

"I can see that," Elizabeth said thoughtfully. "But, Honor, if we don't find a way to keep them from 'Buccaneering' one system after another, won't that have the same effect? Which doesn't even consider the impact on billions of innocent bystanders!"

"When word of what happened at Hypatia gets home, Old Chicago may rethink the whole concept. I don't really *expect* it, but it's possible. In the meantime, I think there may be a better tactical solution than scattering SD(P)s hither and yon, though. Given what *Phantom* and three *Saganami-B*s accomplished in Hypatia, I'm more convinced than ever that the Mark 16 can handle about anything the Sollies throw at us. So I'm going to propose we redeploy the *Agamemnons*. I'd really prefer to use *Nikes*, if we had them, but we don't, and given what Kotouč's people accomplished with no pods at all, I think a division or two of *Agamemnons* should be plenty to rain on any Solly's parade. We've only got a hundred or so of them, and only the Flight IIs have Keyhole, so they couldn't duplicate *Phantom*'s tactics—not fully. On the other hand, the Demonic Duo may have come up with a stopgap solution to that particular problem."

"'Demonic duo'?" Elizabeth repeated.

"Sorry. My personal nickname for the firm of Hemphill and Foraker, Inc.," Honor said. "Either of them alone was bad enough. The two of them together are *scary!*"

"And what have they come up with now?"

It was obvious Elizabeth was trying not to laugh, and Honor grinned at her. Then her expression sobered...a bit, at any rate.

"I suspect the initial concept came from Foraker," she said, "but the final proposal has Sonja's fingerprints all over it, too. Basically, they took a good look at the way our *Saganami-Cs* and *Rolands* have been integrating Ghost Rider into their fire control loops, and they've come up with a refinement. For all intents and purposes, their suggestion is that we use Hermes buoys in conjunction with Ghost Rider. The *Agamemnons* have plenty of telemetry links; their links just don't have an FTL capability. So the idea is that we strap Hermes buoys onto Ghost Rider recon drones and then tractor four or five more buoys just outside an *Agamemnon*'s wedge perimeter and let them talk to each other. Hermes has a *lot* more bandwidth—and more channels—than the standard shipboard grav com, Elizabeth. So if we pair buoys between those tractored to the ship and the ones mounted on the recon platforms then feed the telemetry links through the buoy channels and use the ones on the recon platforms to talk to the missiles..."

She raised an eyebrow as her voice trailed off. Elizabeth looked at her for several seconds, then began to nod—slowly, at first, but with increasing enthusiasm.

"Don't get too excited," Honor warned. "Like I say, it's a stopgap. Neither Ghost Rider drones nor buoys are what you might call tiny, which means they'll displace a lot of missiles. And the entire system's on the...ramshackle side. It won't have Keyhole's bandwidth, even with all the buoys an *Agamemnon* can handle, and it won't provide the additional missile-defense Keyhole's laser clusters offer, either. But it *will* help a lot, and from the shipboard end, most of the refit will consist of software changes, so we should be able to put it into service quickly."

"I understand about getting too excited," the Empress said, "but I like what I understand about the idea, Honor. I like it a *lot!*"

"Well, so do I, actually," Honor admitted. "But even granting that it's mostly software, it'll take time to exterminate the bugs and get it up and running. And while we're doing that, I'm sure we'll find out where else the Sollies have been blowing away innocent bystanders' infrastructure. And that means we'll still have to come up with a way to...reshape their thinking. This 'strap-on Keyhole' will help, but it's primarily *defensive*. We need something more proactive."

"Are you starting to lean towards the idea of reprisals after all?" Elizabeth asked carefully, and Honor shrugged.

"I don't know," she said. "I just don't know. All the arguments against *invading* the League still apply, and the fact that they're already show-ing us at least a few new tricks of their own underscores why that's true. But by the same token, those new tricks—and Commodore Les-sem's comments on their productivity are pretty well taken, too—mean our time window to go for a 'softer' solution is closing on us. We're watching them as closely as we can, but we can't be *certain* they're not going to sneak something radically new into the deck when we're not looking. I'm pretty sure they can't come up with a big enough game changer to keep someone as smart as Pat Givens and her people from telling us about it in time to kick the stuffing out of them in a full-bore offensive; I just hate the thought of doing that one moment before we have to. But there's a point where worrying about future Solarian revanchism comes in what Hamish calls a 'piss-poor second' compared to the need to prevent more Hypatias, Elizabeth. Because somewhere—we don't know where...yet, but *somewhere*, just as sure as we're sitting here—there's another Hajdu or Gogunov with no Kotouč and Petersen to stop her."

Hillary Indrakashi Enkateshwara Tower
City of Old Chicago
Sol System
Solarian League

"I DON'T THINK THERE's any doubt now," Daud al-Fanudahi said just a bit indistinctly around a mouthful of bagel. He shook his head apologetically, sipped coffee from a disposable cup, and swallowed.

"As I say, I don't think there's any doubt now," he repeated, wiping crumbs from his tunic. "We still may not be able to *prove* what they're conspiring about, but the correlations are too damned convincing for them not to be conspiring about *something*."

"I'll agree with that," Simeon Gaddis said. The Gendarmerie brigadier had made one of his rare visits to the Ghost Hunters' lair to participate in today's strategy session. "The problem is that we still can't prove what that 'something' is. We have a shit pot of circumstantial evidence, and the fact that Lawton, Nye, and Salazar are all providing the same slant on their intel *and* that their recommendations are universally to slam the Manties harder ought to make any honest spook—I realize that's something of an oxymoron, in this town—suspicious as hell. Under normal circumstances, I'd be willing to go to an honest prosecutor—another oxymoron, but I do know a handful of them—with what we have. Under the present circumstances, I'm afraid we'd just get whoever we went to killed. We don't have anything concrete enough for me to jump the queue, which means any submission would go up the normal chain at Justice."

"And there's no way in hell these people aren't wired in somewhere along that chain," al-Fanudahi acknowledged rather more glumly. "Or that they wouldn't do whatever they figured it would take to short-circuit the process."

"Even if that weren't true, who could we jump the queue *to*?" Lupe Blanton asked.

"Rorendaal," Gaddis replied without hesitation, and Blanton looked suddenly thoughtful.

The Federal Department of Justice was probably the least important

339

department of the Solarian League's government. Most of the League's member systems had robust local departments of justice; the League no longer required one. That was what a few T-centuries of bureaucratic fiat and regulatory governance that no longer bothered the legislative branch with little things like passing laws tended to produce. Indeed, Justice was so lacking in stature that none of the deputy attorneys general—Justice's equivalent of the other departments' permanent senior undersecretaries—had ever even been considered for membership among the Mandarins.

Of Justice's three divisions, however, the Criminal Law Division had the most power, greatest independence...and least relevance. It was widely acknowledged as the senior division. In fact, Deputy Attorney General Marie-Claire Rorendaal, who headed Criminal Law, was the closest thing to an effective Attorney General the League possessed, given Attorney General Ronayne's total lack of competence. Unfortunately, CLD was charged with the prosecution of *crimes*, which in the Solarian League no longer included malfeasance and corruption. Or, rather, those were still technically crimes, but Criminal Law was prohibited from acting upon them without a referral from the Ethics and Integrity Division. That had a lot to do with why Rorendaal's opinion of Ludovico Mazarello, who headed Ethics, was somewhere south of unprintable. It would have been difficult to decide whether her contempt for his venality exceeded his contempt for her *lack* of venality, but it would have been a very close run thing.

After the Monica Incident, Rorendaal had been on something of a roll. The evidence of criminal wrongdoing on a massive scale had been too great to be suppressed even in the Solarian League. Or, rather, the Mandarins had decided to throw Technodyne Industries under the air lorry to keep anyone from looking too closely in their own direction. The consequence had been to allow CLD to actually prosecute criminal actions by a major transstellar for the first time in T-decades, and Rorendaal had *hammered* Technodyne. In fact, she'd made such headway some of the League's other transstellars had begun to look nervously in her direction on the theory that in the process of nailing Technodyne to the wall she was likely to turn up evidence of their own wrongdoing. God knew there was plenty of such evidence to be found, and she and her dedicated team of professional prosecutors had been building a dangerous momentum.

Fortunately, from the perspective of both Technodyne and those other nervous transstellars, Rorendaal's investigation had been abruptly tabled—only "temporarily," of course—when the confrontation with Manticore turned ugly. She'd protested strenuously, but the crisis had given Technodyne's friends sufficient cover to shut her down. She and her staff continued to assemble evidence, but they'd been systematically starved of funding, personnel, and computer access because of the "crisis," and none of the Ghost Hunters expected her investigation to go anywhere even after the crisis ended.

But even though that was true, she was still the AAG for Criminal Law and the team she'd assembled to take down Technodyne was as pissed off as she was over the abrupt termination of their investigation. If Gaddis went directly to her, bypassing his own immediate superiors—and Mazarello—she and her people would probably take their current evidence seriously.

"Would you really be willing to approach her?" Blanton asked after a moment.

"Not with what we have so far." Gaddis shook his head. Blanton looked a little surprised, and he snorted.

"We just agreed the Other Guys must be keeping a close eye on law enforcement in general, Lupe," he pointed out. "If you were doing something illegal, immoral, and fattening and you were going to worry about any of the AAGs, which one would it be—her, Mazarello, or Illalangi?"

"Point," Blanton said, and al-Fanudahi and Natsuko Okiku laughed. It was not an *amused* laugh, however.

Mazarello was the quintessential corrupt bureaucrat who just happened to possess a law degree. He was a mousy-looking fellow, with brown hair and brown eyes which managed to look myopic despite modern medicine *and* biosculpt. He was, however, an extraordinarily *rich* mousy-looking fellow, courtesy of all the corruption his Ethics and Integrity Division somehow managed not to find. And Uwan Illalangi, despite an impressive appearance, including amber, cat-pupilled eyes as a result of significant genetic manipulation of his family line, had been almost as irrelevant as Rorendaal until very recently.

Illalangi headed the Constitutional Compliance and Conformity Division, which was responsible for assessing the constitutionality of any new regulation before it could take effect. That requirement was mandated by the Constitution, and Illalangi had sworn a solemn oath to discharge his duty without fear or favor. Which meant, in the modern Solarian League, that he drafted whatever memo the Federal Government required for its current purposes, then found a pet judge to sign off on it, if needed. Most of the time it wasn't, as he dutifully certified by citing the appropriate precedents. He was the epitome of a reliable apparatchik, and until the Manticore Crisis, his had been a simple, straightforward sort of task. Given the constitutional crisis provoked by Beowulf's threatened secession, he'd recently acquired a sudden importance—and headaches, not to mention time in the spotlight, he'd certainly never wanted. But it was unlikely, to say the least, that anyone would be worried about *his* turning over any unfortunate rocks.

No, if the Other Guys were keeping a proactive eye on anyone, Rorendaal was that anyone.

"I've known Marie-Claire a long time," Gaddis went on, his expression somber. "If I took this to her, she'd take it seriously, if only because it came from me. And if she took it seriously, she'd open an investigation of her own, which would be a Very Bad Idea. At the moment, her key prosecutors are pretty damned loyal, but you know there'd be a leak somewhere, and that would get her killed."

"Simeon, that's going to be true whenever we take it to her," Weng Zhing-hwan said quietly. "And you're right, she *is* the one we need to talk to about it."

"I know she is," Gaddis replied, his expression going still darker. "And I hate it, because, eventually, we won't have any choice about that. But I don't want to be painting any targets on her a second before we can give her something *conclusive*. A genuine smoking gun, not just suspicions that *might* be supported by all our circumstantial evidence. Something slam-dunk enough she can move so quickly she may actually get the charges in front of a grand jury before they can kill her."

He did not, the others noticed, mention what would happen to all of *them* if Rorendaal was killed before she could impanel a grand jury.

"So we're right back where we started?" Al-Fanudahi looked around the office.

"We've inched farther ahead," Gaddis demurred. "What we've done is build a body of evidence that can point investigators—*official* investigators, I mean—at people we know are dirty. We need something more conclusive—that smoking gun—to *start* the process, though. Something compelling enough to draw up the charging document immediately, *before* the Gendarmerie starts formally beating the bushes looking for more evidence. That's what we don't have."

Al-Fanudahi nodded thoughtfully. Then he inhaled and brought his chair upright.

"In that case, I have another question. Are we at a point now where we go Bryce's way, grab one of these people we 'know are dirty,' and get the truth out of them any damned way we can?" He looked around the office again. "Personally, I'm ready to face prosecution for whatever we have to do to turn this thing off."

"I think we all are," Okiku said. "And I'm ready to sign off on Bryce's suggestion."

"I'm not. Not yet." Gaddis shook his head. "The Outcasts are still chewing data, and they *think* they've nailed down at least two more of Ms. Bolton's 'clients.' They're not ready to confirm that yet, but if they do—*when* they do—then, yes. I think we drag Bolton in here, we put her through whatever damned wringer we need to, and then we take the entire mess to Marie-Claire. Who, being the hardnose she is, probably *will* indict us for kidnapping, illegal imprisonment, violation of civil rights, and anything else you can think of. But"—he smiled crookedly—"at least she'll be very grateful to us!"

"Wonderful." Colonel Weng sighed.

"Actually, what *I* want to get out of her—Bolton, I mean—" Blanton said, "is just who the hell the Other Guys really are. I mean, it *is* conceivable that despite everything we think we know, it really is the Manties."

"There's a tiny difference between 'conceivable' and more-likely-than-the-apocalypse," al-Fanudahi said. "I realize we have to maintain our objectivity, Lupe, but really. The *Manties?*" He shook his head.

"I didn't say it was, Daud. I said it was conceivable that it *could* be, which is damned well the argument the Mandarins will prefer to hear. And it's still *our* responsibility to keep an open mind on that, too. That's why we always call them the 'Other Guys,' isn't it? To remind ourselves not to develop tunnel vision and make any assumptions we can't prove?"

She looked at him, one eyebrow raised, until he nodded, then shrugged and continued.

"My point is that while I don't think it is the Manties, I still find this whole 'Alignment' business awfully hard to accept. Not only would it be harder than hell to keep a conspiracy on that level a deep dark secret for *centuries*, but the whole concept is stupid. The Final War's been over for more than seven hundred T-years, damn it. By this point, any lingering prejudice against genies is a prop for people who want to feel superior to genetic slaves, not a burning issue people give a rat's arse about. Do you *really* think a majority of the human race is still so adamantly opposed to genetically improving the species that somebody with the resources the Other Guys must've required to put all this in motion in the first place couldn't simply have financed a PR campaign to convince the League to revoke the legal prohibitions supporting the Beowulf Code's ban on genetic manipulation?"

She looked skeptical, and al-Fanudahi couldn't really blame her.

"I've wondered about that," he acknowledged. "Like you, I find it hard to swallow. The Manties and Havenites obviously do believe it, though, and they're more than smart enough for that same argument to have occurred to them. I realized that some time ago, so I've been pushing a notion around lately, looking at it from different angles, and I started to wonder. What if the 'Alignment' is actually a bit of disinformation planted on the Manties?"

"Excuse me?" Blanton's eyebrows rose, and he snorted.

"Look, assume someone, for some reason, wants to destabilize the League. I think we could all agree that if that *is* what the Other Guys are after, they're doing a damned good job. And I can think of several plausible scenarios, ranging from a would-be God Emperor hiding out in the Fringe somewhere with designs on galactic hegemony, to a bunch—and I mean a *bunch*—of transstellars who see a chance to make even more money, like Technodyne is doing right this minute, to an independent warlord in waiting who'd like to see OFS pruned back so he can expand his own local power base. Whoever it is, he's using the 'Grand Alliance' as his sledgehammer, so suppose someone like that—someone who knew he'd *need* a sledgehammer—sat down and carefully crafted the sort of 'evidence' he knew the Manties and the Havenites, both of whom have hated Mesa's guts ever since they signed the Cherwell Convention, would jump for. We've had plenty of evidence of how our own so-called intelligence people follow their preconceptions straight down a dead grav shaft rather than consider alternative possibilities. The fact that Manticore and Haven have demonstrated their competency in other areas doesn't mean they're competent in *all* areas."

"So you're suggesting the Other Guys are manipulating the Manties, too," Okiku said thoughtfully.

"I'm suggesting they *may* be," al-Fanudahi corrected. "And it's also possible the Manties are absolutely right. I spend a lot of time dealing with motivations and intentions, Natsuko, and I've read a lot of history along the way. As a way to stretch mental muscles, you might say. So I've seen people just as nutty as the ones the Manties are describing, all the way back to Ante Diaspora history. It's possible this Alignment exists; I just find it *improbable*."

"That's probably fair," Weng Zhing-hwan said after a moment. "And when you come down to it, if the Other Guys *are* manipulating the Manties, they've managed to push them into a position most Solarians figure is somewhere west of insane." She shook her head. "We know about it because a single nutty scientist"—she grimaced as she delib- erately reused al-Fanudahi's adjective—"with obvious mental issues, attested by at least a half-dozen official Mesan sources, somehow fled Mesa in the wake of a nuclear terrorist incident the Mesans say was orchestrated by Manty operatives and poured out his heart to Manty intelligence, revealing the existence of a massive conspiracy no one else in the entire galaxy ever even heard of." She rolled her eyes. "As flimsy evidence goes, that's even more...*outré* than usual."

"Granted. Granted!" Al-Fanudahi waved one hand. "Even if every single thing this Simões had to say is pure distilled truth, nobody's willing to believe it once Abruzzi and Public Information get done ridiculing it. And we *should* be skeptical of it, to say the least. But we have—we, the Ghost Hunters, I mean—have awfully damned convincing evidence the Other Guys do exist. The Manties may have misidentified them, but they *are* out there, Zhing-hwan. And an awful lot of both the pressure to flatten Manticore and the physical support to do that flattening—like Technodyne's Cataphracts—*are* coming out of Mesa or a Mesan connection. Is that more misdirection aimed at the Manties? Or is it evidence the Manties may actually be onto something?"

"Are you deliberately trying to fry my brain, or is that just collateral damage because you've already fried your *own*?" Weng demanded in an exasperated tone, and al-Fanudahi chuckled.

"Neither. I'm just saying that a question we need to keep constantly in mind is, if it isn't the 'Alignment,' who the hell *is* it? And whatever else may be true, the Manties managed to survive the short end of the odds against the People's Republic for the better part of two T-centuries and kicked its arse into the bargain. So they clearly haven't deluded themselves into any fatal missteps *before* this one. I'm simply saying it behooves us to keep our own minds open to the possibility that whoever the Other Guys are, their objective is neither what we thought it was *nor* what the Manties think they've found."

❖   ❖   ❖

"Sorry to be calling so late in the afternoon," Rajmund Nyhus said from Adão Ukhtomskoy's com display. He'd caught the Section Two head just as Ukhtomskoy was heading for the door, and his blue eyes were as unhappy as his tone. "I know it's Friday, too, but I thought I'd better get you up to speed on this before the weekend."

"Up to speed on what?" Ukhtomskoy asked warily. "You've managed to ID your so-called sources in Maya?"

"Not yet. I'm trying to nail down the source of my second report, but there hasn't been time for any response to my queries to come back. Even if there had been, you know how hard it can be getting field agents to come in for interviews...and how unhappy they are about giving up sources when they finally do come in."

Ukhtomskoy's nod was impatient, and Nyhus shrugged, his expression grim.

"Well, there may not have been time for any responses to my

queries, but MacQuilkin—you remember, our senior agent in Sprague?" He paused, and Ukhtomskoy nodded again, even more impatiently. "Well, she's sent a follow-on. In addition to the stringer in Smoking Frog who got the photos of our mysterious Manty meeting with Barregos, she's got several sources in Erewhon. One of them's a senior exec in the shipyards building those locally-financed warships for Barregos and Rozsak. And according to him, they're building one *hell* of a lot more ships than they're telling anyone in Old Chicago about. Not just cruisers and destroyers, either, Adão. He says they're building superdreadnoughts. *Pod-laying* superdreadnoughts, complete with Manty technology. The whole nine meters: FTL coms, stealth, better compensators, those god-awful missiles. The whole shooting match."

"My God," Ukhtomskoy muttered. Then his eyes narrowed. "What kind of corroboration has she got?"

"Nothing concrete yet," Nyhus conceded. "According to her message, she was leaving for Erewhon herself a couple of days after it was dispatched. Which means she's there by now, maybe even on her way back to Sprague. She says she thinks her source can get her close enough to the shipyards for some visual imagery. But if this guy knows what the hell he's talking about, it's not just Maya we have to worry about. If the Manties really are giving Erewhon access to their latest tech, especially after Erewhon already jumped ship to the other side once, then they must have some pretty damned ironclad guarantees it won't be used against *them* this time. And if Barregos and Erewhon don't need it to stand off the 'Grand Alliance,' I can only think of one other adversary they could be worried about."

SEPTEMBER 1922 POST DIASPORA

HMS *Tristram*
In Hyper-Space

"WOULD YOU PASS THE rolls, please, Mr. Harahap?"

"Of course, Captain."

Damien Harahap passed the basket of yeast rolls to Lieutenant Xamar, who passed it on to the small, dark, extremely attractive woman at the head of the table.

"Thank you," Commander Naomi Kaplan said. She took one of the rolls and began buttering, and Harahap hid a faint smile as he sat back in his chair.

He'd been a Gendarme during his career in the service of the Solarian League, not a naval officer or a Marine, but he *had* been aboard Solarian warships upon occasion. None of the really big ones, mostly destroyers and cruisers. That experience was enough to tell him that HMS *Tristram* was much larger than any Solarian destroyer ever built. In fact, she was bigger than some of the light cruisers he'd seen, despite the small size of her complement. Unless he was seriously mistaken, however, she was also incomparably more lethal than any ship—any *other* ship—he'd ever been aboard.

And despite the courtesy of Commander Kaplan's request, he was *not* an honored guest.

No, he thought, *but at least I'm still* alive. *That's something. Quite a lot, in fact.*

He glanced across the table at Indiana Graham, the youthful—and very dangerous—head of the Seraphim Independence Movement. He'd been surprised when Indy decided to "accompany him" to Manticore. Almost as surprised as he'd been when he realized Indy wasn't going to shoot him out of hand and avoid all the bother. Harahap wasn't certain he'd have made the same decision, in Indy's place. On the other hand, he understood why the Manties were determined to get him home in excellent health. What he *didn't* understand was why he was still in the aforesaid excellent health. It was more than two T-weeks since he'd found himself a Manticoran "guest," and he'd expected whatever suicide protocol his recent Mesan employers had implanted to change that state of affairs rather drastically. Unless...

349

"More coffee, Mr. Harahap?" Chief Steward Clorinda Brinkman murmured in his ear, and he nodded.

"Please," he said.

Brinkman refilled his cup, then turned to the attractive—and very young—lieutenant at his left elbow.

"Lieutenant Hearns?"

"Yes, please, Chief."

Hearns's soft accent fascinated Harahap. Her uniform was of a totally different color and cut from that of anyone else around the table, and he'd realized early on that she must be a Grayson, one of the personnel on loan to the RMN from its ally. The fact that she was a woman was rather surprising, given what he understood about Grayson social mores, but what he found especially fascinating was that he'd heard an accent almost exactly like it many years ago, and not from a Grayson. She sounded for all the world like a younger version of Colonel Bronwen Prydderch, one of the few native Old Terrans with whom Harahap had ever been professionally associated. Prydderch had also been one of the more competent people for whom he'd worked, but she'd tended to run on—endlessly—about the beauties of her hometown, someplace called Llandovery on the Old Terran island of England. Although, now that he thought about it, he didn't think that was what she'd called the island. In fact, she'd gotten pretty upset the one time *Harahap* had called it that.

Unlike Prydderch, thank God, Lieutenant Hearns didn't talk much about *her* hometown, but he'd still picked up a few details. Enough to know that, in addition to being one of the vanishingly few women in the Grayson Space Navy, she was also the daughter of a steadholder, which made her the equivalent of a royal princess. That was even more intriguing to someone in Harahap's line of work—or what *had* been his line of work—than her accent. His experience with the high and mighty of the Solarian League didn't include anyone who'd voluntarily risked his own rosy arse for even his own star nation, much less someone else's! That said some very interesting things about Grayson and Manticoran social dynamics.

"Lieutenant Simpkins informs me we'll be arriving in Manticore in about thirty-six hours, Mr. Harahap," Kaplan said as she finished buttering her roll. Harahap twitched internally, but aside from a politely arched eyebrow, his expression didn't even flicker. "I'm sure our intelligence people will be very interested in talking to you."

"Yes, Captain." Harahap allowed himself a faint smile. "I imagine they will."

Indy Graham looked at him rather sharply across the table, and

Harahap gave him a tiny shrug. Unless he was mistaken, that was an edge of concern in Indy's eyes. Rather touching, really. Especially considering the way Harahap had played Indy in the Mesan Alignment's service. Still, there'd never been anything personal in it. He hoped Indy—and his sister Mackenzie, especially—understood that.

"I'll remind you, Sir," Kaplan continued in that same, serene tone, "that you've given your parole. I realize that for a covert operative such as yourself, lying and swearing false oaths go with the territory. I mention this"—she smiled at him, reminding him in that moment of a small, very attractive tiger—"because I'm a naval officer and, unlike covert operatives, I take oaths very seriously. I won't like it if you should happen to violate this one. And if I don't like it, you'll like it even less."

"Understood, Captain." He returned her smile with a rather broader one. "And we covert operatives are very pragmatic sorts. For some reason, we don't think it's a good idea to give someone who probably already wants to shoot us an even better reason to squeeze the trigger. I'll behave, I promise."

✧   ✧   ✧

Abigail Hearns sipped from her fresh cup of coffee and suppressed a headshake of amusement.

Damien Harahap was a very dangerous man, and if he truly was the "Firebrand" who'd orchestrated the anti-annexation movement in Talbott, he was responsible—albeit indirectly—for the deaths of hundreds of Royal Manticoran Navy personnel, many of whom had been Abigail's personal friends. She was pretty sure he *was* that "Firebrand," and whether that was true or not, he was definitely the agent provocateur who'd falsely promised Indiana and Mackenzie Graham Manticoran naval support for their rebellion against their own corrupt system government. Nor was the Seraphim System the only place he'd spread his webs in the service of the Mesan Alignment. God only knew how many people had been killed as a direct consequence of his actions.

And despite that, she actually liked him. A little bit, at least. He was charming, intelligent, and possessed a lively sense of humor. And despite all the carnage in which he'd had a hand, she sensed absolutely no malice in him. Which was probably one of the things that made him so dangerous, actually. He *hadn't* done what he'd done out of malice. It was simply his job—or his *craft*, at least—and he was good at it. She didn't know how he'd become what he was, and she wondered if his ability to manipulate and betray so many thousands of people—millions, really—without any personal sense of malice meant he was a sociopath of some sort.

She didn't think so. She didn't know what to make of him, but she didn't think he was a sociopath. No doubt *successful* sociopaths had to be able to pretend they weren't, but her personal armsman, Mateo Gutierrez, seemed to like him, too, and Mateo was an excellent judge of people. Of course, the fact that Mateo might like him wouldn't prevent the armsman from shooting him squarely between the eyes if he even looked like posing a threat to Abigail or anyone else aboard *Tristram*. On more mature consideration, she decided, Mateo might be willing to shoot to *wound* if the threat was to someone besides her, but that was about as far as he'd be prepared to go.

She looked across the table at Indiana Graham. The brown-haired Seraphimian was actually a couple of T-years younger than Abigail herself, although he carried himself with the assurance of someone much older. Abigail knew she did, too, and probably for some of the same reasons. She'd never imagined leading a rebellion to free her star system from what amounted to social and economic slavery, but she suspected it must have much the same...clarifying effect as knowing you were about to die in a hopeless battle on someone else's planet.

She saw a lot of the same ghosts when she looked into his eyes, anyway.

She'd also discovered that she liked Indy quite a bit more than she liked Harahap. In some ways, he reminded her of a lot of Graysons she'd known. The Seraphim System hadn't tried to poison him every time he drew a breath, but it had offered its own survival challenges, especially after his father was arrested and he and his sister began organizing the SIM. But in other ways, he was very different from anyone she'd ever known back home, and almost equally different from most of the Manties she'd met. Actually, who he reminded her of the most was her friend Helen Zilwicki. Possibly with a little bit of Helga Boltitz thrown in for good measure. He had that same spit-in-your-eye sense of independence, that awareness of where he'd come from, what he'd overcome, and the determination to handle anything the galaxy threw at him or die trying. No one could possibly come from a background more different from her own wealthy, privileged, thoroughly protected upbringing, yet behind those brown eyes was someone she really wanted to get to know better.

And in thirty-six hours, they'd reach Manticore, and he'd leave *Tristram*, and she'd probably never see him again.

There were times she seriously questioned the Tester's sense of humor.

✧　　✧　　✧

Indiana Graham listened to the conversation and tried to decide what he felt.

A part of him was delighted by the thought of handing his good friend Firebrand over to the Manties and their allies. Until Commodore Zavala's arrival in Seraphim with his destroyer squadron, he'd believed Firebrand—he still thought of the covert operative by his codename, not his given name, assuming his given name really was "Damien Harahap," which was far from a certainty—truly was his friend. And that was the reason he couldn't decide how he felt, because another part of him still considered Firebrand just that: a friend. Not simply a friend, but the man who'd provided the weapons which had allowed the Seraphim Independence Movement to succeed. Who'd led SIM strike teams on one high-risk op after another. Who'd risked his life to drag critically wounded SIM fighters to safety under heavy fire on four separate occasions. Who'd sat up late, drinking coffee, while Indy and Kenzie and he studied the maps, tried to decide where to shift their resources. Who'd led one of the three strike teams into Terrabore Prison to rescue Bruce Graham and the other political prisoners held there.

He hadn't had to do all those things. He could have simply washed his hands of Seraphim completely when the moment actually came, and he hadn't manufactured that moment, either. He'd been no more able to foresee the assassination of President McCready or the opportunity it would offer the SIM than anyone else, and no one would have blamed him if he'd opted out of the uprising when it began. No native Seraphimian had fought harder or taken more risks, either. Logically, Indy understood that he'd wanted the rebellion to succeed so he could capture the transportation he needed to get out of the system before the inevitable OFS-summoned Solarian task force arrived. Especially since, unlike Indy or Mackenzie, he'd known there'd be no *Manticoran* task force to stop it.

But he still hadn't had to do it. And that was why Indiana Graham had such . . . mixed emotions where Damien Harahap was concerned. It was also the reason he'd left his father Bruce, his sister, and Tanawat Saowaluk to organize an interim government for Seraphim under the protection of Zavala's other four destroyers while he boarded *Tristram* to accompany Harahap to Manticore. He couldn't have told anyone, including himself, exactly what his motives were, but he suspected one of them was to be Firebrand's friend in court. Which was probably stupid, since whatever might have happened after the fighting began, Firebrand had most definitely been setting Seraphim up to be hammered when it began.

On the other hand, if I wasn't pretty stupid, I'd have been smart enough not to start any hopeless rebellions, wouldn't I? Besides—his eyes drifted to the slender brunette seated across the table from him—*if I hadn't come along, I'd never have met Abigail.*

Mount Royal Palace
City of Landing
Manticore Binary System

HE WAS A VERY *ordinary*-looking man.

In fact, Honor couldn't remember ever seeing one who looked more ordinary. She'd thought that the moment she saw the file imagery, and then she'd thought about it. About how *extra*ordinarily difficult it must be for anyone who'd accomplished all this man allegedly had to look so...innocuous. So completely and utterly forgettable. She could have passed him on the slidewalk, knocked packages out of his hand and helped him pick them back up, and never really remembered him at all.

That's what she'd thought then. Now, as he walked through the door into the heavily guarded conference room, she realized just how wrong she'd been. Not about how he looked, but about how forgettable she would have found him.

It took all her self-control to hide that sudden awareness and sit calmly in the comfortable chair, watching the wary Queen's Own sergeants escort him across the room to the chair on the opposite side of the table. They were courteous but watchful, and she considered telling them they weren't watchful enough. She could taste their mind-glows, knew their professionalism was fully engaged, yet she also knew they'd allowed that surface ordinariness to lull them.

They really had no idea at all who—*what*—this man was. But then, they lacked her advantage, her ability to see beneath the surface with a treecat's acuity.

And, after all, he looked *so* ordinary.

It was just as well her armsmen didn't share that ability of hers. She'd never have convinced them to wait outside the conference room if they'd had a clue about just what this man truly was. She felt Nimitz sharing her impressions, like a beloved echo in the back of her brain, and knew his assessment matched her own. He lay stretched along the top of her chair back, not perched on her shoulder, but she felt the wary tension in the long, sinuous body pressed against the back of her

354

head. Whatever the escorts might have thought, Nimitz was poised, ready to erupt off his perch in a heartbeat.

The man stood behind his chair, head cocked, one eyebrow raised above a mild eye, and she smiled at him.

"Sit down, please, Mr. Harahap," she invited.

"Thank you."

He settled into the chair with a near-treecat neatness, the first real flaw she'd seen in his façade of ordinariness. He'd masked that smooth, trained suppleness quite well walking across the room, but Honor Alexander-Harrington had spent half a century as a practitioner of coup de vitesse. The way he sat, the way he placed his feet so carefully, centered himself perfectly in the chair—those things said quite a lot to someone with her experience.

She tipped back slightly in her own chair, elbows on the armrests, fingers steepled under her chin, legs crossed while she contemplated him. Then she raised her eyes to the noncoms.

"That will be all," she said.

The senior of them started to object, or question her wisdom, at any rate. But she twitched her head in a minute shake before he got his first sentence launched, and he closed his mouth.

"Of course, Your Grace," he said, instead. "We'll be stationed at the door with your armsmen if you need us."

"Thank you," she said, and felt Damien Harahap's faint amusement as he, too, recognized the real target of that last sentence.

The sergeants withdrew, the door slid shut behind them, and Honor returned her attention to the man across the table, studying him thoughtfully for exactly twenty-five seconds by the digital display in the corner of her artificial left eye's field of vision.

"You do realize all the reasons we should just execute you and be done with it, I trust, Mr. Harahap," she said then, pleasantly.

"Oh, I doubt I know *all* the reasons," he replied. "I can think of at least—two dozen? Three?—right off the top of my head, though. I'm assuming your people have decided there's at least a possibility I'm worth more alive and talking than I'd be dead as an object lesson, though. Far be it from me to disagree if you have, Duchess Harrington."

"They told you who I am?"

"No." He shook his head. "The only thing they told me was that I was about to be interviewed by a highly competent interrogator. I admit, I didn't expect a navy admiral. I've been thinking more in terms of, oh, Mr. Zilwicki. Or possibly someone with bottles of chemicals and maybe a rubber hose or two, assuming he was a traditionalist. But—I hope you'll forgive my pointing this out—you and your friend"—he twitched his head at Nimitz—"have attained a certain notoriety in Solarian circles. You almost fooled me, though. Sitting down the way you are, I hadn't realized you were three meters tall."

"Three meters?" She shook her head with a faint smile. "Just under two, actually."

"So I noticed. Nobody reading the Solly newsfaxes would believe it, though. They'd probably wonder where the horns were, too, now that I think about it."

"I suppose someone might wonder the same thing looking at you, if they were familiar with your track record, Mr. Firebrand." She shook her head again. "From our perspective, you've been a very bad boy."

"Would you believe me if I told you it was nothing personal?" he asked, and she cocked her head. His tone was almost whimsical, but underneath it . . .

"Yes, Mr. Harahap. I think I would."

Damien Harahap stiffened. It was a tiny thing, more sensed than seen, and his eyes narrowed ever so slightly.

"Kind of you to say so, anyway," he said lightly. "Somehow I doubt that's going to make a lot of difference to my ultimate fate, though."

"Actually," she told him, "the outcome of this interview will make quite a lot of difference to your 'ultimate fate.'"

"Oh?" It was his turn to cock his head. "I hope you'll forgive me for pointing this out, but aren't you supposed to be a fleet commander? Not a spook, I mean?"

"Like yourself, I'm a person of many parts, Mr. Harahap. As far as you're concerned, what matters at the moment is that in addition to commanding Grand Fleet, I'm a peer of the realm, a Grayson steadholder, the cousin of the Beowulf System Chairman, and a personal friend of both Empress Elizabeth, Protector Benjamin, and President Pritchart. Oh, and also of Chien-lu von Rabenstrange, who's third in line for the Andermani throne." This time, her smile was a treecat's. "My point is that I have a certain influence with people who trust my ability to make judgments about other people's sincerity. I'd advise you to make a good impression on me."

He looked at her for a long moment, and then he chuckled. From his mind-glow, she knew his amusement was genuine.

"Somehow," he told her, "that sounds like a very good idea. So, tell me, Duchess Harrington. How can I start making that good impression?"

✧   ✧   ✧

"Well?" Elizabeth Winton said as Honor followed Colonel Ellen Shemais into the private drawing room. Spencer Hawke and Joshua

Atkins had peeled off at the door, joining the Queen's Own sentries already stationed there.

"Would it be all right if I sat down before we began the cross-examination?" Honor asked her, and most of the treecats present bleeked in laughter. Ariel, Elizabeth's treecat, joined in it, and the empress snorted.

"If you insist," she said, pointing at the armchair across from her own, and Honor sank into it with a sigh. She urged Nimitz down into her lap, hugging him rather than parking him on the back of her chair, and looked around the drawing room thoughtfully.

In addition to Elizabeth and Ariel, Hamish and Samantha were present. So were Patricia Givens and her treecat bodyguard, Thought Chaser, and her civilian counterpart at SIS, Sir Barton Salgado and Crooked Tooth. Thomas Theisman was there with Springs From Above, and so were Thomas Caparelli and Clear Mind, Sir Anthony Langtry and Moon Dancer, and Sir Tyler Abercrombie, the Home Secretary, and his furry bodyguard, Stone Climber. Stone Climber and Samantha were the only female 'cats in the room.

After so many decades when Nimitz had been the *only* treecat in the room, period, the denseness of the 'cat population took a little getting used to.

And there was a *lot* of celery being munched upon.

"Despite what Palace Security and the Queen's Own may have told Mr. Harahap, I'm not really a 'highly competent interrogator,'" she said after she and Nimitz were settled.

"You may not be a highly *trained* interrogator, Your Grace, but you're definitely one of the most *competent* ones I've ever met," Patricia Givens disagreed.

"I'd have to admit *I* wouldn't want to try to lie to you, Honor," Theisman put in. "And neither would any of the other cabinet secretaries, senators, and congressmen who met you in Nouveau Paris. Most of them had reached that conclusion long before we found out you were half treecat yourself, too."

"I suppose that's one way to put it," she conceded as the treecats went off into a fresh round of laughter.

"That's why we all wanted you to talk to him." Elizabeth's tone and expression had turned much more serious. "Our 'cats can talk to us now, tell us what they're sensing, and we all know how useful *that*'s been to people like Admiral Givens and Sir Barton."

She twitched her head in the direction of the SIS Director and Patricia Givens, and Honor nodded. One unanticipated—although it darned well *should* have been anticipated—advantage of the treecat bodyguards was the enormous edge they gave counter-intelligence agents. There still weren't enough of them—treecats were a top-tier predator species; their population densities had always been low—but they'd already made their presence felt in a big way. The vetting process was still in its early stages, but the human-'cat teams had already unmasked no less than eleven spies in the upper levels of the ministries' professional staffs. Four of them had "died of natural causes" when they realized they'd been detected, which left little doubt about who *they'd* been working for. The seven who hadn't died didn't know who their employers had been.

It would have been nice to take someone who *could* confirm the Alignment's existence alive, but those four "natural" deaths had been plenty of confirmation for the members of the Grand Alliance. And at least they were progressively sealing off the leaks they hadn't known about previously.

"But whatever the 'cats can *tell* us, none of us can sense it ourselves," Elizabeth continued. "You can. That's the reason none of us shared a word of our own impressions with you until we'd dragged you down from your flagship and you'd had the opportunity to 'taste his mindglow' yourself. So, now that you have, what's your impression?"

"The first point, I suppose," Honor said thoughtfully, "is that I understand now why he's been so damnably effective. I think probably the only people I've ever met who could compare to him as a covert operations sort, if in somewhat different ways, would be Anton Zilwicki," she extended her right index finger, "Victor Cachat," her second finger joined the first, "my Uncle Jacques," the ring finger rose, "and Kevin Usher."

The silence which followed was profound. Then Theisman stirred.

"That's impressive company, Honor."

"I know. But he's a very dangerous fellow. He's very smart, very skilled, and extraordinarily methodical. Those are dangerous qualities in anyone, but Mr. Harahap is also a . . . call it an honest craftsman, for want of a better term. If he takes a job on—*any* job, not just blowing up star systems—he gives full value."

"You're saying he's a mercenary?" Givens asked, frowning intently, and Honor shrugged.

"I suppose that's one way to put it. On the other hand, when he says none of what he did was 'personal' he means exactly that. Not that his statement was *entirely* accurate. He didn't want to admit it—because he didn't think I'd believe him, I think—but what ultimately happened in Seraphim *was* personal for him."

She shrugged again, her eyes gazing intently at something only she could see as she searched for the right words.

"The truth is—and, again, it's nothing he said; I tasted it *behind* what he was saying—he wanted every single one of the rebellions he helped foment to succeed."

"I find that...difficult to believe," Sir Tyler said slowly. Of all those present, he knew Honor and Nimitz least well, and she tasted his skepticism. His belief Harahap had somehow managed to snow her despite her ability to taste the emotions of those about her.

"I doubt you find it much more difficult to believe secondhand than I did at firsthand," she told him with the off-center smile her artificial facial nerves imposed. "It's true, though. He really did."

"Why?" Theisman asked. "And did that apply to his activities in Talbott, too?"

"I can't tell you why for certain," Honor said slowly. "Can't give you all the reasons, I mean, but at least part of it was that the strategist in him thought the Mesans were missing a bet. He thought that at least a few successful rebellions by people who everyone believed had been backed by the Star Empire, however vociferously we denied it, would hurt us a lot worse in the court of Solarian public opinion. That it would tie into the line Abruzzi's selling everyone about our ruthless imperialist ambitions. But that was only a part of it. I think mostly it was because he despises Frontier Security."

"Honor, he *worked* for Frontier Security," Hamish pointed out.

"No, he worked for the Gendarmerie, which farmed him *out* to Frontier Security," Honor corrected. "And underneath all that serenity of his, so far underneath I'm not sure even he realizes it's there, there's one hell of a lot of anger at OFS." She saw his eyebrows rise at her choice of adverb, "He thinks it's only contempt because they're sloppy and incompetent, Hamish, but he's wrong. What he actually feels is a lot stronger than that...and his reasons are a *lot* more personal than he thinks they are."

"Why?" Theisman asked again.

"Because he comes from the Startman System."

Honor's voice was oddly flat, and her husband frowned as he heard that flatness. Patricia Givens heard it, too.

"Why is that significant, Your Grace?" she asked. Honor looked at her in evident surprise, and she shook her head. "The name sounds familiar, but I'm not making any connections."

"I think it's significant because it's in the Protectorates and Harahap was seven years old when OFS handed his entire homeworld over to StratoCorp," Honor said with that same flat, hard edge, and Theisman's eyes narrowed.

"StratoCorp?" Givens said a bit sharply. "That's not in his dossier!"

"Forgive me, Pat," Caparelli said in a dry tone, speaking up for the first time, "but I was rather under the impression we were *building* a dossier on him."

"Well, yes." Givens looked a bit chagrined. "But that much should already have been in it! If Her Grace could get it out of him this quickly..."

"My understanding is that Commander Kaplan and her people were specifically told *not* to interrogate him on the trip here," Theisman observed. "That would make it just a bit difficult for them to get anything out of him, wouldn't it?"

Givens nodded, and not entirely happily. She understood the reason for Jacob Zavala's instructions; she just wasn't sure she agreed with them. Still, Zavala's argument had contained at least one compelling point. It probably had been better to let Harahap stew in the juices of his uncertain future—assuming the insufferably composed bastard knew how to stew in his own juices over *anything*—without giving him an opportunity to begin building a narrative with people who'd never been trained to interrogate someone who operated at his level.

"Point taken, Sir," she said. "*Both* points, actually." She returned her attention to Honor. "I'm still a little surprised you got that out of him, Your Grace. If you're right about how it shaped him, it's the sort of vulnerability an operative of this caliber would go a long way to conceal from an adversary."

"As you've all just pointed out, I have certain unfair advantages." Honor smiled briefly. "I don't think he realized where he was going till we got there. Either that or it was what they used to call a Freudian slip. For that matter, he obviously didn't know I'd ever heard of his home system." Her smile disappeared. "Most Manticorans haven't."

"I don't believe I have, either," Hamish said. "But like Pat says, it sounds vaguely familiar." He frowned for a moment. "Was it something that might have come up in regard to Lacoön?" he asked then, and she nodded.

"Probably. It's on the far side of Sol, about a hundred and seventy-six light-years from Old Terra." She shrugged. "It never had much in the way of an economy, but it's only about a hundred light-years from the Titania Wormhole and less than twenty-six from Franzeki. That was enough to draw StratoCorp's attention."

Hamish nodded, although he still looked a bit perplexed.

Startman's location, especially its proximity to Franzeki, might explain why it had been mentioned at least peripherally in one of the Lacoön briefs. And most Manticorans who'd ever had to deal with the Solarian League had heard of StratoCorp. Otherwise known as

Stratosphere Services, Incorporated, it had been around a long time. It actually predated the Solarian League itself, although it had been Stratosphere Enterprises when it was first founded. It was also even more acquisitive than most Solarian transstellars, probably because it had fallen upon hard times for a couple of T-centuries. Its survival had been problematical, and it had emerged from the experience under a ruthless, and particularly rapacious leadership team which had set its mark on its corporate personality for generations to come.

He'd never heard of the Startman System—aside from its name— but he knew StratoCorp had been building a portfolio of captive star systems for at least the last three hundred T-years. And although the Franzeki-Bessie hyper bridge was fairly short—little more than 125 LY—the Bessie System was only 30 LY from the Clarence Terminus of the Clarence-Artesia warp bridge, which was almost 370 LY long. For that matter, the Titania-Mullins warp bridge was well over 900 LY long, and the population of the Mullins Cluster systems was expanding rapidly. So, yes, he could understand why something like StratoCorp would want to get its claws into a system near enough to those termini to provide a useful base.

But that didn't explain why Honor knew about it. And why whatever she knew seemed so significant to her.

Honor felt her lips twitch as she tasted her husband's curiosity.

"I know about it because of Uncle Jacques, Hamish," she said. "StratoCorp's been in bed with Manpower for a long time. Among other things, Manpower staged slave ships through Startman on their way to and from Clarence. The people they had in charge of the Startman slave depot were even worse than usual, but they were too far away for the BSC to do anything about. About fifteen T-years ago, though, the Ballroom paid them a visit. It was . . . ugly."

Several of the others nodded in understanding, although Abercrombie seemed uncomfortable at the reminder of a Manticoran duchess's close connections to an outlawed terrorist organization.

"Anyway, Harahap may have been only a child when OFS moved in, but he was old enough to remember at least some of what it was like—for him personally, and his family, I mean—before that happened. And to see what StratoCorp's arrival did to his parents by the time he was twelve. Their system managers are pretty bare-knuckled, even for the Protectorates. Like anyone with a working brain would have, he wanted out, and the Gendarmerie offered him a ticket off-world when he was only nineteen. I don't think he worried very much, at that point in his life, over what he'd have to do to earn it. And then it turned out he has a certain talent."

"He told you all this?" Abercrombie asked, and Honor glanced at him coolly.

"No, he didn't. He didn't have to. Whatever he might *say*, Sir Tyler, he can't control his emotions any more than anyone else. He does an almost scary job of not letting *them* control *him*, but that doesn't mean he doesn't have them. And I just spent six hours talking to him." She shook her head. "Believe me, he doesn't have a clue how much I pulled out of what he *didn't* say."

Abercrombie looked dubious, but Stone Climber made a soft sound in his ear and smacked him very gently on the back of the head. He twitched in surprise, then drew a deep breath and smiled at Honor in what his mind-glow told her was genuine apology.

"I obviously didn't have time to get his complete life story in only six hours," she continued. "As I say, I think I got a lot more than he knows I did, though. So do you really want my impression of who and what he is?"

"Of course we do," Elizabeth said.

"Really?" Honor smiled. "All right, then. I think he's exactly what he told Zavala and Kaplan he is. A mercenary, yes, in the sense that he works for pay, but he really didn't have much choice about taking Mesa's offer." She shrugged. "He certainly didn't go *looking* for it, at any rate. He joined the Gendarmerie to get out of Startman, and he did what he did *for* the Gendarmerie because he was very good at it and because he'd become part of a system where that's what people do." She smiled briefly. "You might want to think about someone named Palane in that conjunction."

Elizabeth's eyes flickered. Then, almost despite herself, she nodded, and Honor nodded back.

"After we found the Lynx Terminus, his superior officer loaned him to Manpower—actually, to the Alignment, although none of them knew that—to destabilize our efforts in the Talbott Quadrant," she went on. "He didn't owe us anything, he had his orders, and he did his job. By the way, he also thinks Nordbrandt's a lunatic and that the sooner we catch her and hang her the better.

"Then, after Terekhov blew that operation wide open, he was a dangerous loose end and someone tried to tie him off. I'm inclined to believe it may really have been Kalokainos." She grimaced. "He didn't want to give me that name, but I was insistent."

"Why would he have wanted to conceal it?" Theisman asked.

"Because I think he has visions of dealing with Mr. Kalokainos in person."

"Because he thinks Kalokainos ordered him killed?"

"No, Tom. Because he thinks Kalokainos had one of his very few close personal friends killed at the same time," Honor said quietly. "In his own way, he's just as Old Testament as a Gryphon Highlander."

Theisman looked thoughtful, and Honor returned her attention to the Empress.

"The Alignment offered him work and an opportunity to stay alive. The pay was good, I'm sure, and Harahap's not the sort to turn his nose up at that. Hardly surprising, given where he spent his childhood and adolescence. But I'm pretty sure it was more the cover against Kalokainos—and maybe the possibility that his new bosses would help him square his account *with* Kalokainos someday—that drew him into Alignment employment. Well, that and the fact that he was pretty sure the Alignment would have snipped the same loose end if he *didn't* accept their offer. The fact that he figured out that whoever his new bosses might be they weren't *just* Manpower didn't hurt, either. I don't think he much liked working with Manpower, even as a Gendarme in Talbott, much less once he'd become a . . . free-agent, let's say. I'm not saying that would have prevented him from taking the job, given all the other considerations—like staying alive—or that he had any objection to working for people who could pay him really, really well. I'm saying that given Startman's history, working for Manpower wouldn't have been high on this man's to-do list without some pretty compelling counter arguments. Mesa and transstellars in general, yes. He had no problem there. But direct association with *Manpower* would never have been his first choice."

Theisman nodded slowly, but Pat Givens frowned.

"That's all well and good, and I don't doubt anything you've told us, Your Grace. But one thing about this bothers me. Bothers me a lot." Honor's arched eyebrow invited her to continue, and the woman who ran the Office of Naval Intelligence shrugged.

"He's alive," she said. "The Mesan operative Van Hale and Genghis turned up on Torch before the assassination attempt had some sort of suicide protocol. From the fragmentary reports we've gotten from Old Terra, Rajampet committed suicide—probably that 'killer nanotech' of theirs—when it looked like his connection to them might come to light. Then there's what happened with 'Ellingsen' and 'Abernathy' on Smoking Frog. For that matter, there's what happened to those four the 'cats helped us scoop up right here in the Old Kingdom. It looks like every agent who knows who she's actually working for drops dead the instant she's found out. I find it difficult to believe the Alignment wouldn't fit a mercenary, not even one of their own people, with the same . . . security software."

"You think he's a plant," Honor said.

"I think he *could* be a plant." Givens shrugged again. "Everything he's told you may be the truth, but what *he* was told, what he was allowed to learn, could have been carefully orchestrated."

"Why?" Theisman asked for a third time.

"I don't have a clue," Givens admitted frankly. "And there's no conceivable way they could've arranged the chain of circumstances that ended up with him in our custody. I'm willing to grant 'genetic supermen' all sorts of esoteric talents, but I'm pretty sure *that* one would be beyond anyone. So I don't really see how they could specifically have aimed him at us. But that doesn't mean they didn't plan on aiming him at *someone*, eventually. So I don't have a theory to propose about their possible objectives at this point. All I've got is a question. Why is this man still alive?"

"I think the answer is Jack McBryde," Honor said, and felt the others' astonishment as all of them turned to look at her.

"I told you this is a smart, capable fellow," she reminded them. "You think he hasn't wondered the same thing? Of course he has! And I think he may have hit on the explanation. From my conversation with him, it would appear, ladies and gentlemen, that he received several physical upgrades when he became a full-time Alignment operative. I think we may want to look carefully at some of the mods they gave him, because they sound pretty interesting and most of them don't have a thing to do with *genetic* modifications. However, he got those mods at the Gamma Center just before they rushed him off on his first op as a full-fledged Alignment employee. And he was scheduled to go *back* to the Gamma Center for additional 'upgrades' when he got back to Mesa. Only the Gamma Center wasn't there anymore, and given the confusion after Green Pines, he wasn't too surprised no one was worried about getting one more agent's benefits package tweaked.

"But according to what Dr. Simões has told us about McBryde's contingency plans, most of the Gamma Center's records went with the base when he pushed the button. Not just the ones on site, either; Simões says he planned to drop an attack into the Alignment's entire secure net." She shrugged. "I think it may have worked. Harahap didn't know anything about McBryde or his plans, but when he didn't drop dead after capture, it occurred to him that all his erstwhile employers might *think* he got a suicide protocol...when he hadn't."

"My God," Givens said softly. "You really think that's what happened?"

"Yes, I do. And if I'm right—"

"If you're right, we really do have somebody who can give us an inside look at this false-flag operation," Elizabeth said. "And someone they're going to assume is *dead*, not a threat. And if he's not a threat, they don't have to worry about covering up anything he might conceivably tell us about."

"As a start," Honor agreed, nodding firmly. "I think we may have the end of a string that leads right into the inner workings of the Alignment. All we have to do"—she smiled whimsically—"is to convince Mr. Harahap he ought to accept the Queen's dollar. And, of course," her smile turned much colder, "see to it that he's an 'honest craftsman' for *us*, too."

Dempsey's Bar
Sunrise Tower
City of Landing
Manticore Binary System

"YOU HAVE REACHED YOUR destination, Sir," the air-cab said.

Indiana Graham stopped craning his neck and swiveling his head like some sort of rotating sensor system as the cab slid neatly to a stop at the hundred and twelfth-floor landing stage and hovered there on counter-grav. The starboard hatch licked open, and he started to ask the vehicle's AI if it was sure they had the right destination, but he stopped himself in time. The cab had doublechecked the address when it heard his off-world accent. He hadn't realized how pronounced that accent actually was until he reached Manticore itself. No one had been rude enough to comment on it aboard *Tristram*, and he'd had other things on his mind for the voyage here. It had been brought rather more sharply to his attention since the shuttle flight from orbit to the city of Landing, however. Not because anyone had deliberately remarked upon it or pointed any fingers at the guy who talked funny, but Manticoran AIs were clearly programmed to recognize accents and dialects that weren't native to Manticore. Not because they couldn't understand the strangers, but because the strangers *were* strangers, and the AIs' programming doublechecked the sorts of things strangers might have problems with—like addresses in an unknown city.

"Thank you," he said, instead. The cab was a machine, but thanking his "driver" was second nature to him, since there were precious few AIs back home. And it didn't hurt anything to stay in practice.

"You're welcome, Sir," the cab replied. "Please, remember Circle City Taxis if you have further transportation needs. And, on behalf of Circle City, have a pleasant day."

Indy chuckled and stepped just a bit gingerly across the half-centimeter wide—and four hundred-plus meter *deep*—gap of empty air onto the Sunrise Tower landing. He moved clear of the debarking area as the air-cab went zooming back into Landing City's meticulously managed airspace. He was several minutes early, so instead of finding the lifts, he strolled over to the landing stage rail and propped both hands on it as he leaned forward and looked out over the largest, most magnificent city he'd ever seen.

This is what Cherubim could've *been like,* he thought, drinking in the mammoth pastel towers.

They rose like ceramacrete mountains from the green belts and parks, the bike trails and walking paths and the broad avenues where ground traffic moved steadily about the giants' feet. The entire population of the Seraphim System's capital could have been housed in one of them—two, at the outside, if they'd wanted to avoid crowding—he thought. Crystoplast glittered and gleamed in the late morning sunlight, some of the towers had smart skins which slowly changed color or portrayed works of art or landscapes from elsewhere in the Manticore Binary System. Jason Bay was an endless, polished expanse of blue marble, swirled with white as it stretched away from him to the south, and the air was like crystal as he drew it deep into his lungs. It was the capital city of what was arguably the wealthiest star nation, on a per capita basis, in the history of mankind. Of course it was going to put anything from a poor star system like Seraphim to shame! But there was more to it than that.

There's a reason *Seraphim's poor,* he thought grimly, his enjoyment of the view dimmed. *McCready and O'Sullivan were homegrown, and scum like that didn't need any outsiders to teach it how to be scum. But it was Krestor and Mendoza who gave them the chance, and it was OFS and the Sollies who stood behind them with a club in their hands. And without Firebrand—*

He stopped that thought short…again. His feelings about the agent provocateur seemed to have become even more ambiguous since they'd reached Manticore. Even before he'd seen Landing, it had been… difficult to process the discovery that his home star system owed its recovered freedom to a cynical ploy which had provided the Seraphim Independence Movement with so many weapons, so much economic support, purely to blacken Manticore's eye when their uprising was inevitably crushed.

If Zavala hadn't turned up, we would've *been crushed, too.* His eyes darkened. *We'd all be dead by now…if we were lucky. Me, Kenzie, Dad, Tanawat—all of us. God knows we got enough people killed, anyway.* His eyes went darker still as he remembered Ning Saowaluk, remembered how she'd died and all the others who'd died with her. *I know that. And I know he was only there because of Admiral Henke and Admiral Culbertson. Henke didn't* have *to decide Manticore was going to save the people who'd thought that was who they'd been talking to all along. And*

Culbertson damned well didn't have to send ships out looking for places that might've happened, either! How many star nations would have done that? Would've diverted naval forces to something like that, gone looking for someone else's fight, when it was already fighting the Solarian League *for its own survival?*

He was pretty sure he could have counted the number on one hand...without using all his fingers. But Manticore had, and Prime Minister Grantville had greeted Indy himself, personally, almost as if Indy had been a visiting head of state and not a rag-tag revolutionary from the back of beyond.

All that was true, yet without Firebrand—without the "Mesan Alignment's" cold-blooded, cynical intervention—there would have been no rebellion when McCready died. Or, if there had been, it would have been short and very, very ugly for the rebels.

So what do *I hope happens to him?* Indy asked himself, abandoning the pretense that he could simply brush any thought of the traitor who'd been one of his closest friends—or who he'd *thought* was one of his closest friends—out of his mind. *The one thing I can count on is that if anybody can land on his feet, it'll be Firebrand! And he's got to have some really valuable intelligence to trade. But from what Abigail was saying, they want his hide for a lot more than just "Operation Janus." And do I want them to collect it because of what he* intended *to do in Seraphim, or do I try to plead his case with them because of what he actually* did *do in Seraphim? For that matter—*

His brand-new Manticoran uni-link beeped, and he shook himself. He'd used up his time cushion standing here staring at the pretty scenery and worrying. If he didn't get a move on, he was going to be late, and that would be a Bad Thing.

He snorted at the thought, squared his shoulders, and headed for the nearest lift shaft, grateful for the discreet signage pointing him toward it and hoping he didn't look too much like a country rube with manure still on his shoes.

❖　　❖　　❖

"Incoming at four o'clock, My Lady," Lieutenant Gutierrez said quietly.

Abigail Hearns twitched ever so slightly, then glanced up at her towering personal armsman with a quick grin. His answering smile was slight but deeply amused, and she shook her head reprovingly at him.

"Teasing isn't nice, Mateo," she said.

"Teasing, My Lady?" Gutierrez's tone was bland innocence itself, but his eyes twinkled at her—for a moment—before they resumed their unending threat search, sweeping the atrium about them. "Wouldn't know anything about 'teasing,'" he added.

Abigail snorted and punched him affectionately in the chest. It was rather like punching a boulder—or a nearoak—and it was probably as well none of her father's steaders were present to see. A steadholder's daughter wasn't supposed to show affection for her armsman openly, and she certainly wasn't supposed to have physical contact—in *public*—with a man who was neither married to nor related to her! Fortunately, they weren't on Grayson and there were no steaders.

Besides, if I could scandalize them just by punching Mateo, think of how many of them would drop dead out of pure apoplexy at the thought of Miss Owens—heir, however distantly, to Owens Steading—actually meeting a man *without any chaperones at all!*

The thought gave her considerable pleasure. In fact, few days went by when she didn't do *something* that would have scandalized those conservatives. The mere fact that she was a serving naval officer would have been enough for most of them without her *doing* a single thing. The amount of time she spent interacting with male officers would have made that still worse. The way she went gallivanting around foreign planets with only Mateo to keep her out of danger—and, of course, to protect her virtue—would have been intolerable. But to actually arrange to have lunch with a man she'd known for less than a T-month in a public venue without a single female companion—!

Oh, the heart attacks would have come thick and fast! And if they'd known what she was *thinking* about the man in question...

I can only hope the tale gets home to Owens, suitably embellished, she thought wistfully, and turned to look in the direction Gutierrez had indicated.

The young man walking towards them, his eyes scanning the atrium, no longer seemed quite as overwhelmed as he had immediately after they'd reached Landing. She was glad. And despite any uncertainty he'd felt at the time, she'd been confident he'd find his feet quickly. He was a lot tougher and more resilient than he realized.

She raised one hand and the movement drew his searching gaze. He looked in her direction, raised his own hand in acknowledgment, and walked quickly across to them.

"Hi," he said. "You didn't warn me how *big* this blasted tower is!"

"Trust me, if *you* think it's big, you should've seen *my* first reaction to it!" She rolled her eyes. "The tallest building in Owens Steading when I was growing up was sixteen floors."

"Really?" He looked at her, obviously wondering if she was pulling his leg, and she glanced up over her shoulder.

"Mateo?"

"Her Ladyship's right, Mr. Graham," the armsman said. "Surprised me a bit when I first reported for duty with the Guard, to be honest. Hadn't realized how...close to the ground they built on Grayson."

"To be honest, we generally tended to build *down*, not up," Abigail said. "Before Skydomes started doming entire cities it only made sense. Everything above ground was exposed to wind and weather. It needed lots of maintenance, even minor breaches could be dangerous, and we needed complete environmental systems, anyway. So we tended to dig deep, instead. Before the alliance with Manticore, major buildings on Grayson usually had more subfloors than aboveground structure."

"I think I'm just as happy I never lived someplace where the planet itself tried to kill me," Indy said after a moment. "It must create an... interesting perspective on wide open spaces. Like the view from the landing platform," he added with a certain feeling.

"Oh, you have no idea!" Abigail laughed. "And *swimming!*" She shook her head. "No Grayson would even think about *swimming* as a form of exercise or relaxation. Before the Alliance, it was way too hard to purify enough water just for agriculture and drinking. No one was going to waste any of it just splashing around in it."

"I imagine so." He shook his head with a chuckle, then looked around the crowded atrium again.

"Which way now?" he asked.

"Mateo will now demonstrate one of the shameless advantages of having a personal armsman whose family is from Trevor's Star," Abigail told him, reaching out and tucking her right arm through his left. "If you would, Mateo."

She waggled the fingers of her left hand in an airy lead-the-way sort of gesture, and Lieutenant Gutierrez snorted. But he also started forging across the atrium.

The press of people parted before him with a certain inevitability. It wasn't so much that any of them seemed to think about it consciously. They just did it, which probably wasn't too surprising when they glanced up and saw two meters or so of armed, uniformed, heavy-grav bodyguard coming their way.

✧   ✧   ✧

It wasn't a long walk, despite the atrium's enormous size. In fact, Indy wished it had been longer when the holo-sign came into sight. It turned out he and Abigail were very nearly exactly the same height, and he smelled the faint scent of what was either very nice perfume or equally nice shampoo as they walked arm-in-arm. He was also very conscious of her slender warmth at his side and of how gracefully she carried herself.

He wondered how much of the way she moved was a product of her rearing.

Another thing he hadn't realized until they reached Manticore and he'd had the chance for a little research was exactly what it meant to be a steadholder's daughter. No doubt someone like that was *taught* how to move, how to comport herself in public. Couldn't have clumsiness reflecting poorly upon a royal family, now could they?

He'd gathered from the very beginning that it meant wealth, privilege, and power, but he'd had no idea how *much* of each it represented. Mostly, he thought, that was Abigail's fault. No one in *Tristram*'s company had treated her as anything other than a naval officer. Aside from Lieutenant Gutierrez's presence whenever she left the ship, there was nothing to single her out as otherwise important in any way. And he defied anyone— especially anyone from a world like Seraphim—to spend five minutes in her presence and file her away as a daughter of power and wealth.

In fact, she was the wealthiest person he'd ever met. She was "only" a daughter—and until he'd researched Grayson, he hadn't been aware of all of the implications of *that*, either—but that didn't change the fact that she could have personally financed the Seraphim Independence Movement—*all* of it—out of her own credit account.

Discovering those minor facts had almost sent him running. What did *he* know about people from her background? How to talk to them? How to act around them? Which fork to use when they ate? The proper way to *address* them, even? What could he possibly have to say to Abigail Hearns, Miss Owens, one of the most nobly born citizens of her homeworld, outside the purely tactical things they'd discussed aboard ship on the way here? And what would anyone who saw a hardscrabble street hand from Cherubim hanging around her say? They'd *know* why he was there, wouldn't they? Of course they would! For that matter, he probably would have thought exactly the same things in their place. And that was the reason he should have run for cover the instant he realized the incredible gulf that yawned between them.

But he hadn't. He couldn't. Well, maybe he could have . . . if *she* hadn't screened *him*. She'd said she'd look him up if she got dirt-side, but he hadn't really expected her to, especially after he'd done that research. He'd filed it away as the sort of polite commonplace someone said to a casual acquaintance on parting.

Only she'd meant it. She *had* screened, and he wasn't certain, looking back, which of them had suggested meeting for lunch. He did remember suggesting that since she knew Landing and he didn't she should pick the restaurant, but he couldn't remember whose idea it had been to pick *a* restaurant in the first place. Now he recognized the sign—"Dempsey's Bar"—and wished she'd picked one farther from the atrium's entrance.

✧　　✧　　✧

"Lieutenant Hearns!" The hostess behind the small stand in the restaurant lobby greeted Abigail with a broad smile. "It's been too long! How long will you be in-system?"

"It has been a while, Lucy," Abigail agreed. Unlike the hostess, whose discreet earbug had undoubtedly identified her from the restaurant chain's database as soon as she walked in the door, Abigail plucked the woman's name from memory. "And I'm not sure how long I'll be in Manticore this time. I don't suppose anybody can be too confident about something like that right now."

"No, you're right about that." The hostess's eyes darkened for a moment. Then she visibly squared her shoulders. "But you're here right now! I don't see a reservation for you, though. Are you meeting someone?"

"No, it's just me and Mr. Graham, here. And Mateo, of course." She rolled her eyes and Lucy chuckled.

"I see. Well, we have an open table fronting the fountains, or I can put you in one of the privacy booths. Which would you prefer?"

"Indy?" Abigail raised one eyebrow at him.

"The table sounds great," Indy said, mentally kicking himself for not holding out for the privacy booth. On the other hand, she'd never said anything about wanting to be *that* alone with him...damn it. If that *was* what she wanted, though, she could always make a counter suggestion and—

"The table it is, then," she said with a crisp nod.

"Excellent!" The hostess beamed. "If you'll come this way?"

Indy decided he'd never been in a restaurant remotely as upscale as this one. The sign might call it a "bar," but it was a far cry from anything to which *he* would have attached that noun. The soft background music, the low murmur of voices from the diners, the gleam of flatware and crystal, and the delicious scents seductively caressing his nostrils all shouted that this was not The Soup Spoon back in Cherubim.

On the other hand, he wasn't here to plot a rebellion, either.

The louder music of living water rose across the background as Lucy escorted them to the promised table, and Indy remembered to pull back Abigail's chair and see her seated before sitting down himself. They'd passed several other unoccupied tables on their way here, and as he sat, he realized why they had.

Their table didn't "front" the fountains; it occupied the end of a sort of promontory, extending well out into something far grander than he'd anticipated when the hostess mentioned "fountains." In effect, they were seated *inside* the fountain—*one* of the fountains; there were three separate clusters of jets—on a crystoplast floor. The streams of water were carefully shaped and directed, splashing back into the catcher basins in a continuous liquid song. He could sense the moisture in the air about them, feel the cool, slightly damp breeze blowing gently across them, yet somehow that had all been arranged without their actually being "rained on" at all.

And it just happened—purely by coincidence, no doubt—that there was another table at the point where the crystoplast under *their* table reached out into the fountain. One where their hostess seated Lieutenant Gutierrez, perfectly positioned to protect their privacy and with an excellent view of almost the entire restaurant.

Lucy beamed at them.

"Please consult the menus," she said, waving one hand at the displays in the table's smart top. "May I go ahead and tell the kitchen what beverages you'd prefer?"

"I'll have an Old Tillman, I think," Abigail said. "In the bottle, please, not a stein."

"Of course. And you, Sir?" she looked at Indy, and he shrugged.

"Still learning my way around," he said. "Should I take it 'Old Tillman' is a beer?"

"Oh, yes, Sir. A product of Sphinx," the hostess said. "It's a hoppy oatmeal stout with just a touch of honey." She held up her right hand thumb and index finger perhaps two millimeters apart. "I've been told the genetic mods oats and hops required to adjust to Sphinx are what give it a hint of almond. It's quite good, really."

"Then by all means let's try it." Indy smiled. "Should I assume the real aficionado holds out for the bottled variety?"

"Only the *true* beer snobs," Abigail assured him, elevating her nose.

"Well, in that case..."

"Two Old Tillmans, in the bottle," Lucy said with a smile, and waved at the menu displays again. "Just signal when you've made your selections, or Jonathan, your server, will be happy to take them in person when he delivers your beers."

She swept them a slight bow and headed back to her station in the lobby, and Indy sat back in his chair, looking around the restaurant.

"This is nice," he said. "Very nice. Is the food as good as it smells?"

"Better," Abigail replied. "The Dempsey cartel runs the best restaurants in the entire Old Star Kingdom. The 'Dempsey Bars' are its flagship chain, named for the very first restaurant the original Dempsey opened here in Landing almost three hundred T-years ago." She smiled, waving her hand around the dimly lit, elegantly furnished restaurant as brightly colored native Manticoran fish with too many long, trailing fins swam gracefully below the crystoplast under their chairs, and shook her head. "This isn't exactly what *I* thought of the first time someone invited me to a 'bar,' either."

"That obvious, was it?" Indy smiled back at her.

"Only because I'd had the same reaction the first time. I got over it, though. In fact, I remember the maître d' teasing me about it the second time I ate there. He said he'd seen a lot of—"

She broke off suddenly. Indy had been admiring a holo-sculpture against the restaurant's back wall, but her abrupt silence jerked his gaze back to her, and his eyes widened as he saw the tears.

"Abigail?" His voice was soft, concerned, and she shook her head sharply. Then she picked up her napkin and wiped quickly, almost angrily, at her eyes.

"Sorry." The word came out husky, and she stopped and cleared her throat. "Sorry," she repeated more naturally. "I was just thinking about that first visit. And how well I got to know Michael, the maître d', and the rest of the wait staff. It was the Dempsey's on *Hephaestus*."

Indy frowned, perplexed. Why would—?

Then he understood. *Hephaestus*. That was something else he hadn't known about before his arrival in Manticore: the Yawata Strike.

He started to say "I'm sorry," but stopped himself before the words were out of his mouth. They would have been too automatic, too dismissive. Or, no, not *dismissive*, perhaps, but too...banal in the face of her pain.

"I can't imagine what that must be like," he said instead, softly, and realized he'd reached out across the table.

"I know it was terrible for the people who were actually here when it happened." Her voice was equally soft, and she took his hand almost absently, her eyes focused on something else far, far away. "But I think it may've been even worse, in a way, for those of us who weren't. We left everything—and everyone—alive and well and we hypered out, expecting *we* were the ones who might be called to action. *We* were the ones who might die. And then we found out. First that the attack had happened. Then, a day or so later, that losses had been heavy." She snorted a mirthless laugh. "'*Heavy!*' I suppose that's one way to put it. We didn't find out *how* heavy for a long time, though. I remember when we found out about the *Kitty*."

Her grip tightened almost painfully, her eyes filled with tears again, and her free hand brushed them away as quickly as their predecessors. Then she blinked, her eyes refocused on Indy, and fell to the two hands on the table as she realized how tightly hers was squeezing his.

"Sorry," she said again. She began to withdraw her hand, but his turned and caught hers in a firm clasp before she could.

"I understand," he said. "Not the scale of it, not how many people you must've lost, not even its unexpectedness. But I understand the *pain* of it, Abigail. I know what it it's like to lose someone you care about. What it's like to feel helpless while you watch someone you love being taken away from you and there's not one damned thing you can do about it. And I know how the memory can...ambush you when you don't expect it. Never apologize for grief. For honoring the memory of people you've lost by admitting how much they meant to you when you had them."

She looked at him for a long, still moment, lower lip quivering ever so slightly. Then she nodded, drew a deep breath, and gave his hand one more squeeze before she gently withdrew her own and leaned back in her chair.

"You're right," she said. "Father Church teaches that the Tester opens his arms to all of us. That death is just another doorway and we should celebrate the lives of those who go on ahead of us, not mourn for them. But not mourning for *them* doesn't mean we can't grieve for ourselves in their absence. For our loss, whatever their gain might be. But it's hard, you know. There's no point in any of us pretending the Yawata Strike didn't happen. I doubt there's a single person in the entire Manticore System who didn't lose *someone*. I know I certainly did, and I know there were people—like Duchess Harrington—who lost almost their entire families. But I'm a naval officer, the head of *Tristram's* Tac Department. It was my job to be there for *other* people, not to break down over my own sense of loss."

"From what I've seen of you, you would've been there anyway, Abigail, whether it was 'your job' or not. It's who you are—*what* you are. What you do." He smiled almost wistfully at her. "For that matter, I watched you doing it on the trip here from Seraphim, and not just by being there for others. There was part of you that really and truly wanted to shoot Firebrand—Harahap, I mean—right where he sat. I could tell there was. You never showed it. Not overtly. You never even said a harsh word to him, because it was your job *not* to, but I knew. I didn't realize why you felt that way—not at first, that was. Not until Bosun Musgrave told me about Monica and New Tuscany. About everything he did to set that in motion." He shook his head. "God, you must *hate* him."

"Not really." His surprise showed, and she smiled back at him. "No, really, I don't. I won't go so far as to say he's one of my favorite people in the universe, but I don't *hate* him. And I really do realize how valuable he could be to the Alliance. Besides, what good would it do me—or anyone else—to hate him? It wouldn't undo anything he's done, and everything that happened to us in Monica, or in Talbott, combined isn't a drop in the bucket beside what happened in the Yawata

Strike. For that matter, when you come down to it, not everything he's done ended up all that badly, now did it?"

"No, I guess it didn't," he acknowledged with a chuckle. "If McCready had gotten herself assassinated the same way and our good friend 'Firebrand' hadn't gotten those weapons to us—or, for that matter, hadn't dug in when the fighting actually started—I'd probably be dead, too. I don't think I'd like that very much."

"I wouldn't like that, either," she said softly. His eyes widened, and her smile grew broader and somehow gentler. "I wouldn't like that at all."

Their gazes held for a moment, and then she looked deliberately back down at the menu display.

"Everything they have here is really, really good." Her tone was much lighter than it had been, almost amused. "I'd never eaten seafood before I arrived here in Manticore, so I think I'll start with the lobster bisque. I think you'd probably like it, too, and maybe the stuffed clams for an appetizer?" She raised her eyes to meet his again. "And if you've never tried it, maybe the Chateaubriand as the entrée. Dempsey's has started using Montana beef. Trust me, it's good."

"Oh, I think I can do that," Indy said. She quirked an eyebrow. "Trust you, I mean."

"Well," she said, eyes bright as she reached for the order button, "that's a good start. Trusting me, I mean."

City of Landing
Manticore Binary System
Star Empire of Manticore

"SO WHAT CAN YOU tell us about this—" the orange-haired man consulted his notes "—Collin Detweiler?" He looked up, his peculiar purple eyes with their vertical pupils showing only mild curiosity. "We're trying to fill in the gaps about the 'Alignment' and all we have about him is a single headshot and a name from...Well, from another source, let's say.'""

Fill in the gaps? Damien Harahap thought sardonically. *What you mean is you people don't have a* clue *who he is and little red ants are eating you alive while you try to figure out what the* hell *the "Alignment" is really up to.*

He leaned back in his own chair, pursing his lips with a thoughtful air. He was still far from certain why he hadn't conveniently dropped dead—conveniently for his most recent employers, that was—although the most likely answer remained the Gamma Center's destruction. It seemed, assuming there was any truth to the Mesan claims, that he owed Anton Zilwicki and Victor Cachat a vote of thanks.

Actually, he'd like to discuss quite a few things with Zilwicki and Cachat. He admired professionalism, whoever happened to have it, and the two of them had ripped a lot of scabs off of things Isabel Bardasano— among others—had very much wanted to stay hidden. Besides, he'd like to compare notes with them about Green Pines, given his post-"terrorist attack" visit to Mendel. Unfortunately, they weren't available. For that matter, he hadn't been able to figure out what their true relationship with their respective star nations' official intelligence services was. It sounded like Zilwicki was essentially a free agent whose primary loyalty was split between the Kingdom of Torch and the Star Kingdom—now Star Empire—in which he'd been born. And it sounded like Cachat was essentially a loose warhead *officially* in the employ of the Republic of Haven's Foreign Intelligence Service...whose directives he followed on the infrequent occasions when they made sense to him.

"I'm afraid I actually only met the gentleman twice, Mr. Jubair," he said after a moment to his current interrogator.

377

"So you said earlier." Antoine Jubair tapped the memo pad on the table between them and smiled. When he did, he showed very pointy teeth, the product of the same genetic manipulation which had given his genetic slave grandfather his dark complexion, bright orange—*orange*, not red or auburn—hair, and catlike pupils. "It would seem both those meetings were rather significant in terms of your...employment, though."

"That's a fair assessment." Harahap nodded and glanced at the tree-cat stretched comfortably across one end of the table. Aside from the angle of their pupils and the fact that they were green, not purple, its eyes reminded him a great deal of Jubair's. Not least because of how unwaveringly they were focused upon one Damien Harahap. Unless he was mistaken, there was more—a *lot* more—intelligence behind them than he'd previously assumed, too.

"There's not a lot I can tell you about him that's what I'd call con-crete," he said. "I never saw any organization charts, much less one with his name on it. For that matter, I didn't catch a name on him at all. And once I'd passed muster with him, I never saw *him* again, either. So please understand that anything I tell you can only be conjectural, based on my one-time impression of him."

He paused, eyebrows raised, and Jubair nodded.

"Understood," he said in the tone of one professional speaking to another one.

"With that proviso, then," Harahap continued, "he's smart—*very* smart—and as ruthless as they come. More than that, he comes equipped with a lot of focus and, I think, genuine commitment to whatever these people are really after, and your imagery doesn't capture how much... call it command presence he has. Or the fact that he has a command *mentality*, as well." Harahap shrugged. "I'd say he's a man who makes *decisions*, not one who takes *directions*."

Jubair glanced at the treecat, who only yawned daintily, showing teeth that were another point of similarity between them.

"That's an interesting distinction," the Manticoran observed after a moment.

"Well, I guess I should admit it's based at least in part on Cherny-shev's attitude towards him," Harahap said.

"That would be Rufino Chernyshev? The fellow who wound up with Bardasano's job?" Jubair asked, and Harahap nodded. He felt a twinge—a tiny one—of regret at having IDed Rufino for the Manties, but the Mesan was a fellow professional. He'd understand. That wouldn't stop him from shooting Harahap right in the head if the opportunity arose, but he'd *understand*.

"Yes," he said. "Neither he nor Bardasano ever used the term 'Mesan

Alignment' to me or in my presence, but assuming your people are right about its existence—and if you are, that might explain some of the things I found puzzling about their strategies—I'm pretty sure Bardasano was in charge of its covert operations. I don't know anything about their intelligence-*gathering* activities, except that from the raw take I studied on the systems they assigned to me, they're tapped into official League sources at very high levels. The intel they provided me was better than the Gendarmerie usually comes up with, and they obviously had sources outside the official ones, as well. How those contacts were established or managed was never part of the intel package, though, so I can't say if she was involved in that side or if she was only their director of operations. From her attitude, from some of the things she said, I'm inclined to think she had executive responsibility for both sides of their shop—intelligence *and* covert ops—but there's no way I could confirm that.

"The important thing, though," he leaned forward, "is that whatever her role may have been, your friend Detweiler was *her* boss. So, if you're right about the existence of the Alignment and it really isn't the 'consortium of transstellars' he and Bardasano tried to sell me, I think he's very probably the 'shadow government' Minister of Intelligence."

"Interesting possibility," Jubair said. "I'll want to come back to that in a bit. But for now, tell me what you can about the shift in Chernyshev's responsibilities after Green Pines. For example—"

✧   ✧   ✧

"I wish I thought we really could turn that man into an asset," Patricia Givens said almost wistfully.

She sat in a secure conference room between Hamish Alexander-Harrington and his brother William, who happened to be Baron Grantville, not to mention Prime Minister of Manticore. At the moment, all of them were watching another installment of Damien Harahap's ongoing debrief by Barton Salgado's Special Intelligence Service. Personally, Givens thought ONI ought to have the lead role, given that it was a naval officer who'd scooped him up in the first place. On the other hand, she had more than enough on her own plate, especially in the wake of Hypatia and the reports beginning to come in from other systems who'd been visited by the Sollies' goddamned "Buccaneers."

"He's a trained, skilled intelligence operative, not a scientist sequestered in a think tank or even doing applied research," she went on. "That means he's already given us at least three or four times more on the operational side than Dr. Simões was able to . . . assuming we can rely on it."

The dappled treecat on White Haven's shoulder produced something that sounded remarkably like a human sigh, and the 'cat on the back of Givens's chair laughed. The admiral looked over her shoulder at her furry bodyguard and frowned, then turned back to the two-leg participants in the conference.

"Despite Samantha's and Thought Chaser's reactions," she said a bit tartly, "I'm not suggesting he's getting any intentional deception past Pounces on Leaves." She twitched her head at the treecat participating in the recorded interrogation. "My problem is that I still can't quite convince myself—not fully—that he isn't some kind of plant, even if he doesn't know it."

"Oh, Pat!" the prime minister sighed. "I swear, you are the most *paranoid* person I've ever met." He considered a moment. "Well, the most paranoid, otherwise sane person I've ever met."

"Part of my job," she pointed out. "Besides," her expression darkened, "don't forget how long these bastards have played every intelligence agency in the galaxy! They got away with it partly because none of us paranoid but sane people were paranoid *enough* to believe in tooth fairies, Easter bunnies, honest politicians—no offense, Mister Prime Minister, Sir—or secret societies of genetic supermen hell-bent on galactic domination." She shook her head. "Honestly, most mornings I wake up and have to convince myself all over again that this 'Alignment' really exists!

"But even though a lot of their success to date stems from the fact that the entire concept is so patently absurd no serious analyst ever thought of looking for it, nobody keeps something this broad, this ambitious, hidden for as long as Simões and McBryde's information suggests these people have been around, without being very, very good. Crazy, megalomaniacal, fanatics too bug-fuck crazy to come in out of the snow, maybe, but good at concealment, misdirection, and misinformation. The fact that I can't *see* any way they could've deliberately planted him on us doesn't mean they couldn't do it. More to the point, it doesn't mean they didn't deliberately mislead *him* as a security measure, just in case he fell into our hands and decided to get talkative."

"You don't buy Honor's theory about that?" White Haven asked mildly.

"I didn't say that." Givens shook her head. "Actually, I think she may well be right about why he's alive. I'm just saying these people believe in defense in depth. Everything we've seen tells me the Alignment's like one of those matryoshka dolls Charlie O'Daley gave Moira last year for her tenth birthday. Every time we take one of them apart, there's something else hiding inside it. I don't see any reason to assume they didn't hide something else inside whatever Harahap knows about."

"Clearly they *did*," White Haven said. "Or tried to, anyway. Nobody ever said anything to him about genetically enhanced conspirators out to overthrow the League. He figured out on his own that they were really after a lot more than they were telling him about, but they were damned careful he didn't find out *what* they hadn't told him. In fact, I think your matryoshka doll's actually a very good metaphor for their entire approach. That's why I also think Honor's right about how useful he can be. He's at least two or three dolls in from the edge. That gives us a lot better starting point for the *next* doll. Assuming she's also right about whether or not we can genuinely turn him."

"Turn him *again*, you mean," Givens's tone was rather pointed, and she snorted when the earl shrugged. "Man's probably getting vertigo by now!"

"Maybe. But I come back to Pounces on Leaves. He and Nimitz both agree with Honor's evaluation of Harahap's basic personality."

"I know, but—"

"Pat, the decision's been made," Prime Minister Grantville pointed out. She looked at him, and he shrugged. "Her Majesty's signed off on it, and so has Tom Theisman for Eloise Pritchart and Michael Mayhew for Protector Benjamin," he reminded her in a reasonable tone. "All of them understand and respect your reservations, but he's way too potentially valuable for us to just park in a holding cell and trot out for occasional interrogations."

"That wasn't precisely all I intended to do with him," Givens said tartly, but it was her turn to shrug. "On the other hand, you're right and I know it. I just would really, really like some way to be sure he doesn't get a better offer from someone *else* down the road, flip again, and sell *us* out the same way he's selling out the Alignment."

"I wouldn't say that's exactly what he's doing," White Haven observed, then chuckled. "Mind you, I can see where an . . . established pattern of behavior on his part might seem like grounds for a certain degree of concern to a professionally paranoid woman such as yourself."

"I can't tell you how relieved I am that you find that amusing, My Lord," Vice Admiral Patricia Givens told the civilian head of her service.

"Oh, I don't find your suspicion or your awareness of the potential risk amusing at all," White Haven assured her. "What I find amusing is the thought of Mr. Harahap's response to the . . . prophylactic measure Honor's suggested to prevent anything like that from happening."

"'Prophylactic'?"

"That's how I think of it, anyway." He smiled at her, then his expression turned—slightly—more serious. "You've met Dame Lisa—Lisa Llorens—haven't you?"

Givens frowned as she rummaged through her memory. Then she

nodded, although, from her expression, she wondered where he could possibly be going.

"I wouldn't say I really know Dame Lisa," she said. "I saw her dance before she retired—several times, really, but to be honest, Simon and Moira both love ballet more than I do. I know she and Honor are close, too, and you're right; I did meet her a couple of months ago, when Thought Chaser and I were on Sphinx. I'm not really clear on what she could contribute to our little problem here, though."

Dame Lisa Llorens had risen to the rank of Second Principal Dancer in the Royal Ballet's Company of Sphinx, a position she'd held for close to twenty-five T-years. That quarter T-century as one of the four best ballet dancers in the entire Star Kingdom—there was no Company of Gryphon, which led to all manner of snarky jokes—had ended with the Yawata Strike, however.

She'd been headed toward retirement well before that, despite the fact that she remained in high demand as a performer and an artist. She and her treecat, Grace, had been deeply involved in Adelina Arif's quest to teach treecats how to communicate with humans, however, and that had been claiming more and more of her time. She'd made her two careers work—somehow—yet the strain had mounted as her heart pulled her in opposing directions. It was probable she would have followed that heart into fulltime work with Dr. Arif under any circumstances, but the Yawata Strike had tipped the balance. The Sphinx Company had been scheduled to perform in Yawata Crossing. A third of the company had already arrived to begin rehearsals and the shuttle delivering Dame Lisa and the rest of the company had been less than thirty minutes out when the tsunami struck...and killed every member of the company already on the ground.

She and Grace had left the world of dance after the deaths of so many people—human and treecat alike, and not just the members of their company—they'd known so well and loved so much, in order to dedicate themselves fully to the rapidly evolving relationship between the 'cats and their two-leg neighbors.

"Well, Honor's put quite a bit of thought into your 'little problem,' too," Hamish said now, "and I think she's come up with a workable solution. She asked Dr. Arif and her team for a nominee, and Dame Lisa and the memory singers came up with one I think will work very well. His name is 'Clean Killer.'"

Givens stared at him for a moment, then burst out laughing.

"His very own treecat *bodyguard?*" she demanded.

"Well, if he's on the up-and-up, he's definitely somebody the Alignment would move heaven and earth to shut up, assuming they figure out he's alive and we've got him," White Haven pointed out. "It would make sense to give him a nanotech-detector to make that as difficult as possible, wouldn't it?"

"Oh, of course it would!" Givens agreed, still snickering as she turned back to the recording. "My, oh my! Remind me to compliment your wife the next time I see her." She shook her head. "I *do* like a woman with a devious mind!"

✧　　✧　　✧

<I do not fully understand why our two-legs are so confused about how to deal with this person,> Clean Killer told Thought Chaser. <Surely if he is a friend to the evildoers who murdered Black Rock and so many two-legs, there is only one thing to do with him!>

<Truth,> Thought Chaser replied, looking across from his place on the back of Crafty Mind's sitting place. <I have observed that two-legs do many things People find difficult to understand. Yet I have also discovered that most often they have good reasons.> He yawned a silent smile at the younger scout. <Not always, of course! And they are two-legs. If the People have learned anything about two-legs over the last hands upon hands of turnings, it is that we will never fully understand how their minds work just because we can taste their mind-glows!>

Clean Killer mind-laughed in agreement. *No one* would ever fully understand two-legs; that was a given. But he didn't need to understand them to know that, just like the People, there were good two-legs and there were evil two-legs, and he knew where his own allegiance lay.

His laughter faded as he considered that, thought about why he was here in this huge two-leg nesting place. A "city" they called it, he thought, forming the mouth-noise carefully in his mind. The strength of so many hands of mind-glows pressed in upon him like some powerful, invisible wind, or perhaps like the heat of the sun in mid-summer. It threatened to crush him, but he had tasted the memory songs of others of the People who had gone among the two-legs. That had prepared him for it, although not so well as he had believed it had before he experienced the reality himself. That first day, he had seriously considered fleeing like a kitten newly escaped from its nesting place, but he had overcome the temptation by remembering why he was here.

His older sister, Silver Claw, had mated into the Black Rock Clan. She had also died with her mate, her kittens, and her entire new clan family when the fire fell from the heavens. Clean Killer had been near the boundary between Black Rock's range and Mossy Tree Clan's. Indeed, he had been mind-speaking with her when it happened, and he would never forget that day. Never forget her scream of terror, brief as the time between two breaths, before her beloved mind-voice vanished into cold, eternal silence, cut away from him forever with the sharpness of one of the singing blades the two-leg hunters and scouts used.

And then, even as he turned to speed madly through the net-wood towards Black Rock's range, the dreadful boil of sun-bright fury had roared up before him and the terrible thunder-rumble and howling wind had raced over him like a mighty storm. The shock had splintered branches all about him, flung him from the net-wood like one more broken twig. Indeed, so far as any of the memory singers knew, no one closer to Black Rock's central nesting place than he had survived, and it had taken him many hands of days to heal from the bones which had been broken, even with the two-leg healers' assistance.

It had taken far longer for his mind-glow to heal.

Heart Singer, Mossy Tree's mind-healer, had told him he could survive the deep, inner wounds of that day. At first, Clean Killer had shut his own mind to him, refusing to believe the older Person. In the end, though, Heart Singer had been right. He *had* survived it, but he would never be the same again. *None* of the People would ever be the same. Clean Killer was not the only Person who had directly shared that single mind-scream from all of Black Rock's People, and by now all of the People—aside from the youngest kittens—had tasted the memory songs of that day. The day Black Rock died, murdered by the evildoers from beyond the sky who had killed so many more of the People's two-legs on that same dreadful day. The memory-singers had mercifully dimmed the worst of the terror, of the agony, in their songs, but it was important that all of the People taste them, know the darkness at their core.

Know their enemies' work and never forget their hatred for the ones who had done it.

Clean Killer needed no memory songs. He carried that darkness with him everywhere. Thanks to Heart Singer it had not devoured him, as it had too many other People, yet he had discovered he could not go back to his everyday life as one of Mossy Tree's scouts. He could no longer roam the net-wood and golden leaf, hunting and warding, guarding the clan from death fangs and snow hunters. Not when he knew that other, far greater threat hid beyond the stars. And so, when the memory singers sent forth the summons, seeking volunteers to venture among the two-legs and to guard them against the threat they could not taste themselves—the other two-legs who the evildoers somehow compelled to slay even their closest friends—Clean Killer, scout of Mossy Tree Clan, was among the first to volunteer. And not just because of his need to protect the two-legs who fought to protect all the people—People and two-legs, alike—of his world. No. He'd volunteered because he hoped that someday, some way, he would come within claw's reach of at least one of the evildoers responsible for such slaughter, so many deaths, and on the day he did...

He supposed that was why Spins for Joy, Speaks from Silence, and Dances on Clouds had considered him as the "protector" for this once-upon-a-time evildoer who claimed now to be a friend. Well, Clean Killer would see about that. He had tasted Pounces on Leaves' memory of People's Eyes conversation with the captured evildoer, and he knew the evildoer had never said anything which was not true, but that did not fully reassure Clean Killer. The People had never even considered saying a thing which was not so before they had encountered the two-legs and learned to understand their mouth noises. There had been no point, since any Person always knew whether or not the Person mind-speaking with him was doing such an outlandish thing. But two-legs were mind-blind—all of them except Dances on Clouds and Cloud Dancer's Joy, her kitten, and—just a tiny bit—Deep Roots and Laugh Dancer, her parents. Not only could they *say* things which were not so, they could not always tell when someone else said such things *to* them, poor creatures. People could deceive or trick other People—indeed, some, like Laughs Brightly, were notorious among all the clans for their ability to do that! But they could not do it that easily, not by simply saying false things. They had to find other ways, more creative ways. Was it not reasonable to assume that two-legs had more than one way to deceive their own kind, as well? Clean Killer had observed that some of the most effective deceptions lay not in the saying of untrue things but in saying things which were entirely true...and did not mean what the other Person *believed* they meant.

He did not expect to enjoy his time "protecting" the evildoer, although the memory song of the two-leg's mind-glow Sorrow Singer had relayed to him from Pounces on Leaves was much less...distasteful than he had initially expected. Pounces on Leaves had a powerful mind-glow for a male. Admittedly, he had been more focused on tasting the truth of the evildoer's responses to People's Eyes questions than on delving deep into the two-leg's mind-glow itself, but the memory he had shared with Sorrow Singer and, through her, with Clean Killer had carried none of the dark, cold evil Clean Killer had always assumed must mark an evildoer capable of destroying Black Rock Clan and so many two-legs.

Perhaps it does not, he thought now, grimly, as the two-leg flying thing swooped downward towards its destination. *But unlike Pounces on Leaves, I will be a hunter stalking that mind-glow, and this evildoer who now says he is prepared to aid our two-legs will not like what happens if I find treachery within him.*

✧   ✧   ✧

Damien Harahap felt more unsettled than he would have admitted as he followed his escort—the Manties were too polite to call her a guard—down the hall. He supposed it was a good thing they wanted to keep him alive, at least until they decided differently, and he doubted they were lying about the "nanotech assassins." He had no more idea than they did about how Bardasano's people might make that work, but it sounded like exactly the sort of thing they *would* make work. So if this treecat they meant to pair him with could keep that sort of unpleasant encounter from claiming the scalp of one Damien Harahap, that was a good thing.

He was less comfortable with why his new protector, Clean Killer—a name which suggested a few unpleasant possibilities of its own—would be able to detect a programmed assassin in time to do something about it. There'd been rumors about Sphinxian treecats' supposed esoteric abilities for a long time, although he'd never been interested enough to chase them down himself. One thing he *hadn't* heard about them, however, was that they'd learned to communicate with humans. If, as Jubair claimed, they were telepaths, able to detect lies—and assassins— their ability to tell someone about it explained why Jubair had been accompanied by his own treecat partner for every session with Harahap. And there was the corollary: a telepath who knew someone was lying would make the most effective "control" for any asset of dubious reliability in the long and murky history of espionage.

Harahap might not have minded that, since he entertained no current plan to be *un*reliable, if he'd felt more confident about a treecat's sense of...self-restraint in the case of any little misunderstandings. Or, for that matter, if he'd believed treecats were the adorable, silken pets they appeared to be. Unfortunately, he believed nothing of the sort. He might not have made a special study of them, but Honor Alexander- Harrington's companion Nimitz was the most famous treecat in history in no small part because of how conclusively he'd demonstrated that however adorable and silken he might be, he was anything but a "harmless pet" when his human was threatened.

And there was that name...Clean Killer.

❖   ❖   ❖

"He's on his way, Ma'am," Commander Lassaline said.

Patricia Givens looked over her shoulder as her chief of staff entered the small conference room. The admiral's expression was an interesting study in contrasts, Lassaline thought. The chief of staff probably understood Givens's ambivalence where Damien Harahap was concerned better than almost anyone else. Lassaline had been her assistant chief of staff for over three T-years before moving into the top slot just after the Yawata Strike. She'd seen—and shared—Givens's anguish in the wake of ONI's total failure to see the sneak attack coming. And, like all of the admiral's staff, she wanted any window into their enemies' operations and objectives they could get. But she was also a career intelligence officer, and she knew how devastating a trusted source that provided bad information could truly be. And she also knew that some of the best disinformation programs had depended upon the individuals providing the information not knowing it was false to begin with.

"Thank you, Terry," Givens said, then smiled with more than a trace of sourness. "I wonder if he's looking forward to this with as much joy and celebration as I am."

"If it's any consolation, Ma'am, I'm pretty sure he's looking forward to it with a lot *less* joy and celebration than you are," Lassaline replied. "Man's got a damned good poker face, but I don't care how good he is at hiding what he feels, he still *feels* it!"

"I know. I only hope Her Grace is right about *why* he feels it. Pull up a chair." Givens twitched her head at one of the other chairs at the conference table. "One way or another, it ought to be interesting."

"You always were a mistress of understatement, Ma'am," Lassaline told her with a smile and seated herself in the indicated chair.

Givens tipped back in her own chair, rubbing the ears of the treecat spilled warmly across her lap, while the three of them watched the smart wall display showing the interior of the interrogation room just down the hall from where she sat.

At the moment, its only occupants were Antoine Jubair, Pounces on Leaves, and Clean Killer, and Givens frowned as she thought about why they were here this morning. It wasn't that she really thought it was a *bad* idea, but—

Thought Chaser turned his head to look at her and a true-hand smacked the fingers which had paused in their rubbing. She twitched slightly and looked down at him, and he smacked her hand again, narrowing his eyes.

"Sorry!" Her frown turned into a smile and she heard something suspiciously like a suppressed chuckle from her chief of staff's direction. She glanced at Lassaline whose poker face at that moment could have given lessons to Damien Harahap. Givens glowered at her for a moment, then started stroking Thought Chaser's ears again, and her smile grew into a grin as he closed his eyes once more and buzzed a contented purr.

He and she had formed nothing like the soul-deep adoption bond between Honor Alexander-Harrington or her husband and their treecats. There were times she wished they had, when she envied those who'd been adopted. Other times, she didn't. She knew Nimitz had represented a very real hurdle, one that could have derailed Honor's naval career before it ever began, despite Queen Adrienne's rules about treecats and their people. And she wouldn't have liked knowing that if something fatal happened to her, Thought Chaser would almost certainly follow her into death.

But if they didn't have that bond, he'd still become what was probably the closest, most reliable friend she'd ever had, and she'd learned to trust his judgment implicitly, at least in most ways. There were human conventions, relationships, and societal mechanisms no 'cat truly understood or probably ever would, though. And she did have concerns about how the species' intrinsic honesty might affect the judgment of someone navigating the murky moral waters of the intelligence community. If telepaths couldn't lie to one another, then how deep an appreciation of human-style dishonesty and deceit could they truly possess? And if—

The door opened, and Thought Chaser sat up in her lap as she brought her chair upright.

✧   ✧   ✧

Harahap followed his keeper into the now-familiar interrogation room, then paused just inside the door as he saw the pair of treecats parked on the table like matching bookends.

They weren't identical, although they had exactly the same coloring and exactly the same grass-green eyes. His was a brain which had been trained to record and file away as much data, even—or perhaps, especially—trivial data, as possible in a single glance. So even though it would have been difficult for him to consciously catalog all the differences between the two creatures, he was reasonably certain he'd be able to tell them apart if he ever saw them side-by-side again. He might have more trouble putting a specific name to either of them in isolation, however. It was rather like looking at a pair of almost, but not quite, identical twins. Seen together, the differences between them could be picked out; seen separately, the similarities would overwhelm the memory of any identifying differences.

The one on the right's Jubair's partner, Pounces on Leaves, he told himself. He found treecats' names a bit odd, but he supposed a telempathic species' naming conventions would have to be a little strange. *So, that's Clean Killer on the left. Wonder if those swirls in his fur are from scars underneath it?*

It was an interesting question, since Jubair had been at some pains to explain that Clean Killer had survived a treecat mass-casualty event during what the Manties called the Yawata Strike. He'd also explained how badly the 'cat had been injured by it. Since Manticore held the Alignment responsible for the attack, Jubair had suggested, not at all delicately, it might be unwise for Harahap to say, do, or even *think* anything that might lead Clean Killer to associate him with the attack.

Sounder advice was never given, Harahap decided. He reminded himself that reading an alien species' body language was likely to yield less than reliable results, but Clean Killer—who, now that he thought about it, looked to be at least twenty percent bigger than Pounces on Leaves—didn't look very happy.

Hadn't realized a treecat's coat could actually bristle, he thought. *Alien species or not, I doubt that's a sign he's just overjoyed as hell to see me!*

✧   ✧   ✧

<*So, this is the evildoer,*> Clean Killer said.

<*It is the one who* used to be *an evildoer,*> Pounces on Leaves replied <*And you should not allow your fur to stand on end, younger brother. It is...discourteous.*>

Clean Killer flicked his ears in mingled embarrassment and humor as he tasted the dry amusement in the older Person's mind-voice. Not that Clean Killer was all that concerned about courtesy at the moment. Still, he was supposed to be protecting this two-leg, not killing it himself.

He pulled his claws back into their sheaths. The bristle of his coat, however, was not a conscious response. He could not make it go away as easily, so instead of trying, he switched his attention to the two-leg.

He was not as tall as some of the other male two-legs Clean Killer had seen since volunteering to help guard the People's two-legs, but Clean Killer saw with a scout's eyes, recognized the way the two-leg moved. The one who had escorted him here was armed, and he was not, yet Clean Killer sensed that he was actually far more dangerous than she. He was poised, balanced, in a way she was not, much as a scout on duty was perpetually attuned to all about him while he flowed through the net-wood, every sense alert for any sign of danger to the clan.

But that was only the two-leg's outer shell. It was not what truly mattered, and Clean Killer's eyes narrowed as he reached out and delved deep to taste this two-leg's mind-glow fully and completely.

✧   ✧   ✧

"Mr. Harahap," Jubair began, "this is Clean—"

Harahap heard the Manticoran, but his eyes were on the treecat, as focused as he'd ever been on anything in his life. He saw the furry arboreal—treecats reminded him of a fusion between a Startman pantera and a scimpanzé, or possibly an Old Earth bobcat and a lemur—crouch ever so slightly, staring at him closely. He could almost *feel* the intensity behind those bright green eyes, he thought.

And then he realized it wasn't a matter of *almost* feeling that intensity, after all.

✧　　✧　　✧

Clean Killer heard People's Eyes mouth noises, but he ignored them for the moment as he dived into the other two-leg's mind-glow. There would be time enough—

He twitched and his eyes went suddenly wide. For an instant, the entire world stood still, and then he launched himself like a long, sinuous projectile straight at the two-leg.

✧　　✧　　✧

"Oh, shit!" Patricia Givens gasped as Clean Killer hurled himself at Harahap, both sets of arms spread wide, long, deadly fingers crooked.

Damn it! If he's been lying to us all along, we need to know, but even so, he's too valuable to let Clean Killer just—!

✧　　✧　　✧

Damien Harahap saw Clean Killer coming, and his arms opened automatically. There was no conscious thought in that moment. There was only *awareness*, and his arms closed again, enfolding that long, slender, impossibly strong body and cradling it against his chest like the most precious thing in the entire universe.

✧　　✧　　✧

"Oh, *shit!*" Patricia Givens snarled in a very different tone as she realized what had actually happened.

Thought Chaser's obviously delighted, bleeking laughter didn't help one bit.

✧　　✧　　✧

"So, what do *you* think we should do about it? If I recall correctly, this was your brilliant idea in the first place," the Earl of White Haven said from his wife's com in what might not unreasonably have been described as a snippy tone.

Honor snorted. She hadn't been able to accept Hamish's screen when the original com request came through, because she'd been in an electronic meeting with the Joint Chiefs. He'd left her a recorded message, though, and she'd found herself laughing out loud as she'd viewed his indignant commentary. Nimitz had thought it was just as funny as she had, but it was obvious her husband remained rather less amused.

"I don't think we should do anything at all about it," she told him now. *Imperator* was currently part of a training exercise just under ten light-minutes from the capital planet, so there was a 9.2-second one-way signal delay, even over the grav com. "Actually, I think it's the best thing that could possibly have happened!"

She sat back, cradling her outsized mug of cocoa in both hands. She waited patiently, and then, approximately eighteen seconds later, she gurgled with delight when she was rewarded with a bug-eyed look White Haven would never have permitted anyone else to see.

"'*Best thing*'?" he repeated in incredulous tones. "Honor, the idea was for Clean Killer to rip his throat out if he turned traitor! How damned likely is he to do that *now?*"

"Hamish, why do you persist in not taking my word for it where Harahap is concerned?" She shook her head, still chuckling. "Believe me, I have no intention of nominating this man for canonization, but he's not exactly an unmitigated monster, either. I told you where I think he's coming from—where he's come from for his entire *life*, for that matter. And now he's been adopted by a treecat. Well, guess what? I did some research before Dame Lisa and I ever made our suggestion about Clean Killer, and in the entire history of the Star Kingdom, no treecat's ever adopted a criminal or a traitor. Dr. Arif and I found three cases in which 'cats had adopted someone who later committed serious offenses, not some misdemeanor nonsense, and *became* criminals, but in each of those instances, the 'cat renounced the bond. Do you really think Clean Killer wouldn't do that if Harahap turned? Or think there's any way he'd leave Harahap alive if it happened?"

She shook her head again.

"There's one—count them, *one*—case of someone who was adopted subsequently being convicted of a major crime—voluntary homicide—and *not* being renounced by his 'cat, but that's it as far as serious offenses are concerned. And, frankly, having looked at the facts of that case—as well as I could; it happened over a hundred and fifty T-years ago—I think it should've been ruled *justifiable* homicide. Of course," she quirked one of her off-center smiles, "the 'cats and I tend to have much the same attitude when it comes to dealing with enemies, so you might want to take my opinion about that with a grain of salt.

"However," her smile disappeared and she leaned a little closer to the camera, "you've been adopted yourself, Hamish. You shouldn't need me to tell you what that means. Since you seem just a trifle upset over this, though, let me recapitulate.

"One." She took her artificial hand off the cocoa cup so she could raise her left index finger, just as she had in the initial discussion of Damien Harahap's mind-glow. "Clean Killer's sister and her entire family were killed in the Yawata Strike, and he came darn close to being killed himself. Two," she extended the second finger on her left hand, "we believe—and Clean Killer agrees with us—that the Mesan Alignment was responsible for the Yawata Strike. Three," she extended her ring finger, "Clean Killer knows Harahap worked for the Alignment—although Harahap didn't know it was the Alignment at the time—and Harahap knows as well as we do that the Mesans are the only ones who could have pulled off the Yawata Strike. Four," she extended her little finger, "despite that, Clean Killer adopted Harahap essentially on sight, after—I remind you—having volunteered to be his 'bodyguard' specifically so he could *kill* Harahap if it turned out he was an unregenerate 'evildoer' after all. And, five," her thumb joined the fingers, "nobody who's been adopted by a treecat has *ever* wanted that treecat pissed off with her, even when the 'cat in question hadn't wanted to kill her before they ever met.

"Which means, love of my life, that whatever worries we might have cherished about what Damien Harahap might have thought or been tempted to do under some unknown future circumstances are no longer relevant." She closed her hand into a fist and smiled again, far more broadly. "We've *got* him now, Hamish. Trust me on that one."

Eighteen seconds later, his expression shifted again, from one of moderate outrage to sudden thoughtfulness.

"You may have a point," he said slowly.

"Sweetheart, I *do* have a point. So why don't you just go tell Pat to unknot her knickers about Mr. Harahap? From this moment on, he has a conscience that hates the Mesan Alignment and all its works at least as passionately as I do, and it's permanently parked in a corner of his mind-glow. He may not be able to sense Clean Killer's emotions the way I can sense Nimitz's, but, tell me—has Samantha ever found it difficult to express what she's feeling to *you*?"

"I think you could safely assume the answer to that question is 'no,'" White Haven said, and the cream and brown dappled treecat on the back of his chair laughed just as hard as Nimitz.

"Precisely." Honor leaned back again, still smiling in triumph. "Believe me, *no one* wants her 'cat...unhappy with her. Dying is the *easy* way out, compared to having your 'cat pissed off at you! So instead of worrying about whether or not Clean Killer will warn us if Harahap starts thinking traitorous thoughts, tell Pat to start concentrating on the fact that we don't have to figure out how to turn him and be sure he *stays* turned anymore." She shook her head yet again. "Clean Killer just took care of that for us!"

George Benton Tower
City of Old Chicago
Old Earth
Sol System

"—AND YOU DON'T EVEN want to know what this is going to look like when the Exchange opens tomorrow morning!" Omosupe Quartermain glared around the conference room at her fellows. "Trifecta's not one of the big players—not like Technodyne or Zumwalt or even De Soto Industries—but when the market finds out what that bastard did, we're going to see the mother of all runs. *Another* mother of all runs! God knows we've seen enough of them since this crap started," she ended bitterly.

Innokentiy Kolokoltsov used his coffee mug to hide a grimace. The strong, hot brew was especially welcome at four a.m. on a tempestuous night when he ought to have been in bed hours ago. The storms rolling in off Lake Michigan lashed George Benton Tower's flanks with seventy-five kilometer-per-hour winds and blinding sheets of rain. Thunder rumbled almost continuously and lightning flickered across the tower's crown like an angry halo, striking its towering lightning rods again and again as it sought the absorbent earth.

It was, he thought, all too appropriate a metaphor for what was happening to the entire Solarian League, and despite the hundreds of cubic meters of ceramacrete isolating this quiet conference room from the storm's fury, the tension about him crackled with its own angry electricity. Quartermain seldom waxed quite so strident, especially this early in the damned morning (or this late at night, depending upon how one wanted to look at it). On the other hand, she'd never been what one might call a fan of Manticore at the best of times, and the news from the Mobius System had hit a nerve. Not just with her, either, he thought, eyes shifting to Agatá Wodoslawski.

"Omosupe's right about that," the permanent senior undersecretary of the treasury said, as if his eyes had summoned her agreement. "We're not going to get hit as hard by the market at Treasury as she is over at Commerce, but that's mostly because interest rates have already tanked." Her expression was at least as bitter as Quartermain's. "It's a hell of a note when the upside is that the situation's already so shot to hell that even something like *this* can't make it worse! Except, unfortunately, that it can...and will. Mobius wasn't that huge chunk of our cash flow from the Protectorates—not by *itself*. But if we don't get some kind of handle on this, we're going to look like an elephant gnawed to death by ants."

Kolokoltsov winced internally at the simile, but he couldn't deny its aptness.

"What *I* want to know," Malachai Abruzzi said, turning icy eyes upon his normal ally, Nathan MacArtney, "is why we didn't hear about any of this before this frigging Terekhov blew the piss out of Yucel's Gendarmes? Not to mention massacring the entire legitimate system government while he was at it!"

"That *is* an apropos question," Kolokoltsov agreed, lowering his coffee mug and turning toward the permanent senior undersecretary of the interior. He tapped the memo on the table smart top in front of him. "According to this, you've been getting reports about Manty provocateurs in the Fringe for months now, Nathan!"

"Without any confirmation," MacArtney pointed out in response. "For God's sake, Innokentiy! There are seventeen trillion conspiracy theories running around in our so-called *intelligence* community! Half of them are from people trying to cover their own arses, and half the rest are from people so scared they see Manties under their own *beds*, much less making trouble in the Fringe! If I brought every one of them to you before we were able to confirm or disprove it, that's all the hell we'd be *talking* about!"

He glared back at the other Mandarins, his body language defensive, but Kolokoltsov had to acknowledge his argument had at least some validity. Maybe not enough to excuse the way this had blindsided them, but some.

"I'm not sure that's a sufficient explanation," he said out loud, his tone cool. "At the same time, none of us have covered ourselves with proactive glory since this all started. So instead of trying to fix blame for why we didn't see it coming, what do we know about it now? I think"—his smile was frosty—"we need to at least know how many arteries have been slashed before we start trying to control the bleeding."

"As far as what actually happened in Mobius is concerned, I think we've got the essentials," MacArtney said, after a moment. "Everything we have so far comes from Captain Weaver's report, so I'm sure there's still a lot to fill in, but I don't expect what she's already told us to change very much."

And we should trust your judgment about that after you never even mentioned the possibility something like this might happen? Kolokoltsov thought sardonically. *I know I just said we've all made mistakes, Nathan, but really* . . .

"And Captain Weaver's said exactly *what*, Nathan?" Wodoslawski asked.

"Actually, I think Omosupe may have a better fix on that than my people do—yet, anyway." MacArtney shrugged. "I've got more background information—more *possible* background information—to help set it into context, but Weaver went to Commerce before she got around to us."

Kolokoltsov didn't—quite—frown as he heard the slight but unmistakable edge in MacArtney's voice, but he felt a vast weariness that owed very little to the lateness of the hour. The ship was foundering under them, and they were still trying to score points about who'd left which porthole open. In fairness, MacArtney did have a point in this case, however.

Captain Josephine Weaver commanded the Kalokainos Lines freighter *Rudolfo Kalokainos*. So far as any of them knew, *Rudolfo Kalokainos* was the only League merchant vessel to have escaped from Mobius, and Weaver had headed directly for Old Terra. According to her, Aivars Terekhov—and, oh, how all the Mandarins had come to *hate* that name!—hadn't even tried to prevent *Rudolfo Kalokainos's* departure, however, so it seemed likely other Solarian and neutral dispatch boats and freighters would soon be spreading the news elsewhere.

It was unfortunate, but scarcely surprising, that Weaver had chosen to report what had happened to her employer before she got around to mentioning it to the federal government. It was equally unsurprising that someone at Kalokainos had promptly leaked the news to the public. Volkhart Kalokainos's personal hatred for everything remotely connected to the Star Empire of Manticore had been legendary even before New Tuscany, and the incredible hit the shipping-based Kalokainos empire had taken since the Manties started seizing wormholes hadn't made him any happier. Not surprisingly, probably, since current estimates said Kalokainos Shipping had lost over eighty percent of its value. So it wasn't surprising the news had leaked so rapidly . . . or that the Gendarmerie casualty count Weaver had reported—which, admittedly, had been bad enough on its own—had been inflated by two or three hundred percent.

Few people had been awake to react here in Old Chicago when the story broke, but two thirds of the planet were up and about when the leak hit the public boards. The instant response had been furious anger, and that fury was certain to increase as the news sank fully home. At the moment, Malachai Abruzzi's people were playing catch-up, trying to get in front and shape the narrative to make sure that growing fury was directed somewhere besides at the people in this room, but they had their work cut out for them.

More to MacArtney's immediate point, however, Quartermain's position in the Department of Commerce meant she tended to hear things from the League's transstellars before anyone else. In this case, the fact that she'd been an executive with Kalokainos Shipping for twenty T-years before becoming a bureaucrat only gave her even better connections.

From her expression, she was less than pleased to have him underscore that point.

"As you say, Nathan, we have a lot of pieces to fill in." Her tone was as chill as her expression. "What we actually know—or *think* we know, at any rate—is that President Lombroso asked Commissioner Verrocchio for support after a violent insurrection broke out on Mobius. According to Weaver, it started in Landing but spread quickly. In response to Lombroso's request, Verrocchio sent Brigadier Yucel and a couple of intervention battalions, along with enough light naval support to control Mobius's orbital space. Yucel landed her Gendarmes to secure the capital and called in orbital strikes on half a dozen towns." Her lips twisted in distaste. "Weaver says that effectively broke the rebellion's back, although the hard-core rebels refused to concede defeat, so Yucel and her people assisted the Mobian planetary authorities in rounding up the diehards. She'd almost completed that part of the operation when Terekhov turned up. He took out the Navy units—Weaver's not sure if they were destroyed or simply surrendered, although she thinks they most likely did, given the odds against them—and entered Mobius orbit himself. He contacted Yucel and demanded that she cease operations immediately and surrender her people. She refused. At which point he devastated a couple of square blocks of downtown Landing with a KEW strike on Yucel's HQ. Weaver says he killed the entire remaining planetary government in the same strike. Somebody named Breitbach wound up running the show planet-side. Weaver says he was supposedly the rebellion's leader and Yucel had him in custody but didn't realize who he was." Quartermain shrugged. "I don't know if that's true or if he's just a Manty mouthpiece, but that's all we *do* know at this point."

Kolokoltsov nodded. That hadn't added a lot to what he already knew, but it certainly defined the parameters of their problem. The political and diplomatic parameters, anyway; he was unhappily certain Quartermain and Wodoslawski would be able to provide far more depressing detail about the economic parameters when they got around to *that* side of the problem.

But apparently Quartermain had provided new information for at least one of the Mandarins.

"None of the newsies have mentioned anything about Yucel's authorizing any kinetic strikes," Wodoslawski said sharply. "Is Weaver certain about that?"

"As certain as she is about any of it." Quartermain shrugged again. "We're dealing with a single report, Agatá. With no way to crosscheck, I can't *guarantee* any of it."

"If the Gendarmes started using KEWs before Terekhov ever turned up, that's not going to play well with the public," Wodoslawski worried.

"Which is probably the reason our good friends over at Kalokainos haven't mentioned it to anyone...yet," Kolokoltsov said. Quartermain gave him a moderately dirty look, but said nothing.

"Can we keep it from coming out?" Abruzzi asked.

"That's really more your bailiwick than anyone else's," Kolokoltsov observed, earning himself an annoyed look from the information undersecretary, as well.

"I don't know, Malachai," Quartermain said. "In the short term, probably. As Innokentiy's just pointed out, *whoever*"—she emphasized the pronoun—"leaked this didn't mention that aspect of it. So presumably they don't have any interest in leaking it later on. Unfortunately, the Manties aren't that reticent. Terekhov already posted his entire com conversation with Yucel on the Mobius System's info net. Weaver brought a copy of it with her. I've viewed it." She shook her head, eyes bleak. "If the woman-in-the-street believes it's accurate, not doctored or edited, it's going to hurt us. Yucel comes off like a frigging lunatic and they've got her threatening to execute prisoners in mass lots if Terekhov doesn't back off."

Kolokoltsov winced. *That* bit he hadn't heard yet.

"Doesn't mean a thing," Abruzzi said. The others looked at him, and he waved one hand in a dismissive gesture.

"It doesn't," he insisted. "My people at Information could whip up that same 'conversation' in fifteen minutes from a standing start. Hell, we've *done* it! So the fact that the Manties are so obliging about sharing it actually offers us a way to attack it. We dig up Yucel's records, demonstrate she's always been firm about completing any mission but always scrupulously observed the relevant laws and regulations while she did it." He smiled. "Trust me, whatever her record's really like, I can make her look like a girl scout! Then we point out how easy it would be to manufacture something like that. We don't usually want to draw attention to that, since it gives malcontents the opportunity to suggest we routinely do it, but in this case we might want to go ahead and produce a clip of our own, showing Yucel giving in the instant Terekhov demands her surrender. Then we put that up on the boards, side-by-side with her threat to start shooting people, and *admit* her surrender was created out of whole cloth. Admitting that won't prevent it from having a certain subliminal impact, and it will conclusively demonstrate how easy it would have been for the Manties to do the opposite."

"That might—*might*—help defuse that threat," Kolokoltsov said skeptically. "But what about the kinetic strikes? What happens when independent confirmation of *those* hits the boards?"

And it will *hit them*, he thought glumly. T*he Manties've been too damned good about hauling "neutral" newsies—even* Solarian *newsies— around with them. Be a bit hard to sweep their imagery of the craters under the rug, Malachai!*

"We don't deny they happened," MacArtney said before Abruzzi could respond.

"You're not serious!" Wodoslawski protested, and Kolokoltsov understood exactly why. Every Solarian citizen knew the SLN *prevented* mass-casualty strikes. That was why there was an Eridani Edict in the first place!

The fact that there'd been quite a few kinetic strikes by the SLN over the centuries was one of those unpleasant little truths which had somehow failed to make it into the same "everyone knows" territory as the Navy's reputation as the guardian of truth and justice in a darkling galaxy.

"Of course I'm serious," MacArtney said impatiently. "Agatá, I understand the possible downsides, but we can't pretend there weren't any KEWs, and not even Malachai's people could convincingly explain why the *Manties* would be bombarding Mobian towns and cities outside the capital. That means they had to come from our ships. But—" he raised his right hand, index finger extended "—they weren't Yucel's idea. They were called in at the urgent request of the legitimate system government and directed at centers of dug-in resistance—urban areas which had been evacuated of all civilians except those the rebels physically prevented from leaving to use as human shields—where the Mobian military and the Gendarmes would have suffered enormous casualties if they'd gone in on the ground." He shrugged. "I admit it was regrettable, and no doubt a lot of innocent civilians were killed, but that was as a consequence of the Lombroso government's decision—and, even more, of the rebels' decision to use those innocent civilians as cover. Brigadier Yucel had been sent to assist the legitimate authorities, and it's well-established that domestic police actions by legal governments don't rise to the level of an Eridani Edict violation unless casualties are truly massive. In this case, they probably didn't exceed a quarter million. A half million, at the most." He shrugged again. "As I say, regrettable, but not our responsibility or our decision. And I expect Malachai's people can do a pretty fair job of arguing that the Manties and their Mobian puppets are vastly inflating the fatalities, anyway."

Kolokoltsov puffed his cheeks, then took another sip of coffee. It didn't help. The bad taste remained as he contemplated MacArtney's glib proposal.

"We can probably make that work—for a while, at least," Abruzzi said, after a moment. "We've already been working on strategies headed in that direction to counter Manty claims once Buccaneer hits its stride. Not the same, of course, because we're not talking about local governments' assistance requests in Buccaneer's case and it's aimed at infrastructure, not mass casualties. But I've got plenty of talking heads on record explaining that Buccaneer doesn't violate the Edict for several reasons, including the argument that it's a legitimate exercise of the federal police power against treasonous Solarian citizens. It's easier to justify the destruction of infrastructure in hostile, non-League star systems, but since we're denying the legality of secession, we should be covered even someplace like Hypatia. Like I say, none of that speaks directly to Nathan's suggestion, but it's all groundwork we've already put in place. Eventually, the Manties' version will gain traction in the opposition 'faxes, but they're still pretty marginalized. And, frankly, the general public has the attention span of a gnat." He raised both hands, shoulder high and palms uppermost. "By the time the other side's version gets disseminated, most Solarians will already have internalized *our* version."

"The other side's version," Kolokoltsov thought. *Even here, he's not willing to call it "the truth." Whoever said truth is the first casualty of war damned well knew what he was talking about!*

Which didn't mean Abruzzi didn't have a point. And as long as the Navy kept collateral casualties to a minimum and the Manties didn't force the task force commanders to resort to Parthian...

"Whether or not we can...mitigate that aspect, Mobius is still an economic and public relations nightmare," he pointed out.

"Economically, yes," Abruzzi replied. "But in terms of public relations?" He shook his head, and to Kolokoltsov's surprise, his eyes glittered with something that looked very much like genuine enthusiasm. "Oh, no, Innokentiy! This time, the fuckers have stepped right into it. They've given us the biggest club we've had since all this started."

"Excuse me?" Quartermain sounded as surprised as Kolokoltsov felt, and Abruzzi actually chuckled. It was not a warm and mirthful sound.

"We've been telling everybody this is all about the Manties' interstellar ambitions, right?" He looked around the conference room, then snorted. "Well, what else do you call a galaxy-wide operation to foment rebellion—*violent* rebellion, the kind that gets millions of people killed—throughout the Fringe in order to generate pretexts for military intervention to set up pro-Manty puppet regimes? I'm sure someone on their side is going to claim this is a purely defensive reaction on their part, prompted by our 'senseless aggression,' but there's no way in hell something like Mobius happened overnight. This had to have been planned in detail, especially given the reports Nathan's finally gotten around to sharing with us."

He joined the others in momentarily glaring at MacArtney, then shrugged.

"What we've got, what we can dust off and send to the boards at the most strategic moment, is evidence—pretty *strong* evidence, that we can make even stronger, depending on how we go about presenting it—that the Manties started organizing this T-years ago. That it's a long-term strategy, one they put in place before Raging Justice, before Spindle, before New Tuscany, before Monica—hell, before *any* open incident." He smiled coldly. "Believe me, by the time my people are done massaging this, there won't be any more questions about the Manties' *real* aims."

Office of the Director of Naval Operations
Gregor Mendel Tower
City of Leonard
Darius System

"SO WHAT CAN I do for you today?" Benjamin Detweiler inquired as his brother Daniel appeared on his com.

"You and Rochelle can meet me and Trudi for lunch, among other things. I might actually be able to entice your two older nieces to join us. Angela, unfortunately, has informed me that her mare has just gone into labor and I'm afraid that when you're eleven, the birth of a new colt is far more enthralling than lunch with a mere uncle."

"It's good to see that your daughter has a proper sense of priorities," Benjamin said gravely. "Dare I ask if she's settled on a name yet?"

"No, but she has narrowed the list. The remaining candidates are Donner, Blitz, Erdbeben, Fulmine, Laser, Molnienosnyj, Nova, Rayo, and Tsunami." Daniel rolled his eyes. "Personally, I'm pulling for Nova or Tsunami, although I have to admit Molnienosnyj rolls trippingly off the tongue."

"I am *so* happy Susanna and Tabitha favored hamsters over horses," Benjamin told him. "There was a lot less drama when a new one came along, and naming them never seems to be quite as...fraught as Angela seems to be making this."

"Go ahead—mock my pain!" Daniel made a rude gesture. "Names for *hamsters*? Somehow, 'Nibbles' doesn't strike me as even in the same league as Erdbeben!"

"No," Benjamin agreed. "But I don't suppose pet names were what you screened to discuss?"

"They aren't. Mind you, if you accept the lunch invitation, Sandra and Lindsey are going to bend your ear about it. Putting up with Angela's quest for the *perfect* name has been a sore trial to them, and their mom and I haven't been as sympathetic to their pain as they think we should've been."

"Can't imagine." Benjamin grinned, then cocked his head. "And so to business?"

"And so to business," Daniel agreed. "There are two or three projects we need to discuss—someplace besides over lunch in a restaurant, I mean—but the main thing is that, as of today, Silver Bullet's ready for production. We still have a couple of bugs to address, but they're mostly software issues. The prototype *hardware*'s performed almost perfectly, and Test and Eval signed off on it yesterday."

"That's great!" Benjamin raised one hand in a thumbs-up gesture. "Faster than I expected, too."

"Well, most of the hardware was pretty much off-the-shelf. We'd already been tweaking the torpedo's drive for you, and the gravitic sensors are out of our own grav com R and D. The biggest problem was power supply, really. My people haven't been able to duplicate the Manty micro fusion plants yet. I think they're on the track, and I'm actually predicting that they'll pull it off in the next T-year or so, but it won't be any sooner than that. Assuming Collin's people don't manage to steal the plans for us. Any chance of that?"

"'Fraid not." Benjamin shook his head, his expression much less cheerful than it had been. "I had a report from him a couple of days ago. Apparently, the Manties are rolling up his networks in a big way. We always knew there was a risk of that—once those bastards Zilwicki and Cachat blew the top off, they were bound to start looking under every rock—but this appears to be worse than our worst-case assumptions. So far, we don't have a clue how they're doing it, and however they're pulling it off, they're obviously working their way down from the top. It seems to be spreading to Beowulf, too, although it looks like it's going slower there. And I'm afraid we took out his best bet for getting us the kind of info your people need ourselves. Oyster Bay killed a *lot* of the agents he'd managed to insert into their construction units."

"I wish I could say I was surprised." Daniel sighed, then shrugged. "Well, knowing something *can* be done is two thirds of figuring out how to do it. I wish we'd been paying more attention to the hardware side of things and less to the political and diplomatic side when Collin set up his networks, but I think we've at least identified the right paths forward for a lot of their stuff. Now it's just a case of hammering through, and God knows we've got enough motivation!"

He smiled with very little amusement, and Benjamin nodded in both understanding and agreement.

Daniel's researchers had yet to duplicate most of the cornucopia of hardware which had flowed out of Roger Winton's long-term prewar R&D. In fact, they hadn't even *identified* all of it yet. As Daniel had just suggested, they were making progress—in fact, their *rate* of progress continued to increase—but they remained far behind and he was unhappily certain the Manties weren't resting on their laurels. Worse, now they were comparing notes with Haven. There was a reason Sonja Hemphill and Shannon Foraker were right at the top of Collin's Assassinate As Soon As Possible list. If there were two navies in the galaxy who understood the need to stay ahead of the technological curve, it was the RMN and the RHN, especially under Hemphill and Foraker. It was unlikely, to say the least, that the Alignment was going to overcome the edge in their hardware anytime soon.

"Well, without micro plants of our own," Daniel continued, "what my people had to do was to throw together a new fuselage big enough to let us graft together the power packs of two Wraiths. It's . . . large."

Benjamin snorted. The Wraith was the Mesan Alignment Navy's equivalent of the Manty Ghost Rider recon platforms, and without Manticore's new stealth systems—and their damned thumbnail fusion plants—building something equally hard to see had been a challenge. The good news was that the spider drive's gravitic signature was incredibly faint compared to conventional impellers, so it didn't require as much stealthing in the first place. The *bad* news was that the drive itself took up a lot of space and its plasma-charged accumulators took up almost as much. From the sketchy information they'd been able to assemble on Ghost Rider, a Wraith was probably at least seventy percent bigger than a current generation Manticoran recon drone. It was also much slower and lacked Ghost Rider's FTL capability, but it was probably at least as difficult to detect, and indications were that its onboard sensors were a bit better even than the RMN's current hardware.

But if Daniel was talking about something big enough to carry a pair of Wraith power packs, then he was talking about something which was probably at least two or three times as big as the MAN's graser torpedo . . . which was already nearly twice the size of a Manticoran Mark 23 MDM. In which case, calling it "large" was something of an understatement, especially from the perspective of the man whose navy would be trying to deploy the damned things.

"How large a 'large' are we actually talking about here?" he asked.

"Try sixty-eight meters long and right on eleven and a half in diameter."

Benjamin winced. That wasn't *quite* as bad as he'd feared, but it was still over ninety percent the size of a Manticoran *Shrike*-class LAC.

"I imagine it's fair to call that 'large,'" he said judiciously.

"The final version's going to be at least a couple of meters longer," Daniel warned him. "That sixty-eight meters is basically the carrier, the graser, and the power supply. We've designed four different nose sections, and I won't know which one we're using until I know how the software tweaks finally resolve." He shrugged. "On the other hand, given that it's already way too big to fire from anything we've got, including *Detweiler's* torpedo tubes, I figure a few more meters here or there won't hurt."

"Probably not," Benjamin agreed. He sat for a moment, eyes gazing into the distance and fingers drumming on his desk while he thought. Then he nodded to himself and refocused on his brother's face.

"Unless we can figure out a way to carry these things externally without anybody noticing them, which seems unlikely, we'll have to swim them out of a standard cargo hold. Will that be workable?"

"Don't see any reason why not." Daniel chuckled. "As a matter of fact, I figured you'd have to do that, so I've got another team busy designing what *looks* like a pair of standard *Rhino*-class heavy-lift cargo containers glued together end-to-end. We can fit one of these things into something that size and even tuck a presser into one end of the container. I figure that would let you drop the '*Rhinos*' with the clock set for the Silver Bullet to deploy itself once the deploying ship's gotten well clear."

"Sounds like a good idea to me." Benjamin nodded again, more enthusiastically. "You say it's about ready for production? How soon are we talking about?"

"Pretty much as soon as we choose the definitive nose section. Call it ... mid-October."

"If you don't mind, I'll add another couple of weeks and call it the *end* of October." Benjamin's smile was tart. "I've been bitten by optimistic schedules a time or two."

"It wouldn't hurt to have a couple of weeks' cushion," Daniel acknowledged. "Have you got any thoughts on how to get them deployed once my pet geniuses hand the design over to Production?"

"Actually, I do. Or, rather, Collin and I do. I didn't realize just how big these things were going to be, but that doesn't matter. I've been operating on the assumption that whatever size they were, they'd be too big to deploy any other way from the get-go. And we just happen to have a Kalokainos freighter tucked away in Warner. So as soon as your Bullets are ready to go, we load them onto one of our streak drive freighters here in Darius and send them to Warner."

Daniel nodded his understanding. Darius was over 130 light-years—and one hyper-bridge translation—from the Felix System, which was just over ten light-years from the Mannerheim Terminus of the Mannerheim-Warner warp bridge. A streak drive-equipped freighter could make that entire trip in less than forty-eight hours.

"Once we get them to Warner," Benjamin continued, "we transship them to the Kalokainos ship and it sails off to Beowulf. It'll arrive covered by a legitimate shipping manifest. Warner seized a bunch of general merchandise consigned to Beowulf when the Manties started shutting down the wormholes, and Beowulf's trade rep's been working on prying it loose ever since. The system government's been dragging its heels, claiming it wants to see which way the plebiscite goes before it releases the goods. The Beowulfers have been arguing that the goods in question belong to private individuals and corporations, not to the Republic of Beowulf, so they aren't liable to seizure whatever the plebiscite decides. Collin has half a dozen people in place in the Warner government, and they've had their thumbs on the delaying-things side of the scale. Once we get the Silver Bullets to Warner and get them loaded, they'll change their tune, and off the ship—it's called the *Star Galleon*—will go to Beowulf."

Daniel frowned, rubbing his lower lip as he did some mental math. Warner to Beowulf was about 103 light-years. For a standard freighter, that worked out to thirty-five days or so, just under twenty-eight subjective days for *Star Galleon*'s crew. So if he made his delivery schedule . . .

"Last week of November or first week of December, you think?"

"Something like that." Benjamin nodded. "Have your projections for in-system deployment changed?"

"Not significantly." Daniel shook his head. "Given the volume we've projected for the Mycroft platforms' locations, they should be fully deployed within twelve days."

"Dwell time projections?"

"That's actually a little better than our original estimates. Given the size of the final platform, we were able to build in deployable solar panels and a trickle charger for the plasma capacitors. They'll be far enough out to limit what the panels can scoop up, but they should have enough power to hold the accumulators' charge for at least eighty days before they fall behind the leakage rate and the capacitors drop below minimum operating levels. The numbers for Beowulf suggest it'll be closer to ninety or even a hundred days, but eighty's a safe minimum estimate." Daniel shrugged. "If the spider wasn't such a power hog, those numbers would be a lot better."

"Then that defines our operational window, doesn't it?" Benjamin drummed on his desktop a bit more.

"I'll have to discuss the final timing with Collin," he said then, "but I think you've given us more than enough flexibility." He smiled warmly at his brother. "On the other hand, we'd probably better get the new schedule off to Gweon pretty quickly. It's only about eight days from Warner to Sol under streak drive, but we don't know how long it'll take him to bring Kingsford around."

"*Will* he be able to convince Kingsford?" Daniel asked a bit anxiously, and Benjamin shrugged.

"Collin says 'probably,'" he said. "The problem is that Kingsford's smarter than Rajampet was, and he's already gotten his hand burned in Raging Justice. Unfortunately, it looks like since the shooting started—and since Kolokoltsov put him in charge of the SLN—he's gotten a lot more wary about the Manties and a lot less enthusiastic for any more of the 'Mandarins'' adventures. The man's an actual Solarian *patriot*, too, which surprised me a bit, since he never seemed particularly averse to picking up a little extra pocket change along the way. He's changed his tune on *that*, too, though. In fact, he's officially terminated his relationships with half a dozen lobbyists whose credit vouchers had access to his ears. That means we can't manipulate him as readily as we'd hoped, which means we can't predict that he'll jump at the opportunity the same way we could have gotten Rajampet to."

"But in that—" Daniel began, and Benjamin waved one hand at the com.

"We think we've found the bait to encourage him, and Gweon will hardly have to lie about it at all. Besides, whatever he may think about our proposal, *he's* not the one calling the shots, ultimately. And he's not a 'Mandarin' himself. He doesn't *quite* have a seat at the high table, and do you really think *they* won't jump at the opportunity? We can give them a pretty powerful military argument, but as far as Collin's analysts can tell, we probably wouldn't actually need to. They can see which way the plebiscite's going to come out just as well as we can, and the political arguments—especially since they've already embraced Operation Buccaneer—should be pretty overwhelming."

"And how do we expect the Grand Alliance to react?"

"Now that, Daniel, is the sixty-eight million-credit question." Benjamin showed his teeth. "I'd say they're likely to react . . . poorly from the Mandarins' perspective, but none our analysts are prepared to predict *how* poorly. The access we've lost in the upper strata of their governments isn't helping, either. We've got a range of opinions, running all the way from immediate reprisals in kind or an actual blockade of the Sol System to an intensification of efforts to bring more and more of the Fringe and the Protectorates over to their side of the ledger. Part of how they respond will depend on the Solly battle plan and any modest tweaks we might add to it, though. My staff's in discussions with Collin's PsyOps people about how we might want to go about that.

"On the other hand," he showed those teeth again, "even if they aren't idiotic enough—or enraged enough—to create a few counter-atrocities of their own, we still come out ahead. If they *are* stupid enough to opt for reprisals in kind, they'll guarantee enough Core World hatred and resentment to keep them occupied for the next fifty T-years, even if they win in the end. But whether they do that or not, it'll definitely hurt their military capabilities in the short term, and all Collin's indications are that they don't see Hasta coming or have a clue about the other info we've fed into Technodyne's R and D. That being the case, they may not realize how their window of technological supremacy is shrinking, and the Solarian League's basic tech and educational system are a hell of a lot better suited to making up the difference between the SLN's capabilities and the Grand Alliance's than the People's Republic's were to making up the difference between the RMN and the People's Navy. I don't think the Mandarins can stay afloat fiscally much longer, but if we can entice the Grand Alliance into genuinely enraging Core World opinion—into lighting something like a real fire in the Solarian League's belly—somebody or something will replace Kolokoltsov and his crew. I don't give a damn what their precious Constitution says. Scare them enough, piss them off enough, convince them this is a genuine fight for survival, and then throw in a hefty dollop of revenge, and whoever kicks the Mandarins out will find the resources to use the League's industrial capacity to build enough 'almost as good' weapons to bury the Manties and their friends. And while they're doing that, they'll go right on shedding Fringe and Verge systems."

Daniel nodded slowly. He didn't like the thought of "counter-atrocities" one bit, but he couldn't refute Benjamin's logic. Except, that was, for the fact that the People's Republic had believed the same thing was true in its favor against the Royal Manticoran Navy. And for the fact that the Detweiler Plan had always called for the League's dissolution, not for driving it even more tightly together against an outside threat.

But that's not what's going to happen, really, he thought. *Ben's right about that, too. Whatever the* Core Worlds *may do, the Fringe and the Verge are going up in flames. At best—from the Sollies' perspective—the League will be busy for decades trying to put out one fire after another while people like Hurskainen and the rest of the Renaissance Faction—and Barregos; let's not forget him!—bite off chunks. We need chaos outside the Core for the plan to succeed, and that means the one thing we* don't *need is Manticore, Haven, and the Andermani combining to put out the fires before the SLN ever gets around to them. And that means the "Grand Alliance" has to go. Either that, or we need it locked in a war against the League that goes on and on and on while we gather up the pieces around the periphery.*

So either way, Silver Bullet looks like living up to its name.

He wished he felt better about being able to collect the credit for that.

"Sounds good," he said, rather more cheerfully than he actually felt, then deliberately shifted gears.

"And now that we have that out of the way, and noticing the time, may I suggest you and your lady join me and *my* ladies for that lunch? I'm thinking in terms of Goryachev's, my treat. Only seems fair, since I'm planning on bringing two adolescent appetites with me!" He chuckled. "You and I can talk about those other projects this afternoon, after we get everyone fed."

"Works for me," Benjamin told him. "Just let me com Roxy. I don't think Susanna's in Leonard this afternoon, but she can probably bring Tabitha along. I'll ping you back in five minutes. That good?"

"As you say, works for me. Talk to you then. Clear."

The Golden Olive Restaurant
City of Old Chicago
Sol System
Solarian League

"AS FAR AS I can tell, Kolokoltsov and the others actually believe their own story, at least as far as first causes go," Weng Zhing-hwan said after the server had deposited her order of *Měnggǔ kǎoròu* in front of her and withdrawn. The savory scent of pork, mutton, and chicken rose to greet her, and she picked up her chopsticks.

"Hard to blame them, really, I guess," Lupe Blanton replied. She'd been in the mood for something lighter than Mongolian barbecue, and she frowned as she picked at the salad in front of her. "Depressing, but hard to blame them. Especially with *dear* Rajmund stirring the pot."

"I know." Weng popped a bite of chicken into her mouth and chewed appreciatively, but her blue eyes were unhappy. "I pulled Yucel's record back when you and I first started worrying about this. Based on what she's done in the past, I can't say anything in the Manties' version of events strikes me as unlikely."

"Zhing-hwan, there *isn't* an official 'Manty version' yet," Blanton scolded.

"Oh, excuse me!" Weng rolled her eyes. "I meant the version the Manties are going to present when they get around to it. You know, the one that happens to be the truth?"

"Oh, *that* one!" Blanton snorted. She sprinkled a little salt onto her salad. "I'm just pointing out that so far all anyone's hearing is our esteemed superiors' version. Which, as you just suggested, wouldn't recognize the truth if it walked in the door."

Weng chuckled, but neither of them found any real humor in the situation.

"It's a given that Abruzzi's lying about it," the colonel said then. "His lips are moving. The thing I find most interesting, though, is the fact that according to Captain Weaver, Terekhov disclaimed any preexisting promises of naval support."

"That's not quite what he said," Blanton objected.

409

"Oh yes, it is," Weng disagreed. "He specifically apologized for arriving so far behind Yucel because nobody on the Manties' side knew anything about the Mobian situation soon enough to be more proactive."

"What?" Blanton lowered her fork and cocked her head. "I didn't see any of that in the com record Weaver brought home."

"No, you didn't." Weng smiled. "On the other hand, and without wishing to cast any aspersions on the gaping holes in Frontier Security's intelligence net, is it possible that—unlike the always-efficient Gendarmerie—*you* didn't have a stringer aboard *Rudolfo Kalokainos*?"

"Wait a minute. You're saying you *did* have somebody aboard that ship?"

"Not exactly," the colonel admitted. "What we had was somebody who knew somebody. *Rudolfo Kalokainos's* purser has a sister in the Gendarmerie. He made it a point to look her up as soon as he could catch a shuttle from orbit. And given the spectacular way all the Mobian crap is likely to hit the Gendarmerie right in the face, the sister kicked his version upstairs fast. She's over in Davenant-Prydmor's Analysis shop, not Operations, but Noritoshi made sure what she had to say got distributed to everyone in Intelligence Command. Well, all the division chiefs and senior analysts, anyway."

"That was a lucky break," Blanton said.

"Nonsense. It was all the result of careful prior planning."

"Say that again with a straight face," Blanton challenged, and it was Weng's turn to snort. Then her expression sobered once more.

"Fair enough," she said. "But the key point is that according to our source—who, admittedly, doesn't have any recorded official com traffic to substantiate it, but who also has no reason I can see to lie about it—Terekhov told Breitbach and his senior lieutenant, somebody named Blanchard, that no matter what Breitbach might have thought, his 'Mobius Liberation Front' *hadn't* been talking to the Manties. Now, Breitbach and Blanchard obviously both believed they'd been in contact with Manticore, and *somebody* sure as hell provided them with heavy weapons and covert support. But if it was the Manties, wouldn't Terekhov have said so? I mean, he was theoretically talking to people who'd *expected* his arrival. Seems to me Manticore would want the credit for being a reliable ally, wouldn't you think?"

"Your source says Terekhov actually *told* this Breitbach that?"

"That's what he says." Weng shrugged. "He was dirt-side when the balloon went up, and he got swept up by the locals early on. His wife's a Mobian. Apparently, the locals arrested him at the same time some of his in-laws were picked up on suspicion. So until he was released by the new regime and allowed to return to *Rudolfo Kalokainos*, he had an inside seat for a lot of what was going on."

"And, as someone with Mobian connections, especially if he spent time in custody as a suspected rebel, a motive to...cast your late, lamented colleague in a less than favorable light," Blanton pointed out.

"Which, I'd argue, is offset by the fact that he's talking to his own sister," Weng countered. Blanton thought about that for a moment, then shrugged agreement.

"I could see Manticore denying any connection to an unsuccessful rebellion it had helped instigate," the colonel continued then. "But a *successful* one? One where the new people in charge think the Manties were in their corner from the very beginning?" She shook her head. "That one I find harder to accept."

"So you see it as more evidence of the Other Guys' involvement."

"I do."

Weng plied her chopsticks as they sat in thoughtful silence. Then Blanton leaned back on her side of the table.

"I'm inclined to agree," she said. "Mind you, I can see an upside for the Manties if they're taking the position that they're so noble they're ready to come to the rescue of people who only *think* they've been talking to Manticore. I suppose that could be a subtle part of their master plan, if they really are behind it and there aren't any Other Guys. I mean, it *would* let them foment unrest and rebellions all over the Fringe and Verge without having to provide real support to most of them." She shrugged. "They turn up for two or three, announce they 'just happened' to hear about what was going on and—being the noble and selfless souls which all the galaxy knows Manticorans to be—rallied to the defense of the people who'd been misled into believing they had promises of Manticoran support. That insulates them against the claim that they're using 'disposable tools,' on the one hand, and gets them all kinds of credit for rushing to the rescue when they're under no moral obligation to do anything of the sort."

"I thought about that." Weng nodded. "And I'm sure that's what someone like our friend Rajmund's going to argue is happening. I don't think it is, though. I keep going back to how *early* this operation started. I'm convinced—I think *all* of us Ghost Hunters are convinced—that the Manties never saw direct conflict with the League coming, even after Monica, until Byng screwed up. And all of us know this crap about 'Manty imperialism' would make really good fertilizer. Manticore had exactly zero reason to start trying to build some kind of interstellar empire. Hell, it already *had* one; it's just that it was commercial, not territorial. The Manties spent centuries building it, too, so if anybody in the galaxy understood how it worked, *they* did. Now Abruzzi and the others want us to believe they decided to destabilize the most successful economic system, on a per capita basis, in the history of humankind by deliberately picking a fight with the *biggest* economic system in the history of humankind?"

She shook her head.

"I could see a policy of destabilizing the Protectorates as a response to an existential threat to their Star Empire's existence, Lupe. In fact, in *Realpolitik* terms, that would make an enormous amount of sense. But this started too early to be a response to *us*. To me, that only reinforces the likelihood that it was the Other Guys all along."

"You're probably right." Blanton reached for her iced tea. "Pity it's going to 'prove' exactly the opposite when it all finally hits the boards."

George Benton Tower
City of Old Chicago
Old Earth
Sol System

"THE PROBLEM I HAVE, Admiral," Malachai Abruzzi said, "is that selling what happened at Hypatia as anything besides a frigging disaster will be just a bit difficult for my people over at Information."

"I'm sorry to hear that, Mr. Abruzzi," Winston Kingsford replied politely.

"We need something to work with," Abruzzi said in a more pointed tone. "The way this is working out doesn't help our narrative one bit."

Kingsford only looked at him, and Abruzzi's face tightened.

"Malachai," Innokentiy Kolokoltsov said, "Admiral Hajdu wasn't sent to Hypatia by himself." Abruzzi transferred his unhappy glare to the Permanent Senior Undersecretary for Foreign Affairs, but Kolokoltsov went on in the same level voice. "Ms. Yang-O'Grady had *primary* direction of the mission. Admiral Hajdu assumed responsibility only after she decided—and formally informed him—that she'd failed in her own mission, at which point the situation was...complicated. We're in no position, at this remove, to second-guess his understanding of that situation. I may agree with you that some of his decisions were...less than optimal, but he was acting within the parameters of his mission as he—and *Yang-O'Grady*—understood it.

"The bottom line is that the two of them were sent to Hypatia to deliver a message. They did that." He grimaced. "We might all wish it had worked out differently, but it didn't, and it's a little unreasonable to insist that Admiral Kingsford, who wasn't even there, pull some kind of magical rabbit out of his hat for us at this point."

"I agree that the way things worked out at Hypatia is...regrettable," Nathan MacArtney put in, "but, overall, Buccaneer's having exactly the effect we needed."

"I think that might be putting it a bit too strongly," Omosupe Quartermain said. MacArtney raised an eyebrow at her, and she shrugged. "It's probably having a *lot* of the effect we wanted, Nathan. I don't

413

think I'd go as far as to say 'exactly' until we've got a lot better read on things. And I can't quite rid my mind of the law of unintended consequences. Of which, I might point out, Hypatia would appear to be a case in point."

"True." Kolokoltsov nodded. "And it's not like we haven't—your people at Information haven't—clearly established that Buccaneer is a response to naked Manty aggression."

That's one way to put it, Kingsford thought from behind a calm and attentive expression. *Not quite the way Hypatia and the Manties would describe it, though. For that matter, not the way the Hypatians are describing it, if you've happened to glance at the news reports from Vivliothékē. And thanks to Hajdu and that idiot Gogunov...*

The initial reports coming back from his task forces indicated Buccaneer was succeeding as a military strategy. Unfortunately, the ultimate object of any military strategy was to achieve *political* ends, and that was looking rather more...problematical. He'd warned his civilian masters that might be the case, although, as Abruzzi's attitude suggested, they'd ignored that warning the same way they'd ignored everything else that might have saved them—and the Solarian League—from its current rolling disaster.

Capriotti's Cachalot strike had gone with textbook perfection, and so had the attacks on Maize, Snyder, Waterfall and Golem. The attack on Kenniac—even closer to Beowulf than Hypatia, although in almost the opposite direction—had been highly successful, as well. The attack on Bryant had been...messier. Vice Admiral Gomez had found a half dozen Manty cruisers in Bryant, although—thank God—none of them had been those overgrown heavy cruisers with the long-range missiles. And they'd been equally lucky in that the Bryant government had previously announced its neutrality and declined to allow the Manties and their allies to station any permanent force in their star system. The Manties had sparred at long range, covering the evacuation of their own shipping in Bryant, which had amounted to no more than a pair of freighters, then withdrawn when System President McGillicuddy pointedly reminded both sides of his star nation's neutrality.

Too bad for McGillicuddy, Kingsford reflected now. *Not that the Manties could've changed the ultimate outcome. It does seem a little ungracious of us to go ahead and trash his star system's entire industrial base after he was obliging enough to run them off for us, though.*

He shook his head mentally at the thought. He wasn't about to tell Kolokoltsov or the others, but he really wished Gomez had shown sufficient initiative to disregard his orders after McGillicuddy had so strenuously defended his star system's neutral stance. Deciding *not* to destroy Bryan's infrastructure after its president had been so adamant about his neutrality and denied *either* side free run of his system might have provided a carrot to go with Buccaneer's stick. But Gomez wasn't the SLN's most imaginative flag officer; his instructions had been unambiguous; and he'd carried them out to the letter. Fortunately, there'd been zero loss of life. In fact, Gomez had held his attack long enough for the Bryantese to evacuate even their pets from their orbital habitats. Not that his "restraint" was likely to earn the Solarian League any friends in the end.

On the other hand, that hadn't been the point of the exercise.

"You may be right, at least about how clearly we've put forward our version of things, Innokentiy," Agatá Wodoslawski said, "and I'll admit it's getting good play with the newsies and boards here in Sol. Whether or not we've convinced anybody else—anybody outside the Kuiper, I mean—is another question, though. And, frankly, I think the other side's claims about Hypatia are likely to undermine our efforts to portray Buccaneer as a measured response to the Manties' initial aggression. Especially given what I suppose you'd have to call the 'end game' there."

"Exactly," Abruzzi said. "Exactly! What in God's name was Gogunov *thinking*, Admiral?"

An excellent question, Kingsford thought, *however*—

"I believe he thought he was obeying his orders, Mr. Abruzzi," he said out loud. "The original time limit, as Mr. Kolokoltsov just pointed out, had been set by Vice Admiral Hajdu... after consultation with Ms. Yang-O'Grady."

He hid a smile behind a carefully grave expression as several of the civilian faces on the other side of the table tightened. Nathan MacArtney seemed particularly irked.

That was nice.

"Vice Admiral Hajdu's orders, in accordance with the directives the Navy had been given, emphasized both the need to make the strongest possible statement in Hypatia's case and the necessity of avoiding additional heavy losses, if at all possible. After all, we didn't want to add to the false impression of Manticoran invincibility."

He couldn't quite keep an edge of acid out of his last sentence. He was so *tired* of losing men and women in enormous numbers because they were so out-ranged by their adversaries. He was a naval officer. He understood people got killed in wars. He even understood that it was his job to spend however much blood it took to achieve the Solarian League's military and political objectives. But what truly pissed him off was that he'd been instructed to avoid heavy casualties not to keep people alive but because—as Abruzzi had put it at the time—"if your people can't keep from getting killed, it's really going to screw up our ability to sustain civilian morale."

"Well, he certainly didn't manage to accomplish *that* bit of his orders," Abruzzi said now, his tone bitter.

"No, he didn't, Mr. Abruzzi." Kingsford's liquid-helium voice was warmer than his eyes as he met the permanent senior undersecretary for information's glare. "Because there were already Manties in-system when he arrived, and he couldn't find them through their stealth."

And because he didn't look *for them, I suspect*, the admiral admitted to himself, *but I am* damned *if I'll give you one bit of ammunition, you prick.*

"When the Manties ambushed him, he had no option but to fight, and I believe his losses speak for how *hard* his people fought. And— again, as Mr. Kolokoltsov observed—he and Ms. Yang-O'Grady were both dead when the shooting stopped. So Admiral Gogunov—originally *ninth* in the task force's chain of command, I might point out—suddenly found himself faced with deciding what to do next. We're not sure if he's still alive. We do know there was at least one survivor from his flag bridge, so he may also have survived and be a POW at this time. Without the chance to debrief him, I can't tell you exactly what he was thinking, but I'd wager that a part of it was the clause in the Buccaneer ops order that emphasized its psychological objectives. His task force had just taken enormous losses. Under the circumstances, he may have felt that allowing himself to be deterred from maintaining the original time limit Vice Admiral Hajdu—and Ms. Yang-O'Grady—had set would have presented the appearance of weakness, and given the Manties a moral and psychological victory."

"Which they damned well ended up with anyway," Abruzzi pointed out, not giving a centimeter.

Kingsford's jaw tightened, but he couldn't dispute that part of Abruzzi's analysis. The Manties had scored an *enormous* psychological victory, and not simply for their own Navy.

"Maybe we can defuse some of that," MacArtney said thoughtfully. "What if we spin Gogunov's refusal to extend the deadline as a reaction to the Hypatians' treachery and the massive casualties his task force had already taken?"

"What do you mean?" Abruzzi demanded.

"Well, I know this is more your bailiwick than mine," MacArtney said in a so-why-didn't-*you*-think-of-this tone, "but as Admiral Kingsford's just pointed out, Vice Admiral Hajdu didn't know the Manties were there, and clearly in much greater numbers than they're prepared to admit. It's obvious neither they nor the Hypatians have any reason to tell us what the actual numbers were, and I'm sure they think understating their own strength adds to their aura of battlefield supremacy."

He grimaced, and Abruzzi cocked his head, listening intently.

"And the reason Hajdu didn't know they were there was that the Hypatian government hadn't told him. Or that they'd invited the Manties in—obviously *before* the referendum vote had been counted. So we have their outright act of treason in attempting to secede in the first place, their treachery in inviting the Manties in, all coupled with their decision to conceal the Manties' presence from Vice Admiral Hajdu and Madhura—I mean, Ms. Yang-O'Grady." He shrugged. "It's obvious the Manties were able to inflict such one-sided casualties only because they had the advantage of total surprise, and Gogunov would have known that as well as we do, just as he knew they had that advantage only because of the Hypatians' duplicity. Under the circumstances, and having just seen so many thousands of his fellow spacers shot in the back by the cowardly ambushers, as it were, he initially overreacted. But whatever he may have *threatened*, he never actually fired on the Hypatian habitats, did he? We might want to consider 'discovering' some com traffic between him and his successor in command—Yountz, was it?—in which he says he intends to relent in the end anyway. If we make it clear he's so furious he wants the Hypatians terrified—that he's looking for some *emotional* revenge in lieu of the wholesale massacre he couldn't possibly justify militarily—it'll actually make him seem more human, more believable. And, of course, in the end, our people not only withdrew from the system but did it *without* destroying the Hypatian infrastructure—which the Manties couldn't have prevented them from doing at that point, whatever might—or might not—have happened to our warships afterward, purely as a humanitarian gesture to a star system which damned well didn't *deserve* it after such unbridled treachery!"

He raised his right hand in front of him, palm uppermost, and arched his eyebrows at his fellows.

"You know, I may just be able to work with that," Abruzzi said, his expression much brighter than it had been.

Kingsford, on the other hand, kept his mouth shut only with difficulty.

He found it hard to believe there'd been only ten Manty ships in Hypatia, although to Thomas Yountz's credit, he'd steadfastly refused to inflate the enemy's numbers to make himself look better in his own report. In fact, based on his tac officers' data, he'd even suggested that some of the nine ships in the initial attack force had been decoys, not real ships. It was hard to believe anyone had drones capable of maintaining a false emission signature that powerful for such an extended time, but the Manties seemed to make a habit out of doing the unlikely, didn't they?

Even assuming they'd had twice the number of hulls Yountz had actually counted, though, that still came to no more than twenty. And unlike the civilians sitting in this room, Winston Kingsford knew what it had taken for a score of ships to walk deep into their enemies' range basket to attack eight or nine *times* their own number, and "cowardly ambushers" had no place in any description of them, however great their technological superiority might have been. He knew he couldn't ' admit his admiration for those men and women, for their courage and their willingness to lay down their lives for the people of someone else's star system. Not in this room. But whatever he or the Mandarins might be willing to admit, the rest of the galaxy—and especially the galaxy outside the League—would understand the Manties hadn't *had* to fight. That they'd *chosen* to sail straight into their own deaths to defend someone else. The consequences for the effort to demolish the Grand Alliance's reputation among the galaxy's neutrals would be very difficult to overestimate.

And that's one of the reasons you had such doubts about Parthian from the beginning, isn't it, Winston? he reminded himself scathingly. *You should never have even* listened *to Bernard and Salazar about that. Take out the infrastructure, sure, but don't kill everybody in sight! If you'd only shut them the hell up fast enough...*

What had actually happened in Hypatia was bad enough, in terms of its probable impact on galactic public opinion, but if Yountz had carried through on Gogunov's threat, if he *had* killed six or seven million civilians...

And it's frigging MacArtney who grabbed Parthian from the civilian side and ran with it, he reminded himself. *With* your *support, Mr. Abruzzi.*

Despite the most intense search he could conduct without going public, Kingsford had no idea who in the Office of Strategy and Planning had leaked Captain Mardyola Salazar's proposal to MacArtney after he himself had categorically rejected it. The *last* thing the Navy—*his* Navy—needed was to be accused of violating the Eridani Edict! Buccaneer would come uncomfortably close to that even without Parthian Shot, which made it particularly important that they not pile avoidable civilian casualties on top of it.

If he ever *did* find out who'd leaked that proposal to MacArtney, he'd turn the guilty party into dogfood. He'd really wanted to think it must have been Salazar herself, but his investigation had fully cleared her. Yet *someone* had leaked it, and the man who ran Frontier Security had been more than desperate—and vengeful—enough to embrace it.

Indeed, he'd clearly hoped there *would* be mega casualties somewhere along the line. And he'd managed to talk his fellow Mandarins into supporting it, as well, despite Kingsford's opposition, on the grounds that without Parthian the SLN would look weak anytime it backed away from a star system protected by an Allied squadron or two.

He'd salved his conscience at the time by hoping his commanders in the field would recoil from killing innocent bystanders in job lots. Thinking about that now, he felt only scathing, richly deserved contempt for his own naivety. No, for his own deliberate self-delusion. It had been an act of moral cowardice to rely on his subordinates' willingness to disobey the orders they should never have been given in the first place. Even if it hadn't been an abdication of his own responsibilities, he should have known how having Parthian in his back pocket would affect the thinking of someone like Martin Gogunov. He'd expected better out of Hajdu Győző when he chose him to command TF 1030, but looking back with bleak honesty, he knew he'd been deluding himself there, too.

But what could I do when civilian command authority made it a direct order, damn it? Maybe I should have resigned instead of smiling and accepting the directive, but who would the five of you have put into the CNO slot if I had? Another Crandall? Another Filareta? Another Byng? God, I hope there aren't two of him in the Service! But whatever my thinking, I didn't resign, did I? And now you want to turn the fact that somebody disobeyed your orders only because someone else had her pulser in his ear into our get out of jail free card?

The thought was bitter as gall, but voicing it would do no good.

"It is true Admiral Yountz could have executed Buccaneer, despite the tactical situation," he said instead, once he was certain he had control of his voice. "It's probable he would have gotten several thousand more Solarian spacers killed, but he could have."

"I think Nathan's onto something here." Kolokoltsov frowned, his eyes narrowed in thought, apparently oblivious to Kingsford's qualifier. "Especially since all the other strikes went so well."

"Aside from Admiral Isotalo's raid on Ajay, you mean?" Kingsford managed to kill the anger in the question, but it was a very near thing.

He still didn't know what had happened to Jane Isotalo and Task Force 1027. Aside from the fact that not a single one of her battlecruisers had come home again, that was. From the handful of Vice Admiral Santini's surviving screening units, it was obvious the Manties had arranged a devastating ambush on the Ajay side of the terminus. Just how they'd pulled that off, especially when Isotalo had been careful to scout the wormhole before taking her battlecruisers through it, was something he'd dearly love to know... and they weren't saying. It seemed likely the same LACs—or whatever the hell they were—they'd used when they caught Santini with his hyper generators down had played a role in the disaster, but there was no way to be sure, and the last thing they needed was to jump to any conclusions—any *more* conclusions—over what Manty tech could and couldn't do.

"Of course, Admiral." Kolokoltsov had the grace to look a little abashed. "No one's forgetting the price the Navy's paid. If it sounded like I was trivializing what happened in Ajay—or Hypatia—I certainly didn't intend to."

"Understood, Sir," Kingsford replied.

"I agree with everything Innokentiy just said." Abruzzi sounded about as sincere as the honesty quotient in a typical Information news release, and Kingsford's answering nod was just a bit brusque.

"What's your overall assessment of Buccaneer at this point, Admiral?" Kolokoltsov asked before Abruzzi could say anything else.

"My overall assessment is that, from a military perspective, it's been reasonably—but not completely—successful, Mister Secretary," Kolokoltsov said in a more formal tone. "Losses were extremely heavy in the cases of Hypatia and Ajay, but we were completely successful, with light to no casualties at all, in the other six Phase One attacks. We hit targets across an arc of well over four hundred light-years and served notice to the Manties and their allies that if they want to prevent additional attacks, they'll have to disperse their naval forces much more broadly. Obviously, that will reduce the threat of what they might be able to do with their 'Grand Fleet.' I'm not in a position to assess the degree to which Buccaneer's having the desired *political* effect. The only thing I can say on that front is that our analysis over at ONI suggests we're probably hardening hostility against the league in the Verge and—especially—the Fringe. But by the same token, we knew that was likely to happen going in."

"What was it that old pre-space philosopher said?" MacArtney said with a harsh chuckle. "Something about it's better to be feared than to be loved?"

"I believe the actual quotation is 'It is better to be feared than loved, if you cannot be *both*,' Sir." Kingsford stressed the conjunction. Slightly. "The philosopher in question was a gentleman named Niccolo Machiavelli," he added as MacArtney's eyebrows rose in surprise.

And the only reason I signed off on Buccaneer in the first place is that you and Frontier Security have damned well made sure we can't "be both" in the Verge, the admiral added with silent, bitter venom. *I only hope to hell we aren't busy making sure the Manties can.*

"At the moment, I'm afraid, we'll have to settle for being feared,"

Kolokoltsov said, as if he'd read the admiral's mind. "And, that being the case, where are we on Phase Two?"

"We're into the prep stage, Sir," Kingsford replied. "To be honest, the decision to divert additional battlecruisers and cruisers to... peacekeeping duties in the Protectorates is cutting into our readiness."

"You have *how* many battlecruisers?" MacArtney asked, bristling instantly. "Something over four thousand, I believe?"

"Five T-months ago, Battle Fleet and Frontier Fleet between them had four thousand four hundred and twelve in active commission and four hundred and sixty undergoing routine overhaul," Kingsford replied in a precise tone. "At that time—as Admiral Rajampet had mentioned upon occasion, I think—we were at least twenty percent understrength for our *peacetime* missions in the Verge and Fringe. Specifically, Mr. MacArtney, in the Protectorates. Since that time, we've lost in excess of four hundred of those ships—and their crews—and given the obsolescence of our superdreadnoughts, virtually the entire burden of fighting this war is falling on that class of ships. We have an additional hundred and eighty or so in the Reserve and we're mobilizing them as rapidly as possible, but they won't even compensate for the ships we've lost since the shooting started." He held MacArtney's eyes coolly. "Under the circumstances, diverting those additional ships to the Protectorates has cut *significantly* into our readiness posture."

"Excuse me, Admiral, but the entire reason we *have* a Navy, is to—" MacArtney began hotly.

"That's enough, Nathan!" Kolokoltsov's sharp tone drew an indignant look from the permanent senior undersecretary of the interior.

"Nobody's arguing that we can afford to let the Protectorates go," Kolokoltsov said impatiently. "That's the reason we're fighting this thing in the first place instead of just taking our ball and going home. But the Admiral needs to be able to tell us the truth, whether we want to hear it or not, and it's not *his* responsibility to justify how we got into this mess in the first place. It's *ours*."

MacArtney locked eyes with him for a moment, then inhaled sharply and looked back at Kingsford.

"Innokentiy's right, Admiral." It sounded grudging, but he didn't flinch. "We don't need to take out our frustration on you for a situation that was none of your making."

It wasn't exactly an apology, Kingsford reflected, but it would do until something better came along.

"I can certainly understand your frustration, Sir," he said out loud. "Trust me, we have quite a bit of that over at the Admiralty right now, too."

"I can imagine." For a change, MacArtney's smile looked completely genuine.

"Given what you've just said about force availability, how badly is Phase Two likely to be delayed?" Kolokoltsov asked, turning his attention back to the admiral.

"That's difficult to say, Sir." Kingsford shrugged. "Our force posture is changing daily, of course. We'd demobilized most of the remaining superdreadnoughts and redistributed their crews to the battlecruisers and lighter units coming out of the Reserve—and to serve as cadre for the new-build battlecruisers as quickly as we can get them built. I've ordered that process reversed—enough, at least, to fully crew a hundred and fifty or so SDs. Deploying wallers for routine system security duties is wasteful, to say the least, especially from a manpower perspective, but one of them ought to be impressive as hell out in the Protectorates, and using them to ride herd on our more restive systems will let us recall the battlecruisers we've already deployed. Since they now constitute our primary striking force, I've *got* to be able to concentrate them closer to hand. It would help, to be honest, if I could stand down the planning and prep for Operation Fabius."

"I think that may be out of the question, Admiral." Kolokoltsov's expression was troubled. "If making a point about Hypatia was important, it's likely to be even more important to make one in Beowulf's case."

And just how well did that "point" work out in Hypatia, Mister Permanent Senior Undersecretary? Kingsford thought bitingly.

"Sir, with all due respect, Fabius would be a death ride."

"That's not the way you seemed to feel a month or two ago, Admiral," MacArtney pointed out.

"A month or two ago, Sir, I hadn't had the opportunity to study the intelligence reports which have come across my desk since. Nor had I had the opportunity to evaluate what happened to Vice Admiral Hajdu. I remind you that there were no fixed defenses in Hypatia and, so far as we know, every missile they fired came out of the *internal* magazines of *cruisers*." Kingsford shook his head. "If Beowulf is covered by superdreadnoughts and pre-deployed heavy missile pods, we'd be lucky to get recon drones close enough to locate targets for even a Parthian launch, much less actually get the birds away."

MacArtney looked thunderous, but Kolokoltsov raised a placating hand.

"No one wants to send the Navy on any 'death rides,' Admiral. And, to be honest, I think that for the moment we might want to delay implementation of Phase Two of Buccaneer, as well. What we've already accomplished is having a significant effect on Core World public opinion. All of Malachai's polls agree on that point. And the Manties' losses are a big part of that."

Really, Mr. Kolokoltsov? And just what "Manty losses" would those be? Kingsford wondered. The ludicrously inflated Allied losses appearing in the official news releases were particularly galling to the man whose men and women had paid such an exorbitant price in blood for the Manties' *actual* losses.

"Under the circumstances," Kolokoltsov continued, "I think it might be advisable to...postpone Phase Two."

"I won't pretend a pause wouldn't be welcome, Sir. It would give us time to build up our stores of the new Cataphracts, and I have a message from Admiral Kindrick about a new weapon system she wants to show me out at Ganymede. The last thing anyone needs to do is to start believing we can come up with a miracle weapon by just snapping our fingers. On the other hand, Technodyne's R and D people seem to think this one—they call it 'Hasta'—may represent a significant enhancement of our combat power, and Kindrick concurs. Given how skeptical of Technodyne's claims she tends to be, that suggests there may really be something to their claims this time around.

"A hiatus in Buccaneer would give me more time to evaluate whatever it is they've come up with and to reorganize our deployments. At the moment, we're still badly off-balance, and the diversions to reinforce the nodal pickets covering both the Protectorates and our frontier with Talbott are only making that worse. The Manties' seizure of so many wormholes is playing as much hell with our naval movements as it is with merchant shipping, and what should be routine deployment orders are...a bit more complicated than they used to be." He grimaced at his own massive understatement. "If I can get all the Phase One units back to base and do a little judicious rearrangement, I can build much more balanced task forces for Phase Two if and when we resume Buccaneer."

"I can see a lot of merit to doing all that, Innokentiy," Wodoslawski said, and Quartermain nodded her head emphatically.

MacArtney—predictably—looked rebellious, but Abruzzi finally nodded, as well, albeit with less enthusiasm than Quartermain.

"So can I," he said. "At the least, it'll give us the opportunity to massage the message we already have out there. It'll let me hear back from focus groups in at least the closer Core Systems, too. Boundary, Faraday, Sebastopol, Lunacy—some of the others." He twitched an unhappy frown. "I hate how fast this whole thing is moving. There's just not time to do enough opinion sampling to establish real trend lines anywhere except right here in Sol, and this time I'm afraid we need to reach a lot broader audience than usual."

Now, *that* was a refreshing admission, Kingsford thought. For as long as he could remember, no one in the federal government had given much of a damn for public opinion outside the Sol System. In fairness, most of the Core World member systems—the only ones that had counted, when one came down to it—didn't much care about federal policy. *They* were insulated against its bureaucratic intrusiveness, so the only opinions that really mattered when it came to formulating those policies were those of the professional governing class and those who made their living from the government, in one way or another.

To be fair, thinking "inside the Kuiper Belt," as a Beowulfan newsie—who'd been almost as annoying in his time as Audrey O'Hanrahan was in hers—had labeled it over two T-centuries ago, worked both ways. The people inside it didn't worry about anyone *outside* it; too many of the people outside it never gave a single thought to what went on *inside* it; and he'd been just as submerged in that mentality as any civilian bureaucrat. Well, maybe not quite *that* deeply, he amended. After all, he and the Navy had been responsible for enforcing federal policy—outside the Core, at least—which meant they'd had to be aware of its real-life consequences. But he'd never given any more thought to *protesting* that policy than any of those fat-and-happy Core World civilians.

Until now.

"So, we're agreed about temporarily halting Phase Two?" Kolokoltsov looked around the conference room until everyone, including MacArtney, had nodded, then turned back to Kingsford.

"I think that's all we really needed to talk about today, Admiral. Thank you for coming and for being your usual clear-spoken self."

"It's what you pay me for, Sir."

Kingsford smiled, but he didn't climb out of his chair yet, and Kolokoltsov arched one eyebrow.

"If I may, I just wanted clarification on one point, Sir," the admiral said.

"Which point would that be Admiral?"

"Fabius, Sir." Kingsford shrugged. "It would help my redeployments even more if I could take Fabius off the front burner. It's using up a lot of staff time over at Strategy and Planning, and trying to build up the reserve for it is tying down over two hundred battlecruisers that aren't available for use anywhere else. And, as I've just explained, barring some totally unforeseen technological development, our ability to execute a Buccaneer-style attack on Beowulf is effectively nonexistent."

"No," Kolokoltsov said firmly, and shook his head when Kingsford opened his mouth again.

"I understand your point—your points, plural, I should say, Admiral. And I fully accept their validity. But I'm afraid there may be circumstances under which we'd have no choice but to commit to Fabius, despite our probable losses and even if the prospect of success was...dim. I know you don't want to hear that. For that matter, I don't want to say it, and I pray we'll never have to *do* it, but the possibility does exist. So I'm afraid we need a plan for it, and I'm sure you'll agree that we also need to continuously update that plan in light of anything we learn about the enemy's capabilities—or vulnerabilities— and in light of any of those 'unforeseen technological developments' you just mentioned. If we have to do this in the end, if we have to send your spacers out on a forlorn hope, they have to at least go with the best, most comprehensive battle plan we can possibly give them."

SNS Maya Sector Bureau
City of Shuttlesport
Smoking Frog System
Maya Sector

"so you want me to believe my ace reporter—the guy who taught me everything I know, I think you've been known to suggest upon occasion—doesn't have a clue what this is all about?" Laura Lochen tipped back in her chair, her heels propped inelegantly on her desk. An enormous Beowulf Manx cat, who rejoiced in the improbable name of Ziggy, lay curled on her blotter, rumbling a purr that threatened seismographs all over the city of Shuttlesport, and the tumbler in her hand was half-filled with amber liquid. Fifteen minutes ago, it had been completely filled. "Is *that* what I'm supposed to believe? Tell me it ain't so!"

"At the risk of tarnishing my halo," Christopher Robin replied, reaching for the bottle which had been three quarters full of the same amber liquid, "I have no idea at all. Zip. *Nada*. *Nichts*. Zilch. Zero. *Rien. Ingenting. Ničego.* Not a—"

"Oh, shut up!" Lochen told him with a laugh. "I swear to God, Chris, you spend more time dredging up obscure languages than anybody else I know. And I also know you only do it to be irritating. At which, may I say, you succeed admirably."

"Why, thank you, Boss!" Robin was ninety-seven T-years old, twice Lochen's age, but she was the Solarian News Services bureau chief here in the Maya Sector, whereas he was simply her senior reporter.

Which suited him just fine, he thought, pouring more Glenfidich into his glass, then recapping the bottle and setting it back on the desk between Ziggy and Lochen's left heel. She was young, sharp, and obviously on her way up, whereas the Maya Bureau was way out in the sticks, by SNS's standards, definitely still in the minor leagues. But that also made Maya an excellent place for future big-league stars to gain experience and seasoning, and that was exactly what Lochen was doing. Personally, he gave her three more years—five, tops—before the home office sent her on to bigger and better things.

He'd miss her, when that happened, but he wouldn't *envy* her. For himself, Robin found Smoking Frog a pleasant beat, far removed from the Core World cesspools he'd covered as a brash young newsy. He wouldn't go so far as to say he was in his sunset years, but he had fewer ulcers and slept far better than he had when he'd been considered one of Old Chicago's top half dozen political reporters. These days, he regarded himself almost more as a coach than a player, somebody who'd made his mark as a starter in the majors and now was content to pass his experience along to the next generation before the fresh line of warriors took up the battle in his place.

He suspected the home office thought of him that way, too—whenever it happened to think of him at all—given the number of younger, upward-bound newsies like Lochen it kept sending out to Maya. He couldn't think of any other reason for it to keep cycling people as good as she was through Smoking Frog. For the last several T-decades, the Maya Sector had been about as quiet and orderly as it was possible for a Protectorate sector to be, notable primarily for the dearth of exciting news it generated.

Up until the recent excitement over Congo and Torch, at any rate, and as far as he could tell, nobody in the home office had been especially interested in the reportage Lochen and her people, including one Christopher Robin, had produced on that.

Probably killed it because they didn't want to be accused of giving the Ballroom good press, he thought now. *Just like them. Lord knows I hated the contortionist act Editorial insisted on when I was covering Old Chicago. Doesn't look like it's gotten any better since, either. Especially with all this crap about the Manties!*

After twenty-three T-years watching the Star Kingdom of Manticore, the People's Republic of Haven, and Erewhon from uncomfortably close range, Christopher Robin knew what *he* thought about the allegations of Manty imperialism and warmongering. Unfortunately, Malachai Abruzzi had made the League's official position on those issues crystal-clear, and SNS wasn't going to buck Education and Information. The editorial board probably wouldn't have disputed Abruzzi's version at the best of times. They certainly weren't going to do it at a time like this.

But at least I don't have to add any fuel to Malachai's bonfire, he reminded himself. He'd known the current permanent senior undersecretary of information back when Abruzzi had been only a particularly ambitious and unscrupulous young apparatchik, and the man hadn't improved with age. *I meant it when I told Laura I don't know what Barregos is up to. Doesn't mean I don't know he's been up to something for the last few T-years, though. I guess somebody who still thought of himself as a* real *reporter would've dug up all the bodies and dumped them in the middle of the town square just to run up the notches on his pulser while he watched the fireworks. That's what a good, crusading muckraker does, isn't it? But with the entire galaxy going up in flames, I will be* damned *if I pile on. Besides, it's* Barregos.

He'd been astounded when he realized how much that last fact weighed with him, because he couldn't remember the last time he'd genuinely admired a Solarian politician. On the federal level, at least; there were probably at least a half-dozen—maybe even a full dozen—honest *local* politicians in various individual system governments, although he reserved judgment on that. His time covering politics in the League's capital city had only refined, tempered, and polished his contempt for the career political bureaucrats who ran it, and he'd learned far too much about the Office of Frontier Security along the way. Yet Oravil Barregos, not simply a career bureaucrat but an *OFS* bureaucrat, had actually earned his admiration and respect. He'd given the people of the Maya Sector good governance—*honest* governance, for that matter, when the best anyone had a right to expect out of an OFS governor was that he'd be an efficient administrator while he stole everything that wasn't nailed down.

Christopher Robin wasn't about to nominate Barregos for sainthood, and he recognized someone who enjoyed the exercise of power when he saw it. God knew he'd covered enough of them in Old Chicago, and most of them had enjoyed their power because of the perks that came with it. Because of the way the monumentally corrupt system churned out wealth, privilege, and ego-polishing affirmation of their *right* to power. Yet there truly were some people who enjoyed it simply because that was what they were really good at, because they knew they could do it better than ninety percent of the human race and they needed an avocation that *challenged* them. And there were even some, although they were the rarest subspecies of all, who enjoyed it because it gave them the chance to serve their communities. To make those communities better places to live, not worse.

Any successful politico had to be a fusion of all three at some level, he suspected, and especially the ego-polishing bit. A shy and retiring wallflower was unlikely to embrace the bare-knuckled scrum of politics, after all. Unfortunately, the vast majority of *Solarian* politicians tended towards the model of the Mandarins and fell into the first of his categories. There was some of that in Barregos, too; Robin knew that. Yet if wealth and privilege were what he truly desired, he could have acquired both in prodigious quantities during his time here in Maya, and he hadn't. So, yes, he almost certainly was "up to something," and Robin privately expected tonight's news conference to be...

illuminating, to say the least. But the bottom line was that at the end of the day, he *trusted* Oravil Barregos.

And because he did, he wasn't about to help anyone in Old Chicago crap on him, *whatever* it was he had in mind.

He lifted his glass in silent toast to the sector governor and smiled as he remembered something one of his own mentors had said to him long, long ago.

"The real trick to slanting a story," she'd told him, "is less the way you record it than what you choose to record—or not—in the first place." She'd smiled over her beer mug and reached for another pretzel. "Leave out the right things, and you can make Buddha or Jesus sound like Attila the Hun without ever misquoting him once!"

So, maybe I'm making Attila sound like Buddha by following the same policy, he thought now. *I suppose it's possible. But I'll take my chances with Barregos. A man has to do* something *worthwhile in his career!*

✧　　✧　　✧

"Good evening," David Willoughby, Governor Barregos's chief information officer and public spokesman, said briskly. "Thank you for joining us tonight."

The news conference—which was going to be rather less of a "conference" than anyone outside the administration suspected—was being recorded for later broadcast throughout the entire star system, and he knew the various talking heads were waiting in their studios to interpret whatever he was about to say. For that matter, most of them were probably quietly—or not so quietly—fuming over the fact that they'd been given no pre-broadcast transcript. That was sufficiently unusual that it should have given all of them a clue something out of the ordinary was afoot, Willoughby reflected. And given the current galactic situation, "out of the ordinary" meant rather more than it did in more normal times.

Despite that, there were only three newsies actually in the studio, trying to stay out of the way of the technical crew as Willoughby faced the smart wall configured into dozens of individual windows, most occupied by someone attending electronically. The vast majority of reporters had stopped physically attending news conferences even before humankind left the Sol System for the stars, and tonight even two or three of the windows were blank, un-tenanted. Willoughby noted who those windows were assigned to and hid a smile as he contemplated them. This was one scoop they were going to be sorry they'd missed.

"I'll get straight to the point," he told his audience—physical and virtual alike. "As all of us know, the galaxy at large has been in what we might charitably call 'disarray' of late. Here in our isolated corner, we've seen very little of it, despite our proximity to both the Republic of Haven and, courtesy of the Hennessey and Terra Haute termini, the Star Empire of Manticore, as well. Our relative quiet has been a vast blessing, and our local affairs—and economy—are in excellent shape, despite the problems the Federal Government is facing. *Maintaining* that quiet, however, has recently become…significantly more difficult, shall we say. In fact, it's become much more difficult than the man or woman-in-the-street has realized."

Willoughby's expression was composed but somber, and Christopher Robin frowned as he leaned forward in his chair, fingers flickering across his virtual keyboard to jot notes and bookmark video clips. He knew Willoughby well. They'd had a quiet dinner and drinks less than two weeks ago at MacAlton's, one of the capital's better restaurants and brewery bars. The other man hadn't even hinted at any significant stories at the time, and he wondered if David had even realized one was coming. With some politicians' spokespeople, that might have suggested a put-up job, a fabricated news item, to Robin, but that wasn't Barregos's style. Besides, Robin didn't think that was David's *official* somber face, the one he donned when the situation went to what the two of them jokingly called Shitcon One. Nor was it the one he used for Shitcon Two or even Shitcon Three. Those were all canned expressions, ready to be trotted out when needed. This looked…genuine. His voice might be calm, his tone even, but there was a tension in its depths and something that might have been excitement flickered in the backs of his eyes.

"The sector government became aware of some of the threats to the sector's security some time ago, even before the regrettable incident at New Tuscany precipitated the present tension between the League and Manticore and its 'Grand Alliance' with Grayson and the Republic of Haven. Certain steps were put into motion at that time to protect against those potential threats to our citizens' lives and property. Very recently, however, Governor Barregos, Lieutenant Governor Brosnan, Admiral Rozsak, Brigadier Allfrey, and Director of Sector Intelligence Wise have become aware of a new, more insidious, and potentially far more dangerous threat to the entire Maya Sector and even our neighboring sovereign star systems."

Robin's eyes narrowed, and he glanced at Lochen. She was tipped back in her chair, keyboard deployed across her lap in her favorite relaxed note-taking posture, but there was nothing relaxed about her eyes, and he gave a mental nod of approval. His protégée's instincts had obviously picked up on Willoughby's body language.

"It's time all of our citizens were made aware of that threat," the press spokesman said. "And to do that—"

He took a half-step back from the podium in front of the cameras, and waved one hand in a gesture which combined respect and introduction.

"Ladies and gentlemen," he said, "the Honorable Oravil Barregos, Governor of the Maya Sector."

Laura Lochen's chair came upright and she swallowed a muffled oath. None of the handouts had even hinted Barregos would be present in person. It wasn't totally unprecedented for him to meet the press in an unscripted environment, but during all his time in the Maya governorship, he'd held less than two dozen mass news conferences, and his individual one-on-one interviews were always booked well in advance. Why was *he*—?

"Good evening, ladies and gentlemen," Barregos said briskly. "I realize my presence was unexpected, but I think you'll soon understand the reason for it. As David's already informed you, tonight's briefing will be broadcast system-wide in one hour. My purpose in inviting you to attend while it's recorded is to give you the opportunity to prepare your own commentaries and coverage before that happens. Please be aware that I am also invoking the Official Secrets Act, however. What I'm about to say is *not* to be leaked, with or without attribution, until it's officially released for broadcast. Please believe that any violations of that restriction will be punished to the full extent of the law, should they occur."

He looked into the camera, his round face and usually deceptively gentle expression stern, and Robin nodded to himself. The OSA gave the government carte blanche to classify anything it wanted to and forbid anyone from reporting on it, and the penalties were draconian. *No one* violated it, especially out here in the Protectorates. He found it interesting that the despotic, neo-barbarian Manties' outdated and oppressive monarchial government had far less authority to dictate to the press. No one had ever been able to explain to him why it didn't when the Solarian League, that noble defender of all that was right, good, and free, *did*.

"I have a statement and an announcement to make," Barregos continued, after giving his audience time to digest his warning. "I will entertain no questions tonight, but we are arranging a press conference here at the Governor's Residence for tomorrow morning. It will be an 'old-school' physical conference. I will take questions only from reporters actually in the room, and private citizens will be admitted to it on a first-come, first-served basis, up to the limit of available seating. Those citizens will also be permitted to ask questions of their own. That conference will be carried live throughout the Maya System and transmitted as expeditiously as possible to every other system in the

Sector. It will also be communicated to Old Chicago and the Federal Government."

A *news conference* would be "communicated" to the Federal government? Robin blinked. Why in God's name—?

Barregos adjusted the display projected above the podium, deliberately allowing the silence to hum for several seconds. It was obvious that was why he'd done it, since once he finished adjusting it, he never looked once at the text only he could have seen.

"Beginning well over a T-year ago," he began, "in light of the increasing uncertainty of the interstellar situation—first with the resumption and intensification of the war between the Star Empire of Manticore and the Republic of Haven, then with the attack by 'parties unknown' upon the Manticore Binary System, and finally with the high state of tension and actual violence between the 'Grand Alliance' and the Solarian League Navy—Admiral Rozsak proposed, and I authorized, certain steps to safeguard our sector as much as possible out of our own resources. It seemed only prudent to us to develop that capability, given our distance from the Core Worlds and the likelihood that the Navy would find itself fully committed—even overcommitted—in distant areas of the Verge and Fringe and be unable to respond as rapidly or as strongly as it no doubt would have preferred to do. The wisdom of our decision has, I think, been clearly demonstrated. Because of it, last October, we were able to successfully defend our neighbor and ally, the Kingdom of Torch, against an Eridani Edict violation which would have resulted in millions of casualties without the intervention of our valiant naval forces under Admiral Rozsak's command."

He looked into the camera levelly, meeting the eyes of his entire audience.

"Their losses were heavy, far heavier than any of us expected or have found easy to live with. Nonetheless, without the measures we'd already taken, Torch would be a cinder today. And, as I said, that, alone, would constitute a full and total justification for those measures. But it would now appear they were even more justified than we previously believed."

Robin caught his lower lip between his teeth. It was an old habit—the way he kept himself from whistling in surprise. He'd expected something significant, but the way this seemed headed...

"About six T-months ago," Barregos continued in that same, level voice, "our intelligence agencies became aware of certain clandestine meetings between individuals in some of our sector's neighboring star systems and an unidentified outside power. Those... surreptitious contacts included Kondratii, Cossack, Meroa, and Cimbri. In no case had the contacts been with the systems' *governments*, however."

Robin's eyes narrowed. Each of those star systems, while nominally independent, was the effective property of one of OFS's favorite transnationals, courtesy of its own local kleptocracy, with Frontier Security looming helpfully in the background.

And there was plenty of unhappiness among their citizens because of their debt-peonage status.

"At the time," the governor said, "we had no insight into what those contacts might have been about, aside from the fact that they appeared to be directed at what one might reasonably describe, with or without characterizing the reasons for their motivation, as discontented elements. That struck us as ominous against the backdrop of tensions spreading across the Verge and Fringe in general. As a consequence, we redoubled our own vigilance here in the Sector and further accelerated the other measures we'd already put into place, but we found no evidence that the outside power in question had attempted to contact or influence any of our own citizens.

"Then, just over three T-months ago, that changed."

He paused, allowing his audience time to stiffen in speculation, then continued levelly.

"We here in Shuttlesport—I personally, in my office at the Residence—were contacted, very quietly, by someone who introduced himself as a representative of the Star Empire of Manticore. This individual had sought a meeting with me to propose what amounted to a declaration—or perhaps the proper noun would be a *reassertion*—of the Maya Sector's independence. A decision to evict the Office of Frontier Security, Frontier Fleet, the Gendarmerie, all the organs of the Solarian League, from the Sector and to renounce our agreed fee payments to the League for services rendered."

"Oh...my...God," Lochen murmured, eyes wide in disbelief, and Robin shook his head. Technically, as Barregos's use of the word "reassertion" suggested, the Maya Sector was an independent association of star systems which had voluntarily accepted a central Solarian administration, managed by Frontier Security under the SLN's protection, to "better regulate" their commerce with one another and with the galaxy at large. And so—*technically*—the sector's member systems were free to withdraw from that administrative network at any time they chose.

Just like every member system of the Solarian League was legally free to secede from the League whenever it chose. Until, that was, someone actually tried to *do* it.

"I did not agree to his proposal," Barregos said into the singing silence. "Nor did I *reject* it, however. It seemed wise to me to determine exactly what Manticore had in mind, since it's difficult to craft a response or a counter strategy without knowing what one is up against. So, I continued my discussions with Mr. Ellingsen—that was the name under which he'd introduced himself to me—and involved Admiral Rozsak, as well, as my military representative and expert. In fact, I wanted Admiral Rozsak, whose intelligence and opinions I deeply respect, to have the opportunity to evaluate both Ellingsen's offer and Manticore's potential motives.

"In the course of those further conversations, Mr. Ellingsen made it clear that it was the Star Empire which had been in contact with our interstellar neighbors. Moreover, he frankly acknowledged that Queen Elizabeth's government believed a declaration of Mayan independence— which they felt the Federal Government would see as a hostile act, especially given the steadily worsening tensions between Old Chicago and Landing—would force the Solarian League Navy to disperse its available starships, thus weakening its ability to attack—or defend itself against—the Grand Alliance. Although he was careful not to say so in so many words, it was evident from what he *didn't* say that the Star Empire's contacts with other star systems extended far beyond the Maya Sector. In effect, he was inviting us to participate in a grand strategic maneuver designed to provoke unrest, resistance, and outright rebellion throughout the Protectorates and among those Verge systems with the closest relations with the League, and the Star Empire was prepared to offer financial assistance, weapons, and naval support to anyone who would produce those things."

He shook his head, his expression even more serious than it had been.

"Needless to say, such a strategy had much to recommend itself from a Manticoran perspective. And let us be fair. Despite our own experiences here in Maya, there are many places in the Fringe, and not a few in the Verge, where armed rebellion against intolerable local conditions would be totally justifiable."

"Holy *shit!*" Lochen muttered. An OFS *governor* had just agreed that actual violent rebellion against League-sponsored local governments, or even *Frontier Security itself*, might be *justified?* When a copy of this got back to Old Chicago—

"Obviously, the citizens of Maya don't face such stark circumstances," Barregos went on. "It would, however, have been remiss of me as Maya's Governor not to learn all I could about Manticoran and Allied intentions and how they might affect my sector and the citizens for whose security and well-being I am responsible. So I continued my discussions with Mr. Ellingsen, and he went so far as to invite Admiral Rozsak to specify how many squadrons of ships-of-the-wall we would require to guarantee our security when we declared our independence and our solidarity with the Alliance. The Star Empire was, in short, prepared to dispatch an entire *battle fleet*, equipped with its latest and most modern weapons, to support us against the SLN."

Robin realized he'd stopped breathing and reminded himself to inhale.

"That was...an interesting offer," Barregos said with massive understatement, "not to mention a clear indication of how serious Queen Elizabeth was about this venture. On that same visit, Mr. Ellingsen brought me a personal recorded message from Sir Anthony Langtry, the Manticoran Foreign Secretary, thanking me for my willingness to listen to Mr. Ellingsen and reiterating the Star Kingdom's firm promise of military support. There could have been no clearer proof that the offer was genuine, real, and sincere."

He paused to take a carefully timed sip of water, then put the glass back down and shrugged ever so slightly.

"Under the circumstances, I was surprised but not really astounded when *another* Manticoran officer arrived clandestinely in Shuttlesport. I was somewhat taken aback by her seniority, however." For the first time, he smiled. It was a remarkably cold, thin smile. "One does not normally expect to see the Second Space Lord of the Royal Manticoran Navy, the commanding officer of Manticoran naval intelligence, in a Solarian sector governor's office."

"*What?*" Lochen's head whipped around and she stared at Robin. "Patricia *Givens* got in and out of Shuttlesport without our catching even a *sniff* of it? Holy Saint Francis, Chris! If I had balls, the home office would cut them off when it finds out we missed *that!*"

"Got right by me, too, Boss." Robin shook his head helplessly. "I mean, she *is* a spook, and a good one. I guess it's not *too* surprising that—"

"And you expect the home office to accept that line of reasoning?" Her expression was skeptical, to say the least.

"Well, no..."

"As I say," Barregos continued, saving Robin from any further response, "I was rather surprised to see Admiral Givens in my office. Not, however, as surprised as I was by what she'd come to tell me and why the Grand Alliance had believed her message was sufficiently important to be carried by someone I would have to take seriously."

Both reporters' eyes snapped back to the governor's face, and he shook his head slowly.

"Admiral Givens message was simple. The Star Empire of Manticore had become aware of what could only be described as a 'false flag' operation directed against it by the same entity they believed was responsible for the 'Yawata Strike' on the Manticore Binary System. In effect, someone else *claiming* to be Manticore was promising naval support—which he, she, or they had no intention of providing—to local resistance or opposition groups in order to foment violent rebellions against Solarian authority or interests in as many star systems as possible. The aim, she said, was to brand the Star Empire with responsibility for provoking bloodshed—bloodshed that would produce *millions* of deaths—as a cynical maneuver whose avowed purpose was to divert Solarian naval power from the direct confrontation with the Alliance. I'm sure all of you can imagine how the Federal Government would respond to that, but this, clearly, was also aimed directly at the Core World person-in-the-street, who would—quite reasonably—see it as a vile and treasonous ploy, only to be expected out of a star nation he's been told has raw, imperialistic designs on every star system within its reach. And, in addition to the fury the operation's instigators were certain it would provoke in the League, they intended to destroy Manticore's diplomatic reputation with everyone *outside* the League, as well. After all, what star system or star nation could ever trust the word of someone who'd deliberately provoked violence and open warfare in so many systems and then stood by and done nothing as the people they'd promised to assist were crushed by the local authorities, with or without League assistance?"

Robin's mouth had dropped open. Now it closed with a snap, and his eyes flared as he realized just how disastrous the consequences of the strategy Barregos was describing would have been for Manticore and its allies.

"Given the fact that Admiral Givens hadn't simply come to me in person but had brought with her conclusive proof of her own identity and a direct message from Queen Elizabeth which, unlike the one 'Ellingsen' had claimed came from Foreign Secretary Langtry, was in the Star Empire's official diplomatic encryption, I had no choice but to believe she was a genuine messenger for Manticore...and that 'Ellingsen' was not. That whoever was behind 'Ellingsen'—and Admiral Givens made it clear that the 'Grand Alliance' believes that that 'whoever' is this 'Mesan Alignment' they've been warning us about for some months now—they were prepared to see our entire sector rise in violent rejection of the Solarian League and be *destroyed* when the Solarian Navy responded in force, we called for the help we'd been promised...and absolutely no one came. *That* was what Ellingsen's masters, whoever they are, *wanted* to see happen here in Maya."

He paused to drink more water, and this time Robin couldn't look away to see how Lochen was reacting. The quiet sound of the glass, when the governor set it back down, seemed deafening.

"Then, just over two weeks ago," he resumed, "Mr. Ellingsen and a companion returned to Shuttlesport for the purpose, as they thought, of confirming our readiness to act as they'd suggested and to finish coordinating the promised 'naval support.' They were, needless to say"—this time his smile was a scalpel—"somewhat surprised when I ordered them taken into custody, instead. However," the smile disappeared, "*we* were surprised when the two of them promptly died right there in my office. According to our forensics experts, both of them died of completely natural causes... within less than a half minute of one another. And the minor shipping disaster which many of you may recall occurred at about that same time was the transport which had brought them to Smoking Frog blowing itself up in orbit. Twelve of Admiral Rozsak's Marines had just completed a lengthy ballistic free flight to board that vessel in an effort to take its crew into custody. All of them"—his eyes were bleak—"died in that explosion. Their next of kin have been or are in the process of being informed of the sacrifice those men and women made for all of us."

He inhaled deeply and squared his shoulders.

"I've given you this lengthy explanation in order to set the context for what I am about to announce. This is not a decision I've taken lightly, nor, to be totally honest, one which I began considering only in the last few months. It represents a response to a storm I've seen gathering for many T-years. I would never have predicted the form in which it's finally arrived, but I've believed—for a long time—that a storm *like* it was inevitable. And because it was inevitable, it was my responsibility to prepare against it, which I have done, with the able assistance of Admiral Luiz Rozsak and a handful of other courageous people. I do not put the measures we've prepared into action lightly, but I believe I have no option other than to do so.

"Understand me, ladies and gentlemen of the press, all of you watching this at home. I do not know—I think *no one* knows—whether or not the 'Grand Alliance' is correct about the existence of this 'Mesan Alignment.' On the face of it, it seems preposterous, ridiculous—*impossible!* But despite that, someone whose purposes are clearly inimical not just to the Star Empire of Manticore, or to the Republic of Haven, but to *everyone*, has attempted to draw us into an act of sector-wide suicide. Whether we call that someone the 'Mesan Alignment' or simply 'Parties Unknown' *does not* matter. What *matters* is that the forces trying to rip apart the entire explored galaxy have just proved even more dangerous than any of us had dreamed. And the fact that the people responsible for this have demonstrated such reach, such *audacity*, seems to me to clearly confirm that whatever we may think of the Manticorans' identification of their foe, they've been *absolutely accurate* from the beginning about the *existence* of that foe and the way in which the Solarian League has permitted itself to be manipulated by it. What I'm telling you tonight, ladies and gentlemen, fellow citizens, is that Manticore has been telling the truth and that some dark, malign force has set itself the task of destroying not simply the Star Empire and its Allies but *anything else*—including the entire Solarian League—which could possibly stand in the way of its own plans, whatever those plans may ultimately be.

"And that our Federal Government is doing precisely...what...it... wants...us...to...do."

The last half-dozen words were spaced out and heavy. He let them fall into a fresh pool of silence, and Robin swallowed hard.

"They are *so* never going to believe this in Old Chicago," Lochen murmured as the governor paused once again. "*Never!*"

"Maybe not," Robin conceded. Then he turned to look at her, his eyes level. "But do *you* believe it?"

She looked back at him for five or six breaths, then her shoulders slumped.

"Yes," she half-whispered. "God help me, I do."

"Then that's two of us," he said almost compassionately. "I—"

"When I realized that," Barregos resumed, snapping their eyes back to the display, "when I realized the government in Old Chicago was proceeding step-by-step towards the cataclysm our common enemy has designed for all of us, I knew what I had to do. Not without fear and trembling. Not without deep regret. Not without realizing how those who disagree with me will construe my actions, my decisions. But while the opinions of others matter, they do not—they cannot—dictate my actions. The only forces that can do that—the three judges to whom I appeal—are history, my own conscience, and the will of the citizens of the Maya Sector.

"And that is why I stand here tonight to announce that I am withdrawing the Maya Sector from its relationship with the Solarian League, effective immediately. All organs of the federal authority in the Sector now pass under local control. I appeal for calm, cooperation, the preservation of records, and the orderly continuation of our judicial, legislative, and regulatory procedures. As of tonight, however, the Maya Sector will become the Mayan Autonomous Regional Sector, an independent association of sovereign star systems."

Robin shook his head in disbelief. In the entire history of the Solarian League, no sector governor had ever declared himself in open rebellion against the federal authority in Old Chicago. The repercussions of Oravil Barregos's decision would rival—might well *exceed*—those of Beowulf and Hypatia's decision to vote on secession, because Barregos was venturing into totally uncharted waters. Beowulf and Hypatia had at least the *letter* of the Constitution on their side, whatever the League judiciary might ultimately decide.

All Barregos had was *moral* authority.

"My friends," the governor said, as though he'd heard Robin's thoughts, "no OFS-governed sector has ever before withdrawn from its relationship with the League, and so there is no legal precedent, either way, for my decision. I have no idea how the Federal Government will respond to it, although"—he actually smiled ever so slightly and shook his head—"I would be astonished if it's reaction is *good*. That, however, concerns me far less than *your* reaction. I've recorded and transmitted a message to every star system in the sector, summoning representatives of their system governments to Shuttlesport. I realize we already have delegates from those systems here in Smoking Frog, but I feel this steps far beyond any decision those men and women could have imagined they would be asked to make when they were sent here to help regulate trade and arbitrate civil suits. As such, I think it fit and proper that delegations specifically empowered to grapple with it should be sent here to do precisely that.

"When those delegations convene in Shuttlesport, I will lay all of my evidence, all of the reasons for my decision, before them. I will ask them to confirm my actions...or to reject them. Should they choose to renounce my decision, full responsibility for my actions will fall upon *me*, not the men and women of the Maya Sector. If, however, as I hope they will, they ratify my decision, then you and I, your wives and husbands and children—all of us—will have embarked upon a journey countless other men and women have made throughout human history. We will have taken our destiny into our own hands and told anyone—Solarian, Manticoran, unknown enemies, *anyone*—that we will chart our *own* path, make our *own* decisions, and that we will never be anyone's tool again. I know it's a frightening thought. I know many of you will find it difficult to agree with me. But *I* have no choice. I have responsibilities, obligations, *duties* which require me to choose a path, and so, I've chosen. In the ancient words of one of the leaders of one of Old Terra's great reform movements, 'Here I stand. I can do no other.'"

He paused, looking into the camera for endless silent moments, then drew a deep breath and nodded.

"Good evening, ladies and gentlemen," he said, and his image disappeared.

Admiralty House
and
Harrington House
City of Landing
Manticore Binary System

"SORRY I'M RUNNING LATE," Honor said as Spencer Hawke followed her through the door and peeled off to park himself beside it. "Last-minute details."

Commodore Mercedes Brigham followed Hawke, her personal tablet tucked under one arm, and Lieutenant Commander Tümmel brought up the rear.

"I can't imagine how anything like that could happen to someone with as much free time as the CO of Grand Fleet," Thomas Theisman said, pointing at the open chairs opposite him.

"There is a special place in the infernal regions for someone who makes mock of a subordinate's difficulties." Honor frowned repressively as she took one of the indicated seats and Nimitz draped himself comfortably across its back. Brigham took the chair beside hers, while Tümmel found a seat among the rows of aides, staffers, and other flag lieutenants parked well back from the table in the outsized conference room.

"'Subordinate'?" Theisman widened his eyes at her.

"I," she pointed out, "am not the Chief of the Joint Chiefs of Staff. Unlike someone else I could mention—in fact, unlike *three* someone elses I could mention—*I* am but a humble fleet commander."

Theisman snorted, although—technically, at least—she was right.

It had taken a while to get the Joint Chiefs formally organized and stood up. It was fortunate their improvised, interim arrangements had worked as well as they had, but nothing the size of the Grand Alliance could operate that way indefinitely. There were too many entirely legitimate differences of opinion and emphasis, and not simply in terms of strategy or tactics. Some body—some organization—had to be formally in charge of ironing out those differences, and thus the Joint Chiefs had been born.

He wondered if Judah Yanakov was as pissed off as one Thomas Theisman by the form it had finally taken.

Behave yourself, Tom, he scolded mentally. *Somebody has to do it, and you knew damned well it was going to be you from the Republic's side. If you didn't want the job, then you should've stayed an honest spacer and never dipped your toe into the cesspool of politics. And at least you know you've got a competent replacement. Not to mention the fact that Pascaline's a lot less likely to shoot you now that she's been let out of jail!*

He chuckled to himself at the thought, but he wasn't sure it was entirely facetious. Admiral Pascaline L'anglais had commanded the Republic's Capital Fleet because she was, in his opinion, one of the best flag officers—quite possibly *the* best flag officer, after Lester Tourville—the Republic had. If anybody was suited to command Task Force 2, Grand Fleet's Havenite component, it was L'anglais, especially since Tourville had been sent off to reinforce Michelle Henke's Tenth Fleet. In fact, she'd been supposed to command it from the beginning while he returned home to run the Department of War. Regrettably, from her perspective, his presence as Grand Fleet's second in command had been required for the confrontation with Filareta, which had delayed her own arrival.

She'd reached Manticore belatedly just over a month ago, and she and Honor had created a crisp, professional relationship based on their respect for one another's competence. It was, unfortunately, true that L'anglais wasn't entirely comfortable with the Republic's alliance with Manticore. She understood its necessity, and she wasn't a Manty-*hater*, but she found it difficult to put a lifetime's hostility between the two star nations completely behind her. On the other hand, Theisman had no qualms about her loyalty or her ability to take orders despite any private reservations she might cherish. She'd been the first People's Navy task force commander outside the Haven System to declare her support for the old Republic after he'd shot Oscar Saint-Just. As for the rest of her qualifications...

Honor's probably right that, bright as treecats are, they aren't necessarily the best judge of human tactical ability, but they pegged Pascaline perfectly when they decided to call her "Warrior." She'll hold up her end when the time comes.

And her arrival had freed him for other duties...damn it.

The Joint Chiefs of Staff consisted of himself, Sir Thomas Caparelli, and High Admiral Yanakov, who had (not without obvious grumpiness) transferred command of Task Force 3, the Grayson component of Grand Fleet, to Alfredo Yu. Each of them had an Assistant Chief of Staff, in his case that was Rear Admiral Alenka Borderwijk, who'd received a long overdue promotion to qualify her for the slot. The position of Chief of the Joint Chiefs rotated among Manticore, Haven, and Grayson on a monthly basis, which was rather more frequently than he'd originally hoped for. He'd been afraid that frequent a turnover would lead to all sorts of slippage and minor but irritating sources of friction, and so it might have, if not for Admiral Allen Higgins. He held the *non*-rotating post of Vice Chief of Staff, and it was his responsibility to maintain cohesion and continuity.

Theisman had been impressed by his competence, but he also understood why Caparelli, White Haven, and Honor had unanimously nominated him for that position rather than for fleet command. Part of it was his undoubted and indisputable ability. He was one of the most brilliant and well organized flag officers Theisman had ever met, and those two qualities didn't always travel together. But he'd also been the Manticoran commander when Operation Thunderbolt rolled over Grendelsbane Station.

It was Higgins who'd been forced to destroy twenty or thirty years of Manticoran investment and building capacity—not to mention the ships under construction in it—when the Royal Manticoran Navy learned the hard way that the Republic of Haven had acquired multidrive missiles of its own. The board of inquiry had endorsed his actions in the strongest possible terms, but that hadn't prevented Higgins from feeling he should have done a better job. That he should somehow have anticipated Havenite MDMs and found a way to prevent the destruction of his own SD(P)s and the sprawling base when not another soul in the Manticoran Navy or its intelligence establishment had even suspected what Shannon Foraker had been up to at Bolthole.

Then there'd been the Yawata Strike. The most devastating attack in the history of space warfare.

And Allen Higgins had commanded Home Fleet.

There hadn't been one damned thing he could have done about that attack, but it had been like watching Grendelsbane over again, only on an infinitely worse scale, and it had...broken something inside him. Theisman was no treecat, but he didn't need to be one to understand why the 'cats had christened him Shadow Heart, and he suspected Higgins's treecat partner, Sorrow Hunter, was what the 'cats called a mind-healer. He hoped so, anyway. Higgins was a good man...and the only person in the entire galaxy who blamed himself for what had happened.

If he could have, Theisman would have put him back on a flag deck in a moment, "back on the horse," as Honor put it. But that, in a sense, was what his command of Home Fleet had been, and the Yawata Strike was barely seven months in the past. Putting him back into space so quickly would have pushed him too hard, too fast.

Besides, we damned well need him right where he is!

"Well, now that our footloose and fancy free fleet commander component is here," he said, "perhaps we can get down to business."

Honor snorted, yet there was some truth to his description. Not the "footloose and fancy free" bit, perhaps, but as the commander of Home Fleet, she did hold a seat on the Joint Chiefs, although she was the only fleet commander who did. Her position—Vice Chief of Staff (Operations)—was a bit anomalous, since she was technically senior to Higgins but wasn't one of the rotating chiefs of staff and had no formal responsibility *to* the JCS. She wasn't certain she approved of that arrangement, but her command represented the Grand Alliance's mailed fist. Keeping her fully informed of the Joint Chiefs' intentions—and soliciting her input into those intentions—was essential, and as long as Grand Fleet remained based on the Manticore Binary System, it was at least workable.

"All right," Theisman continued, turning to Patricia Givens, who now rejoiced in the title of Assistant Chief to the Joint Chiefs of Staff (Intelligence), as well as Second Space Lord, "the floor is yours."

"Thank you, Sir."

Givens touched a control, the lights dimmed, and a file heading appeared on the table's smart top in front of each attendee.

"As you'll see, ladies and gentlemen," she began, "we now have confirmation of the attack on the Maize System." Her expression was grim. "Casualties were minimal, thank God, but the destruction of the Maize infrastructure was pretty much total. That brings to seven the number of 'Buccaneer' attacks of which we know—that includes Hypatia on the 'Buccaneer' list, rather than as a special one-off political operation—beginning with Cachalot."

She paused, looking up and letting her eyes circle the table.

"We have no reason at this time to believe we won't be hearing about still more of them shortly."

She gave that a moment to sink in, then tapped the control in front of her again, and the file header disappeared into neatly tabulated columns of data.

"These are the best numbers we've been able to generate, at this point, for the actual physical damage in each star system," she began. "Commander Lassaline is working to refine them, but for now, they're still based on a lot of estimating and computer modeling. More concrete numbers are still incoming, and Terry will see that all of you are updated as more definite data becomes available. I doubt that what we have so far is likely to change dramatically, however. It's certainly close enough for us to begin evaluating the overall impact, and as I'm sure you'll notice—"

✧   ✧   ✧

"So what do you think?" Theisman asked much later that evening, sitting back much more informally with Honor and Judah Yanakov.

Caparelli had been scheduled to join them for supper at Harrington House, but the Royal Orchestra was performing Hammerwell's "Saganami Rising" that evening. It was a tradition for the First Space Lord and First Lord to attend whenever that happened, which was why he and Hamish alike were running late. Honor hadn't known it was scheduled when she invited the others to supper, and she'd used the fact that her movements were more or less classified to avoid it. Only a handful of people knew she was on-planet, and much as she loved Hammerwell's music, she'd decided she needed a restful night "at home" more. She would have preferred spending it at White Haven, actually, but it turned out that Grand Fleet's CO's "restful night at home" was a bit more tightly scheduled than most. And since Hamish did have to attend the performance...

Theisman suspected Caparelli would have joined them, as well, cheerfully dumping the public appearance duties on his civilian superior. The First Space Lord, Theisman had discovered, was not a fan of classical music at the best of times. Dianna Caparelli, unfortunately for him, was, and she'd put her foot down—*hard*—when her spouse tried to weasel out on her.

Now Theisman sipped from his beer stein—he'd developed a decided partiality for a brew called Old Tillman—and swallowed appreciatively.

"*Is* there another flight of 'Buccaneers' inbound?" he continued.

"I don't know." Honor shook her head, gazing down into her own stein. "I'm inclined to think we've heard about all their 'first flight' strikes by now, despite how slowly news travels. I don't see any reason they couldn't have launched a lot more than just seven if they'd wanted to, though." She looked back up with a shrug. "By our best estimate, they've still got somewhere around four thousand battlecruisers, and they only used eight hundred or so of them between all the strikes we know about. They could've thrown a lot more than that at us."

"Maybe not, Honor," Yanakov said. Unlike the other two, he nursed a glass of Alfred Harrington's prized Delacorte. Now he waved it—gently, with the respect it deserved—for emphasis. "I think Commodore Lessem's point about the implications of the League's ability to produce so many missile pods so quickly is valid, but there's got to be a bottom somewhere, even to Solly productivity. I'm not surprised they can turn them out by the million—or even the *billion*—once they have a finalized design. Look at the rate at which *we* could churn them out before the Yawata Strike, or the way Beowulf's started gearing up to produce the Mark Twenty-Three now. But there has to be a limit, and in addition to simply building the things, they have to physically distribute them once they're manufactured. That ties up shipping and takes up time. *Lots* of time, actually, thanks to Lacoön. For that matter, unless we're prepared to assume Kingsford is as big an idiot as Byng or Crandall, they have to have prioritized the accumulation of enough of them to equip their equivalent of Grand Fleet, and that would take a good sized bite off the top of their stockpiles, too."

"So you're endorsing Pat's argument that they may have exhausted their initial ammunition loadout—or as much of it as they were prepared to expend on offensive operations—and need to pause to restock?" Theisman asked.

"I'm saying I think that could be a *factor* in a decision to pause," Yanakov replied. "I think there could be others, too, though, and like Honor says, if there were more strikes in their first tranche, we should've heard about them by now. That suggests to me that they *have* decided to pause."

"And I can think of several other reasons why they might have," Honor pointed out. "For one thing, if they're hoping to pull us off strategic balance, they have to give us time to redeploy. And they probably want to give other potential targets the opportunity to think things through, for that matter. The purpose of shooting someone as an object lesson is to convince other people to pay attention to it, and that takes time."

"I think that's a very valid point." Theisman nodded. "Besides, I wouldn't be surprised if they want see how this plays to their own electorate. They can dance around the point all they want, but even though they've managed not to kill several million people *yet*—thank God for Admiral Kotouč and Commander Petersen!—there's no way 'Buccaneer' is anything but an Eridani violation waiting to happen. This isn't like what we were doing to each other, Honor, especially with 'Parthian Shot' built into the matrix. I wouldn't be surprised if they want to bring Solly public opinion up to the point of accepting a genuine Edict violation in stages."

"You think they're really stupid enough to push it that far?" Yanakov's expression was grim, and his voice suggested he found Theisman's analysis only too plausible.

"I think it would be difficult to overstate the stupidity—from our perspective at any rate—of which the Mandarins are capable," Theisman said flatly. "If it were, they wouldn't be in such a deep hole already. The only reaction they've shown so far is to dig the damned thing deeper! What makes you think they're likely to abandon that now?"

"I can't think of anything," Honor acknowledged. "On the other hand, and much as I hate saying this, in a lot of ways 'Buccaneer' plays directly into our own overall strategy. I can't imagine anything more likely to engender universal revulsion in the Fringe—*or* to generate Core World backlash, for that matter, once the inner systems start really understanding what's happening."

Theisman nodded, his expression thoughtful. *He* couldn't think of anything more likely to delegitimize the Mandarins—eventually, after far too much destruction and far too many deaths—than Operation Buccaneer, either. Of course, that presupposed it was physically possible to get Core Worlders to actually *think* about what they were being told by Malachai Abruzzi's shills.

So far, the signs were less than encouraging in that regard.

"What *really* worries me," Honor went on, "is that Beowulf finally votes on the plebiscite week after next. I can't help wondering if they're waiting for the vote tally before they launch Buccaneer Two. And if the vote goes the way everyone expects, they're likely to feel a lot more pressure to up the ante."

"You think they'd go after Beowulf directly? With Admiral Truman sitting on the wormhole and Mycroft operational?" Theisman's skepticism was evident, and Honor shook her head.

"Even assuming they don't know about Mycroft—and I'm not about to assume they *don't*—Kingsford, at least, is smart enough to avoid tangling with Alice and her podnoughts. I suppose the Mandarins might overrule him. I could see MacArtney doing that—or trying to, anyway—but I really doubt Kingsford would go along with something that suicidal. On the other hand, all the indications are that they plan to spin Beowulf the same way they did Hypatia—an unforgivable act of treason, committed in blatant defiance of the Constitution, by a dishonest and corrupt system oligarchy eager to throw in its lot with the Star Empire and its neobarb allies in order to share in the loot when the Evil Manties invade the League and burn Old Chicago to the ground!"

She grimaced in distaste, and Nimitz flattened his ears in her lap.

"I'm sure they'd have done that anyway," she said, "but their entire justification for 'Buccaneer' is that they've been *driven* to it. When Beowulf bails—and they know as well as we do that that's exactly what's going to happen—it'll give them the biggest 'proof' yet of how *we're* the ones driving the entire confrontation. And with that justification in hand, do any of us really see them *not* pushing 'Buccaneer' to even bigger and better things? And if they do that, they're going to force us to rethink *our* options as well." She shook her head, her eyes more worried than she would have let most people see. "They really won't like it if they make us do that. I only wish I felt more confident *they* had a clue that they won't."

Naval Station Ganymede
Ganymede Orbit
Sol System
Solarian League

WINSTON KINGSFORD STOOD ON the observation deck, watching Jupiter's Great Red Spot sweep across below him, and his lips twitched in amusement as he contemplated the huge storm's longevity. The entire planet of Old Terra could have disappeared into its maw, and the amount of energy its outermost winds dissipated every single day was staggering. Yet the vortex stubbornly continued to survive, siphoning additional colder and hotter gases to provide fresh energy. Of course, this was the third Great Red Spot since humanity had started watching Jupiter. Debating climate models for the gas giant remained a contact sport even after all these T-centuries, but there was general agreement that there would *always* be a Great Red Spot somewhere on the planet. The longest interval between them had been less than fifty years, and this one was still expanding. Current models suggested it would be good for at least another two or three hundred years. Which meant that even with prolong, a "weather front" would outlast his entire lifetime. It tended to put the ephemeral nature of human existence into an interesting perspective.

Ganymede's smaller companion, Europa, with an orbital period only half as great, sped past between his current perch and Jupiter, and Io, the innermost of the four Galilean moons had just come over the gas giant's flank. The galaxy of constructs orbiting both Ganymede and Jupiter glittered in the reflected light of the planet, and he drew a deep breath and turned from the panorama.

"Never get tired of seeing that," he admitted to Willis Jennings, his chief of staff. "Not the same watching recorded video of it, either."

"No, Sir," Admiral Jennings said, although, for himself, there was no difference at all. Except that it felt colder somehow, perhaps. That had to be purely psychological, given the comfortable twenty degrees at which all SLN habitats were held. For some reason, though, he couldn't shake a sense that the temperature aboard Naval Station Ganymede's platforms was lower than that, as if the surface temperature of the moon—better than two hundred degrees below freezing—had crept outward into the sprawling base.

Nonsense, of course.

"Well," the CNO said, nodding to the commander who'd been assigned as his escort for the visit, "I suppose we should get to it. Lead the way, Commander."

✧   ✧   ✧

Naval Station Ganymede was the largest of the Solarian League Navy's installations, larger even than Naval Station Mars, despite the fact that the Jovian subsystem was less convenient to Old Terra than Mars. Even when Mars was in inferior conjunction with Jupiter, NSG was 550,000,000 kilometers—better than 30 light-minutes—farther from Old Chicago. At its nearest approach, NSM was a mere 46.8 million kilometers from Old Terra, whereas Ganymede was over 558 million away, almost twelve times as distant. One of the Navy's fast dispatch boats could reach Mars through normal-space in less than two hours, given that geometry; the trip to Naval Station Ganymede required well over six. The same dispatch boat could have cleared Sol's hyper-limit in little more than three hours, translated into the Alpha bands, and micro-jumped across the 35 LM between that point and Jupiter's 4.6-LM hyper-limit in only fifteen minutes. It would arrive at the Jovian limit with a relative velocity of effectively zero, however, and need two hours-plus to rendezvous with Ganymede, so the total flight time would actually have been over forty-five minutes longer.

There were times, Kingsford reflected, following his guide, when the old phrase "you can't get there from here" still applied.

Despite that, Ganymede had become a critical node for the SLN long ago. Jupiter's hyper-limit was far shallower than the system primary's, but that didn't explain NSG's primacy. Mars was much closer to the *Solarian* limit than Old Earth, after all. A battlecruiser arriving at the Jovian limit was two hours and thirty-five minutes from a dock at NSG; the same ship arriving at the Solarian limit was only eight minutes farther from a dock at NSM, and Mars was an enormous population node, which Ganymede most certainly was not. Jupiter, however, was the SLN's primary source of reactor fuel, and with such a superabundance of that fuel at hand, it had made sense to locate the Navy's major asteroid refineries and fabrication center in the same place. Ganymede's endless oceans of liquid water had been another major consideration. The "moon" was bigger than many of the galaxy's planets—it was the ninth largest body in the Solarian system, for that matter—with a fully differentiated interior, a molten metallic core, and more liquid water than Old Terra itself. Getting *to* it through so many kilometers of ice had been a significant engineering challenge in the early days of system exploration but posed no particular difficulty these days. And with access to liquid water and plentiful fuel, came an effectively unlimited supply of oxygen and hydrogen.

Given all of those factors, the Navy had decided T-centuries earlier to make Ganymede its primary base for both construction and interstellar deployments while Mars had become a subsidiary, responsible for supporting operations inside the system hyper-limit. That didn't mean the SLN had no other in-system bases or facilities. Given the sprawling nature of the Sol System's orbital infrastructure, there were nodes of naval activity scattered across an enormous volume. The system's civilian-oriented industry tended to be located around Mars, with relative proximity to both the belter refineries and to its consumers, who were heavily concentrated on Old Earth, Mars, and the orbital habitats around those two planets and Venus. There was plenty of additional civilian industry scattered around the asteroid belts, but it did tend to cluster around Mars. Military heavy industry, on the other hand, had long since co-located with NSG in order to be close to *its* primary consumer. Technodyne of Yildun, for example, employed upwards of a hundred and forty thousand roboticists, cyberneticists, nanocists, and construction workers on its Ganymede I platform, alone, without even counting the large R&D component the transstellar maintained where it would be handy to NSG...or vice versa.

Personally, Winston Kingsford had concluded—somewhat cynically, perhaps—that it was more a case of the latter than the former. Technodyne's relationship with the Solarian League Navy had been the dictionary definition of a "sweetheart deal"—or perhaps "incest"—for as long as any current-duty officer could recall. Up until that unpleasantness at Monica, Technodyne's management had tended to think of the Navy as one of *its* subsidiaries, rather than the other way around. In fact, if he was going to be honest, the admiral had to admit that the one thing about the disastrous current situation that warmed the cockles of his heart had been seeing so many Technodyne VIPs sent to prison and then watching their successors scurry around, frantically pursuing the technology the Navy needed not so much out of patriotism as out of *their* need to stay out of prison.

Now, Winston, he told himself. *Be nice. At least they've come up with the Cataphracts. Of course, you'd be a little happier about that if you didn't suspect they must've had a clearer notion all along of what the Manties and Havenites were up to than your own people did. They came up with that response just that little bit too quickly for them not to have seen something like this coming. Which does present the question of why they didn't warn you about it.*

In fairness—on those rare occasions when he was inclined to be fair to Technodyne—he had to admit that even if Technodyne had warned the Navy, someone like Martinos Polydorou, the recently (and forcibly) retired CO at Systems Development, would have ignored it. For that matter, he wasn't certain he wouldn't have ignored it himself, given the dearth of intelligence reports on the new technology being introduced out in the Haven Sector. The SLN had been focused on maintaining the technological status quo for a long, long time. When one had ten thousand superdreadnoughts in commission or reserve and every other navy in the galaxy combined possessed fewer than *one* thousand, one was unlikely to be interested in technology shifts that would make one's existing wall of battle obsolete.

That explains *what we were thinking*, he told himself now, grimly. *It sure as hell doesn't* excuse *it!*

Well, maybe what he was here to look at today might be a step in the direction of fixing things.

He hoped to hell so, anyway.

✦   ✦   ✦

"Admiral Kingsford. Good to see you, Sir!" the slim, brown-haired admiral said as the commander escorted the CNO and his chief of staff into the largest tactical simulator of the Solarian League Navy.

The vastness of the simulator made her look almost tiny—and she truly was sixteen centimeters shorter than Kingsford's own 183 centimeters—but she was solidly muscled and anything but fragile. She was also very young for her rank; even to someone accustomed to third-generation prolong, she looked like someone's teenage daughter, with a deceptively sweet looking face. In fact, Tory Kindrick was about the farthest thing from "a sweet young thing" imaginable, which was why Kingsford had chosen her to replace Polydorou as the head of Systems Development Command. She *was* young for flag rank in the SLN—only fifty-one T-years old—but she was also smart, ruthlessly efficient, and not too worried about making waves, which was why he'd jumped her straight from commodore to vice admiral to give her the rank for her new assignment. She'd hit SysDev like a long overdue typhoon, but she'd also been in place for little more than two T-months and the task she'd inherited was similar to Hercules' stable-cleaning assignment, only worse.

"And it's good to see you, too, Tory," he said, shaking her hand. "Is this trip going to be as interesting as your reports have suggested?"

"I actually think it may, Sir. For a change," she said, and Kingsford chuckled.

If there was a flag officer in the Solarian League Navy who had a lower opinion of Technodyne's management team and philosophy than Kindrick, Kingsford couldn't imagine who it might be. That was another of the reasons he'd chosen her for SysDev. She had a lot of respect for Technodyne's technical capabilities, and he wasn't afraid her attitude towards management would prejudice her against any good ideas the R&D teams threw up, but she was clearly disinclined to cut the transstellar any more slack than she absolutely had to. That made her a highly critical audience whenever the corporate offices sent a glowing prospectus her way.

"I'm still wading through about six or seven petabytes of reports and analyses," she went on as Kingsford released her hand and she shook Jennings's in turn. "This one was marked urgent, though, and I'm inclined to think they got it right for once."

"You said you thought this one might be even more important than Cataphract."

Kingsford's tone made the sentence a question, and she nodded.

"It's not going to be as...tactically flexible, let's say, as Cataphract, especially not if they keep tweaking the Cataphract booster stage's performance."

She waved politely for Kingsford and Jennings to precede her towards the tactical crew waiting for them on one of the simulator's command decks. At the moment it was configured as the bridge of a *Scientist*-class superdreadnought, and she escorted them across to the tactical section. The tac stations were up and manned, Kingsford noted, glancing at the waiting master display. At the moment, it was configured on the system scale, and he saw what looked like a squadron of superdreadnoughts sitting almost motionless at a range of just over three light-minutes.

"But I don't think we should really consider this as much a tactical system as a *strategic* one," she continued as they walked. "Deploying it won't be anything I'd call simple or logistically efficient, but if it works as well in the field as it has in the sims and the test program, it'll be worth the complications."

"Really?" Kingsford crooked one eyebrow, allowing a carefully metered skepticism into his tone, but she nodded firmly.

"Really, Sir. I had my doubts when I skimmed the initial proposal, but the thing is, it actually works, and we didn't have to invent a single new piece of hardware—well, we did tweak a few subsystems we already had—to put it together. The *software*'s a radical departure from anything we ever deployed before, and we've upgraded the computer's core processors to make it work, but we've been through over forty live-fire tests of actual prototype weapons without a single failure. That doesn't mean everything will work as effectively in action, since we've got such piss-poor evaluations of the tech it'll be going up against, but from a systems reliability perspective, it's probably on a par with a Javelin or Trebuchet."

Kingsford felt his other eyebrow rising. For Kindrick, especially where Technodyne was concerned, that constituted not simply a ringing endorsement but giddy enthusiasm!

"So it's a *mature* technology?" Jennings asked.

"Its current components are, Sir," Kindrick replied. "That's not to say it can't be improved upon. I'm looking at ways to upgrade laserheads and final-phase penetration aids, for example. At the moment, we're fitting the Cataphract-B's final stage and Mod-Eleven laserhead, but I don't see any reason we can't improve on that. We ought to be able to replace the current terminal stage with a bigger one; probably as big as the Cataphract-C's, or even a little larger, I'd guesstimate. It'd mean redesigning the base stage's fuselage—might be more accurate to call it a 'hull,' really, given the dimensions we're talking about—but the basic drive and support systems wouldn't even have to be scaled up. Only the physical dimensions of the structure they're mounted in."

"That all sounds good," Kingsford said. "Assuming it really does work. And that it performs as advertised."

"Oh, so far it has, Sir. In fact, you should see proof of that in about—" she checked a digital time display Kingsford hadn't noticed in the corner of the tactical display, counting steadily downward "—another nine minutes."

"Excuse me?"

"I'm afraid we've arranged a little surprise for you, Sir." Kindrick smiled suddenly, making herself look even younger. "The birds are already in flight. The Commander here"—she twitched her head at the tactical officer on the simulator command deck—"was under orders to initiate launch while I was walking you across. They're on their way in right now."

Kingsford looked at her for a moment, then turned to the display. It looked back at him with bland innocence.

"You've got actual live birds out there, on their way in—under *power*—right this instant?" he demanded, never looking away.

"Yes, Sir. They are."

"And how far out are your RDs?"

"Thirty million kilometers, Sir. Halfway to the launch platforms."

Kingsford shook his head. That was hard to believe, even after studying the précis she'd sent him.

Jennings stepped up beside him, then moved to look over the tac officer's shoulder.

"According to this, they're up to thirty-seven thousand KPS and less than five million klicks from the RDs...with almost *four minutes* left on the clock, Sir," he said.

The chief of staff sounded almost awed, and Kingsford didn't blame him.

"I think, Sir," Kindrick said, and when Kingsford turned back to her, her thin, hard smile looked neither young nor sweet, "that this is one the Manties will never see coming. In *every* sense of the word."

Board of Directors Room
Executive Building
City of Columbia
Beowulf System

"WELL, THANK GOD *THAT*'S over!" System Chairman Chyang Benton-Ramirez tipped back in his chair and raised a stein of beer at the holograph floating above it, where the final tally had just been posted. It was not, perhaps, the most Chairman-like posture he might have adopted, but it had been a *very* long night and none of his fellows on the Republic of Beowulf System Board of Directors seemed offended.

"What's that phrase your niece is so fond of, Jacques?" Director of Defense Caddell-Markham said, looking at the small, almond-eyed man sitting across the table from him. "Something about the end of the beginning?"

"She does have a taste for ancient quotations," Jacques Benton-Ramirez y Chou acknowledged. "Can't imagine where she got it. But you've got a point, Gabriel. Except that I'm not sure this is even as far down the road as ending the beginning. Seems to me it's more a case of *ratifying* the beginning."

"A point," Caddell-Markham acknowledged.

"A very *good* point, in fact," a tallish, blond-haired woman said. "I hope no one will be offended if I say, speaking as the Republic's chief attorney, how deeply relieved I am to be out of what I suppose we might charitably call a legally *ambiguous* situation."

Although Devorah Ophir-Giacconi was only sixty-eight, which was very young for a Beowulfan Director, she'd headed the Beowulfan Directorate of Justice for almost nine T-years now. She was smart, a highly respected member of the Beowulf Bar and a stubborn defender of the integrity of the legal process. Which, Benton-Ramirez y Chou reflected, undoubtedly explained her utter disdain for the Solarian League's current state.

"Oh?" He smiled at her. "You mean now that we're all *officially* traitors?"

A chorus of chuckles, some with a slight edge of nervousness, perhaps, ran around the conference room, and Ophir-Giacconi snorted.

455

"Actually, Jacques, I mean now that we aren't traitors *anymore*. Arguably, at least."

"Excuse me?" Konstantin Brulé-Chou raised both shaggy eyebrows. The Director of Human Affairs was almost eight centimeters taller than Ophir-Giacconi, but his legs were actually shorter than hers, and he was very broad shouldered and powerfully built. That probably helped explain his nickname of "Bear," but his heavy eyebrows, low hairline, and big, powerful hands had contributed their bit to its inevitability. "I'd think the fact that we just supervised a vote to secede from the Solarian League definitely makes us traitors, at least in Old Chicago!"

"No," Ophir-Giacconi said. "We were traitors while, as a member of the Solarian League, we were actively aiding and comforting a star nation—arguably, three star nations, really—who are in a state of war against the League. Now we're either an independent star nation or we're rebels, not traitors. There is a legal distinction. Our own judiciary's interpretation is that we just became an independent star nation again for the first time in seven hundred and seventy T-years through the legitimate exercise of our constitutional rights as a member system of the Solarian League. That means that—like any independent star nation—our foreign policy, including any military alliances we choose to make, is our affair and no one else's, so no one can accuse us of treason for whatever we decide. I doubt anyone in Old Chicago's interested in our interpretation, but it is a matter of public record. And as a nitpicking attorney, I'm glad to get out of the moral and legal middleground."

She probably had a point there, Benton-Ramirez y Chou acknowledged. There *was* a certain legal and moral...murkiness to the Republic of Beowulf's actions over the last seven months or so—starting with the decision to warn both Landing and Nouveau Paris about Filareta's impending attack—regardless of how justified its position might be.

It was still difficult for him to realize Beowulf, the primary mover behind the creation of the Solarian League, really, was in the process of destroying it. The grief he felt, sometimes, when he contemplated that, was almost overpowering. But there'd never been an alternative once Innokentiy Kolokoltsov and his fellows refused to acknowledge even the possibility of the Alignment's existence and doubled down on their conflict with Manticore and her allies, instead. The Mandarins' effort to scapegoat Beowulf for the disastrous outcome of Operation Raging Justice had only underscored his star system's lack of options, and the decision to call a plebiscite to consider secession had made itself. Nor had anyone been surprised by the results flashing in the hologram above the conference table, either—except, perhaps, that the margin in favor of secession had been even wider than anticipated.

That was Hypatia, he thought grimly. *My God, what were those idiots thinking? Creating something like "Parthian Shot" is like passing out pulsers to angry children! It's a miracle Kotouč and Petersen were able to prevent Hajdu and Gogunov from killing six or seven million people in an afternoon. And how much longer can we go on dodging that pulser dart?*

"I suppose you've got a point, Devorah," he said after a moment. "I doubt if anyone in Old Chicago's going to bother his head a lot about whether we're traitors or 'just' rebels, should the opportunity for any legal unpleasantness arise, but it is sort of nice to be out of the shadows."

"Definitely." Caddell-Markham nodded vigorously. "And not just because now everyone knows where we stand. Ninety-two percent in favor?" He shook his head. "I know some of the eight percent will refuse to accept the result, and as someone who always thought of himself as a citizen of the League, I can't say I don't understand. But nobody will ever be able to say there wasn't what you might call 'broad support' for our actions. And one of the other things *I'm* grateful we can do now is let Manticore and Haven park some of their wallers close enough in to cover the inner system, not just the terminus."

"Is that really necessary?" Board Secretary Joshua Pinder-Swun asked. Caddell-Markham looked at him, and Pinder-Swun shrugged. "I was under the impression we didn't really need a bunch of capital ships to do that now that Mycroft's operational."

He looked a little nervous, and Benton-Ramirez y Chou wasn't surprised. Mycroft's capabilities as a defensive umbrella were fundamental to almost all of the Grand Alliance's planning. If those capabilities were less than advertised...

"We may not *need* 'a bunch of capital ships,' but that's not the same as saying they wouldn't be good to have," the Director of Defense said. "It's sort of like checking your backup grav pack before you get on your grav ski, Josh. Odds are, you'll never need it. If you *do*, though, I believe the operable adverb becomes that you'll need it *badly*."

"I agree with Gabriel," Director of Technology Saana-Lebel said. The grandson of a Havenite refugee who'd fled the People's Republic, Saana-Lebel had been one of the strongest supporters of the Republic of Beowulf's current foreign policy. "Mycroft is a really extraordinary achievement," he went on, "and I'm more impressed than ever by what both Manticore and Haven—especially Haven, given the state of its prewar educational system—have accomplished. But it's not guaranteed to be leakproof."

"Even if it were, nobody's told the SLN about it," Caddell-Markham pointed out. "It's sort of hard to be deterred by something you don't know exists."

"True." Benton-Ramirez y Chou nodded. "And let's face it. Even if they *did* know about it, they've shown an unwavering ability to walk straight into one buzz saw after another. I have to think even the Mandarins and the SLN can learn if they get enough people killed along the way, but I don't think it's possible to overestimate just how big a stop sign these people really need."

"Agreed," Caddell-Markham said. "Which is why I'm so happy we can move them farther in-system. By this time, even the geniuses in Old Chicago have to've figured out they *don't* want to tangle with Manticoran or Havenite ships-of-the-wall. They might be more willing to take a chance against *our* ships, though, especially if they think they can stack the odds heavily enough in their favor. That's why what they threw at Hypatia—especially the number of missile pods they brought along—scares me. Less for what they could actually accomplish against us than for what I'm afraid they may *think* they could. So if there's a chance it'll convince them discretion really is the better part of valor before we kill another million or two of their spacers, I'm all in favor of waving the biggest stick they *know* we have at them just as threateningly as we can!"

George Benton Tower
City of Old Chicago
Old Earth
Sol System

INNOKENTIY KOLOKOLTSOV LEANED BACK in the self-adjusting comfort of his chair, pinched the bridge of his nose, and blinked weary eyes at the ceiling. It was late—very late—and he felt the midnight stillness in his bones. The outer wall of his office was configured to transparency, looking out over the gorgeous, magical lights of the largest city in human history. Old Chicago's monumental towers marched out into the waters of Lake Michigan like Titans, their flanks glittering with constellations of earthbound stars, and a full moon gazed serenely down like an ancient silver coin.

He couldn't hear the never-sleeping city's voice from the soundproofed sanctuary of his office. Sometimes he could. Sometimes he configured the sound system to feed from the microphones mounted on George Benton's flanks. Usually, though, it was soft music that floated in the background while he worked. Sometimes ancient Pre-Diaspora composers, but more often more modern works. He even had a secret taste for the new Zerschmetterte Musik his wife's nephew had introduced him to, although he'd never admit that by listening to it here in the office.

But there was no music tonight. There was only silence, broken only by the soft bubbling of the meter-and-a-half waterfall tumbling into the koi pond in one corner of the office. It was, admittedly, a soothing noise, but it was so soft it seemed to perfect the silence, rather than break it. He thought about turning on the microphones, or telling the office AI to pick something random from his music library, but he didn't.

There were some things better contemplated in silence.

He stopped pinching his nose, picked up his cup of coffee, and climbed to his feet. He carried the coffee over to the wall, sipping from the self-heating mug—the big liter-sized one he used only on the long nights, when he worked alone and no one could see the depth of his addiction—while he gazed moodily out across the beauty that disguised such an ugly reality.

459

I wonder how many other people have stood looking out across cities like this and wondered what the hell they were going to do next? he thought. *I guess this kind of view is one of the perks of being a big shot. Too bad it doesn't do a damned thing to help you figure out how to un-fuck the worst damned mess you've ever contributed to.*

Oh, how he wished he could lay the responsibility for all of this off onto someone else! In some ways, he could; his fellow "Mandarins"—even they had started using the pejorative that smart-arse O'Hanrahan had pinned on them—had contributed at least as much to the disaster's preconditions as he had. And he could legitimately argue that Nathan MacArtney and Rajampet Rajani, between them, had contributed one hell of a lot *more* than he had. Rajampet, in particular, with his inspired personnel choices like Josef Byng, Sandra Crandall—even Massimo Filareta!—couldn't have done more damage if he'd *wanted* to do. Indeed, there were moments Kolokoltsov almost wished the Manties were onto something with their hysteria about secret conspiracies and genetic supermen out for galactic domination. It would be so comforting to think he and his bureaucratic colleagues were the victim of malign manipulation rather than a bunch of frigging idiots who'd managed to shoot the entire Solarian League in the foot out of sheer incompetence.

But if he'd ever been tempted to believe there was a word of truth in the Manties' and Havenites' "explanation" for their actions, the cascade of reports pouring in from the Fringe—and even the Verge—would have quashed the temptation.

His jaw tightened as the dull throb of rage rippled through him once more and his nostrils flared.

What had happened in Mobius was no longer a single straw in the wind. Dozens of similar situations were being reported. Some of the reports came from systems where carefully fomented unrest had already spilled over into open violence; others were from systems whose panicky OFS administrators—or, in some cases, even more panicky local oligarchs—had simply become aware that someone from outside was stirring the pot. All those people were screaming for help, for support—for the Navy! And as the fresh threat to the Protectorates and their already strangling revenue streams mounted, they'd had no choice but to send that support. To slice it off of Kingsford's available strength. Thank God they'd decided to postpone the second phase of Buccaneer! But those diversions were eating away at the Navy's available battlecruiser strength like acid. Whether this was the Manties' work or not, its effects couldn't possibly have suited their purposes better. And whoever it was, they had to get to the bottom of it. Had to find the guilty parties and stop this sort of crap before it got still worse. That was the reason he'd demanded an independent analysis of every known instance of... artificially induced unhappiness in the Protectorates.

He'd handed that task to Brandy Spraker. Not only was Spraker one of the best analysts Foreign Affairs boasted, but she'd also been openly skeptical of arguments about Manty imperialism from the outset. She had to be aware "Manty imperialism" was the party line, the justification for the League's policy vis-à-vis the Star Empire, but she'd stubbornly refused to toe that line. MacArtney had read a couple of her scathing dismissals and demanded Kolokoltsov fire her and replace her with someone who, as MacArtney put it, "was at least smart enough to figure out water's wet!"

Kolokoltsov had considered pointing out that he wasn't too sure MacArtney was aware of that fact, himself. He hadn't. Instead, he'd simply kept Spraker exactly where she was, doing exactly what she was doing, because even if it was... inconvenient to have her dispute his own policy justifications, even if only in-house, he needed that kind of honest criticism. The last thing he'd wanted to do was to buy into his own cover story!

Especially now. Over the last few T-weeks, he'd found himself wondering if perhaps he hadn't inadvertently told the truth about Manticoran motivations. It had struck him as unlikely, but not nearly so unlikely as the Manties' version of what had happened in Mobius. They actually wanted the galaxy to believe that somebody else, pretending to be them, was running around fanning the fires of rebellion? Ridiculous! No, it was far more likely they truly had been looking beyond the Talbott Sector from the very beginning.

Spraker hadn't believed that. That was the reason he'd assigned the job to her, and she'd delivered her report this afternoon.

"I'm sorry, Sir," she'd said. "I'm really sorry, but... it looks like I've been giving you bad analysis for months now."

"Don't be silly, Brandy," he'd chided her. "The one thing I know for sure is that you've been giving me your *best* analysis."

"Maybe I have," she'd said heavily. "But maybe I haven't, too. Maybe I've just been willfully blind because I couldn't see any sane motivation for the Manties to deliberately go up against the Solarian League." She'd shaken her head. "Maybe I just didn't give enough weight to their analysis of the balance of military power. Maybe that's why I thought somebody as smart as they've always been would never *deliberately* pit themselves against the League. And the truth is, I still can't think of any rational reason for them to do something like that. But I've come to the conclusion that I was wrong."

He'd looked at her, trying to hide his own conflicting sense of dismay and grim, satisfied justification, and reminded himself to go slowly.

"Wrong in what way, Brandy?"

"I won't pretend I'm really satisfied with some of the data we're getting from Frontier Security even now, Sir," she'd said, and he'd nodded. That was another thing he treasured about Spraker. She was thoroughly aware of the way in which OFS and, to a lesser extent, the Gendarmerie tended to "cook the books" in the data and analyses they passed on to Foreign Affairs, and she factored that into her own analyses.

"Having said that, though, I've turned up some evidence—pretty damning evidence, really—of exactly what Nyhus over at Frontier Security's been claiming. Evidence that didn't come from *him*."

"Really?" Kolokoltsov had tipped back in his chair, his eyes intent, and she'd nodded unhappily.

"Yes, Sir. I've verified at least the basic accuracy of his version of what happened in four different star systems, and I've turned up at least two others that fit the same profile but that he never mentioned in any of his reports. That's bad enough, but I've also confirmed that some of them started well over a year ago. In fact, it looks like some of them may have started as much as two T-years ago, or even a little longer."

She'd paused, looking at him, and he'd drawn a deep breath and gestured for her to continue.

"There are at least three that fit that timeline, Sir, including the one that came to a head in the Loomis System ten months ago. In fact, Loomis is a pretty good example of what seems to be going on. When the 'Loomis Liberation Front' went up in flames in January, everyone thought it was the result of purely internal factors. God knows the situation had been festering for quite a while."

An angry light had flickered in her eyes. Despite her position—or possibly *because* her position gave her a far better appreciation than the average Solarian for how it worked—Brandy Spraker was not a great admirer of Frontier Security or the Protectorate system in general.

"Unfortunately, about two T-months ago, the Loomis System authorities captured one of MacFadzean's—she was the Liberation Front's leader—last remaining cell leaders. He's been executed since, but under interrogation, he was very bitter about the false promises of naval assistance they'd been made. Apparently, that was a tightly held secret within the LLF, which is why no one reported it earlier. Either that or somebody on the ground—probably with the local OFS office—had picked up on it and concealed the fact to cover her arse. Wouldn't want to admit they'd missed something like *that* being orchestrated right under their noses, would they?"

"No, I imagine they wouldn't."

"I'm not saying that's what happened, Sir. I think it could've been, though. At any rate, if this guy—his name was MacGill, and he seems to've been the last member of their senior leadership on the loose—was telling the truth, MacFadzean was first contacted by someone claiming to represent the Manticorans as early as May or June of last year. Sir, that was *at least* six T-months before the New Tuscany Incident. So either we have to accept that somebody who knew New Tuscany was coming half a year before it ever happened—more probably at least a full year, really, given the time needed to find MacFadzean and allowing for travel time—orchestrated all of this to make us blame Manticore for it, or else it really has been the Manties all along."

"Is the timetable equally clear for any of the other incidents?" Kolokoltsov had asked quietly.

"According to the Manties' own chronology, someone—of course, they claim it was someone *else*—initially contacted Breitbach's organization as early as July of last year. That's still four months before New Tuscany. Same thing's true in at least four other cases. It might be as many as five, but we can't nail down the sequence at Locklear from what we know now. So unless we're ready to accept that the 'Mesan Alignment' really exists and really has the reach to manipulate not just Fringe star systems but our own naval deployments, it has to've been Manticore all along." She'd shaken her head disgustedly. "Maybe you should get yourself an analyst who can find her own backside, at least if you let her use both hands."

"I see."

He'd gazed at her for a moment, then stood and walked around his desk to her and extended his hand.

"I can't tell you how much I've always appreciated your honesty, Brandy," he'd said. "I know you'll always tell me the truth as you see it. And the fact that you walked into this office to tell me you've decided you'd been wrong only underscores the fact that I can't afford to lose you. I want you to stay on this. And I want you to tell me if you see anything—*anything*—that conflicts with Permanent Senior Undersecretary MacArtney's people's analysis going forward. You're my watchdog, my sentinel. I shouldn't admit this, but I don't fully trust OFS Intelligence, myself." He'd waved one hand. "Oh, I know all the ministries have their own axes to grind, their own rice bowls to guard, but Frontier Security's too willing to think of itself as *the* essential organ of the Federal Government. We can't afford to have their view of their own importance shaping the intelligence narrative. Not at a time like this."

"I understand, Sir," she'd said, "and I'll give you my best. It may not be as good a 'best' as I used to think it was, but whatever it is, I'll give it to you."

"I already knew that, Brandy," he'd said, gripping her hand firmly. "After all, it's what you've *always* done."

He'd meant every word he'd said to her, but now, as he sipped coffee, gazing out over that glittering lightscape, he let the anger flow through him, thinking about it. Thinking about the bastards' sanctimonious superiority. About the way they'd *lectured* him on the difference between their own moral, upright foreign policy and the Solarian League's. The contempt in their eyes and their voices. The *arrogance* with which they'd claimed their pissant little Star Kingdom wasn't simply *equal* to the Solarian League. Oh, no! It was *better* than the League. It intended to *replace* the League as the beacon of hope and progress to which the galaxy should aspire. And the entire time they'd been doing that, they'd been spreading their poison in the Protectorates. It made sense of this entire "Lacoön" strategy of theirs, too. They'd recognized the Federal Government's Achilles' heel, its dependence on the cash flow from the Protectorates and its shipping and service fees. And so they'd started lighting fires all across the Fringe to destabilize the Protectorates and the revenue stream they generated, and then deliberately smashed the League's interstellar economy to finish off that cash flow once and for all.

And the timing even makes sense, he thought bitterly. *We didn't begin to realize how much technological superiority their navy had, but they knew. And they also knew that once we* did *figure it out, we had the basic tech and the industrial base to* bury *them under their own new weapons. But only if they gave us time. And so they set this whole thing in motion, then took advantage of that incredible, frigging stupidity at Monica—and of Byng's anti-Manticore biases—and manufactured this whole damned military confrontation to accomplish their goals before we could rebuild the SLN into something that could* crush *them like the insects they are. And that fucking idiot Rajampet and his good friend MacArtney stepped straight into their trap with Byng, Crandall, and Filareta. Hell, and I went right along with them.*

That, he realized, was what really stuck in his craw. He'd thought he was the one calling the shots, gaming the situation with all his accustomed, polished expertise, because he'd had the entire Solarian League at his back and the League always called the shots. But it hadn't been that way at all. No, the Manties had *played* him, manipulated *him* even more surely than they had any of those poor damned fools in the Fringe, and that was an offense Innokentiy Kolokoltsov would never—*could* never—forgive.

But what could he do about it? They were right about their technological superiority, and Wodoslawski and Quartermain's projections said their basic strategy was working. The government's debt, and the interest it was compelled to pay to borrow more, were spiraling upward like the helium level in the heart of a star. The Federal Government was so huge, so vast, that its collapse would be like a slow-motion shipwreck—initially, at least. Wodoslawski, especially, was warning that when the end came, it would come quickly and catastrophically. That everything they'd done to stave it off as long as possible would only make the ultimate collapse even more devastating. They might be able to sustain the current spending levels for six more months. Perhaps even as many as seven. But then, unless they could come up with some fundamentally new funding mechanism to tap the bottomless potential wealth of the Solarian League, the ship would founder.

And we can't *find a new mechanism,* he thought despairingly. *Any other government in the frigging galaxy could enact new taxes, generate new revenue streams. But not us. We're stymied by the damned* Constitution.

It was right there in Article I. The Federal Government could not, under any circumstances, enact any form of direct or indirect taxation not generated by levies on interstellar commerce and/or specific services it provided. Indeed, it used the very words "under no circumstances."

We need to find some way around that, but how? How do we do it without admitting what we've been doing in the Protectorates all along? Without validating *the Manties' claims about our rapaciousness? In order to convince the Assembly to let us fix the problem, first we have to tell them what the problem* is, *and that's a public relations battle we can't win. Not the way things stand now. Even if we introduced legislation, and even if someone didn't run straight to the Judiciary, it would only take a single vote—*just one—*to kill any statutory authorization to collect taxes. And the last thing we can afford at the moment is to call a constitutional convention to amend Article I. The way feelings are running all across the League right now, not even God knows where* that *would end! But—*

The musical chime of his official com floated across the office, and he turned from night-struck Old Chicago with a frown. He always had to leave word of where he was with his staff, but who'd have the temerity to screen him this late at night?

He stomped across to the desk with ill grace.

"Identify caller," he growled.

"Admiral Winston Kingsford, Chief of Naval Operations," the office computer responded, and his frown deepened. He'd thought Kingsford was all the way out at Ganymede!

"Accept," he said.

"Transmission is a recorded message," the computer told him. "Message length eleven minutes and seventeen seconds."

"Recorded?"

The computer didn't respond to the obviously rhetorical question, and Kolokoltsov's nostrils flared.

"Very well. Play recorded transmission."

"Message commencing," the computer said, and Winston Kingsford appeared on Kolokoltsov's desk display.

"I hope I haven't caught you at an inconvenient moment, Sir," he said, "but if you have a few minutes, there's something I need to tell you about. I expect"—he smiled quickly—"you can always put me on hold until it *is* convenient, but I think this is something you're really going to want to hear."

The CNO stopped speaking for a moment, obviously giving Kolokoltsov the opportunity to pause the record until a better time. Then he continued, his eyes bright and intense.

"I know I'm the one who's warning everyone not to think in terms of magical equalizers," he said. "And I don't think that's what we've got here. But I've just watched a full day of simulations and three live-fire demonstrations of a new system. I caution you that it isn't on the same level as what the Manties appear to be capable of, but, in some ways, it's close. *Very* close. In fact, Sir, it's close enough that—in sufficient numbers—I think it may be an actual game changer.

"They call it 'Hasta,' and I don't want to tell you *too* much about how it works in a transmission, however good our encryption is. But without going into the details of *how* it does what it does, let me tell you a little bit about its potential.

"First—"

OCTOBER 1922 POST DIASPORA

HMS *Imperator*
Manticore Binary System

"WE MEET AGAIN, MR. Harahap," Honor Alexander-Harrington said ironically as Damien Harahap followed the Royal Manticoran Navy captain who'd greeted him in HMS *Imperator*'s boat bay past the pair of tough-looking green-uniformed men stationed on either side of the hatch. The compartment beyond was much more spacious than anything he'd ever before experienced aboard a warship, Solarian or Manticoran, and the long table was covered in a spotless linen cloth and set with glittering tableware.

"Your Grace," he responded, and Clean Killer made a cheerful sound of greeting. That was probably for the Duchess, Harahap reflected, looking at the cream-and-gray 'cat on Harrington's shoulder. He was only just beginning to learn about treecats, but he rather doubted that a telepathic species needed aural greetings when they met.

"If you'll come have a seat, I'll introduce you to my other guests," she invited, waving him towards the table, and he nodded and followed her towards it. It was the first opportunity he'd had to watch her move, and he was struck by the grace of her carriage, despite the weight of *her* treecat. It was even more impressive in a woman—in anyone, really—her height.

And it probably helps that she's from Sphinx, he thought. *All that heavy-grav musculature* has *to make it easier for her to manage the weight!*

According to his research, Clean Killer was larger than most males, but he was still a bit smaller than Harrington's Nimitz, and Harahap had discovered that carting him around was an excellent way to burn any excess calories that might find their way into his system. It wasn't an impossible task, by any stretch of the imagination, and the 'cats clearly had strong opinions about the proper way for their humans to transport them, but he was still getting used to it. It was fortunate they had so many limbs. That let them dig into their human partners' reinforced, claw-proof shirts or jackets to support the majority of their weight low on their backs. That helped a lot, especially with balance issues.

Not that it made the little beasties one gram lighter.

469

Clean Killer made another sound, this one soft and amused, and Harahap felt himself smile as he realized the 'cat had followed his thoughts, or at least his emotions. In fact, he had to wonder where the division between thought and emotion truly began and how treecats perceived it.

There'll be plenty of time—hopefully—to figure things like that out, he told himself, then shook his head mentally. *Who would've thought it? There probably* will *be plenty of time...unless the* normal *risks of the trade catch up with me. With* us.

His smile faded with that thought. Clean Killer rested a hand lightly on the top of his head and made a soft, soft crooning sound in his ear, and the human inhaled deeply.

No one could reasonably have described Damien Harahap's life as uneventful or free of change, and he'd always been a survivor. From his childhood on Startman through his Gendarmerie career, he'd evolved into a tough, smart, competent professional who knew the value of his own skills and took pride in doing the job—whatever "the job" happened to be at any given moment—better than anyone else. At the same time, he'd always been aware that however good anyone might be, there was always someone better...or *luckier*, at least. And because that was true, he'd always known the odds of a long, peaceful retirement were lower in his case than in most.

What he hadn't known—or admitted to himself, at least—was how lonely he'd been.

Mostly, he reflected, that was because a man in his line of work didn't find many opportunities for deep, meaningful friendships. Not the kind that stayed with him, that really *mattered* to him. That was certainly what he'd told himself at the time, and it was true enough. For that matter, he *had* formed a few friendships that fitted that description. Ulrike Eichbauer, for example.

And what had happened to her was exactly the reason he'd let himself form so few of them. That was what he hadn't wanted to acknowledge to himself. What he'd *refused* to acknowledge to himself for so long. And he'd hidden that awareness from others—and himself—by how easily he assumed the *trappings* of friendship. The comfortable conversations, the sense of humor, the easy camaraderie. All of those came so naturally to him that not even he had realized how much they were part of his mask.

Until Clean Killer. Until ten or eleven kilos of silky fur and hard-muscled bone and sinew had inserted themselves into his life in a way no other creature in the universe had ever managed. Until now, when the thought of how likely it was that the risks of his profession would catch up with him someday, as they'd already caught up with Ulrike and a dozen others he could have named, frightened him at last. Not for himself, but for Clean Killer.

The treecat's croon deepened. His soft warmth pressed comfortingly against the side of Harahap's neck, and the human gave himself a mental shake.

I hope this sort of...soulful introspection isn't going to become the norm, he thought. *Last thing* anyone *needs is for the fearless interstellar secret agent to go all soft and squishy!*

✧ ✧ ✧

Clean Killer twitched, bleeking an approving laugh as his two-leg's mind-glow returned to its properly wry, amused flavor. He'd never anticipated that he might one day bond with any two-leg, and certainly not with someone who had labored so long and—apparently—successfully for the same evildoers who had murdered Black Rock Clan. Indeed, if anyone had suggested that could happen, he would have been furious.

Which only shows how little I knew, he thought. *And how little I truly understood the...complexity of the two-legs. No wonder so many People have been drawn to their mind-glows over the turnings! They are so strong, so bright, and so* different! *Perhaps Golden Voice and Thought Chaser are correct. Perhaps they burn so brightly because they are mind-blind. Because they cannot taste one another, no matter how loudly they call out. And perhaps they are so complex—that,* he reflected, *really was the best way to describe it—because they cannot share the way the People do. Perhaps it is only the way in which each of them is shut up in his own little world that leads them to explore thoughts and ideas that would never occur to a Person. People do not* need *complexity, because mind-voices and mind-glows make everything so simple.*

He didn't know about that—not yet. But he did know that Plays with Fire—he had no idea why so many of the other two-legs thought the name the People had bestowed upon his two-leg was so funny, but no other name fitted his mind-glow so well—had been even more alone inside his mind than most two-legs. And he had been that way for far too long. It had produced a rich, strong mind-glow—a strong *person*—but at the cost of more pain than Plays with Fire was prepared to admit to himself.

He wished he could finger-talk with Plays with Fire the same way Laughs Brightly talked with Dances on Clouds, but that would have to wait. Clean Killer had never truly thought about how *long* it took a two-leg to learn any new thing. That, too, was because they were mind-blind, of course. They could not simply taste a mind song about a new thing and make that memory their own, which was perhaps the strangest thing of all about them. Despite his frustration, he had been assured by both Pounces on Leaves and Thought Chaser that Plays with Fire was a *quick* learner, by two-leg standards, and patience was a virtue any scout required.

It was just that sometimes it was more difficult than others to *remember* that.

They followed Dances on Clouds across the large chamber, and the other two-legs rose in greeting.

✧   ✧   ✧

"Ladies and gentlemen," Honor said, "allow me to introduce tonight's guest of honor." Her lips twitched at the double entendre. "This is Mr. Harahap, known to some of you as 'Firebrand.'"

Harahap did a remarkably good job of looking unfazed as her other guests' eyes swiveled to him.

"Mr. Harahap, I know you've met some of these people before, but allow me to introduce, moving to my right around the table, Captain Rafe Cardones, my flag captain; Commodore Mercedes Brigham, my chief of staff; Captain George Reynolds, my staff intelligence officer; and Captain Andrea Jaruwalski, my operations officer. At the foot of the table, we have Commander Megan Petersen, CO of HMS *Arngrim*. I believe you know the next few people, continuing on around the table, but for the benefit of some of my other guests, they are Mr. Indiana Graham, of the Seraphim Independence movement; Lieutenant Abigail Hearns, tactical officer aboard HMS *Tristram*; Ensign Elijah Dimas, who's recently joined *Imperator*'s company; and, last but not least, one of your colleagues, after a manner of speaking—Mr. Anton Zilwicki, late of Her Majesty's Navy."

She paused for a moment, contemplating the eclectic mix with an inner smile, then waved at the empty chair between hers and Zilwicki's. There was a treecat-style highchair set beside it, like the one in which Nimitz was already ensconced.

"Please, everyone," she said. "Be seated."

✧   ✧   ✧

The stewards were smoothly efficient and the supper was excellent, Harahap decided. It was, according to Duchess Harrington, Grayson-style cuisine, which reminded him of a fusion of Old Earth Italian and oriental. In fact, it seemed to have quite a lot of Thai in its ancestry. Given what he knew of Grayson's history, that seemed unlikely. He was almost certain they must have evolved independently, but the curries, especially, reminded him of the delicious food to which Indy and Kenzie had introduced him at The Soup Spoon back in Cherubim.

He glanced across the table as that memory filtered through the back of his mind, wondering if the same thing had occurred to Indy. It was hard to be sure, since Indy's attention was elsewhere, and Harahap suppressed a smile as he realized just how focused he was upon the evening's other Grayson component.

And good luck to him, Harahap thought. *She looks every bit as toothsome as dinner... if in a somewhat different way.*

Clean Killer made the bleeking sound treecats used for laughter from beside him, and the smile he'd suppressed floated across his lips. He still couldn't decide how Indy thought about him these days, but he'd discovered that his new allegiance simplified his own emotions quite a lot. In many ways, he regretted the false pretenses under which he and the younger man had met, but it was a mild regret. He supposed it shouldn't be, but as he'd told Harrington, it had never been personal. In fact, he'd allowed himself to like young Indy and his sister a lot more than he ought to have. He was self-honest enough to admit that he'd have put that behind him, after the SIM was crushed. He would have felt a rather different sort of regret, but he would have brushed it aside, the same way he'd brushed aside so many other... regrettable consequences of his profession. In time—and probably not all that much of it, if he was going to be fully honest—he would have put it behind him and gone on.

It surprised him how genuinely grateful he was that that hadn't happened, but he wouldn't blame Indy a bit for... holding a grudge against the man who'd planned to cold-bloodedly betray him, his family, and his entire planet.

Funny how little things like that can sour a friendship, he thought.

The *Imperator*'s stewards began clearing away the dessert plates under the eagle eye of James MacGuiness, Harrington's personal steward. He was a slender man, rather shorter than his admiral, and obviously a first-generation prolong recipient, judging by the gray in his thinning sandy hair. He was also, according to the scant handful of facts Harahap had been able to glean, both a civilian and independently wealthy, at least by most people's standards, which suggested he was rather more than a "steward."

She does gather interesting people around herself, doesn't he? he reflected, watching as yet another steward poured wine.

Indeed she did, and tonight's guest list was a case in point. In fact—

His thoughts broke off as Harrington touched her glass and looked down the table at the youthful ensign seated between Lieutenant Hearns and the man she'd introduced as Anton Zilwicki, although he looked very little like the imagery of Zilwicki Harahap had seen. Ensign Dimas looked back at her for a moment, then gathered himself visibly, picked up his glass, and stood.

"Ladies and gentlemen," he said clearly, raising his glass, "the Queen!"

Harrington and all her guests came to their feet, reaching for their own glasses. Harahap rose with the others, although he wasn't sure how appropriate they might feel his participation was. Still, one had to be polite, and—

"The Queen," rumbled back to the youngster, and then, before they could resume their seats, Lieutenant Hearns raised her own glass.

"Ladies and gentlemen," she said, "I give you Grayson, the Keys, the Sword, and the Tester."

"Grayson, the Keys, the Sword, and the Tester," the others responded, and then everyone was sitting again and Harrington smiled at him.

"And now that the serious business of eating is out of the way, Mr. Harahap, I suppose we might spend a little time on less important matters, like, oh, your take on the Alignment."

Harahap gazed at her for a moment, then raised one eyebrow and glanced in the direction of young Dimas. Not only was he younger even than Indy, he was the only person present—aside from the not-Zilwicki sitting to Harrington's left—who didn't already know one Dennis Harahap's history. Or some of it, at least.

"Ensign Dimas has been attached to Captain Reynolds's department at my request, which means he has access to quite a lot of information someone his age might not," Harrington told him. "He's very good with computers and he's already made a valuable contribution to our understanding of exactly what's going on here. In fact, I think he may have the makings of a future 'spook,' so I think you may speak freely in front of him."

The ensign had turned an interesting shade of pink as the duchess extolled his virtues, Harahap noticed.

"Of course, Your Grace," he murmured. "just looking at the ensign I can see he has that steely glint that makes a true spy. I see it in my own mirror every morning."

Dimas twitched, then glared...and finally smiled as several of the other guests chuckled.

"I'm astonished you actually recognize yourself 'in the mirror every morning,'" Harrington said. "Considering all the other people you've been, I mean."

"It does get a bit difficult some mornings." Harahap meant for it to come out lightly, humorously, and so it did...mostly.

"I can imagine." Harrington's voice had shifted, as well. It would have been inaccurate to call her tone "gentle," but that was moving in the right direction.

Silence lingered for a moment, and then Harahap shrugged.

"In answer to your question, Your Grace," he said, "I've been giving that quite a lot thought, especially since Clean Killer entered my life."

He reached out to run one hand caressingly down the treecat's spine, and Clean Killer buzzed softly in pleasure. Harahap smiled at him, then looked back at Harrington.

"I didn't know anything about the Yawata Strike before I... made Commodore Zavala's acquaintance, shall we say?" He shrugged "I've learned quite a lot about it since, though." His hand stroked Clean Killer again, his eyes darkening. "Based upon which, I have to say it has all the hallmarks of an Alignment operation: ruthless, efficient, and damn the body count."

His voice had gone colder, harsher, and he looked across the table at Indiana.

"What actually happened on Seraphim was bad, Indy," he said, meeting the younger man's eyes levelly. "What my employers *wanted* to happen would have been a hell of a lot worse. And what happened here jibes perfectly with the sort of minds that could come up with something like Operation Janus."

"And with the sort of minds that could *implement* Operation Janus?"

The question rumbled up out of the massive chest of the mountain dwarf sitting beside Harrington. It was cold, challenging, and Harahap looked into the blue eyes which should have been brown.

"Fair enough, Captain Zilwicki." His own voice never wavered. "And I'm not going to beg for forgiveness, if that was your next question. I may regret the consequences of my actions, but they *were* 'my actions,' and everyone around this table knows it. I agreed to do the job, for whatever reasons, and I did it to the best of my ability. It's easy to express regret, to pretend contrition. In fact, it's something I've done dozens of times, and a good operative learns to do it with consummate sincerity. But I'm not going to do that this time."

"Why not?" Zilwicki challenged, his eyes intent.

"Partly because if I were the one listening to me do it, I don't think I'd believe me, and the last thing someone in my position should do is anything his audience might construe as, if you'll pardon the expression, an attempt to blow smoke up their arses," Harahap said candidly, and Zilwicki's lips twitched. "But, having said that, there are other reasons I won't. I won't because that's the easy, cheap way to dodge consequences." His eyes moved back to Indy. "Because I've looked into too many mirrors, seen too many people, and I've decided I don't like some of them very much. And I won't because Clean Killer doesn't seem to like hypocrisy any more than I do, and I've discovered his opinion matters. And I won't because words are slippery things. I'm sure you know that as well as I do, Captain. That's been my stock in trade for a long time, now. But I've decided that the only way I'm getting out of this alive—and maybe even starting to like my mirror a little more—is to…adjust my modus operandi."

"That's an interesting way to phrase it," Zilwicki said, and now his expression was simply thoughtful, his eyes measuring rather than challenging.

"I'm an interesting fellow," Harahap said with a lightness which fooled neither of them.

"That's one way to put it," Indy said. All eyes moved to him, and he shrugged. "Part of me still wants to shoot you, you know, 'Firebrand,'" he said. "It would be what I think the psychs call 'cathartic.' But you haven't left me *any* simple ways out, including that one. Besides," it was his turn to twitch a smile, "Kenzie would beat me up one side and down the other if I did."

"God bless her tender little heart." Harahap's tone was light, but his eyes had softened, and Indy shook his head with something between a grin and a grimace.

"Actually, as I understand it," Lieutenant Hearns said, and Harahap hid a smile of his own as he realized her left hand and Indy's right were both out of sight under the table, "you didn't exactly volunteer to help a cabal of lunatic genetic supermen take over the galaxy, Mr. Harahap."

"Kind of you to put it that way, Lieutenant," he replied. "And I will admit there was a hefty element of that old cliché about 'needs must when the devil drives.' Or that other one about 'any port in a storm.'" He shrugged. "When well-heeled assassins are out to kill you, you *do* have a tendency to catch the first shuttle out of town and think about destinations later. And I never heard anything about 'genetic supermen' until I fell into my present company. My employers on Mesa certainly never said a word about them!" He shook his head. "But, having said all of that, I didn't tell them to shove the job offer where the sun doesn't shine when they made it."

"If you *had*, you'd be dead," Indiana said, and Harahap wondered if he'd heard the sharpness in his own quick riposte.

"That *would* have been inconvenient," the ex-Gendarme acknowledged after a moment. "And you're probably right, Indy. But don't be putting me up for any medals. I may not have liked all the things I did for Bardasano and Rufino, and I may not have thought I had a lot of choice, but I *did* do them, and I did my best to do them well. I suppose part of that was a sort of craftsman's pride in his workmanship, and part of it was that it was pretty clear they'd arrange a nasty accident if I *didn't* do them well. But never think I didn't like the thought of all the credits they were contributing to my retirement fund."

"I haven't met very many candidates for sainthood," Zilwicki remarked to no one in particular.

"Nor have I," Harrington said with a curious serenity. Harahap looked at her, and she shrugged. "Mr. Harahap, I've hobnobbed with smugglers, spies, freedom fighters, and Ballroom terrorists. Most of us are some shade of gray."

"Indeed we are," Zilwicki rumbled, then startled the others with a sudden, rolling chortle. They looked at him, and it was his turn to shrug. In his case, it was a rather more massive production than the duchess had managed.

"I was just thinking about genetic supermen and changed people," he said, blue eyes twinkling. "I know a batch of what you might call early-model genetic supermen—well, super*women*, in this case—who have developed a whole different attitude where the Alignment is concerned. If *they* can turn over a new leaf, anybody can!"

He smiled for a moment longer, but then the smile disappeared and his eyes turned dark again. He started to say something more, then stopped and shook his head sharply. Clean Killer raised his head, looking at him intently, and Harrington reached across Harahap to lay her left hand on his forearm.

"Sorry." Zilwicki shook his head almost like a man shaking off a punch. "I just got back from doing something I'm sure we've both done upon occasion, Mr. Harahap: getting out of town in the nick of time. Unfortunately, some of my friends didn't."

"Anton, you don't know that." Harrington's voice was soft, almost gentle.

"You're right, I don't. And that's the real problem, isn't it? *Not* knowing?" Zilwicki said, looking at her, and she nodded.

"I know." She squeezed his forearm gently, then sat back in her chair. "But I'm confident we'll be hearing from Admiral Gold Peak and Admiral Tourville pretty darned soon now, so why don't you let the future take care of itself?"

"Sound advice," he said, and returned his gaze to Harahap. "Frankly, one of the reasons Her Grace invited you to dinner was so that you and I could compare notes."

"Really?" Harahap looked back at him for a moment, then chuckled. "I have to say, I really would like to hear about your and Cachat's adventures in Mendel! I got back to Mesa about a T-month after the Green Pines incident. I never put much stock in the official stories—not looking at the blast pattern and remembering the Gamma Center—but

I would *love* to hear your take on it. Especially since that little jaunt seems to be what started the entire ball rolling on this 'Alignment' business."

"Interesting you should say that," Zilwicki said, "because that's where I just came back from. Mendel, I mean."

Harahap's eyes widened and, despite himself, his lips pursed in a silent whistle. Zilwicki had actually gone back into Mendel? Right back to the one place in the galaxy where the only person more hated and reviled than him would have to be Victor Cachat? And if he had, then why—?

The thought broke off as Harahap remembered what he'd said about friends who hadn't "gotten out of town" in time. And then that reference to Admiral Gold Peak and Admiral Tourville...

"Should I assume your Navy—or, possibly, your *navies*, plural—are about to pay a visit on the good people of Mesa, Your Grace?" he said, cocking his head at Harrington, and she snorted.

"You *do* pick up on the sidebands, don't you?"

"It didn't exactly take a hyper-physicist in this case," he pointed out.

"No, I don't suppose it did. And, yes, that is where Anton was until quite recently. It's also, as I'm sure someone with your keen analytical mind will quickly deduce, the reason he looks so little like himself. By my calculations, if Countess Gold Peak and Tenth Fleet haven't already arrived in Mesa, they should be there within the next couple of days."

"And that's when things really get interesting, isn't it?" Harahap asked slowly.

"Exactly," Zilwicki rumbled. "Especially since there'd been an entire string of 'terrorist incidents' before I left." His expression was grim. "Somebody was using Green Pines and the Ballroom as a cover for sinking ocean liners and blowing up amusement arcades. They were leaving a lot of bodies behind, too... and the pace was accelerating when I translated out."

"But if it wasn't *you*—and that whole story never did make sense to me from the get-go—then who was 'somebody'?"

"That's one of the things you and I need to talk about." Zilwicki shrugged. "On the face of things, I can think of only one logical suspect. And my analysis of the casualties suggested some very interesting statistical correlations. You and I need to examine those correlations, and I'd really like to crank your view of the relationship between the Alignment and the official system government into my models. Victor and I had what you might call a worm's-eye perspective on the in-system dynamic. From where we sat, it seemed obvious there was a hell of a lot going on behind the scenes, but there was no way to get any sort of feel for what it was. I realize you didn't spend all that much time on Mesa, at least after you'd become a valued employee," he gave Harahap a brief, tight grin, "but you did get a chance to actually talk to this 'Detweiler,' not to mention Bardasano and Chernyshev, and we've had ample evidence of your...eye for detail, let's say. I want to hear everything you can tell me about them and about their attitude toward the system government. I'm not looking for what they said about it. I'm looking for the implications of *how* what they said and how their actual actions and interactions—with others, not just with you—might let us get at that relationship."

"I'll tell you what I can," Harahap said. "But if you're about to conquer the system, I'd think your investigators on the spot will be able to tell you a lot more—and a lot more quickly—than anything I might have to offer."

"Maybe they will, and maybe they won't." Zilwicki's expression turned grim once more. "Tell me, have you ever heard of matryoshka dolls?"

Harahap suppressed a blink at the sudden non sequitur. Then he shook his head.

"Pity." Zilwicki shook his head. "They make a really good analogy for what I've started to think we're actually up against. But that's okay. Duchess Harrington here's come up with a somewhat earthier metaphor that works just as well."

"'Metaphor'?" Harahap looked at Harrington. "What sort of 'metaphor' would that be, Your Grace?"

"An onion, Mr. Harahap," she said quietly. "I think what we're doing is peeling an onion, and you've been a lot closer to its core than anyone else we've got."

CNO's Office
Admiralty Building
and
George Benton Tower
City of Old Chicago
Sol System

"EXCUSE ME, SIR. HAVE you got a minute?"

Winston Kingsford looked up in surprise as the side door to his private office opened and a brown-haired, brown-eyed rear admiral stuck his head through it. There were very few people with the combination to the private lift that served that door, and even fewer who would simply arrive unannounced. Access to the Chief of Naval Operations was guarded rather more closely than the Sol System's hyper-limit, and those with the temerity to trespass upon it seldom fared well.

There were exceptions to every rule, however, and this was one of them.

"Maybe *one* minute, Caswell." Kingsford tried—without complete success—to put a repressive note into his voice as he waved the rear admiral into the office and pointed at the chair on the far side of his desk. "I have a meeting with Permanent Senior Undersecretary Kolokoltsov in less than half an hour, and I'm running late."

"I know you do, Sir, and under other circumstances, I would have waited till you got back. I think, though, that something I've just turned up may have a bearing on your meeting with him."

"Oh?" Kingsford's expression took on an edge of wariness.

Rear Admiral Gweon—the overdue promotion to go with his position as the CO of Economic Analysis, officially carried on the organizational chart as Section Three: Office of Naval Intelligence, had finally come through—had demonstrated an uncanny feel for apparently disconnected bits of intelligence that wound up being critically important. He gave honest analysis and wasn't afraid to offer an opinion when asked but never gave one if he couldn't provide the argument to back it up. And along with that feel of his for significant bits of intelligence, he'd demonstrated an almost equally uncanny sense of when those significant bits were time-critical.

480

"Yes, Sir. I don't have as much corroboration as I'd really like, but it's solid enough I felt I had to bring it to your attention."

"And can you deliver this new information to me in time for me to make my scheduled appointment with Permanent Senior Undersecretary Kolokoltsov?"

"No, Sir." Gweon met his superior's gaze levelly. "I'm afraid I can't. Not and give you the context that makes me believe this is really important. I mean, *really* important, Sir."

Kingsford considered him for a moment, then sighed and reached for his secure com. A moment later, Willis Jennings appeared on his display.

"Yes, Sir?"

"Screen Benton Tower," the CNO told his chief of staff. "Tell them something's come up and ask Permanent Senior Undersecretary Kolokoltsov if we can reschedule our sixteen hundred. Tell him I could probably be there by—?"

He paused, looking at Gweon, who held up both hands, spreading all five fingers of the left and four on the right. Kingsford's eyebrows rose, but Gweon only waggled his fingers emphatically, and the CNO shrugged.

"Tell him I can be there by nineteen hundred hours, Willis," he said. "Apologize profusely and if they absolutely can't reschedule, tell them you're authorized to deputize for me." He shrugged again. "It's not like they're going to be discussing anything you and I haven't already chewed up one side and down the other."

"Yes, Sir." Willis nodded, but he also hesitated. "Um, Sir, if they ask me what's come up, what should I tell them?"

"Tell them it's an intelligence matter. One I have to jump on as quickly as possible."

"Yes, Sir. Understood."

"Good! Thank you, Willis. Clear."

He killed the link and smiled at Gweon with just a touch of frost.

"And now, Caswell, I think you'd better explain *why* I have to jump on this as quickly as possible. Bearing in mind, of course, that *I'm* going to have to explain that to the Permanent Senior Undersecretary."

✧   ✧   ✧

"I'm terribly sorry I had to reschedule, Sir," Fleet Admiral Kingsford said as he was ushered into Innokentiy Kolokoltsov's office.

The sun had set thirty minutes earlier, and the October sky outside the office suite's clear wall was a mass of thunderheads, rolling in across Lake Michigan. White-crested waves charged across the lake, pounding across the deserted beaches in a wild smother of foam and gray water, and lightning lit the cloud bellies with rose-tinged fire.

It was, he thought, only too fitting a metaphor for the Solarian League.

"I'm sorry you did, too." Kolokoltsov sounded a bit testy. "MacArtney was really pissed, to be honest." The senior Mandarin shrugged. "He had to leave for that conference on Mars, and I think he had a few things he wanted to discuss with you."

"I'm sorry," Kingsford repeated. "I hope Admiral Jennings was able to answer any questions to his satisfaction?"

"No doubt he could have... if Nathan hadn't announced that he'd just hold them until you 'had the time' to meet with us." Kolokoltsov flashed his teeth in a thin smile. "I can't say I was very happy to have you cancel at such short notice, myself, but Nathan was in fine form, even for him."

"I was afraid of that," Kingsford sighed. "Nonetheless, Sir, I think you'll agree with my decision when you hear what the intelligence matter in question was. And, to be honest, if I'd gone ahead and come on schedule, I suspect a lot of the answers I might have given him would've had to be... revisited."

"Oh?" Kolokoltsov sat a bit straighter. Then he stood and waved the CNO to a chair next to the koi pond. On the way there, he snagged a bottle of thirty-year West Glenmore Blended whiskey from the office wet bar.

"Sit," he said, and poured three fingers into each glass. He set the bottle on the coffee table between them, handed one glass to Kingsford and lifted the other with a wintry smile. "I've got a feeling we'll both need this before you're done. Am I right?"

"Actually, you may be, Sir."

"Wonderful." Kolokoltsov dropped inelegantly into a facing chair, took a slow swallow of whiskey, and leaned back. "In that case, you'd best get to it, I suppose."

"Yes, Sir." Kingsford allowed himself a smaller sip, then sat forward, holding the glass in both hands between his knees.

"I was just tidying up my notes for this afternoon's meeting when Rear Admiral Gweon turned up in my office."

Kolokoltsov's eyes narrowed. In his opinion, Caswell Gweon was the best analyst the Office of Naval Intelligence had yet produced. Which, admittedly, wasn't that high a bar, given results to date.

"Admiral Gweon had just become aware of certain facts he felt had to be brought to my attention and then to yours, and he felt it was important for him to set them in context for me. As it happens, I think he was entirely correct about that."

"And to what would those facts pertain?"

"As you know, our sources in Beowulf have been... limited, to say the least, since Caddell-Markham and the others chucked Rear Admiral Simpson out on her ear and then refused Admiral Tsang transit." He grimaced unhappily. "I have to say that, much as that pissed me off—especially the refusal to pass Tsang through to support Filareta—they really did save a lot of Navy lives that day. Of course, those lives might not have needed saving if they hadn't already decided to throw in with the Manties, but give the devil his due, they *did* save them.

"We've finally gotten a bit more information out of Beowulf, however. ONI had a couple of long-term assets in place in the Beowulfan shipyards and military support sectors even before New Tuscany. They were civilians, not BSD personnel, and one of them came home in the last 'exchange cartel.'"

Kolokoltsov nodded, his expression less than happy. The newly independent Republic of Beowulf had arranged a passenger fleet shuttle service to transport Solarian citizens who had no desire to live in a breakaway star nation—including native Beowulfers who'd disagreed with the plebiscite result—back to the Sol System in return for Beowulfers who'd found themselves stuck elsewhere in the League and been unable to get home before the plebiscite. He and his fellows had taken no official notice of them, since that might have required them to take official action against Beowulf, which was likely to be more than a little risky just at the moment.

"Gweon had been involved in running them, since they were there more for economic and general industrial information than anything on the naval side." Kingsford grimaced. "If we'd seen any of this coming, we probably would have 'retasked' them long ago, but we didn't. Anyway, as soon as this agent hit Sol, she made a beeline to ONI to file her report, and when he shared it with me, I understood why. The 'Grand Alliance' is apparently a hell of a lot shorter on ammunition than Harrington chose to imply to Filareta."

"Excuse me?" Kolokoltsov frowned, and Kingsford shrugged.

"I don't doubt there was an awful lot of something floating around out there, *looking* like missile pods when she flashed them at Filareta," he said. "On the other hand, those could've been some more of their damned electronic warfare platforms. At any rate, even if every single 'pod' she showed Filareta was genuine, they probably didn't launch from more than twenty percent of them. We already knew that from the tactical scans they sent us, assuming that data hadn't been falsified. We don't think it was, though, and according to our agent's report, one reason they fired so few at him may be that they didn't have the missiles *to* launch."

"They haven't been shy about using missiles in the other engagements since then," Kolokoltsov pointed out skeptically.

"We haven't *thought* they were being shy about it," Kingsford replied. "But remember, we haven't seen any of their massive pod launches since Raging Justice. At both Hypatia and the Prime Terminus, all the missiles we saw from the Manties seem to have come from internal magazines. And analysis of the tac records from the survivors from both actions indicate that the missiles being used were *different* from the ones used against Filareta. Our analysts suggest they were smaller—which would make sense, coming from internal magazines—with lighter laserheads, fewer lasing rods, and penaids that were somewhat less capable. There's also some indication—from Hypatia, especially—that to reach their full range they required a ballistic phase their pod-launched missiles wouldn't have. I hasten to add that that last point is more problematical than the others.

"What I'm saying, Sir, is that while our observational data is limited, it indicates that the weapons they've been using against us since Raging Justice are different from—and less capable than—the ones they used against Filareta and, as nearly as we can judge, against Crandall. Now, admittedly, they've been shooting at battlecruisers and cruisers, not superdreadnoughts, which might explain some of that, but it's still significant, especially when coupled with the *other* part of our agent's report."

Kolokoltsov looked at him intently, and Kingsford drew a deep breath.

"According to our agent," he said carefully, "the 'mystery attack' on both Manticore and Grayson took out not just the shipyards, but their missile production facilities, as well. We'd suspected that might be the case; our agent's brought back hacked computer files—she was a senior logistics manager for Ivaldi of Beowulf, Beowulf's primary weapons manufacturer, and she seems to have used her access well—that appear to *confirm* it, however. More to the point, according to her—and, again, the files she brought out substantiate this, albeit a bit indirectly—the Republic of Haven is unable to manufacture the all-up heavy Manticoran shipkillers. They're producing *similar* weapons, but the Havenite missiles' performance is lower—*substantially* lower—than the Manties' version. More than that, according to what Ivaldi was told, Haven's general tech base and workforce will require major upgrades before they can even begin manufacturing the Manty missile. They call it 'Apollo,' by the way, and apparently what makes it such a killer is that it incorporates an FTL telemetry link. It's not that it *out ranges* the Havenite missile, although it may; it's that it's many times as accurate at extreme range. But according to the Ivaldi files, it's going to be a minimum of eight or nine months before Haven can begin producing the all up version."

"And the Manties?" Kolokoltsov asked, leaning forward intently as rain began to lash the office's transparent outer wall.

"They've got the workforce and the tech base, but they don't have the manufacturing facilities anymore, Sir," Kingsford said. "Not yet. According to Rear Admiral Gweon, projections are that they won't even be able to begin new missile production in Manticore for a minimum of another three months. Not until January, and probably not until February. Grayson appears to have lost a higher percentage of its work force—that's highly speculative, but the speculation seems pretty solid—in the attack on their Blackbird facilities, and they have more rebuilding to do, as well, which means they're unlikely to be able to step into that gap or shorten it.

"In addition, even after the Manties get the first of their lines back up, it'll be a lot smaller scale than the monster lines they had before they were attacked. That means their initial production rate will be low. Gweon's people estimate that it would ramp up gradually over a ten-month period to perhaps half of what it was before what they're calling the 'Yawata Strike.' Since both he and I have been burned by overoptimistic estimates before, we cut that in half. So, assuming they can get the lines back up as early as January and they can ramp up twice as rapidly as our people estimate, it would still be next May before they were back up to fifty-percent production."

"Do you think that explains why their battle fleet's been so...passive since Raging Justice? They're sitting there in Manticore and Beowulf rather than coming after us because they don't have the ammunition for a standup battle?"

"That's one possible scenario, yes, Sir. In fact, Admiral Gweon suggests it's a *probable* scenario. The fact that they might not have all the missiles they'd *like* to have doesn't mean they don't have more than enough to handle any wall of battle we threw at them, but ammunition expenditures are almost always lower for the defender than for the attacker. So there's a distinct possibility they're standing on the defensive to conserve their current supply of missiles."

"So they won't be moving offensively against us until they can refill their magazines? And they won't have any new missile production at least until January? And they won't have *adequate* missile production until *May?*"

Kolokoltsov's expression had brightened, his eyes gleaming, but Kingsford shook his head.

"No, Sir," he said regretfully, "that's not quite accurate. Oh, it's *probable* ammunition shortages explain their apparent passivity, but I'm not prepared to endorse that theory without reservations at this point. The last thing we need is to get overconfident because that's what we *want* to be true. And even if it is—true, I mean—assuming 'no new missiles until January' would be grossly overoptimistic.

"First, we have reports from agents we've managed to place in Erewhon that suggest Haven is probably closer than eight months to beginning limited production of its own. Their information suggests it could be as little as *five* months, although it's to be expected their initial production rates will also be low. And, by the way, something else I think we need to discuss—and we probably do need Permanent Senior Undersecretary MacArtney's input for this one—those same reports from Erewhon suggest Oravil Barregos and Luiz Rozsak are getting just a bit cozier with Erewhon than *their* reports suggest."

"What do you mean, 'cozier'?" Kolokoltsov asked sharply.

"Sir, we're still evaluating that—or, rather, Admiral Gweon is still evaluating it. From what he's said so far, I don't think there are any glaring warning lights, but given the Erewhonese's treaty with Haven and their long-term relationship with Manticore before that, I do find it...moderately worrisome when a sector governor and his senior naval commander start getting overly friendly with them. Everything Barregos and Rozsak have told us about that relationship makes sense. I'm just not as confident as I was that they've told us *everything* about it."

"Wonderful," Kolokoltsov said again. "But get back to the missile production business. What do Erewhon and Maya have to do with that?"

"Nothing, beyond corroborating our Beowulf agent's report—although their timetable's more pessimistic, from our viewpoint—about how quickly Haven can start building the new missiles. However, even though the Manties' combat patterns seem—or *may* seem—to confirm that they're being careful about ammunition expenditures, the other point in the Ivaldi report is that they have an alternative source for their high-end missiles."

"Beowulf," Kolokoltsov growled, and Kingsford nodded.

"Beowulf," he confirmed. "Specifically, Ivaldi *of* Beowulf. Apparently, the Beowulfan tech base was able to put them into production from a standing start a hell of a lot faster than the Manties could rebuild or the Havenites could upgrade. According to our agent, they *began* production even before the plebiscite, and the numbers are ramping. They aren't anywhere near the peak wartime numbers for Manticore—apparently even Beowulf hit a few snags—but they're climbing."

"That's why the bastards wanted Beowulf so badly." This time, it wasn't a growl; it was a snarl. "They *knew* they needed a new source for their frigging missiles if they were going to stand up to us!"

"That's certainly one interpretation, Sir."

"So cut to the chase, Admiral. What does all this really *mean*?"

"We're still working on that, Sir. There are several imponderables, things we haven't been able to nail down and may never be able to establish with certainty. But what it looks like is that: One, the Manties *appear* to be husbanding their heavy missiles, these 'Apollo' birds of theirs. Two, we have what appears to be pretty solid evidence that at this time, Beowulf—specifically, Ivaldi of Beowulf—is effectively the 'Grand Alliance's' sole source for 'Apollo,' and probably will be for a minimum of three months. Three, Ivaldi will probably be the *primary* source for additional missiles for another five to six months after that, call it until June 1923. Four, at the end of those eight to nine months, however, all three sources combined will be producing almost as many missiles as Manticore alone was producing prior to the Yawata Strike. And, five, from that point on their production rates will bend upwards—bend *steeply* upwards—to a far higher total than Manticore ever produced solely from its own resources.

"And what all that means, Mister Permanent Senior Undersecretary, is that we have a window of three to four months in which they'll *probably* continue to be tactically and operationally handicapped by an ammunition bottleneck. But it also means that by August or September of next year, unless we're able to put matching weapons into production to supplement things like Hasta, our military situation will be hopeless."

NOVEMBER 1922 POST DIASPORA

HMS _Imperator_
Manticore Binary System
Star Empire of Manticore

"BLEEK!"

Nimitz looked up over his shoulder, ears pricked high, green eyes sparkling with triumph, and Honor shook her head.

The brightly lit expanse of _Imperator_'s small arms range stretched out around them. The range was open to anyone on a first-come basis, outside the Marine detachment's regular scheduled practices, but when Admiral Harrington "requested" its use, things changed. Not only was she an admiral, but her personal security detachment was...unhappy, to put it mildly, about allowing her to be surrounded by other people with weapons in their hands. That was especially true since the death of Timothy Meares, and Major Hawke had made it crystal clear that she would be allowed on the range _only_ when no one else was using it. Given the fact that Rafe Cardones had endorsed her senior armsman's intransigence, there wasn't much Honor could do about it.

And, unhappily, she knew Hawke had a point.

So she and Nimitz had the entire range to themselves and one of her old-fashioned targets—what had once been called a "B7 Silhouette," according to her SCA sources—hung in tatters at a range of ten meters. Pulser darts tended to make very small holes, but the target's surface had been coated in a smart skin that glowed bright red wherever it was broken. At the moment, the target looked like someone with a case of old-fashioned measles, she thought critically. There were dozens—more like scores, really—of red dots scattered across it, but no more than a scant handful inside the eight-ring and only three inside the ten-ring.

"That's still...pretty bad, Stinker," she told her furry henchman.

Nimitz's ears flattened indignantly, and she snorted. Then she punched the button that ran a second target out beside the first one and picked up the long-barreled, three-millimeter Descorso pulser she'd inherited from her father on her sixteenth birthday. The military weapon had been heavily customized, and her dad had changed out the grips to fit her hands when he gave it to her. Now it settled into them as naturally as breathing and she raised the weapon in a two-handed stance.

"Like this," she said, and squeezed the trigger.

It whined in full-auto, ripping off a ten-shot burst in approximately 1.2 seconds, and the second target's ten-ring disintegrated into a two-centimeter chasm fringed in livid red. There wasn't another hole anywhere on the paper, and she looked down at Nimitz and grinned as she laid the weapon back down on the bench in front of her.

"Bleek."

There was a certain scolding note in that sound, she thought.

"Not as easy as it looks," she told him. "I'd hoped the holo sight would do the trick, but obviously not. So, it's time for Plan C."

She laid down the Descorso and picked up the other pulser. A few seconds' work with a small magnetic decoupler removed the bulky—relatively speaking—holo sight and she laid it aside. It took her two or three times as long to attach her chosen replacement under the barrel, and she checked her work twice before she looked back down at the 'cat.

"I figure we're getting close to the end of our options, Stinker," she told him. "Now *concentrate*."

He gave her a disgusted look, but he also nodded, and she closed her eyes.

Not even Alfred Harrington had been able to restore Nimitz's ability to mind-speak. He believed he'd made some progress, but he still had a long way to go. The treecats' "distributed brain" was unique in humanity's experience, and no one really understood how its "transmitters" and "receivers" worked even now. Alfred had developed several models and he was confident one of them was correct. The problem was figuring out which one, and in the meantime, the damage Nimitz had taken when he and Honor attacked their StateSec guards on the planet Enki continued to defy his best efforts.

Those efforts had been put on hold—for reasons Nimitz and Samantha understood and accepted—by his return to active duty at Bassingford. In the meantime, the treecats had continued to strengthen their ability to transmit images to one another using Nimitz's intact empathic transmitter. They hadn't realized that channel was available—no 'cat had realized it could be used that way, as an at least partial standalone in place of their regular transmission modes—before Honor and Nimitz forged their own connection. But Honor had never had the ability to actually mind-speak with Nimitz. Their link had been primarily through his tel*empathic* sense—with what she suspected had been a few "sideband" elements from his telepathic *receiver*—and it hadn't been crippled by the damage he'd suffered. It had never been suited to complex exchanges of information, despite its depth, and that wasn't what he and Samantha used it for these days, either. But he and Honor had discovered long ago that they could transmit mental *images* to one another. Nimitz found the sign language Adelina Arif had modified and taught the 'cats far better suited for sharing complex information, even between him and Samantha, but he and his mate had learned to exchange "mind-pictures" the same way he and Honor did, and Samantha had shared that ability with the rest of their species in a memory song.

Now he closed his eyes, as well, concentrating hard on the carefully formed image flowing from his person. The very tip of his tail twitched as he focused on it and they stayed that way for a very long time. Then he bleeked again, softly, and Honor opened her eyes and looked down at him again.

"So, this time you think you've got it?" she asked with more than a hint of skepticism. He nodded firmly, and she arched an eloquent eyebrow. "I believe that's what you thought the last *three* times," she pointed out, and the 'cat sent her a flash of wounded dignity. "Okay, fine," she said. "Put your money where your mouth is, Mister!"

Nimitz gave her the sort of look he normally reserved for chipmunks, and she laughed. Then she tapped controls, running the first silhouette in close to the bench so she could remove it from the clips and replace it with a fresh one. She'd just sent it back out to its ten-meter range when a warning buzzer sounded.

She looked over her shoulder in surprise, wondering who Clifford McGraw and Joshua Atkins were willing to allow onto the range with her, then smiled in recognition as the door opened.

"Anton!" She turned and held out her hand, and Anton Zilwicki gripped it firmly. "I didn't expect you this early."

"Harahap and I finished this morning's session sooner than we expected," he replied, and she nodded.

The decision to keep Harahap aboard *Imperator*—where *no one* was finding out about his existence—and let the analysts who absolutely had to know come to him, had actually been suggested by Commander Lassaline, who had become Patricia Givens's personal Liaison to the ex-Gendarme's exhaustive debrief, but Honor and Zilwicki both thought it was an excellent one. That was why the massive Highlander had become a more or less permanent member of *Imperator*'s ship's company. Now he released her hand and shrugged.

"Never thought I'd find myself actually *liking* 'Firebrand'!" he admitted wryly.

"I didn't exactly expect it myself." She shrugged. "On the other hand, he'd almost *have* to be likeable to accomplish everything he has, wouldn't you say? Besides, who am I to argue with treecats?"

Nimitz made an emphatic sound of agreement. His fingers flickered, and Honor laughed. Zilwicki hadn't learned to read sign, and he raised an eyebrow at her.

"Nimitz just agreed with me," she explained. "And while he was agreeing, he asked when I was going to be smart enough to stop doing it anyway."

"Sounds like a trio of teenagers I used to know," Zilwicki said with one of his deep, rumbling laughs.

"Used to know?"

"Well, I still know them, but none of them are *teenagers* anymore. Not that their doddering old age has made them any less stubborn." He shook his head. "Don't have any idea where they could've gotten *that* from."

"Of course not." It was Honor's turn to shake her head. "Should I assume this morning went well?"

"It did, actually." Zilwicki shrugged his massive shoulders. "Which isn't to say I don't wish to hell we knew more about their internal dynamic. And I can't say I like a lot of what we *are* putting together. Coupled with what Harahap's had to say and what I'd already seen on Mesa, I'm starting to think their 'inner core' is hidden in more depth than we'd expected, even now. We won't know for sure until we can start looking—openly, I mean—on Mesa itself, but if I'm right about what was going on with all those 'terrorist' strikes and they really were pulling key people out, I'm inclined to doubt they plan on leaving much evidence of their existence behind."

"I'm sure they aren't, but how much evidence could they really erase?" Honor leaned her hip against the shooting bench and crossed her arms. "Even if we assume every single soul on Mesa who knows something we'd like to know has been fitted with this suicide nanotech of theirs—and, frankly, I'm inclined to think equipping every possible information source with it would be a nontrivial challenge—something that's been operating this long *has* to leave a physical fingerprint. It can't have been as busy rearranging the galaxy to suit itself as we know it has without requiring a major support structure, Anton!"

"And I'm sure it has—or *had*, at least—one," Zilwicki agreed. "What I'm not sure about is how decentralized that support structure was. A lot will depend on what their end-game strategy is and how long ago they evolved it, Your Grace. Was the evacuation I identified—I *think* I identified—improvised when the military situation went south on them, or was it something they'd planned for a long time? I mean, they have to have their own version of Bolthole tucked away somewhere. What if they've planned all along to shift operations to there when the time is right?"

"You think they could have been planning on vanishing down a rabbit hole from the very beginning?" Honor's eyes were intent, and she frowned. "I never considered that. I guess I'd always assumed they planned on not being found out, in which case they would've gone right on managing their puppets from Mesa . . . until they suddenly realized they couldn't. But do you think it's really plausible that they planned on pulling some kind of Houdini from the start?"

"I don't know." He shrugged again. "I suppose a lot would depend a lot on where 'Planet X' is located—they couldn't coordinate very well from someplace months away from the Core Worlds or the nearest wormhole—but I just don't know. Nobody knows, on our side, at least. And, unfortunately, our friend Firebrand didn't even realize it was going on. Frankly, I think he might have if he'd spent more time on Mesa and less time flitting about the galaxy lighting fuses. His 'whiskers' are more sensitive than most treecats'. In fact, I'm coming to the conclusion he may be part 'cat himself!"

"I wouldn't go *quite* that far," Honor said, although privately, she wondered if Zilwicki might not have a point.

"Maybe not," the Highlander conceded. Then he inhaled deeply with yet another of those mountain-range-in-motion shrugs. "Anyway, he didn't—notice anything, I mean. And Victor and Thandi and I were a bit too preoccupied to dig into it properly. So until Harahap and I can go in with the occupation teams and start digging, there's no way to know one way or the other. But I do think it's possible they planned on—What was it you called it? Pulling a Houdini?—from a very early stage. I'm not saying they expected to *need* it. I'm saying that these people obviously believe in planning ahead and that they're the sort of people who would've figured that if they *did* need some sort of emergency evacuation plan they'd need it *badly*. And that I think it's entirely possible they planned for that contingency even if they never thought they'd actually use it."

"What a perfectly marvelous thought to ruin my morning. Thank you *ever* so much for sharing. Now I've got something *else* to produce bad dreams!"

"As Cathy would say, that's why they pay you the big bucks, Your Grace. Besides, why should I be the only one worrying about it?"

"Even on flagships, people sometimes have accidents, Mr. Zilwicki."

"No, really?"

He looked at her innocently, and she chuckled. Then he looked at the shredded target draped over the shooting bench and his eyebrows rose.

"Not your best work, Your Grace," he observed. "From your reputation, I'd've expected something more like that one." He twitched his head at the silhouette with the eviscerated ten-ring still hanging in the firing lane.

"It's not my work at all," she said.

She lifted the damaged target with one hand and pointed at what had been hidden under it with the other. Zilwicki's eyes followed her index finger...and widened as they saw the miniature pulser.

It was tiny, smaller even than any hideout weapon he'd ever seen, and he'd seen quite a few. For that matter, he'd never imagined a grav driver could be engineered down into something that small.

"Is that what I *think* it is?" he asked carefully.

"*That*," Honor said, "is either a brilliant suggestion or the biggest bit of lunacy I've ever encountered. The jury is still out on which."

Nimitz bleeked an indignant laugh, then made a severe scolding sound as she looked back down at him. She laughed and rubbed his ears affectionately, then returned her attention to Zilwicki.

"One of my armsmen back in Harrington—a fellow named Randy Todd—fell in love with modern small arms the instant we introduced them to Grayson. The Harrington Guard got pulsers before anybody else on the planet, except for Palace Security and the Mayhew Guard, and Randy was Harrington's first master armorer. He was a corporal when he joined the Guard, and he retired last year as Sergeant Major of the Guard. You might say we think highly of him."

Zilwicki nodded in recognition of that last sentence's understatement.

"Anyway, like I say, Randy was in seventh heaven playing around with pulsers, stun guns, vibro blades, the odd grenade launcher—all those toys so dear to an armsman's heart." Major Hawke, who'd been standing against the firing range's rear bulkhead made a sound remarkably like Nimitz's, and she flashed a smile over Zilwicki's shoulder. "He's also just a bit demented," she continued, still smiling at her personal armsman, "and I wouldn't be surprised if he's had this—" she flicked a finger at the tiny weapon "—in the back of his mind for a long time. But when word got back to Harrington that the treecats were providing bodyguards, he decided any *arms*man—regardless of species—should be properly armed. So the lunatic designed 'cat-sized pulsers that actually work."

"Not exactly precision weapons, judging from the results," Zilwicki observed.

"And it probably wouldn't be a good idea for one of the 'cats to accidentally kill a half dozen or so innocent bystanders," Honor acknowledged. "Especially considering who those bystanders would most likely be."

Zilwicki's shudder was only half humorous. Uncontrolled pulser fire at a meeting of the Joint Chiefs—or, even worse, between Empress Elizabeth and President Pritchart and their staffs—definitely constituted a very *bad* idea, he reflected.

"The problem is that treecats have never used missile weapons more complicated than a thrown stone. Bit surprising, really, but they come naturally armed and oriented for what you might call close-quarters battle. And as anyone who's ever seen Nimitz with a frisbee or a tennis ball could probably predict, they're pretty darned accurate when they do throw a rock at someone. But the notion of aiming and controlling something like a pulser is a bit more complex. And judging from Nimitz, it's not something that comes as naturally to the 'cats as it does to humans."

"No?" Zilwicki frowned. "Do you have any idea why not?"

"Not really." Honor leaned more of her weight against the bench and opened her arms to Nimitz, who leapt up into them and pressed his nose against her cheek before turning in her embrace to face Zilwicki. "Some of it's clearly physiological, but not all of it. There are a lot of things about the 'cats we still don't understand, and we're steadily discovering more of them now that the two species are talking to each other.

"One thing we've found is that their thought processes aren't like ours. For one thing, they don't use words—'mouth-sounds'—at all when they communicate. They send...encrypted data packets, I guess. Dr. Arif's assembled a team of "cat psychs' to try and figure it out, and so far it's driving them crazy almost as much as it's fascinating them, but it seems—so far—like a case of their sharing concepts directly, without any need to formulate terms of reference for them. We don't have a clue exactly how a 'cat experiences complex information interchanges with another 'cat, and to this point, they haven't been able to figure out how to explain it to us, either. The best handle I've been able to come up with is that because their exchange is so direct, literally like sharing the other person's very thoughts without the need for any physical interface, all the references we put into nouns, adjectives, adverbs, differentiated concepts—all that stuff—is simply inherent in the original thought. I'm actually inclined to wonder if that helps explain why they don't seem very innovative by human standards. Their information exchange is so complete that the sort of...ambiguity that often sparks a human inspiration just doesn't happen between 'cats."

"That's fascinating." Zilwicki rubbed an eyebrow thoughtfully. "But if that's the case, how do they manage to sign?"

"It took them centuries to figure out that 'mouth-noises' were data packets at all, but once they did, they seem to have realized that us poor, limited two-legs needed a sound tag to hang on the thoughts we couldn't share. From there, they started gradually learning human vocabulary and syntax, at least well enough to comprehend it. I don't think most people have a clue how monumental an accomplishment that was for a species which had never even considered the possibility of differentiated words!

"Apparently, though, the jump to a *written* language and the ability to associate letters or signs with phonemes and the phonemes with 'mouth-noises' was a heck of a lot steeper in some ways. They realized *what* we were doing when they saw us reading, they just couldn't figure out *how* we were doing it. Dr. Arif made the breakthrough when she taught them to associate their own gestures with the words they'd learned to recognize, and most of the signs they use are really more concept than word, if you think about it. They very seldom sign exact Standard English, although the 'cats who spend the most time associating with humans do a lot more of that. But even they tend to think of the limited number of words they spell out more as 'a two-leg thought construct expressed by multiple gestures' rather than the components of a single word."

She twitched a frown.

"I'm not really explaining this as well as I'd like, but that's because there are still so many holes in what we know. And, frankly, Adelina and her teams are *way* ahead of me and Nimitz in figuring it out. I try to keep abreast of their findings, but there's not enough time in a day for everything I'd *like* to be doing after I finish everything I *have* to be doing."

"I can see that. It is fascinating, though. How else do their thought processes differ from ours?"

"Obviously, we're still working on that," Honor said. "One thing we have figured out already, though, it that they seem to have serious difficulties with any sort of math more advanced than very simple addition and subtraction." She snorted suddenly. "Mom always did say I was half-treecat.

"Anyway, getting back to our abundantly perforated target, Nimitz here seems perfectly comfortable with the notion of point-and-shoot. He's just not very good at it"—the treecat reached up and back to smack her gently—"and teaching him *aimed* fire is turning out to be a skosh more difficult than Sergeant Major Todd expected. And, frankly," her tone turned more serious, "it's even more important with something as short barreled as any 'cat-sized pistol. Randy's worked out a pulse *rifle* suited to treecat anatomy, but I'm not turning any 'cat loose with *any* pulser until I'm confident they understand how dangerous they are and that they'll be able to actually hit their targets without killing everyone else in the room."

"Sounds like a very sound approach to me, Your Grace," Zilwicki said with feeling.

"To Nimitz, too, really," Honor replied, hugging the 'cat briefly. "And I *think* we're on the right track. This pulser"—she nodded at the weapon lying on the bench—"is a dedicated range-only version. It can't be fired at all outside *Imperator*'s range, and it won't fire even here unless it's pointed *down*-range. Which is probably a good thing judging by how...enthusiastically dispersed Nimitz's first groups were. But I've been working with Captain Cardones's armorer to modify it, and we seem to be getting better results—for certain values of the word 'better,' at any rate—today. The problem's been getting Nimitz to understand both what a sight picture is and why it's important. That's what we were working on when you arrived."

"Well, by all means continue, Your Grace!" Zilwicki chuckled. "Far be it from me to stand in the path of such a noble scientific endeavor. Especially"—his smile sobered—"one that's likely to save some very important lives down the road."

"My thought, as well," Honor said quietly, and looked down at Nimitz. "Ready, Stinker?"

He nodded firmly and jumped back on to the shooting bench.

He gathered up the pulser with what struck Zilwicki as admirable safety awareness. He was especially careful about where the muzzle pointed and keeping his fingers away from the treecat-adapted trigger guard while he did it.

"I came to the conclusion that a big part of the problem is that the barrel length doesn't give Nimitz enough sighting axis. The way his shoulders articulate, it's difficult for him to even get into a proper sighting posture, and then he's looking down that really short barrel. I tried fitting it with a standard holo sight like the Simpson and Wong on my Descorso, but we just found out that doesn't seem to work for him either. So, we're trying this. You're just in time for the trial run of Plan C. Although, really, by now it's about Plan G, I think. Show him, Stinker."

Nimitz bleeked cheerfully, raised the pulser to point in the general direction of the fresh target, and wrapped both true-hands around the weapon's grip, still keeping the first finger of his right true-hand away from the trigger. He held it there and looked up at Honor, pricking both ears in inquiry, and she nodded.

"Ready on the range!" she announced formally, and he returned his attention to the task at hand.

Nothing happened. Then the miniature laser Honor had mounted under the barrel blinked to life. A small, brilliant dot of light appeared on the target, the pulser whined instantly...and a tiny blotch of crimson dye blossomed exactly where the laser had pointed.

Nimitz bleeked in delight, capering triumphantly on the shooting bench on his true-feet. Zilwicki started to flinch, despite everything Honor had said about the pulser's safety features, but then he relaxed. The cat's elation was obvious, yet despite his glee, he'd carefully laid the pulser back on the bench before he started his war dance.

"Good for you, Stinker!" Honor laughed, scooping him up and burying her face briefly in his belly fur. "Knew we'd finally find the answer! Should've tried this one sooner, I guess."

"Bleek! Bleek, bleek, *bleek!*" Nimitz agreed, and she looked back across at Zilwicki, who was grinning broadly.

"I don't like laser pointers," she told him a bit apologetically. "I've seen them lose alignment, especially external units on rifles. I really want to teach him iron sights, too—everyone needs to know that, even if only for a backup—and I may be able to do that when we move to the rifle. It's just not going to work with the pistol version, though."

"At the range where any of the 'cat bodyguards is likely to be shooting, the laser actually makes a lot of sense," Zilwicki pointed out. "Has more of a 'stop-and-think-about-this' psychological quotient, too."

"Which won't be much against the nanotech." Honor's voice was grim, but Zilwicki shrugged.

"Probably not. On the other hand, I imagine the 'cats will be handy to have around when it comes to garden-variety, run-of-the-mill, old-fashioned assassins, too."

"Now that's probably a very good point," she acknowledged. She smiled almost sheepishly. "You know, I've been so focused on the Alignment that I hadn't really been thinking about what I guess you might call other applications."

"Not too surprising. I have to wonder, though. Did your Sergeant Major Todd ever consider the possibility of just issuing them teeny-tiny stunners? More prisoners and less collateral damage that way, I'd think."

"Actually, we did think about that. Unfortunately, not even Randy could figure out how to build a stunner this small with more than a couple of yards' range. And even if we could, we don't know what the nanotech would do in a case like that. As far as we can tell, the human being who's being controlled is already 'out of the loop' as far as what her body is doing. If she's rendered unconscious, does that shut her down? Or does the nanotech just go right on with whatever it's doing?"

"Forgive me, My Lady," Spencer Hawke put in diffidently, "but I'd vote against trying to stun someone in those circumstances even if we knew the answer. There's a reason most bodyguards don't like being restricted to nonlethal force, because you can never be sure it's going to work. Anti-stun armor's readily available and light enough to be worn under most people's clothing. Besides, not everybody reacts the same way to *being* stunned even when they're totally unprotected." He shook his head, his expression somber. "It's an armsman's job to keep his principal alive, whatever it takes. We'd just as soon never kill anyone, but if someone's trying to kill *you*, then keeping that someone alive—no matter why he's trying to do it, I'm afraid—is secondary or tertiary, as far as we're concerned. Given who the treecats are protecting, I don't think it should be any other way for them, either."

"He's right." Zilwicki shook his head with a chagrined expression. "I should've thought about that myself. I guess it was the spook in me—thinking about data and not the potential consequences of trying to acquire it."

"Well, at least we seem to have solved Nimitz's problem...once he finally got the correlation between the dot on the target and the pulser dart." Honor grinned at the treecat's scolding sound. "Even that wasn't as easy as I expected it to be. And now we have to see if he and I between us can pass it on to Sam so she can start spreading the word to the rest of Her Majesty's Own Treecats!"

Admiralty Building
City of Old Chicago
Sol System

"BE SEATED, LADIES AND gentlemen," Winston Kingsford said as he strode to the comfortable chair at the head of the briefing table.

The men and women attending the meeting—both those physically present and those in the various dedicated quadrants of the enormous smart screen in the briefing table's hollow horseshoe—waited until he'd actually seated himself. Then they settled into their own chairs, and he smiled.

"I'm sure we all have a lot to do still today," he said, "so I'd like to restrict this morning's session to a quick overview. To be honest, one of the serious mistakes we'd settled into before this entire thing blew up in our faces was a failure to keep everybody in the loop. I realize the galaxy is a big place and we've always had a lot of irons in the fire. There's no way we could possibly keep everyone attending today fully informed on everything all of us separately have going on. Can't be done. But what we need to do—and what we haven't been doing—is to have regular meetings at this level in which anything that's risen to the top of our own departmental to-do list gets aired. By not doing that, we've deprived ourselves of the advantage of outside viewpoints that might have had something important to add. I don't know that any of us had anything hidden away in our files that might have warned us this shit storm was coming. I *do* know that none of us realized we did *if* we did, though. People, we can't afford to let crap get past us any longer."

He looked around the briefing room—and the displays—and his blue eyes were cold. The others looked back, and if any of them disagreed with him, at least they had the good sense to keep their mouths shut. Not surprisingly, perhaps, given how ruthlessly he'd weeded the senior officers he'd inherited from Rajampet Rajani. In fact, this was the first time several of the attendees had been present in their brand new roles.

It was unfortunate that some of his remaining ... legacy senior officers were so well-connected he hadn't been able to get rid of them even now. He didn't like that. But most of the names on his short list belonged to people who were at least smart enough to know they were also on his *shit* list, and as the severity of the situation seeped deeper into the minds of their patrons, they could probably feel the ice getting thinner underfoot.

In most cases, at any rate.

He paused a moment to consider two of his happier additions. He'd finally managed to get rid of Karl-Heinz Thimár, who'd headed the Office of Naval Intelligence for far too long under Rajampet, after one of the most vicious bureaucratic turf wars in recent Solarian memory. Thimár's...lack of brilliance had become abundantly clear as the SLN fell deeper and deeper into the crapper, but he'd been so thoroughly in bed with the defense industry that it had been all but impossible to fire him. The one good thing about what the Manties had done at Prime and in the Hypatia System was that it had finally underscored—with surviving raw *Solarian* tactical data no one could argue had been doctored by the Manties—the inferiority of even the Navy's newest weapons. Coupled with Thimár's deep involvement in the Fleet 2000 Program, the "modernization program" everyone now realized had been purely cosmetic, that evidence had been enough for Kingsford to finally boot his incompetent arse out the door. Thimár had found himself not only displaced from ONI but beached, with no ongoing role in the war at all...thank God. At least Kingsford had accomplished that much.

Not, unfortunately, without making himself a lot of new and implacable enemies. Most of them seemed to adhere to the theory that Thimár was being scapegoated for others' mistakes—including those of one Winston Kingsford—and those enemies were waiting almost eagerly for *him* to screw up spectacularly enough to be sacked. He knew that, but if that was the price of doing business, then so be it. And he was determined to get a little competency into place before any impending axes landed on his own neck.

Admiral Heinrich Bergman, Thimár's replacement, was a case in point. Little more than half his predecessor's age, he was also very new to his rank; Kingsford had jumped him over at least a dozen other flag officers, which had undoubtedly made *him* a lot of enemies, as well. Like Kingsford, however, Bergman seemed prepared to worry about that once the shooting was over. He was tall but quick-moving, with brown hair and eyes and one of the darkest complexions Kingsford had ever seen. He was also aggressive and smart, and he was energetically attacking the train wreck Thimár had left him at ONI. He'd held his new position for barely a month at this point, however, and how successful he'd be at clubbing all the alligators remained to be seen.

But at least I've been able to give him some *support*, Kingsford thought, moving his gaze to Vice Admiral Karen Clarke.

Clarke's hair and eyes were even darker than Bergman's, but despite her last name, her complexion was very pale. She was twenty T-years older than her new boss—indeed, she was one of the people he'd been jumped over, and Kingsford had very carefully considered her for the top intelligence slot before settling on Bergman—but if she resented that, she'd shown no indication of it. Maybe that was because she realized she was far too valuable as Rosalinda Hoover's replacement for ONI's Section Two, the Office of Technical Analysis. She wasn't one of the most brilliant officers in the SLN, but she had the sort of clear, incisive mind which might have been expressly designed for taking problems apart and identifying their components, then finding solutions for them one by one. She was one of the most original thinkers the SLN had produced in recent memory, she *was* brilliant as an organizer and manager, *and* she got along very well with Tory Kindrick at Systems Development Command. That was possibly the most vital single connection in the entire Solarian League Navy, under the circumstances, and she and Bergman were chopping their way through the undergrowth in a powerful and effective partnership. If only they'd had less kudzu to cross...

And if only I could get rid of Cheng, the CNO thought glumly. *Why the hell anyone would want to prop* him *up is more than I can understand, but* somebody *sure as hell does!*

Kingsford knew where the *visible* support for Cheng Hai-shwun, the CO of Operational Analysis, was coming from. What he couldn't imagine was why Nathan MacArtney was so damned determined to keep a man who was so obviously incompetent in such a critical position. Everything suggested that someone else had to be whispering in MacArtney's ear, and very compellingly, at that. Worse, whoever it was clearly had influence with Malachai Abruzzi, as well. But why? And what sort of influence could make them support a hack like Cheng at a time like this? MacArtney and Abruzzi knew even better than most how deep a hole the League was in, and MacArtney, in particular, as the Permanent Senior Undersecretary of the Interior, was the one watching the Protectorates erode right out from under him. So what in *hell* could be influencing him to protect someone like Cheng?

Until Kingsford figured that out, there wasn't a lot he could do about the situation at OpAn. The fact that all the Mandarins knew he and MacArtney despised one another—and that Abruzzi wasn't very high on his list of favorite people, either—made it difficult to enlist any of the others' support in this instance. Kolokoltsov was coming around—probably—but even he seemed unable to free himself of the suspicion that personal animosity was at play. Unless Kingsford could provide him with convincing evidence that MacArtney and Abruzzi were being influenced—or coerced—into backing someone they knew was incompetent, he was unlikely to step in.

But even with Cheng still screwing around at OpAn, I've got the critical bases covered, he reminded himself. *God knows I need better analysis of the tac data for Bernard and her people at Strategy and Planning, and it would be nice to have a better feel for what the* hell *the Manties think they're doing. I know it's not what any of the* Mandarins *think they're doing, but that's not a lot of help. Until I can get some kind of handle on the "Grand Alliance's" real war aims, building the best strategy to stop them is likely to be just a bit difficult. But at least with Bergman in the CO's office at ONI and Clarke and Kindrick digging in on the technical side, I've got my best shot at surviving long enough to get rid of Cheng and figure out what the hell is really going on.*

"All right," he said, and made himself smile at Admiral Cheng, "why don't we start with a look at Hypatia." Despite himself, his smile turned a bit thinner and colder. "What can your people at OpAn tell us, Hai-shwun?"

**Presidential Palace
and
Belinda's Bar
City of Landing
Meroa System**

"DO YOU *BELIEVE* THIS shit?" System President Adenauer Kellogg demanded.

It was hard to determine whether the president was more furious or incredulous, Johannes Stankiewicz reflected. Kellogg was a quintessential product of the Meroa System's crony capitalism. Like his fellows, he regarded the star system's economy as his own personal cookie jar—with, Stankiewicz admitted, rather more justification than many. He'd been system president for almost forty T-years now, and the Office of Frontier Security had been his quiet sponsor for thirty-five of them.

Stankiewicz was more aware of that than most, since he'd been Kellogg's OFS "advisor" for the last fifteen T-years, during which quite a few crumbs had come his way from that same cookie jar. As such, he might reasonably have been as furious as Kellogg himself. What he actually felt, however, was much closer to panic. When Old Chicago heard about *this*, the career of one Johannes Stankiewicz was coming to a screeching halt. In fact, he'd be lucky if that was all that happened to him.

"How could your people possibly have missed something like this?" Kellogg went on, directing his ire at Minister of Internal Security Reinhard Freeman.

That, Stankiewicz reflected, was an excellent question...and the one he was certain Old Chicago was going to ask *him*, as well. Unfortunately, Meroa, while a fee-paying member of the Protectorates in all but name, was technically an independent star nation. It was also one where there'd been remarkably little visible unrest since the Argo III Incident of 1898. Because of which, there was no official Gendarmerie presence in Meroa and he'd become accustomed to relying on Freeman and the Meroan Citizen Protection Force for intelligence assessments.

Big *mistake, Johannes*, he thought now.

"We don't know we *have* missed anything," Freeman protested. "All we've got so far is Manticore's and Barregos's unsupported word for all of it! You *know* the Manties have to be looking for any lever they can find, and as for *Barregos*—! Do you really think a man who's in the process of openly rebelling against the League is going to worry a hell of a lot about telling us the truth—or even about whether or not *he* was told the truth!—instead of whatever serves his purpose is best?"

"Colonel?" Kellogg said, turning his glower upon the slight, blond-haired woman seated at Freeman's elbow.

Colonel Jessica Myhrvold commanded the Meroan Citizen Protection Force, the system-wide unitary police force responsible for criminal investigations... when it could spare the time from hunting down any potential threats to the Kellogg regime's authority. Despite her relatively low official rank, she was actually one of the most power-ful members of the Meroan establishment, and the anger in Kellogg's expression wasn't very surprising, given the resources poured into the MCPF. But Myhrvold's hazel eyes met the system president's steely glare without flinching.

"I'm afraid I can't fully support Minister Freeman's argument, Sir," she said.

Freeman bristled visibly and opened his mouth, but Kellogg's chopping hand motion shut it again.

"Expand on that," the president said coldly.

"Mister President," Myhrvold said carefully, "we've actually seen several what you might call 'straws in the wind' over the last eight to twelve T-months. None of them were strong enough to suggest anything like *this* to my investigators, but there's been growing evidence—especially among the belters and miners—that something called the Meroa Resis-tance Movement is out there."

"And why have *I* never heard of this—what did you call it? 'Meroa Resistance Movement'?" Kellogg demanded in an even icier tone.

"I'm afraid I can't answer that question, Mister President," she said.

"Why not?"

"Because I don't report directly to you in these matters," she replied in a painfully neutral tone, and Kellogg's eyes swiveled back to Free-man like twin missile tubes.

"Should I assume from the Colonel's response, that she *did* report this to *you*, Johannes?"

"Well, yes." Freeman was less than happy, and the anger in his eyes boded ill for Myhrvold's future. Unless there was a change in Ministers of Internal Security, Stankiewicz reflected. "But there's always some loudmouth out there, Adenauer! You know that as well as I do. The rabble gets filled up with cheap beer and overinflated egos and mouths start shooting off, and those dimwit belters are the worst of the lot." He shook his head in disgust. "If we spent all our time worrying about lowbrow blowhards, we'd never get anything done!"

And that, Stankiewicz thought tartly, *is probably the reason all of you are about to get the chop, Minister. You really* are *an idiot, aren't you?*

That was probably a bit unfair, which didn't bother Stankiewicz much at the moment. In fact, however, Freeman *wasn't* an idiot. No one would ever accuse him of brilliance, but he didn't have to be reminded to wipe drool off his chin, either. What he was, unfortunately, was a product of the Meroan elite's "bubble."

OFS had seen the same thing again and again in the façade democracies it propped up throughout the Fringe. People at the apex felt unbridled contempt for the people who spent their lives laboring to support their "betters" in the style to which they had become accustomed. After all, if those lesser being had *mattered*, they'd have been the ones making the decisions, right? The fact that they weren't was directly attributable to their inherent inferiority and general stupidity, not the inequality of opportunity.

It wasn't that hard to understand. God knew Stankiewicz had seen the same thinking inside the League. In fact, it was part and parcel of the entire inside-the-Kuiper community...which undoubtedly helped explain why the entire fricking galaxy was blowing up in the League's face.

"Obviously, this is one batch of 'blowhards' we *should* have been worrying about." Kellogg bit out each word like a pulser dart, and Freeman flushed darkly. The system president glared at him for another few seconds, then sat back, laid his forearms on his chair's armrests, and inhaled deeply.

"All right," he said finally. "How things got this fucked up is less important—at the moment—than the fact that they are. And it's not like *all* our problems are homegrown anymore, is it? So the question becomes, what do we do about it?" He bared his teeth in something no one would ever have mistaken for a smile. "Any suggestions?"

✧   ✧   ✧

"Do you *believe* this shit?" Gottfried McAnally demanded.

He looked around the quiet table in the back corner of Belinda's Bar and saw the same stunned expressions on the other three people sitting with him.

"You tell *me*, Boss," Michael van Wyk said. "You're the one who was talking to the Manties. You *really* think it was all a setup?"

"I don't know!"

McAnally raised both hands and waved them in frustration. He was a huge man, over a hundred and ninety centimeters tall, with dark auburn hair, a full—but neatly trimmed—beard, and hard brown eyes. At the moment, those eyes looked even harder than they normally did, but there was an unusual edge of something like uncertainty in their depths.

That was a quality one seldom associated with Gottfried McAnally. He was as pugnacious as he was physically tough, his natural inclination was to go *through* an obstacle, rather than around it, and he generally knew *exactly* what he meant to accomplish. Still, that didn't mean he wasn't capable of subtlety. The fact that he'd built the Meroa Resistance Movement from a handful of hard-core, roughneck asteroid miners who were the next best thing to anarchists into a tightly organized force on the brink of what looked like almost certain victory was a testimony to that.

At the moment, however, there was very little "subtlety" in his expression.

"Calm down, Gottfried," the petite—well, in comparison to him—woman on the other side of the table said. He glared at her, but Seiko McAnally seemed remarkably unfazed by it. Which probably had something to do with the fact that she'd been married to him for the last twenty T-years.

"Stop taking it as some sort of personal affront, and *think* about it," she continued sternly. "I wouldn't want you to get a swelled head or anything, but the fact is that your brain actually works...when you remember to engage it. So, turn it on, fly boy!"

The other woman at the table laughed.

"*That's* the spirit, Seiko!" Belinda McCleskey, McAnally's aunt, shook her finger under his nose. "Listen to your smarter half, boyo!"

McAnally glowered at her, but he also smiled. Reluctantly, perhaps, but smiled, then nodded in acknowledgment of the needed lighter moment.

"That's not a bad notion," he said, after a moment, reaching across to touch Seiko's hand where it lay on the tabletop. "Too bad I don't have any more information or insight than the rest of you do. Yeah, I'm the one who was talking to the 'Manties,' but I kept you three in the loop on all of it. So, come down to it, I guess the real answer is...I just don't know."

The others sat back, chewing on that unpalatable fact. McAnally made himself wait while they masticated, and while he waited, he faced a few unpalatable thoughts of his own. Like the fact that he really didn't *want* Oravil Barregos's envoy to have been telling the truth.

Gottfried McAnally had been only seventeen when his Uncle Leopold,

Belinda McCleskey's husband, and a dozen other men and women died on the Argo III extraction platform. Technically, they'd been occupying it illegally for almost a T-month before the Meroan System Patrol and the Citizen Protection Force moved in. They'd offered no violence to anyone, and they'd caused no damage, but that didn't matter when the MCPF got its orders. They'd been told to make an example. To discourage any of the other contract miners—and the last handful of independents had been forced into indentured contracts over the preceding fifteen T-years—from getting uppity. From demanding safety equipment be regularly inspected and replaced at need. From insisting their contract delivery rates had to at least pay for their reactor mass and let them put food on their families' tables. From suggesting *they* might have any legitimate voice in the decrees Management handed down like Zeus thundering from Olympus.

Obviously, there'd been only one way to make that point, and Belinda McCleskey had buried her husband, the man who'd raised Gottfried McAnally after his own miner father's death in one of those ships whose safety equipment had somehow slipped through the inspection cracks.

McAnally had followed his uncle into the belts, and he was good. He was one of the best, which meant even Management thought about it, at least for a second or two, before they rejected his operational input. Of course, as the nephew of one of the infamous Argo III hooligans, no one would have considered offering him a position *in* Management, but at least they'd been smart enough to let him run his own four-boat mining section however the hell he wanted to as long as it continued coming in a solid twenty percent above quota.

Which, actually, had been incredibly stupid of them, because that squadron of mining vessels had become the core of the MRM.

It had taken him *years* to move beyond that trusted handful of hard-rock asteroid miners, but he had. Oh, but he had! The chance that he'd actually have been able to accomplish anything might not have been incredibly great. Personally, he'd estimated no more than a forty percent chance of throwing out the Kellogg regime, and something more like *five percent* that OFS and Frontier Fleet wouldn't turn up to crush his movement immediately thereafter. Still, he'd figured, a man had to have a hobby.

And then, two years ago, the opportunity for more had suddenly appeared.

He'd come so *close*.

Commodore François Malinowski's System Patrol was a joke, no more than a handful of obsolete light attack craft suitable—barely—for customs patrols, the occasional rescue mission, and escorting transports full of MCPF riot troops to deal with irritating little situations like the one which had occurred on Argo III. At the moment, McAnally had two dozen—*two dozen*—mining boats which had been fitted with strap-on missile pods and lasers. Any one of them was as powerful as two of Malinowski's rattletraps, and no one in the MSP or MCPF had a clue they'd been armed or that McAnally's highly skilled miners had acquired another set of skills along with their weaponry.

His forty percent chance of kicking Kellogg out the airlock had turned into one of at least *ninety* percent. And, far more important than the weapons themselves, he'd been offered the one thing that might let the Resistance make its rebellion stand up: naval support. Not just *anyone's* naval support, either, but the Royal Manticoran Navy's. With the RMN in his skinsuit pocket, he'd known the time had finally come to reclaim Meroa from OFS and its thieving, bloodsucking "elected leaders."

And now this. Now a light cruiser of something calling itself the Mayan Autonomous Regional Sector Navy—and wasn't *that* a mouthful?—had arrived on Merriwell's doorstep less than two local weeks before his uprising was slated to begin. Arrived to announce that McAnally hadn't been talking to Manticorans at all. That he'd been played by someone whose sole interest in Meroa was to see the uprising crushed as catastrophically as possible. Someone for whom the MRM's bloody destruction wasn't even a primary goal, only "collateral damage" in a strategy focused upon the Star Empire of Manticore and its allies.

Oravil Barregos was OFS himself. By definition, that meant he couldn't be trusted. Yet he had a reputation in the Maya Sector of being a different breed of governor, and his cruiser hadn't arrived alone. It had been accompanied by a Royal Manticoran Navy destroyer whose captain had confirmed every single word of Barregos's statement. Who'd gone on the public boards and informed the entire star system that the Star Empire had no idea who might have been planning an insurrection here in Meroa. Who'd further announced that the RMN hadn't promised *anyone* any support and had no desire to see Meroa disintegrate into violence.

But who'd also offered a stern warning to the Kellogg administration.

"Her Majesty's government has had no prior contact with any individual or group of individuals in this star system," the level-eyed woman in the black and gold uniform had said. "The Star Empire has, however, become aware that there are a great many people in a great many star systems who *believe* they've been in contact with Manticoran representatives. And Her Majesty has decided that if any of those individuals who honestly believe they've been promised Manticoran support act on the basis of that promise, the Star Empire will not abandon them to their fates. We do not condone violent rebellion as a means of regime change. At the same time, Her Majesty recognizes that sometimes violence is the only means of regime change available. That decision is not hers to make in someone else's star nation.

"The official policy of the Star Empire of Manticore is that we will not provide active support to any organization that engages in open violence, regardless of who that organization believes may have promised to support it, *if that violence begins after the Star Empire has announced its new policy*. If violence has *already* begun, then the Royal Manticoran Navy—*and its Allies*—stand ready to prevent outside intervention in the star systems where it has begun. And, in star systems where false promises of Manticoran assistance have been used to entice citizens into planning armed rebellion, it is the Star Empire's policy—announced today, in Meroa—to impose a brokered solution to the causes of contention in those star systems. We will not support armed rebellion, but neither will we accept forcible suppression of any group which prepared *for* armed rebellion after being lied to by someone purporting to represent Her Majesty's Government. We will offer the services of Manticoran diplomats in efforts to broker a peaceful resolution in such cases, but we will *not* allow people who honestly believe that we had promised them support be destroyed while we stand by and watch.

"We believe Meroa is one of the systems in which those false promises of naval support were made. We call upon whoever believed she was operating with the assurance of Manticoran naval support to...rethink her position. And the Star Empire wholeheartedly endorses Governor Barregos's suggestion of a multi-system conference where *all* of these issues will be brought out into the open and dealt with.

"We do not expect this to be easy. We do not expect it to be simple, we do not expect it to be dealt with quickly...and we do not believe the status quo in most of these systems is sustainable or that it will survive. Our analysis is that the people we believe are behind this 'false flag' operation chose systems in which internal tensions made rebellion nearly inevitable. As a consequence, we anticipate that there will be enormous resistance, particularly by the individuals and organizations currently in power, to constructive changes in those star systems. We have no desire to forcibly impose our own solutions on those star systems. We will, however, forcibly prevent any outside intervention—for or against the existing regimes—in them. And, assuming that negotiated solutions to the existing causes of contention cannot be achieved under Governor Barregos's leadership, then the Star Empire of Manticore, the Protectorate of Grayson, the Republic of Haven Navy, the Republic of Erewhon, and the Mayan Autonomous Regional Sector will apply whenever economic and political sanctions seem necessary to *compel* solutions.

"No doubt many will condemn this as the raw abuse of power. Others will see it as proof of the Solarian League's endless claims of Manticoran imperialism. We have no designs upon anyone's sovereignty, but if we must use raw power to prevent millions of deaths for which the galaxy at large will hold the Star Empire responsible, then so be it. No one is going to die on Manticore's watch if there is any way in heaven or hell that we can prevent it."

She'd gazed out of the display, her brown eyes like flint.

"I advise every one of you to believe Her Majesty means it."

Hillary Indrakashi Enkateshwara Tower
City of Old Chicago
Sol System
Solarian League

"TALK ABOUT THROWING A cat among pigeons!"

Irene Teague shook her head, her expression grim. None of the other Ghost Hunters currently assembled in their Hillary Indrakashi Enkateshwara Tower hideaway looked a lot more cheerful.

"I hate to ask this, Zhing-hwan," Bryce Tarkovsky said, "but how good is this guy? I don't mean how much you trust him. I mean how *good* is he?"

"Michal Asztalos is about as good as they get," Weng Zhing-hwan replied flatly. "He's young, I'll grant that, but the Gendarmerie didn't make him a major at his age for screwing up."

She paused to look rather pointedly at the oak leaf on Tarkovsky's collar for a moment, and the Marine nodded in recognition of her point.

"I admit I picked him because I trusted him to give me an honest report," she continued, "but I also picked him because I trust his *judgment*. And because I know Michal's *damned* good at figuring out things other people want to keep hidden."

"I think part of what concerns *me* at this point—and what I'm pretty sure is going to bother Daud when he hears about this—is that it doesn't sound like he had to '*find out*' very damned much," Teague said, then shook her head again. "I can't believe Barregos would have just carelessly left this kind of evidence lying around if he was really up to something!"

"I've been thinking about that, too," Lupe Blanton said. The others looked at her, and she shrugged. "I realize what we're talking about is officially more Nyhus's bailiwick than mine. Having said that, my people and I have seen a lot over the years, and we've caught our own people with their fingers in pies they know damned well they shouldn't have anything to do with a lot more frequently than OFS would like to admit. And I've been looking at Barregos's record. Someone as smart and as capable as he obviously is should be at least as good at hiding his tracks as, say, a third assistant legate assigned to an OFS advisory mission in the Protectorates who's been embezzling from the mission's mess funds.

So I think you're right, Irene; Asztalos should've had to work a lot harder to find any genuine evidence that Barregos wanted to hide."

Her tone shifted ever so slightly on the last three words, and Teague looked at her sharply.

"You're thinking he *didn't* want to hide it?"

"I'm thinking he not only didn't want to hide it, but that he and Allfrey took pains to make sure Asztalos found it."

"That's what Michal thinks, too," Weng said. "I brought along his entire memo, and I'm sure you'll all want to view it for yourselves, but Philip Allfrey himself gave him access to the files containing this 'classified' information. He didn't tell Michal it was *in* those files, but he must've had a shrewd suspicion about what Michal was looking for. On that basis, I think Allfrey—which means Barregos, of course—*wanted* this stuff to get back to Old Chicago. Which leads to the additional question of what we do with it now that we've got it."

"Let me be sure I understand this correctly," Colonel Okiku said. "According to Asztalos, there's *documented evidence* in Barregos's files that he was contacted by individuals claiming to be Manticoran who weren't? That these individuals promised him naval support—*massive* naval support—if he'd rebel against Frontier Security and the League? But that he was subsequently contacted by someone he knows really *is* high in Manty intelligence circles, and *she* told him about a false flag operation being run by someone else?"

"That's essentially correct, Natsuko." Weng nodded. Okiku looked at her skeptically, and the Gendarme smiled crookedly at her. "In fact, Michal's pretty sure he could put a name on the individual who's 'high in Manty intelligence circles.' Having read the relevant portion of the documentation he brought with him—I haven't had time to go through *all* of it yet—I'm inclined to think *I* could, too."

"Really?" Okiku cocked her head. "Who?"

"Unless I'm very mistaken, it was Patricia Givens."

Okiku looked blank, but Tarkovsky looked up quickly and Teague pursed her lips in a silent whistle.

"Obviously, the simple but honest cop here is missing something," Okiku observed tartly.

"Pat Givens is the Manticoran Second Space Lord," Teague said. "That puts her about as 'high in Manty intelligence circles' as it gets, since the second space lord is the one who runs their Office of Naval Intelligence. If Asztalos's right, that's about the same thing as Kolokoltsov sending Karl-Heinz Thimár somewhere as his envoy. Except that Givens is at least as good as Thimár is—or *was*, thank God—*bad*." She shook her head slowly. "That puts a bit of a different slant on things.

If Givens is giving *her* word to someone about what's going on, it's got to be the official Manty position."

"Not necessarily." Tarkovsky shook his head, and she raised an eyebrow at him. "Let me preface my next point by saying that *I* think that's what it means, too," the Marine said. "But Givens, unfortunately, *is* one of their most senior spooks. She may be a high-ranking naval officer, as well, but all the Mandarins will look at is the fact that she's a *spook*. They'll point out that assuming the Manties really are behind all of this, she'd have to be one of the people who helped craft the strategy in the first place. As one of its architects, she wouldn't hesitate for a second to lie about it to someone like Barregos, would she? And be honest—if we didn't already suspect the Manties *weren't* behind it, wouldn't we be ready to recognize the same possibility?"

"I think that would depend on how stupid I thought the Manties were," Blanton said slowly, her eyes thoughtful. Tarkovsky looked at her, and she shrugged. "What you're suggesting has something of a split personality, Bryce. On the one hand, the Manties are telling OFS—maybe a bit indirectly, through Barregos, but still OFS—that they don't have anything at all to do with this. On the other hand, they're supposed to be providing naval support to rebellions all over the Fringe, à la Terekhov in Mobius."

"But Terekhov also said Manticore had never contacted the Mobian resistance before it started killing people about the time he 'just happened to turn up' in Mobius to squash Yucel and Lombroso like cockroaches," Tarkovsky pointed out. "Sounds to me like someone could reasonably conclude this was simply another iteration of the same strategy. I could certainly make the case that this is two naval officers reading from the same page—sort of like Capriotti and Hajdu using the same stupid talking points to justify Buccaneer—and that all Givens really wants is to get that side of the story better coverage in the League's 'faxes."

"But this time they're talking to an OFS governor, not the newsies, and not a word about this supposed meeting's made it into the 'faxes or onto the boards," Blanton countered. "If the theory you're suggesting holds water, they've bought themselves the worst of both worlds, in a way. They can't wave away whatever records Barregos might have made, which means—in theory, at least—that OFS has Givens talking covertly to an official representative of the League, face-to-face, for Abruzzi and his flacks at Information to use against Manticore whenever they choose. They have to be aware of what Abruzzi could do with that, probably without even doing a hell of a lot of CGI! But she went ahead and met with him anyway, assuming we've identified her correctly. If he's a good, loyal little sector governor and passes this contact up the chain and they aren't telling him—and, through him, the Mandarins—the truth, that has to come back and bite them on the arse. If they *are* telling the truth, and if they genuinely hope to get it to Old Chicago—or the newsies—by this weird, circuitous route, they're risking a hell of a lot doing it *this* way."

"Which means...?" Tarkovsky asked.

"I don't think someone of Givens's seniority would've been talking to someone of *Barregos's* seniority unless the Manties and their allies wanted something out of him. And notice that Barregos hasn't passed Givens's denial of responsibility—or even a single mention of their *covert* meeting—on to Old Chicago."

A brief, intense silence fell. It lay there for several seconds, then Okiku stirred in her chair.

"I don't like where you're going with that thought, Lupe," she said quietly.

"I don't, either, especially," Weng said. "On the other hand, the possibility that Barregos is up to something Old Chicago wouldn't like is the reason I sent Michal out to have a look around for us in the first place. And, while we're on the subject, I should point out that some of his other contacts suggested Barregos had made 'a major policy decision' just before his ship translated out for Sol. They didn't tell him what *kind* of policy decision, but given who we know he's been talking to..."

"Shit," Tarkovsky muttered, and Weng smiled sourly.

"Oh, this is going to get *so* bad," Teague murmured, and Blanton nodded soberly.

"I think you're right. I think if Barregos wasn't going to give them what they wanted, then he sure as hell *would* have reported the entire exchange to Old Chicago. The fact that he hasn't suggests OFS is going to be hearing really bad news from the Protectorates sometime very soon now."

"Maybe. Maybe even *probably*," Weng said. "But there's another side to this, from our perspective."

"Oh, I can see *dozens* of sides," Okiku said. "I'm just having a little trouble finding one that's good 'from our perspective'! Which of the *un*-good ones—in particular—did you have in mind?"

"Barregos *is* smart," Weng pointed out. "If Lupe's right about his buying into the game on the Manties' side, then he must be convinced they're telling him the truth. And, trust me, this is a man who'd need a *lot* of convincing before he crossed any Rubicons."

"You mean it's more evidence it's really the Other Guys," Tarkovsky said.

"That's exactly what I mean."

"You may well be right," Teague said. "In fact, I think you are. But more immediately, this is going to drive MacArtney and the other Mandarins berserk. Whatever Barregos is planning, he's planning it as the governor of an entire *sector*. Mobius was *one* system, and its contribution to the federal cash flow wasn't all that enormous. Losing it hurt, but I'm pretty sure they've been thinking of it more in terms of encouraging *other* systems to do the same thing. But we aren't talking about single Fringe planets in Barregos's case; we're talking about an entire damned *sector*, and every planet in it produces about twice as much revenue as any other single planet out there. I don't like to think about how the Mandarins are likely to react in *Maya* if he decides to sign up with the 'Grand Alliance,' but I'm almost more scared by how they'll react somewhere else. Daud and I are being asked for a lot of analysis on Beowulf, people."

"*Beowulf?*" Tarkovsky said sharply. "I thought Daud said they'd dropped that piece of insanity!"

"Bryce, nobody tells us what Bernard and Strategy and Planning are actually thinking about! It's not like Operational Analysis needs to know what they're currently planning to give them the best analysis, after all." Teague rolled her eyes. "Besides, even now, nobody really wants to admit Daud was right when none of them could tell their arses from their elbows. They want him to answer specific questions and otherwise keep his mouth shut and stop reminding them—and their *superiors*—what clueless idiots they were. That mindset flows straight down from Admiral Cheng, and nobody between us and him's going to buck it. So, no, nobody's told us what they're contemplating, and no one's likely to *start* telling us anytime soon. But that doesn't mean we can't make some guesses from the questions they choose to ask."

"You're suggesting they're seriously thinking about attacking Beowulf?" Okiku asked in the tone of a woman who very much hoped she'd misunderstood what she'd just been told.

"I'm suggesting they're asking for analysis that only makes sense in terms of some sort of operation against Beowulf," Teague replied. "And I'm saying that after the shit they tried to pull in the Hypatia and everything else that's gone down in the sacred name of *Operation Buccaneer*," the last two words were a snarled obscenity, "there's not a frigging thing I would put past these people. Beyond that, I've got nothing."

"Jesus." Tarkovsky shook his head. "I thought what might be going down in Maya was bad. But if you're right about what Bernard and her trolls are cooking up, that's the least of our worries!"

"Except," Weng pointed out, "for the resonance effect." Tarkovsky looked at her, and she shrugged. "If Barregos and the Maya Sector go up in flames, it's likely to push them over the edge. And if they're already thinking that way..."

Her voice trailed off, and it was very, very quiet in Hillary Indrakashi Enkateshwara Tower.

HMS *Imperator*
Trevor's Star Terminus
Trevor's Star System
Star Empire of Manticore

"MR. ZILWICKI IS HERE, Your Grace," Lieutenant Commander Tümmel announced, and Honor turned from the spectacular starscape outside HMS *Imperator*'s domed dorsal observation lounge.

"Thank you, Waldemar," she said, and extended her hand to Zilwicki. "And thank you for coming so promptly, Anton."

"You're welcome, as always, Your Grace," Zilwicki replied, and she looked over his shoulder at Tümmel.

"That'll be all, Waldemar. But do me a favor. Screen Commander Brantley and Captain Stefano. Make certain Admiral L'anglais knows about the briefing. I'm not sure if she was planning on personally participating in that task group maneuver she'd laid on. If she did, though, she's probably halfway to San Martin right now. Find out. And if there are any scheduling issues involved in getting her—her personally, not a deputy—here for the briefing, get with Commodore Brigham and work them out. Tell the Commodore she's authorized to set the timing on it however she has to to make it work."

"Yes, Your Grace. Understood," Tümmel said, rather more soberly than usual. He braced briefly to attention. "With your permission, Your Grace?"

Honor nodded permission for him to withdraw and returned her attention to Zilwicki.

The Highlander looked back at her, one eyebrow arched. He'd been a bit surprised when Tümmel led him straight into the lounge, because Major Hawke had been standing outside the hatch with Corporal Atkins, not inside it where he could make sure his Steadholder wasn't kidnapped by space elves when he wasn't looking. That was an unusual departure from his standard paranoia, and there was something unusual about her, as well, now that he thought about it. She seemed more... focused than usual, and Nimitz's body language seemed tenser as the treecat gazed intently at him.

"Your Grace?" he said, and she smiled at him.

"I need to make sure there aren't any conflicts with your schedule for that briefing, either," she told him. "I think your input's likely to be pretty significant."

"*My* input?"

"Yours," she replied, then astonished him by reaching out to lay her hands on his shoulders and squeeze tightly. "We just got word from Admiral Gold Peak. Tenth Fleet reached Mesa nine days ago."

Zilwicki stiffened, his face suddenly pale, his eyes huge and dark, and she shook her head quickly.

"Mike got there in time, Anton!" she told him quickly. "She got there in *time*."

She shook him, and despite his massive physique, she had the strength to do it.

"The final assault on Neue Rostock was just about to roll in when she and Lester Tourville turned up." She smiled into his incredulous eyes, the eyes of a man who hadn't truly allowed himself to hope, whatever he might have told the rest of the universe . . . or himself. "The tower's basically rubble, some of your people are banged up—I understand Ms. Tretiakovna's going to need substantial regen—and casualties among the seccies were brutal. But they *held*, Anton." Tears filled his eyes, and her own weren't completely dry. "They held their ground against every damned thing they threw at them, and Thandi Palane—and the seccies—made the bastards pay in blood for every centimeter. They broke Internal Security's back and damned well *gutted* the Peaceforce, and every seccy on the planet *knows* they did, by God! And I understand your friend Mr. Cachat had prepared a little going away present for the moment they were finally overrun. Something involving explosions, I believe." She bared her teeth. "*Lots* of explosions."

"Sounds—"

Zilwicki stopped. He had to, and he realized he'd reached up, covered the hand on his right shoulder with his own hand while he felt the tears flow down his face. He didn't care about the tears, but he had to clear his throat twice before he could continue.

"Sounds like Victor," he husked then, and cleared his throat a third time. "Man always has liked dramatic gestures."

"So I understand."

She smiled, gave his shoulders a final squeeze, and stood back while he scrubbed the tears from his face. He understood Hawke's absence now, he thought as she turned back to the dome, giving him a little more privacy, and he scrubbed again. Then he drew a deep breath and stepped up beside her, looking out at the stars.

"They're really okay, Your Grace?" He hated asking redundant questions, but just this once, he couldn't help it. "*Really* okay?"

"I told you, they're banged up. Frankly, I'm astonished the breakage wasn't a lot worse, given what they managed to pull off and the odds against them. And from Mike's—I mean Countess Gold Peak's—initial reports, they accomplished exactly what you set out to do. I have to say, after listening to your descriptions of him, it's a little difficult to recognize Jurgen Dusek in the heroic, freedom-loving, father-of-his-star-nation-scale revolutionary Admiral Gold Peak describes, but at the moment, he and General Palane have to be the two most popular people on the entire planet, at least in the seccies' and slaves' eyes. Not so much, in the establishment's view of things."

"I imagine not!" Zilwicki surprised himself with a deep, rolling laugh. "I guess they have to be the most *hated* people in Mesa where the 'establishment' is concerned!"

"No."

Her voice had changed, and he heard a sound out of Nimitz. A *dark* sound, somehow, he thought. He looked at her quickly, and his eyes narrowed, for her expression had changed completely. It had turned bitter, that odd focus he'd seen in her was far more pronounced than it had been, and her eyes had gone very, very cold.

"No, the most hated person in Mesa right this moment is Countess Gold Peak," she said flatly. "Because Tenth Fleet carried out an unprovoked nuclear strike—a *series* of nuclear strikes—on the planet after it had surrendered."

Anton Zilwicki was a very fast thinker. Anyone who knew him knew better than to let his massive, undeniably *heavy*-looking physique deceive them about the lightning speed of his brain. Despite which, it took a second or two for what she'd said to register.

"*What?*" he demanded then.

"I'm sure that's going to be the conclusion of everyone in Old Chicago." Honor said grimly. "It already is in Mesa. Certainly where the establishment's concerned, and I imagine even quite a few of the seccies have bought into it, as well. Hard to blame them, I suppose. There we are, orbiting the planet, every ship they've got's surrendered, the ground forces have laid down their weapons, and then somebody hits the planet with over *thirty* nuclear strikes."

Zilwicki had paled. Now his face went absolutely white, and she gave him the savage smile of a wolf.

"In addition to the strikes on the planet, they blew the Lagrange One orbital habitat, as well. According to the Mesans, that killed the next best thing to three million people all by itself, and we don't have any kind of number yet on the *dirt-side* casualties. Mostly because the strikes on the planet were scattered all over the place—some of them in urban centers, some of them in the middle of prairies or on top of mountain towns. One of them on an uninhabited *island*, for God's sake!"

"But why..."

He broke off, and then he put that wolf's smile together with what she'd said about his attending the briefing.

"It's the 'terrorist campaign' writ large, isn't it Your Grace?" he said softly.

"I think that's exactly what it is." Honor's voice was hard as Sphinxian granite. "The dispersal suggests to me that whoever pushed that button was deleting that hard evidence of the Alignment you and Terry Lassaline and Pat Givens and I have talked about. Oh, she didn't overlook the way this is going to play so perfectly into the Mandarins' narrative, either, especially after the Green Pines Incident. I can't even begin to imagine what effect it's going to have on Core World public opinion, but I'm pretty sure that was her *secondary* goal. The primary was to fill in the rabbit hole behind her."

"That's what you want me at the briefing to talk about?"

"Among other things." She nodded. "More immediately, you've been on Mesa itself more recently than anyone else in the entire Star Empire. You can give all of us a better context for Mike's report, and that's particularly important because this is a *preliminary* report. There's bound to be a lot more detail coming along behind, but—for what I imagine are pretty obvious reasons—she needed to inform us about what happened after the surrender as quickly as possible."

Zilwicki nodded in grim understanding. God only knew how the galaxy in general would react to an atrocity like this, but it damned well wasn't going to be good. No wonder Gold Peak had given Manticore as much warning as possible!

"So I want you available to fill in background for all of us," Honor continued. "But, in some ways, I especially want you there for Admiral L'anglais's benefit."

Zilwicki frowned in confusion, and she snorted.

"I've gotten to know Admiral L'anglais a lot better over the last few weeks. I respect her deeply. But she has...reservations about her star nation's alliance with someone it's been shooting at for so long. Admiral Tourville's endorsed Admiral Gold Peak's report. For that matter, he's sent along one of his own, which corroborates hers in every detail. I know Admiral L'anglais will try to view those reports with an open, unbiased mind; what I *don't* know is whether or not she'll succeed. I'm sure Admiral Tourville's input will help with that, but, frankly, carnage on this level as part of nothing more than a deception measure—as something that amounts to a psychological warfare ploy—is hard for *me* to wrap my mind around. I expect it to be harder for her."

Zilwicki nodded.

"I want you to share everything with her—and I mean *everything*, Anton; I'm authorizing you to pull out all the stops—that you and Harahap have been able to put together about the reason for those 'terrorist attacks' and what they may have been concealing. To show her the reasons—the *other* reasons—someone might have done something like this. I'm not sure how much faith L'anglais puts in the existence of the Alignment. I think she accepts that it's real, but I also think she has doubts about its reach and our analysis of its ultimate objectives. I need you to put our case to her."

"Of course, Your Grace. But she must've seen the reports we've already generated."

Zilwicki made the statement a question, and Honor nodded.

"In that case, I don't know how much I can add. We haven't written up my suspicions about any evacuations—not in any official reports, yet—but she'll have seen everything else already."

"You're right." Honor conceded, but then she surprised him with a smile. "On the other hand, there's Sun Catcher."

"Sun Catcher?"

"Sun Catcher's the 'cat who's agreed to help keep her alive." Honor's smile broadened. "They've only been together for a few weeks, but they're already what you might call close. It tends to work that way with 'cats. And L'anglais has figured out that Sun Catcher can—and will—tell her if anyone's lying to her. So while she may have doubts about the honesty of all the anonymous, faceless spooks and policy wonks recording those reports she's viewed, she won't have any about *your* veracity."

Honor shrugged and her smile disappeared.

"I don't know if it'll help, Anton, but I know darned well it can't *hurt*. No matter what we do or say, an awful lot of people will never believe we're not the ones behind those explosions. I know that. But at this particular moment, I can't begin to tell you how much we don't need Grand Fleet's second-in-command to be one of the people wondering if *we're* the ones lying to her."

HMS *Artemis*
Mesa planetary orbit
Mesa System

"ATENNNN-*HUT!*"

Captain Cynthia Lecter, chief of staff, Tenth Fleet, was not a particularly large woman, but her voice was crisp and sharp, and the men and women packed into the large briefing room rose as Michelle Henke, Countess Gold Peak and Tenth Fleet's commanding officer, entered the compartment with her second-in-command at her side.

That briefing room was unusually crowded and its inhabitants' expressions were much grimmer than one might have expected from people who had just conquered an entire star system without firing a single shot.

Of course, that was rather the point, Gold Peak reflected as she and Lester Tourville crossed to the table at the center of the compartment. She settled into the chair at its head, Tourville took the one to her right, and she nodded.

"Be seated, ladies and gentlemen," she invited, and her husky contralto was bleaker than usual.

A rustling sound answered as the assembled squadron and divisional commanders, Manticorans and Havenites interspersed around the table, obeyed the command. She let them all settle, then squared her shoulders and looked around those grim faces.

"I know all of us wish we were somewhere else this morning," she said. "Unfortunately, this bag of snakes wouldn't get any better wherever we were. It looks like we're going to get bitten however we reach into it, but I don't want any rumors or misinformation running around the Fleet if we can prevent it. God knows we won't be able to stop or control whatever's said by the Mesans and the Sollies. I'd at least like to minimize the wilder versions among our own people. However we proceed from this point, there's going to be a lot of contact—there already *is* a lot of contact, and that can only increase—between our people and the Mesans, and I don't want anything from *our* end making that contact any more contentious than it has to be. And to be

524

honest, I'm less worried about our naval personnel than I am about our ground forces, in that respect."

She looked down the table's length to where two of the few people present who weren't in naval uniform sat side by side.

General Susan Hibson commanded the ground forces under Tenth Fleet's control. Her complexion was dark—much lighter than Gold Peak's, but darker than most of the others in the compartment—and at just over a meter and a half, she was the shortest person present. Although she might be accurately described as "small"—possibly even "tiny," by some particularly foolhardy souls—no one would ever make the mistake of applying the adjective "fragile" to her solidly muscled physique. She was just as tough mentally as she was physically, and despite her current, horrendous task, she looked back to meet her admiral's eyes levelly.

General Saartje van Heemskerck, her own second in command, sat beside her. Van Heemskerck was twenty centimeters taller and twenty T-years older than Hibson and a native of the Rembrandt System. In fact, she was Bernardus van Dort's third or fourth cousin, with red hair lightly stranded with silver and gray eyes. She was also the senior officer of the Talbott Quadrant Guard planetary combat forces which had been forwarded to Tenth Fleet's support by Governor Medusa and Quadrant Prime Minister Alquezar. Gold Peak had peeled off a hefty chunk of that troop strength to serve as backup for the new government forming in the Meyers System and the naval forces responding to the Mesan Alignment's false flag operations. She'd hung on to the majority of it, which meant van Heemskerck's current roster strength amounted to just over three quarters of a million men and women.

That was a lot of combat power, and someone van Heemskerck's age and with that many men and women under her direct command might reasonably have found her nose out of joint at the notion of serving under someone who'd never commanded a force larger than a couple of battalions in her entire career. In fact, Gold Peak probably would have reversed her and Hibson's roles under normal circumstances, despite her own deep respect for the Marine. Unfortunately—or fortunately, depending upon one's viewpoint—Henri Krietzmann, the Talbott Quadrant's Minister of War, had raised the Talbott Quadrant Guard Expeditionary Force specifically to serve under the command of the Royal Manticoran Navy and Marine Corps.

Gold Peak wasn't certain she agreed with that policy, but Joachim Alquezar, the Talbott Quadrant's prime minister, had been insistent. The Quadrant Guard hadn't even existed before the Talbott *Sector* had become the Talbott *Quadrant* of the Star *Empire* of Manticore, and it had been created by merging the existing military establishments of all seventeen of the Quadrant's star systems as a means of assisting in the Quadrant's defense. It was still a very new organization, composed of individual "national" units brigaded together, each with its own organization and rank structure, and some of the newly united star systems had been less than fond of some of the other newly united star systems before their joint admission to the Star Empire. Given the opportunity for internal rivalries and potentially disastrous disputes over seniority and authority, Alquezar and Krietzmann had insisted that whenever the Guard was called to active *imperial* service, it must pass under the command of the Navy and Marines.

Gold Peak understood their logic, although she worried about the potential resentment of men and women who—like van Heemskerck— had spent their entire careers in their home star systems' militaries, rising to general officers rank, only to find themselves subordinate to someone—like Hibson—two-thirds their age and junior in rank, to boot. She'd made it quietly clear to Alquezar, Krietzmann, and Baroness Medusa that she questioned the ultimate sustainability of that policy. For the present, however, she was prepared to accept it, especially in light of the still rather tentative nature of the merger of the individual militaries involved.

Fortunately, Krietzmann obviously hadn't picked van Heemskerck at random to command the Expeditionary Force. She was a calm, competent, professional woman, and if she felt any qualms about serving under Hibson's command, Gold Peak had never seen any sign of it.

"The reason I'm more worried about our ground forces than our naval personnel," she continued, "is simply that our ground forces are going to have more contact with the Mesan in the street than the Navy is. They can't help that. That means they're going to be the ones most likely to run into actively hostile situations, and it's essential that we avoid unnecessary escalations. Don't mistake me, though. No, I don't want *unnecessary* escalation, but given the situation dirtside, any sign of weakness or uncertainty on our part would be even worse. A *lot* worse. I'm not trying to create any wiggle room 'ambiguity' here. General Hibson, you and General van Heemskerck have my full confidence, and I have *your* backs. Use your judgment, but be guided by the firm understanding that the preservation of your people's lives is your highest priority, followed by the preservation of public order and the Grand Alliance's authority in the streets of Mendel and every other city and town on Mesa. That would have been a tough enough assignment under any circumstances, given the numbers of seccies and genetic slaves involved and how badly—and how justifiably—many of them want revenge on the pre-invasion system and the people who ran it. It's going to be a hell of a lot tougher now, so it's essential you coordinate as closely as possible with the Navy and with General Palane and her Citizens' Union. And it's also essential *none* of our people— Navy, Marine, Guard, Manty, Talbotter, Havenite, or Grayson—be in any doubt about who *didn't* nuke the planet after it surrendered."

She paused, looking grimly around the compartment.

"It ought to be simple to prove we didn't do it. Unfortunately, the fact that we can't prove who *did* do it means it's very *un*-simple. Even a newsy like Audrey O'Hanrahan is drawing conclusions on the basis of what she knows and what we can't disprove, and I expect that's only going to get worse. The fact that there are undoubtedly people on our side who think we *should* have nuked the planet until it glows won't help, and if anyone—and I mean *anyone*—is suggesting what happened is a good thing, I want that person stepped on. I want her stepped on immediately, and I want her stepped on *hard*. So far—*so far*—we have a confirmed death toll of over five million and still growing. *Nothing* could justify the cold-blooded murder of that many civilians, and I better not hear one single word suggesting something could have. I want that made *abundantly* clear to every single man and woman in uniform. Is that understood?"

Heads nodded all around the table. She let silence linger briefly, then returned those nods with one of her own.

"In that case, Cynthia," she said, turning to, "what do we know at this point?"

"We don't 'know' a lot more than we did, Milady," Captain Lecter replied with neither hesitation nor apology. The chief of staff doubled as Gold Peak's intelligence officer. It wasn't an easy load for one person to carry, under the circumstances, but every time Gold Peak thought about taking it off her, Lecter once again demonstrated that she was far and away the best person for the job.

Both jobs.

"We've sifted through a lot of data and refined what we know," the captain continued, "but most of it only leaves us with more questions. The final count on planetary nuclear detonations is forty-one. In addition to the Lagrange One explosion, there were nineteen more in Mesa orbit and a total of *twenty-three* scattered throughout the outer system. Quite a few of the latter occurred in places where according to Mesa astro control there was nothing *to* explode."

The chief of staff looked around the compartment.

"As the Admiral just said, the confirmed death toll as of two hours ago is five-point-three-two million. I expect it to top six million before we're done, although given the nature of the attack, we won't have anywhere near that many actual bodies to bury." Her blue eyes were dark, her expression bleak. "That's 'only' about one half of one percent of the total system population, and it's heavily concentrated among the full citizens, but more than enough second-class citizens and slaves were killed, as well. I doubt there's a single person on the planet—probably anywhere in the entire system—who hasn't lost at least one friend or family member. And"—her eyes flicked to Commander Dominica Adenauer, Gold Peak's ops officer—"if anyone in the galaxy understands the kind of hatred and bitterness that can generate, it's us."

She paused, letting that sink in, then inhaled.

"As to who did it, we don't know. We've developed certain suspicions, but that's all they are right now. Admiral Gold Peak's requested the dispatch of intelligence teams from Manticore to assist us in figuring out what the hell is going on. Until we get a response, though, it's up to us, and here's what we have so far.

"First, all of those explosions, at least on the planet, were the result of nukes which were already in place, not of anything delivered to the surface from space. Second, every single dirtside explosion, and all the detonations in planetary orbit, occurred in the space of less than ninety seconds, which obviously 'proves' *we* did it."

"Excuse me for interrupting, Captain Lecter, but how does the timing 'prove' anything of the sort?" Vice Admiral Jennifer Bellefeuille asked. The Havenite admiral who commanded Lester Tourville's Task Force 101 sounded honestly curious, and Lecter smiled grimly.

"It's the narrowness of the time window, Ma'am," she replied. "If this were supposed to be a continuation of the 'terrorist attacks' Agent Cachat and General Palane have reported, they shouldn't have been this tight. So the timing clearly indicates that they were intended to implicate *us*—Tenth Fleet, specifically—since we could, presumably, coordinate our mass-casualty attacks more tightly than a batch of terrorists using stolen commercial Mesan nuclear charges."

Bellefeuille nodded in understanding of the point, and the chief of staff continued.

"We are a little puzzled by some aspects of the timing, but I think my people may be chasing shadows in that respect."

"What respect would that be Captain?" The question came from Oliver Diamato, another of Tourville's task force commanders.

"Lieutenant Weaver, one of my analysts, suggests that the pattern was almost too random," Lecter replied. "He plotted the explosions in terms of time and distance from one another, and found a pattern... of sorts. They sort of hopscotch all across the zone in which they occurred, and he has a naturally suspicious disposition. One of the things I like about him." She flashed a quick smile. "He wondered why, if they were on timers, there was that big a spread to begin with. They should have been able to hit tighter than they did, which presumably would have been even more damning in terms of our responsibility for it. But if they weren't going to be simultaneous, why should explosion number one be halfway around the planet from explosion number two with explosion number three less than five hundred kilometers from explosion number one and explosion number four in low-Mesa orbit? That was the first thing he noticed. But then he noticed that—allowing for transmission lag from the surface of Mesa—every explosion *beyond* Mesa orbit *was* simultaneous. So it appears clear, to him, that those explosions—the ones beyond Mesa orbit—where the result of a transmitted detonation signal. If that's true, why weren't the ones on the *surface* of the planet or in low orbit? Why put *them* on timers and then use a transmission to detonate the others?"

I'd have t' say the same question would occur t' me, Cynthia, given that data set," Rear Admiral Michael Oversteegen put in, and Lecter shrugged.

"Weaver is a very smart cookie, Sir, so I haven't written his observation off completely, but the simplest explanation would be that the *transmission* was on a timer. What I mean is that the deep-space charges were command-detonated by a single transmission, but that transmission was sent from a timer-controlled com somewhere on Mesa."

Oversteegen nodded and the chief of staff shrugged again.

"Having said that, the alternate theory—the one Weaver's suggesting, and I should add that even he is suggesting it only as one possibility—is that *all* of them were command-detonated but someone wanted to make damned sure no one could calculate where the detonation command originated by analyzing the timing of the explosions, allowing for light-speed delays, and backtracking a general locus."

"So you're suggesting there was some point, either on the planet or in near-orbit, from which that command was transmitted?" Bellefeuille thought out loud, her expression intent. "Some point the Alignment wanted to prevent us from identifying as its source?"

"I know it sounds bizarre, Ma'am, but as I say, I'm not prepared to write it off completely. I'm just not prepared to *endorse* it without more supporting evidence," Lecter said. No one, Gold Peak noticed with a certain grim humor, considering what was still to come, disputed Bellefeuille's identification of the party behind the explosions. "But it's pretty damned clear that the people behind this were very sophisticated and that it wasn't some hastily improvised response. So it is possible that he's on to something, given how...thoroughly erratic the distribution of the attacks was. And even if he's wrong about *why* they were so erratic, he's right that the degree of erraticness is statistically unexplainable."

"Interestin'," Oversteegen said, his expression thoughtful.

"As I say, it's an intriguing theory, but one I doubt we'll ever be in a position to confirm or positively deny, Sir."

Lecter paused, looking around the conference table as if inviting further comment.

"The third significant point about the explosions themselves," she continued when no one spoke, "is that nobody seems inclined to accept the fact that the charges were clearly already in place." Her expression had turned much grimmer. "The prevailing belief is that they were nuclear strikes delivered from orbit.

"That's ridiculous," Rear Admiral Onasis, BatCruRon 106's CO, said flatly. "Those were *nuclear* explosions, and there's no reason *we* would've been using nukes to take out planetary targets! KEWs would've been a lot simpler, a lot quicker, and a lot *cheaper!*"

"Of course they would, Shulamit," Gold Peak said. Onasis looked at her, and she shrugged. "But any good conspiracy theorist knows why we didn't. It's precisely so we can make the argument that it wasn't us when it actually was."

"But what about the missile traces, Milady?" Diamato asked. "How are we supposed to have gotten missiles to the surface of the planet without *anybody* seeing them coming?"

"You expect *that* to derail a conspiracy theorist, Oliver?" Lester Tourville sounded disgusted, and the treecat draped across the back of his chair made a sound midway between matching disgust and dark fury. "There are plenty of people who're going to point out that we'd taken possession of every Mesan warship in the system. We hadn't gotten around to securing all of their deep-space platforms yet, but do you really think people are going to worry about that? In either case, we have complete control over any sensor data anyone in the system might have recorded, don't we? Of course we do! And since we do, any data we turn over that doesn't show missile tracks has obviously been scrubbed before we turned it loose. Besides, as Shulamit points out, we were close enough to use KEWs. No reason we would've needed to fire up the missiles' impellers to deliver nukes to the bottom of a gravity well!"

"But even without impellers someone should've seen them entering atmosphere, Sir," Diamato pointed out. "Especially on the night side of the planet."

"We thought about that, Sir," Lecter said, "and it's definitely a point worth raising in our own press releases. But we had over three dozen pinnaces in atmosphere, headed for our initial landing zones—for that matter, we had a dozen already on the ground—when the explosions started. That means we didn't have to deliver anything from orbit. We had plenty of platforms close enough to handle everything with old-fashioned free-falling bombs that never reached a velocity anyone would've seen coming, if we wanted to."

Diamato looked incredulous for a moment. Then his expression tightened and he nodded.

"The bastards *will* say that, won't they?" he said in tones of profound disgust.

"Of course they will." Tourville snorted. "Given time, any genuinely disinterested investigation's bound to prove we didn't do it. It's going to *take* time, though, and it's not surprising that newsies who don't like the Grand Alliance very much to begin with, are piling on. Even those who aren't biased against us, like Hanrahan and Shigeru, have to wonder who really did it when all the evidence we can provide that it *wasn't* us is negative and our only alternative villain is an interstellar conspiracy most of them don't even believe exists! Unfortunately, what we're looking at are the *short-term* consequences and the way the Mandarins can use an Eridani violation against us."

"Agreed," Gold Peak said. "Which brings us to another unpleasant point, I'm afraid. Cindy's people have turned up something that actually worries me even more than the way the Alignment and the Sollies can use the explosions against us."

Several eyes widened with apprehension—and disbelief—at the possibility of something *worse* than a purported Eridani Edict violation.

"So far," Gold Peak continued, "we haven't formally recognized General Palane's Citizens' Union as the legitimate government of Mesa. Even with her and Dusek strongly supporting our position in that regard, there are seccies and slaves who are increasingly disgruntled over that lack of recognition. Long-term, that's another element we have to be worried about, because there are a hell of a lot more seccies and slaves than there are first-class citizens, and they've never been enfranchised. They want that to change, and they want it to change quickly, and they're absolutely right to want both of those things. Until we can be convinced the Citizens' Union isn't going to turn into another Committee of Public Safety, though, we're not going to legitimize it."

She glanced at the senior Havenites seated around the table, and Tourville snorted and brushed his mustache with one knuckle.

"If you don't mind my saying it, Milady, you've said quite a few smart things over the last few weeks. *That* may have been the smartest one of all, though."

The other RHN officers nodded in profound agreement, and Gold Peak suppressed a surreptitious sigh of relief. She'd expected—hoped, at least—that they'd respond that way, but the comparison had to be made. Not because she believed Thandi Palane or even Jurgen Dusek was a Rob Pierre or Oscar Saint-Just in the making, but because revolutionary movements had a habit of escaping their initial leaders' control. And because there were so many people on Mesa with so many reasons to want bloody revenge on their erstwhile masters.

"As part of General Hibson's pacification operations, we've established nodal security forces designed to cordon off direct contact between the Citizens' Union and the areas still being administered—under our direction—by the existing civilian authorities of the Mesa System government," she went on. "We've inserted ONI intelligence and Criminal Investigation Division personnel into those nodal forces and also into the various police forces we're now supervising. Much of their function is open and above board and only to be expected, under the circumstances. They're charting the existing law enforcement and administrative landscape for us because we didn't really have time to do that before we moved in. We need to get control of all of those organs of authority as quickly as possible, but we need to learn enough about them to avoid *breaking* the system before we *replace* the system.

"Behind that open-and-above-board aspect of their operations, however, they've also been looking for the Alignment. The bad news—and I'm afraid it may turn out to be *very* bad news—is that they didn't have to look very hard before they found it."

A wave of confusion went through the compartment, and she smiled without a trace of humor, then gestured to Lecter.

"Cynthia?"

"What the Admiral means," Lecter said somberly, "is that so far we've identified literally scores of people who belong to the Alignment. People who readily admit they do, for that matter. And not one of them knows a single damned thing about the Yawata Strike, false flag operations in places like Mobius, political manipulation in the Republic or the Star Empire, or *anything else* actively hostile to the interests of the Grand Alliance or any of its members."

She paused to let that sink in.

"Well, of course no one would *admit* to that, Captain," Onasis pointed out after several seconds.

"Maybe not, Ma'am," Lecter acknowledged. "But it's not just a case of their not admitting it. They're positively *denying* it . . . in front of lie detectors and even in front of the handful of treecats we have with us.

"And the problem is that they're telling the truth when they do."

"Operational security." Onasis shrugged. "*We* wouldn't disseminate that kind of information outside the smallest possible 'need-to-know' bubble, either."

"The details of something like the Yawata Strike, no," Lecter said respectfully. "But that's not what we're talking about here. Oh, nobody *does* know anything about the Yawata Strike—or at least nobody we've talked to so far, at any rate. But nobody seems to know anything about *any* of the Alignment operations we've identified, either. Every one of them agrees there's a Mesan Alignment, and every one of them despises Manpower and the Mesa System government in general. They belong to a 'secret organization' whose sole purpose is to evade the Beowulf Code's prohibitions on the *voluntary* designed genetic uplift of the species *in their own cases*, not the *involuntary* redesign of humanity in general, and they don't give a damn about Solly or Manticoran politics, except that until we started 'lying' about them, they admired our stance against genetic slavery. They're organized and working 'underground' solely because of the opposition they know they'd face from those of us so benighted that we still oppose *any* thought of designed genetic improvement, and they wouldn't dream of imposing their solution on anyone else. And the reason they despise Manpower—aside from the same philosophical objections any reasonably moral human being would share—is that genetic slavery is what they believe sustains the negative image of genetic design and thus poses an additional barrier to what they and their parents and their grandparents have been trying to accomplish in secrecy here on Mesa for generations."

"I'd like t' think you were jokin' about that, Cynthia," Oversteegen said slowly after a long, still moment. "You're not, though, are you?"

"No, Sir, I'm not." Lecter shook her head. "We're seeing a lot of anger—fury, really—out of those members of the Alignment we've identified because of the way in which we've vilified them. Not just because they feel we've accused them personally—and falsely—of having murdered everyone killed in the Yawata Strike, but because if anyone believes us, the way in which we've condemned them, painted them as monsters, can only set back everything they've been trying to do. Worse, by every single test we can apply, they're absolutely sincere when they say that. We certainly can't prove they aren't, at any rate, and if *we* can't—especially with the 'cats to help out—then I can't think of anyone else who could. Or who'd even *want* to, for that matter."

"My God," someone murmured, and Gold Peak chuckled harshly.

"Exactly," she said. Every eye turned to her, and her smile was bleak. "Let me cut to the chase here," she told them.

"First, we've been accused of nuking a surrendered planet in a blatant violation of the Eridani Edict, and we're going to find it damned hard to prove we didn't do it. As Admiral Tourville says, even if we manage to find evidence that would convince an impartial judge, we're not going to find any impartial judges to prove it *to*. For that matter, we haven't managed to convince most Sollies we didn't deliberately enable the Green Pine bomb!

"Second, our belief in the sinister, vile, murderous 'Mesan Alignment' which killed millions of Manticorans—and was directly responsible for all the bloodshed after we resumed hostilities—explains exactly why we nuked Mesa in revenge the instant we had the chance. At best, we're so criminally stupid we've convinced ourselves that this inherently *benign* 'secret organization' is actually a vast, evil, centuries-old conspiracy—one aimed at destroying all known interstellar order, for some reason known only to itself—and set out to conquer and then nuke an innocent planet in some sort of deluded 'self defense.' At worst, we never actually believed anything of the sort, all our allegations have been nothing more than a pretext to justify the raw imperialism of which the Mandarins have been accusing us from the beginning, and we were cynically willing to murder millions of Mesans to create yet another crime against humanity for which we could accuse our version of the Mesan Alignment to justify what we've already done and the fact that we intend to continue doing it."

She paused amid a ringing silence, and her smile turned colder and bleaker still.

"If anyone's prepared to find a bright spot in any of that, please, share it with me now."

Gregor Mendel Tower
City of Leonard
Darius System

THE SILENCE WAS AS cold as it was complete.

It lingered there, poisoning the conference room's perfectly conditioned air, sick with grief... and hatred.

"Damn it," Collin Detweiler said finally, his husky voice thick with pain. "*Damn* it! I told him to get out earlier! I *told* him!"

"Of course you did," his brother Benjamin said heavily. "We *all* did, Collin. But he was too damn stubborn, too thickheaded, too frigging *stupid* to take our advice! And then... and then—"

His voice broke and he covered his eyes briefly with his palms.

"And too damned *loyal*," he went on after a moment, from behind the shield of his hands. "And too damned determined to do his job."

"And he felt too guilty over rushing Houdini," Franklin Detweiler said very, very softly. The others looked at him, and he shrugged. "I didn't say he was wrong to do it. I said he felt *guilty*, and you all know he did. Hell, *all* of us did! And not just because the collateral damage got so much worse when we activated it early."

No one said anything more for a moment. Then Benjamin inhaled deeply.

"You're right," he acknowledged. "Of course you're right. And that was another reason Mom refused to leave without him."

The others nodded, except for Collin. Collin didn't disagree with the others, but his grief—and his inner anger—went even deeper than theirs. He'd been their father's deputy when Albrecht ordered Houdini brought forward. He'd helped plan its acceleration and implementation.

And he was the one whose timing had come up three T-days—*just seventy-two hours*—short of getting their parents off Mesa alive.

He'd be a long time forgiving himself for that. It wasn't his fault. He knew it. And he'd still be a long time forgiving himself.

"None of that would've been necessary if not for the fucking Manties." Gervais's voice was a snarl. "It's that goddamned loose warhead Gold Peak's fault. If she weren't such a maniac, if we hadn't *known*

535

she'd be coming for Mesa as soon as she possibly could, we wouldn't have had to rush Houdini that way and Mom and Dad would be right here on Darius right now."

A sort of sub-aural growl answered him, but Collin shook his head.

"Gold Peak may be the one who actually pulled the trigger, but it wasn't just her. It was her whole damned 'Star Empire' and their goddammed friends. All of them. Elizabeth, Mayhew, Pritchart...and that bitch Harrington."

The growl was anything but sub-aural this time, and Benjamin gave a choppy nod. A hard, honest core of him admitted that everything Manticore and its allies had done was ultimately defensive. That the Alignment itself had set everything leading to Houdini into motion. But that didn't mean Gervais and Collin were wrong. If Manticore and Haven hadn't turned themselves into roadblocks that had to be removed—or at least neutralized—*none* of this would have been necessary. And while it might be unfair to blame *all* their misfortunes on Honor Alexander-Harrington—names like White Haven, Theisman, Tourville, Webster, Terekhov, Caparelli, and Yanakov deserved an honorable mention upon that list—he shared his father's special ire against Alexander-Harrington.

She should've been ours, *damn it!* he thought bitterly. *She would've been ours if not for that stupid,* stupid—

He made himself stop and draw a deep mental breath. The Harrington genome wasn't the only Alpha line the Alignment had lost over the T-centuries. Perhaps it wouldn't have been...mislaid if Richard and Marjorie Harrington hadn't migrated from Meyerdahl to the Star Kingdom all those T-years ago, but it still could have happened. Sometimes a generation simply didn't produce a suitable candidate for one of the covert lines, and when there were no candidates to nominate and groom for their role in the Detweiler Plan, they simply had to let that line go. The risk of giving themselves away if they chose an unsuitable candidate and didn't realize it in time to eliminate him before he learned too much was simply not acceptable. Upon occasion—fairly frequently, in fact—it was possible to monitor a "lost line" and identify a candidate who *was* suitable after another generation or so. But no one could count on that, especially when one of the cadet branches took itself off to the howling wilderness of the Verge...which was exactly what the Star Kingdom of Manticore had been all those T-centuries ago. And so the Harrington genome had simply been written off, although some of its characteristics—the Meyerdahl mods had been an extraordinarily potent starting point—had been incorporated into other alphas. Even the Detweiler genome had profited from it, in fact. But no one had ever imagined the role the Harrington line would play in hampering the Alignment's operations. It was hard to imagine a single human being—aside from Roger and Elizabeth Winton, at least—who'd done more to obstruct their efforts in the Haven Sector, anyway.

No wonder Dad was always so pissed at the way she kept breaking our kneecaps, he thought bitterly. *And now she's the commander of their goddammed Grand Fleet...and Dad and Mom are dead because of* her *damned best friend!*

"All right," he said out loud. "Mom and Dad are gone. I wish—*how* I wish—Captain Abbott had been able to pull them off planet. I know all of you do, too, but I'll tell you right now there's not another person in Darius who feels worse about it than Abbott does. She *hated* it, but she had over two hundred of our other people on board, she was too far from the planet to get Mom and Dad out before Gold Peak was in orbit, and Dad's orders not to try weren't discretionary. I want all of you to understand that—to *accept* that. She's a good officer, one of my best, and I don't want any of us taking out our grief on her or any of her crew."

The others looked back at him. Gervais's eyes were dark, and Benjamin doubted he'd be able to stop blaming Abbott for what had happened. But that was an emotional reaction; even Gervais's brain knew better, whatever his heart said, and after a long, stiff moment, the youngest Detweiler brother nodded.

"Good," Benjamin said, then pinched the bridge of his nose. "And with that said, what do we do next?" He lowered his hand and looked around the polished table. "Suggestions?"

No one spoke for several seconds. It took them that long to disengage their thoughts from their shared grief, but, finally, Franklin stirred.

"I think the most important thing is that we don't waste this," he said. "Mom and Dad died as part of Houdini, but we all know how Dad planned to use the Houdini acceleration. How he'd want *us* to use it now that he's gone. And I hate to say it, but the way it finally played out will probably make that even more effective."

Collin and Gervais nodded, but neither of them spoke. Instead, all four of the others looked at Benjamin, and the oldest of Albrecht Detweiler's sons felt the weight of those eyes. It wasn't the first time they'd all waited for his response to something. He'd been his father's senior deputy for close to fifty T-years. But they were no longer looking at him as Albrecht Detweiler's deputy. Now they were looking at him as Albrecht's *successor*, and for the first time he truly understood the burden his father had carried for so long.

"You're right, Franklin," he said after a moment. "The question is how we go *about* making it more effective, and a lot of that's more up your alley than anyone else's."

Franklin nodded soberly. Benjamin might have been Albrecht's senior deputy and the Alignment's chief for military affairs, but Franklin had been the Alignment's chief political strategist. Of all of them, he had the best feel for the tangled currents of Solarian politics.

"I can tell you this," he said with a certain savage satisfaction, "the Solly newsies will go crazy. Dad's timing was devastating."

You're right about that, Collin thought, eyes prickling with mingled grief and pride. *And I'll guarantee you Dad thought that through, just like he thought everything through, before he pushed the button.*

He and Albrecht had hoped and planned for Houdini's acceleration to get as many as possible of their key personnel safely out of the Mesa System before its final phase. They'd known they couldn't get everyone out, but they'd tried like hell, anyway, and they *had* succeeded in extracting almost everyone on the primary list. They'd gotten out over two thirds of the secondary list, too...but they'd run out of time before they got to the tertiary list at all. Albrecht had feared from the outset that would be the case, and he'd hated it—*hated* it—which was the real reason he'd stubbornly refused to leave before the last shipload from the secondary list. But even under the original Houdini plan, the onion core's physical footprint in the star system had to be erased, as well. Given more time, that could have been arranged much less... spectacularly and with little or no collateral damage, but time had been the one thing they didn't have, and faced by the threat of the Manties' accelerated imminent arrival, Albrecht had improvised brilliantly. He hadn't liked the vastly increased body count his improvisation had to cost, but he'd paid the price unflinchingly, and the advantages it had bought would be difficult to overestimate.

"Franklin's got an excellent point," he said out loud. "When Dad activated Houdini early, all we really expected was to blame the final explosions on the 'Ballroom terrorists' responsible for Green Pines. Since we'd already convinced the Sollies the Manties were behind that—and, hell, Zilwicki *was* the one who unlocked the nuke's security protocols for the damned seccy!—it would've been easy to blame this 'fresh campaign of nuclear terrorism' on the same people. But when the time came, Dad decided to hand us an even sharper sword."

"How?" Daniel asked. Collin raised an eyebrow at him, and he shrugged. "I know what the original plan was, Collin. I'm just curious about your last sentence. How did Dad make it even 'sharper'?"

"The timing on the explosions—that's what you're thinking about, isn't it?" Benjamin asked before Collin could reply, and Collin nodded.

"Under our original rethink of Houdini, those explosions would've been spread out over a period of about thirty-six hours," he told Daniel. "The idea was to have a sort of rolling crescendo to the 'terrorist campaign'—one that really drove home what those Ballroom lunatics were willing to do—with Manticore's enablement!—to punctuate the entire operation. But what he did instead's going to be even more effective."

"How?" Daniel looked puzzled, but it was the puzzlement of a man who realized he almost understood what he was being told.

"The original timing would have made them obviously coordinated but not synchronized 'terrorist attacks,'" Collin explained. "The sequence he actually used—I'm pretty sure I know which one it was, because we'd discussed a half dozen options for the final phase—was for a worst-case scenario, one in which the Manties had somehow figured out exactly what was going on and launched an immediate all-out search for our facilities. It was designed to take out everything before they could find *any*thing...and also to prevent anyone from realizing the initial detonation command came from the island. The explosion under the house will make people look closely at the island, no matter what, but we didn't want anyone realizing an 'uninhabited island' had actually been the central nexus of the entire Alignment. There weren't going to be any other explosions within a thousand kilometers of it, which was likely to make it stand out even more to the Manties' analysts, and somebody sufficiently paranoid to analyze the explosions' sequence might have been able to plot the command's point of origin closely enough to make them really, really curious about just what the hell had blown up in the middle of a nature preserve that was smack in the middle of their plot. Especially since the fact that it *was* 'uninhabited' had to make that particular blast especially suspicious in the first place.

"Under the revised Houdini planning, we were less concerned about that, and before Chernyshev 'tidied up' Marinescu and her crew, she'd...already dealt with most of the tertiary list groups we knew we weren't going to get out. So what we were really worried about were the physical fingerprints, the facilities we'd used where a good forensics team might pull out information we didn't want shared. Most of them—especially the ones we'd co-opted from the system government or the Peaceforce instead of building them ourselves—would have been legitimate terrorist targets, one way or another. But by going with the timing Dad actually used, it's obvious the final series of explosions weren't terrorist attacks at all. No terrorist group could possibly hit that narrow a time window. So the only people who could've done it had to be the fleet that controlled space around the planet. The newsies—and don't forget, we already had O'Hanrahan on-planet to lead the charge against the 'terrorists'—won't be blaming Manty *proxies* now, Daniel. Elizabeth might have been able to deflect at least some of those charges by pointing out that nobody can really control a batch of terrorists crazy enough to use nukes on civilian targets. But it's not 'terrorists' anymore. It's her *own first cousin*, third in line for the Manticoran crown. *That's* who the newsies will blame for this. I'll guarantee it. And when *that* shit hits the fan..."

He sat back with an ugly smile, and Daniel nodded in understanding. Slowly, at first, and then harder and faster.

"I agree," Benjamin said, and there was cold, bleak satisfaction in his tone. "And you're right, Collin. That has to be exactly what Dad was thinking. He's given us a wedge to drive both sides into more extreme positions, if we use it properly, and the more extreme their positions, the less likely anyone is to stamp on the brakes...on *either* side. So the question before us is how we try to shape the Sollies' reaction to all this." He bared his teeth in a smile that was even uglier and far, far colder than his brother's had been. "Assuming Gold Peak wasn't smart enough—or fast enough—to shut down the terminus before word of her Eridani Edict violation got out, they'll be finding out about this in Old Chicago sometime within the next thirty-six to forty-eight hours. With the streak drive, we can get word to our people on Old Terra via Warner within six T-days after that. We won't be able to affect how Kolokoltsov and the others react *initially*, but we're damned well in a position to help...direct their subsequent thinking. And just right this moment, I don't really think *moderation* is the direction we want to go, now is it?"

George Benton Tower
City of Old Chicago
Old Terra
Sol System

"—AND THEN I THINK we need to ask Admiral Kingsford for another update," Innokentiy Kolokoltsov said, tipped back in his chair as Arnold Kilpatrick-Schuster, his senior aide took notes. "I doubt he's got any new earthshattering revelations, but given Hypatia's announcement that it's following through on that merger with Beowulf—and the rumors we're hearing that they're both going to seek admission to the damned 'Star Empire'—I want to be positive we know exactly where the Navy is on Fabius."

"Yes sir," Kilpatrick-Schuster said, jotting the reminder into his pad.

"And that, unless I'm mistaken, actually gets us to the end of the to-do list." Kolokoltsov shook his head. "Hard to believe it."

"What was that you told me about never saying 'we're done,' Sir?" Kilpatrick-Schuster said. "Something about tempting fate, I think?"

"I'm sure I did," Kolokoltsov acknowledged with a rueful shrug. "On the other hand, the one thing I've discovered over the last year or so is that fate doesn't need any tempting. We're going to get hammered by *something* no matter what we do, Arnold!"

Kilpatrick-Schuster grimaced, but Kolokoltsov noted that he didn't disagree. After all—

The com chimed. He glanced at the display, and his jaw tightened as he saw the flashing urgency of a priority com request.

Maybe he shouldn't have been so cavalier about fate, after all.

❖   ❖   ❖

"My God," Omosupe Quartermain said softly. "My God. And this is *confirmed?*"

"If you're asking if it's an official Manty announcement, then no," Kolokoltsov replied harshly. "If you're asking if we're sure it's accurate, then the answer is hell yes."

"But why?" Agatá Wodoslawski said almost plaintively. The other Mandarins looked at her incredulously, and she shook her head quickly.

541

"I don't mean why did they *do* it—though I do think that's an appropriate question. I mean, why did they let the news out at all? Innokentiy, you said they let our legation come home by way of Visigoth, over the hyper bridge. If they'd closed the terminus, our people would still be sixty days out! Why give us the gift of that much time? Surely they could have used two more months to work on some kind of cover story!"

"That's what *I'd've* done," Malachai Abruzzi agreed. "But they probably figured nobody was going to believe them whatever the hell they said." He shook his head, but if he seemed as stunned by the news as anyone, his was the bright, fierce astonishment of someone who couldn't believe the weapon his adversary had just handed him. "Christ. Gold Peak must be an even bigger lunatic than Harrington! There's no way they can clean this one up, Agatá. Somebody probably convinced her it would only look even worse if they were obviously trying to keep the news from getting out. She probably hopes this will convince some particularly credulous idiots they really, really didn't do it. After all, if they had, they'd try to cover it up, wouldn't they?" He shook his head again, this time with the contempt of someone who'd done a lot of "covering up" in his career. "Problem is, they've got twelve-point-six *billion* witnesses who know exactly what they did. No, they've screwed the pooch by the numbers this time."

"They did shut down the Visigoth Terminus to all traffic for five days," Quartermain pointed out.

"Sure they did. And if I was Gold Peak, it'd damned well *still* be shut down," Abruzzi acknowledged. "They've obviously decided to go a different way, but they can get away with calling those five days a legitimate security concern, making sure none of these 'Mesan Alignment' bogeymen *they* claim are behind all of this could sneak out of the system. Once they'd taken over Astro Control and instigated ship-by-ship search procedures, that pretext went out the window, though. At that point, they had to start worrying about how keeping it shut down could only reinforce everybody's suspicions, so they *had* to revert to letting at least as much 'essential' traffic through as they're letting through all the others they've seized."

"I think Malachai's probably right," MacArtney said. "The question is what we do about it. Or *with* it, at any rate."

Kolokoltsov nodded. It wasn't often he found himself in agreement with anything that came out of MacArtney's mouth these days, but this time Nathan had a point.

"Malachai?" he said. "Obviously, you and I have to coordinate closely on this, but you're our information specialist."

"I think it would be impossible to exaggerate how valuable this is from our perspective," Abruzzi replied. "My poll numbers indicate we've been taking a hammering over Hypatia. Maybe not the rest of Buccaneer, but the Manties' version of what happened there's been gaining traction—a *lot* of traction, frankly—even inside the Kuiper. Everything we've heard from nearby core systems suggests even more skepticism about our version there than here in Sol. The people who buy the Manties' story are still a minority, but that minority's been growing, and there's been a slow, steady swing towards viewing us as the heavies. I don't have any kind of reliable numbers on the Shell, but I expect they're worse than here in the Core, and I know they're worse in the Verge. I won't say there's any sizable body of opinion out there that's actively opposed to our policies, but there *is* some of that. What worries me more, though, is that we've never been able to get a broad swath of public opinion *behind* us, at least outside the Kuiper.

"But, even taking the Manties' version of Hypatia, we're talking about destroying only space infrastructure, and there's no *proof* Gogunov really would have destroyed any of the habitats before they were evacuated. Now we've got the high-and-mighty, oh-so-noble Manties—those paragons of interstellar law and guardians of interstellar morality—killing *at least* six million innocent civilians on a planetary surface in what can only be construed as terror tactics. Unlike Hajdu or Gogunov, no one was threatening their control of the Mesa System, so they can't even claim they needed to take out critical targets before they were pushed out of the system by a counterattack, the way *our* admirals could. And what kind of 'critical target' is a ski resort in the middle of the mountains or a frigging beach resort?"

He shook his head, his eyes glittering.

"Believe me, my people won't even have to massage the message. The Manties have just lost any vestige of a claim to the moral high ground. From this point out, at absolute worst, from our perspective, every time they start yammering about how we've 'abused and mistreated' the Protectorates, all we have to do is point at Mesa and we win the debate. And the other thing this does, is to justify *anything* we do from this point forward—short of nuking an inhabited planet ourselves—to stop them. We may have to do some things we regret, take some actions we deplore, but the Manties have just shown exactly what it is we're trying to stop."

He smiled thinly.

"I hate to say it, because I hate the *reason* I'm saying it, but I think Malachai's right," Wodoslawski said. "In fact, I think it may go even farther."

The others looked at her. MacArtney and Abruzzi seemed puzzled, but Quartermain nodded slowly, and so did Kolokoltsov. The permanent senior undersecretary for foreign affairs flicked his fingers, indicating that Wodoslawski should explain her remark, and she turned to the other two.

"We're bankrupt," she said simply. "In fact, the end is coming even sooner than Omosupe and I thought it would. We've got *maybe* three more months—four, at the outside—before we're officially insolvent."

Alarm flickered in MacArtney's eyes, and she smiled even more thinly and coldly than Abruzzi had.

"Don't look so surprised, Nathan. It's not like we haven't been telling you this was coming!"

"No, but—"

"We've been working on contingency plans," she interrupted him. "There weren't any really viable options, but we kept looking anyway. The problem's the Constitution, of course. We need more cash flow, and the League's potential tax base is *huge*. So the cash is there, we just can't *get* it, because if we tried to tap it, it's for damn sure somebody in the Assembly would point out that Article One specifically prohibits any direct Federal taxation. There are people out there who don't care what happens to us or even to the League as a whole. Whatever happens to the League, *their* star systems will still be intact at the end, and no way do they want any precedent that lets us dip into their systems' personal piggy banks. The bottom line is that they're fine with whatever happens, as long as *their* rice bowls don't get kicked over in the process."

MacArtney nodded with a harsh, condemnatory expression which Kolokoltsov, for one, found bitterly ironic. After all, the Mandarins and their predecessors had used that very political fact of life to their own advantage for centuries now.

"Obviously, we've had Constitutional Compliance and Conformity working overtime at Justice, but this time not even Illalangi's been able to find us a loophole. And there's no existing Federal mechanism we could use to collect the taxes even if we tried to impose them by fiat. We'd need the local system authorities to play cashier for us, and if any of them refused and we tried to force them, we'd probably create even more Beowulfs—especially when the military situation looks so bad that a lot of those system authorities aren't so sure *we're* the ones who're going to win in the end.

"But I think the Manties just changed that for us. If we go to the Assembly now, and if we point out that what may be the most powerful naval alliance in the entire galaxy has embarked on a policy of deliberate Eridani Edict violations, we're in one hell of a lot stronger position. For all the Assembly members know, *their* star systems may be next, and if the Manties are willing to kill millions of people in Mesa, even assuming they genuinely believe this lunacy about sinister interstellar conspiracies, who knows where they'll stop? For that matter, if they really do believe it, they're obviously unhinged, which makes it even harder to predict who they'll decide is out to get them next! And what Navy is responsible for *preventing* Eridani violations?"

She looked around the conference room, and MacArtney sat back in his chair, nodding, his eyes beginning to gleam as brightly as Abruzzi's.

"We go to the Assembly," Kolokoltsov said into the silence that followed her explanation. "We tell them this is a situation—an emergency—the Constitution never contemplated. We argue that a Constitution isn't a suicide pact. That when not simply the survival of the Solarian League as a government but of millions—possibly even *billions*—of Solarian citizens are at stake, we *have* to have the wherewithal to protect them. And that means we have to be able to levy direct taxation on those citizens. And if we have to, we argue that the individual system veto right simply cannot be permitted to stand in the way of saving lives on such a scale. We put a motion to amend the Constitution to permit direct taxation before the Assembly and tell them we need an *immediate* decision. That there's no time to call a formal convention and dot all the i's and cross all the t's of the amendment process the Constitution mandates. Hell, all of them know as well as we do that the Founders deliberately designed that process to insure any amendment took *years* to approve, at the very best. That's why there've been so damned few of them! But extraordinary circumstances demand extraordinary measures and there's no time for the individual system governments to be consulted and hold their own constitutional conventions. We have to act *now*—and if anyone doubts that, we just point at Mesa."

It was his turn to sit back, and he looked around the conference table slowly.

"I wish to hell they hadn't killed all those people," he said, and he meant it. "But they just handed us the keys to the kingdom. I'll guarantee you that the Assembly will give us the super majority for the amendment. We may have to do some more preparation, massage a few more delegates, first, but they'll give it to us after this. And Agatá and I have already considered the text very carefully. Trust me"—he smiled very, very thinly—"in all the rush and confusion no one's likely to notice just how broadly it can be interpreted. When this is all over, we won't *need* the Protectorates, people."

Chez Raimond
City of Old Chicago
Sol System
Solarian League

CASWELL GWEON FOLLOWED THE maître d' across the restaurant, nodding in passing to two or three other regulars. He'd been dining at Chez Raimond for several T-years now, and as a newly minted rear admiral, he was clearly among the rising stars of the Solarian League's bureaucracy. That meant he never had trouble getting a reservation whenever he wanted one, and Chez Raimond's security measures were superb. That made the counterintelligence agents of Rear Admiral Yau Kwang-tung's Section Four happy, since it meant they could spend less time worrying about his accidentally spilling confidential information where unfriendly ears might hear.

Section Four's agents were fond of anything that made their jobs easier. Probably because they weren't very *good* at those jobs.

That thought carried Gweon across the restaurant to the privacy-screened booth in the corner farthest from the door.

"I hope this is satisfactory, Admiral," the maître d' said. "Ms. Pelletier's already here."

"This will be perfect," Gweon said with a smile. Then the smile turned a bit impish. "And could you see to it that we have at least, say, ten or fifteen minutes before someone comes to take our order? I haven't seen Ms. Pelletier all day."

"Oh, I think that could be arranged, Sir," the maître d' said with an answering smile. It wasn't the first time Gweon and his fiancée had spent a little time "catching up on the day" before placing their orders.

"Thank you," Gweon said, and the maître d' disappeared into the dimly lit, intimate restaurant as the rear admiral stepped through the privacy screen.

The very attractive red-haired, gray-eyed woman waiting for him looked up. For someone's fiancée, those gray eyes showed remarkably little joy at his arrival, and she nodded her head rather brusquely at the chair opposite hers. One of his eyebrows rose at her expression,

546

but he settled into the indicated chair without asking any questions and took a small device from his tunic pocket. He switched it on, laid it on the table between them, and checked the telltale to be sure it was operating properly, buttressing Chez Raimond's in-house anti-snooping systems. Then he nodded in satisfaction and looked back up at the woman.

"I trust your expression doesn't mean I'm going to spend tonight sleeping on the couch, Erzi." His tone was dry, and a small smile tweaked one corner of her mouth, despite her focused countenance.

"No, you're not," she said. "But I don't know that either of us is going to feel like doing anything much more energetic than that. I just got our latest instructions."

"Oh?"

Gweon sat back. He'd figured something like this was coming when Erzébet screened him and suggested Chez Raimond for dinner. Their apartment was theoretically protected by Section Four's countersurveillance systems. Actually, those countersurveillance systems leaked like a sieve, however. Worse, from their perspective, Section Four itself monitored everything that went on in or around it. So another venue was strongly indicated anytime the two of them needed to talk about their actual employers or instructions from them. He looked at her thoughtfully for a moment, then cocked his head.

"There've been rumors flying around the office since this morning," he said. "Rumors are all I've heard, though. That suggests to me that either rumors are all there *are*, or else whatever the hell's sparked them is critical enough that even I haven't been briefed in on them yet."

"You can forget about its being just rumors," Erzébet told him grimly. "Frankly, I'm surprised you haven't heard more. There must've been some delay in getting the information to Old Chicago."

"Why do you say that?"

"Because they should've heard about it almost a week ago. *Alpha Prime*'s already heard about it and sent us instructions about what to do about it."

Gweon's eyes narrowed. Neither he nor Erzébet knew where "Alpha Prime" was. For that matter, neither of them knew for certain that it actually existed as a specific physical location. But wherever it was, it was also the central nexus of the Alignment—outside the Mesa System, at least.

"Instructions about *what?*" he asked a bit sharply.

"The Manties hit Mesa eighteen days ago," she said flatly. "It was ugly. At least several million people were killed in a series of nuclear explosions on the planet, in planetary orbit, and in deep space. Alpha

Prime's sent us instructions on how they want you to weigh in when Kingsford finally brings you into the loop."

"Several *million* people?" he repeated, his narrowed eyes going wide in shock.

"At least." Her own eyes were bleak. "Alpha Prime either doesn't have a better casualty count or they don't see any reason to share it with us. Actually," she said a bit grudgingly, "I can see some logic to that. They don't want to give us any more details than they have to because that way nobody's going to notice that we have details we shouldn't have."

Gweon nodded silently, still trying to grapple with the death toll.

"Why did they do it?" he asked. "Surely the system government didn't refuse to surrender!"

"I don't know why they did it." There was something just a bit odd about her tone, and he wondered what she knew—or suspected—that she wasn't sharing with him. "It doesn't really matter *why* it happened," she continued. "What matters is what Alpha Prime wants us—you—to do about it when you get called in as an analyst. There are a couple of points they want to make sure get hammered home, especially in light of what you've already told them about the Alliance's missile production rates." She showed her teeth briefly. "Nobody told me, but reading between the lines, I think somebody in Alpha Prime wants a little payback."

Mount Royal Palace
City of Landing
Manticore Binary System
Star Empire of Manticore

COLONEL ELLEN SHEMAIS SEEMED a bit in two minds.

The head of Empress Elizabeth's personal protective detail approved of anything likely to help her keep the empress alive. That was a given. On the other hand...

Honor Alexander-Harrington hid a smile as she and Anton Zilwicki and Damien Harahap followed Colonel Shemais into the conference room in the Mount Royal Palace subbasement. Several of the guards drawn from the Queen's Own and scattered obtrusively about the palace had done double takes as she and her companions passed them and they noticed the harnesses both Nimitz and the treecat who had been named Clean Killer now sported. Humans in general tended to forget treecats had been tool-users even before they met humanity, although their tools had been distinctly Neolithic. But aside from the simple carry nets they wove "in the wild," treecats didn't worry much about the sorts of reasons humans had pockets, especially if they'd adopted a human. After all, *humans* had pockets, which meant a wise providence had obviously provided them to carry anything that needed carrying.

That was the reason the guards' attention had first been drawn to the 'cats' harnesses. It was only after they'd looked—then looked away and looked *back* again—that they realized those harnesses weren't just for the benefit of the carry pouches both of them now had strapped securely against their chests between their shoulders and mid-pelvises. No, they were also there to support the *shoulder holsters* both treecats now wore, as well.

Which explained Colonel Shemais's...mixed emotions. It had taken her long enough to grow accustomed to the notion of admitting Honor's armed *human* retainers to the empress's presence. Getting used to the notion of armed treecats—especially one who'd bonded with a former agent of the Mesan Alignment—would take a bit longer.

Unfortunately for the colonel's peace of mind, the empress's instructions in the matter had been quite clear.

Honor followed Shemais across to the waiting chair at the conference table, trailed by the two intelligence operatives. They waited until she was seated and Nimitz had climbed onto the perch arranged beside her chair. Then they took their own seats, and Harahap's companion took the perch next to his.

"I'm sorry we're a little late," Honor said, carefully not noticing the expressions on several faces which belonged to people who had never heard of Sergeant Todd or treecat-sized pulsers. "We hit a delay at the shuttle pad."

✧   ✧   ✧

Fire Watch, who had been known as Clean Killer until a hand of days ago, looked around alertly. The mind-glows around him were all unusually focused and powerful. Clearly these were two-leg elders, and he was not certain he liked the taste of some of the mind-glows directed towards his person.

<*Of course you do not like them!*> Thought Chaser told him with a mind-chuckle from the perch beside Crafty Mind. <*They do not trust Plays with Fire, and truly, there is little reason why mind-blind two-legs should* trust *him. They cannot taste him the way we do.*>

<*I try to remind myself of that every day,*> Fire Watch replied. <*But they are very strange, two-legs. Stranger than I had realized. And it is not just because they are mind-blind, or because they do not trust Plays with Fire. They have so many* names *for things! I do not understand how they can possibly keep them all straight. Perhaps that explains why their minds work so differently from the People's.*>

<*It is because they must use the mouth-noises for everything,*> Thought Chaser said. <*They cannot simply taste whatever the other one is talking about, and so they must have special names for everything. Like flying things. They must find a way to . . . differentiate between "air cars," "shuttles," "air lorries," and all the hands of hands of things that fly.*>

Thought Chaser took time to shape the mouth noises as carefully as possible. It was not easy to do that in a mind-voice, but it was not—quite—impossible, either. And he was right, Fire Watch decided. The poor two-legs *had* to have so many names for things, and the People had just had to learn to cope with it. Still, he remained uncertain why the name he and the People had bestowed upon Plays with Fire was so amusing to the two-legs. For that matter, he did not truly understand why the name Plays with Fire had bestowed upon him struck of the two-legs as hilarious. He was proud of it! Bonding with a two-leg was almost—*almost*—like bonding with one's mate for life, and so there was great meaning in the two-leg's choice when he bestowed a mouth-noise name he could actually speak out loud. That was why the People who had bonded accepted those names just as they accepted the names other People bestowed upon them at different stages in their lives. But he truly did not understand what amused them so about *his* two-leg name. Laughs Brightly had done his best to explain it, but Fire Watch was unsure about his own understanding of the other scout's explanation. The fact that Laughs Brightly had lost his mind-voice and was able to communicate only through finger-talk made him no more confident about his own comprehension.

<*And while we are thinking of reasons the two-legs might look somewhat askance at Plays with Fire,*> Thought Chaser continued with a mind-laugh, <*I do not think you want to know how Crafty Mind reacted when she learned you and Laughs Brightly had both been given your own "pulsers"!*>

✧   ✧   ✧

"Excuse me, Your Grace, but are those *pulsers?*" Sir Tyler Abercrombie asked carefully.

"Why, yes, Sir Tyler." Honor smiled at him. "They are."

"But—" the Home Secretary began.

"Sir Tyler."

The voice which interrupted him belonged to Elizabeth Winton, and he closed his mouth quickly as he turned his head to look at her.

"Duchess Harrington's kept me and Palace Security fully informed on this matter," the Empress of Manticore said pleasantly. "Both Nimitz and Fire Watch have demonstrated their proficiency with their weapons, and both the Duchess and Mr. Zilwicki have assured me that they've also demonstrated full awareness of those weapons' potential dangers. And that they've demonstrated the safety of their weapon-handling skills to the satisfaction of the commanding officer of *Imperator*'s Marine detachment." She shrugged. "And, finally, both Colonel Shemais and I were fully informed that both Nimitz and Fire Watch would be armed for today's meeting. In fact, it's very likely other treecats will be acquiring similar weapons in the near future."

Abercrombie looked decidedly uncertain about the advisability of the Queen's proposal. The slender, dappled treecat stretched across the back of his chair instead of the perch which had been provided for her, on the other hand, did not. Her ears pricked sharply and she looked at Fire Watch. Harahap's companion gave her a human-style nod, and she buzzed a pleased purr. It seemed apparent that she did not share Abercrombie's reservations.

"To be fair, Sir Tyler, I can understand why you might be a little concerned by this turn of events," Honor said. "On the other hand, I might point out that treecats are *always* armed. That's one of the reasons they're so effective in the protective role they've agreed to assume for humans who might be targeted for assassination."

Abercrombie's stiff body language relaxed a bit at that reminder, and he reached up to rub Stone Climber's ears.

"The difference is that now they have what you might call a 'ranged capability,'" Honor continued, "and it's not unreasonable for people to worry about how well they understand that and about their ability to respect the threat zone. I assure you, I would never have signed off on giving Nimitz a pulser if I hadn't been fully convinced on both those points. And I'll also admit it took a while to get everything resolved to my satisfaction. But don't forget that Samantha is a memory singer. Once Nimitz was able to get the basic concepts across to her—and once I'd worked with her enough to be certain she really had them—she passed them to Fire Watch in a single memory song. And she can do the same for any other 'cat." She shrugged. "So it's really just a case of whether or not we can trust treecats won't resort to lethal force in circumstances where it's not justified, and after three or four hundred T-years, I think they've demonstrated pretty conclusively that we can."

She shrugged again, and silence lingered around the table. Several of the expressions which had been uncertain had smoothed into thoughtfulness, instead, and after a second or two, Abercrombie nodded.

"A valid point, Your Grace," he acknowledged. "Several of them, in fact. I think the notion will take some getting used to, but definitely a valid point."

Someone chuckled, and Elizabeth smiled. But then the empress shook her head.

"I'm sure it will," she said. "On the other hand, it would appear some other things that are going to take getting used to, as well. Like the situation in Mesa."

Any temptation towards humor vanished abruptly, and Elizabeth's nostrils flared. Then she nodded to Pat Givens.

"Admiral, why don't you get us started?"

"Of course, Your Majesty." Givens didn't seem delighted by the command, but she'd known it was coming. The only other person she could have handed it off to was Hamish Alexander-Harrington, and he was in Beowulf at a conference. So she squared her shoulders and indicated the tall, red-haired and green-eyed man sitting beside her.

"For those of you who don't know him—which would include most of you—this is Charles O'Daley. Officially, he works for Sir Anthony." She tilted her head at Sir Anthony Langtry, the Star Empire's Foreign

Secretary. "In fact, he's with Special Intelligence and he's holding down the Director's desk until Sir Barton gets back from Nouveau Paris."

Heads nodded. Sir Barton Salgado was the Director of Special Intelligence, Givens's civilian counterpart. At the moment, he was either in Nouveau Paris, where he'd gone to confer with Kevin Usher and Wilhelm Trajan, or else on his way home. If he'd had any hint of what would be coming from the Mesa System he would have delayed that trip, Honor thought somberly.

"Charlie and I have been comparing notes," Givens went on, "and I'm afraid neither of us have come up with any brilliant insights. Certainly not about anything that's actually happening in Mesa, at any rate." Her expression was bleak. "We've looked very carefully at Countess Gold Peak's follow-on dispatches, and assuming they're as accurate as her reports have always been in the past, we're looking at pretty close to an unmitigated disaster."

"'Unmitigated' may be just a little too strong an adjective," Honor said. Givens looked at her, raising her eyebrows in surprise, and Honor shrugged. "We can get to that in a minute, Pat. I apologize for interrupting."

"No apology's necessary, Your Grace. And I would be absolutely delighted to find that there really could be something mitigating about what's happened there. In the meantime, though, Charlie's analysts and mine are in general agreement that this represents a goldplated gift to the Mandarins. We haven't had time to hear how they're actually going to spin it, but the truth is, they don't have to do a lot of spinning in this case. Our ships *were* in planetary orbit and there *were* scores of nuclear explosions. At the very least, we let somebody get past us to set them off. At worst—and this is what most of the galaxy's likely to conclude—we were either responsible for or at least complicit in them." The Second Space Lord shook her head. "After Hypatia, we were seen as the champions who'd prevented an Eridani Edict violation, at least by anyone with an open mind. Now, though, those same open-minded people really won't have any choice but to wonder whether or not we were even telling the truth *then*, given what we've apparently done in Mesa. Frankly, if we were in their place, we'd wonder the same thing."

Heads nodded again, and this time those nods were as grim as Givens's expression.

"Our analysts all concur that the Mandarins will use this to further their narrative of Manticore and Haven as the imperialist successors of the People's Republic writ large. They're going to argue that even if we aren't red-fanged conquistadors, we're obviously unhinged. The fact that we've found a 'Mesan Alignment' that has absolutely nothing in common with the interstellar conspiracy we've been talking about will only underscore that. We're about to be painted as the people who nuked a star system and killed upwards of *seven* million people, according to Countess Gold Peak's current numbers, as vengeance against an imaginary enemy we invented in our own paranoid fantasies. And that's the most *favorable* interpretation they're going to put on it."

"So it's your sense the Mandarins' version of this will give them the moral high ground?" Bruce Wijenberg's blue eyes were anxious.

"I can't really answer that, Mr. Wijenberg," Givens said.

"I'd say it's unlikely t' give them the high ground outside the Core, Sir." O'Daley, Honor noticed, possessed a drawl just as irritating as Michael Oversteegen's. Fortunately, from the taste of his mind-glow, he appeared to possess an equally sharp brain. Now Wijenberg looked at him, and he grimaced.

"They say the devil's beyond blackenin'," he continued, "and where the League is concerned, that's certainly true outside the Core. Very few Fringers're prepared t' believe a single word that comes out of Old Chicago, unless they're Fringers whose bread's bein' buttered by OFS. Frankly, even they don't *believe* what the Mandarins say, but that doesn't keep them from goin' along with it for obvious reasons.

"The rest of the Fringe and most of the Verge know better than t' take Old Chicago's word that water's wet. At th' same time, public opinion's held that Manticore's word is almost universally good... again, outside the Core. That's what we've almost certainly lost here, at least in the short term. That doesn't mean everybody outside the Core's suddenly goin' t' take the Mandarins' word over ours. It does mean there's goin' t' be one hell of a lot more skepticism and suspicion where we're concerned."

"And *inside* the Core?" Baroness Morncreek asked, her voice soft.

"And inside the Core the Mandarins will use this to beat us—and Beowulf—to death," Elizabeth said harshly before O'Daley or Givens could respond. "They're going to point at it and scream that we really are barbarians, that we've been lying about our reasons for going to war from the beginning, and that with the neo-barbarians at the gate, it's time for desperate measures."

"I'm afraid Her Majesty has a point," Givens said, drawing all eyes back to her. "All of our analyses indicate our basic strategy's been working. We've almost totally disrupted the federal government's revenue streams; the Mandarins have steadily lost credibility; systems outside the League were steadily tilting our direction, especially after the Sollies unveiled 'Operation Buccaneer'; and more and more League member systems looked like they'd be heading the same direction Hypatia did.

All of that was trending directly towards the strategic goal Duchess Harrington articulated at the very beginning: the *internal* fracturing of the Solarian League without active military operations against the Core Worlds on our part.

"Now, as word of this spreads, an awful lot of that momentum will be reversed. People who were trending in our direction are likely to start trending the other way. Worse, this will give the Core Worlds a unifying focus they really didn't have before. That means it will tend to counteract the centrifugal force which had the League starting to shed member systems. And if the League maintains its territorial integrity, even if we force it to accept terms we can live with by military action, the odds are that we'll be looking at a rearmed, reequipped, and much more dangerous revanchist enemy within the next few decades."

"That's probably true in the long term, Pat," Honor said. "But while I've always been aware of the dangers of Solarian revanchism, I've also said I could live with that if it was only a *long*-term problem. I wouldn't like it, but life is imperfect and there'll always be a degree of 'sufficient unto the day,' whatever we do. What concerns me more at the moment are the *short*-term implications."

"Which ones, Honor?" Baroness Morncreek asked. The chancellor of the exchequer's dark eyes were narrow, and Honor gave her one of her crooked grins.

"The same one I'm pretty sure you're worrying about," she said. "As Pat just said, at the moment, the Mandarins have to be on the brink of fiscal collapse. Operation Lacoön and the withdrawal of our merchant marine is only just now starting to really bite the Solarian economy as a whole, but it's decimated the federal bureaucracy's revenue stream. Coupled with what's been happening in the Protectorates, especially since we started actively looking for planets where Operation Janus"— she twitched her head in Damien Harahap's direction—"had primed local revolts, they couldn't possibly sustain a war effort without some alternate source of funding. Now—"

She shrugged, and Morncreek nodded.

"You're right, that is what I've been worrying about," she acknowledged, then looked at the others around the table. "The single point on which the League member systems have always been united in their resistance to Federal authority, since the day their Constitution was signed, is the constitutional prohibition of direct taxation. That's even held true so far in this damned war, for a lot of reasons, including the fact that not one of those Core Worlds has believed for one moment that we posed any true threat to them and *their* citizens. We've had confirmation of that from multiple sources inside the Assembly.

"At the same time, we've always known the League's gross product is literally incalculable. For all intents and purposes, it *has* no bottom. The way things are now—or the way they've been *up to now*, at any rate—the Mandarins have been forced to operate on credit, and by this point their bond issues are effectively valueless, despite the interest rates at which they're being offered. So Her Grace is right—under pre-'Mesan Atrocity' circumstances, the Mandarins' position and war effort was unsustainable. And it was staying that way, because absent some existential threat to the League itself—*or to their own systems' citizens*—the member systems weren't going to relax the stringency of the constitution.

"But I'm very much afraid that what's happened in Mesa and the way it's being reported, even by—or maybe even *especially* by—genuinely responsible journalists like Audrey O'Hanrahan, will be seen as just that: an existential threat. Maybe not to the League itself, but if we're lunatic enough to kill millions of people in one star system in pursuit of a nonexistent interstellar conspiracy, God only knows how many millions of people we'll kill in *other* star systems for equally insane reasons. Under *those* circumstances, I think it's possible—even probable—they'll find a way to tap those other revenue streams. And if they do, time won't be on our side any longer. If they've got the funding to stay solvent, all they have to do is wait us out. If they aren't going to collapse under their own weight, and if we don't take the war to them when they don't, eventually their research and development people will come up with weapons that match our own and they'll have the funding to put those weapons into production in numbers not even the Grand Alliance can match."

She sat back, and a cold, still silence enveloped the conference room.

"I hate to say it, but from the perspective of the Alignment—the *real* Alignment, not the one we're finding on Mesa—it was a master stroke." Langtry's heavy voice finally broke that silence. "I don't even want to think about the kind of mentality that could kill that many people as a *diplomatic ploy*, but it was sure as hell effective. And if we can't even point to an Alignment that bears *some* resemblance to the one we've been telling the galaxy about, I don't see any way to dig ourselves out of this hole."

"That's one reason I brought Mr. Zilwicki and Mr. Harahap this afternoon, Tony," Honor said. The foreign secretary looked at her, one eyebrow raised, and she smiled humorlessly. "I don't think—*they* don't think—what happened was just 'a diplomatic ploy.' Mr. Zilwicki's done some very interesting analysis of data he gathered while he was on Mesa. Since Mr. Harahap has...joined the side of the angels, shall we say, he and Mr. Zilwicki have been working together on that analysis and combining it with certain of Mr. Harahap's observations from inside the onion, one might say. They've reached some tentative conclusions I think we need to share with all of you, and if they're remotely on the right track, I think it's incumbent upon us to get the two of them—and Fire Watch, of course—to Mesa as quickly as we can. The people we're really after have done a lot better job of disappearing down the rabbit hole than I think any of us would have believed was possible, but Nimitz taught me something a long time ago."

"And that is—?" Elizabeth asked when Honor paused.

"It doesn't matter how fast and elusive the rabbit is if the right hunter's on its trail," Honor Alexander-Harrington said coldly. "So I think it's time we sent our own hunting party after *this* rabbit."

Hillary Indrakashi Enkateshwara Tower
City of Old Chicago
Sol System
Solarian League

"NOW THAT'S VERY INTERESTING," Natsuko Okiku murmured as the video clip finished playing. She frowned at the frozen display for several seconds, fingers drumming on the corner of her desk as she thought about it. Then she looked up across the display at Bryce Tarkovsky. "Doesn't *prove* anything," she pointed out, "but it *is* interesting."

"With all due respect, Natsuko, you're damned right it doesn't prove anything," Lupe Blanton said. She sat on the other corner of Okiku's desk, where she'd just watched the video along with the Gendarmerie colonel. "All we've got is a senior naval officer meeting with his fiancée in a public restaurant." She grimaced. "Hardly the sort of thing anybody's going to take to a prosecutor."

"No," Major Tarkovsky acknowledged. "But from what Daud and Irene have picked up about the analysis Gweon's handing Kingsford, I'd say there's a very strong probability he's working for the Other Guys. And that's what makes the fact that Ms. Pelletier 'spontaneously' invited him to dinner right after leaving her financial adviser's offices. Especially since her adviser worked for Nuñez, Poldak, Bolton, and Hwang."

"Which has about three bazillion and twelve other clients, the last time I looked," Blanton pointed out sardonically. "That's what's made it so damnably hard to identify reasonable suspects even after we figured out Bolton was dirty."

"Granted. But we *have* agreed Bolton's dirty, haven't we?"

"I'd say we've decided there's at least a ninety-nine-point-nine percent chance."

"Okay. Then here's what I find really interesting. Bolton isn't in charge of Pelletier's accounts. In fact, she's never handled a single transaction for her. But according to the very discreet eye we're keeping on Ms. Bolton—and the Outcasts ever-handy data-crunching—the two of them have happened to be sitting at the same table in the sidewalk café on

Nuñez, Poldak, Bolton, and Hwang's air car landing at lunchtime no less than eight times. And so far as our surveillance people have been able to determine, they've never struck up a single conversation beyond 'Nice weather, isn't it?'"

The Marine shrugged.

"We've got plenty of footage now of Bolton in social situations," he continued, "and she's really, really good at striking up the sort of conversations that lead to potential client relationships. Pelletier, on the other hand, is obviously well-heeled and she's both intelligent and gregarious. I find it just a little odd that these two intelligent, articulate people, neither of whom has an existing professional relationship, have 'just happened' to run into each other no less than eight times—*that we know of*—and *never* had any sort of extended conversation. I don't know about you, but that strikes me as statistically improbable, let's say. And now, after Pelletier gets a call from her adviser, asking her to personally come by the office, and after she has lunch number nine at which Bolton 'just happens' to share her table, she gets on her uni-link in the taxi as soon as she leaves the café and invites her fiancé to an unscheduled dinner at a restaurant where we've already determined she and Gweon *routinely* upgrade the existing security systems at least seventy percent—but *only* seventy percent; not *one hundred* percent—of the times they dine there."

He looked at Blanton, one eyebrow arched.

"You *don't* find any of that interesting?"

"Um." Blanton frowned thoughtfully. "Okay," she said. "I still don't think it *proves* anything, but it's certainly suggestive."

"I find it even more suggestive in light of...recent events," Okiku put in, her expression much grimmer than it had been, and Blanton inhaled deeply.

"You could have a very good point there, Natsuko," she conceded. "Of course, if you are, then one has to wonder what Pelletier and Bolton *didn't* talk about."

"I think it was a message pass—that that's what *all* these lunchtime encounters have been," Tarkovsky said flatly. "Not hard to pass an encrypted chip without anyone's noticing. And, as you say, Lupe, I have to wonder what was on this one."

"Nothing good," Okiku said even more grimly, and Blanton nodded.

Unless the Ghost Hunters missed their guess, things were about to get very ugly, very quickly. The blows had come hard and fast, although the Solarian public hadn't learned about all of them just yet.

The Solarian woman-in-the-street knew about the Mayan Autonomous Regional Sector's declaration of independence now, and she'd heard Oravil Barregos's allegations about provocateurs *pretending* to be Manticorans. The jury of public opinion inside the Kuiper was very much still out on that issue, though. There were those who believed it validated the Manties' claims about the mysterious "Mesan Alignment." Unfortunately for the Grand Alliance, those people represented a distinct minority, so far as the Ghost Hunters could determine. A much larger chunk of public opinion was more cynical, regarding Barregos's allegations as payback to the Manties, who'd obviously agreed to back him against the League in his campaign to make himself dictator of the Maya Sector. Obviously, his public support for their ludicrous allegations was the price he'd paid for their military support. And a third opinion held that Barregos might be completely sincere, but that the Manties had deceived him so they could use him as their duped talking head to conceal the truth. There were countless variants between those extremes, but those three summed up the more serious contenders.

What struck Blanton as ominous was that the Mandarins had yet to take an official position on which possibility was correct. That suggested something else was in play while they formulated their ultimate stance, and if there was any truth in the trickle of rumors that had leaked to Daud al-Fanudahi and Irene Teague, she was very much afraid she knew what that "something else" was.

"Do you really think it could have been the Manties?" she asked, looking at the other two. "At Mesa, I mean. If the rumors are accurate."

"No." Tarkovsky's reply was instant and unqualified. Both women looked at him, eyes questioning, and he shrugged. "First, if the Manties had wanted to take out targets on the surface of Mesa, they'd never have used nukes. They'd have used KEWs. I can't believe there was a target down there—especially on an 'uninhabited island'—that needed *megaton*-range warheads, and if the rumors Daud's picked up are accurate, that's exactly what someone used. The Manties could've done the same job, assuming there'd been any reason they *wanted* to, with a kinetic strike that was a hell of a lot smaller, a hell of a lot cleaner, and a hell of a lot less likely to be construed as an Eridani violation."

"And if they used nukes specifically so they could make that argument?" Blanton's question was challenging; her tone was not.

"Lupe, this is the *Manties*. I don't give a flying fuck—pardon my language—how Public Information's painting them; they're *Manties*. They just dealt with catastrophic damage and millions of deaths in their own star system as the result of what clearly *was* an Eridani violation. Hundreds of their spacers just *died* stopping *us* from committing one in Hypatia. And they did it largely because this sort of thing would be complete and total moral anathema to the Star Empire. Again, I don't give a *damn* what Abruzzi has to say about them. I know at least a dozen Manties personally, and all of us have had everything they or the Grand Alliance as a whole have ever done under a microscope for months now trying to figure out what the hell is going on. We *know* they wouldn't have done it. And even if they wouldn't have refused to do it on moral grounds, they aren't that frigging *stupid*.

"First, they came into the system as *liberators*. That's how at least seventy-five percent of the population had to view them. Now they—or somebody—has killed millions of people, a lot of whom had to be the very same seccies and slaves who were so happy to see them. You think Gold Peak and her ground force commanders aren't bright enough to recognize how that's going to generate at least passive, and more probably *active*, resistance from the very people who should be *supporting* them?

"Second, that's just inside the Mesa System. *Outside* Mesa, it's likely to be even worse! They've had the moral high ground—outside the Kuiper, at any rate—ever since this started, and that only redoubled after Hypatia and after Buccaneer became public knowledge. Are you ready to suggest Elizabeth Winton and Eloise Pritchart, who have to be two of the smartest heads of state in the entire galaxy, have suddenly turned so stupid they're willing to throw all of that away? For what? What possible tactical objective in a star system they'd already conquered could have inspired them to do something this... this incalculably unwise?"

"But Gold Peak *does* have a reputation," Okiku pointed out.

"So does Harrington!" Tarkovsky shot back. "And I think we're pretty much in agreement that ninety percent of the stories about *her* hot-headedness and vindictiveness are crap, aren't we? So there's some reason we shouldn't think the same thing about what *Gold Peak*'s enemies say about her? And whatever else she may be, she's Empress Elizabeth's *first cousin* and third in the line of succession. I don't care how big a lunatic she is, *somebody* on her staff would have pointed out to her what you might call the 'political downside' of branding her dynasty—personally—with responsibility for violating the Eridani Edict. So, taking everything into consideration, it's not just a case of 'No, she didn't do it'; it's a case of '*Hell* no—she *damned* well didn't do it!'"

Blanton was forced to nod. Unfortunately, she doubted Solarian public opinion would see things quite as clearly as Bryce Tarkovsky did. Or as *she* did. She still tried to remind herself they hadn't *proved* the "Other Guys" weren't really the Grand Alliance, because that was her job. But deep inside, she knew the truth. Or at least *a* truth.

"If it wasn't her, who was it?" she asked out loud. "I know Daud and Irene have hardened in favor of its really being this 'Alignment,' and there are times I find myself agreeing with them. But if this really was the '*Mesan* Alignment,' why in God's name would they kill this many million of their own people?"

"I don't know," Tarkovsky acknowledged. "In fact, I don't have the least damned idea." He was one of the Ghost Hunters who'd accepted the Alignment's existence early on, and his expression was frustrated. "I know one thing, though. This will fit perfectly into the Mandarins' playbook, and I don't think the Other Guys—whoever they are—can have been... unaware of that fact. That has to be a huge part of why they did it."

"Granted," Okiku said. She'd remained solidly on the fence about the existence or nonexistence of the Mesan Alignment, but at the moment she looked like an agnostic inclining towards outright atheism. "Actually, though," she went on, confirming the impression, "I think Lupe's question's pretty damned valid, Bryce. That's an enormous number of people, assuming the casualty counts Daud and Irene are hearing about are remotely close to accurate. If this 'Alignment' is operating out of Mesa, then those explosions *have* to have just killed bunches of people who were friends or family members of people involved in it. I find it awfully difficult to believe that somebody who's operated clandestinely this successfully for as long as the Manties claim they have—or even just long enough to manage everything we've found right here on Old Terra—could have failed to see the danger that represents to their security. If you just killed my grandmother, or a dozen of my cousins, my loyalty's likely to become just a bit strained."

"There's certainly something to be said for that," Tarkovsky granted. "But until we know more about who actually got killed, we're groping in the dark in that respect. Mind you, I can't imagine any way they could've killed that many people *without* killing those friends and family members of yours. On the other hand, I don't pretend to have an accurate map of what the Other Guys are really after or what they might be prepared to pay to get there."

"I can see that, but Natsuko's got a really good point," Blanton said. "And if the Other Guys *aren't* the 'Mesan Alignment,' then they wouldn't be worrying about the collateral damage punching holes in their own security."

Tarkovsky nodded, his frustration more obvious than ever.

"Agreed. But the bottom line is that, as far as the Manties and the Mandarins are concerned, it doesn't *matter* who the Other Guys are. What matters is that the Manties are going to be blamed for it, and that makes me really, really nervous about this meeting between

Pelletier and Bolton. If the official courier boat from Mesa was delayed five days before it was allowed to leave but somebody else got out the same day—and you know *somebody* else had to get out—that's five days in which Bolton's bosses could have sent her new instructions. And I think we're pretty much in agreement that no matter who the Other Guys are, that's who she's working for. So they may have had those 'new instructions' in the pipeline and waiting to drop the instant they heard about this. For that matter, Bolton could've had them for weeks or months, waiting to deliver them until word of what happened on Mesa reached Old Terra. So if she met with Pelletier to pass those instructions on, that means Kingsford's going to be hearing something from Gweon sometime very soon now, and somehow I doubt what he hears is going to make the situation any *better*."

George Benton Tower
City of Old Chicago
Sol System

"THANK YOU, ADMIRAL GWEON," Innokentiy Kolokoltsov said. "I'm sure I speak for all of us when I say we appreciate the clarity of your briefing." His smile was fleeting. "And I'm equally sure you understand why we weren't delighted to hear it."

"I do, believe me, Mister Permanent Senior Undersecretary," Caswell Gweon replied soberly. "And I wish I'd been able to provide a more optimistic picture."

"Accuracy is far more important at this stage than optimism." Kolokoltsov smiled again, a wintry, bleak sort of smile. "We'd had quite enough of that before you came along. Trust me; what we're getting now is better."

Gweon bent his head to acknowledge the compliment. Then Kolokoltsov drew a deep breath.

"I believe that will be all for now, Admiral. Please hold yourself in readiness for additional consultation, however. I don't anticipate having any more questions this afternoon, but I could be wrong."

"Of course, Mister Permanent Senior Undersecretary," the analyst murmured. He gathered up his minicomp and his record chips, stood, bowed to the briefing room's other occupants, and withdrew.

Silence lingered as the door closed behind him. Then Nathan MacArtney cleared his throat.

"May I assume, Admiral Kingsford, that you concur with Admiral Gweon's analysis?"

"Admiral Gweon's analysis *is* my analysis, Sir," Kingsford replied a bit coldly.

"What I meant to ask," MacArtney said, making an obvious effort to control his own tone, "is if you concur with the *implications* of his analysis."

"I think his conclusions are well reasoned," Kingsford said, clearly choosing his words with care. "Assuming our intelligence sources from Beowulf are accurate—and I should, perhaps, point out that Admiral

564

Gweon's been involved in managing those sources for quite some time, which puts him in the best position to evaluate their reliability—then so far as I can tell, his logic is irrefutable and I endorse it fully. If, however, you're asking me what I think we should *do* about those implications, I'm afraid that's a question I can't answer." His eyes circled the conference table and the men and women seated around it. "As I've said from the beginning, any direct action against Beowulf will inevitably have political consequences I'm in no position to assess. Even the military consequences are impossible to predict with any degree of certainty, given the fact that virtually all of our intelligence is from human sources. We don't have hard sensor data to confirm *any* of it, I'm afraid. That doesn't mean it's inaccurate; it simply means it's impossible for me to verify it from any other source. And that, of course, means it *might* be inaccurate."

MacArtney's nostrils flared. He didn't use any words like "weaseling" or "arse-covering," but it was clear what he was thinking, and Kingsford's expression tightened.

"Believe me, Admiral Kingsford," Kolokoltsov intervened firmly, shooting a warning glance MacArtney's way, "all of us appreciate the limitations of the information available to you. You're our senior uniformed officer, though. Based on what Admiral Gweon's said, would Fabius be a viable operation?"

Kingsford sat back, folding his hands on the conference table before him, and considered his next words even more carefully. Kolokoltsov, MacArtney, and Agatá Wodoslawski had now been fully briefed on Hasta and its capabilities. Abruzzi and Omosupe Quartermain had only a more general understanding of the new system, but they, too, grasped its extraordinary reach and stealthiness.

That limited his ability to temporize—assuming that was what he decided to do—and that was always dangerous. Civilian understanding of military capabilities invariably seemed to come in only two flavors. Either they completely misunderstood the capability in question, or else they *thought* they understood it and believed—usually erroneously—they were then qualified to evaluate its effectiveness. And far more often than not, they overestimated that effectiveness rather than exercising a modicum of prudence and *under*estimating it.

He had little doubt where MacArtney fell on that spectrum. He was less positive about Abruzzi, and he couldn't hazard a guess which way Quartermain would come down.

Doesn't matter, he told himself. *Bottom line, they're the civilian government and you're the Navy officer. All you can do is give them your very best estimates and advice and then go out and try to keep their decisions from shooting all of us in the foot. Or someplace more fatal than that.*

"Assuming Admiral Gweon's sources are correct," he began "this new area-defense system, 'Mycroft,' will come online in Beowulf sometime in the next eight to twelve T-weeks, which severely limits the time window in which we might act. We can expect losses on any deep penetration of the system to be catastrophic even without the new control stations; *with* them, any attack will be suicidal. So, even with Hasta, I'd have to unequivocally recommend *against* Fabius after 'Mycroft' is operational. Whatever the potential gains of such an operation, our losses would be catastrophic. Because of that, I could support Fabius only in the window before 'Mycroft' goes operational.

"In that timeframe—*before* 'Mycroft'—it's possible, perhaps even probable, Hasta would permit a successful strike on the Beowulfan missile production facilities. It's not possible to realistically assess the Grand Alliance's ability to detect Hasta after launch. The best we can do is use *our* ability to detect it as a meterstick, and, assuming the Grand Alliance's ability is no greater than ours, the probability of their seeing Hasta incoming in time to take effective counter actions is low. I'm not prepared to quantify *how* low, because no one can. But, given a detection capability approximately equal to our own, I would have to rate the chance of Hasta getting through as excellent.

"The downsides are that we're still likely to take severe losses, although we've been working on an approach that *might* minimize those—and the extreme range at which it would be necessary to launch. At that distance, the attack would be totally dependent upon Hasta's internal targeting systems and software. Those systems and that software are far better than anything we've ever had before and we've spent months testing them—in both simulations and live fire exercises—but they've never actually been used in combat. That means all our projections for their effectiveness have to be theoretical. Moreover, there would no longer be a human element in the tactical cycle, no point at which a human could decide the attack needed to be aborted, and that *significantly* ups the probability of hitting unintended targets. I'd be lying if I said anyone in the Navy would be happy about the potential for disaster that could represent.

"And, in addition, I have to point out that the estimate on when 'Mycroft' is likely to come online is based on...tenuous information. It's the best information we have, and given Admiral Gweon's track record, I'm convinced it's fundamentally accurate. But it's by no means *complete*. It could contain all sorts of unpleasant surprises. In particular, I strongly urge that no one forget that the eight to twelve T-weeks of Admiral Gweon's estimate is *only* an estimate. I believe we'd be far wiser to assume our window is no greater than four to *six* T-weeks and plan—or not plan—accordingly.

"Having said all of that, my considered opinion is that *if* the Grand Alliance's ability to detect Hasta is no greater than our own and *if* we can mount the operation before 'Mycroft' goes operational, the chance of success would be high. I say that only with the understanding that there *will* be some degree of collateral damage in a strike at that range. How *much* there will be, I can't predict, and the Navy will do all in its power to hold it to the barest possible minimum. But I want it clearly understood by whoever authorizes Fabius that collateral damage *will occur*, no matter how careful we are, and that with weapons as powerful as Hasta, any damage will be severe."

✧   ✧   ✧

"I wish just once we could have a military advisor who doesn't qualify every single damned thing he says," Nathan MacArtney groused some hours later. He sat in Innokentiy Kolokoltsov's office and he waved a glass of whiskey for emphasis. "Couldn't just one of them, just once, tell us what will or won't work?"

"Forgive me, Nathan, but wasn't that precisely what *Rajampet* did?" Kolokoltsov's tone was caustic. "I don't believe that worked out all that well, did it?"

"Of course not," MacArtney growled, his face coloring. "But, still, Innokentiy—! He spent way too damned much time putting out sheet anchors to make sure nobody could nail *him* if anything went wrong! What we needed was a firm recommendation. What we got was 'yeah, sure, maybe, if only, well, it *could* work, but—'"

He rolled his eyes, his expression as exasperated as his tone.

Kolokoltsov frowned at the total unfairness of the criticism. It wasn't particularly surprising, coming from MacArtney, but that made it no more pleasant to listen to. And for himself, Kolokoltsov couldn't fault Kingsford's caution. For that matter, it was one of the things he most valued about the admiral. Unfortunately, there were factors which mitigated against caution. Kingsford might know about some of them, but Kolokoltsov doubted the CNO knew about *all* of them.

He sipped his own whiskey, glowering out the windows at the Old Chicago sunset. Too many things were coming together too rapidly. There were too many threats and—conversely—too many opportunities...and too little time in which to examine any of them of them.

Every indication was that the Assembly would approve the amendment he, Quartermain, and Wodoslawski had drawn up, although it was taking longer than he'd anticipated to finish preparing the ground for it. The member systems' resistance to granting the federal government the right to levy actual taxes was set deep in the League's bedrock; getting *anyone's* delegates to sign off on changing that without direct orders from their home systems was a gargantuan challenge. On the other hand, the Manties had given him a gargantuan club. The panic the Mesa Atrocity had awakened among the delegates would be difficult, if not impossible, to overestimate. Few people would have shed any tears if something nasty happened to Manpower; several million dead civilians, the majority of whom probably had nothing at all to do with Manpower, was something else. And the fact that the Manties would openly violate the Eridani Edict, whatever they might claim to the contrary, was terrifying, especially given the dawning awareness that the Grand Alliance's war-fighting technology was decisively superior to anything the SLN had. Under those circumstances, his argument that the Constitution wasn't a suicide pact had found fertile ground. It was going to take some time—possibly at least a couple more months, more likely three—but in the end, they'd give him the majority he needed. Whether or not the system governments which had sent those Assembly members to Old Chicago would feel the same way was another question, but it also didn't matter. Once the amendment was approved, however it happened, getting rid of it again would be a monumental battle, and one in which the federal bureaucracy held all the advantages.

But on the other side of the ledger, there was Barregos's defection and the fact that Kingsford had made it abundantly clear that if the Manties truly stood behind this "Mayan Autonomous Regional Sector Navy" abortion, there was nothing the Navy could do about it, at least in the short term. Nor was Maya the only spot in the Protectorates where unrest was brewing. And, perhaps even worse, it was becoming evident Manticore and the Grand Alliance wouldn't be the only magnet pulling Verge and Fringe star systems out of OFS's grasp and into competing political units. He still had few details, but an entire cluster of independent Verge star systems had proclaimed a new entity that sounded a lot more like a star nation than the simple "collective security association" it claimed to be. His analysts—even Brandy Spraker—were scrambling to put together the details about this "Renaissance Factor," but the name seemed ominous. And everything his people did know about it at this point suggested the Republic of Mannerheim was the driving force behind the Renaissance Factor's emergence. That was worrisome, especially in light of the fact that the Mannerheim System-Defense Force was far more potent than most Verge navies. That meant the Renaissance Factor could provide the sort of regional security umbrella only OFS had previously provided.

And a government run by their neighbors, people from their own region, has to be more attractive to neobarbs in the Protectorates than OFS ever was, he thought sourly, glancing at MacArtney. *And I'll bet Barregos and what's his name—Hurskainen—are only the first snowflakes of winter. If we don't get a handle on this situation soon, prove* our *navy's still the eight hundred-kilo gorilla, despite any temporary setbacks, the process will only accelerate. For that matter, some of the member systems that don't like the new tax amendment are likely to go looking for safe havens outside the League to avoid paying up. And if we haven't established that we can compel them to behave*...

And then there was Gweon's projection of Manty missile production numbers. If they could get in, take out the missile lines, knock the Grand Alliance back on its heels militarily the same way Gold Peak's monumental fuck-up was already knocking it back in terms of public opinion, buy a little time for more developments like Hasta to level the playing field...

"I realize Kingsford wasn't as enthusiastic over Fabius as you'd like him to be, Nathan," the permanent senior undersecretary for foreign affairs said. "For that matter, I'd prefer for him to radiate confidence myself, assuming that confidence was justified. Since we don't know that it is, I'm just as happy to have him tell us we don't, rather than promise us the galaxy on a platter.

"Having said that, though, I don't think we have a choice." He inhaled deeply, his expression bleak, as MacArtney twitched upright in his chair. "Assuming he can mount the operation within his time window—that is, within the next six T-weeks, when we can be confident 'Mycroft' isn't online—I think it may be our best—perhaps our *only*—option. Mind you," he raised his right hand, an admonishing index finger extended, "I'm not saying we *will* launch it. Not at this point. But I'm going to instruct him to begin planning for a modified Fabius, with an execution date no later than the first week or two of January. If we don't start organizing it now, we won't have the option of launching it in that time window, and we can always cancel if that seems advisable when we get closer."

"Of course we can!" MacArtney's tone was as hearty as his expression, but Kolokoltsov wasn't fooled. The permanent senior undersecretary of the interior understood full well that once an operation was committed to, standing down again was always problematical.

And the hell of it, Innokentiy Arsenovich Kolokoltsov thought grimly, *is that the worthless son-of-a-bitch is right.*

HMS *Tristram*
Visigoth Terminus
and
HMS *Artemis*
Tenth Fleet
Mesa System

"THESEUS AUTHORIZES US AS number one in the departure queue, Ma'am," Lieutenant O'Reilly announced.

"Thank you, Wanda," Commander Kaplan replied and glanced at Hosea Simpkins, her Grayson-born astrogator. "Take us in, Lieutenant."

"Aye, aye, Ma'am," Simpkins replied, and Kaplan leaned back in her command chair as HMS *Tristram* nosed into the Visigoth Terminus.

I wonder if Hosea feels as...strange about taking astro control data from Theseus as I do? she wondered, watching Master Chief Andrew Dawson ease her destroyer delicately into the terminus's complex gravitic tides. *Not that Countess Gold Peak had any choice about it, I suppose.*

Rear Admiral Shulamit Onasis's *Reliant*-class battlecruiser flagship floated with the remainder of BatCruRon 106.1, three and a half light-hours from the K8 primary of the Visigoth System, holding station on the Visigoth Terminus. The battlecruisers were dwarfed by the freight and traffic control platforms clustered about the wormhole, but there was no trace of the bustling commerce those platforms should have served, and the majority of the platforms themselves were as empty as the vacuum around them.

There was a reason for that.

Visigoth System Control had flatly refused to cooperate with the RMN in any way after the "Mesa Atrocity," which probably shouldn't have surprised anyone. It certainly hadn't surprised Admiral Gold Peak, unfortunately for Visigoth.

Although the Visigoth Terminus hadn't been on the original list for Lacoön Two, Gold Peak had realized she couldn't leave it in anyone else's hands. If she'd ever entertained any thoughts about that, the Mesa Atrocity would have changed her mind, and she'd politely but firmly taken possession of the terminus within twenty-four hours of dispatching her initial report to Manticore. Now Onasis's squadron, supported by Rear Admiral Gunnar Malbois's BatCruRon 19 of the Republic of Haven Navy, hovered watchfully over the platforms from which the Visigoth System government had evacuated every living human in protest. A constellation of FTL-capable sensor platforms covered a sphere two light-hours across, centered on the terminus, two *Hydra*-class CLACs backed up the battlecruisers, and a pair of six million-ton missile colliers waited to deploy pods at the first sign of a Solarian attack.

Not that even Sollies are stupid enough to try anything like that, Kaplan reflected as the icons of a squadron of LACs arced across her plot, headed out to relieve the outer shell of *manned* platforms at ninety light-minutes. *Even* they *have to realize* nobody's *getting through this terminus without our permission.*

She didn't like the reason that was true, but, under the circumstances, she could live with it.

The first queasy outriders of a wormhole transit tiptoed through her midsection, and she snorted in amusement as another thought struck her.

I so wish I could be aboard Artie *when the Admiral and "Firebrand" come face-to-face at last!*

❖   ❖   ❖

Damien Harahap reached up to stroke Fire Watch's ears gently as the treecat shifted on his shoulder. The 'cat hadn't liked his person's insistence that it would be wiser to leave his pulser aboard *Tristram* just this once, but that wasn't the reason his muscles quivered with so much tension. It wasn't difficult for Harahap to guess why they *did*, however, and he concentrated on thinking soothing thoughts.

That would have been easier if *he* hadn't been so aware of the attitude of the red-haired, green-eyed lieutenant at the lift car's control panel. Young Lieutenant Archer was not one of Damien Harahap's admirers, and it seemed likely her flag lieutenant's attitude mirrored Countess Gold Peak's. That could be...unfortunate.

Fire Watch made a very soft hissing sound, and Harahap shook his head.

None of that, he thought as hard as he could. *We need to make a good impression on the lady. Trust me on that.*

Fire Watch couldn't "hear" him. He knew that. But he hoped the treecat would absorb the "taste" of his "mind-glow." He still had problems visualizing how all of that worked, but the comforting presence glowing just beyond his grasp in the back of his own mind proved it did. Now he opened to that glow, embracing it, and marveled once again at the awareness that there was at least one being in the galaxy who truly and simply loved Damien Harahap despite knowing *exactly* who he was...and exactly what he'd done with his life.

Until Fire Watch had given him that priceless gift, he'd never once allowed himself to realize how desperately—or for how long—he'd wanted it. He didn't expect anyone who hadn't been adopted to understand how the bond worked. For that matter, he didn't *understand* it, himself. But he knew he would die before he allowed himself to fall short of that loving presence's expectations.

No wonder Duchess Harrington seemed so amused by it all, he thought. *If anyone understood just how good a...a moral jailer Fire Watch was going to be, it had to be her. And talk about ironic justice—!*

The lift car came to a halt, the doors opened, and Archer stood to one side with a wave of his hand.

"This way, gentlemen," he said with flawless, if less than effervescent, courtesy.

"Thank you, Lieutenant," Anton Zilwicki rumbled. Harahap contented himself with a nod of thanks. Prudence suggested allowing Zilwicki to take center stage, after all.

Archer led them down the passage to a closed hatch. The neat label read "Flag Officer Briefing Room," and the glowing light on its frame indicated the compartment was in use, but it opened the instant Archer pressed the admittance button.

"Bring them in, Gwen," a pleasantly rough-edged contralto said, and Archer nodded to his guests.

"This way, gentlemen," he said again, and led them into the briefing room.

Eight humans and a pair of treecats waited for them there.

Harahap scanned the faces—human and feline—as he and Zilwicki followed Archer towards the briefing table at the center of the compartment. Admiral Gold Peak was easy to identify, given her coloring and her striking resemblance to Empress Elizabeth. The tall, brown-haired, mustachioed admiral in Havenite uniform to her right had to be Lester Tourville, which meant the treecat on the back of his chair must be Lurks in Branches. Harahap had made a point of learning the name of the Second Fleet CO's treecat companion. The blond captain seated to Gold Peak's left was probably Cynthia Lecter, her chief of staff, and that would make the tall, chestnut-haired senior-grade captain beside Lecter Victoria Armstrong, Gold Peak's flag captain. He wasn't certain who the small, compact Marine brigadier might be, nor did he have a clue about the identity of the Marine master sergeant standing behind Gold Peak with yet another treecat on his shoulder, but he could make a good guess about the two civilians.

"Mr. Zilwicki, Mr. Graham, and...friend, Milady," Archer said by way of introduction, and Gold Peak smiled faintly.

"Thank you, Gwen," she said, then tilted her head. "It's good to see you, Captain Zilwicki."

"I could wish it was under other circumstances, Milady," Zilwicki replied.

"As could we all," she conceded, then turned to Indiana.

"Mr. Graham," she said. "Welcome to Tenth Fleet. Commodore Zavala speaks very well of you, although I'm afraid I don't quite understand—yet, at least—why you've joined us. No doubt all will be made clear in time."

"I hope so, Admiral," Indy said.

She nodded to him, then looked past Zilwicki.

"And this," she said with a noticeable lack of warmth, "must be the infamous 'Firebrand.'"

It wasn't precisely a greeting, Harahap decided, and contented himself with a brief bow of acknowledgment. Fire Watch, on the other hand, flattened his ears at the admiral and Harahap felt his hand-feet's claws sink deeper into the pad on his shoulder.

One of Gold Peak's eyebrows rose slightly, and Harahap suppressed an urge to grimace. If anyone who'd never been adopted herself was going to understand treecat body language, it had to be Gold Peak, given her decades of friendship with Duchess Harrington and Nimitz. And the last thing they needed was for Fire Watch's obvious belligerence to antagonize her.

Further.

Behave! he thought even more loudly at the 'cat.

"However," Gold Peak continued after a moment, dour expression easing into a broad smile, "before we get down to the reason you and I are seeing one another, Captain, I believe there are a couple of people here who'd like to greet you."

The two civilians were on their feet almost before she'd stopped speaking. The man was an improbably handsome fellow, with green eyes and long blond hair, who looked absolutely nothing like the file photos of Victor Cachat Harahap had been shown. The woman was almost as powerfully built—for a woman—as Anton Zilwicki, although she lacked most of his undeniable massiveness, and aside from some extensive facial mods, she still looked quite a bit like the notorious General Palane.

"Anton!" the woman enveloped Zilwicki in a massive hug no lesser mortal was likely to survive. On the other hand, Harahap noted, he was hugging her back just as hard, and his eyes were suspiciously damp.

"Thandi." He shook his head. "It's *good* to see you. I was afraid—"

"Hush." She stood back a bit, just far enough to shake him. "Somebody had to go. You drew the short straw."

"Yes, but—"

"Hush, I said!" She shook him again, harder, and he smiled. Then he looked past her to the blond-haired young fellow.

"Victor."

"Anton."

They stood there, looking at one another for several heartbeats. The silence stretched out, but neither of them moved a muscle until Palane snorted in exasperation.

"You know, it's perfectly all right to admit you're friends. I swear, watching the two of you—!"

Zilwicki and Cachat looked at her in near perfect unison, then back at each other.

"Oh, the hell with it!" Zilwicki said. "Come here, Victor! She's going to get pissed and hurt both of us if you don't."

"Probably got a point," Cachat said after a moment. He stepped towards Zilwicki, holding out one hand, but the Highlander ignored it. He reached out, instead, wrapping both arms around the smaller, far slighter man and hugging him almost as tightly as he had Palane.

Cachat stiffened, his eyes going wide. But then that sharp, green gaze softened and he wrapped his own arms—awkwardly, hesitantly, perhaps, but still wrapped—as far around Zilwicki as he could.

"Now if only I had the holo-pics to post!" Palane said. Both men looked at her again, and she chortled at their expressions. "God, I could charge a fortune! 'Black Victor hugs Cap'n Zilwicki, Terror of the Spaceways!'"

Cachat glared at her, but a rumble of laughter went around the briefing room. After a moment, his own glare turned into a lopsided grin and he shook his head.

"A true professional, accustomed to smooth and subtle operations planned with exquisite care and forethought—as opposed to the crude, smash-and-grab tactics espoused by mere Marines, you understand— would've had a camera ready," he observed.

"And you are *so* going to pay for that one," she assured him.

"I'm sure he will," Gold Peak said. "And from everything I've seen and heard about him, there'll be significant karmic payback when the moment comes. For now, though, I'm afraid we need to turn to other concerns." She indicated three empty chairs, facing her across the table. "Why don't we all be seated again and get down to it. I understand you have quite a few things to tell me, Captain Zilwicki, Scourge"—she grinned wickedly—"of the Spaceways."

✧　　✧　　✧

"—and so, they sent Damien and me out to see what we could dig up," Zilwicki finished his concise, organized brief some forty minutes later. "I'm sure your own intelligence people have been digging like mad, Milady, but the two of us have...a certain set of skills that may give us better shovels. And, to be honest, both of us have very personal motivations to dig up Duchess Harrington's rabbit."

"I see."

Countess Gold Peak, Harahap had observed, had the ability to listen without interruptions. That wasn't always—or even often—the case with senior officers, in his own experience. But she'd sat tipped back in her chair, jotting an occasional note into the pad on her knee, and listened without comment or question as Zilwicki spoke. Captain Lecter had interjected two questions, and the Marine brigadier—Brigadier Hibson— had asked three. Hibson's, especially, had been brief, to the point, and well taken, but Gold Peak had simply listened, soaking it all in.

"Thank you, Captain Zilwicki," she continued. "That was one of the better briefs I've received. And it didn't come at us completely cold. Mr. Cachat and General Palane had already shared your statistical findings with us—after a fashion, at least. I'm afraid neither of them fully grasped the nuances, and *I* certainly didn't." She flickered a brief smile. "Most of *my* math is involved with how to blow things up faster."

"I can, ah, see where those particular math skills might not've been the best ones for absorbing my suspicions, Milady," Zilwicki rumbled with a faint smile of his own.

"Yes," she agreed, but then her smile faded.

"On the other hand," she said, swiveling her eyes to his companions, "I'm rather less clear on exactly why Mr. Graham and—especially— Mr. Harahap are here." Her expression was the antithesis of a smile as those eyes rested on Harahap. "Neither of them are statisticians either, I believe."

"No, Milady," Zilwicki agreed, "and neither of them fit into any neat pigeonholes. Actually, Indy here sort of wrote his own ticket." The young Seraphimian colored slightly, although he met the admiral's gaze with commendable steadiness. "I think at least part of it's his desire to...ride herd on Mr. Harahap. They have a bit of a history," he added with massive understatement. "On the other hand, I didn't have any objection to his attaching himself to the mission, whatever his original motives might've been. He doesn't have anything in the way of formal training, but he's a bright fellow and from all reports he's actually very good—if occasionally a tad overenthusiastic—in covert situations." He shrugged. "Someone like him can always make himself useful, and Duchess Harrington cast the final vote on his inclusion."

"I see. All right, that accounts for Mr. Graham, but to be honest, he wasn't the one I had reservations about."

"I'm not surprised, Milady. But, as I mentioned earlier, Damien"—the use of his first name was not an accident, Harahap reflected—"has skills of his own which can be of great potential value to us. Not only that, his ... previous employment, let's say, gives him a knowledge base no one else has. And, frankly, he has his own reasons to want the Alignment—or, rather, what Duchess Harrington's taken to calling the 'onion core'—dragged out into the open."

"Oh, I'm quite certain he has a 'knowledge base no one else has,'" Gold Peak said grimly. "What I'm not quite clear on is why we should *trust* him—in light of what he was doing while he *acquired* that 'knowledge base,' let's say."

"If I may, Milady," Harahap said mildly, before Zilwicki could respond, "that's a very good question. In your place, I *wouldn't* trust me. But—" he met her eyes "—I think you've had a little experience trusting *treecats*."

"I have, indeed," she allowed after a brief pause. "Treecats don't always understand 'two-legs' and the way their minds work, though. And while they're usually very good with *people*, their understanding of human political and social complexities is less well developed. I have to wonder how that might affect their ability to understand where someone's true loyalty really lies. In short, I can visualize circumstances in which even they could be ... mistaken."

Fire Watch stiffened on the back of Harahap's chair, his ears going flat once again. Harahap reached up quickly, but even as he did, Lester Tourville's companion gave a short, sharp, unmistakably *stern-sounding* bleek. Gold Peak turned towards him, and Lurks in Branches's true-hands started flashing sign far too rapidly for Harahap's still limited proficiency to follow. He did recognize a few of the signs, though. The right-handed "D" tapping the back of Lurks in Branches's left wrist, spelling "duty," and a palm-out "W" at the corner of his muzzle, arcing outward to spell "sing." The emphatic closure of two wiry fingers on a thumb to sign "No," and two hands, each signing "5" near the shoulder, one above the other, pulling out and closing into "S's" to sign "trust." There were dozens of others, including three he'd come to recognize only too well: "Y" hands facing each other and shaking in the sign for "plays"; "A" hands, placed palm-to-palm in the sign for "with;" and palm-up bent "5"s moving upward with fluttering fingers.

He saw Tourville snort and cover his mouth with one hand as that particular trio flashed across Lurks in Branches's true-hands. Even the corner of Gold Peak's lips twitched, as a matter of fact. But aside from that, he had no idea what the Havenite's companion was saying. He only knew it seemed to be taking quite some time to say and that his true-hands were *very* emphatic.

He stopped, finally, and Gold Peak looked at him levelly. Then she glanced at the treecat on the master sergeant's shoulder and arched an eyebrow. The silent question evoked only a single sign—one of the ones Harahap *had* learned to recognize—in response: the nodding "Y" which meant "yes." Gold Peak considered him for a moment longer, then shrugged and turned back to Harahap.

"You have...interesting advocates, Mr. Harahap," she said. "Lurks in Branches was particularly forceful in his assurances. You may have noticed that he seldom uses one sign when half a dozen will do." Lurks in Branches bleeked a laugh, and she smiled slightly. "Alfredo, on the other hand, is a 'cat of very few signs. I think he prefers to let Lurks in Branches expend the calories to get the message across. But the *message*, Mr. Harahap, is that not only do you have no intention of betraying us, but you're personally determined to find the Alignment for reasons of your own. May I ask what those reasons are?"

Her tone was light, almost amused, but her eyes bored into him like paired lasers. It was not, he decided, a moment for prevarication.

"There are several of them, Milady," he said, meeting that sharp-edged gaze levelly. "Some of them I haven't quite figured out for myself yet. One is that the bastards played me, and I don't like that. Another is that I've recently discovered I'm *tired* of rationalizing what I've done, of avoiding the consequences of my actions by simply ignoring them. I can also honestly say I never suspected what the Alignment's true agenda was or how far it went. But the truth?"

He reached out and touched Indy's shoulder without ever looking at the younger man.

"I betrayed Indy, his sister, all of his friends. It was nothing personal, just a job, like dozens of other jobs I'd done before. And I knew I'd be able to leave it all behind when the hammer came down. But then everything went to hell and, for the first time in my career, I got trapped in my own trap. I saw it from the inside, not in my rearview mirror. And I realized I'd let myself like those people a hell of a lot more than I ever should have. They were real for me, people who *mattered*, and I'd been completely prepared to leave them to take the fall because that was the *job*."

It was very quiet in the briefing room, and the shoulder under his fingers was tense. He could taste Indy's surprise almost as if he'd been a treecat himself, but perhaps that wasn't really what was happening.

Perhaps what he was really tasting was his *own* surprise as the words flowed out of him and he realized every single one of them was true.

"I'm no paragon of virtue, Milady. I'm someone who's always taken pride in his abilities and his skills, but I never really let myself think very hard about the consequences of what I used them to do. On Seraphim, I didn't have that option. And that means I don't have it anywhere else anymore, either. Worse, your people—specifically, Duchess Harrington—gave me the chance to—*forced* me to—make a choice. And then there was Fire Watch."

The treecat flowed down from the back of his chair, sitting upright in his lap, leaning back against him while bright green eyes looked defiantly at everyone on the far side of the table.

"The Alignment killed his sister, her family, all of her friends, and he felt her die." Damien Harahap's face could have been carved from granite. "He *felt* her die. I'm still just learning my way around treecats, Milady, but I've learned enough to start to at least dimly understand what that must have been like for him, and no one—*no one*—will ever do that to him or another treecat again."

He was distantly startled by the quiver in his voice, the burning in his eyes, but he never looked away.

"I owe a lot of people a lot of debts, for good or ill," he told the admiral. "I'll be a long time paying them. But I've decided it's time to get started, and I don't know a better place to begin. They tell me treecats always know if a human is lying, and given what I've seen out of Fire Watch so far, I'm inclined to believe it. So let me put this the clearest way I can for them to taste for you. To use Duchess Harrington's metaphor, I've taken Empress Elizabeth's dollar and I owe her an honest day's work. I've always believed in that. But this time I've gone farther. For the first time since I left Startman, thirty-four T-years ago, I have a *home*. I haven't had one of those since StratoCorp took it away when I was seven years old. Now I do, and it's right here." His hands caressed Fire Watch with feather gentleness. "And I will kill *anything* that tries to take it away from me again."

He stopped and cleared his throat, feeling unaccustomedly abashed in the absolute silence, but his eyes held hers without wavering. Then she glanced at Lurks in Branches. He nodded once, emphatically, and it was her turn to clear *her* throat as she turned back to Harahap.

"Well, who am I to argue with a passel of treecats?" The huskiness of her voice betrayed her whimsical tone. "I suppose that makes it a case of 'welcome aboard'...Plays with Fire."

DECEMBER 1922 POST DIASPORA

Solarian Merchantship *Star Galleon*
Beowulf System

"LAST ONE," EVELYN CHERNITSKAYA, first officer of the Kalokainos Lines freighter *Star Galleon*, announced in a tone of profound relief.

Captain Simeon Russo smiled thinly. He understood Chernitskaya's relief, and he was just as happy to be done with the deployment phase himself. Trundling across the Beowulf System, heading in from the hyper-limit to deliver the Beowulfan property the Warner system government had seized prior to the secession referendum, would have been slow in any case. The "cargo containers" which had somehow found their ways overboard in a steady trickle had made it nerve-racking, as well. Ships seldom passed one another closely enough for anyone to have noticed something that small separating from another ship, but this time—naturally—they'd had a relatively close neighbor for most of their voyage towards the planet Beowulf. There'd been little chance of their unwelcome companion noticing anything even if it had been looking in exactly the wrong direction—two million kilometers was "close" only by the standards of a star system's dimensions—but everyone aboard *Star Galleon* had breathed a sigh of relief when the stranger's course diverged towards Cassandra, the Beowulf System's second inhabited planet.

And at least we don't have any more of the damned drone-in-a-boxes on board if the customs people get curious, he reminded himself. *No reason they should, come to that. But they're damned* Beowulfers. *If anyone's likely to do something just to screw us up, without even realizing they're doing it—!*

His smile grew even thinner, then disappeared completely, and he admitted the real reason for Chernitskaya's tension. And his own, for that matter.

It was roughly thirty-five days' hyper travel from Warner to Beowulf, twenty-eight subjective for a starship's crew, but *Star Galleon* was thirty-*seven* days, twenty-*nine* subjective, out of Warner. As their mission orders had required, they'd dropped out of hyper at BS-712-19-6, a planetless red dwarf just over twenty-one light-years short of their ultimate destination on the line from Warner to Beowulf.

The rendezvous had been set up in case their orders required some last-minute modification, and Russo hadn't really expected to find any-one waiting there. He'd been wrong, however. And he'd been equally wrong in his initial assumption that the operation had been scrubbed for some reason. The streak drive-equipped vessel had been consider-ably larger than most of the Alignment's courier vessels, but it had still been effectively four times as fast as *Star Galleon*'s plodding best speed. There'd been time for his superiors to brief him on the disaster in Mesa and transship the additional items. That briefing hadn't told him how many people had actually died, but from the nature of his changed instructions, he was pretty sure he'd like neither the numbers nor the identities of the dead when and if he finally had that information.

And speaking of those changed instructions—

"Contact Beowulf Near-Planet Traffic Control," he told his com offi-cer. "Transmit our manifest to them and ask them if we can expedite unloading. After all," he showed his teeth for just an instant, "we're behind schedule, aren't we?"

Admiralty Building
City of Old Chicago
Sol System
Solarian League

"SO IT LOOKS LIKE both BatCruRon 312 and BatCruRon 960 will be available to Admiral Capriotti, after all, Sir," Vice Admiral Simpson said.

Simpson, recently promoted from rear admiral despite her failure as Rajampet Rajani's messenger to Beowulf before the Raging Justice debacle, had a compact build and brown hair. She was also Winston Kingsford's staff operations officer, and despite what had been a less than spectacular career for someone with her family's connections, she was...solid. That was the best word for her, he thought again: *solid*. She wasn't as smart as Willis Jennings, his chief of staff, but she was methodical and organized. Even better, she made it a point to temper the sometimes extravagant optimism of Fleet Admiral Bernard and the rest of Strategy and Planning's personnel.

Most of whom, he reminded himself now, sourly, *have never seen a shot fired in anger. Or not one that was fired at* them, *anyway*.

"That's good, Marge," he said out loud. "Mind you, I'm sure Vincent and Vice Admiral Helland would like us to find anyone else we can. How's that looking?"

"Beyond the units we've already firmly assigned—and BatCruRon 312 and 960, of course—I'm afraid the cupboard's bare, Sir," Simpson admitted. She didn't look happy about it, but she didn't try to blow any smoke, either. "If we had another month, even another couple of weeks, we could probably scrape up at least two more squadrons—*possibly* three. That's about it, though, after all the diversions to the Fringe."

She was careful about her tone with that last sentence, Kingsford noted with a certain bitter amusement. Well, that was fair. He wasn't particularly pleased by those diversions, either. His move to swap out single superdreadnoughts for divisions of battlecruisers had freed up quite a few of the lighter ships, even if it was a ludicrously expensive way to "show the flag," at least by prewar standards. Unfortunately, it hadn't freed up enough to give him a sense of confidence for Operation Fabius.

Which is probably because you don't want to carry the damned thing out in the first place, Winston. He hid a mental grimace before it ever reached his expression. *There are so many ways this thing can go south on us. And if it does, and if the Grand Alliance reacts the way I'd react, things'll get even uglier. Jesus. If someone had used those two words—"even uglier"—to me about something like the "Mesa Atrocity" even a month ago, I'd've told him he was a frigging idiot! How could anything be "uglier" than that?*

He didn't know, and he didn't want to find out. That was one of several reasons he'd tapped Vincent Capriotti to command Task Force 790. He'd done well with TF 783 and managed to avoid killing any civilians in Cachalot along the way. It was obvious from his post-up reports that he'd realized *why* he shouldn't be killing them, too. Given that track record, he'd been the obvious man for Operation Fabius.

Although he's probably not planning to send me any thank-you notes anytime soon. I damned sure wouldn't be, in his place!

"We'll just have to do the best we can, despite the diversions," he said out loud. "Stay on it, though, Marge. If anything does turn up, I want it transferred to Capriotti's command immediately."

"Understood, Sir."

"Are there any updates on Technodyne's delivery schedule, Turner?" Kingsford continued, turning to Captain Turner Rabindra, his staff logistics officer, who glanced at Simpson from the corner of one eye.

Technically, Rabindra reported first to Admiral Jennings and then to Kingsford himself, not to Simpson, but Jennings had been unable to attend today's meeting and he and Simpson had been working closely together even before the modified Fabius was ordered. Clearly, he wanted to make sure he didn't step on the pecking order, but Simpson only nodded to him and he returned his gaze to Kingsford.

"As of this morning, Sir, they hadn't reported any glitches."

Rabindra's tone was very careful. He was almost as tall as Kingsford, with broad shoulders and an athletic build honed by hours on the null-grav basketball court. Despite that, he somehow managed to project a stereotypical, "supply clerk" mentality, and he hated being pressured for hard delivery dates. It was an attitude which could drive Kingsford to frothing madness, but he tolerated the man because for all of his irritating traits—and despite the rank which had stalled at captain almost twenty T-years ago—he was probably the best logistician the CNO had ever met.

"They're actually projecting slightly better production numbers on the Hastas," the captain continued. "I don't have a hard estimate from them for you yet. They've promised me one before close of business at Ganymede, today. We're going to have slightly *lower* numbers than originally projected on the latest Cataphracts, though."

"How 'lower' are we talking about?" Kingsford frowned. "We're already adding three more battlecruiser squadrons to the original Fabius OB. I'm hoping we won't need Cataphracts at all, but if we do, I don't want our magazines shorted."

"All they've told me so far is 'slightly,'" Rabindra said unhappily. "I sent back a query as soon as they did, but they haven't replied yet. I'll give them another kick as soon as this meeting is over, Sir."

"Good." Kingsford nodded sharply. "We've probably got more than enough early-mark birds to fill any empty spots, but our people are operating at enough of a disadvantage. I don't want them sent out with anything less than the very best we can give them."

"Understood, Sir."

Both staffers nodded soberly, and well they should, Kingsford thought. He'd hammered that point hard enough and often enough, anyway!

"All right, in that case, let's look at our latest projections on the Manty and Havenite ship strengths on the terminus. I know our numbers have to be tentative, but is there any possibility of firming them up by—"

Silver Bullet Q-12
Beowulf System

THE DRONE SLID SILENTLY through the concealing dark.

Silver Bullet Q-12 was far larger than most people's drones, larger even than one of the Royal Manticoran Navy's Ghost Rider platforms. It was, however, at least as stealthy as Ghost Rider as it swept slowly along on its spider drive. In the time since its initial deployment, it had traveled clear across the system without anyone's so much as noticing it.

SBQ-12 was, in fact, one of the last units of the constellation *Star Galleon* had deployed to reach its assigned position. It got there at last, however, and decelerated smoothly to a halt relative to the system's G2 primary. Panels in its radar-absorbent skin slid open, deploying the solar panels designed to sustain the charge in its plasma capacitors as long as possible. They would make it considerably less stealthy, but it was unlikely—to say the least—that anyone would notice it now that it was no longer moving. Once they were in place, reaction thrusters burned briefly, sending the drone into an end-for-end rotation in place, sweeping the exquisitely sensitive gravitic sensors in its carefully designed nose section across its assigned volume of space.

Somewhere in that volume lay the control platforms which made Mycroft possible. The people who'd emplaced those platforms understood their importance, and they hadn't gone out of their way to make them easy to detect. The grav-pulses which made FTL communication possible were difficult to hide, especially from something inside their transmission paths, but the Grand Alliance had deployed a dense shell of Ghost Rider platforms and sensor buoys well outside Mycroft's sphere. They provided the information Mycroft would require if it was ever called to action, but their constant stream of FTL transmissions also provided a background into which the control platforms disappeared.

From outside the sphere, at any rate. From *inside* it...

The Holy Grail of true artificial sentience continued to evade humanity. After so long, only a handful of researchers continued to pursue it at all, but the capabilities of current generation "brilliant software" were more than good enough to convince most people outside that select community that computers truly could think.

They couldn't, and perhaps that was just as well in SBQ-12's case. Its AI wasn't worried about the fact that it had been dispatched upon what ultimately had to be a suicide mission. Nor was it likely to get bored as it listened patiently, patiently, for the signals its designers knew had to be out there somewhere. Mycroft was far too vital to the Grand Alliance for its admirals to take any chances with its availability. If they ever needed it, they would need it on very short notice, and so the system stayed up continuously—watching, waiting, ready to defend the star systems sheltering under Mycroft's wings. And that meant there was a constant stream of readiness signals and scheduled system tests, all of which required FTL pulses. They might be very brief, they might come on *irregular* schedules, but they had to be there.

And because they did, SBQ-12 floated in the darkness, listening with infinite patience...and waiting.

Storage Room 212-05-632
Bramlett Tower
City of Old Chicago
Sol System
Solarian League

COLONEL TIMOTHY LAUGHTON'S HEAD hurt and his mouth tasted incredibly foul.

That was his first realization. Then he realized he was in a room he'd never seen before, seated in a heavy chair with his wrists and ankles secured to it. It was—or had been—a storeroom, he thought, with dust on the floor. Aside from the chair in which he sat, the only furnishings were another chair, this one empty, which faced it.

Not good, he thought, blinking his eyes as he tried to clear his sluggish mind and decide which of the several possible people with reason to be unfond of him had put him here. *Not good at all.*

"Hello, Tim," a voice said from behind him.

His head snapped around, eyes narrowing, but he felt an undeniable surge of relief as he recognized that voice. Unlike several other people who'd been running through his brain, he was pretty sure Major Bryce Tarkovsky was unlikely to put a pulser dart behind his ear in the very near future.

"Br—" He had to stop and clear his throat. "Bryce." The name sounded almost natural the second time, and he smiled. "I thought our poker game wasn't until Wednesday."

"It's not." Tarkovsky smiled back, although his green eyes were very cool.

"I promise I wasn't planning on palming any aces, if that's what this is all about."

"I'm afraid it's not." Tarkovsky strolled around and seated himself in the second chair. "This is more in the nature of a quiet conversation to help me decide whether or not I should turn your sorry arse in."

"Turn it in for what?" Laughton asked. "I mean," he smiled again, tugging against the wrist restraints, "I'm sure there are any number of things. Nobody can keep all the Regs straight. Right off the top of my

588

head, though, I can't really think of anything I've done that requires this sort of response." He tugged at the restraints harder.

"I'm not talking about Regs, Tim. This goes a little deeper than that."

"Where?" Laughton looked back at him with a puzzled expression.

"Tim, I've seen the raw data coming in to you, and I've also seen the analysis going out *from* you. You've been drawing some very strange conclusions. Or perhaps I should say some very *confident* conclusions from very scanty—one might almost say nonexistent—evidence. I'm curious as to why you've been doing that."

"Which conclusions would those be?" Laughton asked, his tone touched by a thin edge of wariness.

"The ones that say the Manties are behind all the unrest in the Protectorates. You know, the ones Oravil Barregos pretty much debunked. The ones which've been contributing so handily to the Mandarins' official line."

"Hell, Bryce!" Laughton laughed. "The Manties *have* been behind it! Isn't what happened in Mesa clear enough proof?"

"Even assuming that really was the Manties—and you're a Marine, Tim; would *you* have used nukes instead of KEWs?—that isn't the same thing as this false-flag operation you've been saying so confidently *had* to be them. And you started saying it at almost exactly the same time Rajmund Nyhus started saying it, which is interesting, because I know damned well *he's* lying out his arse. Like I say, I've gone back and looked at the same raw take you've seen, and unless you have some secret private com link to someone in the Manticore System, there's not one damned thing in it—until less than two months ago, at least—that fingers the Manties for it. But nobody reading your analyses would ever guess that."

"I disagree."

"I figured you'd say that." Tarkovsky leaned back and folded his arms. "But this is a bit too egregious to be a simple matter of interpretation. You've been deliberately cooking your analysis, Tim. Not only that, you've been doing it for months, while a hell of a lot of people have been getting killed. I want to know why, and I want to know who."

Laughton considered him thoughtfully. Technically, the deliberate falsification of intelligence reports was a felony, punishable by a minimum of five T-years in prison. That was the peacetime penalty. In time of war the consequences got considerably stiffer and decidedly unpleasant. On the other hand—

"Bryce, you've been stuck in Old Chicago even longer than I have. You know how the game's played. *Everybody* 'shapes the narrative' in his analysis! For that matter, you do the same thing. Oh, I know you're the squeaky-clean Marine, but tell me you haven't . . . shaded a report or two to favor the Corps's position! Everybody's got a rice bowl he's trying to protect *somewhere*."

"There's a lot of truth to that," Tarkovsky conceded. "But this is different, Tim. This time you've been part of something that's getting millions of people killed, and the people behind it *want* them killed." He shook his head, his expression grim. "I think it's time you stopped helping with that."

"Nobody wants anybody *killed!*" Laughton shook his head incredulously, then cocked it for a second and shrugged. "Okay, maybe the people you're talking about—if they existed—wouldn't *care* if people they didn't know got killed, but nobody's *trying* to stack the bodies any higher than they'd get stacked anyway."

"That's an interesting way to put it. Suppose you tell me who the people I'm talking about—if they exist—might be and let me decide about the rest?"

"You do realize any evidence obtained under duress is inadmissible?" Laughton raised an eyebrow and tugged at his wrists once more. "I only mention it as a point of information, you understand."

"Right now I'm more interested in who they are than in what happens to you." Tarkovsky gave him a fleeting grin. "Truth is, before this, I always liked you, and I'd hate to lose the income stream our poker games represent. But I'm dead serious, Tim." His smile disappeared and his eyes bored into the colonel. "I want to know who you're working for."

Laughton gazed at him for several seconds, considering carefully. He didn't know why Tarkovsky had gotten this sudden bee in his bonnet but, as he'd just said, *everybody* in Old Chicago was in someone's pocket. Timothy Laughton had spent too long seconded to Frontier Security to be unaware of the League's endemic corruption, and it was even worse, in many ways, inside the Kuiper than out in the Protectorates. It was less . . . bare-fanged, perhaps. Less openly acknowledged. But the very fact that no one ever so much as commented on it—certainly no one was willing to undertake the Sisyphean task of doing anything *about* it—only underscored its omni-pervasiveness.

He'd always known Tarkovsky had a quixotic streak, a bit of a Lancelot complex. But surely the major couldn't believe anyone in Old Chicago was likely to work up a sense of outrage for what was no more than a case of business as usual! Even if he turned Laughton in, and even if the "tainted evidence" of a coerced confession didn't automatically get thrown out—and it was true the Navy and Marines had somewhat more elastic standards in that respect—too many other people in this city had too much to lose if people doing "favors" for other people got hammered. So in the end, despite Tarkovsky's rather . . . melodramatic interrogation techniques, he was looking at no more than a disciplinary slap on the wrist.

"Okay, Bryce," he sighed. "You know, all you really had to do was ask about this across a card table. One without a recording device, of course. It's not like there are any deep, dark secrets here."

"So, tell me."

Tarkovsky leaned back, crossing his legs, and Laughton nodded.

"Sure. It's business as usual. I know you don't like the way the system works, but that doesn't *change* it. Back when I was with OFS out in the Protectorates, I got to know quite a few of the players. Shipping lines, transstellars, that kind of thing. So when the situation with the Manties started going south in Talbott, I wasn't surprised when one of those contacts got in touch with me. Look, it was obvious to anybody smart enough to check both hatches on the airlock that Kolokoltsov and the others would screw the pooch, whatever happened. It's not like anything *I* said was going to be a critical component in their ability to bugger things up! But I'll admit that my—let's call them 'clients'—wanted me to do my bit to shape Federal policy. So when they suggested my analyses should reflect the Manties' long-term objectives in the Fringe and Verge I didn't see any way it could hurt."

"And this notion that the Manties were deliberately fomenting unrest in the Protectorates? Was that your own contribution to 'shaping Federal policy'?"

"Um." Laughton pursed his lips thoughtfully. "You know, I'm not really certain about that." He frowned. "It just sort of grew out of the situation in Talbott."

"So all this goes back to Talbott?"

"Of course it does! The Manties pissed off a lot of people when they gobbled up Talbott."

"Including your 'clients'?"

"I'm sure they were pissed off by it, but, trust me, *they* didn't need the annexation of Talbott to want to plant one in the Manties' eye!"

"No?"

"Bryce, I'll give you a thousand-credit slip if you can think of anyone in the entire league who hates the Manties more than the Kalokainos clan does!"

"So you've been working for *Kalokainos Shipping* all this time?"

"Of course I have!" Laughton shook his head. "Heinrich Kalokainos has hated the Manticorans for damned close to eighty T-years, and the only guy I can think of who hates them *more* is probably Volkhart. I have to admit that, in some ways, they aren't the sharpest styluses in the box, though." He shook his head again. "I think they still think the Manty merchant marine can be slapped down to clear the way for their ships. I also think they're out of their minds, but I'm perfectly happy to take their credits if they want to throw them at me."

"Kalokainos," Tarkovsky mused. "Interesting."

"Like I say, Bryce," Laughton said almost compassionately, "it's the way Old Chicago runs. You're probably the last white knight in this entire town."

"Maybe I am," Tarkovsky said. "But I'm a little curious, still. You said you're not certain if you're the one who came up with the notion that the Manties were deliberately stirring up trouble across as much of the Verge as possible. You're sure about that?"

"Sure about the fact that I'm not sure about it?" Laughton snorted. "Yeah, I guess that's one way to put it."

"Nobody pointed you at it?" Tarkovsky put an edge of skepticism into the question, and Laughton frowned.

"What are you getting at, Bryce?"

"I'm just wondering whether or not Shafiqa Bolton suggested it to you."

Laughton stiffened, eyes narrowing in surprise. If Tarkovsky already knew Bolton was his contact with Kalokainos, surely he should've had some idea of who she was working for! He was too good at his job not to have traced that back. So why was he—?

The colonel blinked as his vision blurred suddenly. He shifted in the chair and swallowed again, heavily, at a sudden surge of nausea. What—?

A nova exploded at the center of his brain, and his entire body tensed, then collapsed forward against the restraints.

Hillary Indrakashi Enkateshwara Tower
City of Old Chicago
Sol System
Solarian League

"THE NEXT TIME YOU get a brilliant brainstorm and decide to go off on your own like a loose warhead, stop drinking whatever the hell you were drinking and breathe some pure oxygen! Goddamn it, what the *hell* did you think you were doing? Or am I doing you a disservice? You *are* a Marine after all, so I suppose it's entirely probable nothing as sophisticated as *thinking* ever entered your damned head!"

Simeon Gaddis glared at Bryce Tarkovsky, who looked back without flinching.

"I tend to agree, Simeon," Weng Zhing-hwan said. "On the other hand, and while I'm fully aware this is only likely to reinforce those loose warhead tendencies of his, I also have to think we're ahead of where we were."

"You do, do you?" Brigadier Gaddis turned his glare—stepped down a couple of notches, perhaps—on his fellow gendarme. "Pray enlighten me! How exactly does this light our darkness?"

"I think the timing on that 'aneurysm' tells us quite a lot, Sir," Daud al-Fanudahi said. "He was apparently just fine admitting he'd falsified his analysis, even admitting he'd done it for Kalokainos. But the instant Bryce mentioned Bolton's name, he dropped dead. Somehow I doubt that's a coincidence."

"They've got a point, Sir," Natsuko Okiku said diffidently. Gaddis turned his goaded expression upon her, and she shrugged. "Sir, your own forensic people found the nanotech. It's possible—in fact, I'd say it's *probable*—Laughton never knew who he was really working for, but what happened to him tracks perfectly with what Barregos says happened in Smoking Frog."

"But 'my own forensic people' don't have a clue how the hell it happened," Gaddis pointed out. "'He just died' isn't what I'd call a detailed cause of death. And they don't *know* it was the frigging nanotech that caused that convenient aneurysm of his."

His dutiful subordinate only looked at him patiently, and he scowled. Unfortunately for his mood, she had a point of her own. In fact, so did Tarkovsky, even if his lone-cowboy approach had been incredibly reckless. The brigadier couldn't begin to count the number of ways kidnapping a serving officer in the Solarian Marine Corps could have blown up in their faces. Especially when the serving officer in question died in custody. Fortunately, whatever his other faults, Tarkovsky was a competent tactician. He'd slipped the unsuspecting Laughton a mickey, then transported the unconscious colonel up the freight lift shaft to the abandoned storeroom in Laughton's own residential tower inside a cargo container without anyone seeing a thing. And he'd transported the colonel's body out of the building the same way and spent the better part of two hours flying around Old Chicago and the surrounding countryside to make sure no one had followed him before he contacted any of the other Ghost Hunters.

Okiku had been holding down the fort at Hillary Enkateshwara when Tarkovsky's secure com came in, and despite Gaddis's misgivings about where all this might yet lead, she'd done everything right. She'd dispatched two gendarmes she trusted to collect the container from the loading dock where she'd told Tarkovsky to leave it. And those gendarmes had transported the container to one of the Gendarmerie's less well advertised facilities, whose personnel were accustomed to reporting directly to Brigadier Gaddis in cases with sensitive security aspects.

She'd also instructed the senior medical examiner in that facility to look particularly closely for any sort of biological nanotech. Including—specifically—nanotech designed *not* to be found.

And they'd found it.

That was the key point, he thought, stepping back to perch on the corner of Okiku's desk. They'd *found* the damned stuff.

He settled himself and beckoned impatiently for Tarkovsky to sit behind the facing desk, then drew a deep breath.

"All right," he said. "Let me be very clear about this, Major. If you ever—and I mean *ever*—do anything like this again without previously clearing it *personally* with me, I guarantee you'll disappear almost as tracelessly as Laughton. Is that understood?"

"Yes, Sir."

The major had not said "and it will never happen again," Gaddis noted. On the other hand, he felt reasonably confident Tarkovsky understood he was only half-joking about the consequences.

"That said," the brigadier continued, "Natsuko has a point. The same one, I'm sure, you were making, Zhing-hwan. I wouldn't call it 'proof,' but this is pretty conclusive evidence the Other Guys are, in fact, operating right here in Old Chicago and that they don't want us looking in Ms. Bolton's direction. And as you said, Natsuko, this matches pretty nearly perfectly with Barregos's version of what happened to his 'Manties.' My examiner isn't a genetic specialist, and he's not on the cutting edge of bio-nanotech, so he doesn't have a clue what the stuff he found was supposed to do or how it was engineered. He *does* know it's not only based on Laughton's own DNA but seems to've been designed to be indefinitely self-replicating—until after it kills its host, anyway—which breaks about seventeen provisions of the Beowulf Code. And whoever built it, it's sophisticated as hell."

"Evidence it really did come from Mesa?" Weng thought out loud. Gaddis looked at her, and she shrugged. "Or maybe from somebody *in* Mesa, anyway? After Beowulf, they've got the best geneticists and bioengineers in the galaxy."

"Which makes it tempting to look in Mesa's direction," Gaddis acknowledged. "At the same time, there *are* other highly competent biotechs, Zhing-hwan. Using a technique which would point a finger at Mesa if somebody stumbled across it would have to be attractive to the Other Guys."

"Assuming the Other Guys really aren't Mesans themselves," she replied.

"Assuming that." He agreed, then looked at Tarkovsky. "You say he didn't look nervous or apprehensive at all?"

"Not a bit, Sir. I've uploaded the video."

"I know you have. But you're the interrogator who was actually in the room with him."

"Yes, Sir." Tarkovsky nodded his understanding. "And, as I say, he actually seemed more relaxed as we went along." He shook his head, his expression unhappy. "I have to say, I hate how this worked out in a lot of ways. Tim might've been dirty, but he had a point. Everybody in this goddamned city's 'dirty' one way or another! He clearly didn't think he was any dirtier than anyone else, and he seemed perfectly comfortable ID-ing Kalokainos. In my opinion, he genuinely believed that was who he was working for and figured that between the favors other people owed Kalokainos and the general cesspool of Old Chicago politics, he'd walk away in the end. He didn't have any idea he was about to die."

"That was my impression from the video," Gaddis said. "I just wanted your confirmation. And if he didn't have any notion he was about to die, that probably does indicate he was only a tool, not part of the core effort."

"I think it also indicates we're right that Bolton's a handler for the

Other Guys. In fact, she's probably a pretty *important* handler. However the nanotech killed him, it didn't do it until Bryce brought up *her* name," al-Fanudahi said, and Gaddis nodded.

"At the same time, though," the brigadier pointed out, "we have to wonder how broadly the Other Guys have distributed this 'drop dead' security protocol of theirs. We've already demonstrated that they're really, really good at avoiding surveillance and electronic eavesdropping. If anybody we arrest and interrogate falls over dead the instant we ask any *useful* questions, it's going to be damned hard to build any kind of case we could take to anyone, even Rorendaal and her people at Justice. Any of the Mandarins would laugh us out of their offices if we can't bring them something a hell of a lot solider than this!"

"Agreed." Al-Fanudahi's expression was grim, verging perilously close to despair.

He couldn't dispute a single one of Gaddis's points, but that only made him more desperate. He and Irene Teague had nowhere near full data on "Operation Fabius," but what they did know, they didn't like.

Unless someone had come up with an ultra-secret weapon about which nobody in Operational Analysis knew a damned thing, any attack on Beowulf would be a disaster for the Solarian League Navy. Raging Justice and Hypatia made that much abundantly clear. It was possible—indeed, what they were hearing suggested it was *probable*—that Strategy and Planning believed the SLN *had* come up with some technological equalizer they hadn't mentioned to OpAn. They might even be right. It was hard for al-Fanudahi to conceive of one big enough to actually level the playing field, but they could have found something which offered Fabius at least a chance of reaching its targets.

Even if they had, though, the SLN was still likely to suffer massive casualties, on top of those it had already taken. That was enough to turn his stomach, but there was an even worse possibility. If the Manties hadn't carried out the "Mesa Atrocity," whoever *had* carried it out had demonstrated their willingness to murder millions to further their goals. And if they were willing to murder millions of Mesans, there was no reason to think they wouldn't arrange the murder of millions of Beowulfers, as well. In fact, if the Other Guys really were the *Mesan* Alignment, they'd probably be a lot more willing to slaughter Beowulfers, given the history between them. And what happened if they did? If they managed to kill a million or two citizens of Beowulf and blame it on the SLN? Or, even worse, genuinely used the SLN to inflict those deaths? How would the Grand Alliance react to *that*?

Stories about a new amendment to the Constitution, one designed to solve the League's current fiscal crisis—some from accredited newsies;

most anonymously sourced—were beginning to hit the public boards. Given the atmosphere here in the Sol System, the amendment—if it existed, and he thought it probably did—would probably sail through the rumored truncated ratification process, despite the several serious legal flaws in the procedure. And if the Mandarins were able to tap however deeply they needed to into the enormous economic power of the League, the situation would change radically. The probability of the League's collapse—or, at least, the collapse of its Federal government, which might possibly have restored sanity to its foreign policy—would decrease significantly, and the Grand Alliance would know it was looking at a much longer, much more dangerous conflict.

Whether or not anyone in Old Chicago wanted to admit it, Daud al-Fanudahi knew that so far, the Alliance had exercised enormous restraint. It hadn't wanted this war and it didn't want to fight this war, and he'd come to admire its chosen strategy. The tactician in him might be critical of the way their defensive stance left the initiative in the League's hands, but the strategist in him understood. Their defensive advantage was so great they could afford to let the Solarians come to them, at least where their critical core systems were concerned. They didn't have to seek opportunities to chew up the SLN, and they'd actually done their best to *minimize* Solarian casualties, instead. They'd relied on the "soft power" of economic warfare, done everything they could to encourage the collapse of the political clique driving the confrontation, without killing anyone they could avoid killing. Their immediate strategic objective was clearly to strangle the Federal government fiscally while simultaneously peeling away Protectorate systems and Solarian trading partners until the Mandarins—or their successors—were forced to accept a negotiated peace. That much was obvious. But he suspected their *ultimate* objective was to encourage nothing less than the dissolution of the entire League into smaller, less juggernaut-sized successor states, like the Mayan Autonomous Regional Sector and this new Renaissance Factor coalescing around Mannerheim.

Both of those were *waiting* strategies, though. They were the tactics chosen by the side with minimal ambitions for territory...and sufficient confidence in its own military capabilities to be patient. To let time work for it.

But if there was anyone in the entire galaxy who'd had to face down the challenge of making the hard military calls, it was the Grand Alliance. They *had* to realize the potential downsides of their chosen strategy...and that meant they had to have an alternative strategy in place in case their first approach failed. So what happened if there was another "Mesa Atrocity"—this one in one of the Grand Alliance's systems? One coupled with a sudden improvement in the Mandarins' fiscal situation and the simultaneous use of some new weapon which let the SLN get inside their defenses and kill still more of their civilians? What happened if all of that flowed together and convinced the Royal Manticoran Navy and its allies to start taking the war—*genuinely* taking the war—to the Solarian League for the very first time?

And what happened if they concluded that the League had decided the Eridani Edict no longer applied? If they decided the only way to prevent more mass casualty attacks was to adopt a policy of ruthless reprisal? Prove they would, indeed, exact an eye for an eye and a tooth for a tooth, however many millions of Solarians that killed, if that was what it took for the Mandarins to recognize sanity when they saw it?

If the gloves really come off, who knows where the killing will stop... if *it stops?*

An icy chill went through Daud al-Fanudahi as he stared into that question's hollow eyes and only darkness looked back. Because the single thing he knew was that he *didn't* know the answer.

JANUARY 1923 POST DIASPORA

**White Haven
Planet Manticore
Manticore Binary System
Star Empire of Manticore**

"EAT YOUR PEAS, RAOUL."

Honor's tone was supposed to be firmly commanding. It actually came out about midway between a command, a request, and an admission of defeat, and she tasted Hamish's unbecoming amusement as his offspring shook his head stubbornly.

Again.

"*No*," Raoul Alfred Alistair Alexander-Harrington said with the invincible stubbornness of his twenty-one months.

"They're good for you," she persisted. "Besides, you like them."

"*No*," he repeated, despite the fact that he *did* normally like them, and sent his spoon flying across the dining room table.

"*Raoul*—!" Her own valiantly suppressed laughter eroded the sternness of her tone.

"Want 'paghetti," he announced.

"You're *having* peas," she informed him.

"'Paghetti!" he insisted, and she tasted his very self-centered delight in expressing his independence.

"No spaghetti," she said sternly. A mother, even one who spent so much time in space, had to draw the line somewhere, she figured. "Peas."

"'*Paghetti!*"

"Peas!"

She sat back, crossing her arms, and regarded him with a frosty maternal eye.

"You do realize they can sense fear, don't you?" Hamish asked helpfully.

"You *so* do not want to go there, Hamish Erwin MacGregor Simpson Alexander-Harrington," she told him ominously, never looking away from their son.

"You do seem to be having a bit of a problem, Honor," Emily Alexander-Harrington observed.

Her life-support chair was parked beside their daughter Katherine's

601

highchair while she supervised Katherine's dinner. Which, Honor observed, seemed to be going somewhat more smoothly than their son's. Emily couldn't actually feed Katherine herself, given the fact that she had only limited use of one hand, but she smiled encouragingly at the toddler's green peas-smeared face and got a huge answering smile in return.

Honor would have preferred to put that down to the fact that Emily had the home-court advantage. It was true that the weeks on end that Honor spent aboard *Imperator* limited the time she had with their children. There'd been times—more than she could count—when she'd bitterly resented that as Raoul and Katherine raced from babes-in-arms, to self-propelled quadrupeds, to shaky steps, to determined, hyper-velocity toddlers shrieking with laughter as they dodged around the nursery, playing keep away with nannies and treecats. She'd missed so *much* of that transformation, and she could never get it back again, and she knew it.

You're not the only parent who's ever been stuck aboard ship while her kids grew up without her, she reminded herself sternly. *And you're a heck of a lot luckier than most of those other parents were! You're at least close enough to home that you can get there for visits every couple of weeks. And,* she admitted, *when you* are *here, you can actually taste their mind-glows. That's something no other parent—no other two-leg* parent, she corrected, glancing at Samantha and Nimitz—*has ever been able to do. Something Emily can't do. Or, really, something* else *she can't do.*

Her mood darkened briefly as she watched Sandra Thurston wipe the outer few centimeters of pea paste off Katherine's chin. While Katherine appeared far more amenable to the evening's menu, she still plied her own spoon with more enthusiasm than precision, although, to be fair, peas were less spectacular than the results she could achieve with Raoul's favored "'paghetti."

There was no trace of self-pity in Emily's mind-glow as she watched Sandra do what she couldn't, but that only made Honor more aware of her senior wife's loss. And she seemed so *tired* again. It was almost—

She put that thought aside and returned her attention to Raoul.

"No 'paghetti," she said firmly.

He sat back in his highchair, looking at her stubbornly with almond-shaped brown eyes very like the ones she saw in the mirror, and she tasted the developing mind behind them as it grappled with the problem. His ability to put sentences together lagged considerably behind his ability to comprehend what was said to him. According to the pediatricians, that was to be expected at his age. In fact, his spoken vocabulary was well ahead of the norm. He had at least a hundred words in his mental vault by now, and he was adding at least a half-dozen a day. And he did take a certain delight in using them to affirm his independence.

That, too, was right on the curve, she thought. Of course, some children were more stubborn than others. Raoul definitely fitted into that category. Undoubtedly the fault of his father's genetic contribution.

"No 'paghetti?" he said after a moment.

"No 'paghetti," she confirmed in a no-nonsense, listen-to-your-mother tone.

He cocked his head, and she twitched internally as something... brushed at the corner of her mind—that wasn't the right verb, but that was because there *wasn't* a "right verb" for what she was experiencing—and her eyes widened. She'd thought she was sensing something once or twice before, but she'd never been certain, and each time she'd convinced herself she was imagining things. This time she couldn't, and her eyes slid sideways to Sun Heart, the senior female of the half-dozen 'cats who'd immigrated to White Haven.

In many ways, Sun Heart was Lindsey Phillips's co-nanny where both children were concerned. A "retired" elder of Bright Water Clan, she wasn't a memory singer, like Samantha, but she was over a hundred T-years old and the mother of "hands of hands"—the vagueness of treecat arithmetic could be frustrating—of kittens of her own. Most of them were adults now, which freed her to focus on the two-leg offspring of Death Fang's Bane Clan, and she—and all of Bright Water's 'cats—took their responsibilities seriously. Although Sun Heart tended to spend her nights sleeping on the foot of Raoul's bed, her mate, Bark Master, spent every night on Katherine's to be sure both bases were covered.

Honor had never been able to decide all the reasons the treecats did that. Partly, she knew from her own ability to taste their mind-glows, it was because all of the 'cats loved the kids so deeply. And it was because they were determined that nothing would harm either of them. But there was something else going on, as well. Something she suspected not even the 'cats fully understood. There was a complex, subtle...flow between Raoul and his furry guardians. Katherine was a bright, sunny, incredibly smart little girl, but without that interwoven tapestry. Sun Heart had made it clear to all of the various parental two-legs that both Raoul and Katherine were almost certain to be adopted when they were older, when their mind-glows had settled a bit. But there was more than that at play here, and she suddenly wondered how her own ability to taste the treecats' mind-glows might have looked if she could have seen it from the outside.

Now Sun Heart met her gaze—and the more pointed question of her emotions—with calm, grass-green eyes. Then she flipped her ears in the equivalent of a shrug.

Lot of help that *was,* Honor thought, and Sun Heart bleeked in soft laughter that was echoed from Nimitz and Samantha.

"If you're not part of the solution, you're part of the problem," she told the furrier members of the dinner party. "I think—"

"'Elery," Raoul interrupted with the air of a high-level diplomat offering up a compromise solution.

"You need to eat more than just celery," Honor responded. She wasn't sure whether Raoul really liked celery or if his craving for it owed more to watching the treecats devour it.

Or, she thought, thinking about that subtle flow of mind-glows, *maybe he actually...I don't know...experiences whatever it is they get out of eating it. I've certainly tasted* Mister Gobble Guts's *fondness for it!*

Nimitz bleeked a harder laugh.

"The peas were only one thing you were trying to get down him," Hamish pointed out. "Maybe you've got an opening wedge."

"Bargaining creates a future position of weakness," Honor replied darkly, regarding Raoul with calculating eyes.

"Honor, he's not quite two. You've got *decades* to work on him."

"Oh yes?" She turned to give him a withering glance. "Do you have any idea how hard it was for my mom to get back *any* ground she ever yielded to me?"

"I don't have to. I know how hard it's been for me and Emily!" He shook his head. "I'm just saying that sometimes a canny tactician settles for a partial victory rather than reinforcing failure."

"You two do realize you're *feeding a child*, not fighting a battle?" Emily asked. Then she paused, thought a moment, and shook her head. "Forget I said that."

"Truer words were never spoken," Honor said, returning her attention to Raoul.

"No peas, you get the celery, but you have to eat the mac-and-cheese *and* drink every drop of the milk," she countered. "Deal?"

He pondered carefully, considering every aspect of the proposed compromise. She could tell that the "I'm-a-big-boy" corner of his mind wanted to lay down additional conditions. Fortunately, she had a hole card. The Meyerdahl genetic mods were hard-coded, which meant he'd inherited her metabolism. Debating what he was going to eat might turn into a tussle, but there was no doubt he was going to eat *something*. Keeping the Meyerdahl furnace stoked was a full-time occupation. So she sat back, arms folded, and waited him out. He wavered back and forth for a moment, then nodded.

"'Eal," he said firmly. "But 'elery *first!*"

"Done," she sighed, and reached out to remove a stalk of celery from Nimitz's tray. The treecat bleeked indignantly, and she snorted. "You're so darned amused by all this, *you* can provide the celery," she told him.

Raoul didn't care where it had come from. He grinned from ear to ear, grabbed his prize, and started to chew.

"Now, if only the Sollies were that easy," Hamish said.

"The Sollies don't have a clue about *real* stubbornness," Honor informed him with crushing scorn.

✧ ✧ ✧

"I do wish both of you could get home more often," Emily said as the three of them sat in the garden Hamish had built for her fifty T-years ago. She and Hamish held cups of coffee and Honor sipped from her own cup of cocoa as they gazed up through the cool night air at the stars of Manticore. "And I really wish your schedules would let at least one of you go to Briarwood with me!"

"So do I," Honor sighed, lowering the mug. "They grow up so *fast!*" She laughed with an edge of sadness. "I'm sure every parent who's ever lived said exactly the same thing, but that's because it's true. And I'm missing so *much* of it."

"I know you are, sweetheart," Emily said. "But I think maybe you're also more aware of how much they're growing and changing. I see it happening right here in front of me on a day-to-day basis; you see it after being away, and that probably makes it even more impressive."

"And what was all that business with you and Sun Heart?" Hamish asked.

"You remember how I said it was going to be really interesting seeing how kids raised by treecats turned out?" Honor smiled crookedly. "Well, I think Raoul's determined to prove my point. There's something going on there."

"Only with Raoul?" Emily asked, and Honor glanced at her in the garden's dim light. Emily's tone was only curious, and Honor tasted her mind-glow carefully, then relaxed ever so slightly, for that mind-glow was as tranquil as ever.

"Only with Raoul for *right now*," she said, "but I think he got more than his metabolism from me. And, honestly, from what the 'cats have told Adelina, *I* probably got a head start on whatever it is I've got from Mom and Dad. So it's not too surprising Raoul might be showing signs of something like it. It's a lot earlier than I did, but, then, while it's true I spent as many hours in the woods as I could get away with, I wasn't actually *raised* by treecats, whatever certain people may have said over the years. They got hold of me a little later than that."

Nimitz laughed quietly from the back of her chair, and Samantha joined her mate. Sun Heart had headed off to the nursery with Raoul and Katherine, but Crooked Toe—so named to differentiate him from his twin brother, Straight Toe—another of the male treecats who'd attached themselves to White Haven—lay stretched luxuriously across Emily's lap. One or more of the 'cats were always in evidence wherever Emily went on the White Haven estate.

"I wouldn't be surprised to see Katherine start showing a sensitivity to the 'cats a lot younger than other kids do," Honor went on more seriously, "and Samantha and the memory singers working with Adelina seem to think they may actually be able to figure out how to make two-legs 'hear' memory songs. After a fashion, anyway. From the way they're talking, I'm pretty sure they figure Raoul's going to be their initial success story, but they're hoping Katherine's will be the real breakthrough when she's a little older."

"That would be wonderful to see," Emily said.

Honor tasted an edge of wistfulness in her wife's mind-glow and reached out to lay one hand gently on Emily's. The older woman looked at her and smiled, but neither of them said what both were thinking, and Honor's eyes prickled.

"That *will* be wonderful to see," Hamish said with a firmness which fooled neither of them. Then he sipped coffee with the air of a man changing the subject.

"Willie and I have a meeting with Tony Langtry and Tyler Abercrombie tomorrow afternoon," he said. "Since I have no intention of talking 'business' once we retire for the evening, I thought I'd see if either of my top analysts had anything to offer."

"From the list of attendees, I assume you'll be talking about the Mandarins' version of what happened at Mesa?" Emily said. "Among other things, I mean?"

"You assume correctly." Hamish's tone was rather grimmer than it had been. "It's not like there've been any surprises about how they're trying to use it, but we still have to figure out how we're going to respond to it."

"I'm afraid I don't see much of a way we *can* 'respond' to it, short of going active against their core systems." Honor sighed. "Aside from what we've already said and done, I mean."

"It would help—a lot—if our rabbit-excavators weren't finding so many card-carrying members of the 'Mesan Alignment' who genuinely don't know a damned thing about the Yawata Strike or Harahap's 'Operation Janus,'" Hamish growled. He shook his head. "Every single time one of them opens his or her mouth, newsies like O'Hanrahan point at the fresh evidence that even though there *was* an Alignment, we obviously grossly overreacted to—or totally misinterpreted—our own intelligence data."

"And the fact that we were that far out of touch with reality only makes it even more likely we nuked Mesa in a surfeit of xenophobic, paranoiac incompetence." Emily's tone was as grim as his had been, and he nodded.

"Exactly, love. And every time we say we didn't, the Mandarins point at our denial as exactly what you'd expect out of people desperate to dodge responsibility for their own acts."

"Like I say, I don't see much else we can do at this point." Honor sipped cocoa, then shrugged. "I don't like it, and I wish I had some silver pulser dart, but I don't, because there *isn't* one. Unless you come up with something at the conference, that is." She smiled faintly at him. "You *are* going to have quite a brain trust assembled."

"And so far, not a single one of the brains involved has any better idea of how to respond—short of a you-shoot-my-dog, I-shoot-yours that is *way* too likely to spiral out of control—than the three of us do," Hamish retorted.

Honor nodded, less at what he'd said than at the unspoken portion of his thought. Whether or not any of the people scheduled to assemble at the conference in Beowulf had a better idea of how to respond, they'd have to respond *somehow*. It was their job to figure out how, and just this once, a cowardly part of her was delighted her own responsibilities would keep her far, far away from the decision-making process.

She only prayed they could come up with one which *didn't* involve her and Grand Fleet.

Chairman Chyang Benton-Ramirez, as the chief executive of the system hosting the conference, would have the dubious pleasure of presiding over it, although he probably wouldn't be there for the actual working sessions. He had too much other work on his plate, and he'd undoubtedly head back down to his office in the planetary capital as soon as he decently could after he'd gaveled the conference to order. Which made sense, really. He might as well get on with doing something useful with his time, because if the megaton or two of talent assembling aboard Beowulf Alpha couldn't come up with an answer, nobody could.

"Is Willie going to be able to attend?" she asked now.

"I don't think so. Not initially, at least, although he's planning on making at least some of the later sessions." Hamish shrugged. "President Ramirez and he have several things they need to discuss, and he was already scheduled to visit San Martin before the conference was scheduled." He shrugged again. "To be honest, a lot of this will be assembling information and building models—trying to come up with a range of possible options. So it actually makes sense, in a way, to keep the people who'll have to choose between those options out of the scrum while they're hammered out."

"Keep any of them from getting personally invested in the hammering process so they're genuinely neutral when it comes time to pick. Smart," Emily said approvingly.

"That was Elizabeth's thought." Hamish nodded. "And it looks like Tom Theisman won't be there, either."

"He won't?" Honor cocked her head. "I thought all the Joint Chiefs were attending?"

"All of them except Theisman." Hamish grimaced. "He's decided to ride along personally for Charnay."

"Nobody mentioned that to me."

"Nobody's *officially* mentioned it to L'anglais, either," Hamish told her, and she frowned.

Operation Charnay was an extended exercise scheduled for Task Force Two, the Havenite component of Grand Fleet. Pascaline L'anglais had found several spots of rust she'd decided needed sandblasting, and TF 2 was about to spend two or three arduous weeks in Trevor's Star removing them. For her own part, Honor thought the rust spots were rust *specks*. She was completely satisfied with TF 2's performance, but she wasn't TF 2's CO, either. And the truth was that anyone's performance could always be improved. Since the time of Edward Saganami and Ellen D'Orville, the RMN's position had always been that there was no such thing as too much training.

On the other hand...

"Since you're *unofficially* mentioning it to me, can I ask just why Tom feels his presence is required?"

"I wouldn't say he thinks it's 'required,' but he does think it could be worthwhile. I'm pretty sure L'anglais, personally, accepts what we've told her about Mesa. Having Zilwicki and Harahap personally brief her with treecat lie detectors looking on was one of your better notions, and God knows you've had enough of those over the years!"

Hamish smiled warmly at her, but then his smile faded just a bit.

"Having said that, I'm not sure she doesn't still have a few lingering doubts about whether or not Tenth Fleet—and she includes Tourville in that, I'm pretty sure—may have been...overly hasty in the way it moved on Mesa to begin with. And Theisman tells me Alenka Borderwijk's picking up on a few rumbles from some of TF Two's other senior officers. Below the squadron CO level, they still aren't cleared to be fully briefed on everything we know. Given how little we really do *know*, the fact that they aren't cleared for all of it leaves a lot of room for...unhappy speculation, let's call it. Tom wants a little quality time to do some speculation-squashing."

Honor's nod of understanding wasn't completely happy. She understood what Theisman was thinking, and she could see a lot of arguments in favor of keeping his efforts "in the family," as it were. She was irked by the fact that she'd apparently missed whatever Borderwijk had picked up upon, however. And she rather wished Theisman had mentioned it to her before discussing it with Hamish.

"I'm pretty sure Tom plans on mentioning this to you himself at the Palace tomorrow," Hamish said, as if he'd read her mind. "He only mentioned it to me this morning when I asked him if he wanted to make the trip with me in *Cromarty*."

"Her Majesty's letting you use *Cromarty*?" Honor laughed. "Talk about delusions of grandeur!"

"Excuse me? You think there's some reason why someone of my stupendous seniority and toweringly noble birth shouldn't use the royal yacht?"

"Oh, no. I don't think there's *a* reason why you shouldn't!"

"I see that you are, sadly, no respecter of persons, Duchess Harrington," Hamish said sorrowfully, then chuckled. "Actually, we're going to need something at least *Cromarty*'s size, given all the people and staff will be taking along. Thomas Caparelli, Pat Givens, Victor Dyson, Lucien Cortez, me, Francine Maurier, Tony, Tyler Abercrombie..." He shook his head. "Seems like damned near two thirds of Landing's going to be shut down, and that doesn't even count the other folks we'll be taking along. Michael Mayhew, his ambassador—even the ambassador from Torch!"

"My God, Hamish!" Emily said. "How in heaven's name will you get anything accomplished with that many cooks busy stirring the broth?"

"Oh, we'll be breaking down into subcommittees. I haven't seen the detailed agenda yet, but the actual working committees will be a lot smaller than you'd think just from the guest list. Some of us will have seats on more than one of them, but I think they've actually managed to divide the areas of responsibility logically enough—and keep each subcommittee small enough—it really will get a lot accomplished."

"And each subcommittee will be in the same place if they need some sort of quick feedback from one of the others." Honor nodded in approval. "I hate conferences, myself, but this one's overdue, really. The truth is, we've needed to fundamentally reassess our strategic assumptions from the moment we found out about Operation Buccaneer, and nothing that's happened since has made that any less true."

"Exactly." Hamish nodded. "That's another reason I wish you were going to be there, too. We do need to reassess all of our assumptions, and the truth is that you've got a better grasp of them than ninety percent of the other people I just mentioned."

"Nonsense." She snorted. "I don't think I'd be exactly useless, but at least a dozen of those 'other people' are a lot better informed than I am outside Grand Fleet, Hamish, and you know it. The lot of you will do just fine without my own invaluable input!"

"Maybe, but that won't keep me from feeling *lonely*." He let his voice waver on the final word, and his head drooped mournfully.

"Kick him for me, Honor?" Emily requested.

"My pleasure," Honor assured her, and did so.

"Bullies!" He rubbed his kneecap. "Spouse abusers!"

"Of course we are." Emily looked at him in astonishment. "You didn't understand how that works?"

"Then maybe it's a good thing Honor *will* be the one staying home to mind the store," Hamish said with a laugh.

"I'll try to take that as a compliment," Honor told him. "But I will be sorry not to see Uncle Jacques and Grandmother. Give them both a hug for me. Especially Uncle Jacques."

"I'll pass along the sentiment," Hamish said dryly, "but if it's all the same to you, I think I'll just reserve any hugs for the ladies in my life."

"What? Not for Raoul?" Emily demanded.

"Oh, and for him, too, of course!"

"Wise decision," Honor told him. "A very wise decision."

SLNS *Québec*
Task Force 790
Solarian League Navy

"—SO EVERYTHING LOOKS PRETTY good, Sir," Rear Admiral Rutgers said. "I know all of us would feel more comfortable if we had some operational experience using Hasta against live opposition, but that's sort of the nature of a 'secret weapon,' I suppose." He smiled thinly. "Not much of a secret, if you've used it against the other side before, and I'm all in favor of the element of surprise! That doesn't mean I wouldn't be happier with better projections for how well the Manties' systems might see Hasta coming, but at least we know *our* systems have a hell of a time finding it at any sort of extended range."

Vincent Capriotti allowed himself a small smile of his own. There might be a bit of a kid whistling in the graveyard about Rutgers's humor, he reflected, but the ops officer had a point.

"I'd have to agree with Lyang-tau, Sir," Vice Admiral Helland said. "I understand the ops plan's logic, and the profile's going to keep us from getting in too deep. But we've all had to admit the Manties' stealth systems are better than ours, and we don't have any confirmation their *sensor* systems haven't been improved in tandem with that. Their *missile defense* has damned well gotten a hell of a lot better to keep pace with their range and throw weight! I'd be a lot happier myself if we had a better feel for how likely Hasta *really* is to get in undetected."

The strawberry-blond chief of staff didn't sound happy to find herself concurring with Rutgers, Capriotti noted. Their own Cachalot operation had been a walkover, despite Rutgers's reservations, and she'd done quite a bit of crowing in its immediate aftermath. She hadn't been too heavy-handed about it, but she'd gotten her jabs in, and her initial response when Capriotti had been named to command Operation Fabius had been to see it as the just due of the victors of Cachalot. But that had been when Fabius was basically a contingency plan. One that *might* be executed, but probably wouldn't be.

The ops officer—true to form—had been less impressed than she with their own success, and his relationship with her hadn't improved when they crossed swords over Cachalot's outcome. But that had been before she'd read Thomas Yountz's after-action report and discovered what had happened at places named Hypatia and the Prime Terminus. Before she'd admitted to herself, little though she'd wanted to, that TF 783's success had resulted at least as much from good fortune as from skill. Her breezy confidence had undergone a slight revision since, and now that Fabius had gone from contingency to active operation, she—like Rutgers—was less than delighted by the notion of relying so heavily upon a weapon which had never been tested in combat to attack one of the most heavily defended star systems in human history.

Sure she is, Capriotti thought now. *Nobody ever said Angelica wasn't smart, so it's no wonder she's no happier than Lyang-tau about playing guinea pig with Hasta at* Beowulf, *of all damned places. But face it, Vincent! She may be* worried *about that, but what she's* pissed *about is that we're only a "task force."*

He was forced to stifle an inappropriate chuckle at the thought, yet it was true. Helland was of the opinion that any force committed to an attack of this magnitude and importance ought to be designated a *fleet*, not a mere task force. And as she'd pointed out to him rather snippily—and privately, thank God!—there *were* over four hundred ships in TF 790's wall of battle. Unfortunately, all of them were battlecruisers, not superdreadnoughts, and the Navy had decided long ago that only a force which contained actual ships-of-the-wall qualified as a "fleet." Personally, Capriotti didn't give a damn what they were *designated*. What he cared about was actual combat power—and, he acknowledged, the acceleration to get out from under if things went to hell on them.

And even if Fabius goes perfectly—which no military op in history ever has—speed is still the name of the game, he reminded himself. *If everything works the way it's supposed to, this will be one of the shortest decisive battles in history, and we need fast footwork to make that happen. Of course, if everything* doesn't *go perfectly, it'll be an even shorter battle.*

At which point speed will be really *important!*

And whether they were a fleet or a mere task force, they were also two subjective days—just over three days, by the rest of the galaxy's clocks—out of the Sol System. They'd reach Beowulf early the day after tomorrow... at which point they'd find out just how good Hasta really was.

"I'm glad we seem to be in good shape," he said out loud. "And, to be honest, I'm glad to see everyone seems to be bearing in mind that there are a *lot* of unknowns in the situation. Having said that, I've been giving a little more thought to how we want to deploy our recon platforms, especially to help with the background 'clutter' to hide the Hasta launch.

"Lyang-tau, it's occurred to me that if we deliberately—"

Private Yacht *Anachronism*
Beowulf System

"HONOR DIDN'T WARN ME about your toy, Jacques," Hamish Alexander-Harrington said. Samantha lay sprawled across his lap, and he rubbed her ears gently as he gazed around the flight deck.

"My 'toy,' is it?" Jacques Benton-Ramirez y Chou asked mildly. He arched a haughty eyebrow and the 'cat on the back of his flight couch bleeked in amusement. "I'll have you know I acquired this vessel as a legitimate business expense."

"A *business expense*?" White Haven said. "This has got to be the most...ostentatious thing I've ever seen in my life. I'm astonished the toilet seats aren't plated in gold!"

"I tried that," Benton-Ramirez y Chou told him earnestly, "but it was so damned *cold* every time I sat down I had it stripped back off. You don't think the vibrating near-mink lining is an adequate substitute?"

White Haven laughed and something suspiciously like a chuckle came from the jump seat occupied by Tobias Stimson, but the truth was that his comments weren't far off the mark. Honor's runabout in Grayson was almost as big as *Anachronism*, and considerably newer, but Honor was a naval officer, and while *Jamie Candless* was perfectly comfortable, she was also a no-frills, all-business vessel.

Anachronism wasn't. Or she was about the farthest thing imaginable from "no-frills," at least. She was a rich man's toy, from sleek prow to stern-mounted docking bay. Her décor was sumptuous, her passenger suites gave opulence a whole new meaning, there was an actual waterfall in the luxurious main saloon, and any cordon bleu chef would have traded his first two offspring for her galley.

And that was only her *interior*. The exterior was even worse.

There wasn't a single centimeter of her length that didn't gleam under bright, self-polishing smart paint which displayed a constantly changing color scheme, and the architect who'd laid out her lines for Benton-Ramirez y Chou must have thought he was out of his mind. There was no conceivable need to streamline a forty-nine thousand-ton space-going craft which would never enter atmosphere, but *Anachronism*

613

had not only the needle-sharp, aerodynamic prow of one of Saganami Island's Javelin training aircraft but sharply swept wings—wings that doubled as radiators to dispose of waste heat when her wedge was down, admittedly—and purely decorative vertical stabilizers. She even had false portholes along her sides, above each "wing," and what looked like air intakes for atmosphere-breathing turbines on either side of her bow.

She was, in short, the most ridiculous looking thing he'd ever seen in his life.

"Are you seriously telling me you managed to charge this...this flying brothel off on your taxes?" he demanded now.

"Oh, I did much better than that," Benton-Ramirez y Chou said smugly. "I got the system government to *pay* for all the really good bits."

"You did *what*?" White Haven stared at him in disbelief.

"I got the government to pay for it." Benton-Ramirez y Chou smiled broadly. Then his expression sobered.

"Seriously, Hamish. Somebody in the Biological Survey Corps decided that if my cover was going to be the idle layabout, dilettante diplomat it said I was, then I should look the part. And since everyone knows the Benton-Ramirez y Chou clan is filthy rich—not all of us are, by the way, whatever 'everyone knows'—I should probably buy something ridiculous to help that along." He shrugged. "Well, I'd been an SCA member for twenty or thirty T-years at that point, so when The Powers That Were decreed I should commission something only a rich, bored, totally frivolous idiot would want, I decided to recreate an Ante Diaspora airliner—or everyone's popular impression of one, at least—on a somewhat larger scale. And the BSC picked up the tab. Not the *complete* tab, but the Corps did pay for the cosmetic mods, and they provided the, ah...security features, let's say, out of their operating budget."

White Haven shook his head slowly as he realized Benton-Ramirez y Chou was serious. He really *had* had the audacity to "let" the BSC pay for his toy. And, in all fairness, calling it a "toy" was probably a bit unfair.

A *tiny* bit, anyway.

Hamish Alexander-Harrington was two months shy of his hundred and eighth birthday, and he'd been a professional naval officer for almost ninety T-years. In that time, he'd seen more spacecraft, of every imaginable size, than he could possibly have counted, and Benton-Ramirez y Chou had checked him out thoroughly on the yacht's systems before he'd listed him as the second pilot, which was now mandatory on all impeller-drive craft operating in the vicinity of inhabited planets or their orbital infrastructure. In the process, White Haven had discovered that however ridiculous she looked, *Anachronism* was as well-found and maintained an intrasystem vessel as he'd ever seen. And he'd been impressed by those "security features," too. Like the discreetly concealed lasers whose emitters were hidden in those false air intakes. He'd almost missed the fact that the "auxiliary astrogation plot" was actually a sophisticated tactical plot, built in to help manage not simply those lasers but also *Anachronism*'s two counter-missile tubes and an ECM suite which was probably as good as the one installed in Planetary Chairman Benton-Ramirez's official transport.

Anachronism really did look ridiculous, and no one would ever confuse Benton-Ramirez y Chou's yacht with a *Shrike*, but there were some sharp teeth under all that sheep's clothing.

"Am I correct in assuming that Honor doesn't talk too much about her Beowulf family?" Benton-Ramirez y Chou asked now, smiling as he reached back to scratch Bark Chewer's Bane's ears. Bark Chewer's Bane was the only treecat Hamish knew who was habitually addressed by his initials, BCB. The fact that he seemed so comfortable with it reinforced Hamish's suspicion that the 'cat-psychs were right about the way the treecats exchanged information. He knew what BCB meant in its entirety and was perfectly fine with the "bullet-point" version of it those poor, limited two-legs could manage.

"Not very much, no." Hamish shrugged. "Oh, by *name* sometimes— quite often, in fact—but she doesn't talk about their positions or the offices they might hold. I think the best way to put it is that they're important to her because of *who* they are, not *what*, if you take my meaning."

"I'm not surprised she doesn't have a lot to say about the family name. For that matter, I don't think she even *thinks* about it much, thanks to Allison." Benton-Ramirez y Chou smiled faintly. "My sister was determined to get as far away from any Beowulf 'dynasties' as she possibly could, and she did a damned good job of it. So I'm sure that until she fell into Benjamin Mayhew's clutches, Honor really did think of herself as a simple yeoman's daughter. Not"—his expression sobered slightly—"that anyone who ever knew Alfred or a single thing about his service record ever thought of him as a 'simple' anything." He shook his head. "Not everyone gets to know his twin is married to someone who'd storm the gates of hell—literally, not figuratively—to get her back again."

White Haven nodded silently and heard a very soft sound of agreement from Stimson. He wasn't a bit surprised that Honor's armsmen all thought the world of Dr. Alfred Harrington, and not just because he'd put their steadholder back together again so many times. White Haven himself hadn't known about Dr. Alfred Harrington's Marine career—or how he'd originally met Allison Benton-Ramirez y Chou—until he and Emily married Honor, but her armsmen always had. He didn't know where they'd picked up the information—the whole episode was still classified in two separate star nations—but that didn't seem to have bothered them in the least. Sometimes he thought they must use black magic when it came to ferreting out the information they thought they needed to keep their charges alive, yet none of them had breathed a word about it to *him* until one of Honor's chance comments caused him to ask *her* about it. Now he knew, too, and he'd seen the grim, smiling approval on Andrew LaFollet's face as Honor told her husband about the man her father *truly* was. And given who her parents were, perhaps it wasn't surprising Honor had grown up to be who *she* was.

"Anyway," Benton-Ramirez y Chou went on, "the thing is that we have what are commonly referred to as 'connections.' I'm sure the Alexander family has them back in the Star Empire, too. So it wasn't as hard as it might have been for someone else for me to convince the SDF to sneak the weapons into *Anachronism*. And while I never had any intention of using her operationally, I did take a certain comfort from knowing that if I had to—here in Beowulf, at least—I could. In fact, I had her freighted to Sebastopol for the Gomez Cup Race when we were conducting an op there. Took second place, too, and it really was the perfect cover. The bastards we were after never even saw us coming. Besides," he smiled again, this time devilishly, "building her was so much *fun*."

"My God, if Emily and I had only known about the sad mental state of the family we were marrying into!"

"Don't blame me! *How* long did you know Honor before Emily got the two of you off the decicredit?" Benton-Ramirez y Chou rolled his eyes. "If anybody should've known what you were getting into, it was you." He looked over his shoulder. "Wouldn't you agree, Tobias?"

"No, Sir," Sergeant Stimson said promptly. "Grayson armsmen are the soul of tact. It says so somewhere in the training manual."

"Oh, what a cop-out!" Benton-Ramirez y Chou laughed.

"Nonsense!" White Haven snorted. "What you call a cop-out is simply good, sensible tactics."

He chuckled and gave Samantha's ears another rub, then turned to lay her across the back of his own flight couch as a proximity alarm pinged.

"Impeller perimeter in thirty seconds," he announced.

"Copy," Benton-Ramirez y Chou replied. He gave his own instruments a quick look, then shrugged. "Might as well shut them down now," he said.

He pressed one of the control studs on *Anachronism*'s joystick and the yacht's impeller wedge died. She went ballistic, coasting onward towards the mammoth, growing bulk of Beowulf Alpha, the largest of the many habitats in orbit around the Beowulf System's capital planet, and he sat back in his flight couch.

Beowulf's impeller shutdown perimeter had been pushed out to a hundred and fifty thousand kilometers and maximum approach speed on the approach had been reduced to only fifty KPS, which meant that they were still over fifty minutes out. No doubt the system's work-a-day pilots spent much of their time cursing the "wasted time," but after what had happened in the Yawata Strike, they tended to keep their grumbling to themselves. At the moment, though, White Haven was actually grateful, because it gave him more time to watch their destination grow steadily before them.

Even at half a light-second, Beowulf Alpha gleamed like an enormous gem. Not surprisingly, since it was larger and much more massive than even HMSS *Hephaestus* had ever been, with a sheer size and pedigree that underscored just how ancient the Republic of Beowulf actually was.

Before the Yawata Strike, *Hephaestus's* longest dimensions had almost matched those of Beowulf Alpha, but the original core of Beowulf Alpha had been built over eighteen T-centuries ago. That was over a millennium and a half before *Hephaestus's* first girder had been put in place, and Beowulf Alpha had been growing ever since. Nor was simple seniority the only difference between them. *Hephaestus* had been a fairytale sculpture, a thing of components, sub units, long connecting booms, and massive industrial modules, more necklace and lacework than solid. The space station had been a dispersed tracery of open space and structural elements, growing in every direction—and in leaps and bounds—to meet perceived needs, with new sections added wherever seemed most convenient, completely irrespective of any master plan to coordinate that growth, and assembled in the wild Escher-like geometry of microgravity.

Beowulf Alpha hadn't. Beowulf Alpha had expanded over the centuries in carefully planned additions, each incorporated into the existing structure only after carefully considering its impact upon the entire station, and strict zoning requirements had insured that it was home to very little heavy industry. There was a lot of *light* industry, dedicated to consumer-oriented products, but Beowulf had always tended to segregate its heavier industry—and the accidents which could occur on those sorts of industrial sites—away from its residential areas.

Part of that segregation was inevitable, the sort of thing one might have seen in any star system. In Beowulf Alpha's case, that meant its light industrial modules were located on the long engineering and support booms stretching out from the main platform like the legs of some glittering spider, but the system's resource extraction facilities were almost all associated with the Diomedes Belt and the gas refineries around Enlil, the gas giant seventy-three light-minutes from the system primary. And most of the star system's shipyards and supporting infrastructure orbited the planet Cassandra, eight light-minutes outside the orbit of Beowulf itself, because they were so much closer to both the Diomedes extraction platforms and the hyper-limit.

There was quite a bit of industry in Beowulf orbit anyway—Ivaldi of Beowulf maintained its primary nano farms and molycirc tanks there, for example, and the main production lines for the Mark 23 and Mark 16 had been distributed among Ivaldi's three Alviss platforms—but the really heavy industry was farther out for the most part, handier to the belt and the refineries. The volume closer to the planet was dominated by residential habitats, with Beowulf Alpha as the prime example. Alpha was first and foremost a home for its twenty-two million inhabitants, although it had also housed both Adrienne Warshawski University and the Warshawski Center for Applied Astrophysics for the better part of seven hundred T-years. It was home to close to two hundred other civilian research facilities and laboratories, as well, not to mention the George Benton Center for Interstellar Studies, with a galaxy-wide reputation for the depth and breadth of its scholarship.

It was the GBC which had drawn the conference to Beowulf Alpha. Its facilities—especially its research libraries—were unparalleled, its list of consultable experts was enormous, and it boasted a plethora of superbly equipped conference rooms and communications centers.

And I'm sure *the restaurants and nightclubs just down-station from GBC didn't have a* thing *to do with the choice of venues,* White Haven thought.

"Think we'll be in trouble for being late?" he asked as *Anachronism* drifted onward.

"Nonsense! We're not *late,* just fashionably tardy," Benton-Ramirez y Chou told him, and Samantha and Bark Chewer's Bane bleeked with laughter as White Haven gave him a martyred look.

Actually, he and Benton-Ramirez y Chou had both attended the conference's opening sessions. Afterward, however, they'd accompanied Chairman Benton-Ramirez down to Columbia and then headed out for a family event, not an official function. Among other things, it had been White Haven's responsibility to show off several terabytes of video of Caspar Benton-Ramirez y Chou and Jennifer Feliciana Benton-Ramirez y Chou's newest great-grandchildren, and the great-grandparents in question had been vacationing on a skiing trip to Cassandra's spectacular Freyja Mountains.

Cassandra had a hydrosphere of only thirty-two percent, which made it a dry world by the standards of most inhabited planets, and it was decidedly on the cool side. It was, after all, four light-minutes farther from its primary than Mars was from Sol. It was also, however, far more massive than Mars—or even Old-Terra, for that matter—with a diameter of over 32,000 kilometers, a gravity of 1.5 G and a moon almost half as big as *it* was. That produced a lot of tectonic activity, which, in turn, produced an exceptionally active greenhouse effect which—coupled with its gravity well—had allowed it to retain both a deep atmosphere and an average surface temperature well above freezing. A gravity fifty percent higher than the one in which humanity had evolved remained a deal-breaker for the majority of potential immigrants, despite all grav plates could do, but the skiing really was fantastic, as Benton-Ramirez y Chou had demonstrated to him.

He'd felt more than a little trepidation about meeting Jennifer, however. The redoubtable grand dame of the Benton-Ramirez y Chou clan had been one of the galaxy's very first prolong recipients when she was twenty-seven T-years old. She'd just celebrated her hundred and thirty-fifth birthday, but she remained as vigorous as she'd ever been and she'd been one of the leading geneticists of Beowulf for three-quarters of her life. Given Beowulf's preeminence in the biosciences, that put her in what might be called "elite company." Worse, Jennifer had enjoyed a...tempestuous relationship with her daughter before Allison's flight to Manticore. And that relationship had been made no better over the next fifteen or twenty T-years as Allison proceeded to become on Manticore precisely what she had *refused* to become on Beowulf.

Under the circumstances, Jennifer had concluded—reasonably, in White Haven's opinion—that Allison's refusal to embrace the career her mother had chosen for her *on Beowulf* stemmed solely from the fact that it was the one *Jennifer* had chosen for her. Relations had been...strained, and turning that around had actually been Honor Alexander-Harrington's first major tactical triumph.

Which she had achieved, just over sixty-three T-years ago, by being born as Jennifer's first grand*daughter*.

Given that history, White Haven had been prepared for a formidable, daunting matriarch. What he'd gotten was a silver-haired, exquisitely groomed, charming, obviously brilliant woman with a tennis fanatic's tan and an ironic, biting sense of humor. She was also tiny, as small as her daughter, and her smile as she watched the video of Raoul and Katherine could have illuminated half a planet.

The side excursion had been eminently worthwhile, he thought.

"Tell them we're coming," Benton-Ramirez y Chou said as they finally floated across the actual impeller perimeter, and White Haven pressed the transmit button.

"Beowulf Alpha Flight Control, this is Sierra-Lima-Charlie-One-Niner-Six-Five-Tango, private yacht *Anachronism*, at impeller shutdown perimeter on approach from Cassandra. Strobing transponder now." He touched the transponder stud. "Request approach instructions. *Anachronism*, clear."

"Sierra-Lima-Charlie-One-Niner-Six-Five-Tango, Beowulf Alpha Flight Control. We have your transponder. Your vector looks good. Maintain heading on Approach Charlie Alpha Seven and begin decel at fifteen gravities in forty-four minutes from my mark...*mark!*"

"Beowulf Alpha Flight Control, SLC-One-Niner-Six-Five-Tango. *Anachronism* copies approach looks good. Maintain heading on Charlie Alpha Seven and begin decel at one-five gravities at seventeen-twenty-three-sixteen hours Zulu. I make that time to docking tractor lock of twenty-nine minutes after the hour."

"SLC-One-Niner-Six-Five-Tango, Beowulf Alpha Flight Control confirms," the crisply professional voice said. Then it shifted tone. "Welcome back, Admiral White Haven. Is that idle layabout Jacques making you do all the hard work?"

"Of course I am," Benton-Ramirez y Chou said, raising his voice to be heard. "It's what I do!"

"Ain't that the truth?" The voice at the other end of the com link laughed. "Free for poker tonight, Jacques?"

"Only if you've got money you *really* want to lose," Benton-Ramirez y Chou replied.

"Hah! That'll be the day! I'll screen you when I come off duty."

"Sounds good, Terry. See you then."

"That's affirmative, SLC-One-Niner-Six-Five-Tango. Beowulf Alpha Flight Control, clear."

HMS *Fafnir*
Task Force Thirty-One
Third Fleet
Beowulf Terminus

"ACTUALLY, MARIANNE, I THOUGHT the exercise went very well," Admiral Alice Truman said, as the stewards cleared away the supper dishes.

"For what it was, yes, Ma'am," Vice Admiral Marianne Holmon-Sanders replied a bit more formally than she was in the habit of addressing Truman. "It's just that all my people feel like we're only marking time until they scrap our ships. Like we're not pulling our weight in the defense of our own star system."

Truman frowned at Holmon-Sanders across the table in her dining cabin. The diminutive Beowulfer—she wasn't quite 155 centimeters tall—who commanded Third Fleet's second task force was a solid professional. She might look like someone's pre-prolong teenage sister, but no one who'd ever seen her on a superdreadnought's flag bridge would make *that* mistake. At the moment, however, what she looked most was pissed. Not at Truman, her task force commander, but at the weapons she'd been given. Or at fate, perhaps.

"If your people think you aren't pulling your weight, you're the only ones who do," Truman said a bit sternly.

"Oh, we don't think it's because we're slacking, Ma'am." Holmon-Sanders shook her head. "What we think is that at this moment, all the other members of the Grand Alliance will do any real fighting while we sort of stand there with our thumbs up our backsides and watch." She grimaced. "Let's face it, none of our wallers is even in shouting distance of *your* wallers."

"There's something to that," Truman conceded after a thoughtful sip of coffee. She set her cup down, trapped it in an open diamond formed by her thumbs and forefingers, and frowned down into it. Then she looked back up at Holmon-Sanders.

"Compared to a current-generation Manticoran SD(P), your *Leander* really is obsolescent. No offense, Captain François."

"None taken, Ma'am," Henriette François, Holmon-Sanders's flag

621

captain replied. "The truth is the truth." She shrugged. "I love *Leander*, and I'd hate to give her up, but she's the better part of forty T-years old, and there's a limit to what upgrades and refits can do."

"Especially when someone goes and introduces a revolution in missile warfare and none of the new launchers will even fit," Holmon-Sanders said acerbically.

"Well, yes," Truman acknowledged. "But you're comparing her to current-generation Manticoran, Havenite, or Grayson ships, not one of which is even *ten* T-years old. And I think the point you need to bear in mind is that that's not who you'll be fighting, if it comes down to it. Who you'll be fighting are the Sollies, whose ships are a lot farther behind the curve than yours are. Your ships are *obsolescent*; theirs are obsolete deathtraps. Trust me, if it comes to a shootout with the SLN, your people will hold up your end. Maybe the newer ships will do the really heavy lifting, but your people will be a huge part of our defensive envelope, and with Admiral Foraker's latest version of the Donkey, you've got a hell of an offensive punch, at least in the opening phase."

"I know," Holmon-Sanders said, and snorted. "Actually, I think a lot of it's simple envy! We want our new ships, and we want them *now!*"

"Of course you do. And they're coming." Truman picked up her cup and drank more coffee, then shrugged. "Truth in advertising, though. They won't be here the day after tomorrow."

"I know."

This time it came out as a sigh, and Holmon-Sanders sat back from the table and crossed her legs. She and François knew as well as Truman did why those ships wouldn't arrive next week. The Grand Alliance had rationalized its industrial output ruthlessly, with most of Beowulf's heavy fabrication capacity dedicated to rebuilding the Manticore Binary System after the Yawata Strike. It hadn't ended there, though, because the Alliance's existing SD(P) strength was more than sufficient to handle anything the SLN had, Because of that, the proportion of Beowulf's industry *not* dedicated to rebuilding Manticore had been switched to the fleet support role, not new construction.

Facilities like Ivaldi of Beowulf had begun churning out Mark 23 MDMs, Mark 16 DDMs, Ghost Rider drones, Dazzlers, and Dragon's Teeth, but while ammunition—and spare parts—were critical, future expansion hadn't been totally neglected. Other facilities were producing the components—like micro fusion plants and miniaturized FTL coms—Haven's industrial base couldn't manufacture quite yet, and that was likely to accelerate the delivery of Beowulf System Defense Force's first modern capital ships.

Bolthole's stupendous shipyards had undertaken an ambitious

construction program of SD(P)s, built to a new common Manticore-Haven design. Haven's basic technology in areas like FTL coms and missile tech—Keyhole-Two came to mind in that connection—remained significantly inferior to that of Manticore and Grayson, but Bolthole's *construction rate* was almost as high as Manticore's had been at the peak of its pre-Yawata Strike capacity. That meant there'd be a lot of new hulls remarkably soon, but they'd be completed in what could only be called a barebones configuration. They'd be fitted with engines, life-support, point defense, counter-missile launchers, armor, missile cores and pod rails, broadside weapons, and basic sensors, then transitioned to Beowulf's Cassandra yards for the installation of Keyhole-Two, FTL coms, and current-generation fire control and ECM suites to create an end product fully as capable as the RMN's *Invictus*-class. Spreading production between multiple locations was enough to make any logistician queasy, given the way it multiplied potential failure points. If it worked as planned, though, it would increase building rates by something like thirty percent, provide complete commonality of weapons, support systems, spare parts, and maintenance procedures for all the Allied navies' future construction, and get the first of the new ships into commission at least six T-months earlier than any other approach.

And one quarter of all the ships fitted out here in Beowulf would be assigned to the Beowulf System Defense Force's component of Grand Fleet.

But not tomorrow.

"Leaving aside your unbecoming greediness for new toys," Truman said now, her smile taking any sting from her choice of words, "what's your assessment—your *real* assessment, Marianne—of your people's performance?"

"Well, put that way, I'd say my assessment would have to be...not too shabby," Holmon-Sanders said with an answering smile. "Mind, I want more time for my people to work with yours."

"Not a problem now that Mycroft's operational," Truman said with a shrug, and Holmon-Sanders nodded.

The Beowulf Terminus was critical to the Grand Alliance, and the task of protecting it had been assigned to Task Force 31, the Manticoran portion of Truman's Third Fleet. Actually, she wore two "hats," as the CO of both Third Fleet and TF 31, and her task force covered the terminus mostly because the Manticoran ships had the missile range and firepower to punch out any Solarian attack foolish enough to head its way. Politics and the need to keep "foreigners" out of the inner system had played their own part prior to the referendum, and however much Holmon-Sanders might have yearned for more modern ships, she'd never doubted her own superdreadnoughts' ability to defend the inner system using the towed missile pods her allies had provided. But until Mycroft was able to relieve her task group of that responsibility, opportunities for joint training with the rest of Truman's ships had been few and far between. Now that Mycroft was online and had passed every check with flying colors, she'd been able to pull TF 32, Third Fleet's *second* task force, out of the inner system, join Truman on the terminus, and start joint training with a vengeance.

"With that in mind," Truman continued, "Captain Kovalenko and I have been thinking about the next exercise's parameters. Given the fact that your ships' current configuration gives them a massive initial throw weight but very little in the way of sustained engagement capacity, it occurred to us that we might—"

Her com pinged suddenly, and she stiffened as she recognized the urgent priority signal. She raised her left hand in a "hold that thought" gesture and stabbed the acceptance key with her right index finger.

"Truman," she said. "Talk to me."

"Me, Ma'am," Captain Benjamin Masters, her chief of staff, said tersely from the display. "System Defense HQ just commed. They've detected incoming hyper footprints. They didn't get a good count on the footprints, but the impeller wedges confirms a minimum—I repeat, a *minimum*—of four hundred point sources, most of them battlecruiser range."

Holmon-Sanders inhaled sharply and Truman's stomach muscles clenched. The Beowulf Terminus was 362 LM from the system primary, and Beowulf itself was currently in opposition to the Terminus, almost on the far side of the star. Even with the FTL com, it took over six minutes for a message from System Defense to come this far.

"Where are they?" She heard her own voice ask with what seemed like preposterous calm.

"Opposite side of the system, one-point-three light-minutes outside the limit, two degrees above the ecliptic, Ma'am. System Defense says they're inbound at four hundred twelve gravities from zero-zero-two on what looks like a direct heading for Cassandra. As of the time chop on the message, distance from Cassandra was seven-point-nine light-minutes and current velocity was roughly six hundred KPS. From that geometry, they can cut the limit's chord and make a zero-zero with the Cassandra Yards in just under three and a half hours with turnover at ninety-six minutes and some change."

Truman nodded tightly. The Sollies had timed it well, she thought, because Cassandra was just past western quadrature from Beowulf, with its elongation perpendicular to the direction of the primary, forming a right triangle with the sun. They were well over fourteen light-minutes apart—closer to fifteen, really—so any grief headed for Cassandra was headed *away* from Beowulf. That was the good news. The bad news was that Cassandra was barely four light-minutes inside the hyper-limit and that the Sollies' astrogation had been damned near perfect. They could go for a zero-zero with the planet, spend a couple of hours wrecking its yards, and be back out and across the limit in less than two hours when they were done, barely eight hours after crossing the limit inbound. Or they could blow past in a maximum-velocity firing run. If they did *that*, they could be at minimum range in just over two hours and ten minutes, moving at almost thirty-four thousand KPS, and arc back across the limit in another hundred minutes or so—in and out and back into hyper in well under *four* hours.

The civilian casualties would be horrendous in a successful hit-and-run attack like that, given the limited time to evacuate the yards. Normally, that would have given an attacker pause under both the Deneb Accords and the Eridani Edict, but Solarian restraint hadn't been very noticeable even before the "Mesa Atrocity"; Hypatia and the captured Buccaneer ops orders were proof enough of that. *After* Mesa and the way the Solarian newsies—which really meant Malachai Abruzzi—had portrayed it, "restraint" seemed even more unlikely.

"Light off the impellers and spin up the hyper generators, Benjamin," she said. "And tell Steve to start plotting the jump. I want multiple options for intercepting them on their way out whether they go for a zero-zero or a high-speed run."

"Yes, Ma'am."

"Good. I'll be on flag bridge in ten minutes."

"Yes, Ma'am."

She cut the circuit and turned back to her guests.

"I think you and Henriette had better be getting back to *Leander*, Marianne. It seems we have guests."

"Yes, Ma'am," Holmon-Sanders's smile was two-thirds snarl. "Hopefully it'll all be over before we ever get there."

"That would be the best outcome from our perspective," Truman agreed.

Aside from the two squadrons of *Agamemnon*-class BC(P)s of the ready response force, Third Fleet's hyper generators were powered completely down. The Beowulf Junction lay at the heart of a sensor bubble fifteen light-minutes across that a *microbe* would find difficult to penetrate, and the fixed defenses were...formidable. Under those circumstances, there was little reason to put wear on the hyper generators and nodes by holding the fleet at instant readiness. The ability to stand those systems down was the real reason there *were* fixed defenses, and any admiral worth her beret was grateful for them. But there was, of course, a downside to that, as well: time. Time and situations like this one. It would take a *Saganami*-class cruiser thirty-seven minutes—and an SD like *Leander* or a CLAC like her own *Fafnir* over forty—to bring up their generators and translate. For that matter, except for the ready response squadrons, every ship would have to bring her impeller nodes up from scratch at the same time, and that alone would take forty minutes, so not even the *Saganami* was getting into hyper any sooner than *Fafnir*.

At six light-hours, the transit would eat up another twenty-seven minutes or so in the Beta bands. She could carve four and a half minutes off that by going as high as the Gamma bands, but that seriously increased the chance of scatter when they re-entered n-space. Either way, she was looking at a best-case time requirement of well over an hour before she could be in position to intercept them on their withdrawal, and with their head start inside the limit, it was already impossible for her to actually intercept short of Cassandra. Apollo was long-ranged enough she could bring them under effective fire from *outside* the limit, while they were still at least ninety minutes short of a zero-zero with the yards, but they were already technically in range for a Cataphract launch of their own. Their accuracy would suck at such an extended range, but they'd demonstrated at Hypatia that enough Cataphracts could kill anything, even with a lengthy ballistic phase in its flight profile. They might be as inefficient as a Neanderthal with a club, but if you had *enough* Neanderthals with clubs, that didn't matter. Worse, every minute they had to close the range would tweak that accuracy upward, and she couldn't take those minutes away from them.

Shouldn't matter, she reflected grimly. *This is exactly what Mycroft's for, and those poor bastards don't have a* clue *what's going to happen to them when Admiral McAvoy opens up. Not that I plan to sit on my posterior and wait! If nothing else, we'll probably need all hands for search-and-rescue after the shooting stops.*

She grimaced as that thought brought up pictures of Hypatia, but she made herself put it aside.

"I'll walk the two of you to the lifts," she told her guests, and smiled thinly. "It's on my way, you might say."

Private Yacht *Anachronism*
Beowulf System

"—REPEAT: SYSTEM DEFENSE CENTRAL has declared Code Red," the com said. "Enemy warships have entered the Beowulf System, bearing zero-zero-two, zero-two-five true, range two-two-point-four light-minutes. All vessels and platforms are to implement Code Red procedures immediately. This is not a drill. This is not a drill. I repeat: System Defense Central has declared—"

Hamish Alexander-Harrington killed the sound and looked at Jacques Benton-Ramirez y Chou.

"Jesus!" he said. "I hope to hell *you* know what the Code Red procedures are!"

"As a matter of fact, I do," Benton-Ramirez y Chou said grimly, and punched the com button on his joystick. "Beowulf Alpha Flight Control, Sierra-Lima-Charlie-One-Niner-Six-Five-Tango requests diversion instructions as per Code Red procedures."

He glanced at White Haven and grimaced.

"Terry may be a bit getting back to me, under the circumstances," he said. "Why don't you check in and see if you can dig out any more info?"

White Haven nodded and punched a com code from his uni-link into *Anachronism*'s much more powerful com.

"Hamish?" a voice replied almost immediately.

"What can you tell us, Tom?" he asked.

"Not a hell of a lot more than System Defense," Sir Thomas Caparelli replied. "Our initial reports are still coming in—nobody thought Beowulf Alpha needed to be tied into their secure tactical net—but it looks like they're going for the Cassandra yards. I don't have any kind of hard numbers yet, except 'in excess of four hundred.'" White Haven didn't need to see the First Space Lord's shrug; he heard it in Caparelli's harsh tone. "Sounds like they mean business, but they're headed straight into Mycroft."

"But do they *know* they are?" White Haven asked, looking back at Benton-Ramirez y Chou and Stimson, who were both listening.

"That's sort of the million-dollar question, isn't it?" Caparelli replied. "If they don't now, they're going to find out soon enough, though."

"At least they're not headed for Beowulf. That's something."

"After Hypatia, it's a hell of a lot of 'something,'" Caparelli agreed. "God, I hate to think of a lunatic like Hajdu or Gogunov loose in Beowulf near-space!"

"You and me both. Hopefully, I'll see you soon."

"I'll try to have more info when we do. Caparelli, clear."

"Surely the Sollies have to've figured out we'd have something *like* Mycroft," Benton-Ramirez y Chou said.

"Maybe that's one of the reasons they're going after Cassandra. They don't have to get very deep inside the limit to bring it into Cataphract range," White Haven pointed out. "Hell, for that matter, they're already 'in range' for Cataphracts if they settle for a firing pass without time for evacuation. And let's face it: if they're here to hit the yards, there's no way in hell they could give us time to evacuate and still get out without being intercepted. They'd be cutting it close enough as it is, even without Mycroft. They have to know they can't have more than an hour, *maybe* ninety minutes, before Truman and Holmon-Sanders micro-jump in behind them on their best vector out of the system."

"So what would you do in their shoes?"

"If I were in their shoes, I wouldn't have come in the first place! But, then, I *do* know about Mycroft. Assuming I didn't—that the only things I was worried about were Holmon-Sanders in-system and Truman on the terminus—I'd probably come in on the shallowest penetration profile I could, bend it towards Cassandra, launch at my closest approach, and keep right on running at my maximum possible acceleration."

"You wouldn't just launch from outside the limit and accept a long ballistic phase?"

"Their accuracy would suck at that range, unless they've managed to improve their Cataphracts' onboard systems at least a thousand percent or so from the ones we've captured and evaluated, and I've got to assume System Defense's got a lot of EW capability out there to protect Cassandra. That means the Sollies need to at least be able to give their birds detailed emission signatures on their targets—the kind of tac details their missiles will need to pull targets out of that kind of electronic soup—so they'll have to hold fire at least until they get drones close enough to give them that kind of data. Besides, I know there aren't as many people on Cassandra as on Beowulf, but there are more than enough to constitute an Eridani violation if some of those missiles wander off target. The yards are only—what? Thirty thousand kilometers? Forty thousand?—from the planet. Unless they're completely insane, they'll want to minimize the possibility of smacking a missile or two into Cassandra at point-five cee! Fail-safes and self-destruct systems are really, really good these days, but nobody wants to take even a tiny chance on a six- or seven-gigaton energy transfer to an inhabited planet."

"Nobody who's sane *and* smart enough to figure out water's wet, anyway," Benton-Ramirez y Chou agreed bleakly.

"Well, yes. There is that," White Haven acknowledged, feeling Samantha press against the back of his neck. "And while we're hoping they have at least two-digit IQ's, delaying their launch as long as they can wouldn't just make it more accurate. It would also give the yards longer to evacuate as many people as they could."

"I'm not going to hold my breath waiting for Sollies to—"

"Sierra-Lima-Charlie-One-Niner-Six-Five-Tango, Beowulf Alpha Flight Control," the com interrupted. "Acknowledge your request. You are diverted to beacon Sierra-Oscar-Kilo-Seven-Two-Zero-Zero-Bravo. Repeat: beacon Sierra-Oscar-Kilo-Seven-Two-Zero-Zero-Bravo." The alphanumeric designation came up on Benton-Ramirez y Chou's astrogation display simultaneously. "Confirm destination."

"Beowulf Alpha Flight Control, SLC-One-Niner-Six-Five-Tango confirms destination beacon Sierra-Oscar-Kilo-Seven-Two-Zero-Zero-Bravo," Benton-Ramirez y Chou acknowledged. "Am I cleared for impeller approach?"

"That is negative, One-Niner-Six-Five," flight control replied. "Beowulf Alpha is at Defcon Romeo."

"Flight Control, SLC-One-Niner-Six-Five-Tango confirms Defcon Romeo. Initiating fifty-gravity reaction burn for two minutes."

"Flight control copies five-zero gravities' acceleration for two minutes, One-Niner-Six-Five. Get your head down, Jacques. Beowulf Alpha Flight Control, clear."

Anachronism quivered as Benton-Ramirez y Chou opened the throttle on her main reaction thrusters. Without her impellers, she had no inertial compensator, but her gravity plates handled the acceleration easily. The limiting factor was the amount of reaction mass in her tanks. Benton-Ramirez y Chou could have gone for a longer burn at both ends—or even accelerated and decelerated continuously—and cut the transit time to as little as sixteen minutes, but that profile would have cut into his safety reserve. And the profile he'd chosen gave a flight time only five minutes greater than that. On the other hand—

"I could wish Terry had found us a better destination," he commented sourly. "Between them, though, Code Red and Defcon Romeo didn't leave him a lot of choice. 'Nearest safe point of refuge,' I believe they say. And without impellers, our 'nearest safe point' is way the hell and gone out in the boonies."

"It is?" Samantha had swarmed down into White Haven's arms and he cradled her comfortingly as he raised an eyebrow at his pilot.

"Let's just put it this way—you won't be seeing Admiral Caparelli face-to-face quite as soon as either of you hoped." Benton-Ramirez y Chou twitched his head at the stupendous structure now growing more rapidly before them. "Terry's diverting us to a service lock on one of Alpha's engineering booms. If you really want that face-to-face, you'll have to spend an extra forty or fifty minutes on slidewalks and lift cars. Might be even longer, now that I think about it. Some of the transit shafts to Engineering are pretty bare-bones." He grimaced. "Looks like the Sollies' visit's going to give you a tour of some of Alpha most tourists never get to see."

"I always like to get off the beaten path when I can," White Haven replied, and tried very hard to not think about some of the other potential consequences of "the Sollies' visit."

System Defense HQ
City of Columbia
Beowulf
Beowulf System

"SKY WATCH CONFIRMS ITS numbers, Sir," Admiral Cheryl Dunstan-Meyers, Admiral Corey McAvoy's operations officer said. "CIC makes it four hundred and seven battlecruisers and one hundred and twelve lighter units."

"I'm assuming that's solely from their impeller signatures?" McAvoy said, and Dunstan-Meyers nodded.

"Yes, Sir. I'm afraid so. We're vectoring Ghost Riders in their direction, but they've put out hefty shells of recon drones." She grimaced. "Can't really blame them, given how nearsighted their systems are. They probably want to make sure they're not running into another Hypatia!"

McAvoy nodded. The intruders had been back in normal-space for almost twenty-minutes now, and the very first thing they'd done was launch their RDs. And as Dunstan-Meyers had just suggested, he couldn't blame them, either, after what had happened at Hypatia. Or to Eleventh Fleet at Manticore, for that matter. After the number of buzzsaws the SLN had run itself into, he'd have launched a recon shell dense enough he could damned well *walk* to his target across it, if he'd been the Solly CO.

"Their recon birds aren't as stealthy as ours," Dunstan-Meyers continued, "but that's actually helping them just now. The RDs are 'noisy' enough their interference is knocking back our passives' look at their ships' signatures, and none of our active systems can really see them at all—at least until we can get Ghost Rider into position. As I say, though, Sky Watch is pretty confident."

McAvoy nodded again. Active sensors or no, there really wasn't anything else the intruders could be. Their acceleration numbers were right on the eighty percent level for Solly battlecruisers, which was actually a bit high by prewar Solly standards, since they had to be towing hefty swarms of Cataphracts. Unless he wanted to suppose they'd dropped by his star system to let him blow them all out of space without bothering to bring any offensive punch with them.

631

"What's the status on Mycroft?"

"Uploading the targeting queue now, Sir. Sky Watch estimates eleven minutes to complete the uploads to the master platforms and confirm receipt."

"Good. And Cassandra Defense?"

"The block ships are spinning up their impellers now. They should be at full readiness within another five minutes."

"*Very* good." McAvoy smiled fiercely at her.

The block ships were mostly freighters—God knew Operation Lacoön had idled enough merchantmen!—deployed around priority targets, like critical industrial infrastructure and major orbital habitats, throughout the Beowulf System. Once upon a time, the defense planners would have been relatively unworried about protecting civilian habitats; recent events in places with names like Hypatia had changed that.

The ships mounted no weapons, but they stood ready to form a protective hemisphere around the targets under their protection, interposing their impeller wedges between them and the threat axes from any attackers. They'd been reduced to skeleton crews, and the handful of people still aboard them would be leaving shortly, transferring control of their ships to remote stations dirtside or on the orbital platforms they'd been tasked to protect. It was unlikely they'd be directly targeted, at least in the initial wave of any missile attack, but it was virtually certain one or more of them would eat a missile which had been aimed at the platform it was guarding. Given merchant ships' lack of armor, active defenses, or compartmentalization, even one hit would probably be fatal, but until and unless that happened, it would shield that platform against incoming fire.

"Let me know if there's any change or the instant those bastards launch anything towards Cassandra," the CNO added.

"Yes, Sir."

McAvoy nodded, then looked back at the com display connecting him to Gabriel Caddell-Markham. The director of defense—along with over half the planetary Board of Directors—was aboard Beowulf Alpha for the conference Alpha was hosting. At the moment, Admiral McAvoy would vastly have preferred for all of them—and especially Caddell-Markham—to be right here in Columbia.

"You heard, Sir?" he said.

"I did." Caddell-Markham nodded. "We're keeping tabs up here as well as we can, Corey, but you're the man in the chair. You're authorized to launch whenever seems best to you."

"Thank you, Sir," McAvoy said, and meant it.

He would have launched, anyway, but it was nice to have permission, since the System Defense Force had been under orders to conceal Mycroft's existence as long as possible. Technically, standing orders prohibited Mycroft's use against anything short of "a major attack upon the system's vital infrastructure" without direct authorization from Caddell-Markham, Chairman Benton-Ramirez, or their designated deputies. Cassandra certainly represented "vital infrastructure" and in McAvoy's opinion four hundred battlecruisers ought to represent "a major attack" in anyone's book, but it was like Caddell-Markham to assume the responsibility rather than leaving it on his shoulders.

"In that case, Sir," the Beowulf CNO said, "I'll transmit the launch order as soon as the master platforms have confirmed receipt of their targeting instructions."

Silver Bullet Q-12
Beowulf System

SILVER BULLET Q-12'S COMPUTERS considered the data stream.

Unlike a human being in their place, those computers had felt no emotion at all when the platform's sensors detected the massive hyper footprint of Task Force 790's arrival. They'd simply activated the appropriate programs and continued observing. Of course, one of those programs had begun prepping the massive graser torpedo at SB Q-12's heart, but the computers hadn't cared about that, either. Nor had they cared about the sudden spike in FTL transmissions from the star system's shell of sensor buoys and the tactical chatter between the various System Defense Force installations throughout the star system, although it had switched fully from Standby to Ready in response to them.

Now, however, it noted a sudden spike in traffic between the inner system and the platforms it had been specifically detailed to watch.

It responded.

System Defense HQ
City of Columbia
Beowulf
Beowulf System

COREY MCAVOY WATCHED THE clock. Two more minutes until Mycroft launched, he thought, and felt a distant sort of sympathy for the thousands of Sollies who were about to die. Still, he hadn't come looking to invade *their* star system and—

His head jerked up as an alarm shrilled. He'd never heard that particular alarm, even in a training exercise, and his eyes snapped towards the master status board.

"What the—?"

He froze, staring in disbelief at the readouts.

"Sir—" Dunstan-Meyers began, then stopped and drew a deep breath. "Sir, we just lost Mycroft."

"How?" The single-word question sounded preposterously calm in McAvoy's own ears, and Dunstan-Meyers shook her head.

"I don't know, Sir. We just lost the FTL feed from the master platforms. They were about—"

"Excuse me, Ma'am," Captain Chasnikov, one of Dunstan-Meyers's assistants said.

"What?" the ops officer half-snapped.

"Ma'am, according to Sky Watch, some of the Ghost Riders picked up graser fire right on top of the platforms."

"*Graser* fire?" Dunstan-Meyers repeated. "That deep inside the limit?"

"That's what Sky Watch says, Ma'am," Chasnikov said, and McAvoy and Dunstan-Meyers looked at one another in shock. Then the CNO shook himself.

"Right this minute, *how* they did it matters a hell of a lot less than the fact *that* they did it," he snapped. "Block ship impellers to full readiness *now*. They may adjust position on thrusters, but their wedges do *not* go active without my order!"

"Yes, Sir!" Dunstan-Meyers nodded sharply, pointing at the com, and Chasnikov started speaking urgently to Cassandra Defense.

"In the meantime, Cheryl," McAvoy went on, "upload the targeting queue directly to the pods."

"Sir, that's going to take at least another thirteen or fourteen minutes. We'll have to start from scratch," Dunstan-Meyers pointed out. "And without Mycroft, accuracy's going to be poor, even for Apollo."

"It'll be a hell of a lot better than no accuracy at all," McAvoy grated.

"Yes, Sir."

SLNS *Québec*
Task Force 790
Beowulf System

"WHAT THE HELL WAS *that?*" Vincent Capriotti demanded.

"Sir, I don't have a clue." Rear Admiral Rutgers was bent over one of *Québec's* tactical displays. Now he straightened and shook his head, his expression baffled. "It was some kind of energy fire. The recon platforms got a pretty good look at some of it, but I don't have any idea at all what the hell they thought they were shooting at. Whatever it was, it was scattered all around the hyper sphere."

"You mean all around the half of the hyper sphere we can *see*, Sir," Commodore Schlegel put in. The ops officer turned towards him, and TF 790's staff intelligence officer shook his head. "I've been looking at the distribution of the energy fire we picked up," he said, and looked at Capriotti. "Sir, it matches almost perfectly with ONI's estimate of how the Manties would have to distribute the FTL control platforms Admiral Gweon's sources reported, allowing for the fact that our platforms are only far enough out to see half—a little less, really—of the total hyper sphere."

"You're suggesting they decided to blow up their own control platforms?" Angelica Helland asked incredulously.

"No, Ma'am." Schlegel faced the chief of staff squarely. "I'm only saying that what we've seen correlates exactly with the projected distribution of their fire control systems. And *someone* was sure as hell shooting at *something*." He shrugged. "I don't have any more idea of who or what it might have been than you do."

Helland's expression got no less skeptical, but Capriotti nodded. Not so much in agreement as an acknowledgment of Schlegel's information.

But if it wasn't us, then who the hell was *it? Angelica's right—there's no way the Manties and Beowulfers would take out their own defense systems, and it sure as hell wasn't* us! *But who else would—?*

His thought paused as he remembered another report of graser fire just suddenly *appearing* out of empty space. No, that was ridiculous! He was getting as paranoid as the Manties! And yet...

"How long until the second stages launch?" he asked out loud.

"The Hastas have been ballistic for twenty-three minutes, Sir," Rutgers said. "Call it another twenty-four and a half minutes."

Capriotti nodded and leaned back in his command chair, brain whirling. Up until this point, the ops plan had worked perfectly. And if somebody really had decided to...clear the road for them, the odds of his ships' survival might just have risen. But if there truly was someone with that capability, someone willing to use it *against* the Manties, then was it possible the entire Solarian League truly was being used as that someone's puppet, just the way Manticore and its allies *claimed* it was? And if it was—

"Move up Breakaway," he said, looking at the time display. "Reprogram it for execution five minutes *before* the second stages launch." He bared his teeth. "Five minutes either way won't make a lot of difference to the targets, but given that we don't have any idea what the hell *else* may be going on around here, I'd just as soon start for home a little earlier."

Industrial Annex No. 6
Beowulf Alpha
Beowulf System

HAMISH ALEXANDER-HARRINGTON'S UNI-LINK PINGED, and he paused, raising one hand at Jacques Benton-Ramirez y Chou. The two of them, Tobias Stimson, Samantha, and Bark Chewer's Bane had docked with Beowulf Alpha barely five minutes ago. Benton-Ramirez y Chou had locked up his ship and they'd headed for the nearest slidewalk. From every indication, the Beowulfer's estimate of how long it would take them to get anywhere had been grossly optimistic, the earl reflected. At the moment, they were between slidewalks, passing through an enormous waste recycling plant with Stimson in the lead.

"White Haven," he said, acknowledging the com request.

"Tom Caparelli, Hamish."

The voice which replied carried a harsh undertone of tension, and White Haven's eyebrows rose as he turned to look at Benton-Ramirez y Chou.

"What is it, Tom?"

"The bastards just killed Mycroft," Caparelli said flatly.

"*What?*"

"Happened about four minutes ago." Caparelli sounded as grim as White Haven had ever heard him. "Don't have any details yet. According to Corey McAvoy, though, the control platforms may have been taken out—*may* have been taken out—by graser fire. That remind you of anybody?"

"*Mesa,*" White Haven hissed, remembering the horrific damage the "graser torpedoes" had inflicted during the Yawata Strike. But then he frowned.

"If they could get some kind of silver dart into the system and it was capable of not just taking out the Mycroft platforms but *finding* them in the first place, then why the hell didn't they just go ahead and use them to take out whatever the hell these people are here to attack?"

"There some reason you think I've suddenly become a mindreader?" Caparelli shot back. "How do I know why the hell these people do *anything*?"

"Misdirection," Benton-Ramirez y Chou put in.

White Haven looked at him, and he shrugged with some difficulty. He was a much smaller man than White Haven. That made it more awkward for Bark Chewer's Bane to ride his shoulder the way Samantha rode White Haven's or Nimitz rode Honor's, so he usually carried the 'cat the way he might have carried a human infant, instead. Today, though, he needed both hands to manipulate hatch controls and for handholds when they crossed through zero-gravity sections.

"That's the name of the game for these bastards," he expanded now. "Well, maybe the word I really want is 'deniability.' It's the same thing, really, though. They aren't attacking Beowulf directly; they're only enabling the *Solly* attack. I wouldn't be surprised if nobody in the SLN knew they were going to, either. This way, whatever happens to us will be the Sollies' fault, and even if we figure out someone else plowed the road, the rest of the galaxy will think we're only seeing Alignment bogeyman under our beds all over again."

"I think you're onto something," White Haven said, after a moment's thought, reaching up to caress Samantha as she leaned into the side of his neck. "But I can't help wondering if there's something more to it, as well."

"What kind of 'something more'?" Caparelli asked from his uni-link.

"If I knew that, I wouldn't be wondering about it." White Haven shook his head. "No. I don't know what it is, but we're missing something here."

He frowned some more, then his eyes narrowed suddenly. Samantha twitched on his shoulder, ears flattening, and he cocked his head at Benton-Ramirez y Chou.

"Tell me, Jacques," he said, "if you were the Sollies, and you figured you might get one shot at attacking Beowulf—getting in clean, at least, whatever happened to you on your withdrawal—would you go for Cassandra?"

"That's where the shipyards and the industry supporting the reconstruction work in Manticore are located," Benton-Ramirez y Chou replied slowly.

"But if you were going to get only *one* shot at the apple, would you use it going after the yards or would you use it going after the one thing Bolthole can't produce?"

"I don't like where you're going with this, Hamish," Caparelli said.

"I don't much like it, either." White Haven stood motionless, only the fingers of his raised hand moving as they stroked Samantha. Then he inhaled and shook himself.

"I don't like it, either, and I'm probably being paranoid," he said. "A lot would depend on what they knew or suspected about our production capabilities. We haven't exactly taken out any ads on the public boards in Old Chicago about them, but we also don't know what their people—the Sollies' people *or* the Alignment's people—might have picked up here in Beowulf before the referendum vote. So it's possible. The question would be why they're so busy heading for Cassandra, if that's the case."

"You're right," Caparelli sounded as thoughtful as White Haven. "But what if"—his voice had sharpened—"the Sollies *don't* know about the missile lines but the Alignment *does*? What if there are more of those graser torpedoes—or something like them—in-system waiting to hit us in coordination with the Sollies' attack on Cassandra?"

"Could be." White Haven nodded. "Coordinating it would be a bitch, but they obviously managed to coordinate the strike on *Mycroft*, didn't they?"

"Could've been just a simple as waiting until their strike platforms detected a hyper-footprint on the right bearing," Caparelli pointed out. "For that matter, they could have one of their people aboard any one of those battlecruisers in a position to transmit an execution code. In which case—"

"In which case another transmission code could be headed our way right now," Hamish finished for him.

"Exactly."

"Find Gabriel. Tell him about this." White Haven shook his head, his face like stone. "I hope to hell I'm wrong, but if I'm not, we may be running out of time fast!"

System Defense HQ
City of Columbia
Beowulf
Beowulf System

"I HATE TO SAY it, Sir, but Earl White Haven may have a point." Corey McAvoy's brown eyes were dark, his lips tight. "We're still reprogramming the Apollo pods. It's taking a lot longer without Mycroft—and they're not going to be as accurate—but we should be ready to launch within the next six minutes, and we've got a *lot* of them. That's not going to help us if the bastards've snuck something into the inner system, though."

"Agreed." Caddell-Markham's expression was as unhappy as McAvoy's. "Still, they'd've been taking an awful risk trying to sneak something too deep inside the hyper-limit. I'm not saying they wouldn't have tried, and I'm not saying they couldn't've done it, but I think our chance of catching them at it would have been a hell of a lot higher."

"Which probably means anything coming at us will be coming from outside Beowulf's orbit." McAvoy nodded. "I'd give a couple of million credits to be *sure* of that, but I think we have to go on that assumption. At least the inner-system block ships' impellers are hot under Code Red and Cheryl's already positioned them on the threat axis. She's fine-adjusting their alignment now. I only wish I had more of them!"

"And that we weren't going to lose so many to the bastards' initial launch, assuming they launch against the inner system at all," Caddell-Markham agreed grimly. "If the clever buggers have set something up as a *follow on* strike..."

"The best we can do is the best we can do, Sir. And with your permission, I'll go see about doing it."

Planetary Director's Office
City of Columbia
Beowulf

"SHOULD WE TRY TO evacuate, Gabe?" Planetary Director Benton-Ramirez asked, his expression agonized.

"No real point, Chyang," Caddell-Markham replied from his com screen. "They haven't launched yet, even assuming Hamish isn't just being constructively paranoid and the real threat is to the inner system instead of Cassandra. And if they *do* launch now, there wouldn't be enough time to evacuate enough people to make any real difference. All we'd do would be to create a panic, and probably get quite a few people trampled to death even if there isn't a real threat."

The defense director shrugged. Neither of them commented on the fact that the conference attendees on Beowulf Alpha with him were at the very heart of the massive platform. Anything capable of housing that many million people was enormous, and it had been built in layers, like a vast onion. Despite the best planning possible, that put... kinks into its internal transit systems where lift tubes were truncated at transfer stations. Normally, those kinks were little more than excuses for irritated profanity as traffic stacked up during rush hours, but they could have more serious repercussions. It would have required at least forty-five minutes for anyone in the George Benton Center just to reach the station's outer hab zones, for example. Nor was it remotely practical to build emergency escape pods that could reach that deep; the necessary access trunking made it simply impossible.

Of course, prior to Hypatia, no one would have expected them to be necessary even if they'd been practical. The sort of accident that could take out something Beowulf Alpha's size was about as likely as the unannounced arrival of a dinosaur killer, and until the Yawata Strike—and Hypatia—the Eridani Edict had meant no one had worried about sneak attacks on civilian targets like it.

"I don't like it, and, frankly, I think Hamish probably *is* being a bit overly paranoid," Caddell-Markham continued, "but it is what it is. I think Corey's done just about everything we can do, really." He bared his teeth briefly. "And whatever happens in the inner system, things are going to get a bit lively in the outer system in about—" he consulted his chrono "—another three minutes."

SLNS *Québec*
Task Force 790
Beowulf System

LYANG-TAU RUTGERS SENSED ANGELICA Helland hovering behind him, but it was only a vague awareness. His attention was centered on the tactical information pouring in from the thick shell of recon platforms he'd deployed. The shells—plural—actually. One hemisphere of drones raced towards Cassandra, sweeping the volume ahead of TF 790, while another sped towards the inner system from TF 790's original n-space emergence point. Transmission lag had become an issue on the inner-system flight, but the truth was that any data from them was only icing on the cake. Their true function had very little to do with the gathering of tactical information and a great deal to do with misdirection. In fact, the entire Fabius operational plan relied on misdirection, and it seemed to be working well.

Aside from those mysterious grasers. He'd reworked the numbers a dozen times, and Schlegel was right. Rutgers couldn't prove someone—someone *besides* the SLN—had been taking out control stations, but the locations were right, and he didn't like the implications of *that* at all.

He checked the time again. TF 790 had been in Beowulf space for almost three quarters of an hour. Under the original ops plan, they'd have altered course in another nineteen minutes. Given Admiral Capriotti's revision, they'd change course in only fourteen, and Rutgers was entirely in favor of the revision. In fact, he'd just—

"Status change!" one of his tracking ratings announced suddenly. "Missile launch—multiple missile launches! Range at launch two-zero-five-point-two million kilometers. Acceleration four-five-one-point-zero-seven-six KPS squared."

Rutgers's eyes darted to the tactical plot, and he swallowed hard as CIC's uncaring computers updated it. Hundreds—*thousands*—of missile icons raced outward from a launch point one light-minute outside Beowulf's orbit.

"Sir, they've just fired approximately six thousand missiles at us," he heard his own voice reporting.

645

"Time-of-flight?" Capriotti asked sharply.

"Sir, this is the longest range we've ever seen them launch at. We do know—now—that their birds can incorporate a ballistic phase, just like the Cataphract, but that was from what we think are their cruiser-range missiles. And we still don't know what the maximum endurance on their missile drives is, even for their cruiser missiles. We don't have any idea what it might be for their capital missiles, and if this is a system-defense variant we haven't seen before—"

The ops officer shrugged.

"Assuming they could make the entire run at their present acceleration—and I don't see how anybody this side of God could pull that off—we'd be looking at sixteen minutes from time of launch. As it is—"

He shrugged again, helplessly, and Capriotti tried not to glare at him. It was scarcely Rutgers's fault, but that did nothing about the icy fist closing around the admiral's heart. He sat back in his command chair, looking down at the tactical plot deployed from its base, and his mind raced.

If he'd been in command on the other side, those missiles would have been targeted solely on his battlecruisers, ignoring everything else on his sensors, but would he have concentrated on only *some* of those battlecruisers, or spread his fire among them all? Spread evenly, that would work out to right on fifteen birds per ship, which wouldn't have been enough—for most people's missiles, at any rate—to saturate the individual ships' missile defense. On the other hand, the SLN had discovered the hard way that no battlecruiser was likely to be combat-capable after more than three or four—at most five—hits from Manticoran capital missiles, so they might not feel the need to completely overpower his missile defense. On the *other* other hand, even the Manties had to have some doubts about the accuracy of their fire at this range. So at what point did their faith in their systems and their recognition of Murphy's impartiality intersect? Had they fired this hurricane of missiles at less than all of his battlecruisers in order to get enough concentration for decisive results? Or had they spread their fire evenly? And was this all they had, or had they retained a reserve for follow-up salvos? *He* certainly wouldn't have used everything he had in the *first* launch!

But there was no sign of a second launch—yet, at least. Of course there wasn't, he thought after an instant. Without FTL control platforms closer to him, they couldn't coordinate a second salvo tightly in terms of time. Even with FTL sensor platforms right on top of TF 790, any evaluation of the first strike would take over ten minutes to get back to the first strike's launch point, and without forward-deployed FTL control platforms, it would take several more minutes for any targeting corrections *based* on that evaluation to catch up with missiles streaking towards him.

Even in a worst-case scenario which assumed they really could maintain this monster acceleration all the way to TF 790, he had sixteen minutes—fourteen, now, he noted almost absently—before the first salvo could reach him. If they were going to fire a second one, they'd probably want to have at least ten or fifteen minutes after that for the first strike evaluation to get back to them and any adjustments to their follow-on missiles' targeting orders to catch up before they entered attack range. So if they did launch a second wave, the timing on it would probably provide a window on when the first one was likely to arrive.

Which was all very interesting but didn't solve his immediate problem.

"Execute Breakaway now," he said.

"Executing Breakaway, aye, Sir!" Rutgers acknowledged, and Capriotti looked up from the tactical plot to find Helland standing beside him.

"Still sixteen minutes to second stage launch, Sir," she said quietly.

"Understood. But as far as we can tell, they're busy shooting at us, not anything closer in. And, frankly, by this point, there's not that much they could do to stop the second stages. In which case, I'm a little more concerned about *surviving*, and those twelve minutes might just help that happen, don't you think?"

System Defense HQ
City of Columbia
Beowulf
Beowulf System

"SIR, THEY'VE ALTERED COURSE!" Dunstan-Meyers announced sharply. "They're breaking off their run on Cassandra and they've increased acceleration to four hundred and sixty-eight gravities!"

"I see it, Cheryl."

McAvoy crossed the huge, dimly lit chamber to stand beside the ops officer, watching vectors shift and flow as Ghost Rider reported the Sollies' changing heading, and he frowned as he wondered what the hell they were up to now.

Their initial velocity of six hundred KPS towards Cassandra had increased to 12,236 KPS since their arrival. That meant that, at their initial acceleration, it would have taken them forty-eight minutes just to decelerate to zero and start back the way they'd come. But that wasn't what they were doing. They'd turned directly out-system, instead, at right angles to their current vector, and they'd started their run from so far out that they were still barely six million kilometers inside the limit. With that acceleration, bending their vector that sharply, they could be back across the wall in barely *twenty-seven* minutes.

And if all they're really doing is running the hell away, that's fine, he thought. *Maybe this is a panic reaction. Maybe they didn't expect to see Apollo coming at them at all and now that it has they're headed for the high timber. But it's hard to imagine they could've been that stupid; they had to realize we'd deploy MDMs to cover our critical star systems! The acceleration change does suggest they've just cut loose whatever pods they were towing, though, and they haven't launched a damn thing back at us, which sure looks like a panic reaction, plain and simple. If I were them—and if I didn't care any more about civilian casualties than whatever bastard came up with Buccaneer and Parthian Shot—I'd've launched everything I had before I turned away on the theory that even inaccurate birds had to be more effective than birds that were never launched at all! But they didn't do that. Or at least it sure looks like they just jettisoned their pods without even trying to launch. Does that mean they've decided Parthian Shot was a bad idea? That could make sense after what happened in Mesa, if they want to try to convince people they hold the moral high ground. But it also suggests they really thought they could get close enough to Cassandra to target their fire accurately. So does that mean Hamish was right? Were they as surprised as we were by what happened to Mycroft? Or were they really dumb enough to not anticipate system-defense MDMs at all? Or did they—?*

He shook himself. There was no way in hell he could answer any of those questions. All he could do now was wait and hope the POWs could answer them for him later.

SLNS *Québec*
Task Force 790
Beowulf System

"WE HAVE A SECOND launch, Sir," Lyang-tau Rutgers said quietly, and Vincent Capriotti looked across at him, then checked the time.

Fourteen minutes had passed since the defenders' first launch, and he smiled in ironic amusement. The first launch had gone ballistic six minutes and 65,766,900 kilometers after launch. That sounded a hell of a lot like two separate drives with pretty close to standard endurance, which confirmed quite a bit of speculation back home. No one had any notion—yet—how it might be done, but it certainly sounded like the Manties had managed to graft separate sets of impeller nodes into the same missile body without their eating each other before they were successively brought on-line. Assuming that was what was actually happening, and if the missiles packed in a third stage with identical performance, they should resume their acceleration in roughly three more minutes... and arrive three minutes after that, just over *nineteen* minutes after launch.

At least now I know now how big an interval they figure their FTL systems can handle without the dispersed platforms, he thought almost whimsically. *If they could've closed that interval any, they damned well would've done it.*

"CIC makes it another five thousand, Sir."

"Very impressive," Capriotti replied. "On the other hand, we'll be across the limit and gone by the time they can reach us. I'm sure they can figure that out for themselves, so this is probably intended to encourage us to keep moving right along. And to pick off any cripples, I suppose. But in the meantime—"

He looked at another display.

Beowulf System
19,913,317 Kilometers from Beowulf Orbit

THE HASTAS HAD BEEN launched fifty-seven minutes earlier.

They'd started their journey at an acceleration of a mere 15,000 KPS², barely a crawl compared to the 46,000 KPS² a Mark 23 turned out at even its lowest acceleration bracket. On the other hand, they were far, *far* stealthier than any MDM ever built. In fact, they were no more than the mating of a slightly modified Explorator recon drone with a Cataphracht-C's second stage. They retained all of the Explorator's original stealthiness, and their acceleration rates had been stepped down a bit further to make them even harder to detect. The result was something that was almost impossible to detect, even under acceleration, at ranges lower than seventy to eighty light-seconds. Once it went ballistic, it was effectively invisible even to active sensors at anything above 500,000 kilometers, and Operation Fabius had taken steps to make them even harder to spot by sending a host of regular reconnaissance drones ahead of them, with an acceleration rate thirty percent higher than theirs, programmed to spread out and chatter back and forth.

No one on the other side had noticed that the talkative recon drones' stealth systems were working at no more than eighty percent of normal efficiency, and no one had suspected that their sole purpose was to attract any sensor systems to *their* impeller wedges rather than the weaker, stealthier ones coming along behind. Nor had anyone on the other side realized Vincent Capriotti's battlecruisers hadn't been towing Cataphracts when they crossed the hyper-limit. All their towing capacity had been devoted to the Hastas, and their relatively low acceleration rate after the Hastas launched had been designed solely to convince the system's defenders they *were* towing heavy Cataphract loads for the attack on Cassandra they had absolutely no intention of making. The last thing TF 790 had wanted Sky Watch or System Defense HQ to realize was that it had never intended to penetrate more than 4,500,000 kilometers inside the limit before turning and breaking for the safety of the Alpha bands at ninety percent of maximum power.

Vincent Capriotti had nourished his private doubts about the elaborate deception plan, but it had worked almost perfectly. It wouldn't have been enough to save TF 790 from Mycroft without the unexpected assistance of Silver Bullet. For that matter, it might turn out that it *still* wasn't enough. The ops plan *had* worked to get all the bits and pieces to where they needed to be at the critical moments, however, and there was a certain irony in that. If the Mesan Alignment had realized that would happen, they wouldn't have needed to reveal Silver Bullet's existence...or suggest their direct involvement in Fabius. Unfortunately, Benjamin Detweiler and his planners hadn't known how the original Fabius plans would be modified once Winston Kingsford realized what Hasta could do, and so they'd expected the attackers to require all the help they could get on their run in to the target. And the knowledge that there'd been no way to hide their involvement, whatever happened—at least from the Grand Alliance—had made it even easier for Benjamin and his brothers to decide to...tweak the original operations plan.

The impeller endurance of the interference-running recon drones was measured in hours, even in days if it was husbanded properly. A Hasta's endurance was barely ten minutes. At the end of that brief interval, its impellers went down forever and it sliced onward through the void at a constant velocity of 88,260 KPS, as invisible as the vacuum about it.

But now AIs aboard that shoal of invisible assassins noted that the time had almost come. They checked their targeting criteria and instructions against the take from their own sensors—not nearly so good as a regular recon drone's, but far better than any previous generation of Solarian missile, even the improved Cataphracts, had ever mounted. A few corrections were necessary, and they made them.

Then they began the prep cycle.

System Defense HQ
City of Columbia
Beowulf
Beowulf System

"THIRD STAGE ACTIVATION IN approximately sixty seconds, Sir," Cheryl Dunstan-Meyers said quietly, and Corey McAvoy nodded without looking away from his com connection to Gabriel Caddell-Markham.

What could reasonably be described as "a host" of staggeringly senior spectators had gathered behind the defense director, watching the huge display in the enormous conference room deep within Beowulf Alpha which fifteen minutes or so of frenzied tech improvisation had turned into a repeater for the master plot in System Defense HQ.

"At least they broke off without throwing anything in-system," Caddell-Markham said, watching vectors bend and change. "That's something." He grinned suddenly. "And I am *so* going to give Hamish hell for the heart attack he gave me with that little scenario!"

"Agreed," Sir Thomas Caparelli noted. "Means we're not going to tag them with the second launch, though." He glanced at McAvoy and shook his head quickly. "Not criticizing, Corey! I'd've done exactly the same thing, and you probably will pick off some cripples. And while I'd like to get more of them, I'm all in favor of scaring the ever-living hell out of them, too. The longer and the harder they keep on running, the better I'll like it!"

"I'll second that," High Admiral Judah Yanakov's soft Grayson accent couldn't hide the iron implacability at the core of his voice. "Especially the 'like to get more of them,' I'm afraid." He bared his teeth. "I'm sure Reverend Sullivan will have something to say to me about that the next time I see him."

"Don't worry, Judah," Michael Mayhew, Grayson's senior representative to the conference, told him with a smile. "I've got connections. I'll run interference for you."

"I appreciate it, My Lord," Yanakov said. "On the other hand, I've noticed the Reverend doesn't get diverted very easily."

"He does have a certain way about him," Mayhew conceded.

653

"Excuse me," McAvoy said, eyes scanning the assemblage. "Have we figured out where Earl White Haven and Director Benton-Ramirez y Chou are?"

"We're not sure." Caddell-Markham shook his head, his expression wry. "Flight Control stuck them out in the boonies, and the last time I talked to Jacques—about five minutes ago—he and Hamish were delivering heartfelt maledictions upon one of the freight lift shafts while Sergeant Stimson worked on the control box. I don't think he'd quite gotten to the point of shooting it, but I wouldn't be at all surprised to find out he'd been 'malletizing' it with the biggest damn hammer he could find! At any rate, they were stuck in one of the boom sections between the industrial annex where they got docked and the main habitat. Maintenance promises to get them out 'very soon now,' but the people in charge of doing that seem to be just a little preoccupied." He snorted. "Go figure!"

"Yeah, I don't even have good contact with Hamish's uni-link at the moment," Caparelli said with an even broader smile. "And I can tell you he's going to be *so* pissed when he finds out all of us were watching the master plot at the moment—"

"*Status change!*" Dunstan-Meyers said suddenly, and her face went white. "Oh my God! Missile activation! Many missiles! Range to Beowulf orbit niner-point-three million kilometers! Velocity eight-eight thousand KPS. Acceleration niner-six-one KPS squared. *Impact seven-five seconds!*"

McAvoy stared at her for two heartbeats, then wrenched his eyes to the master plot. At least a thousand missile icons glared upon it, driving in on the inner system. CIC projected their vectors with merciless clarity, and the only good thing was that none of them were headed for the civilian habitats. They were driving in on Ivaldi of Beowulf and the other critical component manufacturers, and it came to him in an instant of total clarity.

A diversion. The entire run on Cassandra was a fucking diversion, *and we fell for it! We fell for it!*

But then he shook himself. They'd never seen *this* coming—and he hoped like hell they'd be able to figure out just how the Sollies had gotten their birds in this close before anybody got even a *sniff* of them—but thanks to the Yawata Strike, they weren't quite mother naked.

"All block ships activate *now!*"

SLNS *Québec*
Task Force 790
Beowulf System

"SECOND STAGE ACTIVATION!" REAR Admiral Rutgers crowed as twelve hundred impeller drives glared suddenly on his display. "They're in, Sir—they're in!"

"I see it, Lyang-tau," Capriotti said, and his smile was fierce. Whatever else happened, they'd gotten their birds inside the Manties' defenses, and—

"Enemy missile activation!" Rutgers announced in a very different tone. "Implement missile defense plan Able-Seven."

Counter-missiles slid into launchers, laser clusters trained out on the threat axis, decoys spun up, and ECM went active. The faces on *Québec*'s flag bridge were tight, tension and fear burred in the staff officers' voices, but there was no panic, and Capriotti's fists clenched on the armrests of his command couch. His estimate had been almost perfect, but at least their attack was going to go in two minutes before the Manty MDMs swarmed TF 790. With any luck, they'd get good evaluation of the strike from all those recon drones before the task force's survivors raced across the hyper-limit.

You knew from the minute they proposed Fabius that it was a high-risk op, he told himself. *You knew it. You just . . . didn't want to expect it to be* this *high-risk.*

No, he hadn't, and he hated what it was going to cost his people, but at least he'd get to see what happened to his targets first.

Of course, you may not have very long to enjoy *it*, he thought mordantly, *but a man can't have everything. And at least—*

"Status change!" One of Rutgers's ratings announced just as the first counter-missiles roared from the launchers. "We're picking up additional impeller wedges in-system—between our birds and their targets!"

Ivaldi Orbital Works No. 1
Beowulf System

"COME ON! COME ON, damn you!"

Jacqueline Somerset-Caruso pounded on the arm of her chair as she watched the block ships' wedges come up. As the manager of Ivaldi of Beowulf's Orbital Works One, she'd long since realized that if the Sollies ever got into Beowulf space *her* facility and *her* people had to be priority targets. But like everyone else in Beowulf, she'd known the Sollies were going after *Cassandra*, not Beowulf.

"*Move* your arses!" she snarled at the unmanned ships positioned to protect the sprawling platform. "Why can't you—?"

They'd been jockeyed into place, along with scores of other block ships, on reaction thrusters to prevent the Sollies from spotting them sooner, and formed up in vast hemispheres, hollow domes several layers thick, with their open ends toward the planet, to protect the most critical infrastructure and the major habitats. In theory, they were placed to intercept any energy fire from anywhere other than the planetary surface, but if they didn't get their wedges fully on line in time...

"In position!" Barney Fetukov-Stimson announced over the intercom. "Block ship wedges are *up* and in position!"

"Yes!" Somerset-Caruso pounded the chair arm even harder. "*Yes!*"

System Defense HQ
City of Columbia
Beowulf
Beowulf System

TAKE THAT, BASTARDS!

Corey McAvoy snarled viciously as the block ship impeller wedges came up. A lot of those freighters weren't going to survive the next few seconds, and he knew it. But they didn't have to survive to do their jobs. And in the meantime...

Holmon-Sanders and Alice Truman had left almost five hundred LACs behind when TF 32 headed off to the terminus. Only about half of them were close enough to intervene in the attack, and even they had poor counter-missile solutions, by and large. But they also had a *lot* of CMs and no reason to conserve them, and McAvoy watched them streak across the display, chewing into the Solly missile stream.

Their interception angle was bad, coming in from the side rather than the head-on approach which gave counter-missiles their best intercept percentages. Considering all their disadvantages, they did quite well, but over seven hundred of the Hasta final stages got by them.

They tore down upon the block ships, but those block ships had no more investment in their personal survival than SB Q-12 or the Hastas themselves. They simply obeyed the remote commands, brought up their wedges, and rolled ship.

They weren't *perfectly* placed, because the damned Sollies had suckered them and everyone had expected the attack to fall on Casandra. But the defenders had known the threat axis, and that meant the block ships were in roughly the right spots to form their curved, defensive shield-wall when McAvoy brought them online... and that there'd been no time or way for Lyang-tau Rutgers to update his attack missiles' profiles to avoid them. At least a dozen of them protected every one of the Hastas' targets—two dozen of them guarded each of Ivaldi's most critical installations and the major habitats—and as they rolled ship, bringing their wedges perpendicular to the Hastas' approach, they built a wall in space. Not a single wall, but a series of them—individual

657

shields, impeller wedges twice as wide as usual as their nodes were ruinously overloaded, stacked in a protective cup around their charges.

Now the surviving Hastas reached attack range.

Their AIs were the most capable any Solarian missile had ever carried. The men and women who'd programmed their attack profiles hadn't anticipated the block ships, but they'd been very clear about what did and did not constitute legitimate targets. The AIs noted that all of those legitimate targets had disappeared, and their vectors altered abruptly as they scattered, dodging wildly in their efforts to avoid the obstacles in their path and reacquire their targets.

Most of them failed. Unable to clear the barricading impeller wedges before impact—and precluded from choosing alternate targets by the targeting commands designed to avoid strikes on the Beowulf habitats—they didn't even fire on the block ships. They simply rammed into those wedges and disappeared forever. But not all of them did.

Corey McAvoy swore viciously as he discovered that "roughly the right places" wasn't good enough against Hasta. His eyes widened incredulously as half a dozen of them squirmed through a chink around Ivaldi of Beowulf's number two nano farm. There was no point defense, no sidewall, inside the block ships, and the nano farm simply disintegrated. Entire modules shattered or went spinning off from the vortex of destruction, and then one of the central power plants exploded and wiped the entire platform—and all five thousand workers aboard it—from the face of the universe. Nano Farm Number One took at least one hit of its own, but that was peripheral. The damage was nothing to sneer at, but it should be easily repaired and it was unlikely to significantly impact the facility's production rate. Far more important to McAvoy at the moment, less than a hundred of its personnel were killed.

And that was it.

Not a single hit got through to the missile production lines!

"Well done, everyone!" Gabriel Caddell-Markham said from McAvoy's com display. "Well done!"

SLNS *Québec*
Task Force 790
Beowulf System

"DAMAGE EVALUATION?" VINCENT CAPRIOTTI demanded harshly.

"Impossible to say, Sir," Angelica Helland answered for Lyang-tau Rutgers. The ops officer was far too busy as *Québec* shuddered to the sawtooth vibration of launching counter-missiles. "We won't know till we hear from the light-speed platforms, and—"

She flipped her head at the tactical plot and the missile icons ripping through TF 790's outer defensive zone. Their covering EW systems were incredible, better even than Capriotti's staff had projected from the Hypatia reports.

Five thousand missiles had launched against TF 790. Five hundred were pure EW and penaid platforms and another 550 were Mark 23-E control missiles, with no warhead of any sort. Of the 3,950 actual attack birds, 3,107 broke past the CMs and hurtled into the teeth of the last-ditch laser clusters at a closing velocity of well over eighty-one percent of light-speed.

The laser clusters took down 1,206 more of them. There was no way for Helland or Capriotti to know it, but their defenses' performance was by far the best any Solarian force had yet achieved against an Allied missile attack.

It just wasn't good enough.

Nineteen hundred Mark 23s broke through everything TF 790 had. Pinpoint precision couldn't be expected at that velocity, especially with no telemetry updates in the last eleven minutes of their flight. But unlike anyone else's missiles, the Mark 23-E control missile had been specifically designed to operate well beyond telemetry range—even FTL telemetry range—of any mothership. The Mark-23s were far more capable even than the SLN's new Hastas, and each Mark 23-*E* in that salvo had formed a separate data sharing node, communicating all across the salvo, sharing the sensor data from its missiles' sensors with all of the others and integrating all of that data into a coherent picture of the battlefield which more myopic missiles operating in isolation could never have matched.

The consequences were cataclysmic.

Access Boom
Industrial Annex No. 6
Beowulf Alpha
Beowulf System

"YES!" JACQUES BENTON-RAMIREZ Y Chou hissed.

He'd finally gotten the undersized com display in the bare-bones compartment tied into the same feed as the far larger display in the Jennifer O'Toole Room—just in time to watch the mailed fist of Corey McAvoy's Mark 23s crash down on TF 790. Of Vincent Capriotti's four hundred-plus battlecruisers, thirty-seven survived to cross the limit outbound. He couldn't tell how many of the ships whose impeller signatures had just disappeared might still survive—more or less—as crippled hulks, but he knew very few of the Sollies who'd just attacked his star system were going home again.

None of which made the casualties Beowulf had suffered any less painful. True, they could have been enormously worse, but what they had were quite bad enough.

Bark Chewer's Bane's hiss mirrored his own. The 'cat didn't have to understand the display's icons to realize what had just happened, and while the two of them might not share Honor's or White Haven's adoption bond, they'd been together quite a while now. He recognized the treecat's vengeful satisfaction as Bark Chewer's Bane sat on the edge of the bare desk beside him, and he reached out to stroke his friend's silken fur.

"They put some thought into this," White Haven said, leaning against the bulkhead behind Benton-Ramirez y Chou and looking over his shoulder while Stimson stood just inside the small compartment's door. Even here, White-Haven thought dryly, Tobias was guarding his back. There wasn't another chair. This was—technically—a satellite management station, but from the looks of things no one had used it in a long, long time. Which, he reflected, given the state of the lift shafts which theoretically served it, shouldn't have surprised him.

"I mean, they put a *lot* of thought into it," he said thoughtfully, cradling Samantha in his arms, as Benton-Ramirez y Chou turned his head to look up at him. "What worries me the most is that they clearly knew exactly what they were gunning for. If Corey hadn't deployed the inner-system block ships despite the fact that we all 'knew' they were going for Cassandra, it damned well would've worked. It's not like we didn't get hurt anyway, I know that, but the truth is we were incredibly lucky, Jacques."

"I know," the Beowulfer acknowledged. "And you're right—they *did* know exactly what to target. The question in my mind is how old their data was. I mean, was it from someone that got repatriated after the referendum, or are they still getting information feeds from right here in Beowulf?"

"Exactly what I was thinking." White Haven nodded. "On the one hand, I guess it really doesn't matter all that much, but I really would like to know. And if there *is* an ongoing information flow—"

"If there is, we need to find it and plug it," Benton-Ramírez y Chou finished for him. "I'd say that's going to be more up my alley than yours, though."

"No argument there." White Haven snorted. "Believe me, all I want to do is to get a damned maintenance crew out here to spring us so I can get started on just that!"

Cargo Container H&L 1007-9-463(h)
Freight Hub No. 7
Bay 16-Beta
Beowulf Gamma
Beowulf System

THE CARGO CONTAINER HAD been parked in its storage slot two local days after it had been dropped off. It had been there ever since, waiting for a representative of Stickel & Lyman, one of Beowulf's larger manufacturers of small craft and shuttles, to collect it. The manifest chip listed its contents as an Archon III cargo shuttle's fusion bottle, which explained its large size and mass. And, obviously, it was exactly the sort of shipment Stickel & Lyman might expect or, for that matter, be sending to someone else.

The only problem was that Stickel & Lyman had never heard of it, and the S&L tracking number in the manifest chip was completely bogus.

In fact, it contained a laser-pumped nuclear bomb.

The security scans had missed it entirely, exactly as the people who'd actually shipped it had expected. It wouldn't have been readily detectable as a weapon under any circumstances, since it contained no radioactive elements and the fusing lasers were a legitimate part of the shuttle power plant. The power supply and the actual hydrogen pellet were concealed inside the bottle itself, and the bottle's walls had blocked the scanning systems.

And so it had sat there, waiting to be claimed by someone who didn't even know it existed.

✧　　✧　　✧

Harold Simmons-Gilchrest listened to the cheering all around him and tried not to spit on the deck. His instructions had been unambiguous, but his control hadn't told him—or hadn't been *able* to tell him, perhaps—exactly when the Sollies would get around to attacking, and he'd been away from his station at the critical moment.

There'd always been a possibility—a probability, really—of that happening, but Simmons-Gilchrest was the third-shift cargo master for the Beowulf Gamma habitat's number seven freight hub. It would have taken someone pretty damned senior to get in his way when he insisted on reporting for duty in the face of such an unanticipated emergency. It was just his misfortune that it had taken over an hour for him to physically get here, which meant he hadn't been able to send the signal at the moment he was supposed to. His control had been emphatic that it would be far better to transmit it while Solly missiles were actually flying, but she'd also said there was at least a little flex in the timing.

He reminded himself of that now as he unlocked the number pad on his console and entered the second of the long, complicated commands he'd been given. The one he'd been told to use if he couldn't transmit until after the Sollies' attack had ended.

He'd been placed in Beowulf over forty T-years ago, and despite the excitement of knowing the Detweiler Plan had finally been launched, his had been a terminally boring assignment. He was confident the intelligence data he sent up the line was valuable, but he doubted it was of earthshaking importance, and he'd come to the conclusion that he was one of the countless agents who'd spend their entire careers on the periphery: valuable, dedicated, conscientious, and with damn-all to show for it at the end of the day. So he'd felt an undeniable surge of adrenaline when his control told him he'd been activated as a vital component of a major operation. She hadn't told him what that operation was, although the fact that it was supposed to coordinate with a Solly attack on the system—assuming the Sollies ever got off their arses and *launched* the damned thing—had underscored its importance. He had no idea what his transmission would accomplish, but whatever it was, he was pretty damned sure the Beowulfers around him would never forget it.

Even if they never knew *he* was the one who'd done it...whatever the hell it was!

He entered the last digit of the code and looked down at his panel for a moment, wondering if he should abort his part of the operation, since he hadn't been able to execute it as the missiles attacked, after all. He was tempted, despite the second code he'd been given. Whatever happened when he sent it, the Grand Alliance was unlikely to blame it on the Sollies, and hadn't that been the purpose of the entire operation?

But he didn't know if all the missiles out there *had* attacked yet, now did he? The System Defense Force might know, but *he* didn't, and if there was another attack inbound and he aborted his part of the operation...

His nostrils flared as he inhaled deeply, and then he shrugged. Wiser heads with far more information than he could possess had come up with the plan and they *had* given him the second code. All he could do was the best he could do. And, he admitted to himself, there was another reason.

If he'd been brought operational for a moment that let him contribute to the Detweiler Plan on the grand stage, he was damned if he was going to miss it!

He smiled at that thought and hit the transmit button.

✧   ✧   ✧

Cargo Container H&L 1007-9-463(h) received the command and implemented it.

Twenty-seven seconds later, Beowulf Gamma, the third largest orbital habitat in the Beowulf System, ceased to exist, along with 9.5 million human beings...including a Mesan gamma line named Harold Simmons-Gilchrest.

System Defense HQ
City of Columbia
Beowulf
Beowulf System

SOMEONE INHALED SHARPLY BEHIND Corey McAvoy.

He could never decide, later, why that single, sharp inhalation sent such a sudden, instinctive stab of dread through him. It wasn't all that loud, and there'd been no reason to expect additional bad news, given the Sollies' decisive defeat. The lives they'd lost had been painful, a higher price than he'd ever have wanted to pay, and yet the admiral's part of his brain—the cold part the human being in him so often disliked—had told him it was a ludicrously *low* price compared to the one which might have been demanded. So, no—there'd been no reason at all for that icy flash that told him not to turn around, not to ask who the sound had come from.

But he was an admiral, and so he turned away from his conversation with Caddell-Markham anyway, and found Cheryl Dunstan-Meyers staring at him, her green eyes huge with shocked horror.

"What?" he asked.

"Beowulf Gamma, Sir." Unlike his, her voice was hoarse, stunned.

"What about it?"

"It's...gone, Sir. It's just—" She shook her head. "It's just *gone*."

Her voice quivered, almost breaking, on the final word, and he looked at her in confusion. What could she possibly—?

Then his eyes strayed to the master plot, and the mental question chopped off brutal, guillotine suddenness.

"*How?*" he snapped instead.

"I don't know, Sir." Dunstan-Meyers was one of the most professional officers Corey McAvoy had ever met, but those green eyes suddenly welled with tears. "I don't *know!*" She shook her head again. "We got all the missiles—I *know* there weren't any left! But...but—"

She broke off, her face pale, and McAvoy looked past her shoulder at the display where almost ten million of the civilians he was supposed to protect had just died.

Planetary Director's Office
City of Columbia
Beowulf

"MY GOD, GABE!" CHYANG Benton-Ramirez's face was bloodless. "My God, my God! What the *hell* just happened?"

"I don't know," Caddell-Markham's dark complexion showed his shock less obviously, but his eyes were stunned looking. "Nobody does! Or not yet, at least."

"But, the missiles..."

"That's the one thing we know it *wasn't*," Caddell-Markham said grimly.

"But if it wasn't—?"

"Our best guess up here—and it's what Corey's working on, too, I think—is that it had to be internal." The defense director's voice was crushed gravel. "Somebody got a bomb aboard. One powerful enough to take out a seven billion-ton habitat. That's the only way it could've happened."

"But who—?"

"It was the Alignment, Sir," Patricia Givens said, standing beside Caddell-Markham with Sir Thomas Caparelli and Judah Yanakov. Michael Mayhew stood on the defense director's other side, his face like iron.

"We can't prove it—yet," Givens continued, reaching up to press one hand to Strong Mind's flattened ears. "It's the only answer, though."

"Not the Sollies?"

"No, Mister Chairman." Givens shook her head sharply. "That's the one thing I'm absolutely sure of."

Benton-Ramirez raised his eyebrows, and the second space lord nodded to the woman standing at her elbow.

"Commander Lassaline, my chief of staff, Sir," she said. "She's been coordinating with your local intelligence people since we got here for the conference." She turned to look at the commander. "You want to take this, Terry?"

"Yes, Ma'am." Commander Lassaline's face was tight with tension, but her eyes were clear and focused, Benton-Ramirez thought.

666

"Sir," she said, speaking directly to him, "if the Sollies had wanted to do this—and if they could've gotten a bomb aboard—they'd never have committed that many ships to an open attack and taken such massive losses. They wouldn't have needed to. For that matter, they would have wanted their navy as far away as possible when the bomb went off. My God, Sir—this is an even worse Eridani violation than the Yawata Strike! Total casualties are already high, even with the surviving block ships already in position to intercept wreckage before it de-orbits and kills anybody dirtside, but in terms of a cold-blooded, deliberate mass-casualty strike on a *nonmilitary* target, this is probably the worst violation since the Edict was promulgated! This single bomb's killed more people than the worst-case estimate for *all* the 'Mesa Atrocity' explosions combined! There is no way—no way in *hell*—the Sollies would've done something like this while they're so busy beating us over the head about Mesa."

Benton-Ramirez nodded slowly. Her analysis made sense, although the reason for such an attack made none. Unless—

"You think they could have intended for this explosion to be simultaneous with the Sollies' strike on Ivaldi?"

Givens glanced at her military colleagues, then back out of the display at him.

"I think that's possible, Sir. Probable, even. I don't know why they'd've done it at all, but it certainly *looks* like it was intended to coincide with the attack. I don't know whether that's because they were looking for some kind of deniability or because they wanted to saddle the Sollies with responsibility for some reason. But I can't help thinking there was something else behind it, as well."

"But *what?*" Benton-Ramirez demanded. He wasn't asking *Givens* that; he was asking the universe, and he knew she realized that, but she answered him anyway.

"I don't know, Sir. I only know we aren't going to like the reason when we find out what it was."

Access Boom
Industrial Annex No. 6
Beowulf Alpha
Beowulf System

"OF COURSE IT WAS Mesa," Jacques Benton-Ramirez y Chou said harshly. "I don't know *why* the bastards did it, but it was damned well them."

Hamish Alexander-Harrington nodded in agreement, his blue eyes colder than ice. The two of them were staying out of the conversation between Chyang Benton-Ramirez and the senior officers in the Jennifer O'Toole Room. It was hard, but they were still stuck on the access boom, with only the small screen Jacques had managed to reconfigure as a window into what was happening. Neither could have contributed much, so they had no intention of getting in the way of people who *did* have something useful to say.

Behind them, Tobias Stimson was methodically smashing the locks off one locker after another. White Haven had no idea what his armsman was up to, but right this minute he didn't care. Like Benton-Ramirez y Chou, he was totally focused on the display screen.

"Of course it was Mesa," he agreed now, cradling Samantha in his arms as the 'cat quivered to the emotions ripping through the two humans. "I think Chyang's question about their intending to synchronize it with the Solly attack probably has a lot going for it, but Pat's right that that's only a part of it." He bared his teeth briefly. "I'm sure it wouldn't break their hearts for us to blame the Sollies. That may even be a big part of why they did it, but I'll guarantee we'll find out that's not what it was *really* about when we finally dig down to the bottom of it. Not really. I can *smell* it."

"Agreed. But what the hell *was* it about, then? Aside from pure viciousness, I mean." Benton-Ramirez y Chou's voice was ineffably bitter as he waved one hand at the tiny display and the expanding sphere of wreckage where Beowulf Gamma once had been. It was hard to believe, but the time chop on the display said it had been barely four minutes since the explosion. "There sure as hell weren't any critical targets on Gamma! Just ten million human beings."

"I know, Jacques." White Haven rested one hand on his wife's uncle's shoulder and squeezed. "I know."

Cargo Container H&L 1007-9-464(h)
Freight Hub No. 19
Bay 8-Delta
Beowulf Beta
Beowulf System

IT WAS VERY QUIET in Bay 8-D.

Like all modern cargo-handling facilities, Freight Hub No. 19 was heavily automated, so there was no one to pay attention to cargo container H&L 1007-9-463(h). Even if there had been, no one would have noticed anything. The crated shuttle fusion plant only sat there . . . giving no sign at all of the clock ticking down inside it.

Under the original operational planning, Beowulf Beta would have died at the same instant as Beowulf Gamma, at a moment coordinated with the Solarian attack. The planners had been unable to predict exactly when that moment would come, which was why they'd been forced to rely on their agent-in-place. But they'd also realized from the beginning that that coordination might prove unobtainable when the time actually came. And so, they'd programmed two separate attack sequences. If they lost the coordination with the missile strike and the detonation command was transmitted anyway, there was no point pretending the subsequent explosions were the direct result of the Solarian attack, and in that case, they had a rather different message to deliver.

Jacques Benton-Ramirez y Chou and Hamish Alexander-Harrington hadn't figured it out . . . yet. If they'd been given enough time, they might have. Possibly not, though. Neither of them had ever met Albrecht Detweiler or his sons. More importantly, they didn't understand what Albrecht Detweiler had done . . . or why. They'd assumed the nuclear detonations covering the end of Operation Houdini had been planned from the beginning, and so they had. What they didn't know was the way Tenth Fleet's arrival had rushed Houdini's final phase, or how bitterly Benjamin Detweiler and his brothers blamed everyone *but* their father for their parents' deaths.

And because they didn't know those things, they didn't understand how hatred and grief and loss—and guilt—had shaped the brothers' response. They were looking for the calculation, the strategic plan, behind Beowulf Gamma's destruction because they didn't realize how intensely *personal* it was.

That was why their brains hadn't yet caught up with the possibility that more than one nuclear weapon might have been smuggled aboard more than one orbital habitat.

Five minutes, precisely, after Beowulf Gamma's death, they discovered that one had.

System Defense HQ
City of Columbia
Beowulf
Beowulf System

ADMIRAL MCAVOY GRUNTED AS if he'd just been punched in the belly—or stabbed in the heart—as Beowulf Beta blew up and took another 11.25 million Beowulfers with it. He wrenched his eyes from the cool, bland lights of the hideous master plot and looked at Dunstan-Meyers. The ops officer sat staring at the plot, frozen, her expression a mask of grief... and failure.

"Cheryl," he said. She didn't even blink. "Cheryl!" he said again, more sharply, and she twitched. Then she shook herself and turned to look at him.

"Yes, Sir?" She sounded rusty, broken.

"Same pattern?" he asked.

"Same *non*-pattern, Sir," she grated and chopped one hand savagely at the plot. "We don't see anything. Admiral Givens and Commander Lassaline have to be right. Those were both *internal* explosions."

"And they may not be the last ones," Caddell-Markham said flatly from McAvoy's display. The CNO looked back at the defense director, and Caddell-Markham's eyes were as bitter as they were level. "In fact, I don't think they were."

"But—" McAvoy began.

"I know we don't want there to be any more," Caddell-Markham cut him off. "For that matter, I know neither one of us wants to think about how they got *one* of these fucking things past us, much less *more* than one! But they obviously did, and I don't see any reason the bloodthirsty fuckers would stop with just two if they didn't have to."

"But—" McAvoy said in a very different tone, and Caddell-Markham nodded.

"Exactly," he said harshly. "If they managed to get more than two through, I know exactly where they'd have wanted to plant the next one. And whatever else they may have had in mind, one thing this *damned* well is is a message. Beta didn't just coincidentally go up exactly five minutes after Gamma."

671

"We've got to get you—*all* of you—out of there!" McAvoy said desperately.

"How?" Caddell-Markham asked quietly, and the CNO's jaw clenched as he looked at the man who'd been his boss for the last seven T-years... and his friend for almost fifty.

"I'm sure the bastards who did this timed it carefully," the defense director continued. "They wanted us to realize it was a deliberate interval, that they'd planned it with malice aforethought. But there's no way in hell we could evacuate any of our other habitats in anything less than a full day, and you know it. There are almost twenty-three million people aboard Alpha. It'd take the better part of a frigging *week* to evacuate that many people, and even the smallest of the others is over four million! All we'd do if we tried to evacuate would be to induce a panic aboard *every* habitat, and God knows how many people would be killed if we did. Besides," his nostrils flared, "they'd just love for our people to be running in terror at the moment they die, and I will be *damned* if we give them that satisfaction."

"But, my God, Sir—*Gabe!*" McAvoy's voice was raw with anguish. "It's not just you! It's *all* of you—all of you at the conference!"

"I know," Caddell-Markham said softly. "Believe me, I know. They couldn't have realized we'd be here when they set this up, but we are, and there's no way to get *us* off in less than an hour, either. Maybe they didn't get another one aboard. I hope to hell they didn't. But if they did, they're damned well not waiting half an hour before they blow it. So if that happens, we're not getting out, either. And, frankly, it would be pretty obscene if we *did* evacuate when no one else could."

McAvoy stared at him silently, and Caddell-Markham inhaled deeply.

"Everybody up here is either talking to his family or recording messages, if they're from out-system. I'm sorry, but I need to talk to Joanna now." He flashed a brief almost-smile. "Hopefully, I'll be talking to *you* again in the not-too-distant, too. If I don't, it's been a pleasure and an honor."

"No, Sir," McAvoy said softly. "No, Sir. The honor's been mine. Now go talk to your wife."

"God bless, Corey."

"You, too, Gabe."

White Haven
Manticore
Manticore Binary System
Star Empire of Manticore

"OH, STOP WORRYING, SANDRA!"

Emily Alexander-Harrington looked worn and tired, but her tone was affectionate as her life-support chair drifted through the air van's hatch. The sky the van had just left was a dramatic ocean of black-bottomed white as a line of thunderstorms approached majestically from the east, and her nostrils flared appreciatively as she inhaled the fresh, clean, rain-is-coming air.

"It's not like it's anything new," she continued, turning her head to look over her shoulder and smile just a bit crookedly as her longtime companion followed her through the hatch. "I don't want to hear any more *fussing* about it, understand? Especially not *today*, of all days!"

"It's just—" Sandra Thurston began, then paused and looked across at Sergeant McClure. Emily's personal armsman looked back at her, and Thurston drew a deep breath. "All right, Milady," she said just a bit sternly. "You won't hear any more 'fussing' out of me, but *only* if you discuss it with Her Grace."

Emily's smile disappeared and her eyes flashed, but Thurston held her ground.

"You *need* to discuss it with her, Milady," she said more gently. "You know you do."

"Honor has enough on her mind," Emily retorted.

"I agree. But you still need to tell her." Thurston shook her head. "I'm not making any horrible predictions!" she added quickly. "But, by the same token, you can't let this blindside her, Milady. I know you too well to think you want to do that."

Emily glowered at her for a moment, but then she drew a deep breath.

"You're probably right," she conceded. "And it's not like there won't be plenty of good news to go with it."

"No, Milady," Thurston agreed, reaching down to rest one hand lightly on her charge's frail shoulder. "No, Milady, it's not like there won't be plenty of good news."

"Well, in that case," Emily said, resuming her progress across the White Haven landing pad towards the front door, where Nico Havenhurst awaited them, "I think the first thing you and I need to do is to take another look at the nursery." She smiled as Sun Heart and Bark Master came bounding across the lawn. "I'm thinking Raoul and Katherine are old enough for toddler beds, and that means—"

She paused, then stopped her chair and turned it to the east, looking back the way they'd come, and her eyebrows rose.

"Jefferson? Were we expecting anyone else this afternoon?"

"No, My Lady." Sergeant McClure had already turned in the same direction and his eyes narrowed as he squinted upward. "We're not."

He pressed the fingers of his left hand lightly to his earbug, never lowering his searching gaze from the incoming thunderclouds, while his right hand drifted towards his holstered pulser.

"Central, McClure," he said, calling in to the Steadholder's Guard command center. "Do we have an ID on the incoming?"

He listened for a moment, then smiled broadly and took his hand away from the pulser butt.

"It's all right, My Lady. It's cleared with Central. In fact, it's the Steadholder."

"Honor!" Emily's weariness disappeared, and she sent her life-support chair drifting back towards the pad. Sun Heart leapt lightly into her lap, hitting the moving target with the casual ease of long practice, and Emily chuckled. She ran her good hand lightly down the treecat's back, and Sun Heart buzzed with pleasure.

The distant turbine whine resolved itself into grumbling thunder and Emily's eyes widened in surprise as its source emerged from the clouds. It wasn't an air car. It wasn't even a shuttle. It was a Condor II, an all-up Navy pinnace, and she saw HMS *Imperator*'s hull number blazoned just in front of its forward hatch as it flared and settled on its counter-grav.

That hatch opened, the landing stairs deployed, and a tall figure in black and gold came down them. Three more figures—these in the green-on-green of the Harrington Guard—came down the steps at her heels, and she paused as she caught sight of Emily, Thurston, and McClure. She stood still for a moment, then squared her shoulders and started toward them, and Sun Heart raised her head and stopped purring.

"Honor! Welcome home!" Emily called.

❖   ❖   ❖

Honor Alexander-Harrington felt her expression tighten. She wanted to stop. She wanted to turn around, re-board the pinnace. She wanted to—

What she did was draw a deep breath and keep walking while Nimitz sat still and silent on her shoulder. Her pinnace's flight crew had violated at least a dozen flight regulations to get her here in time, before the news leaked to the public boards. Before Emily could hear it from anyone else. And she could tell from her wife's happy greeting that she'd made it.

And, oh *God*, how a part of her wished she hadn't.

"It's good to see you," Emily said as she drew closer, and Honor tasted her mind-glow, tasted the ever present edge of sorrow, the weariness that went deeper than the merely physical. There was a bubble of joy and anticipation in it this time, though.

"We just got back from Briarwood," Emily continued. "Dr. Illescue says the fertilization went perfectly! And as soon as we can work it into your schedule, he thinks we should—"

The happy voice broke off as Honor's expression registered. Emily's hand stilled on Sun Heart's coat, and the treecat reached up, her green eyes dark and still, and patted her wrist with a gentle true-hand. Emily's gaze flitted to Nimitz, and her mouth tightened. The 'cat sat hunched on his person's shoulder, the normal mischief in his green eyes quenched, his tail hanging.

"Honor?"

Honor went to her knees beside the life-support chair. She reached out and caught Emily's live hand, leaned forward, pressed her cheek against Emily's shoulder.

"Honor?" Emily repeated, her voice a bit sharper, her hand tightening on Honor's.

"I'm sorry, Emily." Honor closed her eyes. "The Sollies attacked Beowulf. We just heard. *Imperator*'s in Manticore orbit. We receipted the report even before Mount Royal." Her voice seemed to waver for a moment and she cleared her throat. "I don't have the numbers yet," she husked, "and I'm not sure yet how they got past Mycroft. It may be a while before we figure that out. But... but they hit the habitats, Emily. Gamma... Beta—"

Her voice broke, and her shoulders began to shake. Emily tugged her hand out of hers and cupped the back of her head.

"And Alpha," Emily Alexander-Harrington finished very, very softly, tears fogging her own voice, and Honor nodded convulsively, unable to speak.

She felt Emily's hand tighten on the back of her head, felt Emily's grief rising with her own, but then she sensed something else under it, as well. A sudden stab of pain that was more than just emotional, more than just spiritual agony.

"Emily?" She pulled back, tear-soaked eyes wide, sudden tension burring her voice.

"I'm sorry, Honor." Emily sounded hoarse, breathless. "I'm so sorry."

"*Emily!*" Honor felt Emily's mind-glow rising up, wrapped in grief and yet incredibly powerful, filled with bottomless sorrow...and blazing with boundless love.

"Forgive me, sweetheart." Emily's voice was a whisper, fading even as she spoke. "I didn't want it to be like this. I wanted you and Hamish to have each other when—"

"*Emily!*" The cry ripped out of Honor Alexander-Harrington. She wrapped her arms around the frail body, crushing it in her desperate embrace, even as her mind fought to hold onto that blazing mind-glow. "Emily, no! *No!*"

"I love you," the three words were soft, barely a sigh, heard more with heart than with ears, and then that glorious mind-glow went out forever.

Mount Royal Palace
City of Landing
Manticore
Manticore Binary System
Star Empire of Manticore

EMPRESS ELIZABETH III LOOKED at the men and women around the gleaming ferran wood table and thought about the other men and women she would never see again.

What was already being called the Beowulf Strike was less than eighteen hours old, and it was unlikely they'd know the final death toll for several days yet. Probably weeks.

And possibly, she told herself drearily, *and most probably of all, we'll* never *know it.*

Frantic search and rescue operations were underway, although the odds of recovering more than a handful alive were minute. No one would be calling them off anytime soon, though. If anyone understood how that worked, it was a Manticoran who'd survived the Yawata Strike.

But one thing they did know: the Beowulf Strike's confirmed death toll was already over forty-three *million.*

Forty-three million, including Sir Thomas Caparelli, Patricia Givens, Lucien Cortez, Anthony Langtry, Tyler Abercrombie, Francine Maurier, Barton Salgado, Gabriel Caddell-Markham, Jukka Longacre, Joshua Pinder-Swun, Judah Yanakov, Michael Mayhew, and—

Elizabeth's eyes strayed to the stonefaced woman at the far end of the table and the cream-and-gray treecat huddled on the back of her chair. She'd never seen Honor Alexander-Harrington look that way. Never seen those dark eyes so frozen, colder than interstellar space itself. Never seen such dreadful, elemental purpose. Such focus.

"We'll be a while confirming anything, I'm afraid, Your Majesty," Charles O'Daley said somberly. The man who would almost certainly be confirmed as Barton Salgado's successor at SIS let his eyes circle the table, and his aristocratic drawl was nowhere to be heard. "What we *have* confirmed is that the explosions were definitely internal, from devices they somehow placed aboard the habitats. And the timing was a message. It was precise to the second: five minutes between the first and the second detonations; ten between the second and the third. I suppose we're lucky they were able to get only three of the damned things into position." He seemed to settle deeper into his chair, his nostrils flaring. "At the moment, though, it's a little hard to feel *grateful* for anything."

"But was it a Solly operation all the way?" Elizabeth demanded.

"Our people at ONI are split over that, Your Majesty." Rear Admiral Joanna Saleta had been Patricia Givens's deputy at ONI for the last five years. She didn't look happy to be sitting in her chair at this table, but she met Elizabeth's gaze levelly. "The majority is inclined to go along with Commander Lassaline's view that even Sollies would have recognized the insanity of doing something like this. It's not a very large majority, though, given the sorts of things we've seen them do already. And the one thing we do know is that it looks an awful lot like the Sollies, at least the ones who actually *planned* the op, knew about both Mycroft and that someone—and with the graser torpedoes involved, this has Alignment fingerprints all over it—would clear the way for them. We've analyzed their 'attack run,' and it's obvious they never intended a serious strike on the Cassandra yards. They were just occupying our attention, giving us something to focus on so we wouldn't notice the damned invisible missiles they'd fired at Ivaldi.

"That looks like careful coordination. They knew about Mycroft, they figured their friends could knock back the control stations, and they just miscalculated what Apollo could do even without Mycroft before they got clear. For that matter, if they'd started their breakaway move even fifteen minutes earlier, they would've gotten away clean. That's how close it was."

"My people don't feel qualified to analyze the Sollies' ops plan, Your Majesty," O'Daley said. "Having said that, I can't argue with anything Admiral Saleta's just said. I would point out, however, that even if they were deliberately and knowingly cooperating with the Alignment, Commander Lassaline and Admiral Givens may very well have been right that they *didn't* know about the charges aboard the habitats." His face was drawn, his eyes dark. "I want to blame them for it. I want to have a *target*, and I want us to rip its heart out. But there are so many arguments against the Mandarins' doing something like this, something that cuts so sharply against the moral case they've been trying to build against us ever since Mesa. Maybe they didn't have a clue about the bombs. Maybe what this really is is Mesa trying to maneuver us again."

"Maneuver us to do what, Charlie?" Kent McCoury asked. Two of

Sir Anthony Langtry's three senior deputies had died aboard Beowulf Alpha. McCoury had been left home to hold down the Foreign Office in their absence.

"Into overreacting," Countess Maiden Hill said before O'Daley could reply. The minister of industry's voice was cold and hard but a furnace burned in her eyes.

"*Overreacting?*" William Alexander demanded. "How the hell is it possible to 'overreact' to something like *this*, Charlotte?" The prime minister looked almost as dreadful as his sister-in-law, Elizabeth thought. "Someone's just killed forty-three million *civilians*," he continued, "and *none* of this would've happened if not for the frigging Mandarins! Whether or not they put actual bombs aboard those habitats doesn't mean squat. If it wasn't their finger on the button, they were still damned well the ones who made all of this—*all of this*—happen!"

"With the most profound respect, Countess Maiden Hill, I have to agree with Prime Minister Grantville," Alfredo Yu said. The Havenite who'd become a Grayson sat in the chair his Protector's younger brother should have occupied, and his eyes were agates. "We never brought this war to *them*; they brought it to *us*, and that makes them responsible for every single person who's died since New Tuscany."

"I agree with what you've just said, as well, Mister Prime Minister," O'Daley said. "But, like the Sollies' ops plan, I'm not in the best position to evaluate the consequences of hammering the League for this. I think we do need to remember, though, that all our intelligence to date indicates the Alignment is playing a deep game, one it's been playing for T-centuries, and that they've been manipulating entire star nations—*including us*—for a long, long time. I guess what I'm trying to say is that we need to be as sure as we can that they aren't goading us into doing something we'll all wish like hell we *hadn't* done somewhere down the road."

"Mr. O'Daley has a point," Thomas Theisman said heavily. "But there comes a time when you *have* to respond, whether it's the smartest thing you could do from a carefully thought out strategic perspective or not."

Elizabeth forced herself to sit back in her chair. Intellectually, she, too, knew O'Daley had a point. And she knew how valuable someone willing to argue against the consensus of her other advisors truly was. But she didn't *want* him to have a point. It was the Cromarty assassination all over again, on a vastly greater scale. This time *dozens* of men and women who'd been not simply her most trusted advisors and allies for years but personal friends had been wiped away. Blotted out as if they'd never existed. And those personal friends put faces on all those millions of other unknown dead. They made that horrendous casualty count *real* in a way nothing else could have, however hard she might have tried to empathize with the survivors they'd left behind.

She looked around the table again, seeing the rage in Grantville's eyes, the fury behind Alfredo Yu's stony control. Saleta looked just as angry, and so did Theisman. But it was Honor who truly frightened her, because there was no emotion at all in her expression, and Nimitz was as barricaded from Ariel and the other 'cats as Honor herself.

What do I do now? the empress wondered bleakly. *I know* exactly *what the bastards are trying to do, if O'Daley's right and this was a manipulation. They want us to carry out reprisals against the Solarian League, to punish the League—the Sol System—by doing to it exactly what the League would've done to anyone* else *who violated the Eridani Edict. What it* has *done to other people who violated it. Because if we do—if we go storming into the Sol System itself, smash everything in sight, since that's almost certainly where this attack originated—what the Sollies are feeling about us right now will turn infinitely uglier and set itself in ceramacrete. They'll never* forgive *us if we kill millions of people in the human race's home star system, whatever justification we might offer—might actually* have. *It won't matter whether it takes ten years, or thirty, or a* hundred, *either. Sooner or later, they* will *exact their revenge . . . just as surely as we would in their place. That's exactly what we've been trying so hard to avoid from the beginning! But Theisman's right, too. We can't* not *respond to this . . . unless we want the murderous bastards to do it again and again while the frigging Mandarins go right on* enabling *them every step of the way.*

"It doesn't matter," Honor Alexander-Harrington said into the ringing silence. It was the first time she'd spoken, and Elizabeth could hear the ice crystals in that soprano, taste the searing rage under that frozen surface.

"None of it matters," Honor said. "We've been patient. We've waited. We've tried to minimize the death toll, tried to be the voice of sanity. We've *tried* . . . and none of it matters one damned bit to those men and women in Old Chicago. They don't care how much destruction there is. They don't care who dies. And if that's the way they want it, so be it." She looked around the conference room and Nimitz raised his head, his ears flat, his fangs half-bared. "We've always known something might change our strategic calculus. That was always part of our thinking . . . and now it damned well has. I'm through taking the 'long view.' It doesn't matter who did it. What matters is that it has to *end,* Elizabeth." Those icy brown eyes locked with her monarch's. "It has to end *now.*"

Harrington House
City of Landing
Planet of Manticore
Manticore Binary System

"WELL, I GUESS THAT'S everything."

Honor Alexander-Harrington stood in the quiet library. Rain pounded the skylight overhead. It was barely midafternoon, but the overcast day was dark and murky, and somehow it felt cold, despite Landing's warmth. She listened to the rain as she looked around her at all the familiar furnishings, the shelved books, the paintings, the subdued lighting. But she didn't really see any of it, and she looked like a stranger standing in someone else's house, unable to understand how she'd come there.

"If you're sure," her mother said.

Allison stood beside Honor with Katherine in her arms. Raoul was in the nursery. He burst into sobs anytime Honor was in the same room as him, clinging to her with desperate strength. She didn't know exactly how it worked, but there was no question that he was able to taste *her* emotions, whether or not he could truly feel anyone else's. She needed to cling to him as desperately as he needed to cling to her, but she couldn't. She couldn't inflict that on him, not now, not when he was only a baby and no one could possibly explain it to him. And so she'd handed him as gently as she could to Lindsey Phillips and walked out of that nursery, heart breaking at his sobbed "Mama! Want *Mama!*" from behind her. Now he lay exhausted in his crib, and the White Haven treecats huddled around him like guardian gargoyles, somehow blunting the worst of his sorrow and fear. Katherine was subdued, obviously aware something dreadful had happened, yet at least she'd been spared the terrible weight of someone else's grief, and Honor reached out to lay a gentle hand on the little girl's head.

For a moment, something seemed alive behind the frozen flint of her eyes, but then she took her hand from Katherine's head and whatever it had been disappeared once again into the ice.

"I have to get back to the ship. We've got a lot to do, and I don't want to lose the time window."

"If you're sure," Allison repeated with a very different emphasis and Honor looked at her.

Honor had raised every barrier she could against the emotions of those about her. Her ability to feel what others felt wasn't something she could turn off or on. It simply *was*, an inescapable part of who she'd become over the years. She had learned to...adjust the volume, though, and she needed that now. Needed it because the loss and the pain, the fury and the sympathy pouring into her and Nimitz from everyone around them threatened to drag them under. That tide of emotion threatened to break her concentration. Threatened to divert her from the task before her, and nothing could be permitted to do that.

But her mother's very special anguish could not be escaped. The grief over the death of her beloved twin brother. The knowledge of how Jacques's death, especially like this, would hammer all of Alfred Harrington's wounds from the Yawata Strike. The aching sense of loss for a son-in-law and, especially, a daughter-in-law she'd come to love dearly. The knowledge that dozens of other friends, family, must have died aboard the Beowulf habitats with Jacques and Hamish.

And fear. Fear for her daughter.

"I'm sure, Mother." There was no emotion in Honor's voice, but she managed a brief caricature of a smile. It vanished quickly, and her nostrils flared as she reached up to the silent, grieving treecat on her shoulder. "Like I told Elizabeth, this has to end. And I'm *going* to end it, once and for all."

Allison shifted Katherine's weight so she could lay one hand on Honor's arm.

"I know you are, sweetheart." Her voice was calm, almost serene, despite the tears glittering on her lashes, and she shook her head. "I *know* that, believe me. But you come back to me. Raoul and Katherine need you now, more than ever. And your father and I—We'll *always* need you, Honor. So you come back to us."

"Mother, I'll be aboard the fleet flagship." She managed another fleeting smile. "The Sollies don't have a thing that could touch her in a standup fight. Maybe that's the problem. Maybe we just didn't make that clear enough." A very different expression replaced the smile, and her frozen eyes filled with a chill, flickering fire. "That's one of the oversights I intend to set right."

She felt Allison's concern spike higher, but she refused to allow it in, denied it access to the frozen helium of her purpose. She knew what Allison really meant. Knew what her mother really wanted to say was "Give me back my daughter and take away this stranger. Give me back the person who still knows how to love, how to care. Give me back my *child* and give back the mother my grandchildren need."

But Honor didn't know if she could do that.

She didn't know if *anyone* could do that.

She reached out, touched her mother's cheek very gently, and her thumb brushed away one of Allison's tears.

"Take care of Daddy and the babies," she said softly.

"Of course I will."

"I know."

She leaned close, kissed Katherine's cheek, then leaned her forehead against her mother's for a long, still moment.

And then Honor Alexander-Harrington, Duchess and Steadholder Harrington, turned and walked out of that foyer, into the driving Landing rain, down the steps to the waiting air car, without a backward glance.

HMS *Imperator*
In Hyper-Space

"WILL THERE BE ANYTHING else, Ma'am?"

Honor looked up from her plate at the quiet question. James Mac-Guiness stood at her shoulder, holding the carafe of cocoa, his gray eyes dark.

"No, Mac." She shook her head. "No, that's fine. I think we're both done."

"Are you sure?" He tried *so* hard to keep the anxiety out of his voice, but she tasted it anyway.

"Yes," she said, as gently as she could. "I'm sure. Thank you." She reached out to lay one hand gently on his forearm. "That's from Nimitz, too."

"Yes, Ma'am." It came out husky and he set the cocoa on the dining cabin table, then ducked his head. "Just...just buzz if you change your mind."

"I will." She tried to smile at him. She failed. "I promise."

He looked at her a moment longer, then nodded once and disappeared, and Honor looked back at the largely untouched food on her plate. The steak had been perfect, with the cool red center she loved. The salad, the baked potato, the stein of Old Tillman...all the components of one of her favorite meals.

And she'd eaten less than half of it.

She gazed at it for a few more seconds, then sighed and pushed back her chair.

She stood, gathering Nimitz into her arms, and crossed the deck. She stood in the hatch between the dining cabin and her day cabin and looked at the portrait on the bulkhead above her desk. Her mother had taken that picture in the White Haven family chapel. Honor stood between Hamish and Emily, holding Emily's hand, her eyes glowing as Hamish faced Reverend Sullivan and recited his wedding vows. Nimitz rode her shoulder and Samantha perched on Hamish's, and she tasted Nimitz's pain as he, too, looked at the people they would never see again. Despite his thick coat, she thought she could feel his ribs, but that was probably imagination. Both of them *were* losing weight, but it had been less than three days since that last hideous afternoon at White Haven.

She knew why MacGuiness was worried. Just as she knew he, too, was grieving. She wished there was some way, any way, she could ease her steward's—her *friend*'s—pain, but there wasn't. She didn't have it in her. She had nothing in her except a vast, singing emptiness where the people she'd loved should have been. Nothing except the single unwavering purpose left to her. The deadly determination, colder than the vacuum outside her flagship's hull, more focused—and far more lethal—than any warhead or broadside graser.

She had no idea what would happen to her—and to Nimitz—when that purpose, that determination, had been discharged. She didn't care. It was all she and Nimitz had, all the universe had left them. She didn't know what the opposition would be, had less current information on her objective's defenses than she'd had before any other operation in the last ten T-years. But she knew two things. She knew the Sollies couldn't possibly expect her this soon, and she knew she *would* accomplish her purpose, her mission, even if Hell itself stood in her way.

What happened after that could take care of itself.

She stood another long, still moment, looking at that image of murdered love, cradling her beloved dead. Then she set Nimitz gently on the perch beside her desk, sat in her own chair, keyed her terminal, and punched up Grand Fleet's order of battle.

BSDS *Hawthorne*
Beowulf Planetary Orbit
Beowulf System

"SORRY, SKIPPER. I KNOW you don't want any coms that aren't essential, but I think you'd better take this one."

Captain John Neitz looked up from his cup of coffee and tried not to scowl at his executive officer. Commander Badilotti and he had been friends for years, and the XO's eyes were as exhausted as his own. They were also apologetic.

"Why is that, David?" It came out testier than he'd intended it to, and he shook his head in a quick apology of his own. "Sorry."

"No sweat, Skip," Badilotti said. "But like I say, I think you'll want to take this one. It's Christina."

Neitz set his cup in the holder on his command chair's arm and inhaled.

"For once, I think you're right about something," he said with a weary smile, and Badilotti's lips twitched in brief response. Then Neitz looked over his shoulder at the com officer. "Patch it through to my uni-link, please, Carla."

"Yes, Sir."

Neitz leaned back in his command chair. It was one of the most comfortable chairs in the known galaxy, but somehow it wasn't quite capable of feeling that way for a body as tired as his was.

"John?" a beloved voice said in his ear, and he closed his eyes while he savored it.

"Hi, honey," he responded.

"I hate to disturb you," Christina Neitz said. "I know you're all exhausted and going crazy up there."

"There are disturbances, and then there are disturbances, sweetheart." He shook his head, even though she couldn't see it. "Trust me, this is one I don't mind. In fact, it's one I think I *need*."

"It must be like visiting hell," she said softly.

"You got that one right, babe," he replied. "My God, you got that one right."

She was silent for a moment, and Neitz could almost physically feel her reaching across the thousands of kilometers of vacuum between BSDS *Hawthorne* and Columbia. Christina was a senior attorney in the Directorate of Justice, and things must be almost as crazy in her office as they were up here, he thought. Her boss, Devorah Ophir-Giacconi, the Board of Directors' Solicitor, and her senior deputy had both been aboard Beowulf Alpha. He wasn't sure who Ophir-Giacconi's surviving senior deputy was now, but a hellacious workload had to be coming down on Christina, too.

There was a lot of that going around.

Six days. That was how long had passed since the Beowulf Strike. Six days of nightmare labor, and a huge part of that had landed on *Hawthorne*. She was one of the Beowulf System Defense Force's *Whitethorn*-class rescue ships, superbly designed and equipped for search and rescue operations under the most difficult conditions imaginable. But there were only eight of them in the entire SDF... and no one had ever imagined conditions like *this*. No wonder Badilotti—all of Neitz's people—were so exhausted.

No really big chunks of wreckage had gotten through to the planet, thank God. There'd been no major surface strikes, no tsunamis like the one which had killed his third cousin and her family in Yawata. The block ships which had been unable to protect the habitats had at least managed to intercept their broken bones before that happened.

Not that plenty of bits and pieces still in orbit didn't pose potential threats. One of the first things Search and Rescue Command had done was to plot vectors for all the larger chunks of debris. Those which had threatened other habitats had been intercepted first, but scores of others tumbled on new, highly eccentric orbits that swooped low enough to graze the fringe of atmosphere. Those would have to be dealt with soon, as well, before they lost sufficient velocity to nosedive to the surface like the lost hammer of Thor.

Most of the debris threatened no one, though. Not immediately.

And God alone knew how many pieces of that "debris" had once been human beings.

Neitz's jaw tightened at that thought. The debris pattern, coupled with the sensor records of the actual event, made it clear the charges had been placed with vicious forethought. Law enforcement and military intelligence were only starting their relentless assault on how it had been done, but at least a dozen competing theories had already emerged. Personally, Neitz went with what was generally regarded as the most probable. The devices had to have been in one of the central cargo hubs aboard each habitat. It was the only way to account for the wreckage patterns…and those hubs had been located at the cores of the enormous platforms' personnel sections. That was why the bastards had taken that approach, chosen those locations for some innocuous, well-camouflaged crate or container. A cargo canister in one of the open-space orbital holding areas would have inflicted little—probably even no—damage when it detonated. Even one of the long-term controlled condition storage booms would have provided sufficient separation for much of something as massive as Beowulf Alpha was—*had been*—to survive. But not in the cargo hubs. They'd been deliberately located as conveniently as possible to the places where people lived.

"How much longer, honey?" Christina asked in his ear, and his nostrils flared.

"However long it takes." It came out much more harshly than he'd intended. "Lord, I'm sorry," he said a moment later, his tone contrite. "It's just…just that we can't quit. We just *can't.*"

"I know. And I shouldn't push for answers you can't give me anyway. I know that, too." He could picture that small, loving, half-apologetic smile perfectly. "It's just that we *miss* you down here."

"Miss you, too," he said, but he knew what she was really thinking. It had been almost a T-week. An entire T-week. *Hawthorne* alone had recovered over six hundred bodies so far, and that wasn't even her primary mission. He had no idea how many had been recovered by Search and Rescue's small craft, and he didn't want to know. Not really. But that wasn't *Hawthorne*'s job. Her teams were out amid the densest parts of the debris field in her specialized salvage shuttles, threading their way through the thousand-ton chunks of alloy, cutting their way into compartments that might still be intact. Searching desperately for someone who might still be alive.

So far, they'd found sixteen. *Sixteen*…and they weren't going to find any more of them. He'd made himself accept that twenty-four hours ago. Anyone who'd been trapped in one of those compartments had run out of air or heat or power long since.

But that didn't mean they'd stop looking. "No One Left behind." That was Search and Rescue's motto, and they would by God keep the faith. No matter what, no matter who, they'd honor that trust.

"I'm sorry to say that the real reason I commed you is that I just heard from Lizzy," Christina said after a moment, and Neitz frowned. Lizzy—Elizabeth—was their daughter, a student at Hippocrates University. She'd been safely on the other side of the planet when Alpha blew up, so why…?

"Lizzy?" he repeated.

"Yes." Christina paused, almost as if she was gathering her strength. "She just found out Felicia Cummings, Tim Qwan, Katsuko Johnson, and half a dozen of her other friends were at the Broken Arrow concert."

Neitz closed his eyes in sudden pain.

Broken Arrow. He remembered how hard he'd tried to get Lizzy a ticket to the band's live concert. She shouldn't have been going—not with mid-terms coming up this week—but he'd known how badly she'd wanted to. And he'd been bitterly disappointed when he found out he'd waited too long.

Then. Before all forty thousand concert-goers died with the rest of Beowulf Alpha. And Katsuko...Katsuko who'd been Lizzy's best friend since nursery school...

"Oh, sweet Jesus," he whispered.

"I know. I *know*." He heard the tears glittering in his wife's voice. "You know what she's like. She's visiting Katsuko's mom right now, and then she's headed over to the Qwans. She's like you. She has to *be* there for people."

Neitz nodded silently. He knew exactly what his daughter was doing at that moment, despite her own terrible grief.

"I just wanted you to know," Christina went on. "You know she's not going to mention it to you—certainly not while you're still up there. But I figured—".

"You figured I should know before she and I have a chance to talk about it," he finished for her. "Because the last thing either of us need is for me to say something that hurts her all over again. And because you're a good mom and a better wife. We're both lucky to have you."

"Oh, *I've* always known that!" she said with a slightly watery chuckle, and he smiled wearily.

"Well, at least I've finally started figuring it out, too," he said. "Wouldn't want to say I could be a little sl—"

"Priority signal!" Lieutenant Simpkins-Howard announced suddenly from Communications, and Neitz's eyes popped open.

"Gotta run, honey!"

"Go," Christina said. "And promise me you'll try to get at least a *little* rest."

"Love you," he said, instead of issuing any promises he knew he couldn't keep. Then he killed the uni-link and swiveled his chair to face Communications.

"What is it, Carla?"

"It's the Bosun, Sir. *Charlie Three*'s reporting a live suit beacon!"

"A *live* beacon?"

"Yes, Sir!"

Badilotti leaned forward, looking over the sensor officer of the watch's shoulder. Now he straightened and turned to face Neitz.

"That's sure as hell what it looks like, Skipper," he said. "One of Platform Engineering's suits, from the transponder code."

"After this long? Where's it been for the last *week*? It's got to be some kind of sensor glitch."

"Don't know where it's been, Sir, but it's Bosun Lochen." Badilotti twitched a tired smile. "If you want, I can ask him to double check."

"Bad idea," Neitz said, shaking his head.

Senior Master Chief Petty Officer Bill Lochen, *Hawthorne*'s senior NCO, had been in Search and Rescue since the year Captain John Neitz graduated from high school. He was the best wreck-diver Neitz had ever met, which was the reason he and *Charlie Three*, Neitz's most experienced shuttle crew, were the point of *Hawthorne*'s spear. If he said he was picking up a signal, he was picking up a signal.

Which didn't explain why no one had picked it up sooner.

"The Bosun does say it's coming from inside a real rat's nest of wreckage, Skipper," Badilotti continued, as if he'd heard his captain's thought. "In fact, if I had to guess, the problem's how deep it is, how much junk it has to punch through. That's got to be why we didn't spot it earlier."

"What's the status of the survivor?"

"We don't know there *is* a survivor yet." Badilotti's excitement waned visibly. "All the Bosun's got so far is the beacon. He says there's no telemetry, or if there is, it's not getting through, anyway. He's working on it."

"Understood."

Neitz inhaled. No wonder Badilotti's initial exhilaration had faded. Skinsuit beacons were designed to be incredibly powerful, but suit telemetry channels were shorter-ranged and considerably weaker. If the wreckage around it had been sufficient to block it for so long, it was entirely possible there *was* telemetry and it just couldn't get through.

But it was far, far more likely that no telemetry was getting through because there was no one—no one alive, at least—inside the suit in question.

"Stay on it, David," he said after a moment. "And tell Bosun Lochen to keep us informed. I know he will, anyway, but, God, I could use some *good* news for a change."

"Yes, Sir," Badilotti said. "We *all* could."

George Benton Tower
City of Old Chicago
Old Earth
Sol System

"WELL, SO MUCH FOR our wonderful secret weapon," Malachai Abruzzi said bitterly. "How the hell am I supposed to sell *this* as the 'decisive victory' we needed?"

"It's not a complete disaster," Nathan MacArtney objected. "It looks like Hasta worked perfectly. If they'd seen it coming before the last stage lit off, they'd've stopped *any* of them from getting through, and they didn't."

"Oh, that makes it *much* better," Abruzzi half-sneered. "Now you're telling me I'm supposed to tell the public we fired off twelve hundred of these wonderful new missiles, the other side didn't even see them coming until the last second, and we still managed to take out one—count them, Nathan: one—of our *eleven* primary objectives." He shook his head in disgust. "I'm pretty good. Hell, I could sell ice on Niflheim! I don't think I can sell *this*, though."

"No one expects miracles, Malachai," Innokentiy Kolokoltsov told him. "We'll just have to do the best we can with what we've got."

"That's reassuring," Abruzzi muttered. Then he shook himself. "I really, really need Kingsford to give me something to work with."

"I'm sure he will. As soon as he can."

Abruzzi snorted, but he also sat back in his chair, arms folded, and Kolokoltsov tried to be grateful for small mercies.

Fabius had been almost as big a disaster as Kingsford had privately warned him it might. Unlike the CNO's worst-case assumption—based on discovering that the Manties' FTL system defense missiles were already fully operational—almost ten percent of Vincent Capriotti's battlecruisers had survived. SLNS *Québec* had not been one of them, however, and the remnants of TF 790 had reached Sol less than eleven hours ago. So far, no one outside the Navy—and the Mandarins—knew they had or had any idea the Solarian League had once again suffered catastrophic losses.

It would be a while before Kingsford could provide any sort of comprehensive after-action report or meaningful analysis of the attack's results. Without Capriotti—or, for that matter, any of the task group flagships—just pulling together the sensor data was likely to take days. What he called the "hot wash" analysis suggested Abruzzi's dismal summary of Capriotti's accomplishments was likely to hold up, though. Kingsford's face had been bitter on Kolokoltsov's com display as he described the impeller wedges which had interposed themselves between the Hastas and their targets.

"We'd have gotten better results going after something farther from the planet," the CNO had said heavily. "We didn't expect that wall of impeller wedges, and we had to be so careful about our targeting commands to avoid civilian casualties that the birds' tactical options were too limited to work around and get behind them, between them and the planet, for an unobstructed shot. We did find that one hole, and it looks like we probably killed at least a dozen of the ships they were using—more likely twice that many—but if I had to guess, they were freighters. Probably *unmanned* freighters—drones. So aside from the nano farm, I think it's likely we didn't get another damned thing. I'm sorry, Mister Senior Permanent Undersecretary. My people *tried*."

Yes, they did, Admiral, Kolokoltsov thought now. *And a hell of a lot of them* died *trying. But Malachai's right. We* can't *sell this as the win we needed.*

"Anything more on that 'data anomaly,'?" MacArtney asked.

"No." Kolokoltsov shrugged. "Kingsford says his people at Operational Analysis are working on it, but so far 'data anomaly' is as far as they've gotten." He shrugged again. "Frankly, I think Kingsford's pretty much of the opinion that it's a sensor glitch. Only two of Capriotti's recon drones even *think* they saw it...whatever it was."

"Good," Abruzzi said with bitter amusement. "At least I won't have to explain *that* one away. Last thing we need is for people to think the Manties are still producing new 'secret weapons.' Especially when *ours* all seem to suck wind."

"I have to say," Omosupe Quartermain put in, her tone as subdued— and anxious—as her expression, "that I'm a lot more worried about how the Manties are going to react to this than I am about what we tell the newsies."

Trust Omosupe to cut to the chase, Kolokoltsov reflected. And she had a point. The attack on Beowulf had upped the ante all around, and it was unlikely the Manties were very pleased about it. Still, there were a few glimmers in the darkness.

Even from Kingsford's current, partial analysis, it was obvious

MacArtney was right: the Manties had never even seen Hasta coming until the final stages went active. That meant the weapon had performed almost exactly as advertised. If not for the freighters they'd managed to interpose, the strike would have been just as devastating as anyone could have hoped, and the fact that at least some of *their* technology had worked perfectly—that the Manties' monopoly on superior weapons wasn't absolute, after all—was at least a little reassuring. According to Kingsford and Vice Admiral Kindrick, Systems Development Command and Technodyne were working on half a dozen other projects which should begin yielding results sometime within the next eight to twelve T-months. How good those results would be was an unknown, but if Hasta was representative, they might just provide a genuine equalizer, especially if they were employed en masse.

And the preliminary vote on the taxation amendment went our way overwhelmingly, Kolokoltsov reminded himself. *If Neng and Tyrone Reid are right, it'll sail through on the final vote week after next, too. If that happens, we'll have all the money we need to buy anything Systems Development wants! We just have to hang on long enough for that to happen, and the Manties are frigging* history!

He reminded himself of that firmly—*very* firmly. And somewhere under that reassurance, he heard the lonely sound of whistling in a cemetery.

CNO's Office
Admiralty Building
City of Old Chicago
Old Earth
Sol System

THE COM PINGED.

Winston Kingsford snarled at the sound. He'd left strict orders that he wasn't to be disturbed by anybody short of Innokentiy Kolokoltsov himself while he tried to make sense out of the confused reports from TF 790's survivors. And since he'd just finished speaking to Kolokoltsov twenty minutes ago—and since if anyone in the entire Sol System understood why he needed to be left alone to get on with it, that someone had to be Kolokoltsov—he rather doubted this was the Permanent Senior Undersecretary for Foreign Affairs.

Which meant whoever *was* pinging his com was about to acquire a new anal orifice.

It pinged again, and he stabbed the acceptance key angrily.

"What?" he snapped.

"Excuse me, Admiral," Chief Petty Officer Chernova said. She'd been Kingsford's personal yeoman for well over ten T-years, and she sounded remarkably calm in the face of his obvious displeasure.

"I *said*, 'no interruptions,' Marilis," he pointed out ominously.

"Yes, Admiral. I know. But Brigadier Gaddis insists on speaking to you."

"*Gaddis?*" Kingsford blinked. "You mean *Simeon* Gaddis—the Gendarme?"

"Yes, Sir. He says it's urgent. A matter of life and death."

Kingsford started to refuse. He couldn't imagine anything that might be "life-and-death" to the Gendarmerie that didn't come a piss-poor second to keeping his Navy alive! On the other hand, Gaddis wasn't stupid. In fact, aside from a certain quixotic streak where things like corruption were concerned, he had a reputation as one of the smartest people on the block. He was also one of the people who was most likely to have heard the truth about Operation Fabius, not the garbled

694

accounts of victory which had leaked to the boards. That meant he had to know Kingsford was going to be...less than responsive to anything else for a while. From which it followed...

"Well, in that case, I guess you'd better put him through, Marilis," he sighed.

"He's not on the com, Sir," Chernova replied. "He's here in person."

Kingsford's eyebrows tried to climb into his hairline. Then he shrugged.

"In that case, change that to 'I guess you'd better send him in,'" he said, and stood behind his desk as Chief Chernova showed the Gendarmerie officer into his office. Under the circumstances, he decided to dispense with the customary offer of refreshments and twitched his head at the office door. Chernova smiled faintly and effaced herself without another word.

"With all due respect, Brigadier Gaddis," Kingsford said then, waving brusquely for Gaddis to take a seat, "this really had better be *damned* important. I know the boards are starting to talk about our 'great victory,' but to paraphrase King Pyrrhys, another 'victory' or two like this one, and we're all fucked." He showed his teeth in something that wasn't a smile. "So I'm just a little *busy* right now."

"Understood, Admiral." Gaddis nodded. "In fact, that's why I'm here. There are a few things you need to know."

HMS *Duke of Cromarty*
In Hyper-Space

"SKIPPER, I REALIZE WE'RE in a hurry, but Her Majesty's going to be really, really pissed if we break the *Duke*. You do realize that, don't you? And I don't know about you, but I don't like it when Her Majesty is pissed at me."

Captain Steven Firestine looked up from his mug of coffee at Commander Rice. The commander looked back, and his expression showed rather more genuine concern than his tone had.

"I don't plan on breaking anything, Alex," he said mildly.

"People don't usually *plan* on things like that," Rice pointed out. "It just sort of happens. Especially when you've pulled the governors on the hyper generator. I seem to remember reading somewhere that that's what you might call a bad idea."

"I have total confidence in your ability to keep everything on the green," Firestine said. "And, if it should happen that my confidence is misplaced, the Empress's temper's likely be the last thing you'll have to worry about."

Rice looked remarkably unreassured.

"Skipper," he said in a much more serious tone, "if we pick up a harmonic this high in the Theta Bands, there's no tomorrow. And we're right on the edge of bouncing off the Iota wall. My systems are in good shape, but I'd be lying if I said I felt anything like confident about the way we're stressing them."

"Understood." Firestine took a long, slow sip of coffee, then lowered the cup. "Understood. But we're not backing off."

"Sir—"

"You've made your point, Alex. But we're not backing off." Firestine shook his head. "I understand what you're saying, and the truth is, I tend to agree. But there's too much riding on this."

Rice couldn't quite keep skepticism out of his expression, and in some ways, Firestine didn't blame him. If Empress Elizabeth's personal yacht hit the Iota wall, it was unlikely there'd be any survivors. But Rice hadn't been party to Firestine's sickbay conversation. He didn't understand the implications, the reason Firestine was determined to set a new record for the Beowulf-Sol run. He was going to shave every second he could off that passage. And if that meant hazarding his command, so be it.

There were some people you didn't fail, and Steven Firestine was *not* going to be the one who failed this time.

CNO's Office
Admiralty Building
City of Old Chicago
Old Earth
Sol System

THE PRIVATE LIFT CAR slid to a stop, and Caswell Gweon allowed himself a final grimace before putting his professional expression firmly in place. He didn't expect this to be a pleasant conversation. That wasn't the same as not wanting to *have* it, however, and he wondered exactly why he'd been summoned.

The rumors had truly started to fly only about twelve hours earlier, which was fairly remarkable, really, since it was almost four days since TF 790's return. He wasn't sure if those rumors had spurted out of the usual leaks or if other Alignment agents had been feeding them to the newsies, but so far there'd been no mention of any mysterious gatekeepers helping the SLN penetrate Beowulf's defenses.

His own analyses had viewed any official conclusions in that direction with careful skepticism. He couldn't just pretend those two drones hadn't seen *something*, but he'd come down heavily on the "probably just a sensor glitch" side. At the moment, though, the influence his analysis exerted was . . . ambiguous. He'd gotten a lot of credit as the analyst who'd first warned that something like the Manties' new missile defense system was in the course of deployment. On the other side, he'd been hammered over his estimate of how long it would take them to actually put it online. At the moment, at least as long as it was still a matter of "sensor glitches," he could argue they *hadn't* put it online—not the FTL component, at any rate—and that even if they had, his worst-case estimate had been that it might already be in place by the time Fabius actually got there. It would be so much better all around, though, if no one figured out that the Alignment really had been plowing the road for the Solarian Navy.

In the meantime, he needed to start shoring up his position with Winston Kingsford, repairing any damage it might have suffered after TF 790's disastrous experiences. That required opportunities to give the CNO good analysis, demonstrate how engaged he was, and impress him with his general competence, which was why he was glad he'd been summoned even if he expected a certain amount of reaming out.

The lift door slid open and he stepped out of it.

"You wanted to see me, Sir?" he said as Winston Kingsford rose behind his desk and nodded in greeting.

"Actually, yes, I did. Or, rather, *we* did."

The CNO waved one hand, and Gweon's head turned as his eyes followed it. Then his eyebrows rose as he saw the Gendarmerie brigadier and colonel standing just inside the door to the office's public anteroom.

"Caswell," Kingsford said, "this is Brigadier Simeon Gaddis and Lieutenant Colonel Okiku."

Gweon nodded and held out his hand, his expression calm and merely mildly surprised, despite the sudden flurry of questions racing through his brain.

"Brigadier," he said a bit cautiously, shaking Gaddis's hand and nodding across the brigadier's shoulder at Okiku. "Colonel. What can I do for you?"

"Actually, Admiral," Gaddis replied releasing his hand and stepping back a pace. "You can keep your hands where we can see them."

"What?" Gweon's eyes went wide as Okiku produced a stunner and pointed it at him. Something about the colonel's dark, almond eyes suggested that she really, really wanted to squeeze its trigger.

"I'm afraid you're under arrest, Rear Admiral Gweon," Gaddis said coldly.

"Excuse me?" Gweon stared at him, his expression one of shocked disbelief, segueing with perfect timing into outraged innocence. "Under *arrest?*" His voice gained volume. "What *for?*"

"Treason against the Solarian League will do for starters." Gaddis's voice was carved from Ganymedian ice. "We know about you and your fiancée, and our other agents are picking up Rajmund Nyhus and Shafiqa Bolton at this very moment." He smiled thinly. "I'm sure that between them and your other friends, you'll have plenty to tell us about the people you're *really* working for."

Gweon froze. The surprised innocence flowed off his face like water, and his eyes went cold and very focused for just a moment. Then his hands rose to clutch his head, his knees sagged, and he toppled forward.

He was dead by the time his face hit the carpet.

✧   ✧   ✧

"My God, Gaddis!" Winston Kingsford said shakenly, two minutes later, as Natsuko Okiku rose from checking Gweon's pulse and shook her head once. "My God! When you suggested this, I thought you had to be crazy! What do we do *now?*"

"That's the million-credit question, Sir." Gaddis scowled down at the body. "To be honest, I'd really have preferred to take this son-of-a-bitch alive, but as what just happened damned well proves, the odds of our doing that were never good. That's why I was willing to run our bluff and risk his dropping dead as our test case to give you the proof we weren't just lunatics. And, over all, I'd say Barregos's story about what happened when he arrested those 'Manty agents' has just been pretty thoroughly corroborated. But if every one of them drops dead like this bastard, proving who they're *really* working for—and I will absolutely *guarantee* you it isn't the Manties—will be the next damned thing to impossible."

"Jesus!" Kingsford sat abruptly. "The *Manties*."

"The Manties." Gaddis nodded grimly. "They may not have both oars all the way in the water, and so far, it looks to us like they were a hundred percent wrong about what they were going to find on Mesa. But they're absolutely right about the way we've been played, and when that little tidbit gets out—"

Kingsford nodded as his brain began to function once more.

He hadn't believed a word of it when Gaddis began spinning his preposterous tale. Only the fact that he knew Gaddis's reputation—knew the man was one of the very few honest cops inside the Kuiper—had led him to even listen. But as the brigadier laid out his case, one damning bit of circumstantial evidence at a time, his skepticism had begun to erode. To be honest, he'd still thought Gaddis and his fellow "Ghost Hunters" were insane, but if there'd been even the faintest chance they weren't, he'd had to know. And if there wasn't, Gweon and he could have a good laugh about it later.

Of course, that wasn't going to happen now, he thought, looking down at the corpse in front of his desk.

There's still no way the Manties are right about this "Alignment" of theirs, he thought. *Everything coming out of Mesa proves that. But what if whoever the "Other Guys" really are deliberately led the Manties to suspect Mesa? What if the very first card they put on the table was to provide the Manties with a bogeyman they knew the rest of the galaxy would laugh off? Get everyone so invested in dismissing the Manties' paranoid fantasies that any evidence there really was someone pulling the strings would be automatically dismissed right along with it?*

Which is exactly what we've all done.

Ice clogged his circulatory system and he drew a deep breath.

"I'll give you that *someone's* orchestrating all of this," he said, looking up at Gaddis. "You've had longer to think about this than I have, though. Would it be too much to hope you have some damned idea of what the *hell* they're really after? Or some suggested course of action on *our* part?"

"Frankly, Sir, we don't have a clue exactly what the Other Guys are up to or why. Not in terms of their endgame strategy, at any rate. But at least one of their *immediate* goals is obviously to keep turning up the heat between us and the 'Grand Alliance.' We can't decide whether their *primary* target is the League or the Star Empire, but they clearly want us at one another's throats. The lengths they're prepared to go to to keep us that way are what pushed us to contact you, in fact. Captain al-Fanudahi and Captain Teague took one look at those 'data anomalies' from Fabius and realized what they were really seeing. Of course," he smiled thinly, "they had an advantage your other analysts lacked; they actually believed the Manties were telling the *truth* about the Yawata Strike and the existence of someone they damned well *think* is the 'Mesan Alignment.'

"What really worries us, though," his smile disappeared, "are the implications for the Other Guys' reach. Those grasers were killing the Manties' fire control system, and however they did it, they had to have been positioned well before Task Force Seven-Ninety ever arrived. In fact, they had to be *coordinated* with the task force's arrival, which required detailed prior knowledge. In our judgment, that pretty much *proved* the Other Guys had been deeply involved in the decision to launch Fabius in the first place. They couldn't have coordinated their missile-killers into the plan if they hadn't known all about it ahead of time, which strongly suggested they had a significant hand in *shaping* it, and what just happened to Gweon seems to prove that. That's bad enough, but given how thoroughly they seem to have *us* penetrated, we don't know how much reach they may have into manipulating *Manty* decisions. It'd be a hell of a lot harder for them to do that, since the Manties obviously know they exist and have to be trying to protect themselves against penetration, but I'm not going to say it's impossible. And Captain al-Fanudahi's suggested a pretty scary possibility."

"Which is?"

"Our ships were busy withdrawing from the system just as fast as they could run," Gaddis said grimly. "It's for damned sure no one was hanging around to monitor the take from our recon drones. What if something *else* happened in Beowulf? Something like what happened when the Manties moved in on Mesa?"

Kingsford felt the blood drain from his face.

"The only good thing—assuming the Other Guys *have* managed to kill a couple of million Beowulfers—is that the Manties have shown an incredible amount of restraint," Gaddis told him. "So far, at least.

But if the Other Guys keep hammering away this way, that restraint's likely to erode. So I think it behooves us to drag this out into the open as quickly as we can."

"I can't go to Kolokoltsov and the others with this," Kingsford said. "Not yet. Because you're right. If everyone we arrest just dies on us, we'll never be able to prove who's behind this or why they're doing it. If I expect anyone else to believe something *this* insane, I've got to have something more concrete than a stack of dead bodies." He scowled down at Gweon. "You've convinced *me*; the 'Mandarins' have invested a hell of a lot more—including their own survival, probably—in the 'the Manties are paranoid lunatics' argument. They'd deny everything, even to themselves, and fire my arse the minute I told them anything of the sort. If I handled it just right and approached them gradually enough I *might* be able to convince Wodoslawski or Quartermain to listen. Abruzzi and MacArtney would never believe it though. I don't know about Kolokoltsov. He actually might—but even if he would, it doesn't sound to me like we can afford the time it'd take to get *any* of them to accept it."

Gaddis glanced at Okiku and saw his own relief in the colonel's eyes. Discovering Kingsford was clean had been an enormous relief. The evidence that the CNO's brain was beginning to function again was an even greater one.

"Sir, I don't know how much time we've got," Gaddis said, turning back to Kingsford, "but we haven't been able to come up with any ideas that would be much faster than that. The only approach we've been able to come up with is that with you in our corner and provided with the evidence we've turned up so far, it should be possible for you—and us—to begin quietly clearing people we know we can trust. We need to have a...a support structure in place before we go public or I approach Deputy AG Rorendaal and her people."

"Why?" From Kingsford's narrowed eyes, he already knew the answer to his own question, but he asked it anyway, and Gaddis snorted harshly.

"Because anybody else who's even come close to these people is dead, Admiral," he said, his expression grim. "None of us want to end up that way, and I doubt you do either. But there's no point pretending it won't happen if the Other Guys figure out what we're doing. Believe me, we've lived with that for quite a while. And that's why we need to clear as many people as we can. We need to build up a deep enough bench, enough people who have the same information we have, that an *army* of assassins couldn't get us all before we go public and start dragging snakes out into the light and clubbing the sons of bitches to death."

He looked Kingsford straight in the eye.

"Like I say, none of us want to die, but if that's what it takes, then that's what it takes. We know that. And we're willing to take the chance. But if we do that, then we need to do it smart and we need to be sure the Other Guys don't manage to sweep *us* under the rug along with all the other bodies before we get it done."

Kingsford looked at him for several seconds, then glanced down at Gweon's corpse again. Then he looked back at Gaddis.

"Sign me up, Brigadier," he said.

Sol System
Solarian League

THE SCREAMING ALARM YANKED Rear Admiral Bethany Ning-ju out of a deep sleep. She bolted upright in her bunk, reaching for the bedside com key before her eyes were fully open.

"Battle stations! Battle stations!" the strident voice filled every compartment, melding with the alarm. "All hands, battle stations! This is *not* a drill! Battle stations! Battle sta—"

An icicle went through Ning-ju, and the voice cut off—in her sleeping cabin, at least—as her hand came down on the com key and overrode the speakers.

"Ning-ju," she said, swinging her feet to the deck. "Talk to me!"

"Commander Rangwala, Ma'am." The voice on the other end was flat, as hard as an iron bar. If it hadn't identified itself, Ning-ju would never have recognized Daiichi Rangwala, SLNS *Andromeda*'s executive officer. "We're picking up a major hyper footprint, Ma'am. It's right on top of us!"

"Define 'right on top'!" she snapped.

"Under eight million kilometers, Ma'am!"

Ning-ju went white. Eight million kilometers was less than twenty-seven light-seconds!

"How big is it?" she demanded.

"So far we've got over three hundred point sources, Ma'am!"

Ning-ju's mind froze. Three *hundred* point sources? That was...that was...that was *insane*. Her entire squadron consisted of only eight *Mikasa*-class heavy cruisers. But what in God's name could—?

Her heart seemed to stop. There was only one place that many ships could have come from. And they could be here for only one purpose.

"Get on the com! Raise them *now!*"

✧   ✧   ✧

"Your Grace, we have what look like eight Solly heavy cruisers at seven-point-eight million kilometers," Captain Rafe Cardones said. "Closing velocity about thirty-five thousand KPS. Not sure from their vectors what they're doing out here, but we're right on top of them. They've just brought up their sidewalls."

704

"I see them, Rafe," Honor Alexander-Harrington replied.

She gazed down into the tactical plot, never raising her eyes to look at Cardones on her command chair com display, and her flag captain bit his lip. He'd seen her like this—or *almost* like this—once before, the night before her duel with Pavel Young. But, no, he thought. She hadn't been like *this* even then. She'd been focused, lethal, determined, prepared to pay the price of sacrificing her entire career to avenge the death of the man she'd loved, but she'd still been *her*. Still been Honor Harrington.

Today, she was a stranger. A *terrifying* stranger.

"Shall I challenge them, Ma'am?" Lieutenant Commander Brantley asked from Communications.

"No," she said flatly, and looked up from the plot at last. Eyes like frozen brown flint met Cardones's on the display.

"Take them out," she said.

❖   ❖   ❖

Commander Gregoire Koenig exploded from the lift car onto *Andromeda*'s command deck. He hadn't bothered with a skinsuit. In fact, he was shoeless and wore only trousers and a T-shirt, but Daiichi Rangwala leapt out of the command chair at the center of the bridge with enormous relief.

"Captain on the bridge!" the quartermaster of the watch barked.

"As you were—everyone!" Koenig snapped. He flung himself into the vacated command chair and spun it to face his tactical officer. "Status?"

"Still more of them coming over the wall, Sir." Lieutenant Commander Paulson's voice quavered. "We're up to almost five hundred now."

Koenig blanched. CruRon 572 was supposed to be conducting a simple training maneuver in the safest star system in the entire League. None of its units had ever imagined anything like this in their worst dreams!

"The Admiral's on the way to flag bridge, Sir," Rangwala told him. "Should be there by now."

Koenig jerked a choppy nod. As soon as Ning-ju reached her station, they'd have to—

"Missile launch!" Yvonne Paulson said suddenly. "*Multiple missile launches!*"

An icy fist punched Gregoire Koenig in the center of his chest. His eyes sped to the master plot and every drop of blood drained out of his face as dozens of missile icons blazed suddenly upon it. The time-of-flight number flashed its crimson warning, and there was no time to even think about escaping them. *Andromeda*'s hyper generator was completely powered down, and at those missiles' acceleration they would reach his ship in barely ninety seconds.

"Launching counter-missiles!" Paulson said, and *Andromeda* quivered as her launchers spat a pitiful salvo of CMs at that torrent of destruction.

"Get them on the com!" Koenig said. "Tell them we surrender!"

"We're *trying* to raise them, Sir!" his com officer said. "We haven't gotten through yet!"

✧   ✧   ✧

"Ma'am," Mercedes Brigham said very quietly in Honor's ear, "they can't hurt us."

Honor said nothing. She simply watched the missiles track across the plot, and Nimitz flattened his ears and bared his fangs from the back of her command chair.

✧   ✧   ✧

"Strike the wedge!" Bethany Ning-ju barked from Andromeda's flag bridge. "All units—*strike your wedges now!*"

✧   ✧   ✧

Rafe Cardones drew a deep breath of relief as the Solly cruisers' wedges disappeared in the universal FTL signal of surrender. His eyes darted back to his com.

And Honor Alexander-Harrington didn't say a word.

✧   ✧   ✧

"They're still coming, Sir!" Lieutenant Commander Paulson said.

"I see it, Yvonne," Commander Koenig replied, and a strange sense of something very like calm seemed to flow through him. Not relief, just... acceptance. The knowledge that every man and woman of his crew was about to die and there was absolutely nothing he could do about it.

They must be even more pissed off by Fabius than we'd thought, a corner of his mind reflected. *But why? We only hit* military *targets. Sure, nobody on the ones we hit had time to evacuate, but it's not like we violated the Eridani Edict the way* they *did in Mesa!*

✧   ✧   ✧

"Your Grace, they've surrendered," Mercedes Brigham said, and Honor looked at her. Her expression never changed, but there was something almost like... puzzlement in those flinty eyes, as if she wondered what that had to do with anything.

"Your Grace, they've struck their wedges!"

She said nothing, only looked at her chief of staff with those puzzled eyes, and Brigham reached out. She gripped her admiral's shoulders, actually shook her in her command chair.

"Ma'am—*Honor*—they've *surrendered!*"

Their eyes locked, and then, suddenly, Honor shivered. She closed her eyes, her nostrils flared, and her hands tightened like talons on the armrests of her command chair.

"Yes, they have, *damn* them." The knife-edged words were so soft only Brigham could possibly have heard them. Then her eyes opened again.

"Abort the engagement, Captain Cardones," she said clearly, coldly, while Nimitz snarled protest behind her.

✧   ✧   ✧

The time-to-attack range readout flashed downward and every eye on *Andromeda*'s bridge was glued to it. Forty seconds. Thirty-five. Thirty...

No one spoke. There was nothing to say, no further orders to give. The tide of destruction came in ludicrously slowly for a missile engagement, because the range was too short for it to reach anything like maximum velocity. Individual missiles—even Manticoran missiles—would be easy meat for the point defense clusters when they came into range. But there were over five hundred missiles in that salvo. If every single cluster CruRon 572 could bring to bear stopped two of them, four hundred would still get through. And without even sidewalls to protect them...

Twenty seconds. Fifteen. Ten.

Gregoire Koenig drew a deep breath—the last he would ever draw—and held it as his ship's death roared down upon him.

And then, suddenly, every single one of those missiles swerved away from its target, arced wide of the squadron, and vanished in a holocaust of self-destruct commands.

Koenig wouldn't have believed the silence on his bridge could grow even more intense.

He would have been wrong.

That silence lingered for ten crackling seconds. Then his com officer cleared his throat.

"Sir, we have an incoming transmission."

"Put it up," Koenig said.

"Yes, Sir."

The commander leaned back in his chair, vaguely aware his hands were trembling, and a woman in the black-and-gold of the Royal Manticoran Navy appeared on the master com display.

"I am Admiral Harrington, Royal Manticoran Navy," she said, and something deep inside Gregoire Koenig shrank from that soprano scalpel. "I accept your surrender in the name of the Grand Alliance. Be aware that any resistance to my boarding parties will be met with instant lethal force and that my acceptance of your surrender is contingent upon the surrender of your *intact* databases. If those databases are *not* intact, or if any resistance is offered to my boarding parties by *any* individual, I will regard *all* of your personnel as having violated the terms of your surrender and act accordingly."

She smiled, and somehow it was the most frightening smile Koenig had ever seen.

"You won't like it if that happens," she said very, very softly, "but *I* will."

Naval Station Ganymede
Sol System
Solarian League

"THIS IS *CONFIRMED?*" ADMIRAL Maridors Haeckle asked.

"Yes, Sir." Rear Admiral Léonard Pataloeşhti, Haeckle's chief of staff, shook his head, his expression pale. "Captain Tsukatani's the duty officer. He says System Watch Command picked up the initial hyper footprints sixteen minutes ago. They were right on top—I mean, *right* on top—of Admiral Ning-ju's squadron, and the sensor platforms detected a massive missile launch. We don't see any of the cruisers' impeller signatures anymore. They're just...gone."

"Shit," Haeckle said flatly, then shook himself. "Well, I suppose that clears up any little ambiguity about whether or not they're hostile."

Pataloeshti only nodded, and Haeckle sighed.

"All right, Léonard, I guess we'd better get down to the command center. How *many* of them did you say we're talking about?"

"Tsukatani makes it a minimum of three hundred and fifty signatures at superdreadnought range, Sir, but he's pretty sure that's low. Total count for all types is about six hundred, plus fifty-five of what have to be freighters or transports in a separate echelon. Tsukatani estimates the transport group's escort at another sixteen battlecruisers and a pair of superdreadnoughts." It was his turn to sigh. "I don't think this is just a raid, Sir."

"No," Haeckle agreed softly. "No, I suppose not."

HMS *Imperator*
Sol System

"GHOST RIDER'S GIVING US good numbers, Your Grace."

Andrea Jaruwalski crossed to stand beside Honor as she gazed into the master plot. A steady stream of additional icons appeared in it as she watched.

"CIC makes it a total of sixty-two superdreadnoughts and two hundred and six battlecruisers in Ganymede orbit," the ops officer continued, consulting her memo board. "Sixty-one cruisers, one hundred and seventeen destroyers and other light craft, and at least fifty-two tankers, colliers, and major service craft—a million tons or more each—of one sort or another. Might be a couple more of those on the far side of Ganymede, and we don't have a hard count on deployed missile pods yet. We *won't* have one until the platforms get a lot closer, but we've already confirmed over four thousand."

"I see."

Honor heard the distant note in her own voice and tasted the burning concern in Jaruwalski's mind-glow. She knew what caused it. She could taste the same worry in Mercedes Brigham, in George Reynolds, in Harper Brantley and Theophile Kgari. She didn't have to taste Rafe Cardones's mind-glow to know it would have been the same.

They were afraid of her, especially after the near destruction of Bethany Ning-ju's squadron. They were frightened of what she'd become. Even worse, they were frightened *for* her, and that was the truly terrible thing. Because *she* wasn't frightened of who and what she was... and a part of her knew she should be.

Too bad Scotty's not here, a voice said in the back of her brain, remembering another day on a moon called Blackbird. But then she brushed that memory aside. This was a different time and a different place, and she wanted no reminder of that day staying her hand when the moment came.

She turned her head to look at her communications officer.

"How long till the Hermes buoy is in position, Harper?" that distant soprano asked.

"Another twenty-nine minutes, Your Grace," Commander Brantley replied. He paused a moment, then added, "They're trying to contact us by com laser, Ma'am."

"Are they?" Honor smiled thinly. "I think we'll just wait till we've delivered our *other* message and don't have any irritating delays. Besides," that smile turned even thinner and colder, "it won't hurt a thing to let them *sweat* a little before we talk to them, now will it?"

"No, Your Grace. Not one bit," Brantley said, and an edge of satisfaction glittered in his mind-glow, clear and sharp enough to cut even through his concern for her.

Central Command
NSG Able-One
Naval Station Ganymede
Sol System
Solarian League

"STILL NOTHING, ERMOLAI?" ADMIRAL Haeckle asked quietly, and Captain Volodimerov shook his head.

"No, Sir." Volodimerov had been the Communications watch officer when the intruders translated into n-space. "Lieutenant Watson's initial challenge went out five minutes after they completed their alpha translations. That's—" he checked the time "—forty-one minutes. So they could have contacted *us* twenty-seven minutes ago, and by now they've known *we're* trying to talk to *them* for at least twenty-two minutes. Either way, they've had time to reply to us if they wanted to."

Haeckle nodded.

The strangers—they had to be Manties, although they had yet to activate any transponders or identify themselves—were almost exactly nineteen light-minutes from NSG. That was twice the Improved Cataphract's maximum powered range, and he doubted that that spacing was a coincidence. The Manties must have acquired enough Cataphracts to have an excellent grasp of their maximum accelerations and burn times by now. For that matter, they had to be aware that Cataphract accuracy at that sort of distance ranged all the way up from "not-a-chance-in-hell" to simply "really-piss-poor," which made it an ideal range from which to open some sort of conversation with no one getting shot on either side.

But if they'd wanted to talk to him, they could have been doing that for almost half an hour now. Of course, there'd be a nineteen-minute transmission delay built into any conversation, but sooner or later they *had* to say *something*.

He wished he was going to be happy when they did.

Once upon a time—and not so very long ago, actually—he would have been confident of Naval Station Ganymede's ability to stand off any attack. Enough superdreadnoughts could undoubtedly have taken or destroyed the station and all its platforms even then, but no one—except the Solarian League Navy—had *possessed* that many superdreadnoughts. And so, in those innocent days of yore, he would have been much more confident of a happy outcome. Under *current* circumstances...

He glanced at the time display again. His initial report to Old Earth had gone out even before Volodimerov had challenged the Manties, and System Watch Command's sensor reports and analyses were automatically relayed to both Naval Station Mars and Old Terra. But, Old Chicago was just over forty-six light-minutes distant at the moment, so Admiral Kingsford would only now be finding out the capital system had been invaded. It would be at least three quarters of an hour before any response from him could get back to Haeckle, and he wondered what that response would be.

Or if there'd be anyone here to receive it.

"What's our readiness state now, Captain Tsukatani?" he asked.

"We're closed up at battle stations, Sir," Franklin Tsukatani, the Central Command duty officer, replied. "All mobile units report Readiness One on weapons and defenses, and most of the destroyers and cruisers have their impellers online and wedges and sidewalls engaged. The superdreadnoughts will be a while yet, on that. All platforms' Missile Defense is also at Readiness One, and all missile pods have been prepped and brought online." He shrugged ever so slightly. "We're as ready as we're going to be, Sir."

And you're no more confident we're "ready" enough than I am, Haeckle thought. Not that either of them could say any such thing.

"Someone get me a cup of coffee, please," he said instead, and forced a smile that looked almost—almost—natural. "Looks like we may be waiting for a while."

HMS *Imperator*
Sol System

"THE HERMES BUOY'S IN position, Your Grace," Andrea Jaruwalski said, and Honor glanced at the operations officer.

She'd often wondered what Hamish—a stab of exquisite pain went through her with that name—had felt during his attack on DuQuesne Base in Operation Buttercup. This wasn't the same, of course, and in more than one way. She doubted he'd ever truly hated even the Peeps—or any other enemy of the Star Kingdom, for that matter. Not with a deep, visceral, ravening need to wreak death and destruction that burned like liquid oxygen. Not him.

But she wasn't him.

"Launch," she said softly, and turned back to the plot.

Central Command
NSG Able-One
Naval Station Ganymede
Sol System
Solarian League

"MISSILE LAUNCH! *MULTIPLE* MISSILE launches!" Lieutenant Enwright McGill announced sharply.

Commodore Benjamin Schalken turned quickly toward the announcement. He and his System Watch Command personnel had been watching the Manties for over an hour now. The tension of that long wait had been more excruciating than anything he'd ever endured. The passing seconds had become a long, drawn out water torture that he'd known had to be the worst thing that could ever happen to him.

Now, as he crossed to McGill's shoulder, looked down at the lieutenant's display, he discovered he'd been wrong.

"Two thousand-plus incoming!" McGill announced. "Initial velocity twelve hundred KPS, accelerating at four-five-one KPS squared!"

Schalken put a hand on his shoulder and watched the vectors reach out across the display for Ganymede.

✧   ✧   ✧

"Return fire, Sir?" Captain Tsukatani asked, and Haeckle nodded.

"You may engage, Captain," he said formally. "Fire Plan Agincourt."

Tsukatani looked at him for a moment. Then his mouth tightened and he nodded.

"Yes, Sir. Fire Plan Agincourt."

He turned away, giving orders, and fifteen seconds later 120,000 Improved Cataphract pods belched 720,000 missiles at the Manties.

Haeckle watched their icons streak across the plot and looked at Pataloeshti.

The chief of staff looked back, then gave him a small shrug.

Most of their fire plans had envisioned using their pods in much smaller numbers, in carefully planned and metered salvos. Agincourt did not. Agincourt was an all-or-nothing throw of the dice designed to put the maximum possible weight of fire—*all* the Cataphracts Ganymede

714

possessed—into space in a single enormous wave. They couldn't possibly manage all the birds of an Agincourt launch, even with all of NSG's enormous telemetry capability, and he wasn't surprised Tsukatani wasn't happy to burn them all in a single spasm. But the Cataphracts were all they had, and they had to get them off before the incoming fire ripped them to pieces still in their pods.

Seven hundred and twenty thousand missiles—the next best thing to three-quarters of a million of them, over seven thousand per target—represented a terrifying weight of metal. Yet the truth was that neither he nor Pataloeshti truly expected them to accomplish much. Targeting would have been . . . questionable at nineteen light-minutes under any circumstances, the range was far too great for any control link, and given the reported efficacy of Manty EW and missile-defense systems, "questionable" was probably about to become "futile." Which didn't even consider the fact that the Manties were outside even Jupiter's hyper-limit.

But it wasn't like he had a choice. Their own launch had made that much abundantly clear. And so did the com link's total, icy silence.

They didn't even try to talk to us, he thought bleakly. *Not a word. They just came in, blew Ning-ju's squadron to bits, and then sat there for a damned hour, letting us sweat. And the whole time, they were planning on this.*

Maridors Haeckle was one of the Solarian officers who'd never bought the official line about the Mesa Atrocity. He'd met several Manticoran officers, including Admiral James Webster, the assassinated Manticoran ambassador to the League, and none of them had been homicidal maniacs. He didn't know what had happened in Mesa, but he'd been certain he knew what *hadn't* happened, because it had been impossible to imagine those officers deliberately slaughtering millions of civilians.

Now he found himself wondering if he'd been wrong . . . and what was about to happen to the star system of mankind's birth if he had.

✧　　✧　　✧

The Mark 23s raced away from Grand Fleet, accelerating at a steady 46,000 gravities. Six minutes later, still more than 312,000,000 kilometers short of Naval Station Ganymede, their impellers shut down and they drove ballistically onward at fifty-five percent of light-speed.

✧　　✧　　✧

"If ONI's current estimate of Manty missile performance is accurate—and it would be nice if it finally was, given the price Admiral Capriotti paid to get us the numbers—they should light off again in about twenty-eight minutes, Sir," Captain Tsukatani said quietly, and Haeckle nodded.

Their own Cataphracts would take longer. Assuming, as Tsukatani said, that ONI's numbers were finally accurate, the Manties' total time-of-flight at nineteen light-minutes would be on the order of thirty-seven minutes. The Cataphracts' first-stage impellers would burn out sooner and at a lower velocity, which meant their ballistic phase would be 56,000,000 kilometers longer than the incoming birds and that they'd require almost twice as long to cover it: fifty-five minutes as opposed to the Manties' twenty-eight.

Which meant that even though they'd fired within twenty seconds of one another, the Manties' laser heads would reach Ganymede almost twenty-one minutes before his Cataphracts could reach attack range of them.

Central Command Center
Admiralty Building
City of Old Chicago
Old Earth
Sol System

"WHAT DO YOU MAKE of all this, Sir?"

Willis Jennings spoke softly, pitching his voice too low to be overheard even in the Central Command Center buried eighty floors beneath the Admiralty Building. CCC was dimly lit, as always, and had the hush associated in Jennings's experience only with churches and military command centers in the midst of crisis.

"If you'd asked me that three days ago, I might not have been as worried as I am now," Winston Kingsford responded equally softly to his chief of staff's question. "I might've been surprised, even after Fabius, given how hard they've tried to convince everyone we're the aggressors, and I probably would've figured they intended to trash Ganymede as a reprisal for what we tried to do to Ivaldi. Of course, one reason I would've been surprised if they'd tried anything more ambitious is that I would've believed that bastard Gweon's estimate on how 'short of ammunition' they were."

Jennings grunted. Kingsford and Gaddis had come up with a crude but simple technique for testing loyalties. The CNO had called Jennings in, and Gaddis and Okiku had "arrested him," exactly as they'd "arrested Gweon." Instead of dropping dead, Jennings had been coldly furious at having been accused of treason, at which point Kingsford had explained what was actually happening. He'd made no effort to hide how glad he'd been to confirm his chief of staff's loyalty—not simply to the League, but to *him*—and they'd set out to clear as many other senior officers as they could. Finding excuses to get them into Kingsford's office—or somewhere else where they could be "arrested" without any witnesses—wasn't easy, and they'd just about run out of pretexts.

But at least they'd managed to test twenty-six of them, so far . . . and five of them had reacted exactly the way Gweon had.

That was a frightening percentage, but as Colonel Okiku had pointed

717

out, they were beginning with officers in the positions which would have been most valuable to the Other Guys. Under the circumstances, it was only to be expected that the other side would have concentrated its efforts on putting its own people into them, which undoubtedly explained why the percentage had been so high.

Kingsford didn't want to think about how the Other Guys would react when they noticed their people inside the Admiralty's upper echelons were disappearing, and if he was honest, he'd also been more than a little shaken by how efficiently Gaddis and Lieutenant Colonel Weng had made the bodies in question do that disappearing. It made him wonder where—and why—they'd learned to conceal corpses so proficiently.

Not even they could keep someone on the other side from noticing the sudden, unprecedented rate of absenteeism eventually, however. They could, however, hope that each of the recently deceased had been assigned to his or her own unique controller as a security measure. That was the way Kingsford would have done it, anyway, especially for moles in such critical positions, assuming he'd had enough controls to make it work. And if they had, that might mean no one on the other side was in a position to realize how many of their agents had just gone missing. Each control would realize *his* mole had gone dark; he just wouldn't realize so many others had done the same thing, which would mean they probably had more time in hand than he was afraid they did. *Relying* on that could have unfortunate consequences, however.

Still, if Weng Zhing-hwan and Lupe Blanton were correct, they should have at least a brief bubble before the Other Guys could change strategies in response even if they'd already noticed their vanishing moles. As Blanton had pointed out, decision-making and communication loops were the Achilles' heel of any interstellar conspiracy. So, logically, it should take the other side's leadership quite some time—presumably, several weeks, at least—to find out they'd lost track of Gweon and his fellows and do something about it.

Unfortunately, Kingsford rather thought Gaddis and Daud al-Fanudahi had made a lot of sense when they'd pointed out in reply that whoever the Other Guys were, they'd been running their interstellar conspiracy for a *long* time. It was entirely possible they'd learned from experience that successful dinosaurs needed secondary brains at frequent intervals and built in contingency plans at the local level. Whether or not those plans had ever visualized the possibility of having their network rolled up from the top down was another question. No doubt it would have been an entertaining one to debate over a good bottle of whiskey, had it been a purely theoretical possibility.

Under the circumstances, he'd been anything but entertained by the possibility.

And now this.

"If al-Fanudahi and Teague's worst-case scenario for what happened in Beowulf after we left applies, though," he continued, "I don't think they're likely to settle for hitting Ganymede."

"Maybe not, Sir. But Ganymede's not exactly naked, you know. And if they want *more* than Ganymede, they'll have to come inside the limit. When they do, their options decrease. They won't be able to hyper out of harm's way, and we've got a hell of a lot more Cataphracts covering the inner system than Haeckle has out at NSG."

"Do they *really* have to come inside?" Kingsford asked softly.

Jennings raised his eyebrows, and the CNO snorted.

"Capriotti didn't *need* to cross the limit in Fabius," he pointed out. "He only did it to divert their attention from the Hastas, and everything we've seen suggests their fire control is even better than Hasta's. Not as stealthy, no, but considerably more capable when it comes to actually hitting things. So what if they're perfectly prepared to sit outside the limit and just blaze away at the inner system?"

"Sir, there are over a *billion* people spread between the inner-system habitats!" Jennings protested.

"And how many million were spread between the *Beowulf* habitats?" Kingsford shook his head. "I think we'd better all pray they're more concerned about avoiding collateral deaths than *we* were."

Central Command
NSG Able-One
Naval Station Ganymede
Sol System
Solarian League

"MISSILE ACTIVATION!" LIEUTENANT MCGILL sang out, shattering the intense silence. "Enemy missiles have reactivated! Range three-six-point-seven-five million kilometers! Time to attack range, one hundred eighty seconds!"

Right on schedule, Haeckle thought grimly. *So at least ONI did finally get something right. Not that it's going to do us any good.*

He checked the seals on his skinsuit with his right hand as he stood beside Pataloeshti, helmet tucked in the crook of his left elbow. Part of him was tempted to go ahead and helmet up, but that wasn't the sort of example an admiral was supposed to set. Besides, there wasn't much point to it. While the big compartment was buried deep at the heart of NSG Able-One, Ganymede Station's main platform, that was unlikely to be sufficient protection against laser heads as powerful as the Manties and their friends threw around. Putting on his helmet wouldn't help a lot if Central Command took a direct hit of that magnitude. In the event that they took damage but were fortunate enough not to be hit directly—and despite its size, Central Command *was* a relatively small target, compared to the rest of the platform—there ought to be time to don his helmet before it depressurized completely.

It was amazing how long three minutes could be, he thought, watching the plot's icons streak towards them. He felt himself tightening internally, his stomach clenching, his leg muscles trying to quiver with the ancient fight-or-flight reaction. But neither fight nor flight was an option, so he simply stood there, waiting.

✧　　✧　　✧

Counter-missiles began to launch, and Naval Station Ganymede was no mere task force, or even a fleet. It had always been liberally provided with counter-missile launchers, and their numbers had been vastly increased as the SLN began—dimly—to recognize the nature of

720

the threat it faced. Every one of the hundreds of warships in Ganymede orbit vomited counter fire, as well, and literally thousands of counter-missiles streaked to meet the Mark 23s.

But this was an old game for the Grand Alliance, and no other navy in the galaxy could match their missile crews' expertise. Dazzlers flared all along that wavefront of missiles, and Dragon's Teeth sprang to life, filling space with false targets while the real threats bored in behind the Dazzlers.

There were twenty-seven hundred missiles in Grand Fleet's launch. Honor could have fired many times that many, but she'd elected to use only three hundred of her Mark 17 flatpack pods. She was, after all, making a point.

Three hundred of those missiles were Mark 23-Es, following behind their more lethal brethren with no warheads of their own. Of the other twenty-four hundred, Andrea Jaruwalski had dedicated a full quarter as EW and penaid platforms. So there were a total of "only" eighteen hundred actual shipkillers in that tide of death.

Naval Station Ganymede fired well over two hundred *thousand* counter-missiles at them, backed by more than four thousand point defense clusters, most far larger than any mobile structure mounted. They were more powerful, there were more of them, and their software had been continuously tweaked since the Battle of New Tuscany.

And they still weren't good enough.

The defenders killed 811 Mark 23s, but 260 of them were penetration platforms. In the end, 1,249 of the most powerful laser heads ever deployed punched straight through the very best the Solarian League Navy could throw at them. They drove in on their targets and then, in one perfectly synchronized instant, they detonated.

HMS *Imperator*
Sol System

"GHOST RIDER CONFIRMS DETONATION," Andrea Jaruwalski announced. "It looks good, overall, Your Grace, but it'll be a few minutes before the detailed evaluation comes in."

"Good," Honor said. "Time to attack for their birds?"

"Nineteen minutes, Your Grace."

"Rafe," Honor looked at the bulkhead screen tied into *Imperator*'s command deck, "set the translation clock for seventeen and a half minutes from now."

"Yes, Ma'am."

Central Command
NSG Able-One
Naval Station Ganymede
Sol System
Solarian League

HE WAS STILL ALIVE.

That was Maridors Haeckle's first incredulous thought. He was *alive*.

He felt himself inhale, heard the same sounds of surprise sweeping through the rest of Central Command, and turned disbelievingly to his chief of staff.

Pataloeshti was still staring at the plot, trying to understand *why* they were alive, and Haeckle gave himself a shake.

"Status," he heard someone else say, using his voice.

"We're—" Captain Tsukatani began, then stopped. He bent over his own terminal, tapping keys, then straightened and turned to face Haeckle.

"Admiral," he said very carefully, "the main platforms didn't take a single hit. We lost two destroyers and a heavy cruiser, but I think that was a mistake in their targeting."

"A *mistake?*" Pataloeshti repeated.

"Yes, Sir—a mistake. They didn't hit *any* of our other active ships, and with all those battlecruisers and superdreadnoughts in orbit, I don't see how they could have missed them all unless they'd tried really hard."

"But, in that case, what—?"

"It looks like they took out at least ninety percent of the super-dreadnoughts in Reserve One."

"The *Reserve?*" This time it was Haeckle, and Tsukatani nodded.

"They have to have done it on purpose, Sir. Not only that, they punched their birds right through our defensive envelope to reach them, and they didn't have to do that. They brought them into range of our CMs and every one of our platforms' point defense clusters, and with their laserheads' standoff range against targets without even sidewalls, they could've stayed entirely out of our *counter-missile* envelope, far less laser range, if they'd wanted to."

"A message," Haeckle said softly. "They were sending a *message.*"

His brain raced. He hadn't even thought about the thousands of obsolescent superdreadnoughts parked in the twenty-four, equidistantly spaced clusters riding Jupiter orbit with Ganymede. Why should he have? If the Manties had proved one thing, it was that those pre-pod fossils were deathtraps waiting to happen. They knew that even better than the SLN, so why in God's name should they have even considered wasting missile fire on ships which were already inevitably destined for the breakers?

Because it let them prove that they could have killed all of our active *ships just as easily.* The realization went through him like a dagger of ice. *It was a demonstration of just how defenseless we are. And proof that they can snuff out NSG anytime they damned well feel like it.*

He stood there, staring at Tsukatani, then sucked in a sudden breath.

"Abort the attack!" he snapped.

Tsukatani blinked, then darted a look at the tactical board.

"We can't, Sir," he said. "We're seventeen and a half minutes from attack range."

Haeckle swallowed hard. It would have taken *nineteen* minutes for the self-destruct command to catch up with the Cataphracts. And that meant the Manties were going to think he'd missed their message.

He turned sickly back to the plot, watching the icons.

HMS *Imperator*
Sol System

"ONE HUNDRED SECONDS TO attack range, Your Grace."

Captain Jaruwalski seemed remarkably calm about it.

"Translation in seventy-five seconds," Rafe Cardones announced from his command deck, and Honor reached up to caress Nimitz's ears.

Central Command
NSG Able-One
Naval Station Ganymede
Sol System
Solarian League

"SIR, THE MANTIES HAVE translated out!" Tsukatani said sharply, and Haeckle felt himself sag around his bones.

He supposed a true naval officer shouldn't feel such profound relief when his enemies escaped unscathed. Particularly when they did it so tauntingly, waiting until the last minute to disappear into hyper. It was the equivalent of thumbing their noses in his face, yet he'd never been happier to see something in his entire life.

"Let's get a transmission off to Admiral Kingsford," he said. "Append our detailed sensor records."

"Yes, Sir."

Haeckle nodded, then crossed to the command chair he'd ignored for the last couple of hours. Pataloeshti followed him, and he racked his helmet on the side of the chair, then leaned back with a sigh.

"I'd just as soon not do that again, Sir," Pataloeshti said quietly, standing beside him, and Haeckle chuckled harshly.

"It beats hell out of what we might've been doing instead," he pointed out.

"What do you think their next move is, Sir?"

"I suppose that depends on where they jumped to," Haeckle said. "If they did what I think they did, it won't be long."

He smiled thinly and sat back, legs crossed, and waited.

✧　　✧　　✧

"Hyper footprint!" Lieutenant McGill said sharply. "Many hyper footprints, range approximately seven light-minutes."

Alarms sounded—quite unnecessarily, after McGill's announcement— and Haeckle straightened in his chair.

"A little closer than I'd expected, really," he said as he watched the last of the invaders come over the alpha wall and back into phase with the rest of reality almost exactly twenty-two and a half minutes after they'd left it.

It was a dazzling display of astrogation, he thought—a perfectly aligned micro-jump barely seventeen light-minutes long—that left the attackers still almost three light-minutes outside Jupiter's hyper-limit. Of course, it would take fifteen or sixteen minutes for their wallers' generators to cycle and allow them to translate out again, and that meant—in theory—that the Cataphracts still in his warships' magazines could have reached them well before they could escape again.

Except that he was reasonably confident "escape" was the last thing on their mind.

The icons on the plot changed abruptly as every one of those ships strobed its transponder, and his mouth tightened at the fresh—no doubt intentional—display of contempt for the best the SLN could do. Those transponders would have been homing beacons for any missile he decided to fire at them, but they obviously didn't care. In fact, it was more than simply not caring. They wanted him to know *exactly* what they'd brought to the dance, and something with thousands of tiny feet crawled up and down his spine as the hundreds of transponder codes identifying superdreadnoughts of at least four different star nations spangled the plot.

"Sir, we have a com request," Captain Volodimerov said carefully. "It, ah, seems to be coming from a relay less than ten thousand klicks out."

"Put it on my display."

"Yes, Sir."

Volodimerov nodded to one of his techs. A moment later, Haeckle's com display came alive with the face of a dark-haired woman in the skinsuit of a Royal Manticoran Navy admiral. He'd never met her, but he would have recognized her from the intelligence files' imagery even without the cream-and-gray creature glaring into the com from the back of her command chair.

"Good afternoon, Admiral Harrington," he said.

"You recognize me," she replied, less than seven seconds later, despite the vast gulf which still lay between them. "Good. That will save some time."

She had not, he noticed, asked who *he* was. He wondered if that meant she already knew...or that she simply didn't care.

"Listen to me carefully," she continued in a voice which could have been carved from Ganymede's ice, "because I'm only going to say this once. I am prepared to allow you and your personnel to surrender to the Grand Alliance upon the following terms.

"First, you will immediately evacuate all personnel from all active warships and scuttle them. There will be no exceptions. You may transfer as many of those personnel as you desire and have the capacity for to the transports and support vessels also in Jupiter orbit, and I will permit any such vessels to depart unhindered for the inner system at such time as the last of your warships has been destroyed.

"Second, you will stand ready to be boarded by my Marines, and be aware that *any* resistance of *any* type to *any* of my personnel will be met immediately by the use of lethal force. Under the circumstances, the lives and safety of my personnel are my sole concern; preserving the lives of people stupid enough to *threaten* those lives and that safety isn't even on my to-do list. Be certain all of your people understand that, because no warnings will be given."

Haeckle's blood ran cold as he suddenly recognized the ferocious hunger in that icy soprano. He didn't know where it had come from, and it was wildly at odds with the mental picture of her he'd built reading between the lines of media reports and ONI's analyses. But she meant it, he thought. Her Marines *would* shoot without warning.

"Third, your personnel will cooperate in transferring control of your platforms' power, environmental, and engineering systems to *my* engineering personnel," she continued. "Fourth, you will surrender to my control—intact and undamaged—every computer and computer file in your possession. And, fifth, your Systems Development Command— and Technodyne Industries—will surrender every prototype and every system under development, undamaged, with complete documentation."

He swallowed hard. If he gave her what she was demanding, the Manties and their Allies would know everything there was to know about the Solarian League Navy. *Everything*, from secure communications protocols to the very latest R&D. The consequences of that would be—

"You don't have to meet my conditions," she told him. "That decision is up to you. But be advised that if you have *not* accepted my terms within the next ten minutes, I will open fire upon you and no further offer of surrender will be accepted."

The blood ran from his face. She couldn't mean that! She was talking about a massacre!

"And be further advised," she told him very, very softly, "that if you accept my terms and then violate them in any way whatsoever, I will withdraw my personnel from your platforms and destroy every... single...one...of...them."

The creature on her shoulder bared needle-sharp fangs at him, but, somehow, *her* smile was far more terrifying.

"I will await your decision...for ten minutes," she said, and his com display went blank.

George Benton Tower
City of Old Chicago
Old Earth
Sol System

"AND KINGSFORD SAYS HE couldn't do *anything* about it?" Malachai Abruzzi demanded. "Not one frigging *thing?*"

"Haeckle had accepted Harrington's terms before Kingsford even knew what they were," Innokentiy Kolokoltsov said flatly. He sat back in his chair, smelling the panic in the palatial conference room, and his expression was grim. "For that matter, he says that even if he'd known and been able to order Haeckle to reject them, he wouldn't have. Not after her...demonstration."

And not, he acknowledged to himself, after seeing the record of Harrington's icy delivery of those terms. Kingsford hadn't commented directly on that part of his reasoning, but Kolokoltsov had viewed the recording himself, and the way she'd spoken, the look in those almond eyes, had frozen him to the marrow. He'd always thought Abruzzi's efforts to demonize Honor Alexander-Harrington were ludicrous. His propagandists had picked up on every allegation the People's Republic of Haven had ever made against her—from Basilisk Station on—to portray her as some out-of-control murderess in their bid to undermine the woman's towering reputation.

Now he wasn't so certain they'd been lying, after all. The woman in that com message had *wanted* Haeckle to reject her terms. To fight.

To give her an excuse.

And that's who's just taken out the biggest, most powerful naval base in the entire Solarian League.

Without us so much as scratching her paint.

The thought was terrifying, because at that moment, the woman who'd done that was only fifteen light-minutes from where he and his colleagues sat, and if anything in the galaxy was sure, it was that she'd soon be much closer.

"Well, why isn't he doing something to kick her arse back out of the system?" Abruzzi said, as if he'd been listening to Kolokoltsov's thoughts. "Maybe he couldn't stop the gutless bastard from rolling over for her out at Ganymede, but why the hell is he just sitting on his own arse *now*?"

"Because going after her on her terms would be a frigging disaster."

Kolokoltsov's eyebrows rose in surprise and all eyes turned to Nathan MacArtney as he answered Abruzzi's question. The permanent senior undersecretary of the interior glared at his usual ally and shook his head with an obvious disgust whose strength, Kolokoltsov was privately confident, owed quite a bit to his own sense of panic.

"Why?" Abruzzi shot back, chin jutting aggressively.

"Because she left less than ten percent of her fleet to hold Ganymede." MacArtney's tone was flat. "The other ninety percent—and probably ninety-*nine* percent of her firepower—is parked two light-minutes outside the hyper-limit. That means she can pop into hyper anytime she wants to—like any time she sees him coming at her. All she has to do is sit there, wait for him to head her direction, and then rip his arse off with those fucking long-range missiles of hers. And he can't even *touch* her, because she can translate out before anything he fires at her gets there."

Abruzzi glared at him, fists clenched on the tabletop, but there really wasn't much he could say in response. And MacArtney hadn't even added that at her current range, Harrington was four light-minutes closer to Old Earth than she'd been to Ganymede when she fired on it. If she chose to unleash those "fucking long-range missiles" on the inner system, there was nothing she couldn't destroy without ever crossing the limit. The only thing that could possibly stay her hand was the possibility of mega casualties among the Sol System's civilians, and remembering the ice in those brown eyes...

Kolokoltsov's own eyes strayed to the time display. Twelve hours. Naval Station Ganymede had surrendered *twelve hours* ago, and she had yet to say a single word to anyone on Old Earth. The long, drawn out wait clawed at his nerves, exactly as she undoubtedly meant for it to, and it was obvious she was in no hurry to break her silence.

He didn't expect to like it when she finally did.

HMS *Imperator*
Sol System

THE TIMER ON HER uni-link pinged and Honor Alexander-Harrington closed the book she'd been pretending to read. She glanced automatically at the bulkhead chrono, then inhaled and ran one gentle hand down the spine of the treecat huddled in her lap.

Nimitz looked up at her, then rose on his true-feet to wrap his arms around her neck and press his muzzle against the live nerves of her right cheek. He stayed that way for a long, still moment, clinging to her physically almost as tightly as they clung to one another's mindglows, and she closed her eyes as she hugged him back.

Then she stood, climbing out of the comfortable couch, and lifted him, swinging him around to his proper place upon her shoulder.

It was time, she thought. Grand Fleet had been in the Sol System for exactly thirty-six hours, and it was time.

The cabin's smart wall was configured to show the master plot, and her eyes sought out the green icon which represented Naval Station Ganymede's current status as a "friendly unit." Haeckle had honored the terms of his surrender with scrupulous fidelity, and she wished—oh, *how* she wished—he hadn't. The part of her which was still an admiral recognized the enormous prize he'd yielded to her intact. Recognized the stupendous victory she'd accomplished without losing a single man or woman. Knew the intelligence windfall from Ganymede, alone, would have made this operation utterly decisive even if she'd accomplished nothing else.

The admiral in her recognized that. The angel of death only resented it.

She closed her eyes, fighting to balance those two conflicting imperatives. Fighting to remember she wasn't here for herself, or for Nimitz, but for her star nation. For the entire Grand Alliance.

And for Beowulf, the killer corner of her soul whispered. *For Beowulf.*

She looked across the cabin at her wedding picture once again. She walked across to it, reached out and laid a hand upon it. She stood there, lips quivering, then leaned her forehead against it as a single tear leaked down her cheek.

I'm sorry, she thought. *I'm sorry I wasn't there to keep you alive, Hamish. Or you, Samantha. And I'm so sorry I killed you telling you about it, Emily.* Another tear crept down her cheek and she tasted its salt upon her lips. *I'm sorry Nimitz and I will never see or hold or touch any of you ever again. I hope wherever you are you can forgive us for that. And I'm sorry I can't even kill the people who killed you. God help me, I want the Sollies to give me a reason, give me an* excuse, *to punish someone—anyone—for it, and if they do—*

She chopped that thought off. Made herself inhale deeply. Felt the sick hunger guttering along her nerves. If they gave her an excuse, she would take it. She would *take* it and the killer in her soul would drown itself in the fiery elixir of their blood and her vengeance. She knew that. And even in her present state, she knew it was the one thing she must *not* do. But some things were simply more—

She shook herself, leaned harder against the picture.

Even if they give me a reason, she thought drearily, *it won't be the ones who really killed you. They've taken even that away from us, because I'll be killing the wrong people.*

She straightened and caressed their faces—all *three* of those faces— and her own face hardened.

But if they didn't plant those bombs, they damned well created the circumstances that let someone else *do it, and there's a price for that. Oh, yes. There's a* price, *and if they give me an excuse to make that point crystal clear to them I will by God do it. Because one thing I promise all of you: I will collect every penny of that price if I have to burn this star system to the* ground.

She stood a moment longer, looking at the faces of her murdered love, tasting the bitter iron of that promise. Then she drew a deep, deep breath and turned away.

The cabin hatch opened at her approach and Major Hawke came to attention as she stepped out into the passage. He'd known Tobias Stimson for a long time, personally selected him as Hamish's armsman, and that made it personal for him, too, on so *many* levels. She tasted the same murderous determination radiating from him, knew there was no question what *he* wanted to happen next, and she nodded to him.

"Let's be about it, Spencer," she said.

Central Command Center
Admiralty Building
City of Old Chicago
Old Earth
Sol System

WINSTON KINGSFORD ARRIVED IN the dimness of Central Command less than five minutes after his office com pinged. Three of those minutes had been spent in the lift shafts, and he'd paused outside the CCC's entrance to catch his breath. No one needed him arriving obviously out of breath.

Wouldn't do to look like I was panicking, *now would it?*

"Willis," he said as Admiral Jennings turned at his approach to face him.

"Sir," Jennings acknowledged.

"So she's begun to move, has she?"

"Yes, Sir." The chief of staff waved at the enormous holo display. "She's taking her time about it, too."

Kingsford looked at the display and nodded.

Harrington's enormous wall of battle was headed directly towards the hyper-limit at its closest approach to Old Earth. And, as Jennings had said, she was advancing at a leisurely three hundred gravities. At that rate, it would take over an hour and a half for her to actually cross it, assuming that was what she intended to do, and he felt confident that slow, deliberate approach was yet another silent message.

She wants *us to see her coming. To know she doesn't* care *if* we see *her coming.*

Every surviving warship in the Sol System had been gathered in Earth orbit. He had over two hundred superdreadnoughts, backed by four hundred battlecruisers and the next best thing to a million pods of improved Cataphracts, and his sensor platforms had kept her under a microscope, twenty-four hours a day, waiting for exactly this moment. He had enough firepower to shatter planets, been given as much warning—as much time to prepare for an attack—as any system commander in history.

And he knew she'd given him that time *on purpose.*

HMS *Imperator*
Sol System

HONOR WATCHED HER PLOT as her massive formation decelerated once again to rest relative to Old Earth and shoals of LACs erupted from her carriers to form up about her wall of battle. She was exactly one light-second inside the hyper-limit, 231,559,727 kilometers from the planet of humanity's birth, and her eyes were as bleak as her soul.

"In position, Ma'am," Andrea Jaruwalski said.

"Thank you, Andrea."

Honor nodded, then turned her head, looked at Lieutenant Commander Brantley.

"Put me through, Harper."

Central Command Center
Admiralty Building
City of Old Chicago
Old Earth
Sol System

"INCOMING TRANSMISSION, SIR," COMMANDER Pamela Furman, the com officer of the watch announced, and Kingsford turned to face her.

It was almost a relief to look away from the master plot. No, that wasn't accurate. It wasn't *almost* a relief to look away from that horde of crimson icons. Harrington remained outside his Cataphracts' powered envelope, and he wondered how many of the light codes spreading out about her superdreadnoughts represented missile pods and how many of them were the infernally powerful LACs ONI had finally gotten around to reporting to him.

"I assume it's Admiral Harrington?" he said, and Furman nodded.

"Yes, Sir. It is."

"Then I suppose you'd better put her on the main display," he said.

He felt Jennings stir beside him, and gave the chief of staff an ironic smile. Jennings might have a point. Perhaps this was the sort of message he ought to be taking in private, but he doubted it would make much difference in the end.

"Yes, Sir," Furman said, but she also paused, and he frowned.

"Is there a problem, Commander?" he asked, a bit coldly, and she inhaled.

"Sir, Admiral Harrington's contacting you through a com relay less than forty thousand kilometers out. It's actually in a geosynchronous orbit above the Atlantic."

Kingsford stiffened. *Geosynchronous* orbit?

"Should I assume we didn't know it was there?"

"No, Sir. We didn't." Furman's expression was as unhappy as any Kingsford had ever seen, but she met his eyes levelly.

"I see."

Kingsford glanced at Jennings again, and the chief of staff's expression was even less happy than Furman's. And little wonder, the CNO

735

thought. The fresh proof of the Manties' remote platforms' ability to penetrate their sensors at will was chilling. But perhaps he should be *grateful* to Harrington for making that point yet again. Anything that inspired sanity and...restraint on his part was probably a good thing.

"Go ahead and put her through, Commander," he said levelly.

"Yes, Sir."

Kingsford tucked his hands behind him and turned back to the main communications display as it came alive and a face he knew from hundreds of megabytes of intelligence analyses looked out of it.

"Good afternoon, Admiral Harrington," he said.

"Good afternoon, Admiral Kingsford," she replied twelve seconds later. He wasn't really surprised. In fact, he'd expected it. Which made the demonstration of the Manties' FTL bandwidth no less galling to someone whose faster-than-light data transmission was still at least a full T-year from anything more advanced than the dots and dashes of old-fashioned Morse code.

"I've been rather expecting to hear from you," he said now.

"I imagine you have." Her smile was cold, and so thin he could have shaved with it. "And since you have, I'll get straight to the point. You have ninety-six hours to stand down your fleet, scuttle every warship in the star system, blow your missile pods in orbit, and evacuate your deep-space infrastructure. *All* your deep-space infrastructure."

Someone behind Kingsford inhaled sharply, and he felt his own expression tighten, but Harrington's frozen eyes never even flickered.

"And at the end of those ninety-six hours?" he heard himself ask.

"I think you know the answer to that question." Her soprano was hard as battle steel. "You set the ground rules with Operation Buccaneer and Parthian Shot. The Grand Alliance is prepared to assume that since no one in the Solarian League has denounced Admiral Hajdu Győző or Admiral Gogunov's actions at Hypatia, the League is equally prepared to receive the same treatment. Except for the minor difference that I'm giving you long enough you really *can* save your civilians' lives."

"And after we abandon our responsibility to protect Solarian lives and property?"

"Why, at that point, I destroy it," she said, as if it were the most reasonable thing in the world. "Unlike your actions at Cachalot and some other star systems I could mention"—for an instant, that icy control slipped and her eyes flashed with pure, murderous fire—"I'll leave your orbital habitats, even the ones with some industrial capacity—not the ones which are *primarily* industrial, of course—intact. I'll even leave old Earth's and Mars' orbital power collectors intact...which is more than you did in Buccaneer. But the rest of it goes, Admiral Kingsford. Every bit of it."

Her eyes bored into him, and his hands fisted behind his back.

"You're not serious," he said.

"Oh, on the contrary, I'm *deadly* serious," she replied, and her voice had turned soft, almost caressing. "And if you're unwilling to destroy your warships yourself, I'll take care of *that* for you, too. You can just leave them where they are, and I'll take them out from here. Or you can come out to meet me. Unlike the Solarian League, the Grand Alliance has no interest in massacring millions of civilians. But you and your ships, Admiral Kingsford—the *gallant* personnel of the Solarian League Navy—are another matter entirely. So *please* leave orbit and come out to meet me. There's nothing you could do that would make my people happier."

Her eyes bored into him, daring him—*begging* him—to take up her challenge. To take his ships out where she could kill every one of them without endangering a single civilian life. He saw that challenge, understood it perfectly... and something shriveled inside him. Twenty brittle seconds stretched out. Then her nostrils flared, with what might have been contempt or might have been disappointment, when she recognized his refusal to take up that iron gauge.

"I allowed Admiral Haeckle to use his available warships to evacuate his people," that soprano sword said then, "and I'm prepared to allow you to do the same... as long as every one of them is destroyed within ninety-six hours. Is that understood, Admiral Kingsford, or do I need to go over it again?"

Rage wrestled with fear deep within him, but he made himself stand very still. He drew a deep breath, faced the com display.

"I believe I understood you the first time, *Admiral*," he said coldly.

"In that case, I'll be in touch again ninety-six hours from now. Unless, of course, you haven't complied with my requirements and destroyed your fleet within that window. In that case, Admiral Kingsford, you won't *hear* a single thing from me."

That final, liquid-helium promise went through him like a dagger. And then, before he could even think about a response, the display went blank.

He stood very still, looking at the huge featureless screen, then turned his head to look at Commander Furman.

"Contact Permanent Senior Undersecretary Kolokoltsov," he told her. "I'll be in my briefing room. As soon as you reach him, put him through to my com there."

George Benton Tower
City of Old Chicago
Old Earth
Sol System

"WHAT DO YOU MEAN you won't go out and fight?" Malachai Abruzzi barked.

He sat with the rest of the Mandarins in Innokentiy Kolokoltsov's secure communications room, glaring at Winston Kingsford's face on the main display. Kolokoltsov had delayed accepting Kingsford's communications request until the others could join him. It hadn't taken very long, since none of them had ventured far from their George Benton offices in the day and a half since Harrington had arrived. He'd wanted to avoid anyone's thinking he'd cut some sort of private understanding with Kingsford. And, he admitted, he'd wanted to spread the responsibility for any decision he made as broadly as possible.

He was coming to the conclusion—rapidly—that that had been a mistake.

"I mean there are over one-point-three million men and women on my ships-of-the-wall, alone, Mister Permanent Senior Undersecretary, and that I have no intention of seeing them butchered for absolutely nothing," Kingsford said now, his flat voice a cold and level contrast to Abruzzi's quivering fury.

"Then why the hell do we even *have* a Navy?" Abruzzi spat.

"Why, you have a Navy to do all those dirty little jobs you need done in the Protectorates." Nathan MacArtney's face went as dark and congested, as outraged, as Abruzzi's, but Kingsford wasn't done. "You have a Navy you and your colleagues sent into a war it can't win. You even have a Navy you can order to completely destroy the economies of completely neutral star nations. But you *don't* have a Navy so I can murder the men and women under my command because you don't have a frigging clue what *else* to do. Does that answer your question, Mister Permanent Senior Undersecretary?"

"Then we'll fucking remove you from command and put someone with some *guts* into it!" Abruzzi snarled. "And then we'll put *you* in

738

front of a frigging court-martial and shoot your sorry arse for cowardice in the face of the enemy!"

"That's your option," Kingsford said. "And if that's what you want to do, you go right ahead. But you're not going to find another admiral who will do what you want. The Navy's done dying just because the lot of you have been too damned stupid and too damned *arrogant* to listen to the people who have been trying to get you to stop this goddamned war you started—*you*, not *them*—since before it even began!"

They stared at him—all of them—in shock, and he looked back with a face like iron. The silence lingered for several seconds.

"I've already begun the evacuations," he told them then. "And while I was waiting for you to get around to accepting my com request, I accepted Harrington's offer to use the Navy to get everyone out... and promised to destroy every one of my ships within her time limit."

He shrugged ever so slightly while they gaped at him.

"The first evacuees should be arriving dirtside within a half hour or so, and another thing I did while waiting for you to get around to answering me was to contact the Gendarmerie. Their people will assist my Marines in organizing the traffic flow and keeping it moving. I suggest you and the local civilian authorities organize transportation to move the evacuees to other destinations before the spaceports turn into total chaos. As for me, right now, overseeing that evacuation is rather more important than continuing this conversation. Good day, ladies and gentlemen."

The display went blank.

The Mandarins sat staring at one another in silence.

HMS *Imperator*
Sol System

IT WAS ALMOST TIME.

Honor sat quietly in her observation dome on *Imperator*'s spine, watching the time display in the corner of her artificial eye's field of vision tick steadily downward.

Winston Kingsford had complied with her demands. *All* of them. Quite a few of the civilians evacuated from the deep-space infrastructure of the most heavily industrialized star system in the galaxy had found temporary homes aboard the orbital habitats. No doubt they were straining the reserve life-support capacity, but that was fine. One thing habitats had was plenty of redundant life-support. And the fact that Kingsford had used those habitats as emergency staging points said quite a lot about whether or not he trusted her to keep her word.

Of course, it also said he hadn't had much choice about it. Not given the millions upon millions of people he had to move. In fact, she'd granted a twelve-hour extension.

She should have felt elated, victorious; what she actually felt was dead inside. She sat there with the ghosts of her dead, felt them there, knew they were glad she hadn't given in to the darkness. She *knew* that...and she still felt dead, empty...drained.

She wondered if she would feel that way for the rest of her life.

She would complete her mission, do her job, despite that inner deadness, because it *was* her job. Her mission. All she had left. But what would she do afterward? How could she find the strength to heal, to be the mother Raoul and Katherine needed? How would Nimitz find the strength to go on without Samantha? And how could she go on if she lost him, too, to his grief?

The two of them sat there, with Nimitz in her lap, her hands moving slowly and steadily, automatically, on his silken coat while he buried his muzzle against her. She could feel him willing himself towards dissolution, on one hand, even as he clung to her on the other. He was balanced on a knife-edge, waiting—like her—to complete their final mission. But what about after that? She was afraid—so afraid—he would choose to die and leave her even more alone. The thought terrified what was left of her soul, yet she loved him too much to fight his decision, because unlike any other human, she *knew* how deep his pain was. How wounded he'd been.

And because part of her wanted to do exactly the same thing.

And she might. That was what truly ground her soul to dust. She might choose to die herself, even knowing how that would add to her parents' pain, abandon Raoul and Katherine. After all, Allison and Alfred would have the children, and the children would have them. Why shouldn't she lay down the hateful burden her own life had become?

She'd given the orders. Grand Fleet would begin Operation Nemesis in two hours. Nuclear charges—multiple charges, in many cases—had been planted on every major platform outside Mars orbit, and most of Kingsford's ships had already been blown up. Two dozen super-dreadnoughts still plied back and forth between Mars orbit's industrial platforms and the surfaces of Mars and Old Earth, but they would complete their missions and scuttle within the next ninety minutes or so.

Even as she sat here, additional charges were being planted on the inner-system platforms which had been evacuated. Shoals of LACs had been deployed to deal with any dangerous piece of de-orbiting wreck-age. Others had been deployed to take care of platforms which *weren't* being fitted with charges. According to Andrea Jaruwalski's ops plan, everything would be ready within the next thirty minutes. And then, one hour and thirty minutes after that, Honor would order the simultaneous, synchronized demolition of the entire system's industrial infrastructure. She would order the greatest single act of destruction in human history, turn the entire star system of humanity's birth into a funeral pyre for Hamish and Emily. For Samantha. For her Uncle Jacques. And for Pat Givens, Michael Mayhew, Judah Yanakov, Lucien Cortez... all her dead.

And it wouldn't bring a single one of them back to life.

Nimitz pressed harder against her as the tears flowed down her cheeks at last. She felt him fighting to reach beyond his own bleak despair, trying to be there for her, and the greatest military triumph in human history was ashes in her mouth as they faced the dark void of their future. It was—

The com pinged.

She twitched, jerked up out of her thoughts, and it pinged again. Her mouth tightened into a thin, furious line and she reached out, stabbed the acceptance key viciously.

"What?" she snapped.

"I know you left orders not to disturb you, Your Grace," Mercedes Brigham said. "But I'm afraid there's been... a status change."

"Is it Kingsford? Is he trying to ask for more time?" Honor's voice was tight and harsh with anger. "Because, if it is—"

"No, Your Grace," Brigham interrupted. "It's not from the Sollies. The *Duke of Cromarty* just made her alpha translation about a light-minute out from the limit."

A fresh spasm of pain went through Honor as she remembered teasing Hamish about using the *Duke* for transportation to Beowulf. But even more than the pain, she wondered what could possibly have brought *Duke of Cromarty* here. What was Queen Elizabeth's personal yacht doing in the heart of the Sol System, when her skipper couldn't have known before he arrived what he'd find waiting when he did?

Of course, the *Duke* wasn't like most "yachts," was she? She was an *Agamemnon*-class BC(P), fitted with Keyhole-Two and cutting-edge defensive and electronic warfare systems. For all intents and purposes, the Navy had taken a front-line battlecruiser, turned a quarter of its magazine space into luxurious accommodations for the Empress and up to a hundred and fifty or so guests, provided it with a picked crew of combat veterans, and *called* it a "yacht."

But for all the potency of her armament, she wasn't really a warship, so what was she doing here *now*, of all times?

She looked back out at the stars, and debated telling Mercedes to handle whatever it was that *Duke of Cromarty* thought was so desperately important. But she couldn't.

"A light-minute out?" she repeated.

"Yes, Your Grace. But it was a crash translation; she's still carrying a velocity of over sixteen thousand KPS."

Honor winced. For *Duke of Cromarty* to reenter n-space with that much velocity she must have hit her downward alpha translation at maximum velocity. Honor had done the same thing herself, upon occasion, and so she knew what that must have done to the stomachs of every man and woman aboard her.

"Captain Firestine hit it almost perfectly," Brigham continued. "She's decelerating straight for us at five and a half kilometers per second. She'll rendezvous with us in just over fifty-one minutes, and Captain Firestine requests permission to come aboard with urgent dispatches as soon as she does."

Honor frowned. Firestine wanted to *hand-deliver* a dispatch? Why? It made no sense. Then again, nothing else made sense, did it? And—she checked the time again—Firestine would reach *Imperator* fifty-seven minutes before she had to execute Nemesis. No doubt she could deal with whatever brought him here before the deadline. And perhaps she could use the diversion. Maybe it was even a good thing.

Unless Firestine's "dispatch" had been sent because Elizabeth and Willie had changed their minds.

Her mouth tightened dangerously as she considered that possibility. But then she shrugged again. It was unlikely Elizabeth Winton, of all people, could have changed her mind. And if she had—

Cross that bridge when you get to it, she told herself.

"All right, Mercedes," she finally sighed. "Please meet Captain Firestine when he comes aboard. Escort him to my observation done." She smiled wanly. "Tell him I apologize for not meeting him personally."

"Of course, Your Grace. I'm sure he'll understand."

"In that case, I'll see you—both of you—then," Honor said.

She killed the connection, gathered Nimitz back into her arms, and sat gazing out at the stars once more.

✧   ✧   ✧

The admittance signal chimed, and Honor stood, Nimitz cradled in her arms, and turned to face the hatch as she waited for Spencer Hawke to escort her visitor in. But when the hatch opened, it wasn't Hawke who stepped through it, and she froze.

He was as tall as she was, although he leaned heavily on a cane at the moment. His right leg seemed thick and swollen under his uniform trousers. Because it was in a cast or a splint, a corner of her brain realized. His hair was dark, dramatically silver at the temples, and his face was lined with fatigue, pain, worry, and grief. His eyes were bluer than a Sphinx sky, a treecat rode his shoulder . . . and he couldn't be there.

He *couldn't.*

She stared at him, heart thundering, unable to speak—unable to *breathe.* Not a muscle moved, but then her mouth quivered suddenly, and Nimitz reared upright in her arms, green eyes blazing, his mind-glow a forest fire as he, too, tasted their mind-glows. Tasted the fire neither of them had ever expected to taste again, drawing them up, up, out of the dark valley where the two of them had been so cold and alone so long. So focused on one another that they'd never even sensed it coming down the passage towards them.

"Honor," the newcomer said softly, *so* softly.

She tried to reply. She *tried,* and she couldn't. She just . . . couldn't.

The silence stretched out as he stood there, braced on the cane, staring at her. And then—

She never remembered moving, but suddenly she was in his arms, her vision spangled by tears, her face buried against the side of his neck, feeling the firmness of him, tasting the glory of the mind-glow she'd known she would never taste again, and the wonder, and the disbelief, and the sheer, searing *joy* of it smashed over her like the sea.

✧   ✧   ✧

"But...but *how?*" she asked a lifetime later.

They sat on one of the observation dome's couches, arms still about one another. Nimitz and Samantha were curled so tightly together across their laps that it was impossible to know where one 'cat began and the other one ended. But perhaps that was actually the point, because there *wasn't* a spot where one of them began and the other one ended... any more than there was a spot where Hamish began and *she* ended.

"We were lucky," he said softly. "We never actually made it to the conference. When the Sollies turned up, traffic control diverted us to the nearest docking point, way the hell and gone out in the boonies. Jacques figured it would take us forty-five minutes or an hour just to get to the hub, but then we hit a freight shaft that was down. So we were stuck in a supervisor's module on one of the industrial booms."

His eyes darkened in memory...and with the awareness of what would have happened if that freight shaft *hadn't* gone down.

"We had some warning after Gamma blew," he continued. "Fortunately, Tobias was even more paranoid than I was, and Jacques was a lot more familiar than me with Beowulfan platform design and SOP. Tobias found the emergency suit locker even before Beta went up—the damned thing wasn't properly marked and he had to smash open half a dozen before he found the right one—and they were gumbies."

Honored nodded against his shoulder. No one knew where the term "gumby suit" had come from, but it had been applied since pre-diaspora times to the loosely fitting emergency vacsuits designed to accommodate the broadest possible range of human shapes and sizes. They were uncomfortable, and it was far harder to move in a gumby than in a skinsuit, but they weren't designed to be comfortable. They were designed to keep someone alive, at least long enough for someone to rescue her. But—

"They were loose enough we could fit Sam and BCB inside with us—especially Jacques and BCB. The two of them had a *lot* of room." Hamish twitched a brief smile. "It wasn't comfortable, especially for the 'cats, but it worked, and all three of us two-legs managed to suit up before the big one."

His smile vanished and his blue eyes went dark and haunted.

"We knew what it was, of course. According to Captain Neitz, whose people pulled us out, we were less than five hundred meters beyond the total destruction zone. The truth is, we shouldn't have made it, Honor. We really shouldn't have."

Her arms tightened fiercely, and he made himself smile as he hugged her back.

"A gumby only has about twelve hours of endurance," he said, "and all of us got banged up pretty badly by the concussion. Jacques and BCB got hurt worse than Tobias or Sam and me, but I came out of it with a broken leg. You don't want to know about the bruises on my back, either, but at least I took the impact with the bulkhead there, which protected Sam.

"We were all out for a while. I came to first, which was probably a good thing. Jacques's suit had micro tears in three places, and it took Tobias and me a while to find the repair kit and seal them. By then, he'd lost half his air, but he'd also come round, and he was the one who steered us to the access point for the liquid oxygen storage system."

He paused and shook his head, then actually smiled crookedly.

"We umbilicaled to the LOX and the emergency power reserve. That gave us plenty of oxygen and enough juice to keep the suits up, but we wouldn't have made it anyway, without Neitz and CPO Lochen. And it was even worse for the 'cats, in a lot of ways. They didn't have helmets or any way to see a damned thing, and by the time all four of us had been suited up for six damned days, things got pretty...fragrant. Gumbies aren't set up for recycling the way skinsuits are, so waste disposal was a problem and all of us were badly dehydrated by the time they finally found us. Jacques's gumby was out of painkillers by then, too, so it was probably a good thing he was only semiconscious. They've got him in a hospital in Columbia right now and BCB's with him. Both of them will be there for a while, Honor, but they made it. They're going to be fine, and Tobias is out in the passage with Spencer right this minute.

"In the meantime, I...really wanted to see you as soon as I could, so I grabbed the *Duke* and headed after you."

You mean you wanted to catch me, let me know you were alive, before I committed my very own Eridani violation, she thought, tasting his mind-glow, knowing how well he knew her. *That's what you were afraid of. And you were right, love. So* right! *But if you'd known the rest, If you knew what I've already done...*

"I'm glad you did," she half-whispered. "So glad. But, Hamish, Emily—"

"Shhhhh." He held her close. "I know. They told me."

"But what they didn't tell you," she said drearily, "is that I killed her. I killed her, Hamish. I went to tell her you were gone, and I *killed* her. She died in my arms, and I'm the reason she did."

The tears broke loose as she admitted it. As she said the words to someone else. She felt the sudden, instant rejection in his mind-glow, but he didn't know. He hadn't been there. He hadn't seen it happen. He—

"That's enough of that!" he snapped so suddenly, his voice so hard, she tried to jerk away from him. But he wouldn't let her do that. He held her, and she slumped back, hiding her face against his shoulder.

"Honor," he said far more softly, and she heard the pain in his voice, tasted its reality in his emotions, "you didn't kill her. She was already dying. I knew that. She knew that. She just...she just hadn't wanted to tell you."

She stiffened, and he stroked her hair.

"Honor—love—Emily was on borrowed time from the day of that air car crash. We always knew that. Without her life-support chair, she would've—"

His voice broke and he had to stop, inhale deeply.

"We always knew it could happen any time," he said finally. "We always knew. And then there was you. Sweetheart, you never knew her before. I don't think you could have any possible idea, even with that empathic sense of yours, what a difference you truly made over the last couple of years. You brought her so much joy, and Raoul, and you and your mother brought her *Katherine*. You know how much she loved the kids. You know that better than anyone else in the universe, and without you we—*she*—would never have had them. Without you—"

His voice broke again. Then he drew another of those deep, shuddery breaths.

"You went to tell her yourself, before she heard it from anyone else, and that's exactly what I would have expected you to do. To be there for her instead of letting her hear it over a newscast, see it on one of the boards. To be there *with* her when she found out. I wasn't there, but I didn't have to be because *you* were. You say she died in your arms? Then you gave her the greatest gift of all, and I know it hurt, and I know it will *always* hurt, but I envy you because you *were* there when she needed you most, and I can never thank you enough for me, not just for her. So don't you *ever* tell me you killed her! Whoever planted those bombs killed her, just as surely as they killed Tom Caparelli, Pat, Francine and Tony, and Michael Mayhew and all the others."

She trembled, still unable—or perhaps unwilling—to relinquish her guilt, yet deep inside, she knew he was right. She *had* been there, and she remembered the incredible power, the final splendor, of Emily's mind-glow. And as she remembered, she admitted to herself at last that the pain in that mind-glow had been grief—Emily's awareness that she was leaving Honor alone—not fear of death.

Never fear. Not in that dauntless, blazing mind-glow of the woman she'd loved.

And even as she thought that, she realized Hamish was right about who'd really killed her.

"Maybe you're right," she said, withdrawing from his embrace, rising to her feet while Nimitz and Samantha moved to Hamish's lap. She looked down at the three people she loved most in all the universe and she nodded.

"Maybe you're right," she repeated. "And whether or not you are, we have a message to deliver."

"I know." He met her eyes, and his were almost as cold, almost as focused, as hers as he saw the Salamander looking back at him. "I know," he said. "So I suppose there's only one thing left to say." She arched an eyebrow, and he gave her a treecat's smile.

"Let's be about it, Admiral Harrington," he said softly.

HMS *Imperator*
Sol System

HONOR STOOD ONCE AGAIN on *Imperator*'s flag deck, but it was very different from the last time she'd stood there. Now Hamish stood beside her, Samantha on his shoulder, and she savored the mind-glows of her staff and the flag bridge crew. She tasted the lingering echoes of disbelief, and their bright, transcendent joy. Not for themselves; for her.

Her eyes burned as that tide of emotion washed through her, but in an odd way, it only refined and purified her cold, focused purpose. There was still hate deep inside her—and in the emotions about her. The fact that Hamish and Jacques Benton-Ramirez y Chou, Tobias Stimson, Bark Chewer's Bane and Samantha, had been returned to them could not miraculously restore the millions of other dead to life. Perhaps the intensely personal corrosiveness of her own hatred had been dulled. Perhaps she'd been returned to that point where her duty was duty, not an excuse for mass slaughter. But Operation Nemesis was still there, still waiting, and she was just as grimly determined to complete it as she'd ever been.

The master display had been configured to show a panoramic view of the space around Old Terra. She gazed into it, waiting, feeling the anticipation thrum in her nerves. Only another few minutes, and—

"Coming up on the mark, Your Grace," Andrea Jaruwalski said, and she nodded. Then she glanced over her shoulder at Hamish, and her lips quirked ever so slightly.

"In that case, Andrea," she said, never looking away from her husband, "let's be about it."

He returned her smile and she turned back to the display, and this time her voice came out flat and cold.

"Execute," she said.

"Aye, aye, Your Grace." Jaruwalski's voice was harder than steel. "Executing now."

She pressed the button . . . and the visual display erupted with twice a dozen tiny suns. They raced through old Earth's industrial zone, each of them the death beacon of a major fabrication platform. A sphere of fire blazed about the mother world, filling night skies ever so briefly with a spiteful, devastating dawn. A matching sphere, even denser, blazed around Mars, crowned Venus in flame, and answering pyres glared deep in the asteroid belt, rode Jupiter's orbit, rose like beacons of vengeance throughout the length and breadth and depth of the Sol System. And in other places, where no charges had been planted, LAC grasers shredded scores—hundreds—of minor platforms. The habitats of individual asteroid miners, the bunk room habitats of hydrogen refinery crews, communications arrays, observation platforms, monitoring stations, freight platforms, shipyards, servicing facilities, navigation and traffic control stations...every single artificial structure in the entire Solar System—*two thousand T-years* of building and construction and dreams, everything within a sphere eleven light hours across—vanished in that single, dreadful, perfectly coordinated cataclysm.

Everything except the major orbital habitats and the power satellites.

Honor watched those intolerable pinpricks spall the visual display. She listened to the reports from CIC as the tide of destruction rolled through the birth system of the humanity and knew she had just become the most hated woman in Solarian history.

And she didn't care.

She waited ten minutes by the clock, then nodded to Harper Brantley.

"Put me through," she said and looked back to her com pickup.

"Aye, aye, Your Grace," he said. He punched in a command, then nodded back to her. "Live mike, Your Grace," he told her.

She waited another moment, letting her face, her expression, register on the eyes at the other end of the FTL link and the eight Hermes buoys riding in geosynchronous orbit about Earth and Mars. The buoys whose signals cut simultaneously into the feeds of every major news channel in the entire star system.

"I am Admiral Harrington, of the Royal Manticoran Navy," she told the ten or twelve billion human beings watching her at that moment. "I am speaking to you on behalf of my Empress, the President of the Republic of Haven, the Protector of Grayson, and all of our allied star systems.

"For the last T-year, my Empress and her allies have called upon the corrupt bureaucrats running the Solarian League as their personal fiefdom to stop their unprovoked attacks and aggression against our star nations. We have persistently warned against further escalations of the conflict. We and our friends within the League attempted to be the voice of reason. For their effort, my Empress and her allies were called warmongers, imperialists, *war criminals*, and those within the League who attempted to be the voice of sanity were reviled as traitors and threatened with military action, including an operations plan specifically designed to violate the League's own constitutional prohibition against deliberate mass-casualty events. Indeed, only the gallantry of a single squadron of Manticoran cruisers who sacrificed themselves engaging two hundred Solarian battlecruisers prevented the Solarian League Navy from murdering six million civilians in the Hypatia System, alone. Ninety percent of that cruiser squadron's personnel paid with their lives to prevent that act of mass murder.

"During the past year, the Solarian League Navy has suffered literally millions of casualties against our Allied navies. In that time, the SLN has not won a single major engagement. Admiral Crandall's fleet was annihilated or captured to the last ship in the Talbott Quadrant. Admiral Filareta's fleet suffered the same fate in Manticore itself. Naval Station Ganymede, right here in the Sol System, was surrendered without inflicting a single casualty on the forces under my command. Every mobile unit of the SLN, every fleet base, every maintenance platform, every tanker in the Sol System has been destroyed or is occupied by my personnel. And I have just completed the destruction of every deep-space industrial facility in the star system. They are *gone*, as if they had never existed."

She paused to let that sink in, then smiled thinly and coldly.

"I realize many of you believe our allegations about the existence of the 'Mesan Alignment' are either a fabrication to justify our own criminal, imperialist expansion or else the product of the deranged paranoia only to be expected from people who support the abolitionist movement. From people who believe there is actually something evil and depraved in manufacturing human beings as property and then trading and selling them. I know that. My Empress and her allies know that. But we really don't care whether or not you believe us. Not anymore. Except in one way.

"Your corrupt rulers, the Mandarins, have aided and enabled the Alignment from the beginning. Perhaps that wasn't their intention. Perhaps they genuinely didn't believe what we told them. But whether it was their intention or not, the consequence is the same. And whether it was their intention or not, their actions remain equally vile and contemptible, a rank violation of interstellar law and solemn interstellar conventions the Solarian League itself sponsored and guaranteed over the centuries. They dispatched fleets—not squadrons, not taskforces, but *fleets*, containing hundreds of superdreadnoughts—to attack our star systems and our people without even seeking a formal declaration of war. Without provocation. When every shot that *we* had fired was in self-defense.

"The Yawata Strike, carried out—we believe—by the Alignment, killed eight million people, including the total population of the city of Yawata, where ninety percent of my own family lived. The SLN was prepared to murder six million more in Hypatia. And two weeks ago, the SLN attacked Beowulf—the oldest extrasolar colony in the galaxy, the star system which led the fight to save *this* star system's population from extinction after old Earth's Final War, the star system which sponsored the Solarian League's Constitution. And in the course of that attack, over *forty-three million* civilian citizens of Beowulf were killed."

She paused once more, and the flag bridge was as still and silent about her as the vacuum beyond *Imperator*'s hull.

"We have tried from the beginning to *minimize* casualties and loss of life," she said then, her voice like hammered copper. "Until today, until I arrived in the Sol System with my fleet, we had not initiated a single conflict with the Solarian League Navy or any of the League's armed forces. We have stood our ground, we have defended our friends and allies, but we have *not* attempted to take the war to the League as we have just conclusively demonstrated we might have done *at any time*.

"The Manticore Binary System was attacked in a blatant Eridani violation, and the Mandarins' only response—the *sole response* of the star nation whose constitution enshrines a specific obligation to *punish* Eridani violations—was to capitalize upon it. Instead of seeking out whoever had committed it, instead of even so much as verbally *condemning* it, they dispatched Admiral Filareta to complete the Star Empire's destruction.

"Since that time, half a dozen neutral star systems have been attacked, their economies totally destroyed, by the Solarian League Navy. Beowulf has suffered millions upon millions of deaths as a consequence of the aggression of the Solarian League. And in all that time, *we* have not killed a *single* civilian in a *single* League system. Even today, we have not killed a single civilian. We have attempted to use diplomacy. We have attempted to use economic pressure. We have done everything we possibly could to bring this conflict to an end without mass destruction, without mass murders. And our reward has been to have *our* civilians, our *families*, murdered in their millions instead.

"This ends today."

Her eyes glittered, Nimitz rose high and proud on her shoulder, baring his fangs, and her nostrils flared.

"These are the demands of the Grand Alliance, the conditions upon which this travesty will end.

"First, the unelected bureaucrats who created and drove this conflict will be arrested by the League and surrendered to us to be tried for crimes against humanity on a scale the galaxy has not seen in over a thousand years.

"Second, every unit of the Solarian League Navy outside a member system of the Solarian League will be withdrawn immediately. Any unit of the SLN found outside a member system of the League within one month of this moment will be regarded as a piratic vessel, not a legitimate ship of war protected by the Deneb Accords, which the Solarian League Navy has already demonstrated its willingness to ignore. As such, it will be summarily destroyed *and will not be permitted to surrender.*"

She paused a heartbeat for that to sink in.

"Third, the Legislative Assembly of the Solarian League will immediately summon a constitutional convention to meet here, in the Sol System, to write a new constitution for the Solarian League. You will not attempt to repair or amend the abortion which permitted the Mandarins to cause so many millions of deaths. You will write a constitution which places authority—and responsibility—in the hands of elected officials, not unelected bureaucrats governing by fiat and regulation. The Alliance does not care what form that government takes—republic, constitutional monarchy, or any other form is perfectly acceptable to us, so long as it precludes the resurgence of the corrupt, venal, *unaccountable* oligarchy which plunged the galaxy into this bloodbath.

"Fourth, that constitution will guarantee the right of any present member of the Solarian League to leave the League. It will dissolve the Protectorates. It will return ownership of all property of any sort whatsoever it *or any private Solarian entity* may control in any star system of the Protectorates to the government and citizens of that star system. It will disband the Office of Frontier Security. And it will create a process and an established procedure by which any present or *future* member system of the Solarian League may legally secede upon the vote of three quarters or more of its population. And it would be wise of that constitution to take cognizance of the fact that the Alliance will stand sponsor to those secession votes and support their outcomes."

She paused once again and squared her shoulders.

"I have communicated the Alliance's terms and conditions publicly, so that there can be no misunderstanding. So that no one like Malachai Abruzzi can distort them, lie about them. And I also inform you today that the Alliance *will* see to it that those demands and conditions are met.

"We will not put armed forces on Old Earth. We will not invade *any* of the League's member worlds. We will not send our personnel to take the Mandarins into custody. We will not threaten the life of anyone on any League planet.

"We have taken no civilian lives here in the Sol System. We will continue to avoid the infliction of mass casualties. But if these terms are not accepted, if the motion to assemble a constitutional convention has not cleared the Assembly, within one month, I will divide Grand Fleet into four taskforces, and those taskforces will proceed to the next four wealthiest star systems in the Solarian League. When they reach their destinations, they will do to *those* star systems what I have done today to yours. And at the end of another month, if these terms still have not been accepted, they will move to the next four wealthiest star systems. And the *next* four. They will continue doing so until our conditions are accepted... or there are no more industrialized systems in the Solarian League."

She let the threat lie before them, cold and stinking of danger, and then she inhaled deeply.

"Those are the Alliance's terms. The choice to accept or reject them is yours. I advise you to choose wisely.

"Harrington, clear."

George Benton Tower
City of Old Chicago
Sol System
Solarian League

"—AND THE ASSEMBLY WILL never give in!" Nathan MacArtney insisted hotly. "Roll over and play dead for an 'alliance' of neobarbs who just totally destroyed Sol's economy? Who've threatened to treat Navy ships as *pirates* and massacre their personnel? The delegates will *never* agree to that!"

"Nathan's right." Malachai Abruzzi's voice was harsh, his eyes glittering. "We need to fight on. We're closing the technological gap, and they know it. That's the real reason they were desperate enough to try this 'Operation Nemesis' shit! They know damned well that *we* didn't kill all those civilians in Beowulf—if *anyone* killed them; I'm not at all sure they were killed in the first place!—but they're using it as an excuse, and sooner or later, everyone in the League will realize that's all the hell this is. If they're stupid enough to threaten the industrial capacity of every Solarian star system, they'll create so much hatred, so much resentment, public opinion will demand we burn *their* systems to the ground and sow the ruins with salt! We'll turn them into bad memories, and—"

Innokentiy Kolokoltsov tuned them out. He sat at the head of the conference table, and for the first time in his long life, he genuinely had no idea what to do next. Agatá Wodoslawski wasn't present, and he wondered where she was. Perhaps she believed she could find a bolthole somewhere, a way to evade the fate Harrington had decreed for them. A place to hide.

God knew they could all use one.

But there's not one. Not one that's deep *enough, anyway,* he thought. *And especially not since Harrington laid it all out on the public boards that way. There's no one in the entire star system who doesn't know* precisely *what the "Alliance's" conditions are. Or who they blame for all of this.*

Was it remotely possible, he wondered, that the Manties had been right all along about the existence of the "Mesan Alignment" . . . or

754

something *like* the "Alignment," at least? Could it be that they'd actually been telling the truth—as they understood it, at least—in all those diplomatic notes, all those protests he'd so blithely disregarded?

He didn't know the answers to those questions, and if *he* didn't, then how could the man in the street, or even an Assembly delegate, know them?

The answer to *that* question, at least, was childishly simple: they couldn't, and it didn't matter a single, solitary damn.

They couldn't know whether or not the Manties were telling the truth, no. But they *did* know whose heads the Manties had chosen to demand. They did know who the *Manties* blamed.

And they knew who they had to hand over to prevent the Manties and their friends from wrecking the Solarian League from one end to the other.

The only good thing was that Harrington had given them a month. Kolokoltsov knew damned well it wasn't going to take that long for the citizens of the Sol System to decide what they were going to do, but at least they had a little time. Maybe there really was a bolthole they could reach. Maybe—

The conference room door opened abruptly, without warning, and his head snapped up as a Gendarmerie brigadier, accompanied by a Gendarmerie lieutenant colonel and a Marine major walked through it unannounced. He opened his mouth to demand an explanation, then froze as a dozen assault rifle-armed gendarmes and Marines in light body armor followed on their heels.

"What's the meaning of this!" MacArtney's demand was hot, fierce... and frightened.

"My name is Gaddis," the brigadier said flatly. "This is Lieutenant Colonel Okiku and Major Tarkovsky. We're here to place you under arrest."

"*Arrest?*" MacArtney surged to his feet, pounding both fists on the conference table, his face dark with fury. "We'll have you court-martialed! We'll have you *shot* for mutiny! You have no *authority*, no—!"

"We have all the authority we need," Gaddis's cold tone cut across MacArtney's fiery indignation like a sword. "It comes from Admiral Winston Kingsford and Deputy Attorney General Marie-Claire Rorendaal." MacArtney's mouth snapped shut, and Gaddis's eyes glittered. "Attorney General Rorendaal, on the basis of information and evidence laid before her, has authorized your arrest for conspiracy, treason, and mass murder. Given the...uncertain state of the civilian government and its agencies, she's formally requested that Admiral Kingsford and the Navy oversee that arrest."

It was suddenly very, very quiet in the conference room, and Gaddis's smile was a vibro blade.

"Admiral Kingsford, in turn, deputized me. I'm afraid he couldn't be here himself, much as he would have liked to be, because his pinnace is currently en route to HMS *Imperator* where, on behalf of the Solarian League, he will formally accept the Grand Alliance's terms."

Three men and one woman, who up until that moment had been four of the five most powerful people in the Solarian League, stared at him in stunned silence, too shocked even to think, far less protest. Gaddis looked at them for a moment, then turned to Okiku and Tarkovsky.

"Take them away," he said.

MARCH 1923 POST DIASPORA

King Michael's Tower
Mount Royal Palace
City of Landing
Manticore Binary System
Star Empire of Manticore

"SO IT LOOKS—SO FAR—LIKE things are going about as well as they could," Prime Minister Grantville said. He sipped whiskey and shook his head.

"I can't begin to count all the ways this could still go south on us, and I wish to hell we still had Tony to advise us, but I think Carmichael's settling in as Foreign Secretary. He probably knows the Sollies even better than Tony did, and he's pretty damn confident it's going to hold up."

"Thank God," a very pregnant Allison Harrington said quietly. Prolong extended gestation periods, and it seemed that, like Faith and James, her third daughter would be born on Grayson. Now she sat holding Raoul in her lap, between her daughter and her brother. "I was really, really afraid somebody might be stupid enough to go ahead and fight."

"That kind of stupid deserves to be culled before it reproduces, Alley," Jacques Benton-Ramirez y Chou, the newly named Beowulf Director of Defense, said flatly. "Unfortunately, none of the people who currently feel that way are *quite* stupid enough. They're not going to poke their heads out of hiding as long as my long, tall niece here is waiting to whack them right off."

He smiled at Honor with fierce approval. He was still in a gravity float chair, and would be for at least another three or four weeks. His brother-in-law had a pronounced tendency to keep a close eye on him—which, in fact, Commodore Harrington was doing at that very moment—but he was very much a going concern again, and so was Bark Chewer's Bane. Now the treecat yawned, baring needle-sharp canines in Jacques's lap, but Honor shook her head as she bounced Katherine very gently on her knee.

"I'm done whacking off heads," she said, bending over to plant a kiss on the part of the little girl's hair. Then she turned her head and smiled at Hamish, sitting in the chair beside hers while Nimitz and Samantha stretched across the chair backs, before she looked back at her uncle. "Besides, it sounds like I won't have to."

"No, you won't," Elizabeth Winton told her with a warm smile. "I think you've done just about all of that we're going to need for a while."

Honor nodded, making no effort to conceal her relief.

The Solarian Assembly was furious, and it wasn't making much effort to hide that fury, but it was also honoring the terms Winston Kingsford had accepted in the Solarian League's name. The new Constitutional Convention had been officially seated on the last day of February. Not all of its delegates had arrived yet, and it was still very much at the setting-up stage, but all their intelligence sources suggested that the convention meant business. Despite its resentment of the League's igno-minious defeat, its members seemed to genuinely understand why they were there. More to the point, whether they chose to admit it or not, every single one of them knew the task to which they'd been called was centuries overdue. And with the Mandarins' disastrous example so fresh in their memory, it was unlikely they'd repeat the same mistakes.

Of course, she reflected with the resignation of someone who loved history, *that just means they'll find* other *mistakes to make. They're human beings, and the two things humans make are tools... and mistakes. But sometimes we get stuff* right, *too, and there are some really good models out there if they're only willing to do the research. I guess we'll have to see about that.*

Actually, she reminded herself, the odds were better for the Sollies than for some other constitution-writers, because they had a pretty demanding editor looking over their shoulders. The Grand Alliance had meant it when she told the Solarian public the Allies didn't care what form of government the League adopted, but it had also meant it when she told them that whatever form they adopted, *elected* officeholders would exercise the decision-making power... and be held *accountable* for those decisions. That and the secession provision were nonnegotiable, from the Allies' perspective, and the hundred or so ships-of-the-wall still riding Old Earth orbit were a silent, pointed reminder to that effect.

The situation in the Protectorates promised to be more compli-cated, and probably ugly. In some instances—like Chotěboř, Seraphim, Włocławek, Mobius, and Swallow—the local star systems looked to be adjusting well, with a minimum of bloodshed and civil unrest. In other cases... not so much. There were a *lot* of scores to pay off out there in the Fringe, especially on the planets whose native oligarchs had been deepest in OFS's pocket, and OFS wasn't going out of its way to engineer any soft landings. In fact, some OFS governors and managers were clearly determined to make the entire process as ugly as they possibly could.

And it's our *fault, too,* she admitted unflinchingly. *We knew a lot of this would happen when we issued the demand. But I honestly don't see any other way we could have gone. If we hadn't demanded Frontier Security's total and* immediate *disbandment, something that big, with so many people in other people's pockets, would have hung on, claiming it was "winding down as quickly as possible," for* decades. *Maybe even longer.*

Quite a few Manticoran politicians argued that the Star Empire had a moral responsibility to provide the stability the ex-Protectorates needed. That, as the creator of the power vacuum, the Grand Alliance was the only force capable of filling it. Part of Honor wanted—badly—to endorse that argument. She *was* a historian, and specifically a *military* historian, and she knew how poorly it was going to end in some of those star systems. She didn't want to see that...and, she knew, she wanted to avoid the moral guilt for having allowed it to happen.

But the last thing the galaxy needed was for the Grand Alliance to simply replace Frontier Security. And the last thing the *Grand Alliance* needed was to turn *into* Frontier Security. The Office of Frontier Security had started with the best of intentions, and it had taken a while for it to warp and corrode. But it had happened, and Honor Alexander-Harrington had no desire to see her star nation—either of her star nations—start down that dark and twisty road.

Besides, there's such a thing as independence and maturity. Star nations have to learn to walk, just like anybody else, and they need to learn to stand on their own two feet. We won't do them any favors by "casting a protective wing" over them if it prevents them from learning both those things.

And it wasn't like the Grand Alliance was simply going to walk away. It had no intention of intervening to impose outside solutions, but it was prepared to trade with any star system, support any legitimate government, extend economic support and military aid as trading or treaty partner. And it was prepared to whack any hands that got too greedy and grasping where their neighbors' toys were concerned. No doubt there would be an upsurge in piracy and warlordism, but the Royal Manticoran Navy had cut its eyeteeth in the Silesian Confederacy. Any newly independent star systems who were inclined to emulate their erstwhile OFS masters would discover the RMN and its allies had a short way with freebooters and would-be conquistadors. Speaking of which—

"I had a letter from Tom yesterday," she said, looking at Elizabeth, who leaned back on an old, worn, sinfully comfortable couch beside Prince Consort Justin while Ariel and Monroe drowsed with the blissful limpness of treecats stuffed with far too much celery.

"Did you?" Elizabeth asked tranquilly.

"Yes. He said something about 'making the Alliance permanent.'"

She regarded her monarch thoughtfully. "It wouldn't happen you—and, of course, my esteemed brother-in-law," she added, looking pointedly at Grantville "—know what he was talking about, would it?"

Elizabeth glanced at Grantville. The prime minister looked back at her for a moment, then shrugged, and the empress returned her gaze to Honor.

"Actually, it would happen I do. I just wasn't planning on discussing it with *you* yet. Not until you come back from Grayson, anyway."

"Oh?" Honor raised an eyebrow, looking rather more intently at her monarch, and her tone might have held just the slightest edge of suspicion.

"It's fairly straightforward, really," Elizabeth said. "The problem Eloise and I see is how long the *People's* Republic of Haven and the Star Kingdom of Manticore spent being enemies. I think we're probably past the worst of that, but old memories die hard—especially in a civilization that has prolong—and even those who don't actively cherish old animosities don't have a very deep reservoir of what you might call warm and fuzzy memories. Once upon a time the Star Kingdom and the Republic had just that, but that was before the Legislaturalists. We've got some new ones we can build on, but there's a genuine danger zone between where we are now and where we need to be. The fact that a lot of people see the way we cleaned the Solarian League's clock as proof that we're the new-model 'invincible star nation' isn't calculated to help me and Eloise sleep soundly at night, either." She grimaced. "You and Hamish are the historians, but I've read a little history myself. If there's anything in the universe more dangerous than complacency, I don't have a clue what it might be."

"There *isn't* anything—outside political or religious fanaticism, anyway," Honor said glumly, hugging Katherine against her chest and resting her chin lightly on the crown of her daughter's head.

"And it's not made any better by the fact that you brought home everything in the Solarian League Navy's databanks." Elizabeth sighed. "Everybody knows you got it, too, so the complacency brigade is sitting around in a blissful haze contemplating the fact that we know exactly what the League was up to and, therefore, what it's capable of."

"They do remember Operation Thunderbolt, don't they, Your Majesty?" Alfred Harrington asked. "I seem to remember that the despised Peeps managed to overcome a fairly severe technological deficit."

"Honestly, Commodore Harrington, how could you even imagine I'd be so crass and crude as to point that out to them?"

The irony in Elizabeth's tone could have turned Jason Bay into a desert, and Alfred shook his head with a snort of disgust.

"Fortunately, what Her Majesty is calling the 'complacency brigade' is a distinct minority at the moment," Grantville said. "And the same is true—at the moment—for the people who don't see any reason the Republic and the Star Empire need to stay focused and on the same page. What Her Majesty and President Pritchart have been discussing is how we might go about keeping things that way."

"And you've come up with...?" Honor raised both eyebrows at him, and he nodded in Elizabeth's direction, obviously returning the thread to her.

"We're not worried at all as long as Eloise is in office," Elizabeth said. "She and I understand each other, and we intend to stay in very close touch—and Benjamin Mayhew intends to stay in the mix, as well as Oravil Barregos. Unfortunately, she won't *be* in office forever. In fact, the Havenite Constitution limits her to no more than three successive terms." The empress grimaced. "I think that needs to be changed, and I think some of the Constitution's other term-limit aspects—especially the clause limiting a president's term to only five T-years—reflects pre-prolong thinking. Now, the Constitution does allow someone to run for the office again after being *out* of office for at least one term, and I'd say if anyone had a chance of pulling that off, it would be Eloise. Or Tom Theisman, if he wasn't smart enough to stay as far away from elective office as physically possible! And some members of Congress are pressing to amend the Constitution to remove the three-successive-terms limitation specifically so she can run again. Eloise won't hear of it, though. For that matter, I think she'd be highly resistant to running for office again—*ever*—once her three terms are up."

"I can see that," Honor said. "She's a historian, too."

"Quite a bit of that going around lately...thank God," Hamish put in.

"Probably." Elizabeth nodded. "And I can understand why it's so important to her to fully establish—*reestablish*—the rule of law in Nouveau Paris. She and Tom Theisman and all the others paid cash for that, and she's not going to let anyone—even, or especially, *herself*—establish any fresh 'president-for-life' precedents."

"Good for her," Honor said.

"Like I say, from her perspective I understand entirely. From *my* perspective, though, it sucks wind," Elizabeth said frankly. She grimaced. "I have such a *great* relationship with her!"

She paused for a moment, eyes distant, as if considering what she'd just said, then shook her head.

"I really *do* have a great relationship with her," she said almost wonderingly. "Never would've seen that coming, but it's true. And that"—her gaze sharpened once again—"is why I don't feel anything

like confident about the chance of establishing an equally good relationship with whoever succeeds her.'"

Honor nodded thoughtfully, and Elizabeth shrugged.

"So, what she and I are going to do in...oh, a T-year or so, is
to propose a sort of...federated association, I suppose you'd call it,
between Manticore and Haven. We're still at an early enough stage no
one's come up with anything to call it yet, but basically, we'd amend
both constitutions to grant reciprocal citizenship."

"'Reciprocal citizenship'?" Honor repeated.

"In essence, any citizen of the Republic would be a citizen of the Star
Empire, and any citizen of the Star Empire would be a citizen of the
Republic. Where they voted and where they paid taxes would depend
upon the star nation in which they currently resided." Elizabeth smiled
as Honor's eyes widened. "Oh, it'll be more complicated than that, I'm
sure, but that's the basic platform we're after. We'll be looking at building deliberate economic ties, as well, and of course Havenite businesses
and individuals will get the same Junction rates as Manticorans do. As I
say, I've talked about it with Benjamin a bit, too. Grayson intends to stay
independent, for reasons I fully understand, but he's inclined to think
the Graysons may be ready for the same kind of relationship by the time
Eloise and I actually have all the bits and pieces glued into place."

"Um." Honor frowned in thought, then glanced at Hamish. There
seemed to be a certain flicker of amusement deep in his blue eyes, but
he only looked back with a solemn shrug.

"It sounds like it *ought* to be workable," she said to Elizabeth then.
"I'd be more confident if history wasn't littered with things that 'ought'
to have worked. But with a pair like you and Eloise driving it, I don't
doubt the legal framework can at least be created and put into place.
Making it actually *work* has a lot of potential to get...complicated,
though, I'd think."

"I agree," Elizabeth said with a chuckle. "On the other hand, there
are some things we can already put into place to help build the relationship we'll need when the time comes. In fact, I'd planned to discuss
this with *you* sometime in the next few months."

"Did you?" Honor said, and there was no mistaking the suspicion in
her tone—or her eyes—this time as she sampled Elizabeth's mind-glow.

"Well, I wasn't going to *cram* it at you," Elizabeth told her. "But one
of the most essential elements will be keeping our military establishments on the same page. Especially with the Alignment still out there
somewhere."

All trace of amusement faded from her eyes for a moment, and her
nostrils flared.

"I know the hunt for the rest of your 'onion' is really only just getting started, Honor, but I have to tell you, I'm not optimistic about our dragging them back into the open until they're damned well ready to *come* back out into the open."

"I'm not giving up hope, but I'm afraid that's what the odds favor," Honor agreed.

"Which is why we have to maintain a strong military posture. I don't see any way in hell we could maintain the fleet strength we have right now. There are megatons of totally valid domestic reasons to cut naval funding now that the League's not a threat and we've pretty much established we can kick anybody's ass," Elizabeth said bluntly. "Manticore has enough of a naval tradition, and enough interstellar commitments, that maintaining a powerful fleet won't be that great a challenge. Maintaining one as powerful as the one we have *now* is likely to be impossible, though. Oh, we'll keep a couple hundred capital ships in commission. A lot of the others can go into reserve—and unlike the Sollies we *will* rotate ships in and out to keep them up to date—but we're going to need a *lot* more cruisers and battlecruisers than SD(P)s in our post-war fleet. And Haven's navy will probably be under even more pressure to retrench. Partly, I'm afraid, because the Havenite Navy acquired a lot of...negative associations under the Legislaturalists that the Royal Navy's never had to deal with."

Honor nodded again. She'd considered those points herself, more than once.

"So what Eloise and I plan to do is find every way we can to weld the RMN and RHN together at the hip." Elizabeth smiled thinly. "For one thing, we're shipping all the Solarian data you brought home from Ganymede to Bolthole, and we intend to establish a permanent joint R and D facility there." Honor's eyes flared in true astonishment, and Elizabeth's smile grew warmer. "Apparently, Admiral Hemphill and Admiral Foraker have taken a genuine liking to one another." The empress shook her head. "Eloise tells me Tom Theisman's taken to referring to them as 'a congress of geeks.'" She chuckled. "I *think* he means it as a compliment."

"I'm pretty sure he does," Honor said, "but...Lord! I don't know if the galaxy's ready to have both of them working together *permanently*, Elizabeth!"

"With treecats thrown into the mix, too," Elizabeth said with a louder chuckle. "Don't forget that!"

Honor shook her head, and Elizabeth grinned at her.

"Anyway, what we're hoping is that our research establishments will cross-fertilize and we can create a commonality of weapons clear across the board. And, of course, strategic and tactical doctrine to go with it. I expect that'll require at least as much work as the hardware side."

Honor nodded yet again, and Elizabeth shrugged.

"One thing we're planning on is to operate permanently integrated Manticoran and Havenite formations in areas which are clearly of vital interest to us both. There'll be plenty of opportunity to cycle up and coming commanders through those sorts of slots. And we're also thinking about modifying our academies' curricula so that our midshipmen and their officer cadets each spend one full year in the *other's* academy."

Honor's eyes widened with respect for that notion, but then she frowned.

"All that sounds *wonderful*, Elizabeth. And I'm pretty sure our current crop of senior officers could make it work, at least at the macro level. Mike and Lester, for example, or L'anglais and Alice. But it's going to tend to fly apart at what I think of as the *micro*-level. The training level, the level where logistics officers and yard dogs get to stick their oars in. Or the level where people who feel their unspeakable talents were underrecognized when someone like that hack Tourville got the choice assignment and all the glory can do their best to pour sand into the gears. That's one of the things I worry about on the political side, but that's not my real forte. The *military* side, though—" She shook her head. "Tom can probably handle it from his side, at least as long as Eloise is in office, but we've got plenty of arrogant, chauvinistic Manticorans who'll require a little...attitude adjustment from time to time while all this is getting set up. Once it's up and running, maybe not, but in the early stages—?"

She rolled her eyes. Then she stopped, and those eyes narrowed as she tasted Elizabeth's mind-glow.

"Oh, no!" she said sharply. "Don't even *think* about it, Elizabeth!"

"Well, I wasn't going to bring it up," the empress said, "but since you have, there's really only—"

"I said no, and I *meant* no," Honor said flatly. "I'm done, Elizabeth. I told you that."

"I know you did," Elizabeth said in a softer voice.

"Well I *damned* well meant it," Honor said. She tucked her right arm around Katherine and reached out her left to take Hamish's hand. "I've been on active duty since the day I graduated from Saganami Island, and since Basilisk, I've been on active *operations* without any real break—aside from the time I spent on medical leave or hauled off to Cerberus! Oh, and I'll give you the time I spent on the beach after the duel or during the High Ridge fiasco, although I wouldn't exactly call either of those 'restful.' But that's forty-three T-years, Elizabeth. *Forty-three*. And I have a family, and I'm going to spend time with that family."

Her eyes burned, her hand tightened on Hamish's, and she realized her lips wanted to quiver. She blinked back tears and looked quickly at him, tasting his support, feeling his love, then turned back to Elizabeth.

"I'm sorry, Elizabeth," she said softly. "I know how badly you *think* you need me. I can *taste* it. But I've given everything I've got. I'm... tired. And Hamish and I went to Briarwood last week for Dr. Illescue to implant the zygote—*Emily's* zygote. The day I told her about Beowulf, the day she *died*, that was the day it was fertilized."

She shook her head fiercely.

"And I know now, Mom," she said, turning to her mother, "why you said I'd understand why you carried me to term when it was my turn. I didn't have that with Raoul, but I'll have it with this child. With *Emily's* child. And when this child is born, my children—and hers—will have a *mother*."

She turned back to Elizabeth.

"So, I'm sorry Elizabeth," she repeated, her eyes misty, "but there are some things in this universe that are more important. And I am finally going to give them—give the people I love—the time they deserve. *Emily* taught me that, and I'm going to do it."

There was silence for a long moment, and then Elizabeth Winton reached out and laid one gentle hand on Honor Alexander-Harrington's knee.

"Of course you are," she said softly.

✧   ✧   ✧

"Your Majesty," Prime Minister Grantville said with unaccustomed formality some hours later, "I don't think—"

"Don't go there, Willie," Elizabeth said with an off-center smile.

Honor and Hamish and their entire family—two-legs and treecats alike—had departed twenty minutes ago, after a private dinner with the royal family. There weren't that many people Elizabeth Winton could invite over for dinner without its turning into a state occasion or a political horse-trading session, and she deeply treasured the people with whom she could do that.

She didn't need Honor's ability to taste other people's emotions to know Grantville had simply been biding his time, though. Now she faced him squarely, and he gave her one of those stubborn Alexander looks.

"Your Majesty, I understand what she's saying. And God knows I love her. For that matter, there's nobody in the Star Empire who has a better understanding of how much she's already given. How much she's already sacrificed. But we *need* her. We need her as the First Space Lord *everyone* would respect. Not even the most chauvinistic Havenite officer in the universe would dare to... to *disrespect* her. And I can't even imagine a *Manticoran* officer with the testosterone level to argue with her. We have to make this military partnership work, and without *her*—"

"First, Willie," Elizabeth interrupted firmly, "*nobody* is truly irreplaceable. Do I agree with you that she would be the absolutely ideal First Space Lord? Of course I do! The only slot she'd be more valuable in would be First Lord, but I sort of think we'll be leaving Hamish in that one for a while. So, yes. I would really, really like to see First Space Lord Harrington working with First Lord White Haven and Secretary of War Theisman and CNO L'anglais or Tourville to make this work. You cannot *imagine* how much I would like to see that.

"But, second, she's absolutely right about how much she's already given. How much her service to the Star Kingdom and the Star Empire's already cost her. I don't think I could even count the number of times she's almost been killed, and the list of people she cared about who *have* been killed would be enough to give me nightmares if I knew all the names on it. She's lost virtually all of her family on Sphinx, God only knows how many cousins she lost in the Beowulf Strike, and now she's lost Emily. And I owe her. *I* owe her—me, personally, Elizabeth Winton, not just Queen Elizabeth or Empress Elizabeth. That woman has put herself through *hell* for me over and over again, and so this time, Willie—*this* time—I have *her* back for a change. I don't really give a damn how badly we think we need her. You leave her be. That's a direct royal command. And you make sure everyone *else* leaves her be, because I will be the worst nightmare of anyone who doesn't. And, just to be sure we're perfectly clear about this, that means *you*, too. And I don't care if you *are* her brother-in-law. Do you read me on this?"

Grantville looked at her for a moment, but then he sighed.

"You're right," he said. "I just... I just can't *not* want to see her where we need her so badly."

"That's because you're a prime minister," she told him with a crooked smile. "Now, go home—both of you," she reached out to give Tree Master a quick ear rub where he sat on Grantville's shoulder, "and get a good night's rest. Because tomorrow, while she and Hamish are out at White Haven packing for Grayson, you and I are going to be thinking about who we'll grab for First Space Lord since we can't have her. Got it?"

"Got it, Your Majesty," he said ruefully and gave the prince consort a slight bow. "Good night, Your Highness," he said. "And to you, as well, Your Majesty."

"Good night, Willie," Elizabeth said affectionately, and walked him to the door.

It closed behind him, and Elizabeth tucked her arm through Justin's elbow and led him out onto one of King Michael's Tower's balconies. They settled on a chaise lounge, and she leaned back, resting her head on his chest with a sigh of deep content as Ariel and Monroe draped themselves on perches.

"I've got to say, Beth," Justin said. "I really didn't expect you to give up that easily. I mean, I agree with everything you just said, but I really, really didn't expect you to let her go without more of a fight."

"Really?" She rolled her head, smiling at him in the moonlight. "What makes you think I gave up on anything?"

His eyes narrowed, and he frowned down at her.

"But you just said—"

"I said she was right, and I said she deserves to be left in peace, and I said I'd protect her from everyone else." Elizabeth's smile softened and something like sorrow floated in her eyes. "And I will. And it won't matter. Not in the end."

"What do you mean?" he asked. "Why won't it matter?"

"Because I'll need her," Elizabeth said, almost inaudibly. "I'll need her, and when I do, I'll get her back."

"Elizabeth, you're a queen, an empress," he said gently, hugging her tight. "I know you care about her. But it's your job—your *duty*—to put the people you have to have in the places where you have to have them, whatever it costs them. Whatever it costs *you*."

"Of course it is." She looked up at him again. "But I'm not the one who's going to make her come back, *make* her put herself on the line again."

He frowned in confusion, and Elizabeth reached up to touch the side of his face.

"I can—and I by God *will*—protect her from everyone in the damned galaxy," she said fiercely. "But there's one person I *can't* protect her from." Elizabeth shook her head, her dark eyes glistening with unshed tears. "That's the hell of it, Justin. I can't protect her from *herself*. I'll need her, and she'll know it, and that will be all it takes. All in the world. Not because I try to force her into it, but because of who she is."

She arched her neck, raising her head to kiss him, and then settled back once again, her eyes closed.

"Because she's Honor Harrington," the Empress of Manticore said softly. "Because she's Honor Harrington."

AFTERWORD

IT'S BEEN TWENTY-FIVE YEARS since I first sent a very young Commander Harrington and HMS *Fearless* off to Basilisk Station. I didn't expect her journey to last for a quarter century when she and I first set out, but it's been a fantastic voyage from my perspective.

Way back in 1991, Jim Baen suggested that since every book I wrote seemed to spawn sequels, perhaps it would be a good idea to actually *plan* a series for a change, so I came up with ten proposals for possible series. One of them was Honor Harrington. Little did I know when I suggested that possibility that Jim had been looking for someone to write "Hornblower in space" for a long time. I'd already decided that if the series worked, the inevitable comparison was going to be to Forrester's Hornblower novels, which was why Honor had the initials I'd given her, but I really wasn't prepared for how enthusiastically Jim jumped on the proposal.

I wrote the first two novels—*Basilisk Station* and *Honor of the Queen*—back-to-back, and Jim released them about a month apart, which I think played a significant role in the series' early success. But I don't think that was the only reason it succeeded. I think it succeeded because Honor Harrington as a character speaks directly to her readers. She possesses qualities which I—and, I suspect, the majority of my readers—wish we and, especially, our leaders possessed. The greatest of those, of course, is that Honor Harrington takes responsibility. She takes responsibility for her own actions, yes, but it goes farther than that, because she assumes the responsibility of fixing *other people's* problems, not because anyone *else* would have expected or demanded that she fix them. She fixes them because that's what responsible adults do.

You can see that in her from her earliest iteration in *Basilisk Station*, when a young, tactically brilliant, unwittingly charismatic, and politically naïve and inexperienced naval officer finds herself pitchforked into a political and moral minefield with which virtually every officer before her has resolutely declined to deal. It's what follows her throughout her career, and I would argue that it's what generates such unbreakable loyalty in both the people she commands and the readers who have followed her through the last twenty-five years.

This book actually represents the culmination of two separate story arcs. I've explained elsewhere how the timing of the Mesan Alignment got pulled forward as the consequence of a couple of collaborative works with Eric Flint. That meant the originally planned ending for the story arc beginning at Basilisk had to be modified, because that story arc was supposed to end with Honor's death in action against Lester Tourville's fleet at the Battle of Manticore. Her death, and her dying message to Queen Elizabeth, "For God's sake, let it end here," was supposed to bring the war with Haven to a conclusion and cap that storyline. The *next* major story arc was supposed to begin twenty-five or thirty years later, when the Mesan Alignment intruded into the light and Honor's children carried the torch forward while the junior officers introduced in *Shadow of Saganami* provided the ship commanders under whom they and their friends served.

I can't pretend I'm sorry Honor didn't die, because the character became even more important to me than I anticipated she might, and her death, however fitting and purposeful it might have been, wouldn't simply have grieved her fans; it would have grieved *me*, as well. It did create some significant logistical problems, however, including the fact that the Solarian League was supposed to have had another couple of decades to "get a clue" where its technological inferiority was concerned, but I'm actually very satisfied with how the combined story arcs have ended in *Uncompromising Honor*. Although, of course, as anyone who's been reading the books undoubtedly understands, there is still plenty of skullduggery to come where the Alignment is concerned. In fact—

But that would be telling, wouldn't it?

If any single poem sums up Honor Harrington's entire life, it would undoubtedly be Rudyard Kipling's "If." She's grown from that earnest, determined, focused, apolitical professional officer—the daughter of a yeoman, who didn't have a *clue* how politics worked... and even less desire to *find out* how politics worked—into a great noblewoman. Into a head of state in her own right on Grayson, a duchess in Manticore, commander of the Grand Alliance's primary striking force, one of her star nation's leading strategists, and the confidante, advisor, and personal friend of monarchs, presidents, and protectors. She's acquired the poise and the confidence to face the responsibilities that go with who she's become as fearlessly as she ever faced a salvo of incoming missiles, and she's still willing to make the right choice—the *hard* choice—regardless of the personal cost to her. She has, indeed, met with Triumph and Disaster and treated those two imposters just the same, just as she's "filled the unforgiving minute with sixty seconds' worth of distance run."

I'm satisfied with where she is, with *who* she is, and who she intends to be going forward. She didn't die on her "quarterdeck," as I'd originally intended, but like Horatio Nelson, she can say "Thank God I have done my duty." And so, at the end of this book, I've sent her off to the honorable retirement my original plan for the series had denied her, and I'm glad it's so. She deserves it.

Of course, people are already asking me if there will be additional "Honor" novels. *I* may be willing to see her in peaceful retirement; quite a few of her readers aren't. I make no promises, but I very, very much doubt we've seen the last of Honor. I *know* we haven't seen the last of the *Honorverse*, although I'm now at a point which lets me explore some other portions of it that I've wanted to explore for a long time. And in the course of those future explorations, I'm sure Lady Dame Honor Alexander-Harrington, Duchess and Steadholder Harrington, will return to the stage. I doubt the Salamander will find herself in the heart of the furnace again; she's too senior for ship command—even for *fleet* command, in many ways—but, then again, she's also grown *beyond* a simple ship commander, a simple fleet CO. And whatever I may want for her in terms of "peaceful retirement," it does seem unlikely she'll be able to stay there forever.

As Empress Elizabeth says, the time is bound to come when her monarch, her star nation, her *duty* needs her once again. And if that time comes, she'll answer the call of responsibility the way she always has because, in the end, however she may have changed in the course of her journey from Basilisk to Operation Nemesis, at the core of her, she is still who she always was.

She's still Honor Harrington.